The Family

Its Structure and Interaction

The Family

Its Structure and Interaction

F. Ivan Nye
Washington State University

Felix M. Berardo
University of Florida

The Macmillan Company, New York

Collier-Macmillan Publishers, London

To Our Children
Betty Jean Morrison, Lloyd Nye, and Beverly Baynard
and
Benito and Marcellino Berardo

The Macmillan Company
866 Third Avenue, New York, New York 10022
Collier-Macmillan Canada, Ltd., Toronto, Ontario

Library of Congress catalog card number: 72-075151

Printing: 1 2 3 4 5 6 7 8   Year: 3 4 5 6 7 8 9

Preface

Our purpose in this book has been to illuminate the nature of the family through maximal use of sociological research findings and selective utilization of key sociological concepts. Moreover, where it is sufficiently developed, social theory is introduced to explain various patterns of family behavior. For the most part the text focuses on the American family system, for two reasons: (1) the most extensive research on the family has been conducted in the United States, and (2) an adequate depiction of the family in various cultures properly requires sufficient space that a separate volume is necessary to that task. Indeed, several books are currently available which treat the family from a cross-cultural perspective. (Many of these are cited in Chapter 2).

Analysis of family behavior over the years has been accomplished by scholars from a variety of disciplines emphasizing different conceptual frameworks and theories. Even within sociology there exist a number of conceptual approaches to studying the family, each having certain advantages and limitations. Thus, one approach may mirror the reality of some aspects of family life better than another approach, while other types of family behavior or structure may be more clearly illuminated by a third and alternative framework. Consequently, we have taken the position, given the current state of family sociology, that it would be unduly constricting to utilize only one approach to the exclusion of others. Either to choose one framework, ignoring everything done in the others, or to take all research and force it into a single framework would unnecessarily restrict our efforts and certainly distort social reality. Our own thinking has been influenced considerably by some of the concepts in sociology drawn from exchange theory at the micro level and structure-functional and systems theory at the macro level. However, most of the research in recent years in family sociology has been executed utilizing the interactional framework. Therefore, it has a prominent place in this volume, as does much scholarly work based on the developmental framework. (A brief description of these various conceptual schemes is presented in Chapter 1).

We present the family as an institution continuously in the process of change. This occurs both through experimentation from within the family, involving new strategies for performing family roles, and by reactions to changes in the other institutions in the society. The tempo of change has increased appreciably during the latter half of the 1960's and during the 1970's. This accelerated pace is reflected in some of the latest research findings and in legislative and judicial decisions dealing with such matters as women's position in employment and the liberalization of abortion and divorce laws.

The conditions of social change which characterize contemporary American society have raised doubts in the minds of many as to the ability of our traditional family system to meet the needs of its members. Increasingly, one hears or reads that the family is obsolete, or that new or alternative family forms are needed, and that our existing family institution must be changed or modified. However, no comprehensive new institution has yet developed to replace the functions presently performed by the family—one that could take over, for example, the care and socialization of children—and therefore render the family obsolete. Nor does any such institutional innovation appear on the horizon. Therefore, the study of the family remains as important as formerly, but more challenging because of new and changed family roles and different or modified sets of interactions with the other institutions in our society. Thus, the structure of the family itself, and the relevant structural aspects of the economic and governmental institutions, as well as the religious, seem appropriate topics for critical examination.

The crucial functions of child care and socialization have received relatively light treatment in previous texts on the family. We attempt to remedy this, in part, by providing a chapter on socialization, one on adolescence, as well as related chapters on nonmarital sexual involvements and premature marriages. Moreover, most texts give scant attention to the latter half of the family life-cycle. We attempt to correct this through the inclusion of separate chapters on the middle-aged family, the retired family, and families disrupted by death. Other relatively unique coverage includes a full chapter on power within the family and one on the disorganized or malfunctioning family.

We have made a very special effort to communicate with the student. As part of this communicative enterprise, we have explicitly defined the key concepts (Chapter 1) and employed only such special sociological vocabulary as will improve understanding. As another part of the communicative process, we strive to provide a realistic assessment of the state of knowledge concerning a given issue in the field of marriage and the family. If the evidence is contradictory or clearly inadequate the student should know it. Within the reasonable limits of a basic text, we seek to challenge the student to think critically and creatively about the research and theory presented to him. We believe that students should think not only how social behavior can better fit existing social structure, but how social structure might be modified to more fully serve human needs at all stages of the family life-cycle.

A number of people have contributed directly to this volume, many others through their research and theory development. A special note of thanks is due Gordon Streib, who read the entire manuscript in its first draft and whose comprehensive knowledge and critical evaluation brought many fruitful additions and suggestions. One or more chapters were read by Jessie Bernard, Viktor Gecas, Melvin Kohn, and Alice Rossi. Not all of their ideas could be utilized; however, the volume benefited immensely from their critical and constructive comments. Finally, a word of thanks to John Moore, former Macmillan editor, who stimulated us to write a basic text, and to Charles Smith, Kenneth J. Scott, Peter O'Brien, and George Carr, Macmillan editors who collaborated in helping us to complete the task. To Esther Nye and Donna Martsen we are most grateful for typing the various sections of the manuscript, and to Ingrid Goldstrom and Jean Moneo we extend our sincere appreciation for their assistance with the necessary but tedious task of proofreading.

F. I. N.
F. M. B.

Contents

Part II

Prelude to Marriage

Part III

Family Organization and Interaction

Part IV

Family Reorganization and Interaction

xiii

Part V

The Postparental Family

Part VI

Postscript on the Family

Introduction

1

The Sociological Study of the Family

How does the study of the family by sociologists differ from that of a mother who views the family from the perspective of rearing several children or the Boy Scout leader who spends his week managing a grocery store or the newspaper columnist who makes a living writing human-interest stories? First, the sociologist's study differs in that before a sociologist can make a statement about what people believe or what they do, he must prepare or see a report based on a random sample of the people from a particular group. He cannot reach a conclusion based primarily on his experience, beliefs, or observation of the people he knows personally. Conversely, if he has made an adequate study, he *can* make statements, regardless of whether they agree with his own personal feelings or observations. Because this is possible for the social scientist, several researchers can investigate a given problem and, if they have done their task properly, emerge with similar results. Besides the ability to perform such research, the sociologist knows, and the student of sociology learns to know, where to look for the reports of research conducted by others. Research asking the question "what" people do in families and what people think about families and family members is frequently called *descriptive research*.

A great deal of descriptive research will be reported in this volume. A good deal of it is or was surprising when first reported. For example, census reports that the median age at first marriage has declined considerably since 1900 surprised most people. Before these reports, it had been assumed that people were marrying later in order to complete their education. A few people have, in fact, delayed marrying for that reason, but more have married earlier. We shall explore both what appear to be the reasons for and some of the consequences of early marriage in Chapter 9. Likewise, it came as a surprise in 1970 that half of all mothers of school-age children only were in paid employment.

3

Most people were used to the expression "mother's place is in the home" and had assumed that all but a few mothers were devoting their full attention to home and family. This participation of mothers in the provider role will be discussed in Chapter 11.

Sociologists are cautious in deciding *why* some family-related behavior occurs. A newspaper columnist writes an article asserting that the increasing incidence of juvenile delinquency is due to broken homes. He may not know or care whether this assertion is true. The sociologist specializing in such matters, however, knows that the divorce rate remained about the same for fifteen years prior to the mid-sixties, whereas the incidence of juvenile delinquency increased each year. Even if divorces had increased at the same rate as juvenile delinquency, this would not prove that delinquency was caused by broken homes. The increase in both might be caused by some third variable—for example, the increasing proportion of people living in urban areas. Although most sociologists consider it appropriate to seek causes, they recognize the complexity of social phenomena, including family behavior, and make cause-and-effect statements with caution. Again, it is the business of the sociologist to know where to find the research reports of others and to interpret them appropriately, with minimal influence from his own experience or that of his family or friends.

Sociologists have developed a number of concepts that describe with some precision some of the family behavior that has been systematically studied. To select one more-or-less at random, take the concept of the *autonomic family.* This is a loosely organized family in which individual family members exercise a great deal of freedom in pursuing their own interests in their own way. Joint family activities are at a minimum. The control of family members by other family members is minimal.[1] Such a concept illustrates several aspects of family concepts. First, it is a quick means of communication. The sociologist who hears or reads the term *autonomic family* immediately visualizes this type of family, which saves the time of the writer and the reader in going through a paragraph to describe the kind of family to which the allusion is made. Second, although the basic ideas are well understood and communicated, it is not a mathematical formula. Each sociologist who undertakes to define the term will state it slightly differently, but the content will be essentially the same.

Some nonsociologists have questioned the utility of sociological concepts. However, they are as essential for quick and precise com-

[1]P. G. Herbst, "Conceptual Framework for Studying the Family," in *Social Structure and Personality in a City*, ed. by O. A. Oeser and S. B. Hammond (London: Routledge and Kegan Paul, 1954), pp. 126–37.

munication as is the formula for the mathematician or the system of plant classification for the botanist. Some of the marriage texts have stated research findings, implications of research, and hypotheses without the use of sociological concepts. They facilitate easy reading but provide less understanding of what is being said or why. Such bypassing of sociological concepts reduces precision and results in less comparability among the statements made by sociologists.

The use of sociological concepts involves both cost and utility. The cost is in the time of the student and the instructor in developing a sufficient level of understanding and familiarity so that the concept becomes a really efficient means of communication. Once that level is attained, communication becomes more rapid, precise, and meaningful. The use of concepts, however, is a means to an end. Only those concepts that are central to the study and comprehension of the family will receive special attention in this chapter.

Individual Case and Category

The sociology student must comprehend the relationship of the individual case, whether that be a person or a family, to a finding for a social category. For example, the reader will encounter many research findings similar to the following: the divorce rates are higher for marriages in which the bride is under age twenty than those in which she is over twenty, or wives who married before age twenty are more likely to evaluate their marriages as unhappy than those who marry at an older age. Students frequently react to such findings by saying, "That can't be true. I know a girl who married at age sixteen. She isn't divorced and she is very happily married." There is, of course, no contradiction; some young marriages are stable and some marriages at more advanced ages are unstable. However, a significantly larger proportion of young marriages fail, a fact that sociologists feel is worth reporting and discussing. We say (Chapter 9) that each spouse is less likely to be able to play certain key roles effectively at an early age than he or she will later. The fact that some early marriages are stable and evaluated as highly satisfactory by the couples involved, and that some marriages of those who were older are unstable, underlines an important social fact, that there is more than one variable that influences the stability of marriage. If one knows one social fact, such as the age of the spouses, he can predict a little but not much more accurately, the outcome of a marriage than if he didn't know that fact. To use another example, the reader will find a statement that conflict between spouses is more characteristic of those marriages in which the wife is employed than those in which she isn't. Confronted with this finding, some

5

student will say, "But doesn't it all depend on the personality of the two spouses?" The answer is "No." If it did depend entirely on the personality characteristics of the couple, the finding quoted above would not have been discovered. However, if the woman student wants to know whether her own marriage is likely to undergo increased conflict if she becomes gainfully employed, that is another problem. That depends on her capabilities, training, and motivation to work, on how many children she has; on whether she has good care for children while she is working; and on her husband's attitude, his capabilities, and more. Her own family might be characterized by frustration and added conflict, or it might be equally improved by her taking employment, but this does not alter the general finding that, *as a social category,* more employed mothers have high levels of conflict in their marriages than those not employed. This is *not,* however, an appropriate basis for concluding that if she, as one individual, combined the provider role with those of a mother, she would have more conflict in her marriage (Chapter 11).

RESEARCH FINDINGS AND DECISION MAKING Family research is frequently utilized to make two types of decision: individual decisions, such as whether the mother works, and decisions of government, business, and so on. In neither case can research findings dictate decisions, but they may be utilized with profit by those making decisions at any level. For example, couples contemplating marriage before age twenty or thinking of an interfaith marriage might look at the higher divorce rates in those types of marriage and review their values, beliefs, vocational training, or religious beliefs before proceeding. Such differences in divorce rates do not tell a couple *why* young marriages and interfaith marriage are more likely to be unstable, neither do they indicate why or what in these marriages is responsible for their instability (although the sociologist may provide an educated guess by offering his own interpretation, as do the authors of this text.)

It should be obvious that no single research finding, no matter how well proved, is a sufficient basis for making individual decisions. As we have noted, a person may have to evaluate a dozen or more social facts before proceeding taking a course of action. A given research finding can provide *one* of these social facts, better than nothing. Two more points are relevant. Sociology is not counseling. Counseling is an art that draws most heavily from psychology, but also from sociology, economics, biology, and other fields. Further, counselors do not make decisions for individuals. They try to provide information on the many variables relevant to a decision; then the person weighs these against his own values and decides on a course of action. We take the position, a general one in sociology, that social research is useful in individual decisions if the individual realizes the limitations of social research and knows that he cannot make a decision on a complex matter on the basis of one social fact about himself or others.

Family research may be utilized in making governmental or private agency decisions. Sociologists researching the effects on children of the employment of mothers were asked whether such employment was related to delinquency or mental health problems of children. If the answers had been affirmative, there would have been pressure for legislation or agency policies to discourage mothers from entering employment. Because the findings were essentially negative (Chapter 11) that finding probably discouraged sentiment for repressive policies. However, if research had shown a higher prevalence of delinquency and emotional problems among the children of employed mothers, this would not be sufficient grounds for legislation or policies to prevent mothers from working. The society would have to weigh the value of children's problems against the problem of restricting the rights of mothers to perform other tasks besides those in the home. It might have been necessary also to consider what the effects would have been on the quality of teaching in the schools, on the effectiveness of government or efficiency in business, if all women with minor children were prohibited from working. Again, research that produces a relevant social fact is most useful in developing public policy decisions, but it does not and cannot dictate policy decisions. These must come from noting *all* the probable consequences of a change in policy, then weighing these and making a decision. The person who says research is not useful because it, in itself, does not indicate the proper decision, is as wrong as the person who takes a single fact as an adequate basis for a policy decision.

Function

To understand family behavior as a sociologist, it is necessary to use several concepts, most of which are common to the general field of sociology. A few of these that the reader will encounter repeatedly as he proceeds will be discussed and examples provided. One of these is the concept *function.*

The concept of function is used widely in sociology. For an extensive discussion of its use in the sociology of the family, the reader is referred to McIntyre.[2] We shall employ it to mean an activity performed for an institution or for a class of individuals. For example, one of the functions of the family is the socialization of children. The family

[2]Jennie McIntyre, "The Structure-Functional Approach to Family Study," in *Emerging Conceptual Frameworks in Family Analysis,* ed. by F. Ivan Nye and Felix M. Berardo (New York: The Macmillan Company, 1966), pp. 52–77.

performs this function for the children involved, for the family itself (as a means of making it possible to live with children in the family), and for the society as a whole, because unsocialized individuals are a liability and even a threat to society. It is possible to employ the term *dysfunction* in the opposite sense as a condition or activity hindering or preventing services' being rendered to an institution or to a category of individuals. For example, it is possible to say that early marriage is dysfunctional for the training of young men to prepare them for employment.

OGBURN'S LIST OF FUNCTIONS Several decades ago, Ogburn proposed a list of seven major activities that the family performs for individual members, the family as a group, and/or society: production of economic goods and services, status giving, education of the young, religious training of the young, recreation, protection, and affection.[3] This list has proved very meaningful to sociologists as it provides a few categories into which the multitude of activities performed by the family can be placed. The asserted decline in all of these except affection has been accepted by some as an explanation of the increased divorce rate. Others have devised slightly different lists. Later, we shall suggest a sexual function of the family (Chapter 13). It is our feeling that *socialization* is a more effective term than *education*, because it includes all types of informal learning by the child, not just the knowledge that the parent intends to impart. For example, it includes how to dress oneself and much of the language the child learns (Chapter 15).

MANIFEST AND LATENT FUNCTIONS It has been noted that some activities that result from a given course of action are obvious and anticipated (manifest), but that some are unanticipated, unintended, and sometimes hidden.[4] For example, wives have become providers to increase the family income or to follow vocational interests or to meet people and obtain some variety of experience, but as an unanticipated consequence they have increased their power in family decision-making (Chapter 11). Adolescents who marry early to satisfy their sexual interests frequently find themselves with heavy obligations toward children that they never expected or wanted (Chapter 9). It is probable that those who espouse sexual freedom for the unmarried would find that it results in an *unintended* increase in forced marriage and illegitimate births (Chapter 7). Thus, the awareness of latent functions and the ability to anticipate them are important to the student of the family.

---

[3] William F. Ogburn, "The Changing Family," *The Family,* **19** (July 1938), pp. 139–43.
[4] Robert K. Merton, *Social Theory and Social Structure* (Glencoe, Ill: The Free Press, 1957), pp. 19–84.

Role Concepts

Few, if any, sociological concepts have been utilized more frequently or more meaningfully than the concept of role. However, like others, its meaning has varied to some extent among sociologists. We shall explore these differences briefly, then indicate the use of the role concept in this volume. Initially, it may be noted that role refers to the behavior expected of persons who occupy a position, for example, wife.

ROLE OR ROLES? Does one think of the role of a wife or the roles? Both usages are respectable in sociology. Gross and his associates, in their extensive exploration of the role concept, employ it in the singular; that is, a wife-mother has *a* role, which is then divided into role sectors, each of which is the behavior directed toward a category of persons: husband, son, daughter, and others.[5] Another usage has been outlined by Bates, who thinks of several roles as forming each position.[6] For example, the wife-mother has one role as a housekeeper, another as supervisor of her children, another as sexual partner to her husband. This second usage is especially useful in family analysis because of the variety of activities expected of each family member, and because some of these are performed in one family and not in another. Many wives enact the provider role by entering paid employment and many do not. Therefore, we will speak of the *roles* of husband, wife, and other family members rather than *the role*. However, the student should know that some authors employ the term in the singular. They may speak of the changing role of the wife, for example, when more wives obtain paid employment.

HOW ARE ROLES DEFINED? Roles are culturally defined and are passed on to succeeding generations as correct behavior. The socializing agents include parents, older siblings, kin, peer group, teachers, ministers, literature, newspapers, radio, movies, and TV. In highly differentiated societies, such as the United States, some small part of the definition of family roles is incorporated in laws and enforceable by the police and the courts. For example, the grounds for divorce are specified (Chapter 18). Most role behavior, however, is more informally specified and enforced. For example, both parents are expected to discipline and control their children. The parents who fail to do so are regarded with disapproval by neighbors, kin, and friends. This disapproval may be expressed toward the parents in gossip about them, in social ostracism, or in other penalties.

[5]Neal Gross, Ward S. Mason, and Alexander W. McEchern, *Explorations in Role Analysis: Studies of the School Superintendent Role* (New York: John Wiley & Sons, 1958), pp. 60–67.
[6]Frederick Bates, "Position, Role, and Status: A Reformulation of Concepts," *Social Forces,* **34** (May 1956), pp. 313–21.

9

Is ROLE BEHAVIOR NORMATIVELY DEFINED? In order for roles to exist (and probably for society to exist) there must be a consensus on the general definition of roles; for example, parents should socialize and control their children so that they will not become public nuisances. However, the methods for performing these roles are seldom rigidly specified in complex and changing societies. They are sometimes ritualized in small, static societies. In most instances, the means to the end are left to the individuals who occupy the positions. For example, there are numerous strategies for controlling children: physical punishment, deprivation of privileges, love withdrawal, rational appeals, and isolation, plus positive rewards for refraining from disapproved behavior. None of these is culturally (normatively) defined as right or wrong in American society. This seems to be true for most roles. To take another example, there is no normatively defined number of times that couples should engage in sexual intercourse. Mothers are expected to prepare food for their families, but what they prepare and how they serve it is not normatively defined. There are some definitely proscribed behaviors, such as incest. Physical attacks on other family members that endanger their health are prohibited in American society. It may be said that certain specific behaviors are prohibited but few are normatively prescribed.

ROLE EXPECTATIONS Because the specific behaviors for enacting roles are rarely specified, such as how one should discipline a child, there are many possibilities for differing conceptions of what and how these activities should be performed. As the child experiences these in his *family of orientation,* he forms opinions positive or negative concerning specific role-playing. Sometimes these are reinforced by *proscriptions* from a group with which his family is affiliated. For example, some fundamentalist religious organizations forbid dancing, card-playing, or the use of makeup.

Role expectations have proved a fruitful concept for viewing marital conflict.[7] One spouse may expect the husband to make all major decisions, for example, how the children will be disciplined; the other may feel that each should share equally in the decision. Or, in an even more specific instance: one spouse sees it as part of the housekeeping role that the wife prepare the husband's breakfast unless she is ill; the other sees this as optional in the role of housekeeper. In a complex society, there are likely to be many patterns for enacting roles. This diversity can be culturally transmitted or patterns may be transmitted or developed in the course of role-playing. For example, the parent who

[7]William G. Dyer, "Analyzing Marital Adjustment Using Role Theory," *Journal of Marriage and the Family,* **24** (Nov. 1962), pp. 371–75.

tries to control his child by lavishing love and attention on him may change his strategy if the child behaves selfishly and irresponsibly.

ROLE PERFORMANCE Although there are few cultural prescriptions specifying precisely how roles should be performed, there are within a society some criteria on how well a family member performs them. There are excellent providers who earn a relatively high income regularly and poor providers who earn little and are often unemployed. There are women who are excellent housekeepers and those who are not. There are husbands who please their wives sexually and those who make intercourse a burden. Performance in some of the key roles of husbands and wives are thought to explain part of marital stability and the attitudes of spouses toward their marriage (Chapter 19).

ROLE CONFLICT Gross and others have defined two types of role conflict, interrole and intrarole.[8] Interrole conflict involves two roles. The husband who needs to work at his business after dinner on a day on which his wife wants him to attend a card party experiences interrole conflict—conflicting demands of two roles, the provider role and a family recreational role. Interrole conflict apparently occurs most frequently when one plays a role in an extreme manner. For example, men who work evenings and weekends in addition to a regular week are more likely to experience interrole conflict than those who work from 8:00 until 5:00, devoting the remainder of their time to other roles. Intrarole conflict concerns only a single role, but two perceptions of it. To utilize a previous example, if a husband expects that his wife will prepare breakfast for him and she expects to stay in bed, there is intrarole conflict. If one parent expects the children to spend their evenings studying and the other doesn't, they experience intrarole conflict. If one parent expects to employ physical punishment and the other to avoid it, there is intrarole conflict for the parent who must discipline the child. Intrarole conflict is frequent in complex, rapidly changing societies because such societies are characterized by a variety of role expectations.

ROLES AND FUNCTIONS The functions that the family as an institution performs are divided among family members in the form of roles. The economic function in families is encompassed in the provider role customarily enacted by the husband, sometimes paralleled by a provider role by the wife, and in the housekeeper role of the wife. In most farm families, the roles children play include that of provider, as they contribute their labor to farm production. To employ another example, in the socialization function of the family, both parents have roles instructing and disciplining children.

[8]Gross et al., op. cit., pp. 248–249.

11

Norms

Norms are patterns of behavior considered to be right in a given society. In most, if not all instances, these are also the modal or most frequent patterns of behavior, although there are usually deviations from the norms. Because they are considered right, deviations are by definition wrong, and therefore subject to sanctions through legal organizations or from other social groups. The range of approved behavior is often wide. For example, the societal norms define the housekeeper role of the wife as keeping the house clean and orderly. However, the definition of what constitutes a clean and orderly house differs between subcultures and individual families. Usually, there is deviant behavior at either extreme in relation to the norm. Although a clean and orderly house is considered, to a degree, evidence of virtue, if the wife devotes all her time to cleaning and polishing or if she denies free use of the house to her family because its beautiful cleanliness would be endangered, she deviates from the norm in overplaying or overemphasizing the housekeeper role.

Because orderliness and cleanliness in private households have not generally been subjects for legal regulation, the sanctions against deviance are provided by other family members who, in many instances, will not care to live under either extreme, and from kin, neighbors, and friends.

Another example may be taken from the provider role of the father. Currently in American society most adult men work forty hours weekly plus doing a few chores about the home. Again, there is no negative feeling about working perhaps as many as fifty hours weekly or as few as thirty-five. However, most men, if they were to work more than sixty hours weekly, would have little time or energy for their recreational role with other family members or for participation in community life. Their sexual role might also be affected by fatigue and preoccupation with work. On the other hand, most men who work less than thirty hours weekly cannot earn enough to enact the provider role adequately.

Insofar as individuals are concerned, they are not likely to be subjected to sanctions for working less than the norm provided they are playing the provider role adequately or for devoting a larger proportion of the week to their occupation provided they do not seriously neglect their other roles. However, men who devote very little time to the provider role or almost all of it are viewed negatively by society, are likely to play some of their roles inadequately, and are likely to be subjected to sanctions from family and other groups.

The term *normatively defined* is employed frequently in relation to roles. It indicates a degree of consensus on how the role should be played.[9]

Values

The sociology student knows that value judgments have no legitimate place in science; that is, the sociologist should not indulge in them. However, societal values or differing values among subgroups in the society are of great interest to students of society. Values provide general and enduring guides to action. Many sociologists, including the authors, emphasize the hierarchal nature of values. Some values take precedence over others.[10] For example, observers from other societies generally agree that Americans place a high value on material things. As a group, Americans are more likely to be willing to work at night, to move their residences about the country, and to sacrifice leisure time and activities in order to increase their incomes. It is not that they place no value on working convenient hours, on maintaining a stable residence, or on having leisure time, but they place a higher value on being able to afford a new automobile, a house in a good part of town, and nice clothing. American businessmen conducting business in other societies have frequently been frustrated by their lack of materialistic values. High pay is not a sufficient incentive to ensure that employees will appear regularly for work, work industriously through the day, or keep the job after they have earned enough to take care of their present needs for food. In many societies the higher value is placed on time—time for visiting friends, for playing with one's children, for siestas, or for recreation. In other societies, including some in South Asia, religious values dominate all life to the extent that one would rather starve than eat a sacred animal.

A value, then, is an attitude toward objects, relationships, or services, which is hierarchal in nature; that is, some values rank higher and take preference over others. For example, in family activity, the value of security is always relevant. Family members who value security above alternatives will want to invest heavily in life insurance, to choose and retain jobs with tenure or other job protection, to remain in the same community, and to emphasize savings at the expense of recreation or a

[9]For a more complete discussion of the relationship of norm to role, see Bates, op. cit., pp. 313–321.

[10]William Wilson and F. Ivan Nye, "Some Methodological Problems in the Empirical Study of Values," Agricultural Experiment Station Bulletin No. 672 (Pullman: Washington State University, 1966); Robin M. Williams, *American Society,* 3rd ed., rev. (New York: Alfred A. Knopf, 1970), Chapter XI, "Values in American Society."

13

higher level of living. Thus, security, as an example of value, encompasses a variety of activities and guides a large number of decisions. It provides a broad orientation for a society or an individual.

In sociological perspective, everyone above the age of an infant has values; that is, he prefers some classes of things to others. The person who says "X has no values" can only be saying that that person holds none of the values of the speaker.

GOAL AND VALUE As already noted, *value* is a general term; *goal* is specific. A person who places high value on security may have set several security goals for himself, for example, $50,000 in life insurance, a savings account of $5,000, and a retirement income of $500 a month. Not all individuals, however, set such specific goals. Rather, they may try to obtain the most secure position possible, to save as much as they can, and to buy as much insurance as possible. In either event, their actions are consistent with their values. Because value is a high-level abstraction, one way to determine or measure it is by ascertaining goals, then inferring values from them.

VALUE CONFLICT There are a number of family-relevant values, such as the value of security, to which allusion has already been made. In addition, the valuing of a higher standard of living and recreational activity are relevant to all or almost all families. The values of self-improvement and religious activities are important to many. Activities directed toward any of these values require allocations of income and time. The more vigorously one pursues activities related to a value, the more resources must be preempted for those activities. It should be obvious that if one spouse places the highest value on security while the other places the highest value on a current standard of living, there is value conflict, which will be reflected in disagreements over many decisions dealing with whether to spend or save.

Students sometimes question the reality of value conflict, proposing that families can realize all their values. To a degree this is possible, but because values compete for time and income, to realize one fully is usually to ignore others or only direct token efforts toward their realization. Value conflict can exist within an individual or between larger groups, such as political parties, as well as between individuals.

INSTRUMENTAL AND INTRINSIC VALUES Some students of the family have deplored the fact that some of its values have been changing, other students that change has been too slow. The controversy seems to stem from the value of two types of behavior, that which is valued for itself and that which is valued because it is an efficient means to an end. The senior author has termed these *intrinsic* and *instrumental* values.[11]

[11]F. Ivan Nye, "Values, Family, and a Changing Society," *Journal of Marriage and the Family,* **29** (May 1967), pp. 241–249.

For example, in the recent past a high value was placed on filial duty, the willingness of children to care for aged parents. Before Social Security, most people, when they became too old to work, were dependent on others, either on their children or on charity. Small wonder that they tried to have several children and to inculcate a sense of duty toward parents. The alternative was pauperism in old age. Following the enactment of Social Security legislation, supplemented by other business and governmental retirement systems and by increased insurance, few older persons are supported by their children. Thus, in a single generation, the value placed on filial duty has declined dramatically (Chapter 22). *Instrumental* values are pragmatic. They become attached to behavior patterns that are efficient in achieving valued ends. When they are no longer efficient, the value disappears.

By contrast, some conditions or relationships apparently are always valued. Such *intrinsic* values include life itself, health, autonomy or freedom of action, and close relationships. There is considerable debate on whether some family-related behavior, such as premarital sexual intercourse, is intrinsically negatively valued (that is, wrong in itself) or instrumentally negatively valued (wrong because it produces illegitimate children and forced marriages). These concepts are explored in more detail in the final chapter of this book.

Institutions and Groups

It has been said repeatedly that all men are different and as frequently that people everywhere are alike. The same is true with respect to families. No two are quite alike in values, goals, and the relationships that family members have to each other; yet families have much in common, and it would be unlikely that one would mistake a family for some other group, such as a political party.

Each individual family is a group, in sociological terminology. It brings together two or more adults in marriage, each of whom has a unique personality with a somewhat different cluster of values, role perceptions, and abilities. Although most families perform the same functions, it is not surprising that each family is unique in somewhat the same sense that each personality is unique.

The elements that permit one to identify family groups readily in terms of their composition and behavior are termed the *institution* of the family. Although these elements are rather numerous, a few are of central importance. Probably the most obvious are the *positions* in the family, such as husband, father, wife, mother, sons, and daughters. Each of these has a set of duties that are culturally defined. For example, if one says "father," the mind produces an image of a male adult who works to provide for his family and who disciplines his children. The behaviors expected of a father are called *roles.* These roles are normatively defined; that is, there is essential consensus within a society or a subunit of it that these tasks *should* be performed by individuals who are fathers. One could add that there are certain *values* that a father should hold, such as, it is better to be employed than unemployed. Relevant to the concept of institution is the provision of *sanctions* to induce individuals who occupy the positions in the institution to enact their roles appropriately. Thus, institution is a highly abstract concept that communicates the common elements of family behavior without reference to any one family group.

The institution of the family is part of the culture of a society. It is passed from generation to generation by the relevant socializing agents: parents, older siblings, other kin, and, in differentiated societies, teachers and religious functionaries. All or almost all members of a given society have the institution of the family presented in similar outline. For example, in American society it is generally understood that people marry late in adolescence or in adulthood, that couples go through a ceremony, and that the marriage is registered. They understand that husbands are providers, that wives are housekeepers, and that sexual intercourse is part of marriage. However, this framework becomes blurred with respect to the details of role-playing. There is no unanimity, for example, in the strategies of disciplining children or the frequency with which family members engage in recreation. It may be said that these areas of behavior are *not* institutionalized.

FAMILY DEFINED It has been said that sociologists can make any phenomenon appear complicated, and it might seem that defining *family* is a case in point.[12] We favor a broad definition, such as the following: two or more people related by bonds of marriage or blood who customarily maintain a common residence. This is broad enough to cover the *extended* family that includes relatives besides the parents and their own children, polygynous and polyandrous marriages, and partial families of one parent with minor children. There might be some argument whether it would include common-law marriages or partial families composed of a mother and an illegitimate child. The partial family qualifies because mother and child are related by blood. The common-law couple seems to fit the definition also because the open maintenance of a common residence by a couple eligible to marry is recognized by law in many jurisdictions as marriage.

---

[12]For a discussion of the difficulty of defining the family, see William N. Stephens, *The Family in Cross-Cultural Perspective* (New York: Holt, Rinehart and Winston, 1963), Chapter 1, "Is the Family Universal?", pp. 1–32.

The familiar family type, consisting only of parents and dependent children, is called the *nuclear* family. It and *partial* families, usually consisting of a mother and her children, are family types common to almost all societies. A variation of the nuclear family is the childless family, but whether the couple is childless during their whole lives or only for a period before children are born and after they have left home, the couple is, in our thinking, a family (Chapter 2).

Family Subcultures

Within any industrial society or in one characterized by the recent immigration of large numbers of families socialized in another culture, one may expect to find major variations in the norms describing familial roles. Ordinarily, one subculture has a dominant position in the society, and the norms of this segment are identified as those of the society from which those of the other subcultures vary in one way or another. Thus, in contemporary American society, the Protestant, middle-class, white segments are dominant and the norms of this group usually are thought of as the norms of the society. For example, divorce is recognized in American society as a legitimate arrangement for ending nonfunctionining marriages but it is not so accepted by the Catholic Church, which views marriage as an indissolvable contract. If one looks further at the Catholic religious subculture, he finds norms regarding birth control, and a distinctive set of norms dealing with the roles of husbands and wives. These will receive more detailed exploration in Chapter 3.

A subculture, then, is a distinctive complex of norms, values, and attitudes that characterize the patterned behavior, thinking, and feeling of an aggregate of people within a society. Such aggregates, however, subscribe in most respects to the norms, values, and attitudes of the other major social segments of society. For example, in matters of dress, Catholics do not differ from Protestants, Jews, or Mormons. Their subculture is based on religious matters in which dress is not a matter of religious import except for nuns and priests. However, in some religious subcultures, dress does possess religious significance, for example, the long, plain dresses of the Amish women.

Subcultures may add a set of norms and values to those held by the dominant segment of the society or it may reject a set that are held by most of the society. For example, long, plain dresses are obligatory for the Amish women, whereas they are permitted but not required for other women in the society. Although an education at least through high school carries a high value in American society in general, it possesses no value for the Amish, or rather it carries a negative value,

17

as tending to undermine their religious teachings. Occasionally, a subculture comes into direct conflict with the societal culture, as occurred when the Amish group refused to provide the educational facilities for their children required by state law.[13] In instances of such direct conflict, in which the subculture is called a *contraculture,* the society usually insists on modification of the subculture to eliminate the direct conflict; for example, the Mormon Church had to change its position on polygyny before Utah could be admitted as a state.

There are, then, two principal ways in which a subculture differs from the general culture: it can add normative requirements for its members that are permitted by members of the society as a whole, or it can place little or no value on objects or behavior that are highly valued by the general society. Finally, it can place relatively more or less value on certain elements of culture than is characteristic of the society. We shall see later that lower-class families as a category place a lower value on college education for their children than do middle-class families. This does not mean that they reject higher education, placing a negative value on it, but they are less likely to emphasize it in their plans for their children. You will note later the very much higher illegitimacy rates among Negroes than among Caucasians. It is not that there is a positive value placed on illegitimacy, but that its negative value is higher among whites than among blacks. Some of the reasons for this subcultural difference in illegitimacy values will be explored in Chapter 3.

We know, then, that American families have many similarities stemming from a common culture. The student has also observed some differences among individual families say, those of his nearest neighbors at home.[14] To these observations he must add a somewhat more difficult observation: if he views the families of a subcultural aggregate say, middle-class families, or Negro families, he will see more similarities among them than he sees among a random selection of American families.

THE IDENTIFICATION OF SUBCULTURES Sociologists have no complete list of distinctive American subcultures, but most would agree that there are several aggregates that have a sufficiently different complex of values and norms to warrant description. Among these are the social classes, which will be discussed in some depth. Others are based on major religious differences, such as the Protestant, Catholic, Jewish, and Mormon religions. Of these, the Protestant is considered the

[13]William M. Kephart, *The Family, Society, and the Individual,* 2nd ed. (Boston: Houghton Mifflin Company, 1966), p. 204.
[14]For an exploration of the notion that families develop their own subcultures, see F. Ivan Nye and Evelyn MacDougal, "Do Families Have Subcultures?" *Sociology and Social Research,* **44** (May/June 1960), pp. 311–316.

majority religion and therefore is not usually considered an aggregate possessing a subculture. However, the more distinctive fundamentalist Protestant sects to possess definite subcultures. The Negro population, because of its distinctive historical experience in slavery—one that still carries certain castelike status and results in a disproportionate percentage of the black population's being in the lower-lower class—is an aggregate that possesses a broad subculture. Large ethnic groups that have migrated to the United States in recent years, such as Italians, Greeks, and Mexicans, retain part of their original cultures. Remote rural areas give ample evidence of norms and values that differ markedly from those of the metropolis. Some sociologists perceive regional subcultures in the West, the South, the Midwest, and the East. For example, if one lives for a time in the West, then in the South, he can hardly fail to note a difference in the way most wives interact with their husbands or in the way girls are trained in preparation for adult roles. Finally, many, but not all, sociologists observe an adolescent subculture, in which in clothing, in speech, and possibly in values adolescents display modal behaviors and thinking that differ from those of the society as a whole.

To return for a moment to the meaning of *subculture,* we employ the term to describe a distinctive complex of modal behaviors and mental phenomena that are held by a minority aggregate of people within a society. To be more precise, the complex is composed of distinctive norms and values held by the minority aggregate—norms and values not embraced by the society as a whole.

Sociological Assumptions

We have discussed a number of sociological concepts that serve the sociologist in describing social phenomena. The fact that the sociologist employs these concepts sets him apart from other disciplines, such as, for example, psychology, which generally employs concepts internal to the organism. A further distinction in sociological outlook is provided by the *assumptions* that sociologists make about man, social relationships, and social institutions. For example, sociologists assume that *the newborn baby is asocial.* It is neither intrinsically good, in that it has a mechanism that directs it to be kind, merciful, or industrious, nor does its makeup include a cluster of vicious instincts impelling it to violence, deceit, or greed. Obviously, it is capable, after a period of learning, of acting either way, or one way on some occasions and another way on others. By contrast, the psychiatrists who draw heavily from Freud assume the original nature of the child to be antisocial and employ the concept of the id to describe it. The distinction is an

19

important one because if original nature is assumed to be asocial, then the society has a crucial task in the socialization of the child so that he becomes a productive and generally conforming member of the community. Social control, however, is also necessary because knowing what one should do rarely suffices to ensure that he will always, or even usually, act accordingly.

A second assumption of sociologists is that *personality is the product of social experience.* Not long ago, children were thought to inherit personality from their parents and other relatives. "She gets that temper from Aunt Agatha," or "that friendly disposition comes from her mother." Sociologists assume that a friendly disposition or any other personality characteristic emerges from learning from others and from the reactions that others have toward one.[15] This assumption carries the broadest implications for child-rearing. If personality characteristics and functioning are the product of social experience, this places a heavy responsibility on parents and on others who are in a position to influence the experiences of children.

Another assumption, completely accepted by sociologists, is that *specific social structure is relative to a given society.* The concept is called *cultural relativity.* For example, marriage to only one wife at a time is limited to a minority of societies. Or, another example, the custom of allowing the young to choose their own spouses is by no means universal. It should be emphasized that such cultural variability exists in specific behavior patterns rather than in the broader functions or activities of social life. All societies have families, socialize children within them, and so on, but *how* families socialize children may vary extremely from society to society and considerably among subcultures within a society.

Such cultural relativity does not mean that the behavior patterns of a society can be changed at will by individuals in society or that individuals can ignore those they find inconvenient. For example, the more permissive premarital sexual patterns in Sweden are accompanied by exacting laws for support by fathers of illegitimate children and for tax-subsidized housing and day-care centers for children. No major behavior pattern stands alone: each is part of a complex that ensures that crucial social functions will be performed and that the essential needs of the various categories of people, such as children and mothers in the last example, will be met.

Some young people, finding sexual restrictions inconvenient, argue that these can be ignored because some other societies are more permissive. Until a society creates provisions for effective contracep-

[15]Charles H. Cooley, *Human Nature and the Social Order* (New York: Charles Scribner's, Sons 1902).

tion among the unmarried and creates a secure place for those children conceived accidentally out of wedlock, society, through its various institutions, will continue to restrict such behavior. Sociologists, therefore, view the social world as *sets of interdependent behavior patterns within institutions* (the family, for example) *and between institutions.*

The list of sociological assumptions relevant to the family could be elaborated considerably but this discussion should be adequate to indicate the distinct perspective or *conceptual framework* of the sociologist. Additional examples of the family in other cultures are presented in Chapter 2.

Specialized Sociological Frameworks

Sociologists have much in common in the problems that they attack and in the concepts that they employ to describe the structure and functions of social behavior. However, as the sociology of the family has developed into a scientific specialty, a number of distinctive perspectives on the family have developed.

THE INSTITUTIONAL FRAMEWORK The first of these was the institutional approach, which describes what the family typically does and how it does it within a particular society. This approach introduces some order into thinking about the family because it enables the student to look beyond his own family (or his neighbors' families) to some generalization about what families have in common and why families exist. The institutional approach has also been called the historical approach because early family scholars looked backward to see how family functions had been performed in earlier days. An example of such analysis was provided by Zimmerman in describing, in turn, Greek, Roman, and early Western family life. Zimmerman also related these families to some other characteristics of the society, especially to its power and influence on the world scene.[16] This approach to the family treats it as just another institution. One could ask as well: What functions do universities perform and how do they perform those functions, or the church, or government? Also, one could ask how families differ today from one hundred years ago, as one asks how government or education has changed during that period. Although such questions are of considerable interest to professors, they often fail to grip college students because this approach doesn't say a great deal about how individuals act, feel, and make decisions, nor does it cast much light on nonnormative behavior, such as sexual

---

[16]Carle C. Zimmerman, *Family and Civilization* (New York: Harper & Row, 1947).

experience other than in marriage. For a detailed description of this conceptual framework, the reader is referred to Koenig and Bayer.[17]

THE INTERACTIONAL FRAMEWORK The interactional framework developed later, perhaps partially in response to inadequacies in the institutional approach. Burgess is credited with the formal initiation of this approach in family sociology because, in 1926, he referred to the family as a unity of interacting personalities.[18] The research and theorizing that has developed from Burgess's formulation has centered on the behavior, the attitudes, and the values of the individuals within particular families. His formulation enabled researchers to ask such questions as in what proportion of marriages wives are dissatisfied with their marriages or in which social class marital dissatisfaction is most prevelant. Within the formulation, researchers have asked how individuals play familial roles and how they think and feel about what they or other members of the family do. At one time it was felt that the institution of the family was dissolving and being replaced by improvised patterns of interaction between spouses and between parents and children. One leading text carried a subtitle: *From Institution to Companionship.*[19]

It is now recognized that the institution of the family is not dissolving, but changing rather rapidly in its functions, roles, and values.[20] However, the interactionist framework enables the researcher and the student to look inside the family to see more specifically how men, women, and children are playing their family roles, how frequent is the deviation from the norms of family behavior, and so on. In a real sense, the interactional framework is complementary to the institutional and the structure-functional (to be discussed later) frameworks, which emphasize the overall functioning of the family and its interaction with other institutions. For a detailed discussion of the interactional framework, the reader is referred to Schvaneveldt.[21]

THE SITUATIONAL APPROACH Like the interactional framework, the situational approach was developed to analyze the actual behavior of families. It differs from the interactional approach, however, in that it

---

[17]Daniel J. Koenig and Alan E. Bayer, "The Institutional Frame of Reference," in *Emerging Conceptual Frameworks in Family Analysis,* ed. by F. Ivan Nye and Felix M. Berardo (New York: The Macmillan Company, 1966), pp. 78–96.

[18] Ernest W. Burgess, "The Family as a Unity of Interacting Personalities," *The Family,* 7 (Mar. 1926), pp. 3–9.

[19]Ernest W. Burgess and Harvey J. Locke, *The Family, from Institution to Companionship* (New York: American Book Company, 1945).

[20]Clark E. Vincent, "Family Spongia: The Adaptive Function," *Journal of Marriage and the Family,* 28 (Feb. 1967), pp. 29–36.

[21]Jay C. Schvaneveldt, "The Interactional Framework for Studying the Family," in *Emerging Conceptual Frameworks in Family Analysis,* ed. by F. Ivan Nye and Felix M. Berardo (New York: The Macmillan Company, 1966), pp. 97–129.

tries to deal with all the social facts that bear on a given individual's actions at a given time. For example, if an unmarried girl decided to bear an illegitimate child, the situation could be studied with respect to the behavior or attitudes of parents, siblings, teachers, kin, and friends. This approach focuses on the interplay of individual forces in a family. Appropriately, Bossard and Boll, major exponents of this approach, developed the notion that individual families develop cultures, which influence and guide the individual acts of family members.[22] Rallings has recently delineated the framework in detail.[23]

STRUCTURE-FUNCTIONAL APPROACH The structure-functional approach is closely related to the institutional framework. Both study the family as an institution, but the structure-functional approach focuses on the interplay between institutions. For example, this approach attempts to explain the form that one institution takes—say, the *nuclear* family—by the type of economic institutions that are found in that society. For example, Parsons has contended that in a society in which men must be free to move with their jobs or to better jobs, it is necessary that the essential family unit be small—usually husband, wife, and children—so that it can move readily and follow the husband's job.[24]

McIntyre states the scope of functional analysis of the family in this way: "A functional analysis of the family emphasizes the relationship of the family and the larger society, the internal relationships between the subsystems of the family, and/or the relationship between the family and the personality of the individual member."[25] Although, in principle, this approach permits equal attention to transactions between the family and other institutions and interactions within the family, the former is the distinctive element of the approach.

THE DEVELOPMENTAL APPROACH The most recent addition to sociological perspective on the family is one based on time span. It views the family in its changing composition and roles from marriage to death. This long span has been divided into different numbers of stages by different scholars; however, all agree on a minimum of stages: the married couple without children, the couple with preschool children only, the family including school-age children, the couple with no children left at home (sometimes termed *postparental*), and finally the widow or widower following the death of one spouse.

---

[22]James H. S. Bossard and Eleanor S. Boll, *Family Situations* (Philadelphia: University of Pennsylvania Press, 1943), pp. 51, 101.

[23]E. M. Rallings, "The Situational Approach," in Nye and Berardo, op. cit., pp. 130–151.

[24]Jennie McIntyre, "The Structure-Functional Approach to Family Study," in Nye and Berardo, op. cit., pp. 52–77.

[25]Ibid.

The family performs different functions relating to the presence and the age of children in the home. The roles of husband and wife obviously change as children are born, mature, and leave the home. Rodgers has termed these role changes a *role sequence*.[26] Essentially, this framework looks inward to the changes in the internal functioning of the family, but the participation of family members in school, in community organizations, and in recreational activities outside the home obviously shifts with the changes in the family life cycle.[27] This framework has been delineated by Rowe.[28]

Résumé

In this chapter we have presented some of the key concepts that family sociologists employ in describing the family and some assumptions that are distinctive to sociology. There is some overlap, of course, with both psychology and social anthropology. For the student who doesn't enjoy becoming familiar with concepts, permit us to remind him that it probably wasn't pleasant to memorize the multiplication tables, either, but they are useful. Actually, it is of little value just to memorize concepts and assumptions. Rather, the sociologist must understand the phenomena that they represent and must employ this understanding in his analysis of what families are and why they act as they do. True, we could discuss family behavior without concepts and ignore the content of assumptions, but the result is a chaos of facts and intuitive notions from which we must escape if knowledge is to be cumulative and if it is to be communicated systematically.

---

[26]Roy H. Rodgers, *Improvements in the Construction and Analysis of Family Life Categories,* Kalamazoo, Mich., Western Michigan University, 1962, unpublished Ph.D. dissertation.

[27]Ibid.

[28]George P. Rowe, "The Developmental Conceptual Framework to the Study of the Family" in Nye and Berardo, op. cit., pp. 198–223.

Part I

The Family: Cross-Cultural
and Subcultural Perspective

2

Cross-cultural Perspective: Family Structure

Although this text deals largely with family structure and processes as manifested in American society, it will prove worthwhile to precede detailed discussions of our own system by a cross-cultural perspective. An understanding of family life in this country can be considerably broadened by such a view. Like people in other cultures, Americans tend to be ethnocentric concerning their marital and familial arrangements. That is to say, they view such arrangements as natural and correct and, in many instances, the best for meeting their needs. We become so accustomed to our patterns of living that it is difficult for us to imagine existing under any other type of arrangement. We sometimes lose sight of the fact that there have been and continue to be many family forms and functions quite different from our own; that the family institution shows wide variation not only within our own society, but even greater variation from one society to another. Any scientific analysis of the family must take into account these variations and, hopefully, to explain them.

As Kenkel has observed, an intercultural study of the family can, in addition to providing us with more extensive knowledge, achieve several important objectives, including the following:[1]

1. *Develop an Appreciation of Family Diversities and Uniformities.* When we examine the family institution in other parts of the world, we come to recognize not only the degree to which it differs from our own, but also the variety of marriage and family practices that seem to work reasonably well for those societies in which they occur. Moreover, we discover that the people in these societies feel just as strongly as we do that their marriage and family forms are natural and correct. Thus,

---

[1]William F. Kenkel, *The Family in Perspective*, 2nd ed. (New York: Appleton-Century-Crofts, 1966), pp. 6–9.

27

although most Americans would abhor polygyny (indeed, our laws prohibit multiple spouses for either sex) and would reject this form of marriage outright, it is in fact a very widespread practice and in a majority of known societies it is the preferred form of marriage.[2] A study, then, of the norms and values and other aspects of those societies in which divergent marital and family forms are practiced may provide us with insight into the meaning those practices have for the people involved.

2. Develop a More Objective Point of View. It is axiomatic in the scientific community that in order to discover what is rather than what ought to be, the scientist must remain objective. In his attempt to achieve objectivity, he is expected to take a value-free stance with respect to the phenomena he is studying. This is often easier said than done. The scientist is a product of his own culture and consequently has incorporated a set of values that, unless he remains consciously aware of them, may interfere with his perceptions and conclusions. Thus, in the present context, he must learn to recognize that although he may value such things as premarital chastity, marital fidelity, spousal equality, a small number of children, and so on, others may adhere to a different set of values regarding such matters, depending on their socialization and the dominant norms of their culture.[3]

Like other scientists, the student of the family must be aware of those values and sentiments that may color his observations and bias his evaluations of other family forms and practices. A certain amount of scientific detachment is necessary to the required objectivity. As Kenkel has observed, "a greater degree of objectivity can be mustered in the study of temporally and spatially distant families than in the study of the family institution of one's own society."[4] That is to say, most of us are too intimately and emotionally involved in our own family system to view it with detachment and objectivity. Once we have learned to view family forms in distant cultures objectively, however, we may be able to approach our own patterns with a greater degree of objectivity. This is another value of cross-cultural perspective.

3. Develop Greater Sensitivity Toward the American Family. A cross-cultural perspective often sensitizes one to the idiosyncratic features of the family system in his own society. For example, as a student studies the mate selection process in other societies and compares them with his own, he may begin to recognize the unique-

---

[2]George P. Murdock, "World Ethnographic Sample," *American Anthropologist,* 59 (Aug. 1957), p. 686.

[3]For an extensive discussion of the role of values in family research see Harold T. Christensen, "The Intrusion of Values," in *Handbook of Marriage and the Family,* ed. by Harold T. Christensen (Chicago: Rand McNally & Co., 1964).

[4]Kenkel, op.cit., p. 7.

ness of our own dating and courtship customs. As he learns how in certain societies the pattern of arranged marriages fits in with other family patterns he begins to see how our system of independent mate selection is congruent with our emphasis on the autonomous nuclear family.

The cross-cultural perspective brings our customs surrounding marriage and the family into sharper focus as we see them contrasted with those found in other societies. In the process our customs take on new meaning for us.

4. Develop Hypotheses About Marriage and the Family. As one examines the patterns of familial behavior among a variety of cultures he begins to compare them with those that exist in his own society. In this process of comparative analysis, he often begins to develop hypotheses concerning the differences and similarities that he observes. For example, he may notice that in those societies with a large family system fathers tend to be authoritarian, whereas in those societies where the small family system predominates the father tends to be more equalitarian or democratic. This might suggest several hypotheses to him that might help explain the finding. These hypotheses may lead him to see some important links between certain patterns of family behavior, the marriage system, and other aspects of society. "Whether these hypotheses prove to be original or commonplace, testable or untestable, is not nearly so important as the fact that scientific curiosity about the family has been stimulated and an attempt has been made to channel it."[5]

In sum, it is hoped that a cross-cultural perspective will make the student a more perceptive analyst of the family institution. Also, he may come to appreciate the fact that despite the variability between cultures, there are some rather remarkable regularities, or what Stephens refers to as *quasi-universals*—that is, certain family practices that are found almost everywhere.[6] Among these are incest taboos, menstrual sex taboos, social disapproval of illegitimacy, the expectation that marriage will not be entered into for only a short period of time, the recognition of kinship ties beyond the nuclear family, and women assigned the main tasks of housekeeping and men with tasks associated with the provider role.

In addition to the near-universal single cultural traits such as those just mentioned, one also can find near-universal patterned regularities. That is to say, certain customs combine so that if one practice occurs a number of other related practices will also generally occur. Stephens found, for example, throughout aboriginal North America, South

[5]Ibid., p. 8.
[6]William N. Stephens, *The Family in Cross-Cultural Perspective* (New York: Holt, Rinehart and Winston, 1963), pp. 401.

America, Oceania, Asia, and Africa, that if a menstruating woman was required by custom to remain in a menstrual hut, then she also was not allowed to cook for her husband, or to have sexual intercourse, and was restricted by many other rules associated with this menstrual taboo.[7]

Knowledge of such quasi-universal and near-universal patterning of regularities provides us with important insights into man's basic biological and psychological needs and the variable conditions under which given family structures have evolved to meet those needs.

Marriage and Family Systems

Although social scientists have learned a great deal about various facets of family structure and organization, they do encounter difficulties in developing broad, culture-free generalizations about the family institution—generalizations that would be applicable to a wide range of societies. One major difficulty derives from problems of definition associated with the concept of "family" itself. The important question—What constitutes a family?—is not as easily answered as one might suspect. As Murdock notes, "Used alone, the term 'family' is ambiguous. The laymen and even the social scientist often apply it indiscriminatingly to several social groups which, despite functional similarities, exhibit important points of difference. These must be laid bare by analysis before the term can be used in rigorous scientific discourse."[8] An understanding of these points of difference will prove useful when we later attempt to answer another important and related question, namely: Is the family universal? It is often claimed that the "family" is the primary or basic institution of any society; that without the family human society as we know it could not exist; and, therefore, that the family is to be found everywhere—that is, it is universal. Let us take up the task of definition first and then attempt to deal with the issue of universality, for, as we shall see, whether the family is universal or not depends on how the term *family* is defined.

Types of Family Structure

What is a family? Most of us think we know what a family is. But when we set out to define the term clearly and distinguish the family from the nonfamily, we run into problems immediately. This is true not only on a cross-cultural basis but even in our society. A recent

---

[7]Ibid., p. 404.

[8]George P. Murdock, *Social Structure* (New York: The Macmillan Company, 1949), p. 1.

newspaper story captioned "Living Together But Not Related: Is It A Family?" illustrates some of these problems.[9]

It seems that fifteen senior citizens in a Florida community decided to rent a twenty-seven-room mansion, with ten baths and three acres of grounds so that they could create a commune. They formed a legal association called the Share-A-Home Association, and hired a younger couple and their six daughters as servants. The servants also lived in the mansion, as well as three grandchildren, and were paid a salary by the association. The idea was to establish a home where the members could live with freedom, independence, and security, while continuing to manage their own lives with dignity.

Subsequently, a complaint was filed against them, charging a violation of zoning regulations, which defined the area as a single-family neighborhood. It was contended in a suit by the county that the association was really a boardinghouse and therefore should not be permitted in a single-family neighborhood. The association contended it met the definition of a family, contained in the zoning code, as a "single housekeeping unit," and its supporters argued that the oldsters simply wanted to be left alone to function as a family. Each member contributed to the household budget according to his means. Their lawyer argued that there was ample historical basis for regarding the commune as a family unit, stemming back to biblical times. Moreover, he contended that since the zoning laws considered a family to be a group of people living under one roof with their servants, the association must be considered a family.

The county finally agreed to let the presiding judge in the case decide whether in fact the association was a family. The judge visited and talked with the members of the association, was impressed by their cooperative spirit, as well as the happy and warm atmosphere he encountered, and ruled that the association was indeed a family.

It is important to note that this judge's subjective evaluation would be considered technically erroneous by many scholars and laymen who deal with the family. For example, our Census Bureau, which is very much interested in the numbers and types of families in the nation, as well as their living arrangements, might have come to a different conclusion . . . or would it? A census taker arriving at the mansion would attempt to apply a standard set of technical criteria, including the following:[10] (1) *Household*—all persons who occupy a housing unit, i.e., a house, an apartment or any other group of rooms, or a room

[9]Don North, "Living Together but Not Related: Is It a Family?" *St. Petersburg Times* (July 26, 1971), pp. 1B and 3B.
[10]These are somewhat abbreviated versions of the standard census definitions. More complete definitions can be found in any one of numerous publications issued by the Bureau of the Census, U.S. Department of Commerce, Washington, D.C.

that constitutes separate living quarters, i.e., quarters in which the occupants do not live and eat with any other persons in the structure and which quarters have either (a) direct access from the outside of the building or through a common hall, or (b) complete kitchen facilities for the exclusive use of the occupants. A household includes the head of the household, others in the housing unit related to the head, and also the unrelated persons who regularly live in the house. A person living alone or a group of unrelated persons sharing the same housing unit as partners are also counted as a household. (2) *Unrelated individuals*—persons who are not living with any relatives. A *primary individual* is a household head living alone or with persons all of whom are unrelated to him. A *secondary individual* is a person in a household who is not related to the head or to any other person in the household. (3) *Married couple*—a husband and wife living together, with or without children and other relatives. (4) *Family*—a group of two or more persons related by blood, marriage, or adoption and residing together. A *primary family* consists of the head of a household and all other persons in the household related to the head. A *secondary family* comprises two or more persons living in a household and related to each other. (5) *Subfamily*—a married couple with or without children, or one parent with one or more children under eighteen years old, living in a household and related to, but not including, the head of the household or his wife. Members of a subfamily are also members of the primary family with whom they live.

Given the above categories, how would the census taker classify the Share-A-Home Association? Certainly it is a household, which may consist of a single family, one person living alone, two or more families living together, or any other group of related or unrelated persons who share living arrangements. Is it a family and, if so, what kind? Is it the same type of family that the judge had in mind in arriving at his decision concerning the Share-A-Home Association?

These illustrations merely serve to indicate how the seemingly simple task of defining the family can quickly become a rather complicated matter. The point is that there are numerous ways to define this particular unit of social organization. Indeed, the cross-cultural evidence reveals that the number of possible family types and their variations is enormous depending on the classification scheme utilized.[11] Moreover, as we shall see in subsequent sections of this chapter, the variations in family structure and function are closely associated with and influenced by other structural features, including types of marital arrangements, residential rules, and principles of

---

[11]Meyer F. Nimkoff (ed.), *Comparative Family Systems* (Boston: Houghton Mifflin Company, 1965), Chapter 2, "Types of Family," pp. 12–32.

descent or lineage. In the following pages, we want to focus on some of the most common forms of the family present around the world, as well as some of the most significant variations from them that have been observed, so that we may perceive and understand our own marital and familial patterns more adequately.

The Nuclear Family

The smallest and most elementary type of family organization is the nuclear family, typically composed of a husband and a wife and their offspring. In a more technical sense, a nuclear family consists of at least two adults of the opposite sex living in a socially approved sexual relationship, along with one or more of their own or adopted children.[12] This type, of course, is familiar to Americans as our most predominant and basic residential family unit.

Cross-cultural evidence has led some anthropologists to contend that the nuclear family is, in fact, universal. A leading proponent of this view is Murdock, who, for example, after surveying 250 representative societies, concluded that: "Either as the sole prevailing form of the family or as the basic unit from which more complex familial forms are compounded, it exists as a distinct and strongly functional group in every known society."[13] He observed that even in those societies where it is embedded in some larger kinship group, as in polygamous or extended family systems, the nuclear family unit is recognized by other members and the community as a distinct entity, and one that usually occupies spatially separate living quarters.

FUNCTIONS OF THE NUCLEAR FAMILY In attempting to explain this apparent universality of the nuclear family, Murdock proposed that it always and everywhere fulfilled four essential functions necessary to the continuation of any human society. These four functions center around sexual relations, economic cooperation, reproduction, and socialization.[14]

1. Sexual Relations. Sex is a powerful drive with an ever-present potential for disrupting the cooperative relationships necessary to the maintenance of the family and the society. Consequently, all known societies place various restrictions on sexual expression. Through the marital relationship the nuclear family affords sexual privileges to the husband and wife and thereby serves to meet this basic need. Within the family context, sexual gratification tends to solidify the marital bond and at the same time bind the couple into a broader web of family relationships and responsibilities.

[12]Murdock, *Social Structure,* op. cit., p. 1.
[13]Ibid., p. 2.
[14]We draw here from Murdock, ibid., pp. 4–11.

33

It would be erroneous, however, to conclude that sex is the only or even the most important factor for explaining the existence of marriage. In our own society, where the formal sex code prohibits and penalizes nonmarital sexual intercourse, such an assumption might appear to be true. But on a cross-cultural basis, this assumption simply does not hold up. In many of the societies surveyed by Murdock, unmarried and unrelated persons were allowed complete sexual freedom and yet most persons in these societies eventually married. Moreover, in many of these societies extramarital sexual affairs were permitted. Thus, one cannot even assume that after marriage sex operates exclusively to reinforce and maintain the stability of the marital relationship. This in no way denies that sex is an important aspect of marriage. But it does suggest that one has to look for other factors to explain the maintenance of the marital relationship within the nuclear family.

2. Economic Cooperation. The bond established by the marital sexual relationship is further cemented within the nuclear family by economic cooperation between the husband and the wife. Every known human society has developed economic specialization and cooperation between the sexes. This cooperation stems in part from biological differences between males and females and is further patterned according to various culturally learned definitions of what constitutes an appropriate division of labor. Because men are usually physically more powerful they *generally* are assigned the heavier and more strenuous tasks. Women, burdened by the demands of child-bearing, are generally assigned to lighter household tasks and child-rearing activities. The economic services provided by the husband and wife compliment one another, allow them to function more efficiently in their roles, and thereby serve to reinforce the marital relationship.

Economic cooperation not only binds the husband and wife tightly together; it also strengthens the parent-child and sibling relationships within the nuclear family. All human societies tend to segregate economic activities according to age as well as sex. In some societies the economic contribution of young children may be rather minimal and confined to rather light chores around the home, whereas in others their contribution may be extensive. In either event the relationship in the nuclear family is reciprocal. As the child moves from a state of dependency, in which the parents provide for the gratification of most of his needs, toward increasing maturity, he takes on additional tasks and makes greater economic contributions. For example, he may assist in the care and support of younger siblings. Often as the parents grow old they are forced to become dependent and their adult children assume the position of providing care and economic assistance. It is this reciprocal economic aid and material service among the members that helps to account for the universality of the nuclear family.

3. Reproduction. All societies place a heavy emphasis on the reproductive function of the nuclear family. The married couple is expected to produce children and to provide for their nourishment and care. Parents who refuse to perform this function adequately are subject to severe social sanction. Thus, such practices as abortion, infanticide, and neglect are generally kept within certain limits, lest they become a serious threat to the entire community. In some societies, children are so highly valued that the husband is not permitted sexual access to his wife until she has previously established her ability to produce children.[15] In others the husband is allowed to dissolve the marriage when the wife proves to be barren. While the major burdens of child care generally fall on the mother, the father and the other children in the family are expected to share in the tasks associated with the physical care of the young. Thus, the reproductive function further strengthens the bonds of the nuclear unit.

4. Socialization. Closely related to the physical care of the young child is his social learning. In all societies the nuclear family is expected to assume the basic responsibility for the socialization of its children in order that they may eventually be able to function adequately in adult roles. The socialization and education of young children is a demanding and complex process, and it typically requires the collaborative efforts of the parents and the older siblings. Here the father is called upon to play a more active role than is the case for physical care, and a more equal distribution of responsibility between him and the wife becomes necessary. Only the father can convey the knowledge and skills necessary for the assumption of adult male roles. Similarly, the mother can best transmit the training that will prepare her daughter to assume adult female roles. Many aspects of the socialization process will require the combined efforts of both parents, and this shared activity serves to unify family relationships further. While many external agencies or groups may assist in the socialization process, particularly in modern industrial societies, the nuclear family everywhere plays a central role.

In a subsequent section of this chapter, we will again take up this discussion of the nuclear family, because the notion that it is universal and everywhere performs the four essential functions outlined has generated considerable controversy among scholars of the family. At this point, however, we want to turn to other forms of the family that have been found to exist both historically and in the modern world.

---

[15]Ibid., p. 5, cites the Banaro of New Guinea as a people who followed such a custom. He also notes that certain peasant communities in Eastern Europe were reported to allow a father to arrange the marriage of his immature son with an adult woman, with whom the father lived and raised children until the son was old enough to assume his marital rights.

35

Composite Forms of the Family

In the majority of human societies nuclear family units do not stand alone as isolated and independent entities in the community. Rather, they are combined into larger aggregates, or what Murdock termed *composite families.* These composite family types are established either through some system of plural marriages involving multiple spouses or by various extensions of the parent-child relationship. Plural marriages lead to the formation of a *polygamous family,* composed of two or more nuclear families linked together by a common parent. When the nuclear family of a married adult is joined with that of his parents they form an *extended family,* comprised of two or more nuclear families related by consanguineous (blood) kinship ties. Numerous variations of these two basic types of composite families are possible.

POLYGAMOUS FAMILY FORMS In the United States strictly enforced *monogamous union* (the marriage of only one male to only one female) forms the basis of our family system. There are, however, other types of marital arrangements that allow plural spouses and produce a polygamous family system. In some instances we find one husband with two or more wives, that is, *polygyny.* In other cases, the reverse occurs and we find one wife with two or more husbands, and this is termed *polyandry.* Finally, it is possible to have *group marriage,* involving a union between two or more husbands with two or more wives. We shall have little to say about the last two types of marital arrangements. Although group marriage is a theoretical possibility, there is considerable doubt that it ever existed as a societal norm.[16] Polyandry is extremely rare; anthropologists have recorded a total of only four of the world's societies practicing this type of marital arrangement.

The frequency with which each of the above marital types occurs cross-culturally helps to provide some insight into the sexual and the economic as well as the ideological facets of human social organization. Murdock's analysis of a carefully selected sample of 565 of the world's societies revealed that roughly 75 per cent could be classified as favoring polygyny, whereas slightly less than 25 per cent preferred monogamy, and less than 1 per cent sanctioned polyandry. Not a single society in this extensive sample was found to practice group marriage.[17] It has been suggested that this widespread prevalence of polygyny over other marital forms lends support to the long-held thesis that males are generally governed by internal sexual drives and are disposed toward sexual variety much more than are females. Although such a thesis is debatable, nevertheless, if it is generally accepted as

[16]Murdock, *Social Structure, op. cit.,* p. 24.
[17]Murdock, "World Ethnographic Sample," op. cit., p. 686.

valid, then one could argue that monogamous marriages place greater restrictions and stress on men than they do on women.[18]

The cross-cultural evidence clearly shows that among the world's societies, especially those that are preliterate, some form of polygyny is the *preferred* type of marital arrangement. However, the same evidence also indicates that the majority of marital unions in these polygynous societies are actually monogamous! To understand this disparity it is necessary to distinguish between a society's ideal or normative expectations and its actual practices. Most persons in polygynous societies do in fact prefer a polygynous marriage and, if given the means and the opportunity, would elect to enter what they consider to be the most prestigious marital arrangement. In some societies, of course, the privilege of assuming plural wives is reserved to a small segment of persons of high status or to members of ruling families. Consequently, most marriages in such societies are monogamous. But even in those instances in which such restrictions are absent, the majority of the population remains monogamous. Thus, although a society may be labeled polygynous in terms of its preferences, in practice monogamy may and indeed usually does prevail. How does one explain this disparity between the ideal and the real? At least two major reasons have been advanced, one having to do with biology and the other with economics.[19]

1. Sex Ratio as a Limiting Factor. Under ordinary circumstances the natural sex ratio, technically defined as the number of men per one hundred women, tends to approximate one hundred in most societies. Theoretically, this condition of a nearly balanced sex ratio affords most adult members of the society the possibility of securing a marital partner. However, when a man is allowed to take on a second wife, this means that some other man will be denied the opportunity to secure a spouse. Only by creating an unbalanced sex ratio, that is, reducing the number of males, would it be possible for the majority of the men in any one society to have multiple wives. Because an unbalanced sex ratio is rarely a permanent characteristic of any society, this possibility seldom materializes. The result is that although a substantial proportion of the world's societies value polygyny, most of the members of these societies are forced to practice monogamy.

2. Economics as a Limiting Factor. A second and perhaps more obvious reason why the majority of persons in a polygynous society remain monogamous is that most men simply do not have the economic resources required to support additional wives and children. Even in those societies in which polygyny is most pronounced it is principally

---

[18]Nimkoff, op. cit., p. 17.
[19]Murdock, *Social Structure*, op. cit., pp. 27–28.

the older men, who have lived long enough to acquire capital, who are found to have multiple wives. The younger men must content themselves with a single spouse or none at all. Indeed, despite our high standard of living, most American husbands would find it economically impossible to assume additional wives, even if permitted to do so. Thus, although polygyny may be an ideal or normative expectation in a society, this marriage form will remain unattainable for most men in that society, and will be confined to the wealthy or those with the greatest power and prestige.

In any system of plural marriages jealousy, especially sexual jealousy, between co-wives or co-husbands, is always a potential source of difficulty. Compared to polygynous societies, jealousy between co-husbands in polyandrous societies seems to be minimal, although it is not exactly clear why this should be the case. One reason suggested is that in polyandrous societies the man generally has some freedom of choice as to whether he will become a co-husband, whereas in polygynous societies women generally have little or no choice in the matter.[20] In any event, the cultural norms in *both* types of societies discourage the public expression of jealousy.

In addition to public censure, there are several cultural patterns that serve to minimize the jealousy potential in polygamous societies by clearly defining the relative status as well as the marital rights and obligations of the co-spouses. In both polygynous and polyandrous families, there normally is a senior or head wife or husband with special power and privileges who dominates the other co-spouses and supervises their activities. Among many polygynous societies a common pattern is for the first wife to assume a superior social status in relation to all subsequent wives and to have a certain amount of authority over them. Frequently co-wives are provided individual and separate dwellings to minimize friction. Another pattern that helps to allay jealousy is the requirement in many polygynous societies that the husband cohabit with each wife, in regular rotation, for a specified period of time. What is important here is not necessarily whether he likes or dislikes the wife whose turn has come around, or even that he have sexual intercourse with her. What matters is that he sleep in her dwelling during the period called for, thereby preventing public embarrassment, which she would certainly experience if he failed to show.[21] Finally, it should be noted that in polygynous families wives

[20]Stephens, op. cit., pp. 56–57.

[21]Murdock, *Social Structure,* op. cit., p. 30. It has been suggested that among the reasons for the failure of the Mormon experiment with polygyny in the United States was the inability to deal with the internal pressures created by husbands' showing sexual favoritism. A husband tended to cohabit with the most recent addition to his menage to the exclusion of his other wives. Because they all resided in the same household and were in close daily contact, status concerns and jealousy feelings generated by sexual favoritism often prevented Mormon polygyny from operating smoothly.

frequently are allowed to veto the husband's subsequent choices when they feel the woman under consideration is unacceptable. This, of course, will often result in a more congenial group of co-wives who will cooperate with a minimum of friction.

It is not unusual for adult males in American society to view the polygynous marital arrangement favorably, especially because it provides certain sexual advantages that are denied by our strictly monogamous system. It can be argued, however, that polygyny is not necessarily more advantageous than other types of arrangements. As Linton has observed:

Although they may allow somewhat more leeway for the satisfaction of the male's roving sexual interests, the man who will bring a new wife into the family in the face of his established wife's opposition must possess reckless courage. No matter what the public patterns of family life may be, the private patterns seem to be much the same in all societies; most wives know how to reduce their husbands to submission. The husband of several wives inevitably finds himself caught on the horns of a dilemma. Either his wives cannot agree or they agree too well. In the first case he is subjected to multiple, conflicting pressures which leave him no peace. In the second, the wives and children tend to form a closed group from which he is largely excluded.[22]

It is mainly through strict adherence to the cultural norms and expectations that govern the behavior of husbands and wives that such dilemmas are generally prevented from becoming openly manifest or from creating overt family conflict.

Despite the potential for jealousy and conflict, then, patterns of plural marriages appear to operate rather smoothly in those groups that are accustomed to them. Through a combination of early conditioning and rewards, members of both sexes come to view polygamy as normative. Children reared by multiple parents experience a wider range of opportunities for the satisfaction of their emotional and physiological needs than is the case in our own society. An exclusive and intense emotional attachment to one mother and one father, which is characteristic of our monogamous nuclear family system, is less apt to occur. Rather, children reared in a polygamous family system experience a diffuseness of dependency feelings and emotional attachments with respect to several adults. This means that the emotional affect toward any one parent is not very high. As a result of this early socialization experience the children reach adulthood prepared to accept and share a spouse with others.

Finally, polygamous societies generally reward spouses for suppressing jealousies and cooperating with one another. Where plural mar-

[22]Ralph Linton, "The Natural History of the Family," in *The Family: Its Function and Destiny*, rev. ed., ed. by Ruth N. Anshen (New York: Harper & Row, 1959), p. 43.

riage symbolizes economic success and high social status, as is the case in many polygynous societies, wives will frequently encourage their husbands to take on additional wives even when the husbands may not be particularly inclined to do so. In such instances, multiple wives not only raise the status of each co-wife in the family but also reduce the work load of each wife and lessen the demands made upon her time and energies.

It is sometimes suggested that polygamous marriage forms ought to be legitimized in American society. Such legitimization would require rather dramatic changes in our public mores and equally significant shifts in the personal norms and values that guide heterosexual relationships. However, changes in the basic organization of marriage and family structures ordinarily occur in very small increments and over a very extended period of time, during which traditional habits and attitudes are slowly modified. There is little evidence at the moment that such changes are likely to occur on a widespread basis in the United States in the immediate future. Given the current socialization processes that most Americans undergo, few of us are socially or psychologically prepared to participate in a polygamous family form.[23] Thus, the probability is very high that even if the polygamous family form were permitted or condoned, most Americans, as well as western Europeans, would choose to continue the monogamous pattern for many generations to come.[24]

EXTENDED FAMILY FORMS It will be recalled that a second method by which composite family forms are established is through various extensions of the parent-child relationship. Extended families are composed of two or more nuclear families related by blood. It is important to note that when the greatest emphasis is on *blood* ties the family systems are quite different from those in which *marital* ties are given the highest priority. In some societies, such as our own, the major stress is on the marital relationship; it takes precedence over all other familial bonds. Thus, in the United States newlyweds generally follow a *neolocal* residential pattern by moving from their respective parental homes to establish their own households as a separate and autonomous or independent nuclear family unit. Their primary loyalties and obligations are to each other and to their dependent children. This is known as a *conjugal family system.* Conjugal family systems, which normally include only two generations, are highly transitory in nature, because they generally dissolve when the parents die or when the

---

[23]See, for example, Gerhard Neubeck, "Polyandry and Polygyny: Viable Today?" in *The Family in Search of a Future,* ed. by Herbert A. Otto (New York: Appleton-Century-Crofts, 1970), pp. 99–109.

[24]Linton, op. cit., pp. 43–45.

offspring leave home. Given these characteristics, and the fact that member units are not intimately embedded in any larger family aggregate, conjugal families are not the most efficient structures for maintaining family traditions, nor do they provide the best mechanism for accumulating family property that can be kept intact and passed on *in toto* from one generation to the next.[25]

In contrast to conjugal family systems, *extended* family systems emphasize blood ties over marital bonds. When marriage occurs in a society where the most common type of extended family prevails, one spouse retains residence in the parental home and is joined there by the other spouse. The residential pattern may be *patrilocal*, in which case the wife settles with or near the parents of the husband, or it may be *matrilocal*, in which case the husband lives with or near the parents and kin of the wife. Under either residence rule, married couples and their children become intimately embedded in a larger corporate kin group commonly involving three or more generations of blood relatives.[26] This is known as a *consanguine* family system and it has several advantages.

One advantage of the consanguineous family system is that it ensures continuity over generations by linking parental families with new families of procreation. Moreover, compared to the conjugal family the extended family is a more effective structure for maintaining family traditions and for transmitting family holdings intact from one generation to the next. Children in the extended family are exposed to a large network of kin relationships. Other kin are immediately available who can assist the parents in the socialization tasks and who act as models for a variety of adult role behaviors. In times of crisis, such as the death of a parent, other kin are able to substitute in meeting the physical and emotional needs of the young. In many ways the extended family structure offers a sense of security not easily obtained in our own small nuclear family system. The larger family setting affords a psychological cushion against the shocks of crises and acts to promote marital and familial solidarity.[27]

Although there are several variations of the extended family that have been observed among the world's societies, only two will be mentioned briefly here.[28] One variation is known as the *stem* family,

[25]Murdock, *Social Structure,* op. cit., pp. 32–33.

[26]A number of other patterns of residential clustering are possible and have been practiced among the world's societies. For a more detailed description of these "rules of residence" and their relationship to other aspects of family organization, see, Murdock, ibid., pp. 16–17.

[27]Robert O. Blood, "Kinship Interaction and Marital Solidarity," *Merrill-Palmer Quarterly,* **15** (Apr. 1969), pp. 171–184.

[28]For other examples, see Dorothy R. Blitsten, *The World of the Family* (New York: Random House, 1963).

ordinarily comprised of two families in adjacent generations who are related by blood and who by custom share a common residence. An interesting example of the stem type of family is found among the rural Irish, where the pattern is for one of the married sons and his wife and children to reside in the same household as his parents. The typical Irish farm is of such small size that subdividing it among the several heirs is not feasible. Therefore, so that the estate may be kept intact, it is passed on to only one of the adult sons. The father has the authority to decide when and to which son he will turn over the ownership and management of the farm. Usually, though not always, he selects the eldest son, who, upon marriage, moves into the parental home with his wife. The remaining sons are provided with some sort of cash settlement to compensate for their share of the land, whereupon they migrate elsewhere to make a life of their own. Eventually, the eldest married son will similarly relinquish control to one of his adult married sons, so that the cycle constantly perpetuates itself. Stem family organization is thus based upon both blood ties and economic considerations, and serves as a device for keeping the family estate intact from one generation to the next.[29]

A more widely known variant of the extended family pattern is the traditional Hindu *joint* family of India. Here the consanguineous unit consists of the adult brothers and their wives and children residing together in the same household. The Hindu joint family represents a *patriarchal* family system, that is, one in which power and authority are vested in the father or other males. Unlike the Irish stem family, the Indian joint family pools its resources, financial and otherwise. It "has common residence, common property, common worship, common kitchen and a system of mutual obligations between the different units of the family."[30] The composition of this joint family actually shifts as it passes through several phases of the life cycle. Initially, the parental home becomes expanded as the sons marry and add their wives and children to the household. When the parents die, the brothers continue to maintain the extended household, living together with their individual families and siblings. When the siblings have been educated and married, then the joint household is broken up. The property is divided among the brothers and each proceeds to establish a separate household. At this stage they resemble the nuclear family structure characteristic of Western society. Eventually, however, the sons in these nuclear units marry and the joint family pattern is brought into existence once again.

The Hindu joint family represents a system of corporate living and

[29]Alexander J. Humphreys, "The Family in Ireland," in Nimkoff, op. cit., pp. 232–258.
[30]M. S. Gore, "The Traditional Indian Family," in Nimkoff, op. cit., p. 213.

mutual assistance that provides considerable social and emotional security for its members. Those who became sick or incapacitated can count on being supported by the rest of the kin group. The joint family orientation is an integral part of the larger system of values within Indian society. These values are strongly internalized, and even where the household has split up into individual nuclear units, brothers continue to accept the obligations to assist each other's families when the need arises.

Structural Features of American Kinship System

We have noted that from a cross-cultural perspective societies exhibit considerable variations in their kinship structures. It may be useful at this point to outline briefly the main structural features of our own kinship system for purposes of comparison (a more detailed discussion of kinship patterns in the United States is presented in Chapter 16).

At least ten characteristics that help identify our particular kinship system may be identified.[31] First, the incest taboo—which forbids marriage between certain relatives—is pervasive. The incest taboo, of course, is found in one form or another in nearly all societies know to man. In our society, members of the nuclear family are prohibited from marrying one another. In addition, the incest taboo against intermarriage between a person and his mother, father, or siblings is also extended to grandparents, uncles, aunts, nieces, and nephews. Moreover, in two thirds of our states laws exist that preclude intermarriage between first cousins. Second, in our society new family units may be established only through monogamous marriages, that is, the union of one man with one woman. Other forms of marriage, such as polygyny and polyandry, are not permitted. A third characteristic of our kinship system is that "no discrimination is made between paternal and maternal relatives for marriage purposes."[32] That is to say, individuals in American society are not required to choose a mate from kin associations of either the father or the mother. We have an extremely fluid and open mate-selection system (Chapters 5 and 6). Fourth, our descent system tends to be bilineal: theoretically no special preference is given to either the male or the female line. In other words, both the father's and the mother's lines of descent are recognized as equally important. The only exception to this is our patrilineal custom of tracing the family name through the male side of the family.

As Williams notes, these four conditions, which regulate family

---

[31]These are drawn from Robin M. Williams, *American Society: A Sociological Interpretation,* 3rd ed. (New York: Alfred A. Knopf, 1970), op. cit., pp. 56–59.

[32]Ibid., p. 56.

organization and descent, result in a highly dispersed system of intermarriage and kinship. They essentially produce a multilineal descent system. Because relatives can accrue from marriages outside the husband and wife's line, and because relatives from either side are considered equally important in the kinship system, it follows that "from any given individual the ancestral lines can fan out indefinitely in the past, so that any one of many lines of heredity may be emphasized for some purpose."[33] In a recent investigation of American kinship, Schneider comes to essentially the same conclusion, observing that:

One of the first things that anyone who works with American genealogies notices is that the system is quite clear as long as one takes Ego as the point of reference and does not venture far from there. As one goes out from Ego—in any direction—things get more and more fuzzy. This boundary fuzziness, or fadeout, is seen in a number of different ways. Most fundamental, of course, is the fact that there is no formal, clear, categorical limit to the range of kinsmen. Or, to put it another way, the decision as to whether a particular person is or is not to be counted as a relative is not given in any simple categorical sense. One cannot say that all second cousins are relatives, but all third cousins are not. An American can, if he wishes, count a third cousin as a kinsman while a second cousin is actually alive but unknown, or known to be alive but nevertheless not counted as a relative.[34]

A fifth important characteristic of the American kinship system is its primary emphasis on the immediate conjugal family—the husband, the wife, and their dependent children. In contrast to many historical and preliterate societies in which larger kin group ties are emphasized, in the United States the solidarity of the nuclear unit, especially the husband-wife bond, is heavily stressed. This is perhaps particularly the case among our contemporary, urban, middle-class families. As we will note again in Chapter 16, the comparatively low degree of kin solidarity in this country is partly a reflection of this nuclear family orientation. Closely related to the above is a sixth feature of our kinship system—namely, that the immediate family of parents and children tends to be *the* effective and autonomous unit for a wide range of residential, consumption, and social purposes. The nuclear family demands considerable independence in decisions regarding these activities, and it often strenuously resists any interference from other members of the kinship group concerning its autonomy in these matters. Indeed, our society views this independent stance of the

[33]Ibid.
[34]David M. Schneider, *American Kinship: A Cultural Account* (Englewood Cliffs, N.J.: Prentice-Hall, 1968), p. 67.

44

nuclear unit as desirable, correct, and proper. Except perhaps in the case of emergencies, American parents are expected to adopt a hands-off policy concerning the family life of their married children. In our society there are relatively few rights and duties that extended kin can consistently expect of each other or demand one another to observe.

As America made the rapid transition from an agrarian to a predominantly urban-industrial society, the family shifted from a productive to a consumptive unit, and this is a seventh characteristic of our kinship structure. In an earlier period, family and kin were often engaged in a common economic enterprise on family farms or in small shops and stores. With increasing urbanization and industrialization, production moved outside the home to the factories and corporations. Now family income is earned away from home by individual members, who are often employed in highly specialized occupations. The income earned by the nuclear unit is then utilized to meet the consumptive needs of its immediate members.

Because the nuclear family is the primary unit and the kinship system is multilineal, family tradition and family continuity receive relatively little emphasis in our society. This is an eighth characteristic of our kinship structure. The clearest exception to this general pattern is perhaps found among the upper-upper class in our society. Our wealthy "elite" families do appear to place much greater stress on lineage and collateral kinship than those in other classes.[35]

A ninth characteristic that dramatically affects the kinship structure of the United States is our comparatively free dating and mate selection system. Dating and mate selection in our society is carried on relatively independently of kinship controls. The choosing of a spouse is viewed as a personal matter on the part of the couple involved, and they resent interference by parents or other kin concerning this decision. Parents may still be asked to sanction the choice as a matter of courtesy, but such action is often viewed as merely perfunctory. Thus, not infrequently, American parents are not intimately acquainted with the partner their adult child has selected for a mate. (That our mate selection system is not as "free" or as open as one might suppose, however, will be amply demonstrated in Chapters 5 and 6.)

The tenth and final feature that can be identified as characterizing our kinship system is the widespread geographical dispersion of adult children from the parental household. Newly married couples in our society are expected to follow a neolocal pattern of residence, that is, to set up a separate household of their own following marriage. In

---

[35]Williams, op. cit., p. 58., does note, however, that evidence of attempts to maintain kinship linkage may be derived from research that shows that large proportions of children in our families are named after a particular relative.

45

addition, the social and spatial mobility associated with the pursuit of occupational achievement often mean that many couples must live considerable distances from the parental home. This is especially the case among the middle-class segments of our society. Thus, for example, in one study of newcomer families to an east-central Florida region, it was found that two thirds of the people interviewed did not have a single relative in the community, and over two fifths had no relatives within the state.[36]

These, then, are the ten main structural features of the American kinship system. They are systematically interrelated and they influence various facets of family life—mate selection, child-rearing, authority patterns, and so on. Given the heterogeneous makeup of our population, however, variations from these general patterns are also much in evidence (Chapter 4). Nevertheless, on an overall basis, they constitute the most dominant characteristics of our kinship system and the norms imbedded in them have a widespread impact on family structure and process. For example, our incest taboo, which prohibits intermarriage among nuclear family members, produces what W. Lloyd Warner termed a family of orientation and a family of procreation. The family of orientation is the unit into which one is born; it consists of Ego, his parents, and his siblings. When Ego marries, he establishes a family of procreation, comprised of his spouse and their children.

Ego is the only common member of the two families; and in the American case each member of the two families is typically linked by marriage to one other previously unrelated nuclear family. Thus, the two families typically link outward to as many previously unrelated families as there are individuals who marry, and this widening web extends backward and forward indefinitely. The end result is a kinship system structured on an "onion" principle, with successive "layers" arranged symmetrically around the two nuclear families at the center.[37]

It is through the operation of these features of our kinship system that certain structures and relationships are produced that are quite different from those found in many other societies.

Universality of the Nuclear Family

Most social scientists agree that in order for any human society to persist, certain fundamental tasks must be accomplished; if they are not, then the society will disintegrate. These basic tasks that must be

---

[36]Felix M. Berardo, "Kinship Interaction and Communications Among Space-Age Migrants," *Journal of Marriage and the Family,* **29** (Aug. 1967), pp. 541–554.

[37]In Williams, op. cit., pp. 60–61.

done or conditions that must be satisfied have been labeled the *functional prerequisites* of a society. They are, for example, providing for the physiological needs of the society's members, for sexual reproduction, for the socialization of the young, and so on.[38]

In all known human societies, some of these functional prerequisites appear to be performed by the family. In a previous section of this chapter it was noted how this observation led some family scholars to conclude that the nuclear family is a universal or "structural prerequisite," because it everywhere performs certain functions necessary to the maintenance of society. We noted that this position was examplified by Murdock, who contended that in every human society the nuclear family fulfilled the four functional prerequisites of sexual relations, economic cooperation, reproduction, and socialization. Murdock argued that no human society "has succeeded in finding an adequate substitute for the nuclear family, to which it might transfer these functions. It is highly doubtful whether any society ever will succeed in such an attempt, utopian proposals for the abolition of the family to the contrary notwithstanding."[39]

This position—that the *nuclear* family is a structural prerequisite for any human society because it fulfills four functional requisites in every known society—has been challenged by a number of family scholars who argue that there are many societies in which the nuclear family is absent or in which the nuclear family does not fulfill one or more of the four functional prerequisites.[40] The most frequently cited exceptions to the universality of the nuclear family are the Nayars of the Malabar Coast of India and the Israeli kibbutz family system. Let us look at each of these briefly.

THE NAYARS OF INDIA The Nayars are a Hindu caste group residing in southern India. The most thorough study of the Nayars has been conducted by Gough, who, through analysis of various documents and on the basis of informants' reports, has reconstructed the social organization of these people prior to the late eighteenth century.[41] It is the "family" customs of this early period that are said to represent one of the unique exceptions to the near universality of the nuclear family. (The traditional patterns of Nayar family organization that we will be

[38]For a detailed explication of these functional prerequisites, see D. F. Aberle et. al., "The Functional Prerequisites of a Society," *Ethics,* **60** (Jan. 1950), pp. 100–111.

[39]Murdock, *Social Structure,* op. cit., p. 11.

[40]Ira L. Reiss, "The Universality of the Family: A Conceptual Analysis," *Journal of Marriage and the Family,* **27** (Nov. 1965), pp. 443–453.

[41]E. Kathleen Gough, "The Nayars and the Definition of Marriage," *Journal of the Royal Anthropological Institute,* **89** (1959), pp. 23–34; "Nayar: Central Kerala," in *Matrilineal Kinship,* ed. by David Schneider and E. Kathleen Gough (Berkeley: University of California Press, 1961), pp. 298–284.

describing have since been substantially altered through the introduction of a new socioeconomic system.[42])

The traditional Nayars were dominated by a matrilineal system; that is, descent was traced through the female line. Inheritance similarly occurred through the female line. The family structure was a matrilineal joint family, with a typical household composed of a woman and her children, her married daughters and their children, her brothers, descendants through her sisters, and her relations through her deceased female ancestors. The men lived in their own households and visited their wives for only a few hours following the evening meal. The men in Nayar society were part of the militia and spent a good deal of their time away from home engaged in warfare.

Two types of marriages occurred among the Nayars. The first, which was compulsory for all females prior to their attaining puberty, was based upon a "*tali*-tying" ceremony. The *tali* was a gold leaf-shaped pendant on a chain that the selected bridegroom placed around the girl's neck. Because the *tali*-tying ceremony normally involved large expenditures of money it was not unusual for "all the girls down to the baby in the cradle" to be married in this fashion at a single ceremony.[43] After the man and the woman spent four days together, the "groom" departed and the "marriage" was considered terminated. However, the wife was required to wear the *tali* around her neck the remainder of her life, and if her *tali*-husband died she was expected to perform certain death rites. It was quite conceivable that between the time of the *tali*-tying ceremony and the death of the ritual husband, the couple might never see each other again.

Upon reaching puberty a girl was allowed to contract a second type of marriage, known as a *samdbandham* union, with a male either from her own caste or from an appropriate upper caste. Subsequently, she followed a polyandrous marital pattern by taking on additional "husbands." Usually the husbands were acquainted with one another and would take turns visiting with her. (A man could also have multiple wives; thus you have a system in which both polyandry and polygyny were practiced!) The "visiting husbands" were expected to bring gifts to the wife on important festival days, otherwise their obligations were minimal. Most of the usual tasks associated with the husband role were not performed by the visiting husbands; rather, they were assumed by members of the matrilineal household. The *sambandham* marriage lasted as long as the couple desired. A wife could divorce a husband at any time, and if the latter did not visit her regularly or continue to send her appropriate gifts, it was assumed that he had terminated the

---

[42]Joan P. Mencher, "The Nayars of South Malabar," in Nimkoff, op. cit., pp. 163–191.
[43]Ibid., p. 171.

marriage. In any event, it is clear that the husbands in Nayar society were not expected to be permanent members of the matrilineal family system.

Given the above pattern, the biological paternity of any children resulting from *sambandham* unions would be difficult to determine—but this was never an issue. All children were recognized as socially legitimate and "fatherhood" was established as follows. When the wife became pregnant she would name one of the visiting husbands as the father. It made no difference whether he was actually the physiological progenitor of the child or not. As long as he was willing to acknowledge paternity the child was considered legitimate. This assumption of legal paternity by the "father" did not require any obligations in rearing the child. Indeed, the primary obligations of males in Nayar society were to their own matrilineage. A child was incorporated into the wife's matrilineage, was reared by members of her matrilineal household, and had little contact with the man designated as his legal father.

Thus, the Nayar family organization and marriage customs appear to represent a unique exception to the universality of the nuclear family. The relationship of the visiting husband to his wife and children was extremely weak. The husband played practically no part in the rearing of the children. The polyandrous pattern prevented the development of any meaningful ties between the husband and wife. Practically speaking, he made no significant economic contribution toward the support of his wife and children. The point is that traditional Nayar society gave virtually no recognition to a nuclear family unit, in terms of either structure or functions.

As we noted at the outset, this description applies to the Nayars at an earlier point in their history. Through a variety of internal and external pressures, this traditional Nayar family organization underwent considerable modification in adjusting to a developing industrial economy. The pattern of visiting husbands, for example, has practically disappeared, although ties to matrilineal kin still continue to dominate family life.[44]

THE ISRAEL KIBBUTZ The Israel kibbutz and its unique arrangement of family relationships has been posited as another challenge to the presumed universality of the nuclear family.[45] Kibbutzim, which were first established in the late nineteenth century, are collective agricultural settlements. They are characterized by communal ownership of

---

[44]Ibid., p. 189.

[45]Melford E. Spiro, "Is the Family Universal?—The Israeli Case," in *A Modern Introduction to The Family,* rev. ed., ed. by Norman W. Bell and Ezra F. Vogel (New York: The Free Press, 1968), pp. 68–79; Yonina Talmon, "The Family in a Revolutionary Movement—The Case of the Kibbutz in Israel," in Nimkoff, op. cit., pp. 259–286.

virtually all property (aside from a few personal belongings), communal organization of both production and consumption, and communal child-rearing. Today, approximately 3 per cent of the entire population of Israel resides in 235 of such collective villages, which range in size from sixty members in some of the more recently established ones to two thousand in the older communities.[46]

The kibbutz is operated as a single economic unit, governed by a general assembly, and its social and economic activities are implemented through various executive agencies and committees composed of members elected each year. The founders of the kibbutz-type settlement sought to establish a cohesive socialistic community of individuals who would cooperate in overcoming the hostile environment of the arid and barren Israeli frontier and in protecting the frontier. The communal social organization of the kibbutz was originally designed to accomplish these goals. The kibbutz was a revolutionary structure based upon a radical ideology, and its success depended ultimately upon the complete commitment and efforts of all its members. Within this context, the maintenance of family and kinship ties was viewed as an obstruction to the emergent collective enterprise. As Talmon observes:

The formation of families of procreation within the Kibbutz confronted the collective with the problem of internal family attachments. New families are a source of centrifugal tendencies. Family ties are based on an exclusive and particularlistic loyalty which sets the members of the family more or less apart from the rest of their comrades. The new elementary families may easily become competing foci of intense emotional involvement and infringe on the loyalties of the collective. Deep attachment to one's spouse and children based on purely expressive interpersonal relations may gain precedence over the more ideological and more task-oriented relations with comrades. Families are considered divisive factors also because they are intermediate units which interpose and come between the individual and the community. Inasmuch as they act as buffers and protect the individual from the direct impact of public opinion, they reduce the effectiveness of informal collective control over members.[47]

Thus, from its initial inception the revolutionary and collectivist ideology of the kibbutz was antifamilistic, and its founders instituted

[46]Benjamin Schlesinger, "Family Life in the Kibbutz of Israel: Utopia Gained or Paradise Lost?" *International Journal of Comparative Sociology,* **11** (Dec. 1970), pp. 251–271.

[47]Talmon, op. cit., pp. 260–261. This presumed antagonism between family and collectivity was observed in other societies that have sought to develop a communistic social order. Thus, both Communist China and Russia have attempted to "collectivize" various forms of the family. Like the kibbutz, however, the Chinese and Russian experiments appear to have been something less than successful.

mechanisms designed to curtail drastically the functions of the family and to prevent it from consolidating as a distinct and independent unit.

The kibbutz is based upon principles of strict equality between the sexes and a doctrine of free and spontaneous love. Consequently, restrictive norms associated with conventional "bourgeois" morality, such as the demands of chastity, lifelong fidelity, and the double standards for men and women, have been rejected. Premarital sexual relations are permitted without censure. However, the liberal norms regarding premarital activity does not lead to sexual promiscuity. They are counterbalanced by a sexual modesty and reticence instilled in the members through socialization and by the asceticism and collectivism of the kibbutz. Moreover, a variety of practices are employed to deemphasize and neutralize erotic tensions and attractions between the sexes and thereby check their disorganizing consequences.[48]

Marriage is viewed as a voluntary union based upon a sincere emotional attachment of two free people to each other. A man and woman who have developed such a relationship and want to "marry" simply apply for a room. If space is available the request is approved, and they commence living together without the necessity of a marriage ceremony or celebration. The marriage is sustained as long as the couple retains a reciprocal emotional bond and as long as they desire to be together. Thus, either the husband or the wife are free to dissolve the marriage at will. Upon the birth of the first child a formal wedding is performed as a means of legitimizing the offspring.

The wife's equalitarian status is not significantly altered by marriage. She can and often does retain her maiden name. A wife and husband are assigned different jobs in the kibbutz. Indeed, there is a strict prohibition against members of a family working at the same location. Economic interaction and cooperation, therefore, occur at the community level and not directly between couples and their children. Division of labor based on sex is discouraged, and women participate in several occupations that, in our own society, have been traditionally assigned to men only.

The tenets of equalitarianism also govern family role relationships. Both the husband and wife share responsibilities for keeping their small quarters tidy and meeting the needs of the children. Family relationships are essentially democratic, and neither spouse has the

---

[48]Ibid., pp. 265–266, notes a number of such practices. Sexual problems were approached in a rational and objective manner, and the differences and distance between the sexes were minimized. Women were discouraged from enhancing their femininity through personal adornments and adopted male styles of dress and patterns of behavior. Physical shame between the sexes was overcome by the assigning of several single men and women to share the same room. Couples were taught to be discreet in public and to avoid open display of affection in the presence of others.

right to dominate the other. An attitude of permissiveness is taken with respect to children and parent-child interaction is relatively relaxed and uninhibited. Children are encouraged to address their parents by their proper names instead of the kinship terms of *father* and *mother.* Indeed, adults in the settlement refer to all children as "son" and "daughter" thus indicating that they are considered part of the larger community. Family togetherness is discouraged; instead, members are encouraged to participate *as individuals* as actively as possible in communal affairs, and not as members of an independent unit of social organization.

The socialization of children in the kibbutz is a community enterprise rather than a major parental responsibility. From birth on, a child is assigned to children's houses where he eats, sleeps, and studies with others in his age group. The specialized nurses and teachers in the children's houses as well as the peer age group become the dominant socializing agents in the child's life. However, children generally spend afternoon and early evening hours with their parents, and the latter are allowed to come and put their young offspring to bed at night. Moreover, the family is together on Saturdays and holidays, thereby providing further opportunities for parent-child interaction. Despite the fact that the children spend most of their time apart from their parents and under the supervision of others, evidence indicates that family relationships are warm and that children develop a strong and positive identification with their fathers and mothers.[49]

However, it can and has been argued that the nuclear family does not exist in the Israeli kibbutz. Certainly many of the traditional functions associated with the nuclear family structure have been taken over by communal arrangements in the kibbutz. Parents have little responsibility for the care and socialization of their children; there is practically no division of labor between spouses—that is, economic cooperation between them is absent—and parents and children do not share a common residence.

On the other hand, it can and has been argued by others that such examples as the Nayars and the Israeli kibbutzim are not really exceptions to the universality of the nuclear family, because they are only small and isolated groups or communities within societies and are not representative of those societies.

It is important to note that during the debate over the universality of the nuclear family, significant changes have occurred among both the Nayars and the kibbutzim. We noted earlier that with emergent industrialism the Nayars have steadily shifted toward the establishment of nuclear family households. Similarly, as Israel has become

---

[49]For a summary of this evidence see, Schlesinger, op. cit., pp. 255–266.

increasingly urbanized and industrialized, life in the kibbutz has shifted toward a stronger nuclear family orientation and a greater emphasis on kinship ties.[50]

Indeed, on a cross-cultural basis it appears that some type of nuclear family structure is gaining widespread acceptance. In our previous discussion of the conjugal and extended family patterns, we noted that the latter type of structure appeared to have several advantages when compared to the former. Despite such advantages, however, there is some indication that it is slowly giving way to the conjugal family system among the world's societies. Goode, for example, after an extensive analysis of family changes that have been taking place in the West, in Arabic Islam, in Sub-Saharan Africa, in China, and in Japan concluded that: "The alteration seems to be in the direction of some type of *conjugal* family pattern—that is, toward fewer kinship ties with distant relatives and a greater emphasis on the 'nuclear' family unit of couple and children."[51] Family scholars are just beginning to unravel the extremely complex configurations of economic, political, ideological, and other social forces that are operating to produce this change.

---

[50]For a detailed examination and analysis of the factors associated with this shift, see Talmon, op. cit., pp. 269–286 and Schlesinger, op. cit., pp. 266–271.

[51]William J. Goode, *World Revolution and Family Patterns* (New York: The Free Press, 1963), p. 1.

3

Subcultural Perspective:
Social Class and the Family

In any society privileges and responsibilities differ among the segments of the population. In relatively open-class societies in which many positions are achieved rather than ascribed, the concept of social class has been employed to describe these differences. The occupancy of these classes is based partly on individual achievement and partly on the achievements of one's parents, grandparents, and earlier forefathers. Thus, membership in the upper-upper class is based on inherited position. Inherited wealth and one's parents' use of it are significant factors as to whether one will have upper-middle- or lower-upper-class status, and, therefore, one may move "down" from the position occupied by his parents as well as "up." On the opposite end, belonging to a minority group may make it hard to move "up."

Because social class involves differences in income, in prestige, in power, and in security, it involves almost if not all family roles, relationships, decisions on family size, and other aspects of structure and interaction.

In relatively open-class societies, the principal basis of social class (except for the upper-upper class) is occupation. In industrial societies, occupations differ in that some tasks require more training, special talents, or physical abilities. The preparation for these tasks requires varying periods of time, training, experience, and requirements, and different levels of support from families.

THE MIDDLE CLASS In societies in which most productive and distributive facilities are privately owned and managed, the middle class has emerged, including among its members the business owner and manager. Unless the manager inherited his business, he usually has had to defer gratification while he saved resources with which to start a business, not unlike the extended period of training of the professional. In turn, the several occupations provide differential

54

rewards in the income, power, and prestige that are accorded to the worker and shared by the spouse and children.

In general, those with occupations that require extended training and the owner-operator of business, who requires an accumulation of resources, receive larger rewards in the society than those whose occupations do not have these requirements. It might be added that both kinds of occupations require some abilities that are not possessed by everyone in the society, so that entrance into and adequate performance in these occupations is not open to all—an added basis for prestige for those who successfully occupy these occupations. Such occupations form the middle class in a society. The *upper-middle class* is composed of those who receive more rewards, in money and prestige, and the lower-middle class, which receives lower rewards. Compared to the lower class, the middle class is highly rewarded in goods, prestige, and power. Membership in it ordinarily involves a certain level of abilities plus a considerable period of deferred gratification. It exacts some other costs from the middle-class worker because most tasks are more complex and abstract, and because often he is responsible for the work of others as well as his own. It is a "performance class" because if one relaxes his efforts after having gained a place in the class, he slips back into a lower class.

THE UPPER CLASS In contrast to the training and performance basis of the middle class, the upper-upper class is based on inherited wealth or position.

The lower-upper class is composed of people who have recently accumulated wealth or a continuing position of power, such as a commoner who seizes the throne of a country. These people possess affluence independent of their earnings that they can transmit to their children, but they were socialized in one of the humbler classes and do not possess the manner, dress, and friendships within the older aristocracy. Ordinarily, they will not be accepted into the upper-upper class despite their wealth or power. However, their children—or, at least, their grandchildren, who are socialized into the upper class and who will possess the manners, dress, and other aspects of the style of life of the upper class—are likely to be fully accepted into the upper-upper class. Thus, class membership, although it is related closely to power and prestige, is not the same concept. A president of the United States from the lower-middle class may, during his term of office, have more power than any member of the upper class, but this does not mean that he is a member of the upper class, or that he is accepted by it.

The upper-upper class distinguishes itself from the middle class by virtue of "illustrious" ancestors, the assumption being that the longer the family has occupied upper-class status, the more complete its

55

mastery of the upper-class subculture and the more perfect the role performance of its members. Up to a certain length of time, this assumption would appear to be true, because the socialization within the upper class would be more complete if all the relatives and companions of the child had themselves been socialized in the upper class.

The upper class, then, has a different financial base than the middle class. Income may not be more than for many in the upper-middle class, but enough of it flows from inherited wealth so that members of the class are relatively free to work when and at whatever tasks please them, and their children are freed from pursuing vocational types of education. They *do* have a special task in maintaining, and preferably increasing, inherited wealth, which calls for prudent financial management, marriage to others within the same class, and family planning to have no more children than family resources can support from invested wealth.

Most upper-class American men are not idle; most are employed, but they are more independent of their occupations for income and prestige. Upper-class youth attend colleges and universities but not primarily to obtain the vocational training necessary to earn an income. They are more free to study man and his culture in its many dimensions rather than concentrating on some small segment of production, distribution, or services. Likewise, upper-class youth are typically under less pressure to compete in college and are more free to pursue interests other than high academic achievement. As a consequence, youth may pursue the subtleties of dress, food, drink, and music and become knowledgeable about literature, philosophy, and foreign languages. They have the time and the resources to travel, to view selected portions of other societies at first hand, and to cultivate personal acquaintances with upper-class people in those societies. Thus, the upper class keeps itself apart from the middle class by pursuing and mastering the subtleties of culture, to which the education of the middle classes gives less attention.

THE LOWER CLASS Compared to middle-class families, lower-class families average less income, less stability of income, and less prestige. The investment necessary is also less because there are few educational requirements for blue-collar jobs. In general, the jobs involve hand labor, animals, or machines rather than working with people. However, insofar as families are concerned the differences between the upper and lower levels of the lower class are probably more significant than between the upper-lower class and middle class.

The upper-lower class is characterized by skilled labor in such occupations as plumber, carpenter, and machine operator. Many of these jobs require periods of apprenticeship for learning the required

56

skills and for gaining entry to the skilled occupations. Labor is unionized with wages maintained at fairly stable levels. In general, income supplies the basic needs of the family with some left for luxuries or investment. Although income, prestige, and economic security are not generally as high as for the middle class, they are sufficient to maintain the integrity of the family. Because employment is usually by the hour rather than by yearly salary, the upper-lower class is vulnerable to depressions or even recessions, during which the family may have to live on a fraction of its regular income or on unemployment compensation or even public assistance. During periods of economic stability, the family in the upper-lower class leads a life that differs little from that of the middle class.

The occupations of the lower-lower class involve unskilled labor or only such skills as can be learned while the individual is working, involve concrete rather than abstract problems, and do not involve the supervision of other adults—always a complex operation. Income and prestige are lower. The level of mental abilities required is lower than that of middle-class operations. There is usually a surplus of individuals available who can perform these tasks.

As a consequence, unemployment is a condition of life for a proportion of lower-lower-class people, which is not the case for the other classes. Instability of employment is another characteristic of lower-lower-class life. Although some people have positions on which they draw a monthly salary, most are employed by the hour. When their labor is not needed, such as during a slack period in production or unfavorable weather conditions, they may have no employment, which means no income. This kind of unemployment is not due to unwillingness to work but to the nature of production jobs and to the poor bargaining power of unskilled and semiskilled workers. This uncertainty of income means that the provider cannot undertake long-term obligations, such as buying a house or furniture, with the confidence of a salaried person, and results in the necessity of sometimes looking to other sources of financial support—unemployment insurance, "relief," or the "solicitous" help of small loan companies.

We should note that in the lower class three rather different aggregates can be distinguished. Upper-lower-class people, although working on an hourly basis, generally have steady employment. In recent years they have received higher wages so that they have achieved a comfortable standard of living including some luxuries. Also, if their families aren't too large, they can provide some assistance for children who want to go to college.

In the lower-lower class there are two types of families, both below the poverty level. One of these functions "normally" in that the husband works whenever employment is available and the wife cares

57

for the children as adequately as she can, given limited education and inadequate financial resources. An example of this type of lower-lower class family is the migrant farm laborer's family. In this kind of family the husband often is illiterate and has a low level of skills to sell. He must take whatever crumbs of employment are left after the better-educated and -trained people have taken the steady employment. This type of lower-lower-class family performs all the functions of a family as well as it can, but it does not provide an acceptable level of education, diet, and medical care for children or adults. Children grow up without the education and health that they need to become adequate adults.

The other type of lower-lower-class family includes one or more seriously disorganized parents. The family may be in the lower-lower class because of a father who is too disorganized to function as a provider, such as an alcoholic or a mentally ill person, and a mother who is unable to substitute for him as a provider. Of course, some mothers are seriously disorganized also, but it is primarily the capability of the provider that places the family in the socioeconomic structure. Such lower-lower-class families usually require the intervention of a social agency to provide funds and sometimes to protect children from abuse. Elsewhere, it is termed the *malfunctioning family* (Chapter 17).

INDICATORS OF SOCIAL CLASS Social class has been described as a "way of life," but how does the researcher measure such a complex and amorphous set of phenomena? When he makes a statement, such as the following, "Middle-class mothers tend to be more permissive than lower-class mothers," how did he decide which mothers were middle class and which lower class?

In most instances, the researcher will have employed occupation as his indicator. He may have employed as many as ten categories of occupations, but more likely he has utilized only two broad classes: *blue collar* and *white collar.* This division places most of the professional, technical, and managerial jobs in one category and most of the manual-labor jobs in the other. Roughly, this classification also places the more highly rewarded positions in the white-collar and the less rewarded ones in the blue-collar category. True, a few blue-collar workers earn more in a year than some white-collar workers and also some skilled occupations require more training than some sales and clerical jobs, but in general the classification holds. Also, in general, it separates the occupations that are salaried from those that pay by the hour. Because the number of years of education is quite closely related to occupation, it also can be utilized as an indicator of social class, as can income.

Although occupation, income, and education are useful indicators for differentiating the middle and lower social classes, they are inadequate for distinguishing between the middle and upper classes. The upper social class is distinguished by income from sources other than wages and salaries, so the researcher needs *source* of income as a minimum additional criterion for distinguishing upper-class families. The matter, however, is somewhat academic, because upper-class families form a relatively small proportion of the population and are relatively inaccessable to researchers. Most social class research currently available includes data only from the lower and middle classes.

Social Class and Values

Because the social worlds of the social classes—the occupational tasks and the types of socialization required to produce personalities that can function in these tasks—differ, it is reasonable that the relevant values should differ, also. Research evidence suggests that this is true, but to complicate the issue, some values apparently have been changing in recent decades. We say "apparently" because values cannot be observed directly: they must be inferred from what people do or report.

INSTRUMENTAL AND INTRINSIC VALUES It appears that the social classes share some values but not others. They share what we have termed *intrinsic values* (Chapter 1) or *end values*. Whether a person is in the lower, middle, or upper class he is likely to value good health and autonomy (freedom to choose activities, locations, and companions), having people who care for him personally, and being well-thought-of or having a respected place among his fellows. Such values seem to be generally shared by humans regardless of class, age, sex, or cultural context. It appears that these are shared by almost everyone in all social classes.

By contrast, the values placed on activities or attitudes that are useful in achieving the intrinsic values may vary widely, depending on how likely it is that an activity will lead to the achievement of an intrinsic value. The value placed on such activities or relevant attitudes we have termed *instrumental values* (Chapter 1).

Based on this discussion, the value of a college education should be very different for lower-, middle-, and upper-class parents and children. Because a college education is not required for unskilled and semi-skilled positions it has value only in terms of upward mobility—into the middle class. Lower-class parents who are uninterested in their children's entering into middle class occupations, or who actually oppose their upward social mobility, will place a low or even a negative value on their children's entrance into college.

There are several reasons for lower-class parents' negatively valuing college training for their children. The parents are deprived of any

59

labor or income their children might provide, they would probably be expected to contribute to college expenses, and finally they might foresee that middle-class occupations would mean that the children would leave the community and/or drop lower-class associations as they developed new ones in the middle class.

The value placed on higher education by lower-class children is likely to parallel that of their parents. They know they do not need it for lower-class jobs. To value it positively, they must have upward mobility aspirations *and* have received positive reinforcement from teachers and/or parents. Such positive reinforcement is less common for lower-class children for reasons that cannot be pursued here.

Finally, it is likely that the lower-class adolescent must himself provide all the financial resources to defray college expenses. Therefore, his value on a degree must be especially high if he is to attain one.

If the lower-class child values a college degree and his parents value it negatively or if his parents value it positively and the child values it negatively, a basis is provided for parent-adolescent conflict.

Recent research has shown that upper-lower-class parents are more likely (than middle-class parents) to value neatness and cleanliness (mothers' responses), being able to defend himself (fathers' responses), and obedience to parents (both parents' responses). They are as likely to value honesty highly as are middle-class parents (Table 3.1). Honesty, obedience, and neatness were once considered middle-class values. Current evidence shows that many of the middle-class values are also lower-class values, or at least values of the upper-lower class, from which Kohn's sample was largely drawn.[1]

MIDDLE-CLASS VALUES In contrast with the lower class, most middle-class parents value higher education positively. If they are employed in professional and technical positions, they know that a college degree is a requisite for such occupations. Parents want their children to have at least as rewarding a position in society as they themselves have achieved. Because of their higher incomes, they can more easily provide financial assistance for children in college.

Although many middle-class adolescents value college highly, many do not. They start by expecting to achieve a level equal to that of their parents. For many, this requires a high level of effort. Whereas getting to college at all is a major achievement for the lower-class adolescent, the middle-class adolescent is expected to maintain at least average grades and receives positive reinforcement only for superior achievement. Because he has experienced a high standard of living by virtue of

[1]Melvin L. Kohn, "Social Class and Parental Values," *American Journal of Sociology*, **64** (Jan. 1959), pp. 337–351.

Table 3.1
Italian and American Parents' Selection of the Three Most Important Characteristics for Children, by Social Class

| | Italy | | | | United States | | | |
| | Fathers | | Mothers | | Fathers | | Mothers | |
Characteristic	Middle Class %	Working Class %	Middle Class %	Working Class %	Middle Class %	Working Class %	Middle Class %	Working Class %
1. That he is honest	54	54	55	55	52	58	44	53
2. That he has good manners	32*	44*	44	51	24	25	19	24
3. That he obeys his parents well	31*	45*	36*	48*	13*	39*	20*	33*
4. That he acts in a serious way	25	18	18	20	–	3	–	1
5. That he has self-control	23*	11*	16*	8*	20*	6*	22*	13*
6. That he is dependable	23*	13*	21*	10*	33*	8*	24	21
7. That he is able to defend himself	21	14	17*	8*	2*	17*	10	6
8. That he is ambitious	19	17	21	19	17	8	7	13
9. That he is happy	14*	7*	16	14	37	22	46*	36*
10. That he is considerate of others	11	9	10*	3*	35*	14*	39*	27*
11. That he is affectionate	10	12	13	12	2	8	5	4
12. That he is neat and clean	9	14	7*	14*	15	17	11*	20*
13. That he is popular with other children	9	7	6	4	15	25	15	18
14. That he is a good student	8*	24*	13*	24*	7	19	15	17
15. That he is liked by adults	4	9	5	9	–	8	5	4
16. That he is curious about things	3	1	2	1	13	8	18*	6*
17. That he is able to play by himself	1	2	–	1	2	6	1	–
Numbers	(160)	(148)	(263)	(205)	(46)	(36)	(174)	(165)

Computed from Melvin L. Kohn, "Social Class and Parental Values", *American Journal of Sociology*, **64** (Jan. 1959) Tables 1 and 2.
*Social class difference statistically significant at the .05 level using Chi Square.
SOURCE: Leonard I. Pearlin, *Class Context and Family Relations, A Cross-National Study*. (Boston: Little, Brown and Company, 1970). Reprinted by permission of author and publisher.

his parents' efforts, he knows little of the poverty and privation of those with small or no incomes. The middle-class value on higher education is *a means* to obtaining a good position and receiving a superior income, and tends, especially for boys, to be vocationally oriented.

Kohn has noted other middle-class values that seem to be occupationally oriented—a higher value (than in the lower class) placed on being dependable and possessing self-control (fathers' responses), being happy and curious (mothers' responses), and being considerate of others (both parents). These emphasize qualities needed by persons in responsible, autonomous positions, which are characteristic of professional and managerial occupations.

UPPER-CLASS VALUES If we look again at the instrumental value placed on education, this time from the vantage point of the upper social class, the view is different. A college degree is not viewed as a means to a more prestigious position or a higher income, because income is primarily from other sources. The private preparatory school and the expensive, "exclusive" university are not for preparing children for a vocation but for socialization for upper-class life. Both the school and the university provide an insulation against middle-class socialization and the development of middle-class friendships and marriages. Segregation furthers upper-class socialization by cultivating upper-class tastes and proficiency in appearance, conversation, eating, and knowledge of music, the arts, literature, and foreign languages and cultures. The private school and the university also provide social contacts with the children and youth who will become members of the upper class as adults. Thus, education possesses a value perhaps as high as for the middle class but it consists of a different type of education with different objectives.

Perhaps the highest value for members of the upper class is to maintain that class position for themselves and their children. To that end, marriage with persons with ample financial resources, small families, a special type of education, and prudent financial management all rate high as instrumental values.[2]

We have proposed in this section that values differ by social class if reference is to instrumental values or the means by which ends are achieved. Thus, for example, the classes place different values on education. However, intrinsic values do not differ by social class. Such values as autonomy, health, and love are not class related. If one has reference to instrumental values, he finds differences; if to intrinsic, similarity.

[2]Ruth Shonle Cavan, "Subcultural Variations and Mobility," in Harold T. Christensen, *Handbook of Marriage and the Family* (Chicago: Rand McNally & Co., 1964), pp. 559–560.

Social Class Norms and Strains

Behavior required in one social class may not be required in another. To put it another way, there are differences in the norms of the social classes. For example, it is expected of middle-class parents that they financially support or at least assist their children in obtaining a college education. The parent who refused such assistance to the extent of his ability would be criticized. Not so for lower-class parents; some choose to assist their children, but such support is more than can be expected of the limited financial resources of the average lower-class parent. In addition, a college degree is seen as a means of upward social mobility, above and away from the life of parents and friends. It is not characteristic of the norms to require behavior that decimates the group through the social mobility of its young.

It should be recognized that, except for legally enacted laws and such other formal requirements as those spelled out by universities, the norms are unwritten and must be inferred from behavior and comment and the reactions of others. Although the content of norms can, like values, be researched, such research to date has not described the norms in detail; therefore the following statements of class norms should be taken only as appearing to be true at this time.

LOWER-CLASS NORMS Lower-class families have the least resources to invest; therefore less is expected both by themselves and by those in the other classes. Houses may be modest, provided they are comfortable and secure; food is not expected to be elaborate but should provide an adequate vitamin and energy supply. Clothing need not be varied or expensive but should provide comfort and be appropriate to the occasion. Education need not include college or even high school graduation but should provide a good level of literacy. Honesty and good work attitudes and habits are important. In short, the norms of the lower class include the necessary conditions for the safety, the good biological functioning, and the physical comfort of family members. For children, it requires a type of socialization that will enable them to obtain and adequately perform unskilled, semi-skilled, and skilled jobs. For men, the norms require regular employment, if possible; if one is not employed, they require that he be seeking employment and be ready to work whenever employment is available. In the most general terms, the lower class strive to function as self-supporting, self-respecting members of the society, possessing at least the minimal resources for comfortable living and socializing children in such a fashion that they can achieve at least the same result.

It is normative, we think, for families to strive toward social class placement of their children to at least the level of the parents. Many parents strive to help their children to achieve upward social mobility

63

above the class level of the parents. Although this is permissible and even viewed as commendable, it is not a requirement of parents, in any sense of the word, and therefore not normative.

Research, reported by Kohn[3] and Bronfenbrenner[4] emphasizes honesty, cleanliness, and obedience as lower-class values. These we view as necessary for workers who are continually faced by competition from a surplus of unemployed workers. Lower-class jobs require less imagination, initiative, and responsibility than middle-class jobs, but, like any job, diligence, honesty, and an appropriate appearance are likely to make the difference between being employed and promoted and being intermittantly employed or unemployed.

Although these values are normative for the lower class and especially the upper lower class, not all class members are able to conform to the norms. In the lower-lower class, the struggle of day-to-day existence prevents regular school attendance by many lower-lower-class children, which results in illiteracy, which in turn usually prevents them from functioning adequately as adults. Other lower-lower-class families are so disorganized, or are so penalized by disorganized members, that they do not obtain the necessary food, the medical attention, or the housing for a comfortable existence, nor do they adequately socialize their children so that they will be able to obtain these when they become adults. We shall discuss these families in more detail in Chapter 17.

MIDDLE-CLASS NORMS The middle class averages both a higher income level and more stable incomes, because salaries rather than wages are the modal pattern. Also, most middle-class individuals defer some gratifications while they obtain advanced education. These larger and more stable incomes lead to higher expectations in the middle-class level of living. It is expected that middle-class people will live up to "a middle class way of life." Housing should not only be comfortable but look attractive within and without. An automobile becomes not only a means of transportation but an object of beauty. A library and magazines should serve the intellectual interests of the educated parents and stimulate the mental development of the young. Food should be varied and attractive as well as nourishing. Clothing should reflect style and taste as well as comfort. In short, middle-class occupations require more education, are more complex, involve more responsibility, and as a consequence command larger financial rewards. The norms reflect the expectation that these larger financial

[3]Kohn, op. cit., pp. 337–351.
[4]Urie Bronfenbrenner, "Socialization and Social Class Through Time and Space," in *Readings in Social Psychology,* ed. by Eleanor E. Maccoby, Theodore M. Newcomb, and Eugene Hartley, (New York: Holt, Rinehart and Winston, 1958).

resources will be reflected in a more generally desirable level of living. The family whose way of life doesn't reflect such a level of living may be thought to be exercising poor judgment in the use of its resources.

Perhaps more crucial are the norms for middle-class children. Advanced education is viewed as necessary for their placement in the middle class at their parents' level or for upward social mobility. Therefore, children of middle-class parents are expected to devote themselves to their studies and to demonstrate superior academic accomplishment. Parents are expected to provide strong financial assistance for college training.

In college they (especially boys) are expected to achieve superior grades, because they need not only a college degree, but superior grades and indications of superior ability, motivation, and organization in order to obtain the better positions upon graduation. Creative achievements are especially valued, as Kohn has noted, because middle-class occupations require judgment and innovative ability of a high order.[5] Further, any type of hostile behavior, especially involving physical violence (except in athletic competition) is a violation of the norms of cooperativeness and congenial behavior required in middle-class occupations.

In short, middle-class socialization is closely tied to the requirements of middle-class occupations, stressing superior performance in the classroom, creativity, and cooperative and congenial interaction with peers and adults. For the wife, this includes maintaining a way of living that reflects efficient use of the more adequate financial resources of the middle class.

Finally, a word on middle-class conventionality. The middle class has been considered the conforming class. Recent research, however, questions this. For example, Cuber and Harroff's study of the upper-middle class found a typically autonomic family structure with husband and wife pursuing many individual interests and frequently with extramarital attachments—some, but not all, involving sexual relations.[6]

Again, sexual conventionality appears to be connected with middle-class occupations, which deal mostly with people in contrast to lower-class occupations, which deal mostly with things. The bulldozer operator's job is to operate the machine, but the supervisor's job is to organize and supervise people. The conventions describe how people in roles shall interact. The office manager who makes sexual advances

[5]Kohn, op. cit., pp. 337–351.
[6]John F. Cuber and Peggy B. Harroff, *The Significant Americans* (New York: Appleton-Century-Crofts, 1965), p. 104.

65

to his secretary creates a set of personnel problems in the office that reduce his usefulness as an employee. The bulldozer operator with extracurricular sexual interests is for that reason no less useful as an employee. We are not convinced that middle-class individuals are more conventional in their thinking, or even their behavior, but they are more careful in regulating their conduct with fellow employees and even in placing a value on their reputations as conventional people. As a consequence, unconventionality among middle-class individuals is more likely to be expressed away from their own communities and to be hidden, either by distance or otherwise.[7] This guarded quality of middle-class behavior has been termed hypocrisy when compared to the more open, unconventional behavior of the lower-lower class. The difference probably is less in mental outlook than in the requirements of the types of occupations that the two classes follow.

UPPER-CLASS NORMS Upper-class norms are oriented toward maintaining membership in the upper class. Because its basis is inherited wealth, this wealth must be safeguarded through profitable investment, marriage with another with substantial financial resources, and appropriate birth control. Any dissipation of inherited funds, marriage outside the class, or the conception of more children than invested wealth can support would be regarded with concern in the upper class.[8] The position of the upper class is a privileged one in that its members need not invest time in an occupation in order to maintain a superior standard of living. Once invested income becomes insufficient for maintenance, the economic basis of the class position is lost.

As the middle class maintains a style of life superior to the lower class, so is the upper class expected to display the superiority of a life made possible by inherited wealth. As noted before, the upper class utilizes some of its available time to master the subtleties of dress, food, house furnishings, and conversation, and to pursue interesting nonvocational matters. In the norms associated with these, upper-class individuals are expected to display a way of life that reflects the time they have had available to pursue such interesting and time-consuming matters. Through marriage within the upper class, the family not only usually replenishes its finances, but gains another member well socialized in its style of life.

University training is possibly as important for the upper as for the middle class, but high value is not placed on academic achievement,

[7]Hans L. Zetterberg, "The Secret Ranking," *Journal of Marriage and the Family*, **28** (May 1966), pp. 134–143.
[8]Cavan, op. cit., pp. 559–560.

because there is no need to impress a prospective employer. Rather, the private school and the exclusive university further the whole socialization process. In short, upper-class norms cluster about two concerns: maintaining the family in its upper-class position, and maintaining the way of life of the upper class.

Mobility and Other Stresses in the Social Classes

Each social class has inputs from two sources: (1) Children whose parents are members of that class and whose socialization was in that class and (2) children whose parents were socialized in another class but who found placement in this class through upward or downward social mobility or by their occupation. The lower-lower class has some special problems because of the downward mobility of disorganized persons socialized in other classes. Thus, the lower-lower class tends to encompass the social misfits from all the social classes and to include a substantial number of disorganized families.

THE LOWER CLASS Lower-class mobility problems are demonstrated in the upward path of the ambitious lower-class adolescent who obtains a good education or who develops a prosperous business. Such upward mobility usually creates stresses both for the adolescent and for his parents. The upwardly mobile individual strives to function in a world in which he was not socialized, one in which there are different standards of housing, dress, and social intercourse—on matters that were not covered directly in his advanced schooling or in any written regulation.

For his parents, there is likely to be gradual loss of contact with the upwardly mobile person as their individual worlds encompass fewer and fewer common elements. The middle class is geographically mobile, so that the young adult is likely to follow a job to another city or state, further decreasing contact with his parents.

Frequently it is assumed that there is no problem of downward social mobility within the lower class, because the lower class *is* at the bottom of the reward system. However, there is quite a range of incomes and styles of life within this class, and it seems that the plumber's son who finds permanent employment as an unskilled laborer is downwardly mobile, as would be the plumber himself if he became an alcoholic and took up residence on skid row. The stresses on parents and their children of downward social mobility are probably little different if it occurs in the lower class than if it occurs elsewhere. Because parents

67

strive for social class placement to at least their own class level, downward social mobility is likely to be viewed as a failure both of the child and of the parents.[9]

THE MIDDLE CLASS The middle class is faced with both upward and downward mobility, although most middle-class children find placement somewhere within the class. In one community, McGuire found that in the upper-middle class, 88 per cent of the children were placed there with 6 per cent upwardly mobile and 6 per cent downwardly mobile. In the lower-middle class, 73 per cent stayed, 21 per cent moved up and 6 per cent down.[10] For those children who moved out of the middle class the problems appear similar to those of mobile lower-class persons—loss of contact for parents of the upwardly mobile youth, and, for the upwardly mobile youth, existence on the fringes of that strange upper-class world in which wealth and success in one's vocation are not enough and where the subtleties of upper-class life look both too difficult and too trivial for mastery late in life. For the downwardly mobile child, his lack of achievement is likely to be considered failure by his parents, part of which they are likely to assess against their own performance as parents.

It is frequently overlooked that *middle-class status is achieved, not ascribed,* and it is a considerable achievement for *any* child to obtain the training and motivation to function there satisfactorily. This is the basis for a type of middle-class stress—the child has not performed successfully unless he is toward the top of his group. This contrasts with expectations in the lower class, where to pass in school is to succeed, or to be employed steadily is to succeed. Not so for the middle-class and especially the upper-middle-class child. As one successful businessman said about his son, "Oh, he wants to go to Annapolis and have a navy career. I can't see him spending his life pacing a destroyer and drawing $____ per month." To be *only* a naval officer was to be a failure in this upper-middle-class father's eyes. The middle-class parent can in many ways help his children, including financial assistance, personal contacts, and knowledge of the middle-class world. Still the attitude toward levels of reward-for-effort is quite different in the two classes: a given level of achievement

[9]Such feelings of failure, however, are more likely to be mitigated by the offering of biological explanations for failure to achieve at an average level for that class; for example, "It's sad that Tommy just isn't very bright."

[10]C. McGuire, "Social Stratification and Mobility Patterns," *American Sociological Review,* 15 (Apr. 1950), pp. 195–204. Despite the general upward movement in the occupational structure, Blau and Duncan say that "more than one quarter of the sons of white-collar workers are in manual or farm occupations." Peter M. Blau and Otis Dudley Duncan, *The American Occupational Structure* (New York: John Wiley & Sons, 1967), p. 59.

may be outstanding by lower-class standards but mediocre by those of the middle class. In short, the stresses on the middle-class child focus on the high level of achievement usually expected in the middle class.

The pressure on middle-class adolescents may further increase if they internalize these expectations and feel a sense of accomplishment only if they rise faster and farther in class position than did their parent of the same sex.

THE UPPER CLASS In terms of interclass mobility, only downward mobility is possible for the upper-upper class, although for the lower-upper class—the newly rich—upward mobility into full acceptance by the highest class is equally possible. Logically, the lower-upper class is the most unstable of all classes, because one cannot literally be the "newly" rich for more than one generation.

The principal problem of the newly rich, however, is to prevent loss of invested wealth or to increase it sufficiently to keep abreast of inflation and the rising level of living of the other classes. To lose this financial basis of class membership would be to return to dependence on employment or active business management, which obligates one's time and essentially moves one back into the middle class. This does not mean that the members of the upper class don't work; most do, but they may change employment or leave it at will if it becomes burdensome or uninteresting.

Any out-of-class mobility of the upper-upper class is, by definition, a failure. Marriage into the middle or lower class is to be avoided at almost any cost, because it usually dissipates financial resources and brings a member into the family who lacks upper-class socialization. These severe restrictions on marriage reduce the marital choices available and lead with some frequency to marriages based on considerations other than interpersonal attraction. Children experience stress in acquiring and displaying the superior social skills of the upper class and in maintaining the financial basis for class participation.

WOMEN IN CLASS MOBILITY Because social class is based primarily on the amount and the source of family income, it has been assumed that a woman's place in the social class structure depends on whom she marries. This has been and still is usually true. Because it is true, it introduces an element of calculative deliberation into the spousal choices of women that need not be present for men. A girl must not only base a choice on the personal attractiveness of a man but on the occupation he is in or is planning to enter and his prospects in terms of probable size and stability of income. The man who reads the *Wall Street Journal* and who drives a Cadillac or a comparable automobile

69

may have a special interest for the woman who is thinking of marriage.[11]

If we grant the above, what are the other means of social class placement for women? Whereas it appears that men are likely to make their own vocational choices, whether a man can enact that vocational role successfully may be influenced markedly by the support, encouragement, and sometimes the participation of his wife. Therefore, married women may influence their own social class placement to a great extent by their enactment of their roles in marriage.

Finally, in industrial societies, many occupations are open to women and they can, through their own abilities, training, and efforts occupy managerial and professional positions that place them in the middle class. In exceptional cases, a woman may become independently wealthy in her own right and move into the lower-upper class. Finally, women who inherit large fortunes are members of the upper class.

Résumé

In this chapter we have tried to indicate the rationale for viewing the family through a subcultural perspective—in this instance, social class. We have discussed and illustrated the bases for social class ranking and some differences in the instrumental values, norms, and stresses in the social classes. We have *not* here presented the detailed research showing social class differences in family size, the distribution of power between husband and wife, child-rearing philosophies, and the like. These topics will be dealt with specifically in later chapters. What we have attempted to accomplish in this chapter is to alert the student to the significance of social class differences and to prevent any oversimplified assumptions about the general uniformity of families in complex societies. We have illustrated these class differences by showing that the classes have differing instrumental values, such as the value placed on education; that different types of stresses are experienced by children and parents in the different classes; that the lower-lower class has a "deficit" in the resources to provide adequate, stable family life; and that in some respects, each class has its own set of norms. Later (Chapter 10), we shall try to show that some new familial roles have emerged in the middle class that are still generally unrecognized in the lower social classes.

---

[11]Recent research has analyzed marriage as a form of social-class mobility. See Glen H. Elder, Jr., "Appearance and Education in Marriage Mobility," *American Sociological Review,* **34** (Aug. 1969), pp. 519–533.

4

Subcultural Perspective: Ethnic-American Families

In pursuit of a more comprehensive understanding of the family institution—and the role it plays in shaping human lives and destinies—sociologists have found it profitable to examine the subcultural variations in family structure in our society in terms of how they are influenced by social class and ethnic factors. Social class influences were outlined in detail in the preceding chapter and their effects are further noted in connection with many other facets of marriage and family life treated throughout this volume. In the present chapter, we concentrate on the ethnic component within the context of ethnic-American family subcultures. Ethnicity has long been recognized as a particularly potent force in determining family structure and roles. As Stein and Cloward have observed: "Ethnic determinants of behavior are deep and ramified, stemming as they do from cultural patterns which penetrate the individual's values, and his role in life, and define the norms which provide him with a sense of location, identity, and continuity with his cultural group."[1] In short, ethnicity is one of the major societal determinants of family behavior.

Before beginning our discussion of ethnic-American families, we need to provide some definition of what is meant by the term *ethnic group.* For a variety of reasons, traditional concepts that denote ethnicity, such as race and nationality, have often been found restrictive and unsatisfactory for research purposes. Indeed, there has been considerable scientific debate and confusion over their exact meaning and definition.[2] Moreover, a great many prejudicial attitudes and feelings had become associated with such terms, especially with

[1] Herman D. Stein and Richard A. Cloward (eds.), *Social Perspectives on Behavior* (Glencoe, Ill.: The Free Press, 1958), p. 3.

[2] M. F. Ashley Montagu, "On the Phrase 'Ethnic Group' in Anthropology," *Psychiatry,* **8** (Feb. 1945), pp. 27–33.

respect to race.[3] Consequently, social scientists have gradually come to substitute the broader and less emotional term *ethnic group* in making references to human groups that are identifiable by a core of cultural homogeneity.

Within the latter context we can proceed to adopt a definition of *ethnic group* as any group that is defined or set off by race, religion, national origin, or some combination of these categories, as they are found within the national boundaries of the United States. As Gordon notes, although each of these categories forms a distinctly separate aspect of ethnic identification, nevertheless, they all "serve to create, through historical circumstances, a sense of peoplehood for groups within the United States, and this common referent of peoplehood is recognized in the American public's usage of these three terms, frequently in interchangeable fashion."[4] The term *ethnic group* then is a useful designation for this common social-psychological core or sense of grouphood, derived in part from a consciousness of kind among members of a subculture. Thus: "The American who answers Who He Is, answers, then, from an ethnic point of view, as follows: I am an American, I am of the White or Negro or Mongoloid race, I am a Protestant, Catholic, or Jew, and I have a German, or Italian, or Irish, or English, or whatever, national background."[5] It should be kept in mind that it is possible for an individual to have a different pattern of identification for each ethnic identity that he may ascribe to himself or to others, and that each ascriptive alternative may have a different salience at different moments in time.[6]

To sum up, it is the broad definition that we have only briefly outlined that will be used as a guide in subsequent discussions of the multiethnic character of American families and their subcultural diversity. Race, religion, and nationality are all seen as contributing to the development of ethnic group consciousness in a society that is perhaps unique in world history in terms of the pluralistic composition of its population and the diversity of its family systems.

The Immigrant Family

Any sociological analysis of ethnic-American families should logically begin with a consideration of our immigrant heritage, for it is the

[3]Gordon W. Allport, *The Nature of Prejudice* (Garden City, N.Y.: Doubleday and Company, 1954), especially Chapter 7, "Racial and Ethnic Differences," pp. 107–128.

[4]Milton M. Gordon, *Assimilation in American Life* (New York: Oxford University Press, 1964), p. 27. See also, E. K. Francis, "The Nature of the Ethnic Group," *American Journal of Sociology,* **52** (March 1947), pp. 393–400.

[5]Gordon, op. cit., p. 26.

[6]Daniel Glaser, "Dynamics of Ethnic Identification," *American Sociological Review,* **23** (Feb. 1958), pp. 31–40.

source from which contemporary ethnic cultures have been derived. Sociologists occasionally remind us that, strictly speaking, there are no native Americans, that we all are, in a sense, immigrants. Our forebears came to this country—some voluntarily, others not—from another continent, and there are those who would contend so did the ancestors of Sitting Bull, Pocahontas, and Cochise!

It has been estimated that between 1820—when the federal government first began to collect and publish official immigration statistics —and 1965, more than 43 million immigrants came into the United States, over 35 million of whom were from Europe.[7] The European exodus is generally viewed as consisting of two different waves of population movement: the so-called old and new immigrants. It is generally agreed that together they constituted the largest intersocietal human migration in recorded history. The old immigration period spanned most of the nineteenth century and involved an influx of about 19 million people into this country. The majority of these early immigrants were from northern and western parts of Europe, where culture patterns were sufficiently similar to the white, English-speaking, and predominantly Protestant colonies to enable them to adapt to the Anglo-Saxon culture. The assimilation of these early groups occurred within a comparatively short period of time and with relatively little of the tension and conflict that was to characterize the experience of later immigrant families.

Beginning in the latter part of the nineteenth century and continuing into the second decade of the twentieth century, another massive influx of immigrants from eastern, central, and southern Europe occurred. This new wave of immigration represented a greater and primarily non-English-speaking culture and one that was in sharp contrast to that of the native and early immigrant families. Mostly uneducated and of peasant background, they were generally considered to be of "inferior stock" and their alien customs were viewed with open disdain. This attitude is clearly reflected in one of the published works of a professional educator writing during this period. He stated:

These southern and eastern Europeans are of a very different type from the north Europeans who preceded them. Illiterate, docile, lacking in self-reliance and initiative, and not possessing the Anglo-Teutonic conceptions of law, order, and government, their coming has served to dilute tremendously our national stock, and to corrupt our civil life. The great bulk of these people have settled in the cities of the North Atlantic and North Central States, and the problems of proper housing and living, moral and sanitary conditions, honest and decent government, and proper education have everywhere been made more difficult by their presence. Everywhere these people tend to settle in

[7]U.S. Bureau of the Census, *Statistical Abstracts of the United States: 1967,* 88th edition, (Washington, D.C., 1967), p. 96.

73

groups or settlements, and to set up here their national manners, customs, and observances. Our task is to break up these groups or settlements, to assimilate and amalgamate these people as a part of our American race, and to implant in their children, so far as can be done, the Anglo-Saxon conception of righteousness, law and order, and popular government, and to awaken in them a reverence for our democratic institutions and for those things in our national life which we as people hold to be of abiding worth.[8]

As a consequence, the adaptation of newcomer families was considerably more difficult and their efforts at assimilation involved much more conflict and tension than those in preceding generations. Moreover, the ethnic cleavages that emerged out of the clash between members of the old and the new immigrations in some significant respects still persist to this day.[9] As Wattenberg has observed about the quality of that fabled receptacle, the American melting pot: "[I]t is a happily inefficient one. It has succeeded only in melting immigrants into productive Americans, but fortunately, it has had difficulty melting the cultural differences out of the immigrant or his descendants."[10] As we shall see later in this chapter, however, a rather extensive assimilation process has taken place over the years.

Massive immigration from Europe (and Africa) was effectively terminated through restrictive legislation enacted during the twenties, with the introduction of the so-called national origins system. This new immigration policy—which discriminated against eastern and southern Europeans—remained in effect, with only minor modifications, until very recently. The result, of course, was a dramatic decline in immigration. In 1960, for example, the United States was admitting one eighth the number of immigrants that it used to. In 1965 a new immigration policy was adopted that eventually removed many of the inequities of past legislation. Immigrant quotas established earlier were subjected to a new preference system that allowed the shifting of unused allotments of previously favored high-quota countries to low-quota nations. In 1968, the national origins system was eliminated entirely, and all nations outside of the Western Hemisphere were allotted a total of 170,000 immigrant visas on an essentially first-come, first-served basis, with the maximum for any one nation set at 20,000.

The vast majority of the most recent newcomer families to migrate to the United States come from within the Western Hemisphere—Mexico, Puerto Rico, Canada, and Cuba. Of these, the Mexicans and the Puerto

---

[8]Ellwood P. Cobberly, *Changing Conceptions of Education* (Boston: Houghton Mifflin Company, 1909), pp. 15–16, as quoted in Gordon, op. cit., p. 98.

[9]Ralph L. Kolodny, "Ethnic Cleavages in the United States: An Historical Reminder to Social Workers," *Social Work,* **14** (Jan. 1969), pp. 13–23.

[10]Ben J. Wattenberg and Richard M. Scammon, *This U.S.A.,* (Garden City, N.Y.: Doubleday and Company, 1965), p. 47.

Ricans are the most conspicuous in number. During the decade of the fifties, for example, more than 350,000 Mexicans migrated to this country, most of whom located in the western and southwestern states. During this same period, 667,000 Puerto Ricans arrived and took up residence primarily in the northeast—more than eight out of ten situated within the boundaries of New York City. Throughout the decade of the sixties large numbers of both groups continued to arrive each year. In varying degrees these newcomer families have been undergoing similar processes of assimilation that previous generations of ethnic-Americans had experienced. Their arrival extends the culturally heterogeneous patterns of marriage and family life already present in our society. Moreover, they and preceding ethnic groups significantly influence the broader social structure in a variety of ways.[11]

Complete analysis of all the ethnic-American families that could be distinguished is, of course, not possible within the short space of a single chapter. Consequently, to illustrate the wide range of variations that do exist we shall concentrate on two family types—the Italians and the Negroes. These may be viewed as representative of two major elements of ethnicity noted earlier, namely, nationality and race. A word of caution about *the* family systems we will be discussing. Our descriptions represent modal types or central tendencies in the family behavior patterns of these two ethnic groups. In reality, there is considerable diversity within each of these family systems, reflecting in part certain intracultural differences that existed between villages and provinces in Europe and Africa and that were transmitted to this country via immigration, as well as their own unique assimilative experiences and encounters.

The Italian-American Family

In numerical terms the Italians represent perhaps the largest ethnic group in American society during the past half century. At the last census they constituted over 13 percent of the more than 34 million people of foreign white stock in the United States (persons born in a foreign land or having at least one foreign-born parent), followed by the Germans, the Poles, and the Irish, in that order.

Despite or perhaps because of their large numbers, it is generally

[11] As Glazer and Moynihan point out: "Ethnicity is more than an influence on events; it is commonly the source of events. Social and political institutions do not merely respond to ethnic interests; a great number of institutions exist for the specific purpose of serving ethnic interests. This in turn tends to perpetuate them." Nathan Glazer and Daniel P. Moynihan, *Beyond the Melting Pot* (Cambridge, Mass.: MIT Press, 1963), p. 310.

agreed that the Italians have maintained a stronger adherence to their ethnic identification and, therefore, have not assimilated as rapidly into the dominant American culture as most other segments of foreign white stock.[12] A number of other and more specific reasons have been advanced for their slower rate of assimilation, including: language difficulties (although the majority migrated from the same general region, they spoke several distinct dialects, depending on the village or province from which they came, thus impeding intergroup communication); a low level of occupational skills (the majority were in fact quite illiterate and unskilled, consequently they entered this country at the very bottom of the occupational structure as day laborers); religious differences (at variance with the values of the established American Protestant regime); and a presumed inferiority as a race derived from prevailing stereotypes about non-Nordic groups (they were often referred to as "swarthy," "dirty," and not infrequently, "nonwhite").[13]

The bulk of the Italians who migrated to the United States were small-village peasants from southern Italy, including Sicily. For example, of the 2.3 million who came between 1899–1910, all but 400,000 were from that general region. They arrived from an agrarian, semi-feudal background. Life in their homeland had been family and village centered and the attitudes of persons from different villages or provinces was one of mutual suspicion and antagonism. Men and women were expected to marry someone from their own village, and any heterosexual relations with outsiders were not generally condoned. Indeed, the southern Italian villager exhibited an "extraordinary suspiciousness of everyone and everything outside of his family and blood relatives."[14] This strong family loyalty served as a source of strength in his efforts to adapt to a new social environment, but it also tended to impede his assimilation into American society.

Like many other eastern and southern European immigrants, the early Italians tended to settle in the urban areas of the eastern seaboard in isolated neighborhoods populated by kinsmen and friends they had known in the old country. "The most important social division for them in their new home came to be that between those who spoke their language and those who did not."[15] People from the same villages clustered together in the same residential areas and native Americans soon came to identify these ethnically segregated neighborhoods as "Little Italies." (Urban concentrations of other immigrant groups were similarly labeled.) Ethnically segregated communities, formed in part

[12]Michael Lalli, "The Italian-American Family: Assimilation and Change, 1900–1965," *The Family Coordinator,* **18** (Jan. 1969), pp. 44–48.

[13]See the discussion and references on this point in Kolodny, op. cit., p. 19.

[14]Glazer and Moynihan, op. cit., p. 184.

[15]Kolodny, op. cit., p. 19.

by a rather natural inclination to be with one's own people, and partly as a defense against rather inhospitable native Americans and established old immigrant groups, formed a haven of security in which could be found persons of similar language, customs, and values. Here, the newcomer families could generally benefit from kinship reciprocity and could obtain information and assistance regarding employment, housing accomodations, and so on. These ethnic islands served a useful function by acting as social-psychological cushions for anxious inhabitants rebuffed by the harsh realities of becoming socially integrated into a larger society in which "prejudice against the new immigrant was not considered at all unrespectable,"[16] and was practiced on a widespread scale.

Frequently, the migration of young men was brought about through the encouragement and assistance of *padroni*—relatives and leading fellow townsmen who had become established in the United States and who were often paid commissions by American employers to recruit laborers from abroad. Unfortunately, the *padroni* often exploited their young charges for personal financial gain.[17] In addition to functioning as middlemen between employers and the new arrivals, the *padroni* enacted a cluster of related roles: they financed immigration, provided employment opportunities (often they were the straw bosses or foremen on the jobs), acted as informal legal advisors, interpreters, and scribes. The new arrivals, unable to speak English and unsure of themselves in a strange culture, became highly dependent on *padroni,* who in turn often used this dependency to their own advantage. "The *padroni* were often godfathers to the immigrants whom they assisted, and godparenthood was given great importance in southern Italy. Thus the *padrone* was able to trade on the respect and reliance of his godsons; although, according to tradition, godparents were supposed to assist their wards altruistically."[18] The exploitation of immigrants by the *padroni* eventually diminished with, among other things, the passage of state laws to control their activities, more direct hiring by American employers, and the greater Americanization of the immigrants themselves.[19]

The early Italian immigrants were a relatively youthful population and included large numbers of single men and married men who had

[16]Kolodny, op. cit., p. 19.

[17]Glazer and Moynihan, op. cit., pp. 190–191. Not infrequently, for example, the *padroni* pocketed money entrusted to them by the illiterate immigrants for saving or for transmission to relatives in Italy.

[18]John S. Macdonald and Leatrice D. Macdonald, "Urbanization, Ethnic Groups, and Social Segmentation," *Social Research,* **29** (Winter 1962), p. 44.

[19]Humbert S. Nelli, "The Italian Padrone System in the United States," *Labor History,* **5** (Spring 1964), pp. 153–167.

come without their families. Some came with the specific intention of remaining just long enough to earn enough money to enable them to return to their homeland, purchase a piece of land, and, if they were single, get married and begin to raise a family. Others returned to Italy after a time only for the purpose of finding a wife or, if already married, to bring the wife and children back to America. Still others, of course, brought their families along with them in the initial emigration from Italy. In any event, the majority of their marriages, following the European tradition, had been or would be arranged. Although many of the men were single when they came to the United States, they seldom intermarried with native-born citizens or older immigrant groups. Eventually, most either returned home to wed or sent passage fare to bring their "proxy" wives to the New World. Until they did marry, however, many of these young men boarded with relatives and friends. Although taking in lodgers was practically unheard of in southern Italy, in the United States it apparently became a common means of supplementing the meager incomes of immigrant families.[20]

The strict courtship pattern that prevailed in Italy was transplanted to the United States. Heterosexual interaction among unmarried persons was usually restricted to group events or activities such as occurred on holidays, special occasions, and the like. If a couple exhibited a special interest in one another it was generally assumed they were seriously interested in becoming engaged and getting married. Moreover, any form of premarital sexual intimacy was strictly forbidden. Indeed, virginity among Italian daughters was rigidly guarded as a matter of family honor and both father and son assumed the responsibility of protecting the daughter's virtue until she was properly married.[21] Custom required that the couple obtain parental permission—especially from the girl's father—to become engaged. If approval was given (and it usually was), a formal announcement was made and the wedding took place within the year.

The European immigrant families were comparatively large and characteristically patriarchal in structure, with the wife and the children almost completely subordinated to the will of the husband.[22] So it was with the first-generation Italian family. The Italian father was highly authoritarian and a strict disciplinarian who ruled the home with a stern hand. Although not lacking affection for his offspring, he showed little hesitation in employing verbal or physical punishment as a means of controlling their behavior. Indeed, the parent-child relation-

[20]Macdonald and Macdonald, op. cit., p. 44
[21]Stein and Cloward, op. cit., p. 4.
[22]W. Lloyd Warner and Leo Srole, *The Social System of American Ethnic Groups,* Yankee City Series, Vol. 3 (New Haven, Conn.: Yale University Press, 1945) Chapter 6.

ship typically encompassed a mixture of overt expressions of both affection and discipline.

Children were expected to display a respectful obedience of adult authority in general and of parents and older persons in particular—especially older persons associated with the family through kinship or close friendship ties.[23] Moreover, they were required to assume adult responsibilities at a relatively early age.[24] Sons were especially pressured to seek early employment in order to supplement the limited family income. The ideal son was expected to hand over his entire weekly earnings to the father—a practice that was to meet increasing resistance as the youth became Americanized. The period of extended childhood that characterizes the contemporary middle-class child in America was never experienced by his immigrant predecessor.

The firm paternalistic stance of the Italian father was counterbalanced by an affectionate and protective mother who often intervened in behalf of the children. At the same time, however, the immigrant Italian wife played an extremely dependent role with respect to her husband. Separated from the kinship and friendship bonds that pervaded the rural Italian village, she became sharply confined to the home in the United States. Seldom allowed to venture beyond the boundaries of the neighborhood and burdened with the supervision and care of the relatively large family characteristic of lower-class immigrant groups, she found herself isolated from the larger urban community of which she had become a part. Lacking little if any command of the English language and uncertain of her position in the new society, she often reacted by adhering tenaciously to traditional ethnic customs because they provided her with a sense of security in what was often perceived to be a bewildering and sometimes hostile community. On the other hand, her husband and her children, primarily through his occupation and their school, were almost immediately thrown into daily confrontation with American institutions and mores. For them the maintenance of their ethnic identification and cultural patterns became acutely problematic as they encountered a variety of forces consciously or unconsciously designed to promote rapid social assimilation.

Coming from a rural village background and possessing little in the way of formal education, the Italian father usually entered the occupational system as an unskilled laborer. Even at that level, however, obtaining and holding a job became a formidable challenge. In addition

---

[23]Lalli, op. cit., p. 47.

[24]Adolescence as a distinct age-grade was practically nonexistent in Italy and at comparatively young ages boys and girls were becoming fully productive members of their family units. Thus, immigrant parents held similar expectations for their children in the New World.

to being handicapped with learning a new language, he had to contend with the open antagonism of both "native" and older immigrant workers who viewed his presence as an economic threat to whatever job security they had achieved. He discovered that his foreign tongue, his customs, and even his food preferences and eating habits were often used by others to stereotype him as an object of resentment and to keep him from fraternizing with other workers.[25] Forced to compromise in varying degrees with the realities of adjusting to a complex and competitive work world, at home he would continue to insist on retaining a cultural pattern of family life similar to the one he had known in Italy. In the home and in the ethnic neighborhood he could regain a sense of belonging and a renewed confidence in his abilities to resist the pressures of assimilation he had encountered in the larger community. For his children, however, adherence to family values and loyalty to the Italian way proved a more difficult task.

The integrated family life of the transplanted southern Italian was transformed and subjected to disruptive internal conflict as its children became increasingly engaged in the American community. The initial confrontation occurred in the streets. There the second-generation Italian child's contacts with more Americanized peers and native-born children made him uncomfortably aware of his cultural differences. Uncertain of himself and anxious to be accepted by new-found friends, he grew increasingly receptive to pressures from them to speak English and to adopt new modes of dress and behavior. Under the influence of the peer group the Italian child began to internalize a set of values and norms that sharply conflicted with those that prevailed at home. The processes of acculturation had begun and were to be further accelerated through the impact of the school system.

Generally speaking, southern Italian immigrant parents were not prepared to cope with either the idea or the necessity of formal education for their children. In their villages in the old country schools were viewed as a privilege of the land-owning class:

the peasant's child (should the parents have the strange idea of sending him) was unwelcome. Education was for a cultural style of life and professions the peasant could never aspire to. Nor was there any ideology of change: intellectual curiosity and originality were ridiculed or suppressed. 'Do not make your child better than you are,' runs a South Italian proverb.[26]

Given this background, immigrant parents viewed with suspicion and considerable ambivalence the compulsory school attendance laws in America. They did not readily understand the emphasis in this

[25]Kolodny, op. cit., p. 17.
[26]Glazer and Moynihan, op. cit., p. 199.

80

country on achieving social mobility through formal education. From their Old World frame of reference a family could only hope to improve its material circumstances through a combination of hard work and good luck. It is important to note here that the Italian ethic highly valued activity on the part of family members that served to promote the welfare of the family as a whole. This contrasted with the American ethic, which emphasized the pursuit of activities related to self-advancement.[27] Thus, parents often resented the time spent in school by any one of their children, time they felt he might use better in assisting at home or working to help support the family. This clash between ethnic parental values and those of the larger society was often reflected in high rates of truancy and drop-outs among working-class Italian youth. Moreover, the relatively low value placed on formal education eventually lead to a significant underrepresentation of Italians among the college and university youth. Thus, the social mobility of second-generation Italians was impaired by the child's acceptance of the parental conception of the school system as threatening and nonutilitarian.

Despite initial resistance, the American school system played a crucial role in promoting the social assimilation of immigrant children. Through daily instruction in the classroom second-generation Italian children soon surpassed their parents in acquiring a proficiency in English. Teachers encouraged them to accept the middle-class orientation toward personal initiative and self-reliance and to push their level of aspirations beyond the boundaries set by the family. The schools exhalted the virtues of democracy and equalitarianism, which, in many respects, were inconsistent with, as well as threatening to, parental values and traditional Italian family organization. Increasingly the young person felt much tension from his efforts to satisfy the contradictory norms of two competing value systems. He was caught in the dilemma of inviting criticisms for being too foreign in the schoolroom and too American in the home. Indeed, the home-versus-school dilemma reflected the major problem of the second-generation Italian-American, namely, how to inhabit two social worlds simultaneously and without conflict.[28] An eventual resolution of this problem was sought by many through a repudiation of much of their ethnic heritage in favor of the norms, values, and customs of the new society.

As Italian children grew older and extended their sphere of extrafamilial relationships they were increasingly eager to become more fully integrated and identified with American culture. In the process of

[27]Ibid., p. 196.
[28]Irving L. Child, *Italian or American? The Second Generation in Conflict* (New Haven, Conn.: Yale University Press, 1943).

adopting the attitudes of the larger community, they gradually came to perceive their home life as unnecessarily restrictive and a potential source of embarrassment. They felt ashamed of their parents' "foreign" ways and their awkward "broken" English. Conflict erupted in the home as the growing adolescent began to resent the authoritarian stance of the father and the demands for filial loyalty to Italian customs and traditions. "When the son and the daughter refused to conform, their action was considered a rebellion of ungrateful children for whom so many advantages had been provided. The gap between the two generations was widened and the family spirit was embittered by repeated misunderstandings."[29]

With recurrent defiance of parental prerogatives family conflict gradually intensified, frequently to the point of open hostility. The young adolescents, and particularly the sons, responded typically by escaping to the streets to seek security in neighborhood peer groups. Through the activities of the street gang they could satisfy needs for independence and autonomy of action and at the same time gain companionship and a much-desired sense of belonging. Indeed, many of the friendships established during this period were carried over into adulthood. Within the context of the gang subculture young Italians could find temporary refuge from the restrictions of the home and the larger society and at the same time engage in a variety of exciting and contrary behavior.[30] The gang had its own normative system, which sanctioned behavior often at variance with the mores of middle-class American society. It was through the activities of this kind of teen-age clique, for example, that many young Italians had their first encounters with the law and their initial experiences with premarital sex. Although parents generally disapproved of such activity, they found it extremely difficult to counter the freedom and the attractions of the street life. As youngsters began spending more and more time outside of the home, parents sensed a growing inability to control and manipulate the lives of their progeny. This period of intense conflict reflected the acculturative process by which teen-agers would eventually attempt openly to introduce into the family situation their newly acquired American values and expectations and parents would react by attempting to reinforce the Old World family patterns.[31]

As the second generation approached adulthood they exhibited an

[29]Marcus L. Hansen, "The Third Generation: Search for Continuity," in Stein and Cloward, op. cit., p. 140.

[30]William F. Whyte, *Street Corner Society, The Social Structure of an Italian Slum* (Chicago: University of Chicago Press, 1943).

[31]Paul J. Campisi, "The Italian Family in the United States," *American Journal of Sociology,* **53** (May 1948), pp. 443–449.

overt reluctance to adhere to traditional Italian customs, particularly those governing courtship and mate selection. Having been exposed to the relatively free dating system of American society they began to challenge parental insistence on close supervision of their heterosexual interactions as outmoded and an unnecessary intrusion. Moreover, they began to resist the general admonition against dating non-Italians. During this period of awkward transition of generational values a pattern developed that constituted a blend of Italian and American dating customs. Lalli has described this pattern with respect to attendance at various social events:

Dates were not specifically arranged. Young men and girls would make their appearance as members of separate groups knowing well exactly who would be there. Although such meetings were "accidental," a young man would often have the opportunity of taking a girl home. If the relationship developed to the point where a date or two was arranged in advance and the young man called at the girl's home—there was a strong presumption in the Italian community that an engagement would soon be made.[32]

This system gave the appearance of adhering to ethnic protocol and at the same time permitted the young adults to achieve greater freedom in establishing heterosexual relationships. (A similar pattern associated with the dating process apparently has tended to persist among Italian-Americans currently residing in the working-class neighborhoods of large metropolitan centers in the United States.) By the time sons and daughters reached adulthood and married, forms of compromise in other areas of family life had emerged to diminish the potentially disruptive effects of intense parent-youth conflict and hostility and to promote an accommodation between the generations.[33]

[32]Lalli, op. cit., p. 46.

[33]Campisi, op. cit., pp. 448–449, cited a number of factors that helped bring about a new stability between the generations, including:

the realization on the part of the parents that life in America is to be permanent; the adult age of the offspring; the almost complete dependence of the parents on the offspring, including use of the children as informants, interpreters, guides, and translators of the American world; recognition on the part of the parents that social and economic success can come to the offspring only as they become more and more like "old" Americans; the conscious and unconscious acculturation of the parents themselves with a consequent minimizing of many potential conflicts; the long period of isolation from the Old World which makes the small-village culture and peasant family seem less real; the decision by the parents to sacrifice certain aspects of the Old World family for the sake of retaining the affection of the children; the acknowledgment by the children that the first-generation family is a truncated one and that complete repudiation of the parents would leave them completely isolated; the success of the first-generation family in instilling in the offspring respect and affection for the parents; and the gradual understanding by the children that successful interaction with the American world is possible by accepting marginal roles and that complete denial of the Old World family is unnecessary.

The majority of second-generation adult Italians were perhaps not sufficiently confident in their new independence or adequately comfortable with the American ways of life to completely break away from the influence of ethnic customs and traditions. Despite their objections to parental pressures, most of them confined their serious dating to and selected their marital partners from the Italian population. Even among those marrying "outsiders" the custom of obtaining parental consent was generally adhered to. Moreover, married couples typically took up residence either in the ethnic neighborhood in which they had been reared or nearby in the same community. It was not uncommon during the Great Depression for such couples to double up with parents until they could accumulate enough resources to establish separate households. Indeed, it wasn't until the World War II period and thereafter that significant numbers of Italian families began to move away from the ethnic neighborhood and the surrounding area. Among those who eventually managed to achieve both residential and social mobility, dating and courtship practices gradually approximated those of middle-class American society.

Marriage and family life among the majority of second-generation Italians was, in the main, tradition oriented, but with some noticeable modifications produced by the acculturation process. Although the family remained essentially patriarchal, the husband assumed a less rigid authoritarian posture in the home and a more tolerant attitude regarding the obedience and the discipline of his children. Although spousal roles continued to be performed on a fairly segregated basis, the new wife was considerably less submissive to and dependent upon her husband than had been the case in the past. The fact that both generally had had more education than the parent generations and, indeed, had often attended the same schools, indirectly affected the character of the marital relationship. Because the wife's facility with the English language was now equal to that of the husband's, her position in the home was improved. Moreover, she could and did venture beyond the boundaries of the ethnic colony with a sense of familiarity and confidence relatively unknown to her mother, often to find employment in the larger community. Being able to make an economic contribution to the household expanded her feelings of independence and provided her with greater leverage in a still predominantly patriarchal family structure.

Generally speaking, however, most couples confined the greater part of their informal activities to the more comfortable relationships in the Italian community. Thus, a study of a Boston working-class neighborhood in the late fifties showed that Italian-Americans conducted most of their daily social life within the context of a peer-group society based on long-established ties with selected relatives and friends of the same

84

age, sex, and life-cycle status.[34] More specifically, it was found that husbands and wives spent almost as much time interacting with siblings, in-laws, and cousins of the same age and sex as they did with each other. In essence, a pattern of sex-segregated peer-group relationships involving kin and close friends and formed early in childhood was continued following marriage. This was especially noticeable among working-class Italians who generally experienced a minimum of residential mobility.

Although the large family still commanded respect, second-generation couples tended on the average to have fewer children than those of the first generation, even though the second-generation couples were often under pressure from their parents to produce many grandchildren. Child-rearing patterns showed greater diversity than in the past because of increasing acculturation and a gradual attainment of improved socioeconomic position. The majority of husbands, however, were still heavily concentrated in working-class or blue-collar occupations and their households were "adult-centered," that is, "run by adults for adults, where the role of the children is to behave as much as possible like miniature adults.'[85] Youngsters were expected to be quiet and passively obedient in the home and to behave so as to please the adults. At the same time they were allowed to act their own age outside the home among their peers and relatively free of parental supervision or guidance—provided they didn't get into trouble. As Gans noted, these "second-generation parents have accepted the need for education through high school, but they—like their own parents—have continued to maintain the traditional demand that within the household the child must obey parental rules.''[36] But when their own (now third-generation) child enters adolescence he too—like them before him—rejects the requirements of traditional conformity to ethnic norms and values in favor of a more Americanized style of living and greater personal autonomy, both within and outside of the home.

Actually, the assimilative patterns manifested by third-generation Italian teen-agers varied according to earlier modes of adjustment that

---

[34]Herbert J. Gans, *The Urban Villagers, Groups and Class in the Life of Italian-Americans* (New York: The Free Press, 1962), pp. 36–41. Gans notes that such peer group affiliations are rather universal among the working class and can be found in other classes. However, they seem to be especially intense and more family oriented among the Italians.

[35]Ibid., p. 54. Gans contrasts this pattern with "child-centered" families, which are more prevalent in the lower-middle class and in which parents tend to subordinate their pleasures in order to provide children whatever they think they need or demand, and with the "adult-directed" families of upper-middle-class groups, in which parents similarly reorient their own priorities to guide their children in a direction they consider desirable.

[36]Ibid., pp. 64–65.

had been adopted by their parents.[37] Some parents had largely rejected the Italian subculture and had actively sought complete integration into American society. To the extent that they succeeded their children exhibited few if any Italian cultural characteristics. Such parents often moved out of the ethnic colony altogether and some changed their names. Teen-agers in these families were reared as Americans and have become progressively indistinguishable from their non-Italian peers. Some parents chose to resist acculturation into American society and instead sought to maintain and reaffirm identification with the Italian subculture. Teen-agers of these families have experienced considerable conflict and uncertainty both within and outside the home as the forces of social change and acculturation have increasingly penetrated their neighborhoods and weakened the Italian subculture. In many areas the distinctly Italian neighborhood has undergone a major transformation as increasing numbers of Italian-Americans have moved up in the social scale and have been replaced in the slum areas by more recent, Spanish-speaking immigrants and Negroes.[38]

The majority of second-generation parents, however, have exhibited neither of the two patterns described above. Instead, they have gradually sought to become Americanized while still retaining ties with the Italian subculture. Their teen-age offspring have experienced much less culture conflict than their parents and have managed to maintain certain aspects of their ethnic identification while at the same time assuming typical American characteristics and adopting American customs of dating and courtship. Although much less so than in the past, these families tend to be concentrated in the lower socioeconomic classes, and teen-age behavior and activity are often more reflective of lower-class norms and values than of ethnicity.

The Italian-American Family: The Future

With each succeeding generation Italians in America have slowly and somewhat reluctantly moved away from the traditional ethnic culture. The process for the majority has been gradual, for the strong family, kin, and neighborhood ties among Italians have especially resisted the forces of change. Given the hardships and the complications of living in a strange and visibly antagonistic urban community, the early immigrant family was a highly stable unit. Divorce was not allowed and marital separations and desertion were relatively rare.

[37]This section draws heavily from Francis A. J. Ianni, "The Italo-American Teen-Ager," *The Annals of the American Academy of Political and Social Science,* **338** (Nov. 1961), pp. 70–78.

[38]Distinctly Italian neighborhoods have, of course, by no means completely disappeared from the American scene. Glazer and Moynihan, op. cit., p. 187, for example, point to the Italian districts of New York and note that "it is striking how the old neighborhoods have been artfully adapted to a higher standard of living rather than simply deserted, as they would have been by other groups, in more American style."

Responsibility toward one's family obligations was the predominant rule of life and a basic source of strength. Despite numerous frustrations engendered by the conflicting demands of two cultures the second generation upon maturity also established a fairly stable family system. Although they had begun to break with Italian tradition their high rates of marriage to other Italians indicated that in many respects they remained committed to its norms and values.[39] But ongoing processes in the larger society and the forces of acculturation have gradually brought about manifest changes in the social context of Italian-American family life.

These changes are most pronounced in the third generation, among whom, for example, only a rapidly diminishing minority are willing to learn or are able to communicate in the ancestral tongue. In increasing numbers they are leaving the old communities to take advantage of the educational and occupational opportunities available elsewhere— often with the blessings of their parents. Their movement into the mainstream of American society has been both physical and cultural.[40] As a result the third generation has shown a greater propensity to interact with and even to intermarry with non-Italians than previous generations.

The contemporary Italian-American family differs from generations past in both its structure and its relationships. The large patriarchal system with its adult-centered orientation has been gradually replaced by a smaller family system, a more equalitarian husband-wife relationship, and the child-centered characteristics of the American middle class. Even among the lower class the third generation is just "slightly more patriarchal than other lower class families but still strives toward the 'democractic family' ideal."[41] As the modern Italian family has increasingly absorbed the attributes of middle-class America it has also become more vulnerable to disruption and divorce than was the case among previous generations.

Italian-American families continue to experience various aspects of successful assimilation, but their ethnic consciousness and identification have by no means disappeared. Despite the achievement of general social acceptance over the past fifty years, intermittent encounters with subtle prejudice and discrimination remind them that many others in the society continue to view them as "different." Recognition of this

---

[39]For evidence of the low intermarriage rates of second-generation Italians, see, for example, Ruby Jo Reeves Kennedy, "Single or Triple Melting Pot? Intermarriage Trends in New Haven, 1870–1950," *American Journal of Sociology,* **58** (July 1952), pp. 56–59; August B. Hollingshead, "Cultural Factors in the Selection of Marriage Mates," *American Sociological Review,* **15** (Oct. 1950), pp. 619–627.

[40]Francis A. J. Ianni, "Residential and Occupational Mobility as Indices of the Acculturation of an Ethnic Group," *Social Forces,* **36** (Oct. 1957), pp. 65–72.

[41]Ianni, "The Italo-American Teen-Ager," op. cit., p. 76.

fact was partly responsible for the formation in the late sixties of the American-Italian Anti-Defamation League, which encourages members, among other things, to "join the fight to put an end to defamation, discrimination and slurs that stigmatize and offend the integrity, reputations and character" of the 22 million citizens of Italian descent in the nation.[42] Italian immigrants arriving in the United States in the seventies soon discover that ethnic labels are still pervasive and ethnic consciousness is still very much in evidence.

Black American Families

In numerous and crucial respects the experience and the development of Negro or, as some would prefer, black (we shall use both terms interchangeably) families in the United States represents a sharp contrast to that of Italians and other ethnic groups who came to the New World. Indeed, the distinct historical circumstances that helped to shape the Negro family system in America have been unusually complicated and in some ways without parallel in comparison to other segments of our multiethnic society. The fact that they originally came here from Africa rather than Europe, that they were forced into a system of extended slavery and essentially isolated from their traditional culture, that they were and continue to be the large physically visible minority in the nation, and that for three and a half centuries they were generally excluded from full participation in the larger society are just a few of the historical factors that have significantly influenced the structure and the functioning of Negro families. As with other groups, only perhaps more so, the distinctive patterns of contemporary black American families are intimately connected with the historical, economic, and social conditions encountered by generations past.

The first Negroes to become permanently settled in the New World were purchased from a Dutch ship that had arrived in Jamestown, Virginia, in 1619. Twenty in all, they were sold to the local colonists to become indentured servants and, presumably, had the same legal status as the white indentured. Under the system of temporary servitude they could earn their freedom after working for their masters a specified number of years or sometimes through conversion to Christianity. But only a small proportion of Negroes were ever given the opportunity to gain freedman status and even those who did found it difficult to avoid the harsh restrictions later applied to persons under slave status. The economic potential of Negroes as a permanent source of cheap labor

---

[42]Also organized in the late sixties, the American Italian Historical Association consists of scholars and laymen devoted to encouraging and facilitating research on the Italian experience in America.

was soon recognized and exploited. The first statutory recognition of slavery in the United States occurred in Virginia in 1661. The other colonies soon followed suit, and by the time the colonies achieved their independence, institutionalized chattel slavery had become a legal fact as well as a way of life perpetuated by generations to come.[43] Prior to the Emancipation Proclamation of 1863, there were almost $4^1/_2$ million blacks in the United States—nearly 4 million in the South alone—the great bulk of whom were enslaved.

The Negro Family Under Slavery

A unique aspect of the historical development of Negro family life in America was its almost total discontinuity with African culture. The black people brought to North America actually represented a variety of complex and distinct African cultural backgrounds. However, unlike the later immigrant groups from Europe and elsewhere, they were effectively prevented from reestablishing and maintaining the traditions of their African heritage in the New World by conditions associated with the slave system. This disruptive process had its beginnings in Africa, where slaves were often separated from their families and tribal kinsmen subsequent to being transported to North America. Upon arrival in this country they were indiscriminately sold to the highest bidder and widely scattered among the plantations, farms, and cities, thus becoming further disengaged from their families and their culture. In their new environment slaves were discouraged if not explicitly forbidden from practicing traditional customs and forced to adopt the ways of their owners. Over generations their African heritage would become but a dim memory.

Through forces of circumstances they had to acquire a new language, adopt new habits of labor, and take over, however imperfectly, the folkways of the American environment. Their children, who knew only the American environment, soon forgot the few memories that had been passed on to them and developed motivations and modes of behavior in harmony with the New World. Their children's children have often recalled with skepticism the fragments of stories concerning Africa which have been preserved in their families. But, of the habits and customs as well as the hopes and the fears that characterize the life of their forbearers in Africa, nothing remains.[44]

These and other circumstances of early slavery made it extremely difficult for Negroes to develop a stable family system in America. For one thing, the initial imported slave population consisted predomi-

[43]Alphonso Pinkney, *Black Americans* (Englewood Cliffs, N.J.: Prentice-Hall, 1969), pp. 1–3.
[44]E. Franklin Frazier, *The Negro Family in the United States,* rev. and abridged ed. (Chicago: University of Chicago Press, Phoenix Edition, 1966), p. 15.

nantly of young males. On many of the early plantations the ratio of black males to black females was nine to one.[45] This extraordinary imbalance in the sex ratio, which would continue to exist until the middle of the nineteenth century, was perhaps partly responsible for the development of casual rather than permanent sexual liaisons. Moreover, the sexual impulses of the slaves could now be expressed without the restraints typically imposed by traditional tribal customs and mores. In addition, the normal sex drives of the slaves were frequently exploited by their white owners for economic advantage. Under the law as well as in fact persons in bondage were considered a form of property and therefore could be traded or sold like any other property. Thus, some owners engaged in the practice of breeding their slaves in a manner similar to that used with livestock. Young black males in their prime would be selected to act as "stallions" and women were encouraged if not coerced into promiscuity in order to reproduce additional slave offspring who could be turned into economic assets.[46] Nor was it uncommon for the owner to further increase his "holdings" as a consequence of having sexual intercourse with some of his female slaves.

Despite the above circumstances an unknown proportion of slaves, usually house servants or artisans, were allowed to enter into monogamous unions and have families. Their marriages, however, lacked the legal foundations and sanctions that ordinarily protected marital and familial relationships. That power rested in the discretion of the owners, who could and sometimes did separate and disperse entire families to further the owners' economic interests. Of course, practices varied considerably among slaveholders and undoubtedly many were kind and considerate toward their slaves, even encouraging some to establish permanent marriages and to develop a stable family life. Moreover, differential treatment of field slaves and house slaves was common.[47] The latter usually enjoyed higher status in comparison to those slaves relegated to field work. Through daily and personal association with the slaveholder's family the house slaves were provided an opportunity to assimilate many of the ideas, sentiments, and values of the owners. Indeed, house servants often formed a strong identification with their masters, adopting their religion, language, dress, manners, patterns of family life, and so on, and exhibiting a deep devotion and loyalty to them. Typically the Negro female servant was charged with the major care-taking responsibilities for rearing the owner's offspring, and as a result of this experience close emotional

---

[45]Andrew Billingsley, *Black Families in White America* (Englewood Cliffs, N.J.: Prentice-Hall, 1968), p. 51.

[46]Frazier, op. cit., pp. 18–20. He cites evidence of owners ordering their blacks to "get married," that is, reproduce or else face the threat of being sold to a slave trader.

[47]Ibid., pp. 24–29.

attachments between black and white children frequently emerged. Sometimes the relations between the children became so intimate that the master would feel it necessary to intrude and redefine the "proper" social distance between the two races. Slave husbands and fathers attached to the household were encouraged to assume prominent roles in their family affairs. Given these conditions, it became possible for some house-slave families to develop considerable stability and organization.[48]

In contrast, among the vast majority of slave field hands it was extremely difficult and often impossible to establish and maintain any semblance of marriage and family life. Generally they were under the supervision of an overseer, a person often recruited from the poorer white class, whose primary role was to enforce strict discipline and obedience and to derive maximum productivity from the slave laborers. There is considerable evidence that the widespread cruelty of impersonal overseers greatly contributed to the institutionalization of uninhibited brutality toward field slaves on the plantations.[49] Marriage among the laborers was viewed as uneconomical and often was prohibited. The development of affectional bonds between males and females was discouraged and sexual promiscuity allowed to promote the breeding of additional slaves. Thus, males were not allowed to marry or to assume familial responsibilities. Even when such ties were established, husbands and fathers were frequently sold or traded off to breed elsewhere, leaving the wives and mothers and children behind. "Since children were economic assets to the owners, the female slave could look forward to having children in substantial numbers and possibly a succession of mates rather than a permanent spouse. Children, then, were frequently born into a family consisting of mother, other siblings, and quite possibly maternal aunts and grandmothers."[50] It was within the context of these dramatic conditions of slavery that the Negro matricentric family pattern emerged which has persisted in modified forms up to the present day.[51]

---

[48]But as Frazier reminds us, their destinies were always subject to the will and economic aspirations of their master and to that extent family life remained threatened and insecure. Ibid., pp. 31–33.

[49]Pinkney, op. cit., p. 10.

[50]Stuart A. Queen and Robert W. Habenstein, *The Family in Various Cultures* 3rd ed. (Philadelphia: J. B. Lippincott Co., 1967), p. 317.

[51]In recent years evidence has accumulated that suggests that the matricentric pattern is not peculiar to contemporary Negro Americans but is equally prevalent among lower-class white families, that the pattern is more a function of socioeconomic or class position than race. Eric Josephson, "The Matriarchy: Myth and Reality," *The Family Coordinator*, **18** (July 1969), pp. 268–276; Herbert H. Hyman and John S. Reed, "Black Matriarchy Reconsidered: Evidence from Secondary Analysis of Sample Surveys," *Public Opinion Quarterly*, **33** (Fall 1969), pp. 346–354; Ludwig L. Geismar and Ursula C. Gerhart, "Social Class, Ethnicity, and Family Functioning: Exploring Some Issues Raised by the Moynihan Report," *Journal of Marriage and the Family*, **30** (Aug. 1968), pp. 480–487.

THE SLAVE MOTHER: SOURCE OF STABILITY Although the system of slavery was by no means kind to either sex, it is clear that during its existence it served in various ways to undermine particularly both the status and the personality development of the Negro male. Viewed by his master as a mere economic utility, he was generally denied normal opportunities to become a significant role model in the family structure. Especially among the field laborers, the husband and father often appeared as a transitory figure, someone the children saw only briefly and rarely identified with. Under the peculiar institution of slavery, the Negro father "was not the head of the family, the holder of property, the provider, the protector."[52] These circumstances, combined with the more favorable treatment of the female and her normal maternal attachments, led the slave mother to assume the major responsibilities of rearing offspring and providing them with parental affection. For these and other reasons previously discussed, it was the Negro mother who emerged as the dominant and most important figure in the slave family.[53]

THE "FREE" BLACK FAMILY DURING SLAVERY We noted earlier that a small class of free Negroes had existed in the United States since the middle of the seventeenth century. At the time of the first census they numbered approximately sixty thousand, and by the time of the Civil War their population was approaching one-half million. A number of sources contributed to the steady growth of this group, including the following: (1) manumission, that is, formal liberation of slaves continued; (2) the children of free blacks also inherited free status; (3) mulatto children born of free black mothers were free; (4) children of free black and Indian parentage had free status; (5) mulatto children born to white servants and mothers were free; and (6) freedom was gained by slaves who managed to escape.[54] The free blacks generally concentrated in urban environments, where they were able to enter a variety of occupations that afforded them some measure of security and independence and where they could participate in a social life centered for the most part around churches and fraternal organizations. Although the free blacks always occupied a precarious and circumscribed position throughout slavery, many of them managed to obtain some formal education, to engage in a number of skilled and professional occupations, to become property owners, and even to achieve positions of wealth. Indeed, many free Negroes became slave owners! Often, however, this involved the purchase of their wives from slavery, as well as relatives and friends.[55]

---

[52]Kenneth M. Stampp, *The Peculiar Institution* (New York: Alfred A. Knopf, 1956), p. 343.

[53]Frazier, op. cit., p. 32.

[54]Ibid., p. 143.

[55]Pinkney, op. cit., p. 17.

Family life among a large group of these free blacks reached a relatively high degree of development and stability during the slave period. This was especially the case among those who had managed to accumulate some property and wealth. Anxious to emphasize their superior position, they often adopted the manners and mores of upper-class whites. In many ways they attempted to lead a separate existence to prevent their being identified with the Negro masses. Their family structure was essentially patriarchal in nature with the husband dominating the lives of his wife and children. This class of free blacks practiced a style of family life that was distinct from that of the majority of Negroes and that has been continued among contemporary middle- and upper-class groups.[56]

Emancipation and the Negro Family

It is generally agreed that the Civil War and the Emancipation created widespread social disorganization among the Negro population. Although there is little doubt that the vast majority welcomed their new freedom, it is also true that they were not prepared for it. They lacked the usual normative and institutional guidelines for directing their lives and were without the necessary facilities for caring for themselves. Thus, many of the newly freed slaves found their lives under daily threat by the lack of the basic essentials for survival. Indeed: "For tens of thousands of Negroes, emancipation meant the freedom to die of starvation and illness."[57]

Those groups of Negroes that had managed to achieve some measure of economic security and family stability during slavery were not significantly affected by the new freedom. But the large majority of the loosely structured and unstable black families experienced considerable disorganization under the stresses associated with the Emancipation. It will be recalled that a legalized formal marriage system was denied slaves and that they were generally not encouraged to assume familial responsibilities. The casual marital and familial practices and relationships that did characterize the slave period were often dramatically severed as hundreds of thousands of ex-slaves took advantage of the opportunity to break loose from the plantation system. Single men left their kinship ties behind as did many husbands, who deserted their wives and children to strike out on their own to test their newly acquired status. Many wandered about the South and eventually other regions of the country seeking work and adventure. During this period men frequently formed casual sexual unions of limited duration, eventually abandoning these temporary attachments to continue wandering in search of new encounters elsewhere.[58]

[56]E. Franklin Frazier, *Black Bourgeoisie* (Glencoe, Ill: The Free-Press, 1957).
[57]Billingsley, op. cit., p. 69.

The general irresponsibility and sexual promiscuity of the Negro male that prevailed following the Emancipation and during the Reconstruction period were particularly harsh on the Negro wife and mother. At least under the slave ·system she could potentially achieve some degree of safety and economic security through the slave owner's interest in protecting his property. Suddenly she was placed in a position of having to depend on the Negro male for the support and protection of herself and her children. But he was in general neither prepared for nor willing to accept these obligations. Thus, the Negro mother often "found herself saddled with the burden of supporting *and* rearing the children, while the Negro male availed himself of sexual privileges, at the same time repudiating any economic responsibility for family maintenance."[59] Consequently, the mother-child relationship remained the primary basis for family life among the masses of ex-slaves. As we shall note later, this mother-centered pattern still characterizes a significant proportion of contemporary lower-class Negro American families—although for different reasons than those mentioned thus far.[60]

Impact of Migration and Urbanization on the Negro Family

At the close of the Civil War well over 90 per cent of all blacks were still located in the rural South. Beginning with the Emancipation, however, a pattern of geographic mobility was set into motion that ultimately was to have profound ramifications for Negro family life as well as American society as a whole. Up to the turn of the century the migration of ex-slaves was primarily to the towns and cities of the South. Thereafter the black population shifted increasingly toward the North and to a lesser extent to the West. Thus, in 1900 about nine of every ten Negroes still resided in the southern region. By 1920, however, this proportion had decreased to 85 per cent; in 1940 it had dropped to 77 per cent, and by 1960 it had further declined to 60 per cent. One hundred years after the end of the Civil War only about 54 per cent of all Negroes were residing in the South. In 1965, more than 38 per cent were living in the North and over 8 per cent in the West.[61]

[58]Frazier, *The Negro Family in the United States,* op. cit., Chapter 13. He also notes that many Negro women took to the road during this period and that some black mothers deserted their children as part of the mass exodus from the plantations.

[59]William M. Kephart, *The Family, Society, and the Individual,* 2nd ed. (Boston: Houghton Mifflin Company, 1966), p. 209.

[60]Bernard questions whether the Negro matricentric family ever typified the plantation and postslavery periods and argues that it emerged out of conditions associated with the urban environment. See Jessie Bernard, *Marriage and Family Among Negroes* (Englewood Cliffs, N.J.: Prentice-Hall, 1966), pp. 19–23.

[61]Figures derived from various U.S. Census Reports. See also T. Lynn Smith, "The Redistribution of the Negro Population of the United States," *Journal of Negro History,* **51** (July 1966), pp. 155–173.

Periodic failures in the southern economy, labor shortages and job opportunities in the North, the cataclysmic social changes produced by two world wars, racial prejudice and discrimination, and a host of other social forces provided the impetus for this massive redistribution of the black population, the effects of which are still being felt today.

It is important to note that the black migration was essentially a movement of millions of individuals and families from rural to primarily urban environments. For example, in 1910 three fourths of all Negro families were living in rural areas, whereas today this pattern is completely reversed with nearly three fourths now residing in urban areas. Indeed, we now have the interesting situation of the nonwhite population's being more urbanized than the white population. Moreover, the steady stream of migration was overwhelmingly directed toward the large industrial and metropolitan centers of the country, particularly in the North. Again, in 1910 none of our major cities had up to 100,000 Negroes, whereas today at least eighteen cities contain over 100,000 black residents. The rapid urbanization of the Negro American has been phenomenal, and if current trends continue, they will eventually constitute a majority of the population in several of the metropolitan communities in America.

Nearly all of the early migrants had little choice but to settle in the dilapidated housing of the deteriorated slums of the cities. Their rapidly increasing numbers eventually overflowed into surrounding neighborhoods, provoking both dismay and open antagonism among the white middle-class residents. Racial discrimination and exploitation in housing and employment subsequently produced a pattern of residential segregation that would increasingly lock the Negro family into urban ghettos for decades to come.[62]

THE NEGRO FAMILY IN THE CITY The thousands of early migrants who crowded into northern cities were predominantly young males, uneducated and unskilled. A significant number were also married men who had been lured northward by promises of better jobs and wages by zealous labor recruiters who usually paid their transportation fare—but not that of their families. Consequently,

the period of estrangement, both for the men in the cities of the North and for their families left behind, exerted definite strains on family solidarity and organization. Many men took longer than their families thought necessary to send for them; some families managed to arrive in the Northern communities without waiting to be sent for, sometimes to the surprise and embarrassment of

[62]Karl E. and Alma F. Taeuber, "The Negro Population in the United States," in *The American Negro Reference Book,* ed. by John P. Davis (Englewood Cliffs, N.J.: Prentice-Hall, 1966), pp. 96–100.

the husband who was waiting to send for them. Some families never joined their husbands and fathers until years later. Some never did.[63]

The strange, impersonal, and often hostile urban environment, the extremely overcrowded and squalid conditions of the slums, and low occupational status and poverty—all of these effected further disruption of this already weakened and loose-knit family system. Lacking the ordinary institutional supports and traditional community controls, the Negro family became increasingly disorganized when confronted with the bewildering and anonymous urban world. The earlier pattern of casual sexual contacts continued, resulting in a high proportion of illegitimate births. Widespread desertion and divorce became increasingly common, leading to a high proportion of female-headed households. High rates of delinquency and crime further reflected the irregularity of family life and the personal and social pathology that prevailed in these early black communities. The urban Negro family was rapidly on the way to becoming a major social welfare problem and, to a considerable extent, has remained so to this day. (Negroes have increasingly joined the welfare roles, and although they constitute only 11 per cent of our population, they receive one third of the nation's expenditure for public aid, education, and housing.) Indeed, perhaps no other family system has gained such widespread national attention over the past decade than the Negro family.[64] The pervasive civil rights movement of the sixties called anew to public attention the long-standing adverse conditions of black families in the United States, especially those in the lower-income strata of our society.[65]

Contemporary Negro Families

From the initial disruption of the African family system under the conditions of slavery to the rapid urbanization of the majority of the black population in the United States, Negro family life has undergone a constant process of change and acculturation. Among the approximately 24 million Negroes currently residing in our nation, one finds a variety of forms of family organization, reflecting their different ways of adapting to the social forces emanating from the larger society and from

[63]Billingsley, op. cit., p. 78.

[64]Daniel P. Moynihan, *The Negro Family: The Case for National Action,* Office of Policy and Planning Research, U.S. Department of Labor (Washington, D.C.: Government Printing Office, 1965).

[65]Elizabeth Herzog, "Is There a 'Breakdown' of the Negro Family?" *Social Work,* **11** (Jan. 1966), pp. 3–10. Among other things, she suggests that perhaps no other document gave the problems of the Negro family greater currency than the well-known Moynihan report, already referred to, by shocking Americans into new recognition of old and unpalatable facts concerning the social, political, economic, and educational disadvantages that have persistently impeded the development of a stable family life among black Americans.

the conditions of existence to which black people in particular have long been subjected.[66] Racial prejudice and discrimination, inadequate education and income, unemployment and underemployment are just a few of the conditions that the contemporary generation must overcome as they strive to establish a more stable family system.[67]

The achievement of a higher socioeconomic position is essential for gaining the level of social mobility that enables the development of a stable family system. There is ample evidence that the structure and the function of modern black American families is more significantly associated with their socioeconomic status—occupation, education, and income—than with any other factor, including race. Although Negroes have made noticeable advances over the past few decades, nearly all of the gains have been made by the rising Negro middle class. The majority remain at a noticeable disadvantage in comparison to white Americans on almost any measure of social and economic status.[68] A long history of deprivation, segregation, and discrimination has taken its toll on both the individuals and the families of the black communities. Currently, for example, less than one third of all whites terminate their formal education with the completion of elementary school or less, whereas more than half of all blacks do so. At the other extreme, the number of whites completing four or more years of college is more than double that of Negroes. The Negro unemployment rate is double that for whites and their median income is a little over half that of whites. Of all the Negro families in the United States, nearly two thirds are living at the poverty level. Thus, although a certain proportion of blacks have managed to achieve high status, Negro families as a whole are predominantly lower class. As Herzog has noted:

It seems more likely that differences between low-income white families, beyond that explained by income alone, may be attributed primarily to post-slavery factors of deprivation and discrimination affecting every facet of life: occupation, education, income, housing, nutrition, health and mortality, social status, self-respect—the documented list is long and the documenting references myriad.[69]

In attempting to cope with the multitude of social forces that have historically impinged on their lives, Negro Americans have manifested

[66]For an extensive discussion of the diversity of family types that can be identified among contemporary black Americans, see Billingsley, op. cit., especially Chapters 1 and 4.

[67]Daniel P. Moynihan, "Employment, Income, and the Negro Family," *Daedalus,* **94** (Fall 1965), pp. 745–770.

[68]U.S. Department of Labor, Bureau of Labor Statistics, *The Negroes in the United States: Their Economic and Social Situation* (Washington, D.C.: U.S. Government Printing Office, 1966).

[69]Herzog, op. cit., pp. 3–10.

various patterns of family life. In the remaining pages, we will present in some detail three major patterns of family organization that have emerged. There are, of course, many others. As we noted at the outset of this chapter, discussions of "the" Negro family—or any other ethnic-American family—refer only to modal or central tendencies in subcultural behavior. In reality there is considerable diversity within "the" Negro family system. Not only do black families differ by class and income, but even at the same socioeconomic level a variety of family forms may be observed.[70]

THE URBAN MATRICENTRIC FAMILY The lower-class Negro matricentric family has roots in the traditional matriarchal family of the past and subsequent adaptations to the disruptive postslavery migration and urbanization experiences described earlier. These families are primarily concentrated in the poorer central-core sections of our large industrial and metropolitan cities. Their efforts to perform normal family functions effectively are often seriously impeded by economic insecurity, the chronic disabilities associated with ghetto life, and the failure of a significant proportion of adult males to become permanently integrated into the occupational structure. A pattern of intermittent employment and/or low wages is common, and males are not predisposed to take on the additional burdens required by the assumption of family maintenance responsibilities. Moreover, the Negro woman and wife generally experiences greater occupational opportunities, making her a more dependable source of steady income. Unable to function effectively in the provider role, the husband finds his position as head of the household increasingly challenged and undermined. The subsequent frustrations and marital conflict often result in his resorting to excessive drinking, extramarital sexual encounters, and outright desertion. Out of this set of circumstances emerges a household unit centered primarily around the wife, her children, and often her mother, that is, what some sociologists have designated the *adaptive urban matricentric* Negro family.[71]

Mate selection and family formation in this subculture are usually preceded by several stages of heterosexual interaction governed by

[70] The diversity and complexity of family life among lower-class Negroes often comes as a surprise to the uninformed. Billingsley, for example, describes at least three types: (1) the working nonpoor, whose families manage their lives well both economically and socially; (2) the working poor, who constitute the vast majority of the black lower class; and (3) the nonworking poor, who comprise a relatively large number of economically dependent families. Types 2 and 3 encompass nearly half of all black American families and also account for nearly one fourth of all poor families in the nation. Andrew Billingsley, "Family Functioning in the Low-Income Black Community," *Social Casework,* **50** (Dec. 1969), pp. 563–572.

[71] Our presentation of this family type follows closely that of Queen and Habenstein, op. cit., pp. 325–338; and Lee Rainwater, "Crucible of Identity," *Daedalus,* **95** (Winter 1966), pp. 172–216.

98

peer-group associations. Rainwater found that adolescents become absorbed into their peer-group societies in their early teens and remain involved even after first pregnancies and marriages. Both sexes become deeply committed to their respective peer groups, whose standards of behavior reflect wide exposure to and emulation of adult Negro activity. More so than is true in many white slum communities, Negro adolescent "behavior more often represents an identification with the behavior of adults than an attempt to set up group standards that differ from those of adults."[72]

Participation in street activities and games provide the boys and young men with opportunities to gain status and enhance their self-concepts. Often these games take the form of verbal contests in which those who can convincingly describe their sexual prowess and exploitation of females receive much admiration. The male peer-group norms essentially define all women as legitimate sexual targets, and individual members are rated in terms of their ability at "rapping" females with a persuasive "line" and their success at physical seduction. Thus, young men aggressively and competitively pursue as many sexual conquests as possible in order to build up their "reps." The girls are aware of and to some extent share these norms of the peer group and are constantly exposed to this seductive orientation in heterosexual interaction. However, they experience some ambivalence over actually engaging in sexual intercourse, which stems from a desire to avoid being taken advantage of or getting into trouble. Therefore, girls generally attempt to restrict coitus to those few males to whom they are genuinely attracted.

Despite their efforts, as well as parental admonitions and precautionary warnings regarding the potential consequences of sexual involvement, a great many girls eventually find themselves pregnant and become unwed mothers.[73] Although marriage is considered in these situations the girl often decides against it either because she doesn't feel ready to assume parental responsibilities yet or because she thinks the young man involved would be inadequate as a husband.[74] Moreover, he ordinarily is under no great pressure to marry her. In most such instances the girl continues to reside at home with her mother, the latter assuming the major responsibilities for rearing the child. Other siblings in the household are also available to lend a helping hand. Given these ready resources to relieve her of the burdens of child care, the unwed mother is able to take advantage of the opportunity to

[72]Ibid., p. 183–184.
[73]Ibid., pp. 185–187.
[74]For a recent investigation of this problem, see Hallowell Pope, "Negro-White Differences in Decisions Regarding Illegitimate Children," *Journal of Marriage and the Family,* **31** (Nov. 1969), pp. 756–764.

resume active participation in the peer-group society. As she has more children and perhaps marries, she may eventually find it necessary to settle down at home and assume more fully the maternal functions. "It is in the easy attitude toward premarital pregnancy that the matrifocal character of the Negro lower-class family appears most clearly. In order to have and raise children it is simply not necessary, though it may be desirable, to have a man around the house."[75]

For both sexes formal marriage is approached with considerable ambivalence. The girl is reluctant to leave the relative security of her home, which places few restrictions on her behavior, to gamble on the uncertainties involved in establishing an independent household. Moreover, her observations of the marriages of friends and relatives have led her to be generally pessimistic about a man's ability to enact adequately the role of husband and provider. The male similarly has mixed feelings about a commitment to marriage. Liebow has described the attitudes of many of these men.

Although he wants to get married, he hedges on his commitment from the very beginning because he is afraid, not of marriage itself, but of his own ability to carry out his responsibilities as husband and father. His own father failed and had to "cut out," and the men he knows who have been married have also failed or are in the process of doing so. He has no evidence that he will fare better than they and much evidence that he will not.[76]

Thus, lower-class Negro men and women enter marriage with considerable pessimism and rather minimal expectations that the relationship will prove sufficiently stable and gratifying.

As the new husband encounters the restrictions of the occupational world on his chances to earn a living, he soon recognizes the difficulty of being able to provide for his spouse and children. Even when he is managing the breadwinner role he has serious doubts—as does his wife—about the likelihood of his continuing to do so. A large proportion of Negro wives find they must seek work following marriage in order to meet family needs. In the face of mounting problems associated with the husband's employment difficulties, she eventually finds herself burdened with widening responsibilities for managing the household, socializing the children, and providing for the economic maintenance of the family. In the process, respect for the husband declines, his status in the household is threatened, and his marriage

---

[75]Ibid., p. 188.

[76]Elliot Liebow, *Tally's Corner, A Study of Negro Streetcorner Men* (Boston: Little, Brown and Company, 1967), pp. 210–211. However, as Liebow and others have noted, in spite of constant exposure to antimarriage sentiments from peers and others most lower-class Negroes eventually do marry—often impulsively—although many husbands subsequently abandon the home for varying periods of time.

and family life become increasingly vulnerable to disruption.[77] Liebow has described the reactions of the husband in these terms: "Sometimes he sits and cries at the humiliation of it all. Sometimes he strikes out at her or the children with his fists, perhaps to lay hollow the claim to being man of the house in the one way left open to him, or perhaps simply to inflict pain on this woman who bears witness to his failure as a husband and father and therefore as a man."[78] Increasingly, he seeks escape in the diversions of street-corner adventures, where he finds temporary sanctuary from the troubles at home and pressures from the larger society. Drinking, infidelity, and other outside involvements generate further strain and conflict in family life. Mounting marital discord, which often erupts into violence, finally reaches a breaking point for the couple. Eventually the wife insists that the husband leave or, as often is the case, he simply deserts the family. In either event the marriage has failed and the couple part ways, the husband often becoming one of the succession of partners taken by another woman whose mate had abandoned her, his own ex-mate in turn accepting one or more men to replace him.[79]

It is generally agreed that the urban matricentric family pattern will continue to persist in the lower class until significant changes in the larger society allow Negro males to gain the education and training necessary to earn a decent living. Moreover, they must be provided with occupational opportunities so that they can confidently assume the provider role as heads of their families. In the meantime, research has shown that some of these families in the inner city of our large urban centers have shown an impressive capacity to adapt to the social, political, and economic deprivations of their environment and to develop a rather strong sense of family. Further study of these families will lead to further understanding of the lower-class Negro family.[80]

THE URBAN BLACK PROLETARIAT FAMILY We have noted that there is considerable diversity among black families both within and between the various social class groupings. Not all lower-class families suffer the disabilities associated with the matricentric pattern described in the previous section. Indeed, it needs to be emphasized that nearly three fourths of all Negro families are headed by men and only one fourth by women. Moreover, the majority of lower-class Negroes live in

[77]Rainwater, op. cit., pp. 190–192.
[78]Liebow, op. cit., pp. 212–213.
[79]Ibid., pp. 219–222.
[80]For summaries of this research. see Billingsley, "Family Functioning in the Low-Income Black Community," op. cit. pp. 563–572; Robert E. Staples, "Research on the Negro Family: A Source for Family Practitioners," *The Family Coordinator,* **18** (July 1969), pp. 202–209.
[81]Frazier, *The Negro Family in the United States,* op. cit., Chapter 21. Billingsley, op. cit., would designate this family type as the "working nonpoor."

nuclear families with both parents present, and most of them are self-supporting. The latter types are more accurately referred to as industrial working-class families or what sometimes has been characterized as the *black proletariat family*.[81] Historically, the formation of this family type gained impetus through the labor shortages created by World War I, during which large numbers of blacks were able to secure jobs in the industries of the North. Since then a growing proportion of working-class Negro husbands and fathers have managed to penetrate the semiskilled occupations and several skilled occupations available in the urban industrial economy. Many have found steady employment as longshoremen, miners, stockyard workers, truck drivers, construction workers, auto mechanics, and so on.

The black proletariat family in many ways shares the life style, the norms, and the values of stable working-class families in the urban white community. At the same time, they face additional problems directly associated with racial discrimination. Many who are able to afford better housing find it difficult to escape the confinements of inferior neighborhoods created by long-established patterns of residential succession and segregation—patterns that persist despite open housing legislation.[82] Even when these families do manage to secure more adequate living quarters they are often forced to pay exorbitant rent costs for the privilege. Meeting the price commonly requires taking in lodgers or sending wives and household relatives to work in order to supplement the family income.[83] On the other hand, some working-class black families like and prefer remaining in their present communities. In this respect they are similar to members of other ethnic minorities who have developed strong sentimental and cultural attachments to their old neighborhoods.[84]

The structure of family relationships in these families resembles that of their white counterparts. The husband's authority as the acknowledged head of the household is conditioned by his ability and his success in achieving steady employment and regular wages. In some instances traces of the traditional female dominance are present and, should the husband fail in the provider role, the wife and often her

[82]Residential succession refers to the mobility pattern of Negroes moving into old neighborhoods formerly occupied by whites. Taeuber and Taeuber, op. cit., for example, found that more than two fifths of the dwelling units occupied by Negro families in the North in 1960 had been inhabited by white families a decade earlier. Their studies show that residential segregation is widespread throughout America "regardless of the relative economic status of the white and Negro residents." Also see Taeuber and Taeuber, *Negroes in the Cities* (Chicago: Aldine Publishing Company, 1965), p. 36.

[83]Frazier, op. cit., pp. 342–343.

[84]Billingsley, *Black Families in White America,* op. cit., p. 92.

mother may move to challenge his authority. The most common pattern of authority, however, is what Billingsley terms expanding equalitarianism, in which couples jointly participate in decision-making.[85]

The socialization of children in contemporary working-class black families varies and is influenced by the social and economic resources available to them and the institutional pressures to which they are subjected. Some of the parents, for example, have been found to manifest a high degree of commitment to middle-class norms of child-rearing and to express deep concern over the education and welfare of their children. They attempt to provide adequate supervision and care and actively encourage their children toward conformity and achievement in the larger society. Other parents in these lower-class families similarly verbalize concern for the well-being of their children, but their own needs for self-improvement and respectability are often given greater priority. The preoccupation of parents with their own aspirations and satisfactions often results in the neglect of children.[86]

As Negro Americans have found greater opportunities to become more fully integrated into the various sectors of the economy, the number of black proletariat families in the nation has gradually risen. They increasingly seek to dissociate themselves from the life style and the social pathology that characterize the masses of impoverished blacks in our urban ghettos. As the Negro worker assumes the role of industrial worker, he assumes the responsibilities for family maintenance and accrues greater authority in the household, and "as the isolation of the black worker is gradually broken down, his ideals and pattern of family life approximate those of the great body of industrial workers."[87]

ACCULTURATED BLACK FAMILIES: THE MIDDLE CLASS We have noted that there is considerable diversity among black families in the United States both within and between social class groupings. This is no less true of the Negro middle class. Billingsley, for example, depicts at least three types of families within this stratum: the upper middle class, which is composed of educated professionals and businessmen; the "solid" middle middle class, comprised of white-collar clerks and salesmen; and the "precarious" or lower middle class, consisting of skilled artisans and small businessmen. Each group is distinguishable in terms of educational, occupational, and income levels as well as on

---

[85]Ibid., pp. 143–144.
[86]Billingsley, "Family Functioning in the Low-Income Black Community," op. cit., pp. 563–572, cites evidence that shows that child neglect and abuse are *less* common among lower-class black families than among white families living in similar economic circumstances.
[87]Frazier, op. cit., p. 355.

103

the basis of family life styles and the security of their hold on middle-class status.[88]

Historically a small but distinct group of Negro middle-class families visibly emerged in the nineteenth century. Their superior social status was based primarily on their racially mixed ancestry and a heritage of long-established family traditions sustained by economic stability.[89] With increasing occupational differentiation among the black population, however, these criteria diminished as the primary basis for social status. Occupational differentiation resulted in a significant expansion of the black middle class to include larger numbers of families whose social position was more apt to be determined by the extent of their education, occupational achievement, and income. This newer and growing middle class of black families is perhaps most representative of what Queen and Habenstein have designated as the *acculturated middle majority* Negro family.[90]

The acculturated black families have gradually incorporated the cultural norms visible among the middle majority of white Americans. They accept the monogamous marital pattern as most appropriate and the ideals associated with permanent marriage. They have embraced the concept of a small nuclear family residing in its suburban dwelling and managing its domestic affairs free from external, including parental, intereference. Both the husband's close relatives as well as those of his wife are included in a network of effective kin. Although these families generally place high value on privacy, they are willing to take in parents who are no longer able to manage on their own.

Mate selection among acculturated black families often follows the standard pattern of casual dating, going steady, engagement, and finally a ceremonial marriage attended by friends and relatives of the couple. However, because of a disproportionate sex ratio, black females sometimes encounter certain complications in the mate selection process. Sometimes they become attached to a male who looks like a good prospect in terms of a stable personality and occupational potential and discover that he will give serious marital consideration only to light-colored or mulatto women.

Although children are desired, the acculturated black couple has developed some commitment to an ideology of planned parenthood

[88]Billingsley, *Black Families in White America,* op. cit., pp. 131–137; He estimates that these three groups constitute about two fifths of all Negro American families. Depending on the indicators and definitions used, other investigators have posed estimates ranging from 20 to 30 per cent.

[89]Frazier, in his *Black Bourgeoisie,* op. cit., pp. 112–149, was highly critical of this early middle class for its emphasis on the superificial emulation of the conventional morality and materialism of the white middle-class culture.

[90]Queen and Habenstein, op. cit., pp. 320–325. The remainder of this follows their description of this family type. See also, Bernard, op. cit., Chapter 2.

and therefore tends to restrict the size of the family. Unlike the situation observed among matricentric families, the socialization of children is a joint responsibility shared by the husband and the wife. If both parents are working—and they often have to in order to maintain a middle-class status and life style—they are more likely to use baby sitters or day-care facilities than parents to look after the children. Parents attempt to encourage and inculcate high levels of educational and occupational aspirations in their children and are willing to plan and make sacrifices in order that such aspirations may achieve reality. Evident among these families then is "a joint dedication of husband and wife to establish a stable family, to prosper economically, and to bring forth a succeeding generation of children who will suffer fewer of the disadvantages experienced by their parents."[91]

Acculturated middle majority blacks have demonstrated that given adequate resources and opportunities they develop and sustain a highly stable family system as well as a warm and satisfying home life. The black infant born in the seventies is apt to experience less difficulty in becoming a middle-class Negro American than his parental ancestors, but the extent to which he will be able to maintain that status will be determined largely by the willingness of members of the white majority, whose institutions he increasingly comes into contact with, to provide supportive and integrative roles.

---

[91]Queen and Habenstein, op. cit., p. 324.

Part II

Prelude to Marriage

5
Dating and Mate Selection

Dating is a significant part of the life of young people in societies with an open choice of marital partners. Most American youth begin dating during their fourteenth year and, since the median age at marriage in the United States is twenty-plus for girls and twenty-two-plus for boys, typically both are engaged in a long period of heterosexual interaction prior to marriage.[1] It might be added that because the divorce rate is now above one in three marriages, a large proportion of both sexes will, sometime after the termination of a marriage, again engage in dating and other premarital interaction.

Most writers have tried to distinguish between dating as casual heterosexual activity, implying no permanent relationship, and courtship, in which couples engage in a process of spouse selection. Others have opposed this dichotomy on the grounds that it has become increasingly difficult to tell whether casual dating or an early stage of courtship is involved. Merrill has described modern dating as follows,

For many young people, the distinction between dating and courtship has therefore lost much of its meaning. In their minds they are still dating, whether their goal is emotional maturation, group prestige, personal education, or mate selection. Only the participants in dating are often sure of what they are doing, and even there is sometimes lack of agreement.[2]

[1] Alan Bayer, "Early Dating and Early Marriage," *Journal of Marriage and the Family,* **30** (Nov. 1968), p. 629.
[2] Francis E. Merrill, *Courtship and Marriage* (New York: Holt, Rinehart, and Winston, 1959), p. 108.

Complications arise where one person may view the interaction as dating but the other as courtship.

Casual Dating

Despite the difficulty in classifying heterosexual interaction into dating and courtship categories, it still seems possible to make a meaningful distinction between them as well as between casual and steady dating. Casual dating can be viewed as activity undertaken for the rewards that can accrue from a single event. One decides it would be more pleasant to attend a movie with a girl than alone or with a group of his own sex, or he decides he wants to attend a dance that requires a date. He doesn't bother to reflect whether or not he would want to marry that person or even whether he would want to go steady.

Even in a first or only date, one of several or a combination of motives may be involved. If it is one of the first dates the person has had, it is likely to be exciting to be out with one of the other sex, regardless of which person it is. Dating involves a new set of social relationships and behaviors. Any date may involve an intrinsic reward, too, in that one is attracted to someone of the opposite sex and therefore wants to be with him.

Dating—even one date—may have status value. To have a date means that someone finds you attractive, or at least acceptable. The assumption that dating is exciting or fun adds to the desirability of dating. Early studies stressed that to date frequently added to one's desirability as a dating partner.[3] To be dating has frequently been considered to be desirable without reference to the person dated. Dating is normative behavior during late adolescence, and parents and peer group become concerned about the nondater and try to help him get started.

Steady Dating

Steady dating in high school may be based on unusual similarity of interests or other strong attractions, or it may be primarily a security strategy. In some instances the couple feels that each has found the person best suited to his interests and needs. In others, they find a mutual security system, which provides for a partner to events that require a date, such as school dances. Even at dances that permit or encourage "stagging," the risks of having no one to dance with are eliminated by having a "steady." Besides the obvious advantage of a predictable date, going steady reduces the insecurity in the competition for approval from the other sex and serves as a minimum social and psychological security system not unlike that of marriage.

---

[3]Willard Waller and Reuben Hill, *The Family: A Dynamic Interpretation* (New York: The Dryden Press, 1951).

110

Going steady doesn't necessarily involve an advance toward marriage. It probably does if the couple and their reference groups define their age, education, and economic prospects as those that make them eligible for marriage. Because most mid-adolescents are considered too young to marry, going steady at that age is not usually viewed as a step toward marriage. However, if the relationship produces emotional intensity and physical intimacy, it may result in an unintended marriage—one that we term a *precocious marriage* (Chapter 9). Going steady, then, may have a variety of meanings. It may be essentially a desired status—having someone with whom to attend recreational events and avoiding appearing to be alone—either in one's own perception or in that of the peer group. Or it may be the most convenient arrangement—the best date that appears readily available. Finally, it may be the companionship of the most attractive, interesting, and rewarding person that one has met. If the latter is the case and if the couple are of an age defined as appropriate for marriage, going steady may mark a definite stage in the courtship process.

Courtship

If courtship can be distinguished from dating, then the distinction is best made in terms of intent, because much courtship behavior cannot be distinguished from that in dating. Neither is the age of the participants an adequate criterion because the age range of daters extends from preadolescence to past retirement. As we have defined dating as an activity engaged in for its immediate rewards, courtship can be defined as an activity directed toward marriage with a given individual. Therefore, dating may shift to courtship at any time, provided one views himself and the dating partner as eligible to marry. One might well begin the evening dating and end it courting! Likewise, one of the couple may only be dating whereas the other has become interested in marriage, and, therefore, is courting. Where boys are dating girls their own age, it often happens that the boys are still defining the activity as dating while the girls have become interested in marriage. This is frequently true of college students in their sophomore and junior years and often causes tensions between the limited interests of the boys and the more general interests of their dates.

Dating and Courtship in Cultural Perspective

The conditions under which youth associate with each other prior to marriage are, like other social behavior, culturally defined. Many societies permit or even encourage extensive association before marriage, whereas others take great precautions to prevent it. Whether a society takes one or the other position is related to the type of family structure. If the marriage is the principal basis of the family (conjugal

111

family type), then mixing of the sexes is permitted and encouraged, but in societies in which the significant structure of the family is the blood relationship between parents and children, siblings and other kin (consanguine type), such premarital mixing is often severely restricted. Goode has drawn the issues somewhat more precisely in basing such restrictions on the degree of economic or social interest of parents and other kin.[4] If large financial exchanges are involved at marriage or if a marriage brings two families together in extended social interaction and/or if the prestige of each family is largely affected by marriage, then such unions are likely to be arranged primarily by the parents, rather than the young people themselves. Where this is the situation, parents take great care to ensure that the young people have no opportunity to fall in love with an inappropriate person. The young are sex segregated or in some societies married before they reach puberty.[5] Incidentally, we have seen this behavior in American society in the upper class, because inherited wealth is involved (Chapter 3).

By contrast, societies in which the married couples have limited contacts with their parents after marriage and few continuing responsibilities on either side, the choice of marital partners is largely left to the individuals involved. Parents attempt to discourage marriages that they perceive as likely to fail, but usually stop short of trying to dictate marriage to a particular individual. American parents have, in general, encouraged dating during the middle and late adolescent years based on the assumption that a considerable acquaintance with the other sex will lead to a better choice of a marital partner. Moreover, some parents feel, too, that the competitive advantage of their children is increased by dating experience. Therefore, many American parents not only permit early and extensive dating but feel concern if their children do not show interest and develop skills in dating. However, as we have noted, the opposite is true in societies in which kin have a strong continuing financial or social "stake" in the couple.

Functions and Dysfunctions of Dating

It has already been noted that dating has several rather different functions. Because of biopsychological attractions between the sexes, dating for most participants is generally an interesting, stimulating, and often exciting activity. It might be said to be *intrinsically* rewarding because of these attractions. As such, it is unnecessary to show that it is *instrumental* in facilitating the achievement of other goals. A related function is to permit certain types of recreation that require a partner,

[4]William Goode, "The Theoretical Importance of Love," *American Sociological Review*, **24** (Feb. 1959).
[5]Ibid.

especially dancing. (Actually, most current dancing would seem to be quite possible without a partner!)

However, some behavioral scientists see dysfunctional consequences in dating. Willard Waller was one of those who viewed dating as primarily dysfunctional. He viewed it as a period of dalliance before youth considered themselves ready to engage in serious courtship. He developed the famous Rating and Dating Hypothesis, which suggested that during the dating period one attempted to improve his own social standing by dating only those of the same or higher prestige. For example, girls from prestigeful sororities preferred to date men only from fraternities of equal or higher prestige, would rather not date in a low-ranked fraternity, and would usually refuse dates from men living in dormitories. Other characteristics of a good male date included being prominent in activities, having ample spending money, being well dressed, being a good dancer, and having access to an automobile. The characteristics of a good female date included having good clothes, having a smooth line, being a good dancer, and being popular. In Waller's view, the date was a means to an end, which led each sex to attempt to exploit the other.[6]

Two later researchers failed to substantiate Waller's findings;[7] nonetheless, he may have been essentially correct in the particular social setting that he researched. For example, his data came from the era of the Great Depression. At that time marriage in college was almost unheard of and almost impossible for economic reasons. Therefore, his sample of students were interacting in an almost ideal dating situation, unmixed with courtship interests, values, and behaviors. Smith and Blood, on the other hand, sampled postwar campus behavior during a period of high prosperity characterized by a large number of student marriages. Besides the high level of prosperity, older ex-servicemen with incomes from the G.I. Bill were in college, providing a marriageable group of men. In this latter setting, dating and courtship attitudes, objectives and behavior became thoroughly mixed. The student, when making a date, could not be totally unaware of the possibility that the encounter might develop into a more enduring relationship. To some extent this has become true of the later years in high school as well as for college and out-of-school youth. It may be, then, that the phenomenon of Rating and Dating such as Waller described occurs in a pure dating situation in which marriage is such a remote contingency that it is ignored in choice of date and in dating interaction. Moreover, Rogers

---

[6]Willard Waller, "The Rating and Dating Complex," *American Sociological Review*, 2 (Oct. 1937), pp. 728–734.

[7]William M. Smith, Jr., "Rating and Dating: A Restudy," *Marriage and Family Living*. 14 (Nov. 1952), pp. 312–317; and Robert O. Blood, Jr., "A Retest of Waller's Rating Complex," *Marriage and Family Living*, 17 (Feb. 1955), pp. 41–47.

and Havens, in a later study, provide some support for Waller's concept. Their data, taken from an Iowa State University sample, show that prestige classes entered into all phases of mate selection from casual dating to mate choice, itself: ". . . students date, pin, and become engaged within their own prestige group."[8] They observe that their data involve the actual behavior of youth, whereas the Blood and Smith studies reported verbalized values. Scott also adds support in describing the college sorority system as a device for insuring that the daughters of middle-class families will not marry beneath them.

Each sorority, for example, has dating relations with one or more fraternities, matched rather nicely to the sorority on the basis of ethnicity and/or class. (A particular sorority, for example, will have dating arrangements not with all fraternities on campus, but only with those whose brothers are a class-match for their sisters.) The sorority's frantically busy schedule of parties, teas, meetings, skits, and exchanges keeps the sisters so occupied that they have neither time nor opportunity to meet men outside the channels the sorority provides.[9]

Although Scott's description reflects more the values of parents than of youth themselves, such values probably have some relationship to those of the daters themselves.

A later study by Larson and Leslie adds strong support for the Rogers and Havens position. They found that steady dating, pinning, and engagement occurred mostly within status categories, with men from high-status fraternities dating, pinning, and marrying girls from high-status sororities. The tendency toward homogamy, they find, increases with the seriousness of the commitment. These studies lead us to formulate the generalization that youth verbally reject the idea of preferring to date, pin, and become engaged to others in high-prestige groups but, in practice, those who have higher prestige do, in fact, more often date, pin, and become engaged to others who have similar prestige. This is congruent with Exchange Theory, which assumes that in interaction, as in the economic marketplace, individuals get as much as their own assets permit.[10]

Besides the exploitation that Waller felt was common in dating, concern has recently been voiced that early dating tends to result in early marriage. There is evidence that early steady dating *is* related to early marriage.[11] This relationship is explored in Chapter 9.

In addition to these problems are those encountered by those who

[8]Everett M. Rogers and A. Eugene Havens, "Prestige Rating and Mate Selection on a College Campus," *Marriage and Family Living,* 22 (Feb. 1960), p. 59.

[9]John Finley Scott, "Sororities and Husband Game," *Transaction* 2 (Sept.–Oct. 1965), p. 12.

[10]Richard F. Larson and Gerald R. Leslie, "Prestige Influences in Serious Dating Relationships of University Students," *Social Forces,* 47 (Dec. 1968), pp. 195–202.

[11]Bayer, op. cit.

wish to date but are unable to do so and therefore feel that they are failures in dating interaction. The uncertainty, anxiety, frustration, and resulting problems in adequate ego development probably are considerable. The assumption that extensive dating improves one's competence in choosing a spouse and that interaction with the other sex prior to marriage develops skills in interacting in marriage is a plausible but untested article of faith. It forms one of the principal bases for pressure on youth to begin dating early and to continue once they have started.

Dating Roles

In American society, dating for older adolescents is normatively prescribed. Parents, friends, and people in general believe that at least older youth *ought* to date. The adolescent who does not is considered a deviant, and parents, siblings, and friends try to help and/or coerce the older adolescent into participation in dating. The person himself may have internalized these expectations and feel inadequate or nonconforming if he is unable or unwilling to date.

Broderick has outlined the substantive content of male and female dating roles. He describes the core of the male role as to press for physical and emotional intimacy, while the female role is to press for commitment from the male. For each increase in intimacy allowed, an increase in commitment is expected. For example, petting intimacy may be exchanged for an agreement to go steady. Traditionally, as physical intimacy increases, an exchange of commitment occurs until the final one in which the commitment of marriage is exchanged for the intimacy of sexual intercourse.[12] The exchange can be halted at any point at which one or the other is unwilling to make an increased investment in the relationship. The relationship can be broken at any time, but ordinarily it cannot be reversed so that the couple interact at a lower level of exchange.

Broderick suggests that the differentiation of roles by sex is related to the vulnerability of the female to pregnancy. An emotional and finally a legal commitment provides security for the female and for children born to the couple. It would seem however, that commitment from the male would provide such protection only if he is old enough to marry and able to enact the provider role.

The preceding seems a useful description of dating and courtship roles, especially in the initial stages. In the more advanced age stages, some women wish to have intercourse before marriage and manipulate the emotions of their partner to result in intercourse. At some stage the man may decide he wishes marriage and may try to persuade his partner to become his wife. Moreover, advances in contraceptive

[12]C. B. Broderick, "The Courtship Process in America," unpublished manuscript.

practices among the unmarried and the liberalization of the abortion laws may change these roles. Women may become more aggressive in seeking increased intimacy and less concerned with obtaining increased commitment from their dating partners.

Theoretical Perspective on Spouse Selection

In societies in which the decision of whom to marry is made primarily by the couple involved, it is of considerable interest why they choose to marry one rather than another person. The lay answer is a simple one—that they fall in love with someone and that is the reason for marrying that person. Although simple, the answer is by no means adequate. Not all love affairs lead to marriage and some marriages occur in which one (or both) is not in love with the other. It also raises the question of why people fall in love and with one particular person rather than another.

Complementary Needs

Winch, drawing on need theory, hypothesized that individuals in their attempts to satisfy their needs, select spouses who will supply a type of behavior or a set of characteristics that are the opposite of their own. For example, individuals who have a high need for dominance tend to select spouses with a high need for abasement, or those with high needs for recognition select those with a high need for deference.[13] Winch suggests this relationship: "The need-pattern of B, the second person or the one to whom the first is attracted, will be complementary rather than similar to the need pattern of A, the first person." It should be noted that Winch hypothesized this relationship occurs between personalities rather than between social characteristics. He recognized that research had shown that Catholics were more likely to marry Catholics, highly educated men to marry highly educated women, blacks to marry blacks, and the like. This principle of homogamy has been shown conclusively, at least within American society. The theory of complementary needs, on the other hand, sought to explain why, within a field of eligibles (a set of persons culturally defined as appropriate for one to marry), A marries B rather than C.

Several studies, including Winch's, have tested his formulation. One independent study provides some support, but four have failed to

---

[13]Robert F. Winch, "The Theory of Complementary Needs in Mate Selection: An Analytic and Descriptive Study," *American Sociological Review,* **19** (June 1954), pp. 341–349. His list of needs is taken from H. A. Murray et al., *Explorations in Personality* (New York: Oxford University Press, 1938).

support it. Therefore, its usefulness in explaining and predicting marital choice is doubtful. Contrary to Winch's hypothesis, four studies offer evidence of homogamy in personality characteristics in opposition to the idea of complementary needs.[14] The most recent of these, Murstein, presented considerable evidence in support of homogamy of personality characteristics in finding that couples similar in neurotic tendencies, self-esteem, and sex drive progressed faster toward marriage than couples dissimilar in these characteristics.[15] These recent studies are consistent with some research prior to Winch's formulation that showed homogamy in personality characteristics as well as in social characteristics. For example, in a study of 1,000 engaged couples, Burgess and Wallin reported, "Of the 42 personality traits studied, 14 showed a greater than chance expectation for homogamous union of engaged couples."[16] In no characteristic—personality, social, or physical—did they find statistical evidence that opposites attract.

Filter Models: Kerckhoff and Davis

One research, which provided some support for Winch's formulation, resulted in the development of what is usually termed a *filter model.* Kerckhoff and Davis, in developing this model, suggest that social homogamy (race, social class, religion, and the like) provides the first filtering process by tending to facilitate dating within homogamous categories and discourage it between people from differing social categories. Thus, social homogamy is the first filter. The second is value consensus. Those who have more similar values move faster toward marriage than those who have more value conflicts. However, value conflict did not, at least in their sample, lead to breaking the dating relationship, only to retarding the progress of the relationship toward marriage. Finally, among those who had dated longer, those couples whose needs were more complementary were progressing faster toward marriage than those whose needs were not. This, they suggest is the third filter.[17] However, a study by Levenger, Senn, and Jorgensen, testing the Kerckhoff and Davis model, fails to support it.[18]

---

[14]Charles E. Bowerman and Barbara R. Day, "Test of the Theory of Complementary Needs," *American Sociological Review,* **21** (Oct. 1956), pp. 602–605; James A. Schellenberg and Lawrence S. Bee, "A Reexamination of the Theory of Complementary Needs in Mate Selection," *Marriage and Family Living,* **22** (Aug. 1960), pp. 227–232; Bernard Murstein, "Stimulus–Value–Role: A Theory of Marital Choice," *Journal of Marriage and the Family,* **32** (Aug. 1970), pp. 465–482; and George Levenger, David Senn, and Bruce Jorgensen, "Progress Toward Permanence in Courtship: A Test of the Kerckhoff-Davis Hypothesis," *Sociometry,* **33** (Dec. 1970), pp. 427–433.

[15]Murstein, op. cit.

[16]Ernest W. Burgess and Paul Wallin, *Engagement and Marriage* (Chicago: J. B. Lippincott Co., 1953), pp. 208–209.

[17]Alan C. Kerckhoff and Keith E. Davis, "Value Consensus and Need Complementarity in Mate Selection," *American Sociological Review,* **27** (June 1962), pp. 295–303.

[18]Levenger, Senn, and Jorgensen, op. cit., pp. 427–433.

117

Filter Models: Murstein

Drawing from Kerckhoff and Davis, Murstein developed a slightly different filter model, that of stimulus, value, and role. It does not address the matter of social homogamy but moves immediately to an open field in which individuals of opposite sexes are in the same spatial area and can observe one another. At this point they are exposed to various stimuli, such as physical appearance, abilities, social prestige, and whatever other characteristics may be known initially that are relevant to one's interest in persons of the other sex. If these stimuli attract them to each other, they may date. This is the first filter, stimulus. After the couple decide they have sufficient interest in one another to talk of matters of personal interest, they begin to compare their attitudes and values. These discussions may involve sex, marriage, education, travel, work, and a variety of other topics. Murstein proposes that their movement or lack of it toward marriage is affected by the apparent fit or lack of it between their values. This is the second filter, value. The third involves discussion and/or other means of perceiving role behavior. What does one expect of the other sex in the marriage relationship? This perception is furthered by actual behavior in dating roles as well as in verbal communication about marital roles.[19] If one accepts social homogamy as an implied first filter, then attraction, value agreement, and role congruence add up to a four-stage filtering process. This model implies that those couples who survive the four stages are likely to marry.

A Propinquity Model

Propinquity studies have not utilized the filter concept, but they, and especially the review of a whole group of such studies by Katz and Hill, imply a filtering process. These studies have shown that most people date and marry those who live near them. The principal question is whether people marry those near them because of the economy of meeting and interacting with them, or because those living nearby are more likely to possess similar social characteristics. Hill and Katz concluded from fourteen of these studies that: (1) People marry within a field of eligibles that is culturally defined. For example, middle-class girls prefer to marry middle-class men. (2) "Within normative fields of eligibles, the probability of marriage varies directly with the probability of interaction." (3) "The probability of interaction is proportional to the ratio of opportunities at a given distance over intervening opportunities."[20]

[19]Murstein, op. cit., pp. 465–482.
[20]Alvin W. Katz and Reuben Hill, "Residential Propinquity and Marital Selection: A Review of Theory, Method and Fact," *Marriage and Family Living*, **20** (Feb. 1958), pp. 27–36.

Two points should be made with respect to this formulation. First, people do not necessarily interact most frequently with those who live nearest—even those who "are in their field of eligibles." People who work in the same unit, attend the same church, or engage in the same recreation may be brought into more contact than those who live in the same residential area. Therefore, the probability of interaction involves more than distance between residences. Second, the "field of eligibles" probably differs in degree as much as in kind. An individual may be unattractive on the basis of one characteristic but very attractive on the basis of another. Therefore, the boundaries of a field of eligibles are difficult to establish.

Exchange and Maximum-Profit Models

In the decision that a woman wishes to marry a given person are included three more limited decisions. The first is whether she would rather be married than single. Married status, although conferring some privileges, involves relinquishing others and imposes the obligations of sexual intercourse, child care, housekeeping, and others. Given marriage to the individual in question, she must decide that it is more profitable to take the status of spouse and relinquish that of single person. Second, if she knows more than one person of the other sex who might be available as a spouse, she must decide that she prefers this one over any of the others. At that time she may lack a full picture of the potential of some of these as spouses, either as to availability or as to their ability to enact marital roles. The third decision is whether this man is probably the best candidate who is likely to appear. The question is a logical one, whether or not most women today think in those terms. Reminiscences of older people frequently include sad cases of permanently unmarried women who "had several good opportunities to marry but were too particular." Whether most women currently in the marriage market think in such concrete terms would be an interesting research question.[21]

Edwards has provided a formulation that illustrates a part of the process of decision-making in an open-choice society, as follows:[22]

---

[21]We have utilized women in this discussion because we view them as having more complex decisions to make. Probably most men need only consider whether they prefer being married to the woman they are courting or remaining single. They are considering primarily a sexual and emotional relationship. In contrast, for women, at least until the present, being married has been an occupation, and in choosing a husband the woman is bargaining for an income level, a status in the community, and sometimes a residential area in which she will live in addition to a sexual and emotional relationship. Nonetheless, although the variables are less complex for men, we believe the profit model is applicable for men as well as women.

[22]John N. Edwards, "Familial Behavior as Social Exchange," *Journal of Marriage and the Family,* **31** (Aug. 1969), p. 525.

119

1. Within any collectivity of potential mates, a marriageable person will seek out that individual who is perceived as maximizing his rewards.

2. Individuals with equivalent resources are most likely to maximize each other's rewards.

3. Pairs with equivalent resources are most likely to possess homogamous characteristics.

4. Mate selection, therefore, will be homogamous with respect to a given set of characteristics.

Edwards suggests that the criteria relevant to homogamy are changing and that such traditional characteristics as race, religion, and social class are likely to be replaced by others more directly relevant. "Increasingly, interpersonal skills and personal assets are the crucial resources for cross-sex transactions."[23]

Murstein suggests that the tendency to marry people like oneself is explained by two facts. Each wants as many socially desirable characteristics as he (she) can obtain: physical attractiveness, education, interpersonal skills, and whatever other characteristics are seen as desirable. This fact prevents most people from seeking as mates people obviously less attractive than themselves. However, as they seek spouses with considerably more assets than themselves, their risk of rejection and failure rapidly increases. People of equal attractiveness in the coin of the marriage market therefore usually provide the best "bargain" in courtship interaction.[24] Commitment as a reward and the conditions and consequences of such exchanges have been explored by Blau.[25]

There are some general exceptions to the homogamy model that, however, seem to fit into a maximum-profit model. For example, women generally have preferred to marry men a few years older than themselves instead of men of the same age. The homogamy model would suggest preference for the same age. However, women have stated that men a little older are better established in their jobs or professions and are more dependable and adequate providers. The same explanation is provided for their preference that the husband have more education. One study showed that only 1 per cent of women preferred a husband with less education, 18 per cent preferred the same amount, and 81 per cent preferred that he have more. However, men (82 per cent) preferred wives with the same education as themselves.[26]

[23]Ibid., p. 523.

[24]Murstein, op. cit., pp. 465–482.

[25]Peter M. Blau, *Exchange and Power in Social Life* (New York: John Wiley & Sons, 1964), pp. 76–85.

[26]Paul H. Landis, *Making the Most of Marriage* (New York: Appleton-Century-Crofts, 1955), pp. 308–309.

Such findings run counter to the idea, frequently advanced by psycho-analysts, that men want to marry women they can dominate.

Discussion of Maximum-Profit Model

The most frequent objection to the maximum-profit model is that people are not that rational in making decisions about whom they will marry. They do not attempt to date everyone of the other sex in order to obtain the most attractive spouse. Even among those with whom they are acquainted, most do not attempt to explore the personality of each in detail with possible matrimony in mind. Such an exploration is probably impossible with present dating practices. However, most youth do date a number of people before becoming engaged and undoubtedly draw some comparisons among them as to their desirability as spouses. Perhaps more central to the issue is Thibaut and Kelley's comparison level. This is the level of desirability that one feels that he deserves.[27] The girl who accepts a date with a relatively unattractive man may be told "You can do better than that." One's comparison level may be the average attractiveness of those of the other sex, but as he is able to obtain an estimate of his own desirability, his comparison level may rise above or stabilize below that of the average member of the other sex. How one fixes his comparison level depends on his observation of eligible partners and his success or lack of it in attracting them. One can decide whether or not he wants to marry on the basis of his date's attractiveness with respect to his own comparison level. Ordinarily he would not proceed toward marriage unless the prospective mate was at or above that level. If it appears that he could have a choice among several eligible partners, all of whom rank above his comparison level, he would, according to this model, choose the one who would seem to offer the most profit in marriage.

The companion concept, the comparative level for alternatives, is also useful. One may feel that he deserves an attractive spouse but none may be available. Others may not share his evaluation of his own rank or he may find it necessary to live somewhere where there are no attractive, available members of the other sex. If he prefers being married to being single, he may marry below his comparison level. In this instance his comparison level for alternatives was lower than his comparison level. The opposite situation undoubtedly exists in which numerous potential spouses are above his comparison level, but he places a higher value on remaining single than on marrying. Presumably, many priests find themselves in this situation.

Current mate selection literature suggests that both affective elements

[27]John W. Thibaut and Harold H. Kelley, *The Social Psychology of Groups* (New York: John Wiley & Son, 1959), p. 21.

121

(liking, love) and rational elements, such as are described by the concepts of the comparison level and the comparison level for alternatives, are usually involved in spouse selection in societies in which the couple are the principal decision-makers. However, some think about and respond to the other in terms of affect, whereas others think in more rational terms in evaluating marriage. These alternative routes to marriage are shown in Figure 5.1.

In Figure 5.1, at the start, the original date may be profitable or unprofitable. If the latter, the relationship develops no further. If profitable, it can be evaluated in terms of affect—"I like him" (a statement of affect) or "He is an excellent dancer and easy to talk with" or "We like to do the same things." Either of the latter are a little more specific, rational reactions and probably place the dating partner above one's comparison level for a date. In either instance, dating is likely to continue. After additional dates the relationship is either likely to be terminated or increase in commitment. Termination can come, in terms of affect, from finding some aspects of the other's personality one doesn't like. One or both decide their emotional reactions to the other are not positive enough to support a further permanent commitment. If they become negative at that point, the relationship will be terminated, but if the relationship involves a mixture of neutral and positive

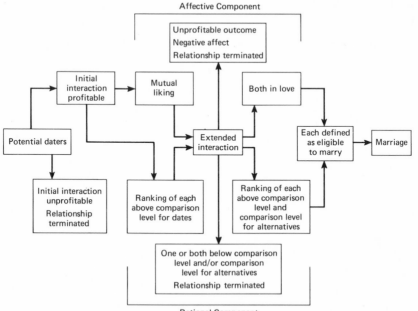

Figure 5.1. Affective and rational components in spouse selection.

122

elements, it may continue until some external circumstance increases the cost of continuing the relationship or someone appears whom one of the couple likes better.

Along the rational route to marriage, after a period of extended interaction, each is likely to determine whether this person is the most profitable candidate likely to appear. If the evaluation is negative one may terminate the relationship to be free to look for and explore other alternatives or may be content to continue the interaction until a better-qualified candidate appears. Lovers' quarrels can be viewed as evidences of unacceptable exchanges. The male may press for the rewards of physical intimacy whereas the female finds granting it too costly. One may want the reward of the security of an exclusive relationship, whereas the other wants the rewards of continuing to "play the field." If so, the relationship may become unprofitable. When a more rewarding alternative appears, the relationship is terminated. However, if no more rewarding candidates offer themselves, and both members of the couple feel it unlikely that any will, then, provided both are defined as eligible to marry, the marriage probably will occur.[28]

In showing alternative paths to marriage, it is necessary to remember that in actual experience both affective and rational components enter into the decision-making of most individuals. Also, although most individuals move through a considerable time period of increasing involvement, an occasional person makes the decision almost instantly through "love at first sight" or a "rational" decision that this partner provides exactly what one wants in a spouse. Finally, it is probably not uncommon for one member of a dating pair to be oriented primarily to the affect components, whereas the other is primarily rationally oriented.

Love as a Behavioral Concept

Much has been written about love, but a precise, generally accepted definition is yet to be formulated. We shall define it simply as a strong emotional attachment toward a person, thing, or experience.[29] For present purposes, we are interested in a strong emotional attachment between persons of the opposite sex who might be, or become, eligible to marry. It is this emotional attachment that is considered the proper

---

[28]"Probably" because an occasional person places a higher value on single than married status. Such a person would remain single even though "in love" or having rationally decided that he had found the person best suited to him as a spouse.

[29]Adapted from Goode, op. cit., p. 41.

basis for marriage in societies with free choice of marital partners. That it is considered the principal but not necessarily the only basis is shown by one study that showed that about 20 per cent of engaged persons felt that it was acceptable to marry without being in love.[30]

The Genesis of Love

Writers employing exchange and profit theory offer the propositions that we like those who reward us (provided their demands on us are not too great, so that the relationship shows a profit).[31] We love those who consistently provide a large profit to us. It is profitable to be liked or loved, so that we tend to love those who reciprocate our sentiments. From this perspective, love is a product of a consistent profit in a relationship. However, humans are also capable of anticipating rewards; for example, enjoying sexual intercourse, having security in a relationship, living in a home of their own, and having whatever else they hope to gain in marriage. Thus, love can be a product of rewards received or anticipated. Romantic love includes the anticipation of rewards in addition to any currently received. Love at first sight would involve anticipated or possible rewards in the future without the necessity of having received any. Conjugal love, by contrast, is the product of having been rewarded by one's spouse over a period of married life. Although future rewards are not excluded, they are not necessary to this kind of attachment (conjugal love).

Romantic Love

We have advanced an explanation of love as the result of a profitable relationship or the anticipation of one. However, in the Western world it has usually been conceived of otherwise—as something mystical, mysterious, and essentially unexplainable. Merrill says,

Romantic love presumably strikes like a bolt from the blue. 'Love at first sight' is the signal for serious courtship to begin. This phenomenon involves 'a quick recognition that one individual is actually beloved because that person seemingly fits the clarified, though often unconscious, ideals of another being'. The conditioning of our culture provides the basis for this reaction, for the individual has been taught to expect precisely this experience.[32]

Pointing to the broad cultural basis of romantic love he states, "Romantic love is the principal prerequisite to marriage in the United States. Courtship and marriage without romance are considered unthinkable, ridiculous, and a little immoral. . . . Romantic love is necessary to the

[30]Burgess and Wallin, op. cit., p. 394.

[31]George Homans, *Social Behavior: Its Elementary Forms* (New York: Harcourt Brace Jovanovich, 1961).

[32]Francis E. Merrill, *Courtship and Marriage* (New York: William Sloan Associates, 1949), p. 25.

124

public welfare."[33] (It should be clear that Merrill in these remarks was describing societal thinking, as he perceived it, not his own evaluation.)

In possibly the most serious effort to explain romantic love in contemporary society, Waller suggested, "Love of a person is a striving toward her, a striving biological in origin, cultural in pattern; it is a striving which is blocked."[34] Thus Waller viewed romantic love as stemming from blocked sexual needs. His analysis is only a short step from an exchange explanation in that the male's sexual needs, stimulated by clothing, the mass media, and freedom of contact in dating, but unmet because of proscriptions against intercourse outside marriage, create an expectation of huge sexual rewards in marriage. This is obviously an oversimplification because men and women expect to gain other rewards from marriage and, presumably, all of the anticipated rewards are involved.

Whatever the genesis of romantic love, the belief that it is both a necessary and a sufficient basis for marriage is an important element in spouse selection. It frequently leads couples to ignore differences in nationality, religion, age, race, or social class in the belief that love will dissipate or render trivial the differences in role definitions, in abilities to perform roles, and in the values usually associated with such social entities. Under this assumption even obvious personally held differences in values, goals, and role perceptions and/or deficiencies in role performance can be ignored as inconsequential or self-correcting.

Love as a Basis for Marriage

Most Americans feel that love is the principal basis for marriage, that one shouldn't marry without it, and, if both individuals are eligible for marriage, that they should marry if they love each other. If love develops from extensive interaction, this seems reasonable. If a courting couple consistently reward one another over a period of time so that they love each other, it is a reasonable prediction that this will be true after marriage—that they will continue to love each other and enjoy their marriage. However, qualifications seem necessary. We have noted that love is possible partly or entirely based on anticipated rewards following marriage. Because future relationships are rather difficult to predict, love based entirely or primarily on anticipated future rewards may be unrealistic—that is, the spouse may not behave as anticipated. Most dating interaction involves only one familial role, recreation. It is difficult or even impossible to predict how rewarding the behavior of the spouse will be in enacting the roles of provider, housekeeper, child

---

[33]Ibid., p. 23.
[34]Willard Waller and Reuben Hill, *The Family* (New York: The Dryden Press, 1951), pp. 118–119.

125

care, and other familial roles. Even the evaluation of recreational experience may be distorted by the excitement of sexual stimulation, never fully dissipated by intercourse. The same recreation enjoyable in the dating context may be boring, or otherwise unsatisfactory after marriage.

All research has agreed that marriages following a long acquaintanceship show a much higher success rate than those following a brief acquaintance. These findings can be explained by the assumption that a long-time, comparatively varied association, which has produced a rewarding relationship prior to marriage, is more likely to result in a stable, durable love relationship after marriage. Therefore, the lay public and the sociologist can agree that love in a continued relationship is a relatively good predictor of a happy marriage.

The rationale for marrying someone one doesn't love is about the same. If the relationship has been extensive and hasn't resulted in love, then the interaction apparently has been unrewarding in some or all respects. To enter a long-term, exclusive, contractual relationship in these circumstances appears nonrational.

Finally, marriage to a complete stranger might result in a love or a hate relationship. In societies in which parents arrange the marriage and the couple are married before becoming acquainted, the expression is common "Love comes after marriage." Sometimes!

Discussion

The dating behavior that leads to a decision to marry seems to involve parts of several of the models just described. There is no doubt that youth are more likely to date and marry those who live near them. Likewise, they are more apt to date those with similar social characteristics, such as race, religion, and education. There is some support also for the belief that they are more likely to marry those psychologically and physically like themselves.

Which individuals they meet, date, and marry, however, seems to involve a considerable element of randomness or of accident and idiosyncrasy—such things as who one sits near in a class or who one works with in the same unit in a business or a school. Having met and dated, the decision whether to marry depends first on whether the couple consider themselves as eligible to marry (age, education, economic prospects). If they are eligible, then each one's comparison level for a spouse seems to be critical. If either falls below it, the marriage is unlikely to occur. If both are above and believe they are in love, a marriage is likely but not inevitable (see the more detailed discussion in the preceding section).

126

To sum up, Americans expect to fall in love before marrying. Love has been explained as the result of a consistently profitable relationship between two people. If they are marriageable, love is affected by their anticipation of a profitable relationship after marriage as well as the experience in the dating relationship. Disillusionment occurs in marriage if the marital relationship fails to deliver the rewards and/or involves larger costs than expected prior to marriage. Marriage without love between people who have been dating for a period of time is hazardous because if the relationship has not been profitable during dating, it is apt to result in an unprofitable marriage. Love at first sight is viewed as the anticipation of huge future profits. If marriage results immediately from love at first sight, there is little basis for forecasting whether the marriage will be profitable or unprofitable. Love may follow marriage in arranged marriages, but there is no assurance of it.

Formal Engagement: Final Stage in the Courtship Process

Although some form of engagement or betrothal is found in nearly all human societies, both its meaning and its functions have varied considerably over time both within and between societies. Among the early Hebrews, for example, betrothal was essentially a contract to wed. The betrothal ceremony in effect marked the initiation of marriage, even though the union might not be consummated for several months or years later.[35] Although ancient Germanic law similarly equated intent to marry with actual marriage, in practice the situation was often ambiguous. For couples with high status and property the law insisted on formal betrothal, an endowment, and a solemn wedding ceremony, but for those of lesser standing these details were omitted. There was a certain degree of confusion and sometimes disagreement as to whether betrothal signified merely an intent to marry or whether it meant the actual recognition of a marriage already established through cohabitation, in which case the wedding ceremony was simply a confirmation of a union already consummated. This confusion over the meaning of betrothal persisted through the early centuries of the Christian epoch. In time, the betrothal either became insignificant or was united with the wedding ceremony, although the custom of premarital cohabitation was continued, particularly among the lower classes.[36]

[35]Willystine Goodsell, *A History of the Family as a Social and Educational Institution* (New York: The Macmillan Company, 1923), pp. 64–65.
[36]William Graham Sumner, *Folkways* (Boston: Ginn and Company, 1906), pp. 405–406, 412–413.

127

With the advent and spread of Christianity the notion of an engagement as a solemn and binding pledge to marry emerged and took hold. Until recently, this particular conception was predominant among many Western societies, including that of the United States. Engaged couples were, in the eyes of the community, obligated to marry and were morally committed to do so. Failure to honor this commitment became legally punishable through the instigation of breach-of-promise suits, whereby aggrieved parties could secure certain damages suffered by their voluntary withdrawal from the marriage market, their subsequent loss of status, the mental and emotional duress experienced as a result of being jilted, and the loss of opportunity to marry someone else.

Although precise figures are sorely lacking, breach-of-promise actions apparently were much more prevalent in the past than they are today.[37] Currently, about one third of our states no longer even recognize such litigation. One reason for this decline, of course, has been the shift in the fundamental meaning of the formal engagement away from an emphasis on a solemn pledge to marry toward a recognition of this period as the final stage in the courtship process—as a time for testing under intimate conditions the congruence and compatibility of a couple's personalities, interests, and values. This change in turn reflects the influence of a variety of social forces that have been at work in our society, including the growing acceptance of equalitarian norms and the changing status of women.

The historical experiences of different societies then has produced wide variations in systems of engagement and the functions they perform—each system reflecting the total configuration of social institutions within which it occurs. As Kuhn has observed, however, despite these variations all institutionalized arrangements concerning engagement function to meet at least two basic human needs: "that of having group sanction and approval when one begins to take on an adult role as a mature member of the group," and "the necessity of cushioning the sharp transition from youth to adulthood and parenthood, from the state of single irresponsibility to that of married responsibility, by some intermediate and transitional stage."[38] Within this context of human needs, engagement takes on significance both for the couple involved and for the larger society of which they are a part.

---

[37]Ray E. Baber, *Marriage and the Family,* 2nd ed. (New York: McGraw-Hill Book Company, 1953), pp. 53–56, However, "good old-fashioned" breach of promise suits still occasionally make the headlines. See "Once Again into the Breach," *Time* (March 3, 1967), p. 50.

[38]Manford H. Kuhn, "The Engagement: Thinking About Marriage," in *Family, Marriage, and Parenthood,* ed. by Howard Becker and Reuben Hill (Boston: D. C. Heath & Company, 1948), pp. 280–291.

128

Form and Content of Engagement

In many societies around the world both the forms of and the functions served by engagement are rather rigidly patterned and prescribed. In the United States, however, these elements are relatively undefined, particularly among our middle class. In our society much of the manner and meaning of engagement is left to the individual-couple definition.[39] Consequently, across the nation one can observe alternative patterns in the form and content of the engagement process. Waller and Hill took cognizance of this variation in their early efforts to delineate several types of American middle-class engagements in terms of two variables, the time span and the provisions for becoming a unified pair.[40] The *short but sweet* engagement typically lasts from two to six months and seldom provides the couple adequate opportunities to achieve the necessary interpersonal preparation for the forthcoming marriage. The partners feel they are deeply in love and are anxious to consummate the marriage. Although the details of the wedding plans are shared with the wider public via a newspaper announcement, and although the usual round of showers and stag affairs are squeezed in, little time is actually devoted by the couple to seriously exploring and becoming sufficiently acquainted with one another's personalities, goals, and aspirations.

The *short but brittle* engagement may be of similar duration, but instead of culminating in marriage it is broken off because of various difficulties or disillusionments encountered by the couple during this period. Some couples discover their attraction is merely superficial; others become separated following engagement and are unable to sustain interest or commitment; still others submit to parental pressures to break off the relationship. More often, major cultural divergences and personality differences become apparent and lead to the decision to terminate the engagement. Thus, in the Burgess and Wallin study of one thousand engaged couples, nearly half of the women and one third of the men reported one or more previous engagements. Moreover, one fifth of these couples later broke the engagements they were involved in at the time of the study.[41] Some family specialists are inclined to view these and similar findings as evidence to support the usefulness of the engagement period in screening out persons who would make unsatisfactory marital partners: "the short but brittle engagement may save the waste inherent in a short but brittle marriage."[42] Burgess and Wallin's finding that couples who have serious problems would seem to add further credence to this viewpoint. At the

---

[39]Ibid., pp. 281–283.
[40]Waller and Hill, op. cit., pp. 221–224.
[41]Burgess and Wallin, op. cit., Chapter 9.
[42]Waller and Hill, op. cit., p. 222.

129

same time, it can be argued that the engagement period does not really provide a cold appraisal of a couple's compatibility for marriage. Udry, for example, notes that many aspects of marriage, such as child-bearing, generate disagreements and conflicts that are impossible to ascertain during the engagement. He takes the position that "the absence of instrumental requirements in the relationship, the ability of strong erotic needs to help the couple 'solve' engagement problems, and the general recreational nature of engagement activities keeps strains and disagreements at a minimum for most people and does not really 'test' the relationship."[43]

As with many other controversies among family scholars, there is some truth in both of these positions. As Udry notes, most couples who become engaged have, in their minds, made a definite decision to marry rather than a decision to simply "test" their relationship. The testing aspect, however, is a latent function of the engagement period that operates with extremely important ramifications, regardless of whether the couple are aware of it. The very act of becoming engaged changes both the nature of the couple's interaction with each other and their interactions with family, relatives, and friends. The couples find themselves being treated differently than they were prior to the engagement in a variety of ways. Slater has caught the flavor of this change in the following passage:

As the marriage approaches there is a rapid acceleration of the involvement of the families of the couple in their relationship. Increasing stress is placed upon an awareness of the ritual, legal, and economic significance of the relationship, and the responsibilities which must be assumed. . . . Much of their interaction during this period will thus concern issues external to their own relationship, and there will be a great deal of preoccupation with loyalties and obligations outside of the dyad itself. Guests must be invited, attendants chosen, and gifts for the attendants selected. The ceremony itself has the effect of concentrating the attention of both individuals on every *other* affectional tie either one has ever contracted.[44]

Under the pressured circumstances and intimate social context of the engagement process, couples come to perceive differences in one another's total personality in ways not experienced at earlier stages of the courtship process. If this changed perception produces uneasiness and much dissatisfaction, couples are less hesitant than in the past to break the engagement. Given our current mores, they are also less reluctant to become engaged later on to someone who has also been previously engaged.

[43]J. Richard Udry, *The Social Context of Marriage* (Philadelphia: J. B. Lippincott Co., 1966), p. 263.
[44]Philip Slater, "Social Limitations on Libidinal Withdrawal," *American Journal of Sociology,* **26** (Nov. 1961), pp. 296–311.

The long but separated engagement is often associated with situations in which, for various reasons, one of the couple must of necessity leave the community—to complete academic or professional schooling, to fulfill military or other governmental service obligations or job commitments, and so on. Prior to the separation, which may last for a rather extended period, the couple decide to become engaged and to postpone the marriage until a more opportune moment when they can be united. Under such circumstances the actual processes of engagement must of necessity be achieved through the mail or by telephone. The length of the engagement here would not seem to accomplish the same positive functions that it might under more normal circumstances. Intimate courtship and reality testing via air mail is rather limited in producing the kinds of premarital adjustments needed in this stage of the relationship. "Couples so engaged," Waller and Hill feel, "have achieved adjustments mainly at the letter-writing level, which would be functional in marriage only to a couple in which the husband plans to become a salesman, lecturer, actor, or musician who expects to be away from home a large part of the year."[45] Often, when such separated but engaged couples are finally reunited they discover they have maintained very superficial conceptions of one another and that a real difference exists between the self they communicated through the mail and their actual selves. Sometimes they marry immediately upon the return of the absent partner and only later encounter this difficulty. Still others discover through the separation that although for some people "Absence makes the heart grow fonder" in their particular case it turned out to be a matter of "Out of sight out of mind"! The long but separated engagement makes it difficult to develop the type of intimacy necessary to uncover significant personality and sociocultural differences.

Couples sometimes find themselves entangled in a *long but inconclusive* engagement, in which they have somehow drifted into patterns of adjustment that effectively postpone the marriage indefinitely. Family loyalties and obligations, inability to resist parental interference or disapproval, overconcern with achieving a safe economic base for the marriage, and other factors consistently intrude as reasons for putting off the wedding date. Couples may become embarrassed or annoyed as friends begin to inquire, perhaps indirectly, about the delay or when an implication is made that questions their motives for forestalling the marriage. Often this prolongation of the engagement serves to build up considerable sexual tension and continued continence becomes increasingly painful. Consequently, this type of engagement is especially vulnerable to violation of the premarital sexual restrictions or a sudden termination of the relationship. The

[45]Waller and Hill, op. cit., p. 223.

long but inconclusive engagement is sometimes the result of the fact that one or both of the partners no longer desire to marry but simply cannot bring themselves to face up to this and sever the relationship, for fear of hurting the other or embarrassing their families. In any event, a continuation of "things as they are" only further heightens the possibility of further strains emerging.

Waller and Hill posit the *long-enough-to-verify-readiness* engagement as perhaps the most functional of all the types they delineate. It may span anywhere from six months to two years, on the average, depending in part on the length of time and the adequacy of the couples' preengagement relationship. Typically, young persons who fall into this pattern have recognized early in their relationship that they are more than casually interested in one another. Consequently, well before a formal engagement period, the couple have been involved in testing, exploring, and discussing their compatibility as potential marital partners. Frequently, this pattern is characteristic of college couples, who move from an initial friendly campus companionship, through a period of mutual discovery and growth, to eventual engagement. Although they may marry while still in college, it is not unusual for them to delay the wedding until one or both have graduated. In either event, the couple are less likely than those involved in other types of engagements to move into the marital relationship until they feel psychologically as well as socially prepared to make such a commitment. These couples are more apt to exhibit a pragmatic approach to marriage and their engagements tend to be characterized by a good deal of conscious planning and rational experimentation.

In light of this discussion, it should come as no surprise that the early marital prediction studies found the reasonably long engagement to be the most strongly associated with marital happiness and success.[46] Both Terman and Landis, for example, found engagements of six months or less to be associated with poor marital adjustment. Burgess and Cottrell found a similar association for betrothal periods lasting under nine months. In general, these studies show that engagements of two or more years are the most strongly associated with marital success. Locke's comparison between happily married and divorced groups points in the same direction. He found that the happily married group had had the longer engagements. The notion that there is a

---

[46]Lewis M. Terman, *Psychological Factors in Marital Happiness* (New York: McGraw-Hill Book Company, 1938), p. 199; Ernest W. Burgess and Leonard S. Cottrell, *Predicting Success or Failure in Marriage* (Englewood Cliffs, N.J.: Prentice-Hall, 1939), p. 168; Harvey Locke, *Predicting Adjustment in Marriage: A Comparison of a Divorced and Happily Married Group* (New York: Holt, Rinehart and Winston, 1951), Chapter 12; and Judson T. and Mary G. Landis, *Building a Successful Marriage*, 2nd ed. (Englewood Cliffs, N.J.: Prentice-Hall, 1953).

relationship between length of engagement and divorce-proneness receives additional support from Goode's study of 425 divorcees living in Detroit.[47] His analysis showed that a relatively short engagement was characteristic of these couples—more than 70 per cent were engaged six months or less.

Again, it is necessary to point out that these findings must be interpreted with care. Length of engagement, per se, although shown to have predictive power in terms of eventual marital success, tells us little about *why* short-term engagements tend to carry the higher risks of marital failure. As noted earlier, it is generally presumed that the longer engagement provides greater opportunities for a couple to become acquainted and to discover as far as is possible whether they are suitably matched for marriage. It might be argued that such functions often may be served by a lengthy preengagement acquaintance. Indeed, there is some evidence to suggest that preengagement acquaintances involving couples who have known each other for some time and who have experienced an extended going-steady period may be as functional as the long engagement.[48] Surprisingly, however, it has also been found that couples who have already come to know each other well through a lengthy acquaintance are also more likely to prefer a long engagement![49] In the final analysis, of course, the question is not how long a couple have been engaged but whether they have become sufficiently acquainted to make a rational judgment about their potential as permanent mates. As one sociologist has observed: "Getting really acquainted is the most valuable outcome of any engagement, and in nearly all cases getting acquainted takes time."[50]

Premarital Sex During Engagement

In Chapter 7, we shall examine in considerable detail the relationship between levels of personal commitment and the degree of sexual involvement in heterosexual relationships. Here we want to note that the engagement situation presents special problems. Because it involves the highest level of overt and emotional commitment, it is particularly conducive to increasing sexual intimacy and it thus becomes a problem for many couples. Although the sex codes allow considerably more intimacy during engagement than at earlier stages of the dating-courtship process, nevertheless, premarital intercourse is

---

[47]William J. Goode, *Women in Divorce,* originally published as *After Divorce* (New York: The Free Press, 1956; paperback edition, 1965), p. 78.

[48]Burgess and Cottrell, op. cit.; Landis and Landis, *Building a Successful Marriage,* 5th ed. (Englewood Cliffs, N.J.: Prentice-Hall, 1968), Table 2, p. 79.

[49]Goode, op. cit., pp. 80–81.

[50]Paul H. Landis, *Making the Most of Marriage,* 5th ed. (New York: Appleton-Century-Crofts, 1970), p. 332.

133

still not formally condoned by the mores. In addition, concern with violating the societal moral code, fear of pregnancy, worry that premarital coitus would tarnish the honeymoon and the marital experience, and a host of other factors contribute to a couple's anxiety over the issue of sex during engagement. Indeed, although they may not openly admit it to themselves or to others, some couples elect a short engagement as a means of coping with their rising sexual tensions.

At the same time, it must be noted that research has shown that a rather significant proportion of all engaged couples have traditionally disregarded the cultural mores regarding premarital intercourse. (For specific data, see Chapter 7). The physical intimacies that occur between most engaged pairs tend to propel them rapidly toward complete sexual union. Moreover, among certain segments of the contemporary marriageable population, there has emerged a growing attitude that essentially rejects the customary inhibitions imposed by the mores. Thus, in one study of four hundred senior college women it was found that 94 per cent approved of sexual intercourse with a fiancé.[51] Moreover, 98 per cent of these women felt that the average female senior at that college would also approve of such activity. These responses no doubt reflect in part a growing courtship ideology that truly meaningful heterosexual relationships cannot be developed without the inclusion of sexual intimacies. This ideology will be examined in greater detail later on in this text.

Married couples who have had premarital intercourse during their engagement period have been asked whether they felt the experience had strengthened or weakened their relationship. In the Burgess and Wallin study over 90 per cent of the husbands and wives who had been sexually intimate prior to marriage indicated that they thought it had strengthened their relationship. Such responses, however, must obviously be interpreted with caution. Undoubtedly there are particular engaged couples who can and do participate in premarital intercourse without damaging their total relationship.[52] Whether premarital coital experience would *in fact* serve to strengthen the relationship of *most* engaged couples remains an open question. The Burgess and Wallin study, for example, also showed that those engaged couples in their sample who were currently having sexual relations had lower engagement success scores than those who were abstaining.[53] Moreover, a number of studies discussed in this text have failed to demonstrate that

[51]Harrop A. and Ruth S. Freeman, "Senior College Women: Their Sexual Standards and Activity," *Journal of the National Association of Women Deans and Counselors,* 29 (Spring 1966), pp. 136–143.

[52]Lester A. Kirkendall, *Premarital Intercourse and Interpersonal Relationships* (New York: The Julian Press, 1961), pp. 199–200.

[53]Ibid., pp. 354–355.

premarital intercourse is positively associated with marital adjustment or marital happiness.

Despite the emergent liberal sex codes apparent in American society today, premarital coital activity typically still takes place surreptitiously. Given the clandestine nature of this activity, often such sexual encounters are fraught with fear of discovery, worry, and guilt, as well as the woman's fears regarding exploitation. Such an atmosphere is something less than conducive to providing a couple with realistic indications of their mutual compatibility or to testing their sexual harmony. Moreover, as Kuhn has pointed out it is erroneous to assume that because a large proportion of engaged persons violate the premarital intercourse restrictions no negative consequences will ensue from such behavior.

On the contrary, whenever two people break this code and go on to the culmination of the sex act they take upon themselves the entire responsibility for its consequences. Should pregnancy result or should they be apprehended, they are treated in much the same way they would be if there were no such divergence between code and general practice. The everybody's-doing-it argument may be influential in bringing about the breaking of the code, but after the code is broken this argument often recedes from consciousness while the code demands and receives its pound of flesh in the form of a feeling of guilt. Codes are curious, because they are both outside and within each of us, and while it is often possible to evade the external aspects of a code, it is very rarely possible to avoid the internal consequences of such evasion.[54]

On the other hand, it seems quite possible that should the mores shift sufficiently to support the cohabitation of engaged couples, then such activity might provide a realistic testing of the pair bond among potential mates. Until American society reaches that point, however, the aforementioned risks remain to be contended with. And whether a particular couple is willing to take those risks depends primarily on the compatibility of their own value systems regarding premarital sex.

Engagement as Marital Role-Rehearsal

It is useful to conceptualize the engagement process as involving a rehearsal for marital role-playing. For example, the decision-making required to sustain marriage and family life is approximated through experimentation with mutual problem-solving on the part of engaged couples. Should they rent an apartment or place a down payment on their own home? Should they have children, and if so, how many and when? Will the wife be employed outside the home? Should they practice birth control, and if so, what type of contraceptive will they

---

[54]Ibid., p. 298.

135

utilize? In their discussions of these and a multitude of other questions requiring conscious and mutual planning, the couple gain some idea of their capacity for joint functioning as husband and wife. It is during engagement that the more serious conversations concerning marital role-performance and expectations occur. The extent to which couples at this stage are able to resolve differences and find areas of agreement will give some indication of their potential for marital-role compatibility.

There are, of course, limitations on the effectiveness of this premarital rehearsal for role compatibility. Rehearsing a role is one thing—playing it for real is another. Moreover, it should be recognized that marital-role definitions and expectations frequently change over time—sometimes immediately following the wedding! One cannot always predict the unforeseen circumstances that might occur following the marriage ceremony. Certain decisions made during the engagement may be abandoned or implemented, depending on the unique marital and familial experiences of the couple. After the wedding one or both partners may discover that for any number of reasons they are unable to meet adequately the role expectations of the other. Given these and other contingencies, perhaps the more critical evaluation to be made during the engagement period is the extent to which each partner possesses the quality of adaptability, that is, "the capacity of the person to change his roles, his attitudes, and his behavior in order to adjust to those of other persons or to a new or modified situation."[55] Burgess and Wallin have suggested that this quality may be among the major personality factors associated with marital success. Adaptability is a rather complex attribute involving a number of components, including empathy, flexibility, command of the appropriate attitudes and roles, and the motivation to adjust.

However, adaptability is, in part, the ability to make the best of the mistakes one has made in spouse selection. The person who has married someone with a value system opposite to his own will have to be highly adaptable to avoid the breakup of his marriage, yet the marriage will not be as satisfactory for either spouse as it would have been if they both embraced the same values or had married someone else whose values largely coincided with their own, because each value difference requires one or the other to give up a desired activity or goal. In contrast, shared values provide shared goals, toward which each can work with the other. Adaptability is an ability to compromise. All marriages require some compromises, but those that require too many yield little profit to either marital partner.

---

[55]Burgess and Wallin, op. cit., p. 623.

6

Dating and Mate Selection II: Mixed Marriage

In the previous chapter we have seen that there is a tendency toward homogamy in mate selection. This has been clearly shown with respect to social characteristics, but with increasing evidence that "like tends to marry like" also with respect to personality characteristics. This seems to contradict the commonly held idea that opposites attract, or if they do, that they are likely to think better of it before a decision is made to marry. Later, we will present research and theories supporting the idea that differences in role perceptions and in value differences are major factors in divorce.

However, many people of marriageable age do not view heterogeneous marriages as especially problematic. One study of a university sample disclosed that over half would not hesitate to be a party to a marriage with someone of another religion.[1] In this chapter we will explore what kinds of social characteristics seem to warrant the term *mixed marriage* and the research and theorizing that these types of marriages have inspired.

Which Types of Heterogeneity Are Relevant to Marriage?

Individuals vary in an infinite number of ways but most of these ways do not seem to affect the patterns of one's behavior or the evaluation that one places on another. For example there are blue, brown, green, and a variety of other eye colors, but it hasn't occurred to

---

[1]Judson T. Landis, "Religiousness, Family Relationships, and Family Values in Protestant, Catholic and Jewish Families," *Marriage and Family Living*, **22** (Nov. 1960), pp. 341–348.

anyone to consider the marriage of a blue-eyed woman to a green-eyed man as a mixed marriage and therefore an alliance that might be fraught with special problems. Neither has it occurred to anyone that the marriage of a chubby person to a thin one is to be considered a mixed marriage. To date, the marriage of members of different political parties is not considered a mixed marriage. By contrast the marriages of a Protestant to a Catholic or a Jew, of an American to a Japanese, of an American Negro to an American Caucasian, and probably of an upper-class American to a lower-class American are regarded as heterogeneous or mixed marriages. For the moment, it is the social characteristics of individuals and their behavioral patterns that are to be analyzed. Heterogeneity in personality will be considered later.

RACE Although physiological characteristics in general are not considered to be the bases of mixed marriage, those that are the bases of race are, especially skin color. The color of the skin is often made synonymous with race, as mention is frequently made of the white, the black, and the yellow races. Race apparently becomes significant only as it is correlated with social class, caste, or ethnic differences, such as language, religion, and other customs. For example, the Negro-Caucasian racial differences are significant in the United States primarily because the Negro has been placed in a lower caste, and to the extent that he has been able to free himself from the caste, has most often found placement in the lower social class. This has resulted in a different and less efficient socialization for Negro children and a less advantageous position in adult life insofar as income and prestige are concerned. However, race is especially significant because the individual is unable to escape identification with it no matter what he may do or how much he may achieve. The physical characteristics of the Negro make identification simple and provide a basis for repression and discrimination against him because of his racial membership independent of his effectiveness in his occupation or the attractiveness of his personality.

In South Africa race is even more significant because in addition to caste membership, ethnic differences also attach to race. The Negro has a native language that is different, a different religion, and a complete set of customs, all of which are significant social differences. In addition, the Negro is a majority group there, and any semblance of equal treatment would result in the Caucasians losing political and economic control of the society.

In contrast, in the former colonial areas settled by the French and the Spaniards—in Latin America and much of Africa, in Hawaii, and elsewhere—the significance of race has been minimized but not obliterated. In these areas, the explorers, the colonial planters, and the administrators married native women and reared children with mixed

138

racial inheritance. In these areas, no caste system obtained, obviously, because castes by their nature forbid intermarriage. However, race became associated with social class, with the Caucasians at the top of the class pyramid, those of mixed parentage in the middle, and the native negroid or mongoloid people at the bottom. The degree of skin coloring took on class significance with preference in marriage and in economic life accorded to a degree on one's light or dark complexion. In these societies race never was a bar to intermarriage but remained a basis for the relative desirability of individuals in the marriage market.

ETHNICITY: NATIONALITY AND RELIGION Ethnic differences are customary ways of thinking and behaving that are characteristic of one group and not others. Political boundaries coincide with the limits of a given political organization. Because political boundaries frequently coincide with language boundaries, also, this frequently adds to their significance as does a psychological identification with a nation. For example, France is coterminous with governmental organization (the state), the French language, and an identification with French history, literature, and customs. By way of contrast Great Britain, Canada, and the United States share a common language, similar although not identical political, economic, and religious institutions. Therefore, nationality possesses a minimum of ethnic differences for those nations in relationship to each other. Where their citizens intermingle, nationality is not related to social class. Thus, nationality may possess little significance. Few would regard the marriage of an American to a Canadian as a mixed marriage.

By contrast, the marriage of an American to a Turk would involve differences not only in government, but in language and religion and in economic and familial institutions. These differences pervade the norms of the two nations and would provide contrasting normative patterns in almost every part of the couple's life.

Ethnic differences are found within complex societies as well as between them. For example, Switzerland contains three major languages and large populations of Catholic and Protestant church members. Canada is bilingual and includes very large numbers of both the Catholic and the Protestant religions. Nationality may be said always to be associated with a degree of ethnic difference but differences are greater between subcultures within some nationalities than between other countries.

Nationality differs from race in mixed marriages in that it usually is not visible. Russian scientists or diplomats at conferences could easily be mistaken for Americans. Likewise, another language can be learned, another religion adopted, and other ethnic changes made. These changes are not simple or quickly accomplished but they are possible. Thus, the American girl who marries a German can obtain German

139

nationality, learn to speak German, learn to understand and participate in German politics, and become accustomed to Germany's distinctive food and customs. In contrast the Negro man who marries a white woman cannot become a white man. The marriage is permanently and obviously mixed.

SOCIAL CLASS Is there enough difference between the socialization of children in the lower and the upper classes to warrant calling marriages of individuals from the two as mixed? There are differences in socialization stemming from some obvious differences in circumstances. The upper-class child need not be trained to earn a living and therefore can be educated to understand and appreciate art, music, foreign languages and culture. The lower-class child, if educated beyond the years required by law, is likely to enter a vocational or business curriculum. In dress, the upper-class child learns the subtleties of fabric and tailoring, whereas the lower-class child will focus on economy. The upper-class child views the world from the assured position of wealth and prestige; the lower-class child is an outsider trying to find ways of securing a share in the goods and services ascribed to the upper class and achieved by the middle class. These differences could be elaborated considerably.

It is clear that social class differences bear more resemblance to national than to racial differences. They are neither entirely obvious nor permanent. They also differ from ethnic heterogeneity in that although religious differences are qualitative in nature, social class differences are more in terms of degree. For example, Catholics and Protestants disagree on religious issues, on birth control, and on divorce. The French and the Japanese speak different languages. The upper and the lower social class speak the same language, even though the upper-class child is likely to have a larger vocabulary.[2] There are no religious differences per se, and they are influenced by the same fashions. They share the same intrinsic values. The differences are largely in how well they are prepared to undertake life's tasks, in how they interact with associates, and the like. The capable and perceptive lower-class child learns many of the subtleties and elaborate behavior of the class above him. The capable and perceptive child reared in the middle class can learn to function acceptably with upper-class people. However, for the child socialized in the lower class to move suddenly into the upper class through marriage usually involves such differences in dress, social interaction, political outlook, and other behaviors and attitudes as to constitute a mixed marriage in the sense of racial and religious intermarriage.

---

[2]The differences in language are dramatically illustrated by Shaw's play *Pgymalion,* in which a girl from the slums is taught the language, dress, and behavior of the upper class.

140

These observations hardly hold for marriages between spouses socialized in the lower and middle classes, for several reasons. First, the two blend at points. The skilled blue-collar worker on a salary lives, talks, and plays much as does the lower-salaried white-collar worker. They share not only the intrinsic values of the society but such instrumental ones as the values placed on honesty, cleanliness, punctuality, and friendly cooperative relations with fellow workers and neighbors. Perhaps more important is the achievement characteristic of the middle class. Any lower-class boy who can obtain a Ph.D., an M.D., or other advanced training and is efficient in his work is ipso facto a member of the middle class. This achievement aspect of the middle class in an open-class society ensures that a large transfusion of lower-class youth enter the middle class in every generation. Furthermore, a large proportion of the children reared in the middle class have parents socialized in the lower class. This lessens the differences in the styles of life between the middle and the lower class. It seems doubtful that marriages between lower-class youth and those socialized in the middle class should be characterized as mixed marriages, despite some differences in the socialization characteristic of the two classes.

EDUCATION Education involves a narrower or more limited part of people's lives than does social class. Because education beyond the high school level becomes increasingly specialized, the area of knowledge and training in which the spouse is competent becomes increasingly limited, although increasingly competent within that specialization. It is a rare pair of spouses that share that specialized training even if both are college graduates or beyond. It is probably the knowledge of general applicability—of man, of social organizations, of other societies, and of the physical world about—that is relevant to the question of homogeneity.

However, indirectly, education seems to affect participation in political life, with a larger proportion of the better educated likely to register, vote, and participate in political campaigns. More favor an active foreign policy and oppose the extension of security and welfare programs. Education also influences, to some extent, the choice of friends and what has sometimes been termed the "style of life"—tastes, interests, hobbies, and leisure activities.

Education is also related to the choice of religious denomination. The highly educated are more likely to find that the "liberal" churches provide a congenial place for worship and social interaction. Less-educated persons are more likely to find a fundamentalist denomination congenial to their needs and tastes.

The most obvious impact of education is on one's occupation. If both spouses are employed, those whose education is greatly different are likely to engage in different types of occupations, manual or mental,

141

that require different levels of abstraction in their thinking. This difference in education reduces the amount of stimulation and interest that each can provide for the other in this area of life. If the spouses have the same amount of education their thinking is more likely to be at the same level of abstraction.

It appears that although not much attention has been directed to mixed educational marriages, there is some basis for believing that the socialization provided by a liberal college education is likely to be reflected in one's patterns of participation in several institutions and in his choice of friends. The difference presumably is increased if one is a college graduate and the other has less than a high school education.

AGE DIFFERENCE Three aspects of age difference may provide a basis for thinking that certain types of age differences in spouses should be regarded as mixed marriage: difference in ability to perform roles, different role definitions because of cultural change, and social disapproval of certain combinations of ages of the spouses.

Differences of the magnitude of a generation between spousal ages frequently span periods of considerable change in the definitions of roles. For example, following World War II there was a strong swing in thinking in the direction of permissiveness in rearing small children. Two decades earlier the norms sanctioned restrictive parental practices, whereas two decades later the pendulum had swung back to more restrictive and directive parental practices. Persons attending college would be likely to have very different concepts depending on when they attended. Similar changes have occurred with respect to the employment of mothers. It is accepted now but wasn't, except under unusual circumstances, two decades ago. The older spouse is more likely to have one set of normative definitions, the younger another.

Age differences may be relevant also to roles that require joint activity, such as sexual relations and many types of recreation. It is clear that age is related to sexual activity. Couples engage in it less frequently as they grow older and typically they indicate a preference for less frequent sexual activity. This decrease in sexual activity corresponds both to research findings and to common-sense assumptions. Even the notion derived from Kinsey's research that teen-age boys should marry women thirty-five to forty years old appears based on a misconception. It is the *proportion* of her sexual experience that results in *orgasm* for the wife, not the frequency of coitus or her preference for frequency, which reaches its high point in early middle age for married women. Women want intercourse less often with advancing years. They have it less frequently, and the total number of orgasms they have declines between the ages of twenty and forty-five. Only the *proportion* of intercourse in which they reach orgasm increases. As physical energy declines with older age, it is probably

142

generally true that the aging spouse will want to curtail his physical activity in various recreational activities, whereas the younger spouse is likely to prefer to be active. In other roles, the abilities of one spouse may not fit the needs of the other. For example, an older man married to a young woman may have minor children to support at retirement age.

Norms defining the relative ages of spouses are relevant because approximate ages are evident. In small communities, kin and acquaintances know the ages of young people because of such events as their graduating from high school, consuming alcohol in public places, or voting. On the average the husband is three years older than his wife in current American society. It has been estimated that six out of seven men are the same age or older than their wives. Even a few years' difference may seem significant if the wife is the older.

The obvious reason for the male to be somewhat older is his provider role. The extra years enable him to complete his training and obtain successful work experience in an occupation. The utility for the male of marrying a woman younger than himself is less obvious. It apparently has been centered on the greater beauty of young girls. This may be debated today as body and facial care and abstention from rough work enable women to keep their physical attractiveness until advanced years. A less obvious advantage of the wife's being younger is her greater participation in sexual intercourse. Both her preferred frequency and her participation decline steadily after twenty-five. Her capacity for orgasm also declines after forty-five.

Countering these arguments in part is the much greater longevity of the woman. Currently, wives three years younger than their husbands can expect to be widows for several years.

Part of the significance of age is in its visibility. Of course, the impact of age on appearance has been so dampened by improved diet, exercise, and beauty aids that a few years' difference is likely to escape notice, perhaps as much as ten years. However, beyond a certain point, the physical indications mark a marriage with widely different spousal ages as mixed and may draw unfavorable notice from others. Research has not established the difference in ages that constitutes a mixed marriage in this sense. We think it might be ten years or more if the older is the wife, or whatever dfference is great enough so that it is apparent that the wife is older; perhaps a generation's difference if the husband is older.

Religious Intermarriage

Intermarriage between members of different religious faiths has been widely discouraged but rarely prohibited. Where two or more faiths are

143

found within one political unit, such as the United States (see Figure 6.1), such intermarriage is frequent. Adequate data have been unavailable because both religion and marriage have been regarded by some as private information that should not be collected for national statistics. However, the Census Bureau in 1958 did publish a report that included data on intermarriage. It showed 2,353,000 intermarriages between Protestants, Catholics, and Jews (Figure 6.2). Unfortunately, these data are believed by sociologists who have conducted research on intermarriage to underestimate seriously the actual frequency. If those reared in one of the faiths, but not active in it, are included, the figure would be

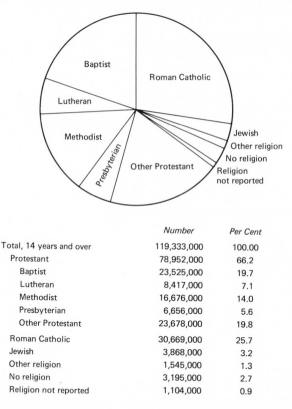

	Number	Per Cent
Total, 14 years and over	119,333,000	100.00
Protestant	78,952,000	66.2
Baptist	23,525,000	19.7
Lutheran	8,417,000	7.1
Methodist	16,676,000	14.0
Presbyterian	6,656,000	5.6
Other Protestant	23,678,000	19.8
Roman Catholic	30,669,000	25.7
Jewish	3,868,000	3.2
Other religion	1,545,000	1.3
No religion	3,195,000	2.7
Religion not reported	1,104,000	0.9

Figure 6.1. Religion Reported by Persons 14 Years Old and Over. Note: Religious censuses are conducted at irregular intervals. The above were the latest national data available. [Source: U.S. Department of Commerce, Bureau of the Census, "Religion Reported by the Civilian Population of the United States, March, 1957," *Current Population Reports: Population Characteristics,* Series P-20, No. 79, February 2, 1958.]

144

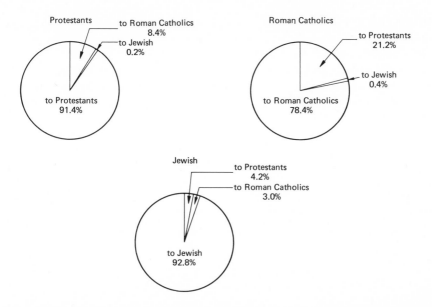

Figure 6.2. Ingroup and Outgroup Marriages in the United States. [Source: U.S. Department of Commerce, Bureau of the Census, "Religion Reported by the Civilian Population of the United States, March, 1957," *Current Population Reports: Population Characteristics,* Series P-20, No. 79, February 2, 1958.]

much higher. Thomas suggests that the proportion may be nearly 30 per cent for Catholics.[3]

WHAT DETERMINES RATES OF RELIGIOUS INTERMARRIAGE? The proposition that the smaller the religious group, the larger the rate of intermarriage has received widespread statistical support. It appears to be true, other variables being equal. That these are not always equal is suggested by the low intermarriage rate of Jews (Figure 6.2). According to the most complete figures available 66 per cent of the American population is Protestant, 25 per cent Catholic, and only 3 per cent Jewish.[4]

The rationale for the proposition is that the smaller the proportion a religious group is of the population, the fewer the potential marriage partners of the same faith. This has been found to be true in studies of the same faith: in states where the proportion of Catholics is low, the intermarriage rate is high. Where Catholics comprise a large proportion

[3]John L. Thomas, *The American Catholic Family* (Englewood Cliffs, N.J.: Prentice-Hall, Inc., 1956), pp. 167.

[4]U.S. Department of Commerce, Bureau of the Census, "Religion Reported by the Civilian Population of the United States, March, 1957," *Current Population Report: Population Characteristics,* Series P-20, No. 79 (Feb. 2, 1958).

of the population intermarriage rate is lower.[5] This is not true of every faith. The Jewish population is only about an eighth that of the Catholic, but the intermarriage rate is much lower. This lower rate may be partly a function of the size of the faith: smaller groups feel their identity is more threatened by intermarriage than do large ones. In addition, the Jewish people have an ethnic identification that goes considerably beyond religious beliefs. It appears that permanent rejection of the intermarried couple by the Jewish extended family (relatives) is not uncommon.[6] Although both Protestants and Catholics discourage intermarriage before it occurs, rejection of the intermarried couple following marriage is infrequent. The fact that probably about one Catholic marriage in three is interfaith is both an indication that sanctions are not extremely severe and also a reason why such sanctions cannot be severe.

The greater frequency of Catholic intermarriage might be taken as an indication of greater permissiveness on the part of Catholics toward interfaith marriage. It is true that they are more permissive than Jews, but Catholic parents and the Church have actively discouraged intermarriage. The Church has in the past required a marriage contract stipulating that all children be reared as Catholics, renouncing the option of divorce and of birth control, and promising not to influence the Catholic partner to change his faith. It has in the past refused to recognize marriages that have taken place without the marriage contract.

Protestant churches and parents have also vigorously discouraged interfaith marriage. However, the lower proportion of Protestants intermarrying is not a reflection of greater opposition to such marriages. As many Protestants intermarry as Catholics, but because the total number of Protestants is greater, the proportion is smaller. One way to assess the propensity of each faith to intermarry is to compare the proportion of its members who do intermarry to the proportion of all spouses available who are of other faiths. If we take the proportions intermarrying in Figure 6.2 as about equally understated and therefore appropriate for comparisons among themselves, the following are obtained. The Catholics comprise 25 per cent of the population of the United States. If there were no special preference for Catholic spouses, 75 per cent would marry non-Catholics. The figure reported is about 22 per cent. Therefore, Catholics are a little more than three times as likely to marry Catholics than would occur by chance. Jews form about 3 per cent of the population, so randomly they would marry 97 per cent

[5]Harvey J. Locke and Mary Margaret Thomes, "Interfaith Marriages," *Social Problems,* **4** (Apr. 1957), pp. 329–333.

[6]Albert I. Gordon, *Intermarriage, Interfaith, Interracial, Interethnic* (Boston: The Beacon Press, 1964), Chapter 7, pp. 174–219.

non-Jews. The figure given is about 7 per cent. Therefore, they are about fourteen times more likely to marry a Jew than would occur by chance. Because Catholics and Jews together make up about 29 per cent of the population, random marriage would produce that per cent of interfaith marriages for Protestants. However, the entire picture is, of course, a little more complex. Jews proportionately marry more Catholics than Protestants, because Protestants are almost three times as numerous as Catholics; Jews should marry almost three times as many of them whereas they marry only a few more (Figure 6.2).

ATTITUDES OF YOUTH TOWARD INTERFAITH MARRIAGE The unmarried appear, in general, unaware of significant differences in family life between major faiths. One study in a large public university found that 55 per cent of the students queried said that if other things were equal they would not hesitate to marry across religious lines. Catholics showed the greatest willingness with 72 per cent willing to ignore interfaith differences compared to 51 per cent of the Protestants. Jews were least willing to marry outside their faith, but there was a large difference between the proportion of the devout (12 per cent) and the indifferent (60 per cent) who would do so.[7] It is not known whether such samples of college students in state-supported universities are representative of youth in general.

If it is assumed for a moment that the above are roughly representative of youth, it is interesting to speculate on why Catholics might be more favorable toward intermarriage than Protestants. First, regarding Protestants as potential spouses increases the number available by some 250 per cent, but for Protestants the increase is only about 40 per cent. In the past, of possible importance, too, was the antenuptial marriage contract that protected all of the Catholic's rights to his own religion and to rearing his children as Catholics. In contrast, the contract placed the religious interests of Protestants in jeopardy.

Because only 6.4 per cent of marriages, about one in sixteen, are listed as intermarriages, (Figure 6.2) there is a vast difference between the attitudes of young people when they are reacting in terms of generalities and the decisions that they finally make with respect to whom they will marry. Serious discussion between courting couples, information and advice from parents, peers, and clergymen of all faiths presumably all are involved in reducing the one in two who would consider interfaith marriage to the one in sixteen who enters one.

RELATIONSHIP TO STABILITY Some of the most provocative data relative to family stability have come from studies of interfaith marriages. These have consistently shown a much higher divorce rate for intermarriage than for intramarriage. Typical of these is a Landis study

---

[7]Landis, op. cit., pp. 341–348.

of parents of college students that found a divorce rate of 4.4 per cent for couples both of whom were Catholics, 6.0 per cent for both Protestants, and 17.9 per cent for Catholic-Protestant marriages. The highest rate of these was for the interfaith marriages in which the wife was Protestant, the husband Catholic. The rate was substantially lower for wife Catholic, husband Protestant interfaith marriages. Data from the entire state of Iowa have been analyzed by Burchinal and Chancellor[8] (Figure 6.3). These are for survival rates for the first seven years of marriage. Divorce rates would certainly increase substantially by the time these couples have been married twenty-five years. Whether the increase will be proportionate between categories is not certain. Some combinations may include more latent stresses, such as the religious training of children, which may produce an increasing proportion of divorces later. It should be noted that desertions are not recorded in these data. These are believed to be more frequent among Catholic marriages because of the impediments placed in the way of ending an unsatisfactory marriage by divorce. The Burchinal and Chancellor data provide some additional information in giving the rates for divorce between Catholics and several major Protestant denominations. Note that survival rates are considerably higher for Catholics marrying Lutherans and Presbyterians than Methodists and Baptists. Because the survival rate for homogeneous Methodists is 91.4 per cent and for Baptists, 89.8 per cent, it appears that this is not due only to higher divorce proneness within these denominations. Viewed another way, the difference between the rates within the denomination and in mixed marriages with Catholics is Lutherans, 3.6 per cent; Presbyterians, 1.2 per cent; Methodists, 7.6 per cent; Baptists, 8.2 per cent. These figures indicate greater stresses in some Catholic-Protestant combinations than in others. No information is available on divorce rates between members of fundamentalist Protestant denominations and sects and Catholics.

The Iowa data provide at least a partial answer to the question of whether intermarriages between Protestant denominations are reflected in higher divorce rates. The answer appears to be negative. The survival rate for homogeneous Lutheran marriages was 94.1 per cent, for mixed Lutheran 93.0 per cent; for homogeneous Presbyterian 91.0 per cent, mixed 94.6 per cent; homogeneous Methodist 91.4 per cent, mixed 92.9 per cent; homogeneous Baptist 89.8 per cent, mixed 90.0 per cent.[9] These differences are trivial and about as frequently favor the mixed Protestant as the homogeneous Protestant marriage.

Finally, studies have shown a very high divorce rate both for

[8]Lee G. Burchinal and Loren E. Chancellor, "Survival Rates Among Religiously Homogenous and Interreligious Marriage," *Social Forces,* **41** (May 1963), p. 200.
[9]Burchinal and Chancellor, op. cit., p. 358.

Catholic-nonreligious marriage and for marriages in which neither party has a religious affiliation. To what extent special stresses are created between couples in which one is religious and the other is not is not known. Religiousness of any type appears to be associated with marital survival.[10]

A latent issue is involved in whether interfaith data should be presented in terms of proportions ending in divorce, as has been the case in most earlier studies, or in terms of the proportion of unbroken marriages, as in the Burchinal and Chancellor study. Critics have raised the issue in pointing to the fact that a large majority of interfaith marriages survive. The issue can be clearly illustrated from the Burchinal and Chancellor data (Figure 6.3). The survival rate (for seven years) of all Protestant-Catholic marriages was 78 per cent. This is only 8 per cent lower than for homogeneous Protestants and 18 per cent lower than for homogeneous Catholics. Such differences might very well be ignored as not very great. However, if one analyzes divorce rates, the differences are impressive. The number of divorces in the mixed Catholic-Protestant marriages is over four times as great as in the intrafaith Catholic marriages and over 60 per cent greater than the intrafaith Protestant marriages. Similarly, the survival rate is only 5 per cent higher for Catholic husband-Protestant wife than for Catholic wife-Protestant husband, but if the divorce rates are analyzed, the

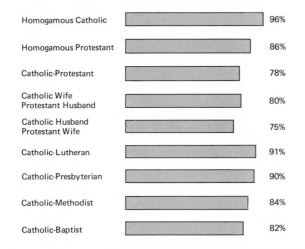

Figure 6.3. Marriage Survival Rates, By Religious Affiliation, Iowa, 1953–1959. [Adapted from Lee G. Burchinal and Loren E. Chancellor, "Survival Rates Among Religiously Homogamous and Interreligious Marriages," *Agricultural and Home Economics Experiment Station Bulletin 512* (December, 1962), p. 758.]

[10]Landis, op. cit., p. 403.

149

difference is 25 per cent. Despite the possibility of discussing these data either as survival or divorce rates, it is possible to reach a conclusion, namely, that the probability that either interfaith or intrafaith marriages will survive is better than that they will end in divorce, but the chances that interfaith marriages will survive are less. Stated negatively, it is not that interfaith marriages have a poor chance to survive, but their chances are poorer than those of intrafaith marriages.

The fact of the higher dissolution rates of interfaith marriages does not, in itself, establish causality. It has been contended that those who would contract an interfaith marriage are likely to be high marriage risks regardless of whether they contract an interfaith or an intrafaith marriage. Some supporting evidence has been offered by Heiss, who found the intermarried couples were somewhat more likely to have nonreligious parents, to have greater conflict with their parents, and to come from less integrated families.[11] Apparently most Jewish participants in interfaith marriages are from liberal and reformed rather than orthodox groups. Slotkin found many of them to be emancipated, rebellious, marginal, and adventurous types.[12] There is, however, considerable contrary evidence. It will be recalled that, in one survey, as much as 70 per cent of the youth sampled said that they would be willing to marry outside their faith. Such a large proportion of a population cannot be atypical. In addition, studies of religious problems in intermarriage reveal many sources of conflict and tension not present in intrafaith unions.[13] The sociological bases of these problems will be explored.

RELIGIOUS DEFINITION OF FAMILY ROLES A religious ideology goes far beyond defining the relations of man to deity; specifically it defines man's relationships to man. Nowhere is this definition of roles more pervasive and prescriptive than in the institution of the family. The Catholic Church is quite explicit in naming the father as head of the family and the principal source of power and authority. It is equally explicit in relegating the wife to a set of tasks within the household. It further specifies the roles of both husband and wife by forbidding birth control devices. It proscribes divorce. It prescribes obedience as the proper posture of the child. In the past it has controlled the food to be eaten on certain days. It has prescribed 10 per cent of the family income as the appropriate contribution of the family to the Church. It has partially financed a system of parochial schools and colleges for the

---

[11]Jerold S. Heiss, "Premarital Characteristics of the Religiously Intermarried in an Urban Area," *American Sociological Review,* **25** (Feb. 1960), pp. 47–55.

[12]J. S. Slotkin, "Jewish-Gentile Intermarriage in Chicago," *American Sociological Review,* **7** (Feb. 1942), pp. 34–39.

[13]Gordon, op. cit., Chapters 4 and 11.

150

purpose of indoctrinating its children. Parents are expected to send their children to these schools if possible.

Although the roles of Protestant husband and wife are not spelled out quite as specifically as are those of Catholic spouses, there are some definite expectations and these differ at each point from those of the Catholic Church. Protestantism stresses the responsibility of each individual and tends to be equalitarian in the husband-wife and more permissive in the parent-child relationships. Nowhere is the husband singled out as the head and authority in the household. Obedience is not in the vocabulary of the Protestant woman. Use of contraceptive devices and divorce are left to the preferences and consciences of the spouses. Although Protestant churches favor tithing, it is to their own congregation, not to a central organization as in the Catholic Church. Likewise they have no objection to the establishment of parochial schools but have no interest in supporting Catholic parochial schools.

For parents, one of the most crucial roles deals with the socialization of children, including religious training. Parents can be one or the other faith, agnostics, or atheists, but they can hardly ignore religion entirely. If each parent is active in his own church, the child cannot identify religiously with both. Current research suggests that the mother is the more influential, whatever her faith. One study reports on the religious training of the children as follows:[14]

1. Mother took full responsibility, 36 per cent.
2. Parents permitted children to choose, 27 per cent.
3. Responsibility equally divided between parents, 20 per cent.
4. Children alternated between churches, 7 per cent.
5. Father took all responsibility, 4 per cent.
6. Some children attended one church, the others the other, 3 per cent.

This suggests that the faith of the mother, rather than the antenuptial contract, is more influential in determining in which church the child shall be socialized. Scattered research indicates that somewhere between 40[15] and 50[16] per cent of children of Catholic-Protestant unions are reared as Protestants. Another study concludes that as many as 60 per cent of the children of interfaith marriages are active in no church.[17]

[14]Judson T. Landis, and Mary G. Landis, *Building a Successful Marriage*, 4th ed., (Englewood Cliffs, N.J.: Prentice-Hall, Inc., 1963), p. 202. Research quoted was conducted by Alfred Prince.

[15]Thomas, op. cit., p. 164.

[16]Judson T. Landis, "Religiousness, Family Relationships, and Family Values in Protestant, Catholic and Jewish Families," *Marriage and Family Living*, **22** (Nov. 1960), p. 344.

[17]Carle C. Zimmerman and Lucius Cervantes, *Successful American Families* (New York: Pageant Press, 1960).

151

These data warrant one conclusion and show another to be unwarranted. The first is that the ante-nuptial agreement is ineffective, because it appears that probably about as many children are reared Protestants as Catholics. Therefore, the antenuptial agreement is violated as frequently as it is honored. Its chief function would seem to be to provide a source of tension between the spouses, their kin, and the faiths involved. The conclusion that must await more systematic research is how effective religious socialization is in interfaith marriages. One study showed 5 per cent identifying with no faith, another that 60 per cent were unaffiliated or inactive members. We do not know which, if either, of these figures is correct.

Gordon found competition between spouses for the identification of their children even where one spouse had never been active in his faith.[18] Such inactive members apparently feel an identification with their faith as a social entity. A Jew still feels he is a Jew even if he never worships; the same is true of Protestants and Catholics. Parents want their children to be *identified* with the same groups that they themselves are. Because there have been strong rivalries and not infrequently conflicts between the major faiths, this desire for identification is frequently buttressed by some feelings of antagonism toward the other religious groups.

PRESSURE AND SANCTIONS AGAINST INTERMARRIAGE Intermarriage violates no legal statute, yet encounters strong resistance and results in the loss of social relationships. Even in the period preceding more serious commitments, interfaith dating provokes comment. As couples seriously consider marriage, they encounter stronger objections from friends, family, and church. Couples attracted to each other frequently devalue the seriousness of role conflict by asserting that religion is a personal matter and that each can believe what he wishes. It is interesting that this would probably be true if religion involved only a person's relationship to the deity, but as we have observed, it deals in a quite comprehensive manner with man's relationship to man and even more especially with man's relationship to woman. Two *contrasting* sets of definitions of man's relations to woman spell role conflict. Furthermore, the major faiths have created large social institutions to serve religious needs and to socialize the young. These are committed to oppose any social relationship, such as intermarriage, that threatens the effective exercise of that faith.

Even those who are relatively uninitiated in the understanding of family functioning are aware of role conflicts of some seriousness in interfaith marriage and therefore exercise some restraining influence on any friends who contemplate intermarriage. Family members have a

[18]Gordon, op. cit., Chapter 11.

larger stake in a possible interfaith marriage; first, because of greater concern for the well-being of a child or sibling, but also because of an anticipated continued interaction with the family member and his spouse over the years. The continued interaction between parents and married children and between married siblings continues to be a major part of the social life of couples, even in a society as mobile and individualistic as America's (Chapt. 16). It is even more crucial in nonindustrial societies. The lack of acceptance of the married child's spouse or continued or serious friction between parents and the child's spouse reduce visiting and mutual help between the generations or between the married siblings.

The identification and interaction with grandchildren may be affected even more. For the grandparents to whom religion is important, the socialization of the grandchildren may prevent relationships from ever developing. There is neither the same amount of opportunity nor the societal prescription to associate with grandchildren that there is to interact with one's own children. How crucial grandparent-grandchild relationships may be is not known. However, sociologists have viewed the isolation of the individual and the nuclear family with some concern, feeling that they provide too little security, both affectional and economic.[19] The alienation of grandparents from grandchildren because of religious differences might be of more than incidental significance. Whether or not such alienation has consequences for personality functioning, it is a source of concern and a basis for opposition of parents to the intermarriage of their children. The opposition of siblings and other kin have similar bases in concern for the extra sources of frustration and conflict that they anticipate and the probability of lessened interaction with the married sibling afterwards.

The opposition of the various faiths to interfaith marriage takes several forms. First, the possibility always exists that one spouse will change his faith to that of the other and that one faith will lose an adult member and the possibility of additional members from the children of the marriage. This is not a random matter in which losses and gains cancel out. Some faiths systematically gain or lose by interfaith marriage.[20]

Although some faiths consistently gain membership from interfaith marriage, all oppose it. Two reasons for this appear to be dominant. It is believed that religious conflict in the family is likely to result in less participation in religious worship and activities by the couple and less or no religious identification for their children. That both happen is a

[19]David Riesman, Nathan Thayer, and Reuel Denney, *The Lonely Crowd* (Garden City, N.Y.: Doubleday & Co., 1953).
[20]Donald H. Bouma, "Religiously Mixed Marriage: Denominational Consequences in the Christian Reformed Church," *Marriage and Family Living,* **25** (Nov. 1963), p. 431.

153

matter of record, but how frequently these results occur is not known. If the alienation and/or inactivity of children of interfaith marriages is as high as 60 per cent, as Zimmerman and Cervantes think, this result will be of increasing concern to those entrusted with the religious socialization of the young.

The various faiths are also concerned with the effective functioning and stability of the family and they view interfaith marriages as a source of conflict and instability. Finally, the faiths could be concerned with interfaith marriages as a source of friction or a barrier to social intercourse among families within the congregation.

Although all faiths oppose interfaith marriage, they vary considerably in the sanctions they impose on those who consummate such marriages despite their opposition. Among Protestant churches and now in the Catholic Church there are no organizational punishments for the member, but he may feel the disapproval of the members and the clergy. Orthodox Jews forbid intermarriage unless the mate accepts the Jewish religion. Those who otherwise intermarry are liable to excommunication.[21] It probably is no accident that the sanctions are harshest in the faith that comprises the smallest proportion of the total population and the mildest in the majority faith.

SOME UNRESOLVED ISSUES Although the research literature on interfaith marriage is considerable and is continuing to accumulate, it is inadequate in some respects. Most of the samples are drawn from college students or their parents or other nonrandom samples. Such samples do not provide a reliable set of statistics with respect to the attitudes of youth toward intermarriage, the kinds of religious socialization that children of such marriages receive, or outcomes in terms of the religious activity of the parents or, eventually, of their children. This is not to devalue what has been done but to point to the need for national probability samples for data in which complete confidence can be lodged. Also, parallel studies of intrafaith and nonfaith families would be required to place interfaith marriage in perspective.

Interracial Marriage

Interracial marriage has been a matter of concern in most racially mixed societies. The concern of the race in the higher status and power positions has been to prevent interracial marriage. The concern of the race in the subordinate position has been ambivalent in these societies. On the one hand the concern is not to become involved in marriages in which the member from the subordinate race is likely to be rejected by

---

[21]Gordon, op. cit., p. 178.

the superordinate race; on the other, the subordinate race has objected to the prohibition of interracial marriage as one more evidence of racial discrimination.

The functions of the prohibition of interracial marriage have been stated succinctly by Merton:

Endogamy is a device which serves to maintain social prerogatives and immunities within a social group. It helps prevent the diffusion of power, authority and preferred status to persons who are not affiliated with a dominant group. It serves further to accentuate and symbolize the "reality" of the group by setting it off against other discernible social units. Endogamy serves as an isolation and exclusion device, with the function of increasing group solidarity and supporting the social structure by helping to fix social distances which obtain between groups. All this is not to imply that endogamy was deliberately instituted for these purposes; this is a description in functional, not necessarily purposive terms.[22]

Although the prevention of interracial marriage may not be purposive with respect to all the above, recent racial relations in the United States and South Africa suggest that the objectives of reserving power and privileges to the white race are reasons that are well understood by the white caste. Merton's argument might be elaborated slightly to add that such segregation makes it unnecessary for the upper caste to identify itself with the high levels of poverty, disease, and ignorance that mark racial groups that have been forced to occupy the lowest level in a caste pyramid. Notably absent from Merton's and other sociological analyses are the reasons that intermarriage must be prevented to protect the "purity of the race" or to prevent the "mongrelization of the races."

There has been no evidence whatever that mixing skin color or hair type in marriage has any more harmful biological effects than the intermarriage of tall and short or green-eyed and gray-eyed people. A few earlier social scientists and others have even talked of the "hybrid vigor" of the children of interracial marriages. However, there seems no more evidence or compelling logic for this notion than for the one that states that mixing the hues of skin color is in some way detrimental. A further reason for suspecting the motives as well as the accuracy of those who oppose intermarriage on biological grounds is the willingness of the superordinate caste to mix the races through sexual intercourse between the males of the higher and the females of the lower caste. American scholars agree that a large majority of American Negroes have some white ancestors. That this is simply another

[22]Robert K. Merton, "Intermarriage and the Social Structure: Fact and Theory," *Psychiatry,* **4** (Aug. 1941), p. 368.

prerogative of the higher caste is shown by the vigilance that whites have shown in preventing intercourse between Negro men and white women. This does not contaminate the blood any more than intercourse between white males and Negro females.

Although there is no biological reason to oppose interracial marriage, once a caste system has been in effect more than a generation, the differential socialization of the young and the occupational and other differentiations in adult life produce social and psychological differences in the races that are significant social facts. Such differences, plus the fact that race is an obvious and unconcealable difference and one that cannot be changed, lead to the identification of interracial marriage as one of the most significant types of intermarriage.

FREQUENCY OF INTERRACIAL MARRIAGE Compared to interfaith marriage, interracial marriage in American society has been rare. Although the former has been reported at 6.4 per cent of all marriages and many sociologists believe it may be double that, it has been estimated that the latter involves probably no more than one half of 1 per cent.[23] This very low rate has been due in small part to segregation of the races, so that propinquity increases the odds one will marry within his own race. However, the reasons are primarily social pressure and legal obstacles to intermarriage. As late as 1966, nineteen states prohibited interracial marriage. Earlier the figure had been much higher. In 1967 the Supreme Court decreed such laws unconstitutional, but prior to that date such laws, concentrated largely in the South, played a part in minimizing the number of interracial marriages that were consummated.

Such laws, however, cannot be credited with the major reasons for low intermarriage rates, because such marriages were legal in about three fifths of the states and no state except Hawaii has had a rate that approaches the average for interfaith marriage. The major reasons must be sought in intense social pressure against this type of intermarriage. This pressure will be discussed in a later section.

Statistical data on the incidence of interracial marriage are not plentiful; however, some data are available for five states and somewhat more adequate information for Los Angeles County, where race was recorded on marriage licenses from 1948 to 1959. All of these data support two generalizations: (1) interracial marriage is only a tiny fraction of what it would be if youth chose their spouses without regard to race, and (2) the rate of intermarriage is increasing.

As the largest population group, more whites are involved in interracial marriages than other races; however, proportionately they intermarry less (Table 6.1). Although 87 per cent of the male popula-

[23]John H. Burma, "Interethnic Marriages in Los Angeles, 1948–59," *Social Forces,* **42** (Dec. 1963), p. 156.

Table 6.1
Percentage of Males and Females of Selected Groups, Los Angeles County, 1960; Percentage of Males and Females Intermarrying, 1948–1959, and Index of Proportion of Each in the Population and Intermarriages

	Males		Females	
Group	Per Cent of Total Population	Per Cent of Total Population Intermarrying	Per Cent of Total Population	Per Cent of Total Population Intermarrying
White	87.51	35.98	90.61	63.98
Negro	7.33	27.60	7.73	10.12
Japanese	1.29	7.02	1.24	13.42
Chinese	.36	5.83	.27	4.94
Filipino	.31	23.95	.14	7.50

SOURCE: John H. Burma, "Interethnic Marriage in Los Angeles, 1948–1959," *Social Forces,* **42** (Dec. 1963), p. 159. Reprinted by permission.

tion of Los Angeles County was white, only 36 per cent of the intermarrying men were white, less than half what would have been expected if each group intermarried at an equal rate. Note that white women were much more likely to intermarry, providing almost two thirds of the interracial brides. Negro men intermarry at four times the expected rate but Negro women at only a little above their expected rate. Japanese intermarried at about six times the expected rate, Chinese at about fifteen times, and Filipinos at about seventy-five times their expected rate. The intermarriage rate is greater for Japanese women than for men but lower for Chinese and Filipino women than for men (Table 6.1). It should be noted that most of the Filipino intermarriages are not truly interracial, because two thirds of the men are estimated to have married Mexican women. Both Mexican and Filipino populations are mixtures of Caucasian and Mongolian racial stocks.

An interesting question is whether the minority racial groups are more likely, in proportion to population, to intermarry among themselves or with the white majority. Barnett analyzed California data to answer this question. He found that, proportionate to their numbers, Chinese and Japanese were about five times more likely to intermarry than to marry Caucasians. Of course, Chinese-Japanese is internationality rather than interracial marriage. He found Negro-Mongolian intermarriages rare, with only forty reported over a four-year period. He found that the proportional frequency of Caucasian-Mongolian intermarriage was about three times greater than for white-black intermarriage.[24]

[24]Larry D. Barnett, "Interracial Marriage in California," *Marriage and Family Living,* **25** (Nov. 1963), pp. 424–427.

The principle already observed in interfaith marriage—that the smaller the proportion a minority group is of a population, the greater is the intermarriage rate—holds for interracial marriages. Stated another way, the greater the proportion of youth of marrying age who are members of the out-group, the higher the intermarriage rate. Whites intermarry the least frequently, then Negroes, with Japanese, Chinese, and Filipinos showing higher rates. The correlation is not, however, perfect. It was noted that Jews have a lower intermarriage rate than Catholics and Japanese higher than Chinese for the whole state of California; however, if one looks at the Los Angeles data, where Chinese are a much smaller minority, the rule holds, because they have a much higher intermarriage rate proportionately there than do the Japanense.

The smallest racial category listed in the California analysis was the American Indian. Almost half of Indian marriages were interracial, most of them with Caucasians. This is the highest interracial marriage rate reported.[25] The Indian data support the generalization that the smaller the minority group, the greater the likelihood it will have a high rate of intermarriage. Male and female American Indians were about equally likely to be involved in interracial marriages. Only one marriage was recorded between one of them and an Oriental Mongolian.

TRENDS IN INTERRACIAL MARRIAGE In 1949 in Los Angeles County there were only 187 interracial marriages, which was 5.8 per 1,000 or about one half of 1 per cent. The rate increased steadily over the following ten years to 631 in 1959 or 1.6 per cent of the total marriages that year. This is clearly a gain, and that interracial marriages are on the increase is supported by data from Hawaii, Michigan, and Nebraska. As in the case of the divorce rate, there are two ways to view this increase. The rate of intermarriage increased 300 per cent in ten years. However, *intra*marriage declined only from 99.5 per cent of all marriages to 98.4, a decrease of about 1 per cent. Although recent statistics point to increases in intermarriage, early studies found a decline in Negro-white intermarriage.[26]

Current students of interracial marriage are cautious in projecting into the future the rapid increases of the recent past, partly because previous decades have sometimes shown *decreases,* partly because the intermarried are such a tiny fraction of all marriages. Trends that still involve less than 2 per cent of a population may involve people with attitudes and values somewhat atypical of the society as a whole. However, there are some reasons for anticipating a continued increase,

[25]Ibid., p. 426.
[26]Louis Wirth and Herbert Goldhamer, "The Hybrid and the Problem of Miscegenation," in *Characteristics of the American Negro,* ed. by Otto Klineberg (New York: Harper & Row, 1944), pp. 276–301.

although probably at a slower rate. Heer found that intermarriage within California was positively associated with relative lack of residential segregation, a higher proportion of Negroes in white-collar occupations, and a lower proportion of Negroes in a population. He presents evidence that residential segregation has been declining and that the proportion of Negroes employed in white-collar occupations has been increasing. Also, the Negro population is dispersing from its original primary concentration in the South into the northeast, north-central, and western regions. Continued dispersion presents the Negro of marrying age with an increasing proportion of single youth who are non-Negro. With the acculturation of the Chinese and the Japanese, less segregation and greater geographic dispersion appears inevitable for them, also. Heer also cites evidence that supports a belief that a more permissive attitude is developing toward Negro-white intermarriage.[27]

One additional variable that would be predictive of increased Negro-white intermarriage would be a decrease in the differences in income for Negroes and whites. Median incomes have been about one half as high for Negroes as for whites. To date, this gap has shown only a slight trend toward closing. This appears to be potentially the most significant variable. The attainment of equal income would be accompanied by better education, better health, better housing, broader opportunities for travel, and eventually equal prestige with the other races.

HYPOGAMY IN NEGRO-WHITE INTERMARRIAGE It has been noted that white females are much more likely to marry Negro men than white males to marry Negro women. This came as something of a surprise to early researchers. White men have had more opportunity for contacts with Negro women and the notion has had a degree of acceptance that men want to marry women they can dominate. It was also believed that white women would not want to marry Negro men because of generally lower incomes and lower status of Negroes. This marriage by women into a lower caste instead of a higher one has been termed *hypogamy.* The companion term, *hypergamy,* the marriage of women into a higher caste, is not involved here, because the preponderance of Negro-white intermarriage follows the hypogamy pattern.

When it became clear that Negro-white intermarriage was predominantly hypogamy, Merton hypothesized that such marriages were likely to involve upper- and middle-class Negroes with white women from lower-class levels. Thus, there would be a "barter" of high caste position of the woman for high social-class position of the Negro. The woman is compensated for loss in the caste relationship by higher

[27]David M. Heer, "Negro-White Marriages in the U.S.," *Journal of Marriage and the Family,* **28** (Aug. 1966), pp. 262–274.

income and status by social class.[28] Later research, however, has not substantiated the belief that the social-class position of intermarrying Negro men is higher than that of the white women they marry. They are likely to be at the same social-class level.

We think that Merton's idea of barter is correct, but that he hypothesized the wrong social characteristics. The woman obviously loses something by marrying into a lower social caste. Also, if she is perceptive, she knows she loses something by intermarriage itself. What she gains, we suggest, is marriage itself. Although there is no clear status differential between single and married men in American society, one does exist for women. The Negro man gains status by acquiring a white wife, the white woman by gaining married status. It is true that almost any young or middle-aged white woman can find a white husband, if she is nonselective, but most of the pool of unmarried white men are among the uneducated, the unemployed, the criminal, and the mentally inadequate. By being willing to marry into a lower caste, she may obtain a husband who is her educational and intellectual equal and who is able to perform the roles of a husband adequately. It might be added that it has been difficult for intimate relationships to exist between white women and Negro men outside of marriage. Social pressure has been strongly against it in the white community. For the white woman, sexual relationships outside of marriage are doubly hazardous, because if she should bear an illegitimate child, the racial characteristics would be apt to identify the father as a Negro.

White men who marry Negro women also give up something by marrying into a lower caste. What can Negro women provide in return that could not be obtained from white women? A man does not gain prestige simply from being married. White men have often been able to establish emotional and sexual relationships with Negro women outside of marriage, so that marriage is not a requisite of such relationships as it has been for the white woman attracted to a Negro man. Negro women have, in the past, gained status by having a white man obviously attracted to them. They have been able to engage in sexual relationships without marriage because illegitimacy has been an accepted part of Negro life, except in the higher social classes. A child with a white father would have some advantages in that a light skin has been a mark of high status.

In a marriage of a white man to a Negro woman, the man has been in a position to confer two structural gifts, married status and a higher-caste husband. She has had none to offer in return. Her "barter" item has been to engage in sexual intercourse without demanding marriage, and this has been the more frequent pattern. Because some of this type of

---

[28]Merton, op. cit., p. 372.

160

intermarriage occurs, there must, of course, be reasons. Regardless of race, some individuals are attracted to others. Such attraction in some cases is strong enough to overcome the difficulties of interracial marriage.

CAUCASIAN AND MONGOLIAN INTERMARRIAGE Intermarriage of Caucasians with Chinese- and Japanese-Americans involves two races of approximately the same status level. Of the two nationalities, the Japanese have perhaps enjoyed a little higher status as representatives of a modern and efficient society. Too, the Japanese have been ready to accept American customs and have found materialistic American values compatible. There are no "Japantowns" in the major cities. The Chinese have settled in segregated areas of the larger cities and waged long battles to maintain Chinese customs, food, languages, and religion. These differences may explain the lower rate of intermarriage of the Chinese than Japanese with Caucasians. In California, the Caucasian spouse was more likely to be the husband. This is especially true for the Japanese: the rate for Caucasian husbands and Japanese wives is almost twice the opposite.

Differences of this size merit speculation and, hopefully, research. If the role differences are examined, it is found that the Japanese woman centers her life about her husband and renders many personal services to him that are contrary to role definitions of white American women. Men cannot fail to be somewhat flattered and pleased to be so important to their wives. Insofar as husbands are concerned, American men are socialized to equalitarian family patterns, to be aware of their wives' needs, to make relatively fewer demands upon them, and to expect them to exercise more freedom of movement and activities. In contrast, the Japanese male expecting the wife to center her life about his and the American woman expecting an equalitarian and autonomous status would be likely to find these role definitions frequently in conflict.

STATUS DIFFERENCE IN INTERRACIAL MARRIAGE History is filled with the conquest of part of one race by another. Following such contests the successful race establishes a pattern of authority over the other, accompanied by the preemption of high levels of living and the more agreeable and prestigeful occupations. The lot of the conquered is poverty, ignorance, disease, and lives subservient to the dominant race. Rarely have two or more races lived in one nation in a relationship of equality. This is true, at least approximately, for the Japanese, Chinese, and Caucasian Americans, who came voluntarily, but not for American Indians and Negroes. Major status differences in intermarriage most frequently lead to the rejection by the superordinate race of the couple or at least the spouse from the lower status race. Although they are usually accepted by the lower status group, they may wish to identify with the higher, and they usually want their children reared as members of the higher status race, in which they are usually not accepted. This has been true of most Negro-white American marriages.

One result of the major socioeconomic differences between Negro and white races has been the segregation of Negroes in the slum areas of the large cities. Part of this segregation has been due to the need of Negroes for inexpensive housing, but even the Negroes with higher incomes, who could afford good housing in attractive housing developments, have been prevented from living there by restrictive covenants agreed on by those who develop the subdivisions and by the social pressure exerted by the white owners in the areas into which blacks would like to move. Therefore, even the area of the city in which one may live is involved in this type of interracial marriage.

The status difference is less of a problem in societies in which there has been a free intermarriage between races, such as Latin America and French Africa, because race is essentially a variable rather than divided into two separate categories. Although biologically race is a variable in the United States, there is a discrete separation; one is a black or he is not when it comes to identification and interaction with his own and other races. In intermarrying societies, a spouse may be evaluated to some degree on the color of her skin, but she is not accepted or rejected on that basis.

FAMILY ROLE DIFFERENCES BY RACE Because racial differences usually coincide with nationality and religious lines, races usually possess different cultures. Even when this is not true, as with the Negro in American society, the caste and class differences are so great that a substantial subculture is created. We shall illustrate these differences here without attempting to explore them exhaustively.

Although a great deal has been said about the crucial roles of the black mother, it is from those of the father that these differences originate. In the relegation of the Negro to an inferior position in American society, part of the heritage is unemployment. American society, except during major wars, has had a labor surplus. The black man with less education and training, largely excluded from skilled and white-collar occupations, has always had more than his share of unemployment and underemployment. A rough estimate is that unemployment is twice as high among black men and that those employed are paid half as much. Given this inadequate base for the male provider role, more and more of it had to be taken by the mother and frequently by government or other relief agencies. Although the husband was still expected to be a provider, for a large proportion of black men this was not possible. For others, their pay was so low and employment so irregular that welfare payments were a better source of support than a man's earnings. Given this situation over time, the socialization of the

162

black boy developed differently from that of the white boy. Whereas the white boy is taught that he has to work and be the principal support of a family, the black boy is faced with four major models: black men who support families, men who are partial providers along with their wives, families supported by welfare agencies, and families supported by the female members. Education and occupational training for boys have been less valued in the black community because of the obstacles that adult black men have for generations faced in the adult occupational world.

The provider role for black women has expanded to fill the vacuum in the provider role left by black men. For example, whereas about 51 per cent of white mothers with school-age children were in paid employment in 1971, 61 per cent of black mothers of children of that age were in the labor force.[29] This has led, also, to a degree of female domination of the family quite different from the white family. Blood and Wolfe found a considerably larger number of families in which the wife was dominant than in which the husband exercised more power.[30]

The partial loss of the provider role by the Negro male has led to a high degree of family instability, common-law marriage, and very temporary unions. For example, among Negro families with family incomes less than $3,000 only 24 per cent of children in 1969 were living with both original parents. However, the proportion rises to 91 per cent in Negro families with incomes over $10,000.[31] In instances in which males cannot consistently play the role of providers, women have less reason to insist on a legal and stable marriage as a prerequisite for sexual intercourse. The outcome of marriage may be to provide one more mouth to feed—a large male appetite. The presence of an unemployable male in the house may be a disturbing factor within the family and the neighborhood. As a consequence of the marginal position of the husband as a provider, divorce, desertion, and illegitimacy characterize the Negro family to a much greater degree than the white family.

The roles of children are influenced, also. Less emphasis is placed on achievement in school or on completion of a maximum number of years of training. Although there have been a few places in professions and business open to Negroes, these have been too insignificant to serve as goals for the mass of Negro children. The instrumental values placed

[29]F. Ivan Nye and Lois Wladis Hoffman, *The Employed Mother in America* (Chicago: Rand McNally & Co., 1963), p. 15.

[30]Robert O. Blood and Donald M. Wolfe, *Husbands and Wives, The Dynamics of Family Living* (Glencoe, Ill.: The Free Press, 1960).

[31]U.S. Bureau of the Census, *The Social and Economic Status of Negroes in the United States, 1970,* Current Population Reports, Series P-23, No. 38, (July 1971).

163

on education, cleanliness, punctuality, and responsibility in performing work tasks have been less, because the payoff for these virtues has been unpredictable. Frequently the Negro has found the fact of his race has barred his advancement regardless of his training or ability.

More role differences could be presented, but it suffices here to illustrate the major family role differences between blacks and whites. These differences frequently become the basis of role conflict as roles are enacted in black-white interracial marriages. It should be clear that the differences noted are in degree rather than in kind.

The differences in role definitions between Chinese or Japanese and white families are of a different origin. The husbands are the principal providers and marriages are even more stable than those of the white population. The differences are not so much in who performs key family roles or in the effectiveness with which they are performed but in *how* they are performed. The value placed on education, work training, cleanliness, and the like are similar, although probably greater in the Oriental groups. Still, the "how" provides some bases for role conflict, especially between white women and Oriental men. The latter are heads of the household in a way that Western men have rarely experienced. This subservient relationship of wives to their husbands seems to be quite acceptable to American men! Strauss found less than anticipated conflict in his study of Japanese war brides.[32] Because these women were reared in another culture and their kin were still in Japan, the potential for conflict would seem to be greater than for marriages in which both spouses were reared in the same society. The potential for conflict between Caucasian brides and Oriental grooms would seem to be much greater. The typical white female is not about to treat her husband as her lord and master.

SOCIAL PRESSURE AND SANCTIONS In societies in which races occupy caste positions or follow nationality and religious lines, the opposition to interracial marriage is immediate and intense. It has been suggested earlier that the intensity of opposition can be traced to the facts that racial intermarriages are obvious to all and that race is not a characteristic that can be changed by any kind of achievement on the part of either spouse. Social pressure from peer groups, kin, and the community is strong against marriage or its preliminary stages of dating and courtship. The strong opposition comes from members of the race in the higher caste or class position but is frequently felt from the subordinate race also. Frequently it is prohibited by law, as has been the case in many American states.

---

[32] Anselm L. Strauss, "Strain and Harmony in American-Japanese War-Bride Marriages," *Marriage and Family Living*, **16** (May 1954), pp. 99–106.

Unlike opposition to most other types of intermarriage, that involving race is unlikely to cease after marriage. Again this appears to be related to the obviousness and immutability of the racial differences. The spouses in an interreligious union can meet opposition by retreating from active participation in any church or by one spouse's changing his religion. In a mixed socioeconomic marriage, each spouse can learn behavior appropriate to the other class. Although behavioral differences may be learned, physical characteristics cannot be changed.

Where interracial marriage is legal, the principal sanction is the termination of social relationships. Frequently the couple will not be received by the parents of the race of higher prestige. Peer-group relations are likely also to suffer some restriction as some of the friends of the spouse of the superordinate race fail to establish a social relationship with the interracial couple. Although it would be an error to think of these terminations of relationships as purposeful punishment, they do deprive the couple of relationships with people that they otherwise would have. Couples partially compensate for these losses of relationships by finding couples who have no objection to interracial marriage.

STABILITY AND PERSONALITY FUNCTIONING This section is included primarily to draw attention to the subject as an area for research. Very little is known even concerning the characteristics of people who marry across religious lines. They are older on the average and they are more likely to have been married before, according to Burma.[33]

In one of the few attempts to deal with the divorce rate in interracial marriage, Monahan analyzed such marriages for the whole state of Iowa. His data showed the following divorce rates for inter- and intraracial marriages among blacks and whites:

White wives—black husbands	16.8
White wives—white husbands	19.4
Black wives—white husbands	35.1
Black wives—black husbands	39.1

These data suggest that the mixed marriages involving white wives and black husbands are comparatively stable, while those involving black wives and white husbands are comparatively unstable—more than twice as unstable as the opposite combination.[34]

These descriptive data are provocative but do not tell us why one type of interracial marriage between blacks and whites is relatively

[33]Burma, op. cit., pp. 164–165.
[34]Thomas Monahan, "Are Interracial Marriages Really Less Stable?", *Social Forces,* **49** (June 1970), pp. 461–73.

stable while the other is not, nor, of course, does it say anything about the level of satisfaction of either spouse in interracial marriages.

A rather different picture of the stability of interracial marriage is provided by data from Hawaii. There, most marriages involve Caucasians and Orientals. The socioeconomic level of the two races is approximately equal and intermarriage appears to be generally accepted, because in 1961–1963 the proportion of mixed marriages was reported to be 37.0 per cent of all marriages. Because so many large minorities are present and Caucasians constitute less than half of the population, the stereotyped relationship between dominant and subordinant races can hardly be said to exist. Under these unusual circumstances, the major problems believed present for mixed racial marriages do not appear to be present. The divorce rate for 1964–1966 is reported as almost identical for intra- and inter-racial marriages, 22.5 and 22.1 per cent, respectively.[35] Sociologists have consistently maintained that there is nothing in the color of the skin, the texture of the hair, or the shape of the eyes that could in itself affect personality or social relationships. It is the prestige, economic, and value configurations frequently associated with race that transform it into a social variable. These seem to be absent in Hawaii with the result that interracial marriages there appear no more hazardous than others.

The clinical literature is rich in recording behavioral and emotional malfunctioning in the children of interracial marriages. An especially frequent source of frustration is the desire of the child to identify with the race of higher prestige. In most instances, intimate and enduring relationships with it have not been possible.[36] It would be easy, however, to overevaluate the evidence of personality disorders attributed to parents from different races. All children have problems in relationships and in identity. It is easy to attribute these to an obvious fact such as that of interracial parentage. Even so, it appears that children of black-white marriages are subject to some deprivations in relationships, some role contradictions, and uncertainties in role definition that are attributable to interracial parentage; therefore, the incidence of personality malfunctioning might be expected to be higher among the children of such marriages. Such deprivations and contradictions would be expected to be less for Chinese- and Japanese-Caucasian families and perhaps nonexistent in Hawaii. "Did they live happily ever after?," as Burma puts it. Some did, undoubtedly, but much more systematic research must be conducted before answers can be presented in precise terms.

[35]Robert C. Schmitt, "Age and Race Differences in Hawaii," *Journal of Marriage and the Family,* **31** (Feb. 1969), p. 49.
[36]Gordon, op. cit., p. 333–334.

Other Intermarriage

AGE DIFFERENCES We have suggested that great age differences could constitute intermarriage in two ways: 1) if there had been sufficient cultural change between the time the two spouses were socialized so that they learned materially different definitions of the roles of husband, wife, and children; or 2) if large differences in age produced sufficient physical differences so that the ability to enact recreational, sexual, and occupational roles became materially different for the spouses. This matter has attracted little empirical research. Terman related marital happiness scores to differences in age of spouses with the rather interesting finding that wives had the highest happiness scores who were married to men four to ten years younger than themselves. The scores of these husbands, however, were about average. The husbands having the highest scores were those who had wives twelve or more years younger than themselves. The wives in this group had only average or a little below average scores. In marriages in which the husband was three to five years older than the wife, both had the same scores, slightly above average.[37] It appears from this research that both sexes are somewhat happier with spouses considerably younger than themselves. However, divorce rates appear to be lower for marriages that approximate the societal norms. Hawaiian data show divorce rates to be lowest for marriages in which the husband is one to four years older, next lowest if spouses are the same age or if the husband is five to nine years older. Rates are much higher if the husband is more than twenty years or the wife more than ten years older than the spouse.[38]

EDUCATION The question was raised earlier whether great differences in the education of spouses might constitute intermarriage because of their different perceptions of the world, the different levels of abstraction in their work, and the types of friends with whom they would like to interact. Data are not available to test these ideas adequately; however, Terman related differences in the education of spouses to marital happiness scores. He stated his findings as follows: "Husband with more education than their wives tended to fall in the dissatisfied group. When education was equal, husbands tended to fall in the satisfied group. Where the wife's education was greater than her husband's, the tendency was for the wife to be less satisfied than average, the husband better satisfied than average."[39]

MENTAL ABILITY Terman is again the principal source for differ-

---

[37]Lewis M. Terman, et al., *Psychological Factors in Marital Happiness* (New York: McGraw-Hill Book Company, 1938), pp. 183–185.

[38]Schmitt, op. cit., p. 49.

[39]Terman, op. cit., p. 191.

ences in mental ability of spouses. Wives with husbands with intelligence greater than their own tended to have high scores, those with inferior husbands low scores, those rated equal average scores. For husbands, those much superior to their wives had low happiness scores as did those markedly inferior to their wives. Those equal to their wives were most likely to have high scores.

These studies shed little light on the question of whether marked differences in age, education, or intelligence should be considered intermarriage. The data do suggest that all those are relevant to attitudes of spouses toward their marriage. The mechanism would appear to be effectiveness in role-playing. In general, wives do appear to react favorably to husbands who are superior in all these characteristics. Husbands seem to react best to equality but where there are differences, there is some evidence that husbands prefer wives superior rather than inferior to themselves.[40]

Although a good deal of information has been collected concerning intermarriage, especially interfaith marriage, it should be clear that only a good start has been made and that more remains to be done than can be reported to date.

Concluding Note

In this chapter, differences in role definition and values between ethnic groups, social classes, and other categories with distinctive subcultures have been explored as these relate to mate selection, interaction between spouses, and child-rearing. It should be recalled, however, that great differences also exist within these categories. In fact, such differences are greater than between categories. Role perceptions and value formation are the result of personal experience. However, the nature of that personal experience is affected to a degree by the ethnic or social-class part of the society in which one is socialized and interacts in adult life.

If spouses were randomly selected from differing ethnic and social-class categories, the likelihood of experiencing role and value conflicts would be appreciably greater than if randomly selected from within the same social category. Likewise reference group opposition to the marriage is predictably likely to be greater to socially heterogeneous than to socially homogeneous marriages.

It should be noted that the degree of relevant heterogeneity in some of the kinds of marriages discussed is changing. Recent actions of the Catholic Church recognizing the legitimacy of Protestant marriages and modifying the marriage contract, and the Ecumenical Movement, in general, which seeks cooperation among religious groups are likely to

---

[40]Ibid., p. 193.

reduce relevant religious differences. Even more significant are changes in the status of blacks, chicanos, and American Indians. These changes are resulting in higher incomes, a larger proportion of these groups in higher status occupations, and an improved status in American society in general. These changes, if they are carried to their logical conclusion of full equality in income, education, and occupational position, will probably result in the disappearance of most of the relevant social differences among the races within a society. However, the separatist position taken by some militant minority leaders may result in discouraging interracial marriage, at least for a time. The relative influence of these social changes in the immediate future cannot, at this time, be accurately assessed. However, we venture a prediction that the long-term results will be greater social homogamy in the society and a resulting increase in racial intermarriages.

7

Sexual Relationships Between the Unmarried

Few issues in American society continue to generate as much public and private interest—as well as concern—as the sexual attitudes and behavior of the unmarried. Once strongly tabooed as a topic for general discussion, the premarital-sex question or the so-called sexual revolution are now so widely written and talked about—in various forms of the mass media, in popular and scientific literature, and informally—as to have become almost commonplace. Illustrative as to how far American culture has moved in the direction of greater permissiveness in this area is the appearance in the sixties of several Broadway shows and movies in which the actors appear completely nude and enact various stages of lovemaking, including copulation. This led one national magazine to conclude that our society was being bombarded on an unprecedented scale with coital themes and that sex, through the media, was becoming a "spectator sport."[1]

The changing sex habits of the American people have apparently become a subject not only for mass consumption but a serious area for empirical investigations as well. In the sixties: "The public seemed finally to be accepting the legitimate nature of sexual research and although controversy over sex will likely never cease, the battle for open discussion has been largely, although not fully, won."[2] This new freedom regarding sex has evolved over several decades and, although far from complete, it has carried our society a long way from the highly restrictive norms of an earlier era.

One small but perhaps significant indication of this trend toward a more open examination of the sexual mores can be gleaned from

---

[1]"Sex as a Spectator Sport," *Time* (July 11, 1969), pp. 61–66.

[2]Ira L. Reiss, "Introduction," in Ira L. Reiss (Guest Editor) "The Sexual Renaissance in America," *Journal of Social Issues,* **22** (Apr. 1966), p. 2.

changes that have occurred in textbooks, such as this one, commonly utilized in courses on marriage and the family. Under the more restrictive social climate of the past, such books never or rarely contained an entire chapter on premarital sex.[3] Today, in contrast, if a text on marriage and the family was published without including such material, it would risk being severely criticized and would probably be rejected by most instructors as inadequate. (Indeed, it appears somewhat fashionable these days for textbook writers to include at least two chapters on the subject!)

Similarly, college and university students enrolled in courses about the family normally expect the professor to devote considerable attention to nonmarital sexual relationships. Again, should the teacher fail to meet this expectation, he would in all likelihood find the students both disappointed and critical of a course that avoided a subject of such obvious relevance to their lives. And with good reason. Contemporary youth find themselves living in a society undergoing a transitional period of morality with respect to sexual relationships. In seeking to identify and develop a personal code to guide their decisions in this area, they encounter a confusing variety of competing and conflicting value systems, ranging all the way from absolute proscription of all sexual activity outside of marriage to complete sexual freedom; ranging from what Rubin has termed *extreme asceticism* in the sexual realm to completely permissive sexual anarchy.[4]

In an earnest search for personal guidelines, young persons often look to teachers and "family experts" for objective evaluations of, as well as advice on, the major sex codes present in contemporary society. Not infrequently, however, teachers and others serve only to compound further the existing confusion by providing selective interpretations in line with their own particular biases. For example, one analysis of the treatment given premarital intercourse in textbooks on marriage and the family revealed that several authors had neglected or misinterpreted much of the available empirical evidence. Their comments reflected an implicit and erroneous assumption that "premarital intercourse is almost always a lustful, selfish, and promiscuous relation, barren of affection and tenderness."[5]

It has been observed that social and behavioral scientists often exhibit no greater degree of consensus on the issues involved in

[3]For an analysis of changes in emphasis that have occurred through time in family textbooks, see Reuben Hill, "The American Family of the Future," *Journal of Marriage and the Family,* **26** (Feb. 1964), pp. 20–28.

[4]Isadore Rubin, "Transitional Sexual Values—Implications for the Education of Adolescents," *Journal of Marriage and the Family,* **27** (May 1965), pp. 186–187.

[5]Ira L. Reiss, "The Treatment of Pre-Marital Coitus in 'Marriage and the Family' Textbooks," *Social Problems,* **4** (Apr. 1957), p. 334.

171

premarital sex than the general public. Even among the most competent professional scholars of the family, it is difficult to achieve unanimity on the pros and cons of nonmarital sex simply because they view the problem from divergent moral and ethical commitments.[6] Because of such differences it is not unusual for sociologists examining the same body of findings from research to come to disparate conclusions and recommendations.[7]

It should be stressed, therefore, that decisions concerning the propriety of a given sexual act or standard *cannot* and should not be made by sociologists or any other scientists. In the final analysis, the decision as to whether a particular form of sexual expression is right or wrong "must be based upon one's individual values. Whether one's values are the best is a question on which sociology may help but cannot resolve."[8] What the sociologist *can* do as a scientist is to provide objective analysis regarding the consequences of certain forms of sexual behavior, to explain the relationships between these and related forms of sexual expression, to examine the effects of relevant variables on sexual attitudes and activity, to supply information as to the trends in this area, and to make a competent assessment of the sociological significance and implications of these trends. Such are the major aims of this chapter.

The Control of Sex

Every society known to man makes some attempt to regulate the sexual behavior of its members, although the type of activity sanctioned as well as the degree of control exerted varies considerably both within and among societies. Moreover, among the majority of the world's societies,

the point of departure for the regulation of sex is not sexual intercourse *per se* but one or more other social phenomena with respect to which sex is important, notably marriage, kinship, social status, reproduction, and ceremonial. Instead of a generalized sex taboo, what the ethnographer and the

---

[6]For a good illustration of these divergent viewpoints, see Lester A. Kirkendall, "Sex Education of Adolescents: An Exchange," *Marriage and Family Living,* **22** (Nov. 1960), pp. 317–22, and in the same issue, Thomas Poffenberger, "Individual Choice in Adolescent Premarital Sex Behavior," pp. 324–330.

[7]Hyman Rodman, "The Textbook World of Family Sociology," *Social Problems,* **12** (Spring 1965), pp. 445–456. "There are many forks along the road of family sociology, and most of them are taken by different travellers, with varying goals, interests, and values. As a result, the student of family sociology must be on the alert" (p. 448).

[8]Ira L. Reiss, *Premarital Sexual Standards in America* (New York: The Free Press, 1960), pp. 85–86.

historian encounter is a series of sex restrictions, permissions, and obligations in relation to these other phenomena.[9]

Cross-cultural studies show that in the majority of societies around the globe, some type of nonmarital sexual relationship is permitted or tolerated. Apparently, the United States is among that small minority—about 5 per cent—of all known societies whose *formal* codes have traditionally prohibited *any* kind of sexual involvement outside of marriage. That large numbers of our population frequently violate the formal code has long been obvious,[10] and we shall examine the nature and extent of deviations from our sexual mores later in this chapter.

Compared to more complex societies, the more simple societies of the world generally exhibit a more tolerant attitude toward premarital unions. Murdock's analysis of the premarital controls among more than 150 such societies showed that premarital license prevailed in 70 per cent of the cases; among the remainder the taboo fell mainly on the females and appeared "to be largely a precaution against child-bearing out of wedlock rather than a moral requirement."[11] In a related study of 110 societies, Brown found that among the varieties of sexual activity that were considered deviant, premarital affairs and intercourse with a betrothed partner were least likely to be forbidden or punished (whereas incest, abduction, and rape were most often tabooed and brought on the severest punishment).[12] Moreover, her analysis led her to conclude, among other things, that: "Punishments tend to be more severe for those sexual deviations which involve greater numbers of individuals, transgress marital bonds, and contain elements of aggression, than for deviations which involve fewer individuals, concern single persons, and lack aggressive content."[13] This study also showed, as one might expect, that societies vary in their perception of the severity of a particular sex act. Incest and homosexuality, for example,

[9]George P. Murdock, *Social Structure* (New York: The Macmillan Company, 1949), p. 263.

[10]It is important, however, as Reiss reminds us "to keep in mind the difference between the code a society *formally* or *ideally* holds to and the *informal* or *operational* code which is much closer to actual behavior. A society may have a *formal* standard of abstinence for all and an *informal* standard of freedom for men." Reiss, *Premarital Sexual Standards in America,* op. cit., pp. 28–29.

[11]Murdock, op. cit., p. 265. Stephens, on the other hand, found that the most frequently mentioned reason for greater premarital sex restrictions on females was the premium placed on virgin brides, "which often seemed extraordinary and rather quaint in view of the sexual freedom in some of the societies concerned." William N. Stephens, *The Family in Cross-Cultural Perspective* (New York: Holt, Rinehart and Winston, 1963), p. 246.

[12]Julia S. Brown, "A Comparative Study of Deviations from Sexual Mores," *American Sociological Review,* **17** (Apr. 1952), pp. 135–146.

[13]Ibid., p. 146.

173

were interpreted by some societies as injurious to the entire community and therefore harsh penalities were imposed on those engaging in such behavior. In other societies, these identical acts were not viewed as disruptive to the whole community and consequently received less severe sanctions.

An adequate anthropological or sociological explanation for the apparent differential interpretations of identical sex acts is not readily available.[14] Obviously, there is the historical development peculiar to each society involved. Like other customs, the sex mores of a people emerge gradually from their particular experiences in social interaction.

Sumner has pointed out that the mores are mass phenomena which have evolved gradually. First, the individual reacts to a problem in a random fashion. As the individual hits on a bit of adjustive behavior, it is incorporated into a habit system. Other individuals may imitate his behavior, or may independently chance upon the same behavior, until gradually more and more individuals are responding consistently in a similar fashion. In this way, folkways are created. As they become settled and carry the conviction of rightness, they evolve into mores, which are eventually reinforced by [sanctions]. . . . However, when one observes cultural phenomena, it is almost impossible to indicate the precise points on the continuum of behavior at which random acts become habits, at which similar individual acts become collectively folkways, and at which the folkways are transformed into mores.[15]

Whatever their origin, the sex codes of a society provide definitions and guidelines for appropriate behavior and expectations. Where the sexual mores become fully crystallized, they tend to produce a high degree of consistency and predictability in heterosexual relationships, thereby contributing to the general stability of these societies.

PREMARITAL SEX CODES: THE WESTERN HERITAGE The sex mores that currently prevail in America are the result of a long and varied historical process and actually contain elements of sexual morality that can be traced to the Hebrew, Greek, and Roman heritage of Western civilization. The ancient Hebrews, for example, had a formal proscription of premarital and extramarital coitus, but informally practiced a double standard that placed greater restrictions on females. A similar code existed among the Greeks, who, although generally relegating

---

[14]Indeed, the related question of why the regulation of sex is relatively more strict among civilized than primitive communities is equally difficult to answer. Udry has argued that: "No one, as far as is known, has formulated any explanatory principle of the occurrence or non-occurrence of premarital restrictions in societies. From the present vantage point, it appears to be largely a matter of historical and cultural accident that a society is permissive or restrictive." J. Richard Udry, *The Social Context of Marriage* (Philadelphia: J. B. Lippincott Co., 1966), pp. 128–129.

[15]Brown, op. cit., p. 143.

174

women to an inferior position, nevertheless created and supported institutionalized forms of prostitution including the *hetaerae,* a class of supposedly sophisticated and, in some instances, highly influential courtesans.[16] Like the Hebrews, the Romans placed a high value on female virginity and at the same time exercised a double standard, and, like the Greeks, they patronized a prostitute class.

The Greco-Roman patterns of sexuality were eventually displaced by the ascetic morality of Christianity, which places a general taboo on all sexual activity except marital intercourse, which was grudgingly tolerated as a sort of evil necessity for reproduction. In their determination to overcome pagan eroticism and the wanton customs of marriage and divorce, as well as other aspects of what was then considered a decadent Roman morality, the early Christians eventually "developed a fanatical fixation about the glory of virginity, the evilness of woman, the foulness of sexual connection, and the spiritual merit of denying the flesh and repudiating love."[17] The end result was a widely accepted definition of sex, particularly premarital sex, as lustful and sinful. Within this framework the repression of one's sexual urges became the core value underlying an ethical way of life. These and other standards of ascetic Christian morality survived through the Middle Ages (during which the phenomena of romantic love emerged). They were clearly manifest in the prudery and extreme sexual taboos of the Victorian period of nineteenth-century Europe, which were eventually transplanted to the New World.

The early New England Puritans placed harsh restrictions on premarital relationships and a high value on premarital chastity. Punishments for sexual deviance were varied and severe, ranging from public branding and confessions to fines and imprisonment. But despite the strongly supported community norms that censured premarital sexual experiences, historical records indicate that considerable violation of the sex mores occurred. Indeed, Hunt's review of this period led him to conclude that fornication was "the most prevalent and most popular sin in New England."[18] In contrast to the single standard of abstinence inherent in the formal sex codes of Colonial New England, the southern colonies favored a double standard, at least among the wealthy class. Upper-class southern women were expected to maintain complete abstinence, whereas sexual promiscuity on the part of upper-class

[16]For a description of the *hetaerae,* see Morton M. Hunt, *The Natural History of Love* (New York: Alfred A. Knopf, 1959), especially "The Noble Companion," pp. 33–42.

[17]Ibid., p. 104.

[18]Ibid., p. 235. Actually, the early Puritans had a rather favorable concept of *marital* sex, which in many ways was similar to our own. The reference to strict "puritanical" sexual attitudes that Americans frequently make comes from later Puritanism, which was strongly influenced by the nineteenth-century Victorian emphasis on respectability and gentility. See Hunt, pp. 234 and 252.

175

males was generally condoned.[19] The sexual exploitation of white and Negro lower-class women by white aristocrat males was another aspect of this double standard; such liaisons apparently received tacit approval from both the legal and the religious institutions. In general, the penalities imposed on southern colonists for premarital incontinence were less severe than those exacted in New England: "no death sentences, no scarlet letter, and no pillory."[20] Although the influence of the southern colonies on modern sex ethics has not been as pervasive as the Puritan heritage, nevertheless they contributed those special sexual and family values that still partially characterize the contemporary South.

Many of the restrictive Puritan concepts of sexuality have survived to the present day. The premarital chastity norms in the New England colonies derived from a theological base and gained their strength and support from religious values. "The archetypical Puritan colonist was completely dedicated to his religion and felt an intense zeal to reform and to order everything in light of God's demand upon him. The Puritan values prevailed for almost three-quarters of a century in New England and during that period were, in effect, the laws of the land."[21] Indeed, many of our laws pertaining to sexual behavior reflect traditional religious moral beliefs. For example, our religious and political institutions still adhere to the ideal of premarital chastity.

That the prevailing attitudes of the American public toward sexual expression in general and toward premarital sexual involvement in particular have been primarily negative hardly needs documentation. But for some time now there have been strong social pressures at work to produce changes in our traditional sexual standards. The extent to which these values have been altered is the subject to which we will now turn.

PREMARITAL SEX STANDARDS IN CONTEMPORARY AMERICA Perhaps the most comprehensive sociological analysis of premarital norms in the United States has been provided by Reiss. He suggests that sexual behavior is of two basic types that blend into one another along a continuum: (1) body-centered, emphasizing primarily the physical aspects of sex, and (2) person-centered, stressing the relationship to the

---

[19]Stuart A. Queen and Robert W. Habenstein, *The Family in Various Cultures,* 3rd ed. (Philadelphia: J. B. Lippincott Co., 1967), pp. 290–293.

[20]Ibid., p. 292.

[21]Robert R. Bell, *Premarital Sex in a Changing Society* (Englewood Cliffs, N.J.: Prentice-Hall, 1966), p. 18. As Bell points out:

For the most part the religious taboos against sex continue to be very strong in the American society. The more general values of religion are important to an understanding of the more specific religious views about premarital sex. Religious values about premarital sex are part of the broader values that see lawful monogamous marriage as the only acceptable means for sexual pleasure and procreation. Therefore, all other forms of sexual behavior are defined as wrong (p. 44).

176

person with whom the sex act is performed.[22] Reiss observes that certain of our sexual standards lead to body-centered intercourse, which is essentially unaffectionate, whereas other standards lead to person-centered and affectionate intercourse. He further suggests that the sexual attitudes of most contemporary Americans can be placed in one of four principle categories:

1. *Abstinence*—premarital intercourse is wrong for both men and women, regardless of circumstances.
2. *Permissiveness with affection*—premarital intercourse is right for both men and women under certain conditions when a stable relationship with engagement, love, or strong affection is present.
3. *Permissiveness without affection*—premarital intercourse is right for both men and women regardless of the amount of affection or stability present, providing there is physical attraction.
4. *Double standard*—premarital intercourse is acceptable for men, but it is wrong and unacceptable for women.[23]

The double standard is still recognizable as the predominant informal sexual standard in the United States, indeed, in the Western world. It reflects the ancient tradition of male dominance and associated concepts about the inferiority of women. It encourages a pleasure-seeking and body-centered type of sexual behavior for males and chastity for females. Obviously, such a standard is self-contradictory—if all women are forbidden from engaging in premarital intercourse, this by definition precludes similar behavior on the part of men! Historically, this ancient dilemma was partially resolved—as we noted earlier in this chapter—by the creation of a prostitute class, which, while providing a sexual outlet for men, would still allow the majority of women to remain virginal. With the passage of time, definitions of the kinds of women with whom it was permissible to have premarital coitus were expanded to include girls from lower-income classes and from different racial, ethnic, and religious groups. One strategy developed to justify male promiscuity was to define certain types of women as "bad" and thereby make them legitimate objects of sexual exploitation.[24] The presence of these rationalizations among white, lower-class males was vividly demonstrated a quarter of a century ago by Whyte's analysis of the social and sex life of the Italian

[22]Reiss, *Premarital Sexual Standards in America*, op. cit., pp. 79–80.
[23]Ibid., pp. 83–84. Reiss makes a further distinction between what he terms the *orthodox* and the *traditional* double standard. The former dictates complete adherence to the double standard; the latter makes exceptions for certain women who engage in premarital intercourse if they are in love or engaged (p. 97).
[24]Ibid., pp. 98–100.

"corner" boys of a Boston slum district. These slum youths either implicitly or explicitly classified women according to various categories of sex experience (good girls, lays, one-man girls, promiscuous, prostitutes), their physical attractiveness (beautiful or ugly), and their social and ethnic group position (superior, Italian nonslum, Italian slum). As Whyte observed, the

corner boys are continually talking over the girls that they know and others that they have observed in terms of these categories. Consequently, a high degree of consensus tends to arise in placing the individual girl in her position in each category. The men then know how they are supposed to act in each case; and the observer, equipped with this conceptual scheme, is able to predict how, as a general rule, the men will attempt to act.[25]

The Pecksniffian character engendered by the double standard is perhaps especially evident among those groups of males in our society who view nearly all members of the opposite sex as "fair game" while simultaneously showing contempt and disgust toward nonvirginal women. "The contradiction here is derived from the fact that double-standard men believe non-virginal women to be 'bad' and therefore desire to marry virgins. At the same time, however, their sexual standards make them constantly strive to render as many women non-virginal as possible."[26] This so-called virginity paradox emerges from any number of studies of premarital sexual relationships. Ehrmann, for example, found that 53 per cent of the males in his southern university sample wanted to marry a virgin, yet 65 per cent of them had engaged in premarital coitus.[27]

Under the impact of a variety of social forces, such as the feminist movement, the development of effective contraceptives, and so on, the double standard has greatly weakened in recent years. There is a spreading belief that this standard is contrary to many of our equalitarian ideas of justice and fair play, and that it conflicts with our beliefs about the worthwhileness of all individuals. Nevertheless, the double standard is still very much a part of American culture, because it supports traditional notions of male dominance not only in the sexual sphere but in many other areas of heterosexual relations.[28]

[25]William F. Whyte, "A Slum Sex-Code," *American Journal of Sociology,* **49** (July 1943), p. 29. Among these slum males, the most desirable woman for premarital coitus was a girl of old American-stock background and blonde, thus showing a preference for girls from a higher social and ethnic category.

[26]Reiss, *Premarital Sexual Standards in America,* op. cit., pp. 104–105.

[27]Winston Ehrmann, *Premarital Dating Behavior* (New York: Holt, Rinehart and Winston, 1959, Bantam Edition, 1960), pp. 31, 237. The latter page shows how these figures have varied from study to study and from one time period to another.

[28]Reiss, op. cit., pp. 114–116.

Permissiveness without affection, it will be recalled, involves body-centered coitus with an emphasis on the physical and pleasurable aspects of the sex act. Although the growth of this ultraliberal position may have been given some impetus by the rational and equalitarian trends in the United States, it has the smallest number of ostensible supporters of any of the major standards mentioned earlier. Scattered and inferential evidence suggests that this standard receives greater acceptance among certain lower-class groups characterized by chronic unemployment, marital instability, and fewer restrictions on non-marital intercourse. It also derives some support from a minority of more sophisticated persons who argue that coitus is as natural and necessary as eating and breathing and that the physical pleasure obtained from the sex act gives it sufficient justification. Obviously, love is not a prerequisite here and persons adhering to this code require no interpersonal commitments as to future obligations from the partner involved. Because of its body-centered orientation and its lack of stress on affection, it is unlikely that liaisons based on this standard will ultimately lead to marriage.[29]

The permissiveness-with-affection standard is thought to be more popular than permissiveness without affection, but less so than the double standard. Here premarital coitus is approved for both sexes provided a stable and affectionate relationship exists. In addition to the affective requirement, however, this code also requires that the participants maintain a mutual concern for each others reputations and emotional well-being. Research has documented the existence of adherents to this standard among college students and it may have wider acceptance among educated middle-class groups than among other segments of our society. Because of its equalitarian stance, the permissiveness-with-affection standard is essentially consistent with our cultural values of justice and individual respect. It incorporates our notions of love and monogamy and basically disapproves of promiscuous sexual behavior. For these reasons it is perhaps less likely to invite public or social condemnation than, for example, the permissiveness-without-affection standard. Like the latter, however, it conflicts with other cultural notions concerning female subordination, the value of virginity, and traditional religious precepts that support a

[29]Ibid., pp. 117–125. Reiss suggests that the permissiveness-without-affection standard has never gained widespread acceptance in the United States because it runs counter to many of our traditional values, including female subordination, and the value placed on virginity and sexual intercourse. Moreover, it is antithetical to many of the precepts of our major religious traditions. He does note, however, that other aspects of this standard are logically integrated with American culture: it provides sexual equality, avoids the "virginity paradox," and unlike the double standard it is not as apt to produce guilt feelings.

179

formal code of abstinence and prohibit premarital copulation. As the strength of such values has declined over the years, permissiveness with affection has been able to gain more widespread acceptance as a premarital standard, especially among the younger middle and upper classes.[30]

The formal single standard of abstinence, which rejects premarital intercourse for either sex, was superimposed on a predominantly double-standard Western world by Christianity. It eventually emerged as a cultural ideal in America and has long been supported and reinforced by our formal sex mores. This standard views coitus as too important to be allowed outside of the marital relationship. The extent to which earlier generations *actually* adhered to this code is unknown, but research on the premarital behavior of persons born in the twentieth century indicates that a considerable proportion of the population deviates from the abstinence standard.[31] The well-known studies by Terman, Kinsey, Burgess and Wallin, and others suggest that nearly half of the white female population in the United States have experienced coitus prior to marriage. Even larger proportions of the white males are apparently nonvirginal at the time of marriage, although the figures vary by social class.[32]

Moreover, many males and females who in principle accept the abstinence standard still engage in a wide range of sexual intimacies just short of actual intercourse. Such people often believe that as long as they refrain from "going all the way" they will enter marriage morally pure. They are "technical" or, to use Reiss's term, "promiscuous" virgins. Nevertheless, adherence to the abstinence standard—even if at times only technically—provides a feeling of comfort, security, and respect for many persons because it affords a sense of abiding by the approved formal standard in the United States, and they avoid the possibility of pregnancy.

Reiss contends that both abstinence and the orthodox double standard have gradually but noticeably weakened under the impact of major social trends, especially the influences of expanding equalitarianism and the widespread dissemination of contraceptive knowledge, both of which have encouraged the growth of more permissive standards. With the growing entrenchment of more liberal codes a return to the "old morality" is highly unlikely. Indeed, Reiss believes that the more person-centered coitus and the permissiveness-with-affection standard will come into increasing dominance in American society,

---

[30]Ibid., pp. 126–145.

[31]Ibid., pp. 195–217.

[32]Alfred C. Kinsey, Wardell B. Pomeroy, and Clyde E. Martin, *Sexual Behavior in the Human Male* (Philadelphia: W. B. Saunders Company, 1948), pp. 549–552.

with large numbers of college students taking the lead in this direction.[33]

While the Reiss formulation discussed above merits the careful attention of the student, it is also desirable to point to some problems in it. First, the concept of a double standard in sexual behavior for men and women is vulnerable. The idea of a double standard is that people who are identical in capacities are treated differently—behavior permitted to some is denied to others. Men and women are different in the extremely important respect that women can and do become pregnant, whereas men cannot. At some future time this difference may be rendered unimportant by completely effective and universal contraception, but until that time the consequences of sex outside of marriage are tremendously different for the two sexes. Therefore, for parents to socialize the sexes differently and to be more restrictive in controls over the sexual activity of girls hardly qualifies as a double standard. Likewise, the concepts of "permissiveness without affection" and "permissiveness with affection" may not be the most significant differences involved. The "with affection" category seems to be important primarily because it includes a commitment of the couple to each other and especially of the man to the woman. Because attraction is always involved in a decision to have intercourse, the first category might be conceptualized as "attraction without permanent commitment," or more simply, "permissiveness without long-term commitment." One study calls this category "casual attraction." The second category would be "permissiveness *with* long-term commitment," Little is known about the psychology of sexual intercourse without long-term commitment, but the presence or absence of commitment is important should a pregnancy occur.

Finally, some reservations can be voiced concerning the utility of the concept "body-centered coitus." Intercourse, with the possible exception with prostitutes, always has considerable psychological importance. One may feel elated, guilty, happy, reassured, disappointed, or whatnot, but coitus with a different person is always a psychological as well as a physiological experience. To term intercourse that does not occur within a long-term commitment "body-centered" fails to tell the whole story.

While the permissiveness-with-affection (or permissiveness-with-some-security) standard is still not generally condoned by the public mores, the cumulative evidence reflecting its increasing popularity over the past quarter of a century is convincing, if not indisputable. Smigel and Seiden's analysis of data from various studies based on college students and spanning the period from 1940 to 1963 led them to

[33]Ibid., p. 239.

conclude that the United States is "witnessing the decline, but not yet the fall, of the double standard," and that "the percentage of both men and women who accept increased permissiveness with affection as their standard has increased."[34] Subsequent research completed in the late sixties has provided additional confirmation of the trend toward a more permissive sex code among college students.[35]

The most recent study of premarital standards reports on a sample of 2,230 unmarried undergraduates from twenty-one geographically representative colleges and universities in the United States: seven were in eastern states, five in middlewestern states, three in southern states, and six in western states. In addition, this investigation obtained comparative data from large and "typical" universities, one each in Canada, England, Norway, and Germany.[36] One of the questions asked of these students was "What kind of relationship should prevail before a male and female should consider coitus as personally and socially acceptable?" The responses (Tables 7.1 and 7.2) revealed several interesting similarities and differences concerning premarital sex standards among contemporary college youth, including the following:

1. While traditional values are adhered to some degree in all countries, the newer and more liberal code is also very much in evidence. European students clearly express a more permissive attitude than their counterparts in the United States, who, in turn, are somewhat more permissive than the Canadians. Compared to the other nationalities surveyed, the English showed considerably more willingness to accept premarital intercourse and under a variety of relational conditions. For example, more than any other nationality, the English felt that "going steady" and being "casually attracted" were appropriate conditions for intercourse among persons between the ages of fourteen and seventeen.

2. There is considerable variation both within and between the sexes

[34]Erwin O. Smigel and Rita Seiden, "The Decline and Fall of the Double Standard," *The Annals,* **376** (June 1968), pp. 6–17. The studies examined were as follows: L. Rockwood and Mary E. Ford, *Youth, Marriage, and Parenthood* (New York: John Wiley & Sons, 1945), p. 40; Judson T. and Mary G. Landis, *Building a Successful Marriage,* 3rd ed. (Englewood Cliffs, N.J.: Prentice-Hall, 1958), p. 215; Winston W. Ehrmann, *Premarital Dating Behavior,* op. cit., p. 189; Ira L. Reiss, *The Social Context of Premarital Sexual Permissiveness* (New York: Holt, Rinehart and Winston, 1967), pp. 25–27. Summary findings of related research are also included.

[35]This more recent evidence may be found in Reiss, *The Social Context of Premarital Sexual Permissiveness,* op. cit., Chapter 7; Judson T. and Mary G. Landis, *Building a Successful Marriage,* op. cit., 5th ed., 1968, Chapter 11; Vance Packard, *The Sexual Wilderness* (New York: David McKay Co., 1968), Chapter 11; Eleanore B. Luckey and Gilbert D. Nass, "A Comparison of Sexual Attitudes and Behavior in an International Sample," *Journal of Marriage and the Family,* **31** (May 1969), pp. 364–379. The latter is based on an analysis of the Packard findings.

[36]For detailed descriptions of the selection procedures and sample characteristics, see Packard, op. cit., Chapter 10; Luckey and Nass, op. cit., pp. 364–365.

182

in their attitudes toward premarital intimacy. Within each of the countries represented, men generally expressed a much less restrictive standard than women, regardless of age. For example, whereas about 87 per cent of the American women viewed nonmarital intercourse as inappropriate below age eighteen, only 68 per cent of the men took this position. Women of all nationalities generally voiced much greater support than men for the standard of coitus "only if married." Canadian women in particular were found to be the most conservative group in the entire sample. Interestingly, the widest discrepancy between the sexes concerning the restriction of intercourse to marriage occurs among Canadians who are twenty-one years of age or older, whereas English males and females eighteen years of age and over exhibit the least amount of disagreement on this point.

3. In general, permissiveness increases with age in all countries and for both males and females. Thus, for example, the conservative Canadian women mentioned above gave no approval to coitus outside the married or engaged relationship for ages fourteen to seventeen, but twenty-seven per cent approved when the age was twenty-four or over. Similarly, only 4 per cent of American college females supported coitus for those fourteen to seventeen years old who were neither married nor engaged, but 30 per cent gave their approval for the twenty-four years and older group. This tendency toward greater permissiveness with increasing age has also been noted in previous studies, and provides further evidence of increasing liberal standards on the part of college students.[37]

4. It is quite clear that a significant proportion of today's college youth no longer support the traditional requirement that spouses be virginal on their wedding day.[38] Packard, for example, found that only half of the male and female college students in his U.S. sample responded affirmatively to the question: "Do you feel ideally that it is still true that a man and girl who marry should have their first full sexual experience together?" When a further inquiry specified that the first coital experience of both partners should occur only after marriage, male support dropped to 35 per cent and female support to 47 per cent.[39] In line with past research, there were significant regional variations in the responses: 66 per cent of the men and 73 per cent of the women at midwestern schools said yes to the initial question, compared to only 39 per cent of the men and 40 per cent of the women

---

[37]See, for example, Reiss, *The Social Context of Premarital Sexual Permissiveness,* op. cit., pp. 25–27, 140–143.

[38]For a summary of findings from previous researches on the percentages of males and females in college who state a willingness to marry a nonvirgin, see Ehrmann, op. cit., p. 237.

[39]Packard, op. cit., pp. 168–169.

Table 7.1

Age Level and Type of Relationship Viewed by Males as Appropriate for Considering Coitus

Type of Relationship	Ages 14–17				18–20			
	United States	Canada	England	Norway	United States	Canada	England	Norway
Only if married	67.6	80.3	28.7	55.7	33.5	38.6	9.6	17.6
Officially engaged	10.7	5.3	13.9	27.9	14.8	15.7	15.8	17.6
Tentatively engaged	6.7	3.6	7.9	6.6	15.5	15.7	15.8	35.1
Going steady	8.5	3.6	26.8	6.6	20.5	15.7	28.1	16.2
Good friends	2.1	3.6	5.9	1.6	8.1	8.6	9.6	5.4
Casually attracted	4.4	3.6	16.8	1.6	7.6	5.7	21.1	8.1
	100%	100%	100%	100%	100%	100%	100%	100%
(N)	(469)	(56)	(101)	(61)	(540)	(70)	(114)	(74)

Table 7.2

Age Level and Type of Relationship Viewed by Females as Appropriate for Considering Coitus

Type of Relationship	Ages 14–17				18–20			
	United States	Canada	England	Norway	United States	Canada	England	Norway
Only if married	86.5	94.6	43.1	78.4	58.6	62.0	16.4	40.0
Officially engaged	7.7	3.6	13.8	10.8	16.7	15.5	17.8	13.3
Tentatively engaged	2.1	1.8	13.8	5.4	11.7	14.1	9.6	22.3
Going steady	2.5	0	12.3	2.7	9.7	5.6	35.6	20.0
Good friends	0.8	0	9.2	0	1.2	2.8	9.6	0
Casually attracted	0.4	0	7.8	2.7	2.1	0	11.0	4.4
	100%	100%	100%	100%	100%	100%	100%	100%
(N)	(530)	(56)	(65)	(37)	(580)	(71)	(73)	(45)

SOURCE: Eleanore B. Luckey and Gilbert D. Nass, "A Comparison of Sexual Attitudes and Behavior in an International Sample," *Journal of Marriage and the Family*, **31** (May 1969), p. 371. Reprinted by permission

	21–23				*24 and Over*		
United States	Canada	England	Norway	United States	Canada	England	Norway
23.4	16.0	11.0	7.2	18.9	12.1	13.1	7.5
15.0	18.7	8.4	13.0	13.9	12.1	7.6	9.0
16.1	21.3	12.8	20.3	11.5	16.7	11.2	16.4
19.0	20.0	32.1	31.9	18.1	22.7	25.2	23.8
14.3	12.0	12.8	8.8	13.9	16.7	9.3	17.9
12.2	12.0	22.9	18.8	23.7	19.7	33.6	25.4
100%	100%	100%	100%	100%	100%	100%	100%
(566)	(75)	(109)	(69)	(501)	(66)	(107)	(67)

	21–23				*24 and Over*		
United States	Canada	England	Norway	United States	Canada	England	Norway
46.0	45.8	13.7	26.0	38.3	39.7	13.5	24.4
19.2	22.3	12.3	10.0	17.4	20.6	9.5	11.1
15.4	23.6	8.2	24.0	14.0	12.7	10.8	13.3
13.6	6.9	31.5	30.0	19.2	17.5	24.3	37.8
3.2	1.4	19.2	4.0	6.1	6.3	16.2	2.3
2.6	0	15.1	6.0	5.0	3.2	25.7	11.1
100%	100%	100%	100%	100%	100%	100%	100%
(624)	(72)	(73)	(50)	(557)	(63)	(74)	(45)

185

at eastern institutions. The sexual conservatism of midwestern students and the more liberal views of eastern students has emerged from much of the related research on premarital standards and behavior.[40] That the decline in the value placed on premarital chastity is not limited to the United States is demonstrated by data displayed in Table 7.3. Luckey and Nass, in analyzing these and other data from this cross-national investigation, conclude that "the double standard of sexual morals is definitely on its way out, and students are not greatly concerned about the first sexual experience being in marriage or being with the partner who eventually becomes the spouse. Even having several sexual partners before marriage was not judged particularly detrimental to the marriage."[41]

Researches completed between 1952 and 1967 on American college campuses have uncovered a number of reasons reported by students as to why they have chosen to *retain* their virginity, and to operate within a more conservative sexual code. The reasons generally line up in the following order of frequency: (1) wanting to wait until marriage, (2) family training, (3) religious beliefs, (4) fear of becoming pregnant, (5) fear that premarital sex will hinder marriage, and (6) fear of social ostracism.[42] Instructive here is Freedman's study of the sexual attitudes and behavior of seniors at a women's college in the East. They were asked, "What is the value of virginity?"[43] Almost none of the responses were in terms of abstract moral or ethical considerations. Instead, the majority of these women gave a wide variety of personal or interpersonal reasons for drawing the line at premarital intercourse, many of them similar to those previously listed. Some indicated fears of pregnancy, others felt the guilt or loss of self-respect incurred might damage the relationship with the men involved, and still others felt that virginity was important to the establishment of a good marital relationship. Freedman sensed a certain caution or inhibition underlying many of these explanations, and suggests they are only surface manifestations of more complex and deeply rooted sentiments inherent

[40]See, for example, Reiss, op. cit., pp. 74–75; Harold T. Christensen and George R. Carpenter, "Timing Patterns in the Development of Sexual Intimacy: An Attitudinal Report on Three Modern Western Societies," *Marriage and Family Living,* 24 (Feb. 1962), pp. 30–34; "Value-Behavior Discrepancies in Premarital Coitus," *American Sociological Review,* 27 (Feb. 1962), pp. 66–74.

[41]Luckey and Nass, op. cit., p. 372. Data not shown here also reveal that with the exception of England, women in all countries more often supported the double standard than men, and North American women did so more frequently than their European counterparts.

[42]For a summary of the proportion of college students mentioning these reasons in the separate studies, see, Landis and Landis, 1968, op. cit., pp. 168–169.

[43]Mervin B. Freedman, "The Sexual Behavior of American College Women: An Empirical Study and an Historical Survey," *Merrill-Palmer Quarterly,* 11 (Jan. 1965), pp. 33–48.

Table 7.3
Percentage of Male and Female in Cross-national College Sample Responding
to Selected Questions on Their Attitudes Toward Premarital Coitus

Questions	United States		Canada		England		Norway	
	M	F	M	F	M	F	M	F
No Response								
Do you think it is reasonable for a male who has experienced coitus elsewhere to expect that a girl he hopes to marry be chaste at the time of marriage?	68.4	53.4	71.1	56.2	59.7	54.5	71.8	66.1
Would it trouble you to marry a person who had experienced coitus with someone else before becoming involved with you?	29.8	61.2	31.0	46.0	46.4	58.4	47.0	58.0
Yes Response								
Do you feel a person can have numerous sexual affairs and still bring a deep, enduring emotional commitment to the person he or she married?	52.1	52.9	63.2	46.7	55.7	51.0	58.8	43.5

SOURCE: Adapted from Luckey and Nass, op. cit., pp. 368–369, Tables 5–7.

in the American middle-class character, such as conservatism, willingness to defer gratification, and so on. Apparently, these women were
only vaguely aware of the influence of these deeper sentiments of
caution, control, and inhibition as underlying motivations for maintaining a virginity standard.

Permissiveness and Adult Role Responsibilities

Because previous research has demonstrated chronological age to be
influential in determining under what conditions the younger generation would consider premarital coitus to be appropriate, this factor is
worth examining in greater detail. The ultimate and perhaps most
important question raised by the preceding discussion is whether the
greater permissiveness of contemporary youth—measured at one stage
in the life cycle—will persist or change as they mature and assume
adult and family role responsibilities. Although adequate longitudinal
data are not available for answering this question directly, some
indirect evidence may be provided by Reiss's cross-sectional comparison of the attitudes among single and married adults. That premarital permissiveness shifts as one moves from a single status to the
assumption of various types of parental roles seems to be apparent in

Table 7.4. According to the table, permissiveness decreased sharply with the advent of marriage and continued to decline gradually as the proportion of teen-age children in the family increased. Moreover, as family size increased the decrease in permissiveness became more accentuated. In short, "As the relation to the courtship process changes from that of participant to that of responsible observer, one's premarital sexual permissiveness tends to decrease."[44]

What Reiss's findings suggest is that permissiveness on the part of college students attains its highest point on one curve at almost precisely the same time that parental permissiveness reaches its lowest point on another curve! The now-conservative parents may indignantly refuse to endorse standards favored by their children that the parents themselves and perhaps other members of their generation adhered to at an earlier point in their own life cycles. Thus, what appears to be a "generation gap" concerning sexual standards today is not a reflection of hypocrisy but is more aptly described as a manifestation of differences in role perspectives and responsibilities.[45] The implication here is that when the currently permissive generation eventually occupies the various parental role positions and obligations, they may feel compelled to attempt to modify their children's behavior even though they themselves participated in similar activity when they were young adults.

Thus far in the chapter we have been discussing the *attitudes* of various catagories of people concerning nonmarital sexual intimacy. It is well known, however, that discrepancies often exist between the attitudes persons express and their actual *behavior*. We have seen that within the context of social change a new set of values regarding premarital sexual intimacy has emerged in contemporary society. Some idea of the extent to which these newer attitudes reflect behavioral changes that might have occurred already can be gained by an examination of the reported incidence of sexual activity among various groups over the past quarter of a century. Before we begin such an examination, however, some words of caution are in order. As in the case of nonmarital standards, much of the research on sexual behavior has been largely derived from a specific segment of the American public, namely, the white, middle-class, college-educated population. Conse-

[44]Reiss, *The Social Context of Premarital Sexual Permissiveness,* op. cit., pp. 145–146. Contrary to popular lay beliefs that parents of girls are more restrictive, Reiss found that the level of permissiveness of parents was little affected by the sex of their children. He did, however, find a relationship between the sex of the children and the *intensity* with which parental permissiveness is felt. Fathers tend to become more intense about their permissive feelings as the number of female children increases, and mothers become more intense as the number of their male children increases.

[45]Ibid., p. 143. The reader is cautioned here that the data being described refer to changes that occur among individuals as they assume various parental role positions. They do not describe the differences between persons of the post-World War II generation and their parents' generation. Smigel and Seiden, op. cit., p. 260.

188

Table 7.4
Premarital Permissiveness Among Adults by
Marital and Family Status

Marital and Family Status	% Highly Permissive
Single	44
Married	
No children	23
All preteen	22
Preteen and older	17
All teen or older	13

SOURCE: Adapted from Reiss, *The Social Context of Premarital Permissiveness,* op. cit., p. 142, Table 9.2.

quently, the extent to which one can legitimately generalize from the results of these studies in many instances is limited. There is, for example, ample evidence that populations not generally represented in these studies exhibit considerably different sexual norms and patterns.[46] Moreover, even among college students one finds wide variations from one campus to another and from one region to another, with respect to both attitudes toward and prevalence of nonmarital intercourse. In addition, much of the research completed in this area, especially some of the earlier investigations, contained a number of methodological weaknesses. Although we need not get into these weaknesses in any detail here, it is necessary to remember that they call for rather cautious interpretations of the results. Finally, it must not be forgotten that what we will be discussing is the *reported* incidence of premarital sexual activity; the extent to which these reports reflect actual behavior is subject to various margins of error. Keeping these types of precautions in mind, we turn now to an examination of the incidence of premarital sexual activity in the United States as well as selected other countries in the Western world.

Premarital Intercourse: Incidence and Patterns

Scientific studies of human sexual behavior were undertaken in the United States during the first half of the twentieth century, but apparently drew little attention outside the academic and intellectual communities. It was not until the late Dr. Kinsey and his associates at the Institute for Sex Research published their findings in the period prior to and following the middle of the century that the public at large was made dramatically aware of its sexual norms and conduct.[47] The

[46]See, for example, Lee Rainwater, "Some Aspects of Lower Class Sexual Behavior," in Reiss, *The Sexual Renaissance in America,* op. cit., pp. 96–108.

[47]Alfred C. Kinsey et al., op. cit. Alfred C. Kinsey, Wardell B. Pomeroy, Clyde E. Martin, and Paul H. Gebhard, *Sexual Behavior in the Human Female* (Philadelphia: W. B. Saunders Company, 1953).

189

now-famous Kinsey reports have been subjected to professional criticism on a number of statistical and methodological grounds (their superiority to previous studies could not be challenged.)[48] No subsequent studies of sexual conduct have provided the quantitative detail and knowledge about sexual activity contained in the Kinsey volumes. They have become established as the benchmark against which all subsequent evidence is compared. Thus, in this section we will make frequent reference to the Kinsey findings as well as to other major studies generally recognized as being representative of the outstanding research in this area.

PREMARITAL INTERCOURSE: MALES We have previously noted that the sex codes that developed in Western societies typically provided greater latitude for male sexual expression. It comes as no surprise, therefore, that every study ever published on the subject has shown the prevalence of premarital coitus for men to be substantially greater than that of women. Kephart has estimated, on the basis of figures from major studies completed between 1938 and 1959, that in the United States perhaps "70 per cent or more of the single (white) male population indulges in sexual intercourse prior to marriage."[49] The percentages vary, of course, from study to study, reflecting the social characteristics of the groups involved, the region of the country in which they are located (southern males generally report the highest incidence of premarital coitus), and so on. Research completed in the late sixties suggests a slight upward trend among college males in the average cumulative incidence of nonmarital coitus.[50]

Kinsey found that male sexual activity is closely associated with educational level. Specifically, males who leave school early commence sexual activity at earlier ages and exhibit higher incidences of premarital intercourse. About 67 per cent of those males who entered college had coital experience prior to marriage; among those who went

[48]Critiques and commentaries on the Kinsey reports are voluminous. For a sampling, see Jerome Himelhoch and Sylvia F. Fava (eds.), *Sexual Behavior in American Society: An Appraisal of the First Two Kinsey Reports* (New York: W. W. Norton & Company, 1955); William C. Cochran, Frederick Mosteller, and John W. Tukey, *Statistical Problems of the Kinsey Studies* (Washington, D.C.: The American Statistical Association, 1954); Albert Ellis, *Sex Life of the American Woman and the Kinsey Report* (New York: Greenberg, 1954); Seward Hiltner, *Sex Ethics and the Kinsey Reports* (New York: Association Press, 1953).

[49]Kephart, op. cit., p. 333. The precautions mentioned at the outset of this section must be kept in mind. Kephart is aware of these and warns that the 70 per cent figure is only a rough approximation and must be used cautiously because most of the incidence figures are based on college students. The lower classes are underrepresented and their premarital coitus rates are presumably even higher.

[50]Packard, op. cit., p. 160, notes that 51 per cent of Kinsey's "younger generation" college males reported they had experienced premarital coitus by age twenty-one, whereas 57 per cent of Packard's twenty-one-year-old collegians reported such experience.

190

through high school but not beyond, 84 per cent; and among those who never got past grade school, 98 per cent.[51] High school and college males in American society are more apt to express their sexual drive through heterosexual petting than in actual intercourse, whereas among the less-educated, lower-class males the reverse pattern prevails. Illustrative here are Kinsey's figures on men who reported having petted to orgasm: grade-school level, 16 per cent; high-school level, 32 per cent; and over 61 per cent of college males not married by age thirty.[52]

Perhaps the most dramatic change to occur in male sexual behavior is a significant decline in the use of the prostitute as a sexual outlet. Ehrmann, summarizing this trend, has commented, "The dramatic change, or revolution, in the premarital sexual behavior of Americans in the last forty years is characterized by the marked increase in petting and coitus among social equals, especially among engaged couples. This has meant a decrease in the activities of males with prostitutes and an increase in the premarital petting and coital experience of other girls and women."[53] Thus, 22 per cent of the college-level males in Kinsey's study had patronized a prostitute by age twenty-one, whereas two decades later only 4 per cent of the twenty-one-year-old male collegiates in Packard's sample had engaged in such activity.[54] Prostitution has been on the decline for some time, and frequency of intercourse with prostitutes is at its lowest among college students. It is, however, comparatively more important as a sexual outlet for men in the lower educational and occupational classes.[55]

PREMARITAL INTERCOURSE: FEMALES The Kinsey study revealed that a significant shift in the incidence of premarital intercourse had occurred between the generation of American women born prior to 1900 and those born in the following and subsequent decades. Whereas 27 per cent of the women born before 1900 had experienced premarital coitus, almost 50 per cent of those born between 1900 and 1909 were nonvirginal at the time of marriage.[56] This new level of coital activity has remained essentially the same for subsequent generations of women; for those born between 1910 and 1919 the premarital in-

---

[51]Kinsey et al., *Sexual Behavior in the Human Male*, op. cit., pp. 549–552.

[52]Ibid., p. 537.

[53]Winston Ehrmann, "Some Knowns and Unknowns in Research into Human Sex Behavior," *Marriage and Family Living*, **19** (Feb. 1957), p. 19.

[54]Packard, op. cit., pp. 163–164.

[55]Kinsey, *Sexual Behavior in the Human Male*, op. cit., pp. 599–603. Perhaps of interest here is Kinsey's observation that many of the groups interested in controlling nonmarital sexual activities have concentrated their efforts on prostitution, despite the fact that it accounts for less than one tenth of all types of nonmarital sexual outlets for the male population.

[56]Ibid., p. 298.

191

cidence figure was 56 per cent; for those born between 1920 and 1929, 51 per cent.[57] Apparently then, the greatest changes in the actual incidence of premarital intercourse for American women occurred during and immediately following World War I, reflecting the adult sexual practices of women born in the first decade of the twentieth century. The dramatic changes documented by Kinsey are essentially in agreement with those reported earlier by Terman in his analysis of a much smaller sample of married persons.[58] The importance of the evidence from both of these investigations is that the evidence was not restricted to college women—as was the case with so much of the research in this area—but referred instead to females of all educational and class levels. Most sociologists today agree that there is no evidence to date to indicate that the premarital coital activity reported by Kinsey for the *total* female population has undergone any significant change over the past two decades. As we shall see, however, some debate has developed over the nonmarital intercourse rates for contemporary college women.

The finding that about half of all white females in the United States enter marriage nonvirginal can be somewhat misleading without further amplification. Kinsey's data show that a considerable proportion of this behavior occurred in the year or two immediately preceding marriage.

Among the married females in the sample who had pre-marital coitus, 87 per cent had had at least a portion of it with men whom they subsequently married. Some 46 per cent had confined their coitus to the fiance. This means that 41 per cent of all the females who had had any such coitus had had it with both the fiance and with other males. Some 13 per cent had had it with other males but not with the fiance.[59]

Similarly, where approximately 51 per cent of the women in Terman's study reported premarital coital experience, approximately 33 per cent of this group had done so with their future husbands only.[60] In sum, a

---

[57]Ira L. Reiss, "Standards of Sexual Behavior," in *The Encyclopedia of Sexual Behavior,* ed. by Albert Ellis and Albert Abarbanel (New York: Hawthorne Books, 1961), p. 999.

[58]Lewis M. Terman, *Psychological Factors in Marital Happiness* (New York: McGraw-Hill Book Company, 1938), p. 321. Terman's data show that 74 per cent of the females born between 1890 and 1899 entered marriage virginal, but among those born between 1900 and 1909 only 51 per cent were still chaste at marriage. His data on men show a similar trend, the male rates of virginity for the two time periods decreased from 42 to 33 per cent.

[59]Kinsey, *Sexual Behavior in the Human Female,* op. cit., pp. 292–293.

[60]Terman, op. cit., p. 321. Somewhat comparable figures have been reported by Ernest W. Burgess and Paul Wallin, *Engagement and Marriage* (Philadelphia: J. B. Lippincott Co., 1953), pp. 311 and 330–331. This study of 1,000 engaged couples and a followup interview with 666 couples who had married showed that 68 per cent of the men and 47 per cent of the women had had premarital intercourse.

192

large proportion of women who engage in premarital intercourse restrict such activity to the man whom they will eventually wed.

We noted earlier that for men the prevalence of premarital coitus declines as the level of education increases. For women, however, this relationship is reversed: 30 per cent of those who stopped their education at the grade-school level, 47 per cent at the high school level, and 60 per cent of the college-educated females have experienced coitus prior to marriage. This pattern reflects in part the greater influence of age on the premarital activity of females; the proportion of women reporting premarital coitus increases with age, regardless of the level of education.[61] The female pattern is also influenced by age at marriage: the younger the age at which a girl married, the more likely she was to have had premarital coitus.[62]

PREMARITAL INTERCOURSE: THE COLLEGE STUDENT One reads a great deal in the popular press these days about the radical "promiscuity" of the younger generation, implying that sexual behavior in the United States, especially among college students, has changed drastically in the last two or three decades.[63] Some sociologists, on the other hand, argue that although sexual attitudes have become increasingly liberal and permissive, there is no statistical proof of any dramatic change in behavior since the patterns established in the twenties, and that, "what has been occurring is a change in attitudes to match the change in behavior of that era. The actual behavior may thus be much the same, but a much larger percentage of these people today are people who no longer look upon their behavior as wrong and have more fully accepted person-centered coitus and petting."[64] The trend, they suggest, has been toward a new single standard of permissiveness with affection (and security). Bell, for example, argues that contemporary youth approve of and accept sex outside of marriage *provided* it is coupled with love.[65]

The college student is of particular interest in the debate among those studying changes in sexual mores and behavior. As noted by Reiss and others, college students constitute the avant-garde, so to speak, of the emerging liberality of our sexual codes and therefore provide some indication of the trends in premarital intimacy that might occur in the next few decades. For example, a 1969 Time-Harris poll of 1,600 "representative Americans" revealed that significant shifts in traditional attitudes toward sex had occurred since their previous survey in 1964, and that it was the young, college-educated, and more affluent

[61]Kinsey, *Sexual Behavior in the Human Female,* op. cit., pp. 293, 333.

[62]Ibid., pp. 295–296, 337.

[63]"The Morals Revolution on the U.S. Campus," *Newsweek Magazine* (Apr. 6, 1964), pp. 52–59.

[64]Reiss, *Premarital Sexual Standards in America,* op. cit., p. 233.

[65]Robert Bell, "Parent-Child Conflicts in Sexual Values," *Journal of Social Issues,* **22** (Apr. 1966), pp. 34–44.

193

Table 7.5
Per Cent College Males and Females Experiencing Types of Sexual Behavior

Types of Sexual Behavior	United States		Canada		England		Germany		Norway	
	M	F	M	F	M	F	M	F	M	F
Light embracing or fond holding of hands	98.6	97.5	98.9	96.5	93.5	91.9	93.8	94.8	93.7	89.3
Casual goodnight kissing	96.7	96.8	97.7	91.8	93.5	93.0	78.6	74.0	86.1	75.0
Deep kissing	96.0	96.5	97.7	91.8	91.9	93.0	91.1	90.6	96.2	89.3
Horizontal embrace with some petting but not undressed	89.9	83.3	92.0	81.2	85.4	79.1	68.8	77.1	93.6	75.0
Petting of girl's breast area from outside her clothing	89.9	78.3	93.2	78.8	87.0	82.6	80.4	76.0	83.5	64.3
Petting of girl's breast area without clothes intervening	83.4	67.8	92.0	64.7	82.8	70.9	69.6	66.7	83.5	58.9
Petting below the waist of the girl under her clothing	81.1	61.2	85.2	64.7	84.6	70.9	70.5	63.5	83.5	53.6
Petting below the waist of both man and girl, under clothing	62.9	57.8	64.8	50.6	68.3	61.6	52.7	56.3	55.1	42.9
Nude embrace	65.6	49.6	69.3	47.6	70.5	64.0	50.0	62.1	69.6	51.8
Coitus	58.2	43.2	56.8	35.3	74.8	62.8	54.5	59.4	66.7	53.6
One-night affair involving coitus; didn't date person again	29.4	7.2	21.6	5.9	43.1	33.7	17.0	4.2	32.9	12.5
Whipping or spanking before petting or other intimacy	8.2	4.5	5.7	5.9	17.1	17.4	.9	1.0	5.1	7.1
Sex on pay-as-you-go basis	4.2		4.5		13.8		9.8		2.5	
(N)	(644)	(688)	(88)	(85)	(123)	(86)	(112)	(96)	(79)	(56)

SOURCE: Adapted from Luckey and Nass, op. cit., pp. 374–375.

people of our society who expressed the most liberal views.[66] Moreover, there is some evidence that new sex norms are emerging at the various stages of dating and courtship, at least for some college students. Bell and Blumberg found that "on the dating level necking is the norm for females and petting for males. During going steady and engagement, petting seems to be acceptable for both sexes. This would suggest that the young people both act and accept a higher level of intimacy than has generally been suggested by courtship norms."[67]

Some idea of the range and extent of premarital sexual activity among contemporary college youth is provided by the percentages in Table 7.5. The United States sample consists of juniors and seniors from twenty-one colleges and universities across the nation. Because of the structural differences in the educational institutions of other countries, the foreign students were selected on the basis of age. However, the mean age for all the males and females in this study was 21.1 and 20.9, respectively. Some of the findings worth noting here are:

1. The proportion of college males reporting premarital coitus ranges from 55 per cent in Germany to 75 per cent in England. Fifty-eight per cent of university males in the United States have experienced premarital intercourse.

2. The proportion of college females reporting premarital coitus ranges from 35 per cent in Canada to 63 per cent in England. *Forty-three per cent* of the university females in the United States report that they have experienced premarital intercourse.

3. English males report the greatest involvement in advanced stages of sexual intimacy (general petting, nude embrace, coitus), and German males exhibit the lowest rate of involvement in these behaviors.

4. English men and women report the highest participation in sadomasochistic practices coupled with sexual intimacy. English male students patronize prostitutes the most and Norwegians the least. Only 4 per cent of American college males engage in sex on a "pay-as-you-go" basis.

5. Compared to the other countries represented, American and Canadian students report a more conservative pattern of sexual behavior.

DECLINING VIRGINITY AMONG COLLEGE FEMALES? Research over the past quarter of a century has generally placed the incidence of nonvirginity among college women at 25 per cent or less.[68] This was the case in Freedman's 1965 published report, based on a study of the

[66]"Changing Morality: The Two Americas," *Time* (June 6, 1969), pp. 26–27.
[67]Robert R. Bell and Leonard Blumberg, "Courtship Stages and Intimacy Attitudes," *Family Life Coordinator,* **8** (March 1960), p. 63.
[68]For a review of research on the sexual behavior of college women, see Packard, op. cit., pp. 140–146, 497–500; and Freedman, op. cit., pp. 43–46.

college careers of forty-nine women who graduated from an eastern woman's college just prior to 1960. The incidence of premarital intercourse among Freedman's graduating seniors was 22 per cent, which he considered to be "consistent with the findings from other studies which are almost unanimous in reporting the incidence of nonvirginity among college women to be 25 per cent or lower."[69] This, essentially, was the picture up to 1960. However, as we have seen from the more recent data presented by Luckey and Nass (drawn from Packard's study) in Table 7.5, *43 per cent* of the juniors and seniors in U.S. colleges and universities now experience premarital coitus. If this figure is accurate, it represents an increase of about 60 per cent in the coital activity of college seniors since 1960.[70] The Luckey-Nass figure is buttressed by a related investigation completed in the mid-sixties by Harrop and Freeman of eight hundred senior college women that showed that *55 per cent* had experienced premarital coitus.[71] These investigators conclude that theirs and other studies have shown that college women have had coitus in the following percentages: freshman, 15 to 20 per cent; sophomores, 30 to 35 per cent; juniors, 40 to 45 per cent; seniors, 50 to 60 per cent; and graduate students, 60 to 70 per cent. The girls in this study almost unanimously rejected a rigid standard regarding sexual behavior. They felt that the type and extent of a woman's sexual behavior should depend on the particular circumstances and the intimacy of the relationship of the couple involved. More than three fourths thought a girl's sexual activity was strictly her own business and saw nothing wrong or distasteful in a woman's engaging in intercourse with a willing and decent partner.[72]

It is difficult to reconcile the higher-incidence figures of the most recent research with the lower rates reported in past studies. Is it then true that contemporary college women are, in fact, experiencing much more extensive sexual intercourse than in any previous generation? The evidence suggests that they indeed are, but this conclusion must be

[69]Ibid., p. 43. A more recent study of college students enrolled in sociology, psychology, and anthropology courses at the University of Georgia reports no major changes have occurred in the incidence of premarital coitus and petting since the findings reported by Kinsey in 1948; Ira E. Robinson, Karl King, Charles J. Dudley, and Francis J. Clune, "Change in Sexual Behavior and Attitudes of College Students," *The Family Coordinator,* **17** (Apr. 1968), pp. 119–123. The investigators do not, however, report sexual activity according to student class standing, i.e., freshman, sophomores, and so on.

[70]Only four of the nineteen schools enrolling women in the Packard study reported incidence rates similar to those of Kinsey, Freedman, and others; and in six of these nineteen schools *more* than 50 per cent of the females reported they had experienced premarital coitus. Packard, op. cit., pp. 162, 186.

[71]Harrop, A., and Ruth S. Freeman, "Senior College Women: Their Sexual Standards and Activity," *Journal of the National Association of Women Deans and Counselors,* **29** (Spring 1966), pp. 136–143.

[72]Ibid., p. 140. The investigators also found that a similar proportion of college men took this position.

offered with some precautions. There is considerable evidence that the prevalence of college female coitus is considerably dependent upon the type of relationship and stage of commitment she has with a male at the time such behavior occurs. For example, in Ehrmann's study of one thousand college students at a coeducational institution in Florida, he found that: "Female sexual expression is primarily and profoundly related to being in love and to going steady. (*This is probably the single most important empirical finding of this research.*) Male sexuality is more indirectly and less exclusively associated with romanticism and intimacy relationships."[73] Similarly, Freedman's findings led him to suggest "that when college women engage in intercourse they usually do so with men with whom they are emotionally involved," and that his study "supports Ehrmann's finding that premarital intercourse among college women is usually restricted to the future husband."[74] That coital activity of female coeds is directly related to specific stages in their relationships to men is illustrated by data from Landis's survey of patterns of premarital behavior among 3,189 students from eighteen different colleges in 1967. He found that among those women who were not dating at the time of the study, 15 per cent had had premarital sexual relations; for those casually dating, the proportion rose to 20 per cent; and among those women engaged 44 per cent reported premarital intercourse. Thus, Landis concludes "that as commitment to marriage increased the percentages engaging in more intimate physical behavior increased."[75] Other studies have similarly confirmed that with each progressive step in the dating and courtship stages there is a concomitant rise in the level of sexual intimacy.[76] In short, premarital intercourse is most apt to occur among college women where there is love or affection plus an understanding or commitment to marry. The majority of college females still view promiscuous sexual behavior as immoral and unwise.[77]

A reasonably conservative conclusion that might be drawn from all of the preceding discussion is that the incidence of premarital in-

[73]Winston Ehrmann, op. cit., p. 337. Similarly, in a study of over 1,800 London youngsters between the ages of fifteen and nineteen, Schofield found that "Girls prefer a more permanent type of relationship in their sexual behavior. Boys seem to want the opposite; they prefer diversity and so have more casual partners. . . . there is a direct association between the type of relationship a girl has achieved and the degree of intimacy she will permit." Michael Schofield, *The Sexual Behavior of Young People* (London: Longmans, Green, 1965), p. 92.

[74]Freedman, op. cit., p. 43.

[75]Judson T. and Mary G. Landis, *Building a Successful Marriage,* 5th ed. (Englewood Cliffs, N.J.: Prentice-Hall, 1968), p. 167.

[76]See, for example, Robert R. Bell and Leonard Blumberg, "Courtship Intimacy and Religious Background," *Marriage and Family Living,* **21** (Nov. 1959), pp. 356–360; "Courtship Stages and Intimacy Attitudes," *Family Life Coordinator,* **8** (March 1960), pp. 60–63.

[77]Robinson, et al., op. cit., pp. 119–123; Freedman, op. cit., pp. 33–48.

tercourse among college women has gradually risen from the preceding period of stabilization following the major changes of the twenties. The exact extent of this increase is difficult to gauge adequately for the nation as a whole, because of the wide fluctuations that appear under the influence of region, religion, whether it is a public or a private university, and so on.

Modern college students clearly view sex from a different, more liberal and more tolerant perspective than their counterparts of preceding generations. Under the impact of growing equalitarianism and an emphasis on individualism, community morality is being replaced by the notion that a person's sexual behavior is his business and dependent primarily on his own moral and ethical code.[78] There are indications that "following one's own bent openly and unapologetically has become a criterion of moral conduct."[79]

Offensive Premarital Sexual Aggression

In American society it is generally assumed as a normative pattern that males will pursue the aggressive role in areas of sexual intimacy. That is to say, men are expected to initiate sexual activity and women are expected to limit and control the extent of that activity. This is normally the case throughout all stages of a relationship, although as the couple develop greater levels of interpersonal commitment it is not unusual for the female to play a more significant role in initiating sexual activity. In any event, it is also generally assumed that the male will tend to press for greater degrees of erotic intimacy unless discouraged or prevented from doing so by the female.

In our culture, then, females supposedly have the choice of limiting male advances at any particular stage of sexual intimacy, from allowing kisses to consenting to actual intercourse. As many young women have discovered, however, this control over the situation is often difficult to maintain. The autonomy, isolation, and fluidity that characterizes the American dating system, "creates a condition in which offensive male sexual aggression may occur, or in which either male or female may become involved in unwanted sexual activity, through either duress or a sense of obligation."[80] Thus a study of male sexual aggression by Kirkpatrick and Kanin, based on questionnaire responses from 291 female college students, revealed that 56 per cent had been offended at least once during the academic year at some level of sexual intimacy. "The experiences of being offended were not altogether associated with

[78]Ibid.

[79] *Time,* "Changing Morality: The Two Americas," op. cit., p. 27.

[80]Winston Ehrmann, "Marital and Nonmarital Sexual Behavior," in *Handbook of Marriage and the Family,* ed. by Harold T. Christensen (Chicago: Rand-McNally & Co., 1964), p. 604.

198

trivial situations as shown by the fact that 20.9 per cent were offended by forceful attempts at intercourse and 6.2 per cent by aggressively forceful attempts at sex intercourse in the course of which meaningful threats of coercive infliction of physical pain were employed."[81] Related studies by Kanin and by Ehrmann have also confirmed the prevalence of offensive episodes of forceful male aggression and unwilling involvement in sexual behavior among high school and college females.[82]

The cooperative and independent investigations of Kirkpatrick and Kanin have shown that the more serious types of erotic aggression, such as petting below the waist, attempted intercourse, and attempted intercourse with violence, happened most characteristically to young women involved in the more permanent type of relationships such as regular daters, pinned persons, or engaged persons.[83] This, of course, is contrary to the notion that confining one's dating to the same male provides security against offensive erotic advances, or that an emotionally intimate relationship necessarily results in self-discipline by the male.

In many instances, sexually aggressive behavior by males occurred without warning. A fourth of the offensive episodes reported by one sample of females happened abruptly and without any prior consent to sex play on their part.

The evidence suggests that among the less involved dating pairs offensive behavior may be a consequence largely of poor communication, the male's beliefs concerning female responsiveness, and other factors, such as incorrect information about the dating partner, which lead to a faulty definition of the situation. Offensiveness reported occurring among the more serious pair relationships, on the other hand, indicates exploitation resulting from emotional involvement.[84]

Some other findings from this study are worth noting. Sixteen per cent of the total number of aggressive acts reported by these girls took place while the male partner was "under the influence of alcohol." Moreover, alcohol seemed to contribute to a greater likelihood of

[81]Clifford Kirkpatrick and Eugene Kanin, "Male Sex Aggression on a University Campus," *American Sociological Review,* **22** (Feb. 1957), p. 53.

[82]Eugene Kanin, "Male Aggression in Dating-Courtship Relations," *American Journal of Sociology,* **63** (Sept. 1957), pp. 197–204; "Reference Groups and Sex Conduct Norm Violations," *Sociological Quarterly,* **8** (Autumn 1967), pp. 495–504; Winston Ehrmann, op. cit., pp. 303–313.

[83]Kirkpatrick and Kanin, op. cit., p. 56; Kanin, "Male Aggression in Dating-Courtship Relations," op. cit., p. 200.

[84]Ibid., pp. 201–202. The findings for this study are based on responses from 262 first semester university women of whom 163 reported offensive and displeasing sexual episodes during their senior year of high school and the summer preceding college entrance.

aggression occurring at the more advanced stages of erotic intimacy. In addition, it was found that seven out of ten aggressive sexual episodes took place in an automobile, which offers both seclusion and escape from social controls. Moreover, as Bell has pointed out:

So long as the boy is the physical aggressor, he is not always going to allow the girl to stop the relationship when she chooses. A common belief among many young men is that a girl often says "no" when she really means "yes," that she must make some pretense of resisting the intimacy as a kind of face-saving device. Some of the differences in male reactions result from the inconsistencies of the "no"—some girls say "no" and mean it, while others really mean "go ahead."[85]

Two primary group influences have emerged from research that seem to be strongly associated with *not* being offended; namely, parental warnings about male sexual aggression and the presence of older brothers.[86] Young girls who had been admonished by parents concerning male erotic aggression were less likely to have been offended than those who had not received such warnings. Older brothers apparently play a role similar to that of the parents in cautioning their sisters about the possibilities of male sexual exploitation. Moreover, interaction with an older brother may provide sisters with a better understanding of male expectations concerning dating behavior, which perhaps leads to a greater tolerance of male sexual advances.

The question arises as to what factors might predispose a young man to engage in the type of deviant behavior that has been referred to here as male sexual aggression. A partial answer to this question is provided by a recently completed study involving a random selection of 381 undergraduate, unmarried men at a large, coeducational, midwestern university.[87] One fourth of the men in this study reported that they had made forceful attempts at intercourse that were both offensive and disagreeable to their dating partner. It was found that a young man's peer group significantly influenced his tendency to become sexually aggressive. As shown in Table 7.6, when compared to nonaggressive males, the aggressive men are much more apt to report that friends exerted some pressure on them to seek premarital sexual experience. Further indication of peer group influence emerges from the fact that

[85]Robert R. Bell, op. cit., p. 103.

[86]Kanin, "Male Aggression in Dating-Courtship Relations," op. cit., p. 199. The presence of an older sister does not, however, seem to have a similar protective influence on younger sisters.

[87]Kanin, "Reference Groups and Sex Conduct Norm Violations," op. cit., p. 495. It should be pointed out that the aggression under discussion does not include attempted sexual assault of strangers nor could the acts be labeled as carnal assault or attempted rape. Sexual aggression was defined as "the male's quest for coital access of a rejecting female during the course of which physical coercion is utilized to the degree that offended responses are elicited from the female."

Table 7.6

Degree of Pressure Exerted by Friends to Seek Premarital Sexual Experience

Degree of Pressure Exerted by Friends	Nonaggressive Males N = 254 %	Aggressive Males N = 87 %
Great Deal	2.4	4.6
Considerable	2.6	18.4
Moderate	20.5	29.9
Little	31.5	33.3
None	42.0	13.8

SOURCE: Adapted from: Eugene J. Kanin, "Reference Groups and Sex Conduct, Norm Violations," *Sociological Quarterly,* 8 (Autumn, 1967), p. 497.

about 50 per cent of the aggressive men felt that admitting their virginity to their friends would lead to a loss of status, compared to 28 per cent of the nonagressives. Moreover, "males having associates who exert strong pressure for seeking sex experience are those most unable to admit to sexual inexperience without resulting loss of status."[88] However, the majority of sexually aggressive males were, in fact, less likely to be virgin than their nonoffending counterparts; 67 per cent of the former had experienced premarital coitus, compared to 38 per cent of the latter. (Interestingly, despite their more extensive sexual experience, aggressive males were more apt to feel dissatisfied with their premarital sexual activity.)

Another indication of peer-group influence derives from the observation that aggressive sexual behavior is much more pronounced among fraternity members (46 per cent) than among independents (30 per cent). The acquisition of a sexually aggressive orientation is not, however, primarily a consequence of fraternity associations, because it is apparent at an earlier stage in the life history of the male. The majority (62 per cent) of the erotically offensive university men studied by Kanin, for example, were manifesting such aggression while still in high school. When such men reach the college level, they tend to gravitate toward reference groups whose values concerning erotic behavior are compatible with their own, namely the social fraternities. Within this context, it has been argued that while fraternities do "serve to embellish old values, provide new vocabularies of motive, modify norms, and provide new norms," regarding erotic behavior, their primary function in this area is to support and sustain earlier acquired sexual values.[89]

---

[88]Ibid., p. 498.

[89]Ibid., pp. 500–501. For a more recent study of the influence of reference groups on sexual behavior, see Alfred M. Mirande, "Reference Group Theory and Adolescent Sexual Behavior," *Journal of Marriage and the Family,* **30** (Nov. 1968), pp. 572–577.

Under what conditions do males consider the type of offensive sexual activity we have been discussing as justifiable? Although a variety of justifications are no doubt available, many university men apparently rationalize that such behavior is justified when the woman involved is perceived by themselves or their friends as being a "teaser," a "gold digger," or just plain "loose." As Kanin observes, such

qualities sufficiently stigmatize and make the female a candidate for sexual advances that some males will even proceed on hearsay evidence from their associates. The definition of a female as being sexually experienced is sufficient in some male groups—particularly where the double standard prevails—to render her a legitimate target for any type of sexual approach. Her prior experience is seen as qualifying her as public property for all interested males and cancels her prerogative to accept or reject sexual partners.[90]

Rationalizations for aggressively offensive behavior are inherent in the vocabulary of the male subculture and are readily transmitted to individual members to serve as a basis for justifying their erotic activities. Kanin views this as an adjustive function of male reference groups in that such ready-made justifications allow a man to engage in deviant sexual activity without subsequent guilt and damage to his self-concept.[91]

In this section we have been emphasizing that many young women encounter offensive male aggression during premarital dating. It needs to be stressed, however, that on the majority of dates, no such behavior occurs; that most couples in fact desire and enjoy the various forms of premarital erotic activity. "The system of testing, rejection, accepting, and adjusting to the sexual and other aspects of the male-female relation forms an integral part of the newly evolved sex codes of conduct of the youth culture, which serves to give some stability to the premarital relations of the sexes and to help them select a future spouse."[92] Moreover, although we observed at the beginning of this section that it is generally agreed that the aggressor role is essentially a male function in our society, it is no longer as exclusively confined to men as was the case in previous generations. Indeed, although the male continues to play the dominant role in initiating sexual activity, there is evidence of considerable and perhaps increasing sexual aggressiveness on the part of contemporary young females.[93]

[90]Ibid., p. 502.

[91]Ibid., pp. 502–504. For a vivid discussion of these rationalizations among white lower-class males, see William F. Whyte, op. cit., pp. 24–31. For a related treatment of Negro lower-class males, see Elliot Liebow, *Tally's Corner* (Boston: Little, Brown and Company, 1967).

[92]Ehrmann, "Marital and Nonmarital Sexual Behavior," op. cit., p. 605.

[93]Ehrmann, *Premarital Dating Behavior,* op. cit., Chapter 6.

Consequences of Premarital Intercourse

Despite the emergent permissiveness and liberality of the younger generation regarding premarital sex, the attitude of the public remains primarily one of condemnation. Long considered a violation of the mores, premarital intercourse had traditionally been viewed by society as a form of deviant behavior leading to a variety of negative consequences: venereal disease, premarital pregnancy, abortion, illegitimacy, premature marriage, premature heightening of sexuality, promiscuity, feelings of guilt, shame, or regret, unfavorable influence on the courtship relationship as well as subsequent marital adjustment, and so on. Such consequences raise a number of personal and social issues and therefore sociological researchers have attempted to ascertain their actual prevalence among persons who have experienced premarital intercourse. The results of their studies, although sometimes difficult to interpret, suggest the effects of premarital coitus are not always as extensive or as disturbing as one might have been led to believe.

1. Feelings of Guilt or Regret. Research reveals that the overwhelming majority of persons who have experienced premarital coitus do not suffer intense feelings of guilt or regret their behavior. In the Kinsey studies, for example, 77 per cent of the married women and 69 per cent of the unmarried women who had engaged in this activity reported they had no regrets whatsoever, and an additional 12 per cent of the former and 13 per cent of the latter expressed only minor regrets. (Interestingly, Kinsey found that among those women who had remained virginal, 22 per cent admitted they had abstained partly because the opportunity for engaging in coitus had not yet arisen.) The Kinsey data also show that the longer a person is involved in premarital coital activity, the less likelihood there is of her feeling regretful over it.[94] As might be expected, even higher proportions of the males in Kinsey's sample felt no regret over their coital activity.[95] A similar lack of negative feelings was reported by Burgess and Wallin in their study of engaged couples: 84 per cent of the women and 96 per cent of the men who had had intercourse reported that they felt no guilt over their behavior. Indeed, over 90 per cent of those couples who had been intimate reported that it had strengthened their relationship.[96]

Indeed, there is some indication that a majority of those who have had premarital intercourse found the experience quite pleasurable. In the Freedman study of upper-middle-class college females the predominant attitude among those who had engaged in intercourse was one of

---

[94]Kinsey et al., *Sexual Behavior in the Human Female,* op. cit., pp. 316–321.
[95]Kinsey et al., *Sexual Behavior in the Human Male,* p. 562.
[96]Ernest W. Burgess and Paul Wallin, *Engagement and Marriage* (Philadelphia: J. B. Lippincott Co., 1953), pp. 371–375. Relevant here is Kinsey's finding that women who had intercourse with their fiancés only were least apt to express regret.

enjoyment and satisfaction, particularly among those with a more serious emotional relationship with the men involved. Moreover: "None of the students who had engaged in intercourse reported that they had not enjoyed the physical and sensuous qualities of the experience. None of these young women, moreover, expressed feelings of sinfulness or guilt. None seemed to feel that they had transgressed basic moral or religious codes."[97]

That a certain proportion of the unmarried who "surrender" their virginity subsequently experience some degree of anxiety or apprehension cannot be denied.[98] However, the argument that such feelings in the long run will have deleterious emotional consequences for the majority of the participants remains doubtful. The fact is, as far as research has been able to determine, most young people are content with the status quo when asked about their sex life. If anything they display a desire for greater coital experience.[99]

2. Effects on Marriage. The question of whether premarital intimacy has unfavorable consequences for marriage has been investigated at three related levels, namely, the effects of premarital intercourse (1) on extramarital intercourse, (2) on marital intercourse, and (3) on overall marital happiness. Let us take up the last level first.

(a) Terman's study of California couples, completed over three decades ago, revealed a slightly higher rate of marital happiness among couples who had entered marriage virginal, a somewhat lower rate among those reporting intercourse with their future spouse only, and the lowest marital happiness among couples who had had intercourse with their future spouse as well as others.[100] Similarly, in Locke's comparison of happily married couples with divorced couples, a greater proportion of the latter admitted having had premarital coitus.[101] In a somewhat more sophisticated analysis, Burgess and Wallin divided a group of married couples into those who had had premarital intercourse and those who had not, and compared them in terms of an engagement success score. They found that a greater proportion of the virginal group registered in the high success categories (the differences between the two groups in terms of "average"

---

[97]Freedman, op. cit., p. 39. The Freeman study, op. cit., p. 140, reports that just under half of both men and women feel some guilt, in descending order, for homosexuality, masturbation, sexual intercourse, petting to climax, petting below the waist, and petting above the waist. It is difficult to interpret their findings, however, because the proportions feeling guilt or shame for each of these behaviors is not presented.

[98]Bell and Blumberg, op. cit., pp. 60–63.

[99]Freedman, op. cit., p. 37; Freeman, op. cit., p. 139.

[100]Terman, op. cit., p. 325.

[101]Harvey J. Locke, *Predicting Adjustment in Marriage: A Comparison of a Divorced and Happily Married Group* (New York: Holt, Rinehart and Winston, 1951), p. 133.

204

success scores, however, was relatively small).[102] Burgess and Wallin went on to compare the couples in their sample in terms of overall marital adjustment. As in previous studies, they found that virginal couples had the highest probability of marital success and couples with a premarital coital history of multiple partners had the lowest probability of marital success.

It must be pointed out, however, that in both the Terman and the Burgess and Wallin studies, the difference in the marital happiness scores between virginal and nonvirginal couples was relatively small. Indeed, the investigators caution that their findings do not necessarily prove that premarital coitus, in and of itself, leads to later marital difficulty.[103] Kirkendall has similarly noted that "the negative effects on marital adjustments attributed to premarital intercourse *per se* have probably been greatly exaggerated in our culture."[104] Nevertheless, the evidence to date does suggest that premarital chastity, particularly on the part of the female, is associated with slightly greater marital happiness.[105]

(b) Over the past quarter of a century, a number of researchers have attempted to trace the effects of premarital intercourse on *sexual* adjustments in marriage. Burgess and Wallin were unable to find support in their analysis for the notion that premarital coitus has adverse consequences on general sexual adjustment in marriage. They did, however, find that when women who had had premarital intercourse were compared with women who had not, the former showed a much greater capacity for achieving orgasm in marriage.[106] A similar relationship between premarital intercourse and postmarital orgasm was reported by Kinsey. More specifically, the Kinsey data showed that nonvirginal women were more likely to achieve postmarital orgasm provided they had experienced premarital orgasm. Although Kinsey was unable to determine whether the greater orgastic response in marriage by nonvirginal females was a "product of some selection which leads the innately more responsive females to engage in premarital coitus in which they reach orgasm, or whether the correlations between the premarital and marital records represent causal relation-

[102]Burgess and Wallin, op. cit., pp. 353–356. The investigators caution that their findings do not prove that premarital coitus has a negative influence on engagement success. For such proof, couples' adjustment to one another would have to be measured before as well as after the occurrence of intercourse.

[103]Terman, op. cit., p. 329; Burgess and Wallin, op. cit., pp. 369–370.

[104]Lester A. Kirkendall, *Premarital Intercourse and Interpersonal Relationships* (New York: The Julian Press, Inc., 1961), p. 227.

[105]A similar conclusion emerges from a large-scale study in England. See Eustace Chesser, *Women* (London: Jarrolds Publishers, Ltd., 1958). Interestingly, the majority of nonvirgins in this study did not want their daughters to follow their example.

[106]Burgess and Wallin, op. cit., pp. 362–367.

ships," he felt that the selection factors were perhaps more responsible.[107]

The most recent evidence in this area has been reported by Kanin and
Howard, who analyzed the relationship between premarital coitus and
honeymoon sexual satisfaction.[108] They found that among women who
had indulged in premarital intercourse with their future husbands, 71
per cent reported satisfactory sexual relations during the first few
weeks of the marriage, compared to only 47 per cent of those women
who were still virginal when wed. Indeed, it appeared that those who
had the most frequent premarital experience had the greatest sexual
satisfaction during the honeymoon period. A paradoxical finding was
that a greater proportion of the premaritally experienced women also
reported more early sexual difficulties. The investigators suggest that
such problems possibly result from premaritally experienced women's
entering marriage with higher expectations for postmarital sexual
adjustment. Despite such difficulties, however, a much greater proportion of the nonvirginal women (87 per cent) than the premarital
abstainers (32 per cent) found their honeymoon sexual experiences
satisfying. Kanin and Howard also found that postmarital difficulties
were partly dependent upon whether or not orgasm had been achieved
during premarital intercourse. Among those wives who had experienced orgasm through premarital coitus, only 28 per cent reported
sexual difficulties in marriage, compared to 47 per cent of the wives
who had failed to achieve orgasm during premarital coitus.

When the wives in this study were asked to evaluate the influence
they felt their premarital activity had on their immediate postmarital
adjustment, it was found "that the more advanced the intimacy level,
the more likely the subjects considered it 'beneficial' for the attainment
of early marital sex adjustment."[109] Thus, 58 per cent of those women
with premarital coitus experience felt it had helped their marital sex
life compared to 54 per cent of those reporting only heavy petting, and
34 per cent of those who restricted their premarital activity to light
petting. On the other hand, a significant proportion (42 per cent) of the
nonvirgins declined to attribute any beneficial effects to their premarital experience. Nevertheless, the overall evidence from this and the
other studies cited strongly suggests that marital sexual satisfaction
among females is closely associated with premarital orgasm.[110]

[107]Kinsey et al., *Sexual Behavior in the Human Female,* op. cit., p. 386.

[108]Eugene Kanin and David Howard, "Postmarital Consequences of Premarital Sex
Adjustments," *American Sociological Review,* 23 (Oct. 1958), pp. 557–562.

[109]Ibid., p. 561.

[110]Indeed, Kinsey et al. found a similar positive relationship between premarital
petting and marital coitus; specifically, girls who had never petted to the point of orgasm
before marriage were much less likely than those who had to achieve orgasm during the
first year of marriage. *Sexual Behavior in the Human Female,* op. cit., p. 265.

(c) In the United States the negative sanctions on extramarital intercourse—otherwise known as marital infidelity or adultery—have generally been even greater than those associated with other nonmarital intercourse. The reason for this, of course, is that extramarital liaisons, in addition to involving deception and subterfuge, pose an obvious and real threat to established marriage and family relationships. Nevertheless, as we note in Chapter 13, a significant number of husbands and wives in America have indulged in extramarital sex.

It has often been argued that nonmarital sex is detrimental to the marriage institution because it tends to promote adulterous behavior later on. Some support for this argument comes from Kinsey's data on the relationship between premarital and extramarital coital experience. Specifically, he found that wives who had engaged in premarital intercourse were much more likely to commit adultery than wives who had remained virginal until marriage. Overall, 29 per cent of the women in the Kinsey study who were premaritally experienced were later involved in marital infidelity, compared to 13 per cent of those women who had entered marriage as virgins. Similarly, by age forty, 39 per cent of those married women with premarital experience had had extramarital relations, compared to 20 per cent of those wives without premarital coital experience.[111]

3. Premarital Pregnancy. One of the major reasons advanced for restricting intercourse is to avoid the risk of premarital pregnancy. That the risk is real has been made apparent by a number of studies over the past few decades that have shown that approximately 20 per cent of all first births in the United States are premaritally conceived.[112] Sociologists estimate that between a third and one half of all high school marriages involve premarital pregnancies. And although college females are not as likely as less educated girls to become premaritally pregnant, they are—as every college and university has learned—by no means immune. Despite her supposedly greater sophistication: "By her own description, the average college girl is 'pitifully naive' about conception and 'even less informed about contraception.'"[113] And in

[111]Ibid., p. 427. Although Kinsey et al. also found a relationship between premarital and extramarital coitus among males, the data are somewhat difficult to interpret because of confounding influences of education, age, and years of marriage. See *Sexual Behavior in the Human Male,* op. cit., pp. 586–590. Moreover, Kinsey found that the males in his sample showed unusual reticence regarding their extramarital activities, and he felt that a certain proportion of them were not entirely candid in providing information about extramarital affairs.

[112]Kinsey et al., *Sexual Behavior in the Human Female,* op. cit., p. 327; Thomas Monahan, "Premarital Pregnancy in the United States," *Eugenics Quarterly,* 7 (Sept. 1960), pp. 133–147; Harold Christensen, "Child-Spacing Analysis Via Record Linkage: New Data Plus a Summing Up From Earlier Reports," *Marriage and Family Living,* 25 (Aug. 1963), pp. 272–280.

[113]Gael Greene, *Sex and the College Girl* (New York: Dell Publishing Company, 1964), p. 160.

spite of the advances in contraceptive knowledge, only a minority of college women who engage in premarital intercourse utilize the "pill." A majority depend instead on less reliable contraceptive methods, and some make no plans for using contraceptives whatsoever. Thus, on the basis of their 1967 survey of the coital activity of college students, the Landises "predict that for some years to come much premarital coitus that occurs will continue to be unplanned and unprepared for."[114] It is perhaps worth noting in this connection, that over two fifths of all illegitimate births in the United States occur among women under twenty years of age.[115] However, the *rate* of such pregnancies is *higher* for women aged twenty to twenty-four.

There are other negative consequences associated with premarital pregnancy that need to be mentioned. That young, premaritally pregnant brides have substantially higher divorce rates than young, non-pregnant brides has been rather well established. Christensen's analysis of marriages involving premarital conceptions showed that such couples have a divorce rate double that of couples in which the wife was not pregnant prior to marriage.[116]

In the face of the preceding evidence, it is hard to deny the possibility of negative consequences resulting from premarital intercourse involving conception. The availability of highly reliable contraceptives does not guarantee that they will be utilized.

Contraceptive techniques *in practice* have been, and still are, too risky—especially for the advantaged girl with everything to lose and only an unwanted child to gain. Even among middle-class married couples practicing birth control, there are large numbers of "accidental" children. Attempted use of contraception among guilt-ridden, poorly informed, and inexperienced couples would often misfire; the number of accidental pregnancies among the unmarried is enough to keep parents fearful and daughters apprehensive.[117]

Premarital Sex Norms and Conduct: What of the Future?

There is little evidence to suggest that promiscuity among the young on any significant scale is likely to occur in the very near future. As

[114]Landis and Landis, 5th ed. 1968, op. cit., pp. 174–175. For example, of 704 women who had engaged in coitus in a "love relationship" that was later broken, a full one fourth had taken no precautions to avoid conception.

[115]It should not be overlooked that the largest incidence of illegitimacy occurs among women over twenty years of age. Moreoover, the greatest increase in the illegitimacy *rate* over the past quarter century has occurred among women between ages twenty-five and thirty-four. Arthur A. Campbell and James D. Cowhig, "The Incidence of Illegitimacy in the United States," *Welfare in Review,* 5 (May 1967), pp. 1–6.

[116]Ibid. See also Samuel Lowrie, "Early Marriage: Premarital Pregnancy and Associated Factors," *Journal of Marriage and the Family,* 27 (Feb. 1965), pp. 48–56.

[117]Hallowell Pope and Dean D. Knudsen, "Premarital Sexual Norms, the Family, and Social Change," *Journal of Marriage and the Family,* 27 (Aug. 1965), p. 318.

Freedman has reminded us, the morality of an earlier generation is deeply imbedded in American culture, and continues to have a tight hold on those who followed.[118] We have noted how as the young enter marriage and assume the adult role responsibilities associated with parenthood, their attitudes regarding premarital sexuality become increasingly conservative and more in line with traditional morality. This is not to say, however, that the standards of contemporary parents in this area are no different from those of preceding generations. They are. The modern American parent, for example, is much more apt to support the notion that an equalitarian norm ought to prevail in sexual relationships.

Certainly the old norms of complete sexual abstinence prior to marriage and the double standard have both been considerably weakened under the onslaught of the massive social changes that have taken place over the past several decades. But the effects of these changes on actual sexual behavior are perhaps too often overstated. We would be more inclined to agree with the assessment of the current situation offered by Smigel and Seiden, namely:

If there has been a sexual revolution (similar to the 1920's but ideologically different) it is in terms of frankness about sex and the freedom to discuss it. Women have demanded and have achieved more education, more independence, and more social rights; one of these is the right to choose a partner for sex. Men are accepting many of these changes in the status of women and are tempering their insistence on what have generally been considered male perogatives, for example, the right to demand that a bride be a virgin.[119]

[118]Ibid.
[119]Ibid., pp. 262–263.

8

Adolescence and the Transition to Adulthood

Why a chapter on adolescence in a family text? First, adolescents live in families, parents are normatively responsible for them, and their interaction with their parents is frequent and significant, both to themselves and to their parents. Second, the roles adolescents play in their families of orientation differ radically from those they will play after they marry and establish their own families. If the adolescent makes the transition to accurately perceiving and successfully playing adult roles, he is likely to fulfill the expectations of his spouse in marriage and is likely to be able to meet his own needs. If the transition is unsuccessful, his family life is likely to reflect this inadequacy. Finally, adolescence is regarded as a problem in American society. Although this is not a book about social problems, such problems raise interesting and even crucial intellectual issues for the sociologist. Why do current methods of socialization and social control fail to achieve the objectives of the society? What, if anything, is wrong with the social and psychological theories that have been applied to the socializing and controlling of adolescents?

CULTURAL PERSPECTIVE In the earlier studies of adolescence, it was thought to be a period universally marked by turmoil within the individual and confusion in his relationships with others. This assumption came naturally to early behavioral scientists, who looked about them, observed such turmoil in Western societies, and decided that it must be a normal characteristic of adolescence. This conclusion was shattered by Mead with her study of adolescence in Samoa.[1] In Samoa she found the adolescent years a serene period of life in which young people made a smooth and relatively uneventful transition from childhood to adulthood. Her observations have been corroborated by numerous other studies of adolescence in simple, static societies.

[1] Margaret Mead, *Coming of Age in Samoa* (New York: William Morrow & Co., 1928).

As we look backward some five or six decades in American society, we see that adolescence was quite different from adolescence in the second half of the twentieth century, and in many respects more like adolescence in Samoa. We see that youth worked not only in school or principally in schools, but also in the home, in fields, shops, and family businesses, in sharp contrast to the use of time by their contemporary counterparts. With productive work in or outside the household, there was a recognition of the youth as a valuable member of the family. Making an important contribution to the family, they shared three of the most pervasive and crucial adult roles, namely, provider, house-keeper, and child-care roles. With work involvement came a full utilization of time and energy with little left for social or antisocial activities. Successful work experience at home brought confidence in being able to obtain employment and earn one's way in or outside the family.

The labor of youths was highly valued by parents, and the man with no children to help him was often an object of pity. It has been asserted that children were an economic asset, and that is probably true of adolescents who were strong enough to do an adult's work, but who were not paid for their labor. Children were also valued as insurance against poverty and want in their parents' old age.

The picture should not be painted all rose-colored, however. Although youths worked, they did not *necessarily* enjoy that activity, and conflict did occur. Some revolted against being unpaid workers with no share in their earnings. The phenomenon of running away from home to escape this type of relationship was not uncommon. There is no reason, however, for thinking that all or most children revolted against their parents. Mead does not record revolt as characteristic of youth in Samoa. It is more likely that revolt occurred against the cruelty of parents or the failure of the father to permit an adolescent to share in making decisions related to his work or in profiting from it.

WHAT IS ADOLESCENCE? Physically, adolescence seems to have a beginning but no end. It is usually marked from the start of menstruation and the development of the breasts and the broadening of the hips in girls and the attainment of near adult height and the broadening of the shoulders in boys. These are called the secondary sex characteristics. Although these developments occur at slightly different ages among individuals, they usually occur during the thirteenth or fourteenth year. It is more difficult, perhaps impossible, to mark a physical end of adolescence. In principle it would be the attainment of full adult size, weight, and strength. Such attainment, however, is both difficult to measure and lacking in significance. Most boys of sixteen or seventeen are strong *enough* to perform provider roles, and both girls and boys of that age are capable of conception. Although the attainment of near adult strength and child-bearing capacity are changes of great

211

significance, the physical changes from late adolescence to early adulthood are both minor in magnitude and socially inconsequential.

To the sociologist, the roles played are more important than the physical changes, although there is some correspondence between the physical and the social. The view of adolescence in modern industrial society has been essentially in negative terms. In general terms, Hollingshead's definition goes to the heart of the matter: "Sociologically, adolescence is the period in the life of a person when the society in which he functions ceases to regard him as a child and does not accord to him full adult status, roles, and functions."[2] Adolescents are young people who have nearly attained physical maturity but who have not: (1) entered a full provider role or, if female, (2) married. Strictly speaking, the provider role is the more definitive. A young man who has taken full-time employment, who has held full-time employment successfully for a time, and who has full control over his earnings is usually regarded as an adult whether this occurs at age seventeen, twenty-five, or even later. Increasingly this is true for girls, also. The expression "he (or she) is on his own now" applies to the youth who has successfully enacted the provider role. Currently, it is an unusual parent who does not at the same time recognize the right of such persons to make their own decisions and seek their own destiny.

Is EVERYONE MARRIED AN ADULT? It is difficult, although not impossible, to visualize a married adolescent. However, there are couples who, for example, marry in high school and live with one set of parents and thus have changed their roles little. Parents continue to support them and can continue to exercise much control over them. Ordinarily with marriage—even those involving very young persons—the couple usually does attempt to occupy the provider role and so establish a claim to independence and adult status. Moreover, many men and some women establish themselves as adults by occupying the provider role before they marry, and some live out their adult lives without marrying.

Therefore, one can say that adolescence begins with the changes that make it physically possible to play adult roles. It typically ends as a youth occupies adult roles, especially that of provider, or, frequently in the case of women, marries a man occupying the provider role and begins to play complementary roles.

In some societies adolescence does not occur, because youth are recognized as adults at puberty and enact adult roles as soon as they are physically mature enough to play such roles. This also occurs for some individuals in societies in which most youth go through an adolescent

---

[2]August B. Hollingshead, "Adolescence: A Sociological Definition," in *Selected Studies in Marriage and the Family,* ed. by Robert F. Winch and Louis Wolf Goodman (New York: Holt, Rinehart and Winston, 1968), pp. 382.

stage. For example, it is often true for the oldest son in a fatherless home or the oldest daughter in a motherless family. Under such circumstances, the youth of fourteen or fifteen years enacts the roles of the missing parent and is accorded much of the authority and responsibility that the parent would have had. In a sociological sense, he was never an adolescent, because he assumed adult roles as soon as he gained the physical stature that permitted him to do so.

Two qualifications to the above are needed. The adult roles of married women do not primarily include that of provider and more often the girl leaves adolescence by virtue of marriage to a man who can and does play that role. However, her adult roles as housekeeper and supervisor of children can be effectively played only if her husband adequately enacts his role as provider. The other qualification is that youth who enact the provider role must have control of the income or products from it. Thus, the apprentice may work full time and produce a good deal, but his product is not his own, so he has not achieved full adult status.

To recapitulate, adolescence may be regarded as a period that has a physical beginning with the attainment of nearly adult physical size and capacity. It ends for males when they successfully and fully occupy the provider role and for females when they marry a man who plays the provider role or when they themselves fully occupy the provider role. Adolescence is socially defined in that it *does not occur* in societies in which youth attain physical and social adulthood simultaneously, nor do all individuals experience it in societies in which adolescence is normatively defined. Within a given society, different categories of individuals experience differing periods of adolescence. In general, one remains an adolescent as long as he is a full-time student because it is difficult to occupy the provider role while one is fully occupied as a student. Thus, adolescence for most American youth begins at thirteen or fourteen and lasts until at least the eighteenth year. Although youth ordinarily occupy adolescent roles until they complete their education, dropping out of school at an early age does not necessarily result in achieving adult status. Steady employment at a living wage is unavailable to many youths who have dropped out of school at sixteen or seventeen. These have quit their student role without being in a position to occupy the adult provider role.

For college students, adolescence may extend as long as one remains a full-time student. The married student, of course, poses another problem of definition. What of the male college student who marries and is supported primarily by a wife employed full time? She is an adult, but is he? We feel that he has also left the adolescent status in that the couple is independent in the same sense that they would be if

213

he were the provider. This leads to the conclusion that at marriage both spouses either remain adolescents (dependent) or achieve adult status. The essence of independence seems to be the control of sufficient economic resources by persons or couples to maintain themselves at a level of living acceptable to themselves.

ADOLESCENCE IN DIFFERENTIATED SOCIETIES Adolescence has emerged as an important social phenomenon in modern industrial societies, which are characterized by a need for highly trained and educated workers. This training requires that youth stay out of the provider role so that they may devote the greater part of their time to education. Most advanced industrial societies formalize this requirement by prohibiting children from full-time paid employment and requiring that they attend school until they have attained a given level of education or a certain age level. Part of the rationale for these regulations is based on the fact that industrial societies usually have a surplus of unskilled labor and a shortage of highly educated and skilled labor. Furthermore, the entry of adolescents into the unskilled labor market would undercut the wage levels of adults who must support families. There has been one major exception to the prohibition of full-time employment of children and young adolescents—that of agricultural work. Children of migrant laborers have worked along with their parents harvesting farm crops. Their education has been neglected correspondingly, producing adults who do not have the education and the technical skills necessary for successful competition in a highly differentiated society.

ADOLESCENCE AS DISCONTINUITY IN SOCIALIZATION It has been asserted that in modern, industrialized societies adolescents are essentially "surplus people." There is no productive place for them in urbanized society. They will be needed later—provided they are well educated and socialized to be productive and essentially conforming adults. In the meantime, and this may be five to eight years, there isn't much for them to do. They are required to be in school during early adolescence and there is strong social pressure for them to stay there until the economic system is ready to absorb them into production. However, even if they are in school, the school day is short and requires or permits little physical activity. Furthermore, because the social structure of modern urban-industrial society does not provide an alternative to adolescents' being in the school, standards have been lowered to retain as many as possible within its doors. Very often, therefore, little intellectual effort is required of the adolescent to stay in school as well as almost no physical effort.

The lack of productive labor and the minimum demands of the school have left a large surplus of time and energy to the adolescent. This has been defined as playtime to be utilized in whatever manner

214

the adolescent can improvise. The definition of adolescent roles as largely play has serious consequences for adult roles, which require most of one's time and energy for work. There is serious discontinuity between adolescent and adult roles.[3]

Finally, current adolescence provides little immediate gratification to reward competent role-playing. Some gain distinction by virtue of excelling in their classes, others by excelling in athletics or school politics, but the latter usually divert the time and effort of the adolescent from his role of student. For many, gratification from school attendance must await one's completion of his schooling, at which time he is likely to have more choice of positions, including some that pay better by virtue of the fact that they require considerable education. This delay in rewards for the adolescent of fourteen may be four years, eight years, or even longer if his training includes a graduate degree. These special characteristics of the roles of adolescents pose some complex problems in the socialization and social control of adolescents, which form much of the content of parent-adolescent relationships.

ADOLESCENT SOCIALIZATION AND SOCIAL CONTROL As already noted, American society tends to view the modern adolescent as a problem. This is true to a degree in other industrial societies. It is relevant to the family in that the family is held responsible for the behavioral problems of adolescents, and increasingly parents are holding themselves responsible for the antisocial behavior or the deficiencies in role performance of their children.

Another problem in social control is the development of a permissive attitude toward adolescent behavior and a fear of the consequences of frustrating adolescents. Sebald has shown that at times this takes the form of reverse socialization, with parents deferring to adolescents: "Examples of the 'educational' literature of teen-agers concerning the 'upbringing' of their parents can be found in volumes or articles with such titles as 'Why Parents Act the Way They Do' or 'How to Deal with Parents and Other Problems.'"[4]

With disheartening regularity, the Federal Bureau of Investigation reports increases in juvenile delinquency of six to eight per cent per year—a rate far in excess of population growth. Although these figures lack precision because of inadequacies in reporting, there is no particular reason to think that they overstate general increases in delinquent behavior. Such increases have been attributed to "breakdown of the family" with the implication that parents are negligent or

[3]Ruth Benedict, "Continuities and Discontinuities in Cultural Conditioning," *Psychiatry,* 1 (May 1938), pp. 161–167.
[4]Hans Sebald, *Adolescence: A Sociological Analysis* (New York: Appleton-Century-Crofts, 1968), p. 62.

215

unconcerned about the conduct of their children. Although precise data are not available to substantiate the notion, it can be argued that parents are *more* concerned and therefore more conscientious than those of several decades ago (Chapter 15). This is probably true because an increasing proportion of parents realize the impact that they have on the personalities and behavior of their children. In fact, the tension and guilt feelings this awareness produces in parents sometimes reduce the effectiveness of their role-playing as parents.

What family behavior contributes to delinquency? Like most interesting sociological questions, not all the answers are in, but research provides some insights. Recent research on juvenile gangs in Chicago stresses the lack of socialization in such commonplace skills as how to eat, what to wear, and how to carry on a casual conversation.[5] The researchers felt that the lack of competence in interaction handicapped these boys in satisfying their needs through legitimate activity. Ordinarily, such skills are learned in the family. The lack of these skills in many gang boys could have been due to the absence of these skills in their parents, to lack of contact with their parents, or to the failure of their parents to inculcate skills that they themselves possessed.

Another way in which parents seem to have contributed to delinquent behavior is through excessive parental permissiveness. Sears, et. al., found that children with permissive mothers displayed the most aggression.[6] On a more general level, group membership often requires behavior unpleasant to an individual and necessitates foregoing activities that would be pleasurable. Children who have not had appropriate requirements made of them in the family can be expected to have more difficulty accepting the requirements of their roles in school, peer group, and community. Nye found that strict but not excessive discipline was associated with infrequent delinquency.[7] Similarly, Glueck and Glueck found that firm but not harsh discipline was associated with low delinquency rates.[8] Close affectional ties and easy and frequent communication between adolescents and parents have also been found to be related to low delinquency rates.[9] It is evident that the strictness of control over adolescents and the type of affectional relationship between parents and adolescents have something to do with delinquent behavior. It has been widely believed that some variations in family structure, especially the broken home, are a causal

[5]James F. Short and Frederick L. Strodtbeck, *Group Process and Gang Delinquency* (Chicago: University of Chicago Press, 1965), pp. 219–221.

[6]Robert E. Sears, Eleanor E. Maccoby, and Harry Levin, *Patterns of Child Rearing* (Evanston, Ill.: Row, Peterson, and Company, 1963), pp. 265–269.

[7]F. Ivan Nye, *Family Relationships and Delinquent Behavior* (New York: John Wiley & Sons, 1958), p. 82.

[8]Sheldon and Eleanor Glueck, *Unraveling Juvenile Delinquency* (New York: The Commonwealth Fund, 1950), p. 132.

[9]Nye, op. cit., Chapters 8, 16, pp. 69–78, 142–154.

factor.[10] Research provides only limited support for this belief. It is true that more children from broken homes are committed to reform schools, but it *isn't* clear that they commit greater numbers of more serious offenses than do adolescents in unbroken homes. However, it *is* evident that conflict between spouses is related to the delinquent behavior of their children.[11]

Is there any way that adolescent roles can be meaningfully related to the high rate of delinquency? In earlier decades in Western societies, and still in nonindustrial ones, the principal role of the adolescent was economic, with immediate and tangible rewards for both the youth and his parents. It occupied his time and expended his energy. Today, the principal role is student with, for most students, rewards deferred for half a decade to a full decade. There may be no rewards at all accruing to the parents.

Other increments in delinquency can be explained in terms of how parents play their roles, in the types of relationships between parents and adolescents, and in the functioning of the educational and legal organizations in the society.

SCHOOL DROPOUTS American society has come to consider early termination of formal education as a problem for the society and for most individuals, especially for the adolescent who appears to possess a high level of intelligence. This has not always been true. In a society in which most employment was in unskilled occupations, there were ample opportunities for the person with little education. However, as industrial societies moved into what we would term the Scientific Era, the demand for highly educated and trained personnel increases and for the unskilled decreases. Few highly trained individuals are unemployed; many of the uneducated can find little employment.

We have already indicated some reasons why adolescents find high school and college unrewarding. Effort is required and other uses of time must be forgone during the school day. For a few, the rewards of intellectual achievement and of the recognition and appreciation of teachers and parents are sufficient, but they are a minority. Others see major, if deferred, rewards awaiting after the completion of education. But for many neither of these sets of motivations is sufficient.

Studies of school dropouts have regularly shown the influence of parental attitudes on the values and plans of adolescents.[12] Generally, this influence has been explained in psychological terms, but it should be remembered that most adolescents are entirely or mainly supported by parents as long as they remain full-time students. A negative parental attitude toward education may mean no support.

---

[10]William J. Goode, *Women in Divorce* (New York: The Free Press, 1956), p. 17.
[11]Nye, op. cit., Chapter 5, pp. 41–52.
[12]These have been reviewed by Sebald, op. cit., pp. 430–457.

Parents play this socializing role in several ways. Most middle-class parents place a high value on formal education. They see it as highly instrumental in their own occupations in reaching positions of higher income, and they encourage their children to continue their education as far as abilities permit. Consistent with this attitude, parents are willing to provide financial support without expectation of repayment. The convictions of middle-class parents concerning the value of education is so strong that if the adolescent is reluctant to stay in school, most parents will apply pressure to keep him there.

One variant from the generally supportive and mildly coercive role-playing of middle-class parents is the extra-competitive parent. Nothing less than the highest achievement level for his child will satisfy him. He takes the school to task for not demanding a higher level of performance from students. One institutional response to this set of values in conjunction with such values in a broader segment of the society has been the creation of honors programs in the public schools and universities in which high performers are put together and made to work harder. The outcome of such parental role-playing and educational response is not clear. In some instances it places excessive burdens on the student, resulting in a loss of commitment to intellectual activities.

Typically, lower-class parents offer less support for a continuation of the adolescent's education. Few of them have higher education, and they see it as less necessary for unskilled or semiskilled workers.[13] Usually these parents are unable to offer much financial support for college education. In the lower-lower class even support of an adolescent in high school may prove a severe strain on family resources. For the self-employed family, the labor of an adolescent may increase family income appreciably. *This is especially* true of migrant labor families. Because social classes are quite well segregated spatially, and even more so in social interaction, the adult models the lower-lower-class adolescent contacts are likely to be truck drivers, mill workers, or small business people who stand out with relatively good incomes and prestige in the lower class. They "made it" without a higher education, so such education seems unnecessary.

Despite a complex of characteristics of the lower-class family that discourage the continuation of the lower-class adolescent to high school graduation and into college, many parents do play a supportive role. They see higher education as the means to more stable, more highly paid occupations and, to the limit of their resources, encourage their adolescents to stay in school.

---

[13]Jackson Toby, "Orientation to Education as a Factor in the School Maladjustment of Lower-Class Children," *Social Forces,* **35** (March 1957), pp. 259–265.

218

Social structural changes bring a new urgency to the need to keep adolescents in school, not only for positive reasons but because the dropout is a delinquency risk and much more likely to appear and reappear on relief roles. The United States government has recognized the value of a well-educated citizenry by appropriating massive amounts of money to support education. In the Communist societies, the government has gone much further in actually providing stipends for university students. Not all governmental actions, however, do support a greater participation in higher education. Most universities are increasing their tuition rates, which raise the barriers to higher education for adolescents from lower-income families. This illustrates the point that families are not independent systems and the actions taken in the political and educational organizations directly affect adolescent behavior, as do the actions of parents.

AN ADOLESCENT CULTURE? One of the explanations advanced for problems in controlling or even communicating with adolescents is that they have their own culture. Coleman dramatizes the problem in his book, *The Adolescent Society*.[14]

Adolescents do not form a society in any usual sense of that concept, but it may be argued that they are a social subcategory that possesses a subculture. It is evident that a large number of them show distinctive behavior in their dress, in music, in dancing, and in a partial language. Coleman believes the issue of whether they have a "culture" rests on whether their values and objectives are different from those of the adult world. His data on this point show that more high school boys would choose to be jet pilots or nationally recognized professional athletes than to be atomic physicists.[15] Coleman assumes that their teachers would place the choices in the other order. However, it is not clear whether high school teachers necessarily represent the value choices of the society as a whole, either.

There is some doubt whether it is appropriate to term the distinctive behavior and thinking of adolescents as a subculture for two reasons. First, it has a transitional population of people who are in the category for only a relatively few years. Most of life's experiences—marrying, rearing children, earning a living, for example—do not occur in this phase. The second reason is that other data fail to support the idea that the intrinsic values of adolescents differ markedly from those of adults. Another earlier study with a large sample produced the concept that the adolescents were "the cool generation," not in rebellion against dominant values and norms, in fact, perhaps *too* conforming to fit the stereotype of rebellious youth. The study reported that seven in eight

[14]James S. Coleman, *The Adolescent Society* (New York: The Free Press, 1961), p. 2.
[15]Ibid., p. 27.

219

were church members and that half attended church regularly. They found a higher value on security than on taking risks. About 85 per cent of those in high school wished to attend college.[16]

What, then, of the concept of an adolescent subculture? Satisfactory, perhaps, if the concept is defined loosely; however, the term *cultural segment* would be a little more precise. The distinctive dress, music, dance, and language is worthy of note, but it doesn't form an alternative to the culture patterns of the society as a whole. It would probably be as appropriate to talk of the culture of childhood or of middle age or of retired people. Each is a distinctive and meaningful "slice" of the culture based on the age and the point in the family life cycle, as is the adolescent cultural segment.

ADOLESCENT ESCAPISM Industrial societies are accustomed to rebellious youth and to escapism on the part of some individuals. However, with the advent of the "beatniks" and then the "hippies," escapism became a major phenomenon of late adolescence. Both groups were marked by withdrawal from educational, provider, and other roles.

It is not obvious at this time what causes this widespread escapism.[17] It is believed that these "social dropouts" come mainly from middle-class backgrounds. Perhaps many middle-class parents hold aspirations for their children that are too burdensome; perhaps a combination of permissiveness and unconditional support of their children encourages them to resist responsibility. Escape seems to be from responsibility more than anything else—the responsibility to work regularly, responsibility as spouses and parents, the responsibility to care for one's person and clothes—even the responsibility to view the world realistically instead of escaping through drugs.

The escapist phenomenon illustrates the opposite reaction to socialization problems from that posed by the juvenile delinquent, that of the individual who can't or won't play the roles expected of a person of his age and sex. Sociologically, this can be termed *role refusal.* The adolescent who says that work is for "squares" or that, although he is willing to work, he will do it only at the times and at the types of jobs he chooses, is refusing to accept the role of provider—the most crucial male role. In a sense, the high school dropout also characterizes role refusal. Perhaps it should not be surprising that the school dropout frequently becomes the juvenile delinquent, the drug addict, the adult criminal, or the chronic occupant of a place on the relief roles. Of course, the school dropout who is employable and who finds and

[16]David Gottlieb and Charles Ramsey, *The American Adolescent* (Homewood, Ill.: The Dorsey Press, 1964), pp. 105–111.

[17]June Bingham, "The Intelligent Square's Guide to Hippieland," The New York Times Company, 1967. Reprinted in *Marriage and the Family,* ed. by Mayer Barash and Alice Scourby (New York: Random House, 1970), pp. 383–399.

retains regular employment simply changes from one legitimate role (student) to another (employee).

Recent extensions of reinforcement theory by Thibaut and Kelley provide conceptual tools for a partial understanding of adolescent escapist behavior. In brief, they point out that individuals seek to maximize their "profits" by participating in acitivites with low costs and high rewards. Costs include any type of effort, unpleasant mental states, and forgone activities—rewards include any goods, services, relationships, or mental states found desirable by the individual.[18] From this perspective, adolescents who abandon the student role find, or expect to find, a larger profit by leaving that role. If they leave it to take full-time employment, or in the case of a girl, to marry and assume a housekeeper role, they are merely indicating that the new role or roles are more profitable, either because of lower costs or higher rewards. However, the escapist—the "dropout from society"—expects to increase his profits by being nothing in terms of roles. He reduces costs by discontinuing attendance at school and ceasing to do any schoolwork. Costs are lowered, too, in that he now has almost unlimited time available to invest in other activities. If the student role has subjected him to mental stress, this is removed.

Given rather obvious reductions in costs, what happens to rewards and, therefore, profits? Under certain circumstances these may not decrease and may even increase. If parents continue to feed, clothe, and provide him an allowance, there is no reduction in material rewards. If they are accepting of his withdrawal, they may even increase the attention and support that they give him. If society or some major segments of it also accord him a respectable status and, as needed, provide public assistance and medical care, his rewards may not decline. The creation of a subculture provides a supportive social group. Finally, cheap and relatively mild drugs may provide an interesting and satisfying diversion from a life that otherwise might become drab and uninteresting.

Under a certain set of conditions the profits of a considerable number of adolescents may have been increased by escapist behavior. However, any change toward less acceptance and support of escapism by either the parents or the society reduces the rewards and profits in this behavior. However, considerable proportions of dropouts from society "drop back in" after a period of time in escapist communities. They find that the kind of life possible without regular employment is too limited to, in the long run, meet their needs. Efforts to reduce escapist behavior can involve increasing costs and decreasing rewards for dropping out or by increasing profit for enacting the student and, later, the provider role. This will be discussed in the following section.

[18]John W. Thibaut and Harold H. Kelley, *The Social Psychology of Groups* (New York: John Wiley & Sons, 1959), Chapter 2, pp. 9–30.

221

Pathological Social Structure

Adolescents have been called "surplus people" in that many technologically advanced societies either feel little need for them or seem not to know what to do with them. Although they are excluded from paid employment partly to protect their health and to provide them time to complete their education, they are also excluded partly to protect the jobs of adults from adolescent competition. As already noted, school requires only about half of the adolescent's day and almost none of his physical energy. The balance is usually free time, but the recreational resources and leadership are not available to channel this time and energy into enjoyable, socially harmless or productive activity.

It has not been recognized that adolescents are essentially adults not children, and they have the needs of adults. Society can deny these needs and treat adolescents like big children, it can give them resources without any productivity on their part, or it can provide part-time work for them so that they can earn what they want to spend. The latter arrangement is the more productive one and provides an early socialization toward work that makes the transition to full-time employment in adulthood easier. The provision of part-time employment for adolescents would require some innovation in the economic institution of capitalistic economies. Such part-time employment is now characteristic of the Communist societies.

Another innovation that might ameliorate some of the social malfunctioning of society for adolescents is to regard the student role as a full-time occupational role. This would call for a somewhat longer school day and year and would provide a stipend for students. Such a stipend could be graded to school performance with better school performance better rewarded. A stipend is already provided in Communist colleges and universities. This provides some economic resources to adolescents and increases the dignity of the student role. An improved recreational program could be provided as an outlet for physical energy.

To date, most technologically advanced societies have denied sexual experiences to adolescents (Chapter 7). The technology now exists that, if socially approved and made entirely available to adolescents, would permit sexual experience to them without the high costs of pregnancy and venereal disease. Social innovation is possible in this area, too, but whether it occurs will depend on the values of the society and its perception of the comparative costs of continuing the present institutional arrangements compared with those of innovations that meet sexual needs.

PARENT-CHILD CONFLICT Davis, in an early and relatively comprehensive analysis, specified a number of reasons for parent-youth

222

conflict, including differences in biological functioning among the young and the old, differences in social perceptions based on greater or less experience and on changes due to cultural change, that is, different content in socialization during the childhood of the parents and the childhood of their children. Because cultural change is rapid, and becoming more rapid in American society, this could account for the high level of parent-adolescent conflict in contemporary American society.[19]

Without disputing the relevance of Davis's points, we feel the matter is basically the lack of institutions to serve youth rather than the changes in them. The United States as an urban society with adolescents excluded from the work force and sent to high school and college dates no further back than 1920. Youth are found in all societies but adolescents as a social phenomenon are essentially a creation of Western industrial societies, which have not yet created the institutions to serve them. Although the school serves some of their needs, it does not for most adolescents provide day-to-day rewards commensurate with the costs to them. Most adolescents "don't like school." In other words, they find it unprofitable.[20]

There is no institutional provision for meeting sexual or therapeutic needs, and the provisions for recreation are inadequate. Only a few adolescents can enact a provider role meaningfully in non-Communist Western societies.

It appears that the conflict between parents and adolescents is essentially one between the society and a very large segment of its population for whom it makes little or no provision. Parents happen to be in the unenviable position of having responsibility for adolescents and attempting to keep them quiet and participating in the school system until the adult world has a place for them. Therefore, parent-adolescent conflict must be expected to be a major phenomenon in Western industrial society until such time as the school is transformed into a profitable institution and institutional provision is made for other adolescent needs.

Transition to Adult Roles

Unfortunately, adolescence provides little work experience except in the student role, and in that role many adolescents work very little. Despite automation, marital and parental roles are primarily work roles. This is true of adult roles, even if one never marries. The end of adolescence usually is defined as when one completes his education

---

[19]Kingsley Davis, "The Sociology of Parent-Youth Conflict," *American Sociological Review,* 5 (Aug. 1940), pp. 523–536.

[20]We are aware that this is a complex issue deserving a more detailed exploration. However, space for such an exploration can be provided only by a book on adolescence.

and/or marries. With some exceptions, married people are expected to support themselves economically and to exercise self-control over their social behavior.

It appears that the transition from childhood and adolescence—which provide little or no work experience—to adult roles that require it, is intrinsically traumatic. Exceptions are found among adolescents who have worked on farms or in a family business or "worked their way through college" and among students who have worked hard at their studies. Lack of work experience represents, in general, inadequate socialization for adult life. However, given these circumstances, some youth enter the adult roles of provider and housekeeper before marriage and obtain the adult socialization necessary to enact these roles adequately *before* they marry and have children. These youths are already enacting key family roles before marriage. If marriage precedes socialization into these roles, then such socialization must occur after marriage. In this circumstance, there is little time for trial and error in enacting these roles. Any initial inadequacy in provider role-playing, especially, is likely to result in dependency on one or both parents or on public assistance, and may result in dissolution of the marriage. Therefore, entry into the provider and housekeeper roles prior to marriage seems to be closely related to stability in marriage in industrial societies. More of this in Chapter 9.

In conclusion, a rapidly changing society has created adolescence but it has not effected creative innovations in the social structure to permit adolescents legitimate means to meet their needs, which resemble more nearly those of adults than of children. When they become involved in delinquency or sexual problems, an accusing finger has been pointed at their parents, but the fault lies in the failure of societies to innovate in the other institutions, with the economic system being especially critical in this instance.

9

The Timing of Marriage

One of the few dependable and unchallenged statistics concerning marital stability in American society that sociologists have produced is based on age at marriage—young marriages have higher divorce rates. Yet, youth have needs for sex and companionship that have not usually been satisfied short of marriage. For girls, marriage to a person attractive to themselves is a major goal in life. In this chapter, the interplay between the unmet needs of adolescents and the requirements of the conjugal family for adult role-playing by spouses will be explored.

Recent Trends

In the United States from 1900 to 1960 the trend has clearly been toward earlier marriage for both sexes. Since then, age has increased somewhat. The median age for first marriages declined from twenty-six to twenty-three for men and from twenty-two to twenty for women. The direction of the trend was consistent over this period, but the change was slow from 1900 to 1940, although quickening very rapidly from 1940 to 1950 for whites. In fact, as much change occurred in the decade between 1940 and 1950 as in the total of the previous forty years. Since 1950, the rate of earlier marriage has again slowed for white girls. Inconsistent change in the age of black brides over the fifty-year period can be discerned, while the increase for black men is small and irregular.

For white men, the increase in early marriages has continued. From 1950 to 1960, the percentage of eighteen-year-olds marrying increased from 3.7 to 5.5 per cent. For nineteen-year-olds it increased from 9.2 to 12.9 per cent, and for twenty-year-olds from 17.5 to 24.4 per cent.

For blacks, the trends are quite different, with no increase in early marriage for girls, and for boys an increase both slight and irregular.

Because these trends are diverse for white boys and girls, let us review them briefly. Little change occurred for either sex until after 1940. Then a rapid increase in early marriage occurred for both sexes. This was followed in the decade 1950 to 1960 by a small increase for girls, about 5 per cent, but for boys this decade was a period of more rapid increase in early marriage. This picture can be seen in more detail in Table 9.1, which shows the proportion married for each age by sex and race.

This trend toward earlier marriage stopped in the decade of the sixties. The obvious reason for this halt was the disparity in the number of girls seventeen to nineteen to boys twenty to twenty-three. The birth rate increased suddenly in 1947. By 1966, this larger cohort of youth had reached an age at which many girls marry, but there was no substantial increase in the number of boys three years older whom they would normally marry. If these girls were to marry in the same proportion they had in former years, they would have to marry boys their own age. Comparatively, few boys of eighteen are ready to marry. The result has been a decline in the proportion of girls marrying in their teens. Whether this is a permanent halt to the trend in early marriage or just a pause cannot be forecast with certainty.

Recently, much attention has focused on early marriage, but "early

Table 9.1
Per Cent Married by Age of the White 15–20-Year-Old Population

Age	Females						
	1910	1920	1930	1940	1950	1960	1971
15	1.1	1.3	1.1	1.0	1.0	2.3	*
16	3.4	3.8	3.9	3.4	5.6	5.6	*
17	8.1	9.1	9.1	8.0	12.7	12.0	*
18	15.9	17.9	17.7	16.2	23.2	24.5	16.7
19	24.6	27.4	27.4	24.1	36.8	40.5	29.2
20	35.1	37.2	36.7	35.4	49.5	54.8	42.0

Age	Males						
	1910	1920	1930	1940	1950	1960	1971
15	0.1	0.2	0.1	0.1	0.6	0.6	*
16	0.1	0.3	0.2	0.3	0.6	0.9	*
17	0.3	0.8	0.6	0.6	1.2	1.9	*
18	1.2	2.4	1.9	1.9	3.4	5.4	4.4
19	3.4	5.9	5.2	4.9	8.8	12.9	11.5
20	7.9	11.5	10.5	9.9	17.5	24.4	19.2

*Data not comparable.
SOURCE: Adapted from Bureau of the Census, *Population Characteristics* for the respective years.

marriage" has been defined in several ways—as under eighteen, under nineteen, and before high school graduation. Because of different rates of maturation and very different social roles for men and women, as well as differences in the median ages at which the sexes marry, we shall regard as early a marriage that occurs before the nineteenth birthday of a woman or the twenty-first birthday of a man.

The variations in the operational definitions of early marriage suggest that we should identify the image in the mind of the person employing the term. It appears that this image may be one of three: the marriage may be early in the statistical sense that only a small proportion of marriages occur that early; it may be early in a normative sense in that it occurs earlier than is generally expected in the society; or it may be viewed as falling in a problematic category—that is, because of age, one or both mates probably lack the capabilities for enacting the marital (and sometimes, of course, the parental) roles involved. Whichever definition is employed, the age should be about two years younger for girls than for boys.

It is worthwhile to distinguish the marriages of the smaller group of girls marrying before age seventeen and boys before nineteen as "very early marriages" or "deviantly early." Both terms, of course, must be viewed in the context of contemporary American society because such ages would not be early in some societies, including those of the Mohammedan world.

The marriages at seventeen or eighteen for girls and nineteen or twenty for boys we shall consider precocious marriage in American society. These are marriages occurring barely within the normative period for marriage, but calling for the playing of adult roles by youth who are hardly prepared to play such roles in our society.

REASONS FOR MORE EARLY MARRIAGES To return for a moment to the data, awareness of the increase in early marriage comes as a surprise to most of the American public, which had assumed that marriage was increasingly delayed because of the greater numbers completing high school and attending college. In this assumption, several facts must have been overlooked. The self-employed man required a period of years to acquire the assets to establish his business. In many families, the young man was required to work for his parents until his twenty-first birthday. By contrast, today a young man is considered free to marry as soon as he has a job or, if a student, as soon as his wife-to-be can obtain a position.

Even more frequently overlooked is the fact that most early marriages do not conflict with the completion of the husband's education. A majority of men do not attend college, so in most instances a marriage on the boy's nineteenth birthday or later would come after he had completed his education. Even for boys attending and graduating from

227

college, a marriage at the average age for all males of almost twenty-three years would not conflict with education. On the other hand, some part of that relatively small proportion planning to obtain graduate degrees may well delay their marriages to reach that goal.

Other plausible reasons offered for the lower age at marriage include greater sexual stimulation through the mass media and from early and frequent dating. More difficult to document is the change in socialization of girls with respect to sex. Earlier generations of mothers frequently presented sex in marriage as a necessary evil, a pleasure for husbands only, devoid of pleasure for women—even distinctly unpleasant. We, of course, cannot know whether such views truly represented the experience of Victorian wives or instead were voiced only out of respect for accepted Victorian sexual mores. However, the socialization of girls toward sex today appears to have much less negative and more neutral and positive content. In this social context, early marriage probably appears desirable to girls for sexual as well as social reasons.

Even descriptive research and education based on earlier marriages may encourage early marriage. One marriage textbook employs the heading, "The Lengthening Shadows of Spinsterhood or Bachelor-hood." The fact is presented that at age twenty, 93 per cent of single women will marry; at 30, 48 per cent; and at 45, only 9 per cent. The implication is that if one doesn't hurry up and marry while at a tender age, all the marriageable men will be married. Ignored is the fact that of divorcees aged thirty, 94 per cent will remarry. The idea that texts and courses in marriage and the family inadvertently promote early marriage, however, should be regarded as a hypothesis with only the most limited support.

Other hypotheses concerning social changes relevant to early marriage include the belief that Americans are becoming more individualistic and therefore less willing to postpone or forego gratification, including sex and marriage. This seems to be true in American society as the state gradually assumes the insurance functions that the family carries in nonindustrial societies; that is, the elderly, the crippled, the widowed, the orphaned, and the mentally ill may be cared for by the society as a unit rather than by the individual family. The responsibilities placed on family members are correspondingly decreased and the individual freed more and more to pursue his individual goals and gratify his own needs.

The increased anonymity of urban life with its increased loneliness has also been cited as a reason for early marriage. For the single person living by himself in the city, it seems likely that life is lonely, with none or too few intimate and durable relationships. College students away from home sometimes voice this feeling of loneliness. Whether the

228

concept applies to "deviantly early" marriages is more doubtful, because most young spouses have been living at home with their families prior to marriage, rather than living by themselves.

The reader has probably noticed the tentativeness in this discussion of societal changes productive of more early marriage. Some of this tentativeness is due to paucity of descriptive research. Urban living probably is lonelier than life in a rural community and young Americans are probably typically more individualistic than their parents, but conclusive evidence is not at hand.

Consequences of Early Marriage

Early marriage has attracted attention recently because of a number of consequences attributed to it by both laymen and sociologists. These have centered on the greater instability of early marriages and the dissatisfaction or the negative affect reported by spouses. Unfortunately, we do not have entirely adequate data on divorce rates by age at marriage. Each state keeps its own (or no) records of marriage and divorce, and the objectives of the National Census do not include answering such questions. Some data gathered in the Census are, nonetheless, relevant. Glick has summarized these as follows:

For women who first married before they were 18, the proportion remarried was about half again as high as those who first married at 18 or 19; in turn, those who first married at 18 or 19 was about half again higher than those who first married at 20 or 21. Perhaps even more impressive is the finding that the proportion of remarried women among those who first married below the age of 18 years was about *three times* as high as that for women who first married between the ages of 22 and 24 years.[1]

The divorce rate continues to decline as the age of the bride increases up to thirty years, but the decline is slower after age twenty-four. Elsewhere it has been stated that *half of all marriages* involving brides under the age of eighteen end in divorce.[2] This generalization concerning teen-age brides should not obscure the great differences in divorce rates between those who marry at ages eighteen or nineteen and those marrying even earlier.

It is evident that the dissolution rate is much higher for the younger 50 per cent of marriages, but what of the "quality" of the marriages—does it in some sense compensate for the high rate of legal

[1]Paul C. Glick, *American Families* (New York; John Wiley & Sons, 1957), p. 111.
[2]University of California, Continuing Education in Medicine and Health Science, "The Uncertain Quest: Teen-Age Marriage and Divorce," a conference held at the University of California Medical Center, San Francisco, Apr. 16, 1966.

dissolution? A number of studies have asked husbands and wives how well satisfied (or how dissatisfied) they were with their marriage. Among women who had married at ages sixteen to eighteen, only 18.7 per cent rated their marriages as good compared with 58.1 per cent of women who had married at age twenty-eight or later. Presented another way, the proportion well satisfied with their marriages was more than three times as great among those marrying late as among those marrying early.

The same general relationship between age at marriage and satisfaction in marriage is found for boys. However, a larger proportion of boys marrying young, ages nineteen to twenty-one, rate their marriages as satisfactory (28.8 per cent). For men, those marrying at ages twenty-eight to thirty provide the largest proportion of well-satisfied husbands, 60.9 per cent.[3] It is evident that early marriages provide less positive and more negative affect than those that occur in the middle or late twenties. Girls, who are credited with being more eager to marry early, are even more likely than boys to regret that action.

Currently, increased concern is expressed for the children of early marriages. Many children are involved because a high proportion of very young couples are less efficient in their use of contraception. The "life chances" of the child of an early marriage are less for several reasons. His chances are high of having only one parent or a step-parent as the result of divorce. In the event of a divorce he may have *no* parent on a regular basis, because a young mother may not be able to provide economic support and/or care and supervision while she is working. Many children of young broken homes are cared for on a temporary basis by grandparents or other relatives and passed back and forth from mother to other relatives and perhaps eventually to foster parents. If the young marriage stays intact, the low incomes typical of early marriage reduce the child's chances for good housing, education, and medical care.[4]

NEED SATISFACTIONS BY EARLY MARRIAGE What are the needs satisfied by early marriage? The most obvious one is the reduction of sexual tensions. Most marriages accomplish this, although there are differences in the sexual interests of spouses, so that the desires of one or the other—more frequently the husband—are not entirely met. There is also one dysfunctional aspect of early marriage as a means of meeting sexual needs. There is a considerable relationship between the total

[3]Paul H. Landis, *Making the Most of Marriage* (New York: Appleton-Century-Crofts, 1965), pp. 322–323. Data is derived from research conducted by E. W. Burgess and L. S. Cottrell.

[4]The effects of early marriage on children is an area requiring research. We know a lot of children are involved, but how many? Following divorce, many children find themselves passed about from family to family, but how many (Chapter 20)? Many families or the remaining portions of them have to be supported by ADC or other public-supported programs, but how many?

interaction in the marriage and the pleasure couples experience in the sexual relationship. Because early marriages are more characterized by conflict, dissatisfaction, and divorce, a large proportion of couples in early marriage experience little pleasure from their sex life. One young wife commented, "So this is what I've waited for so long. It's the most overrated activity I've ever heard of." This is not to deny that early marriage reduces sexual tensions and that for some it probably adds a great deal of pleasure.

Married college students frequently cite both the added companionship that marriage provides and the greater maturity it produces. For single people living apart from their families there seems to be a need for companionship. However, if the sexual element is separated from companionship, it would appear that a roommate or a person to share an apartment would meet much of this need.

Roles attached to the positions of husband and wife have traditionally been defined as *adult* roles involving earning a living; "budgeting", making decisions about where one is to live, choice of friends, and many other decisions and responsibilities. To the extent that older adolescents accept and fulfill these role expectations, they mature rapidly. Although they mature quickly, their development may not be as full as it would be if marriage were delayed. Rather typically, the wife terminates her education to take whatever type of employment her limited training can provide. The husband may take a part-time job, which results in less time devoted to his studies and perhaps in a termination of his training before he has reached the limits of his potential.

CORRELATED EFFECTS If it appears that most of the consequences of early marriage are negative in terms of American values, it is necessary to consider whether all of the negative consequences can be attributed to early marriage per se or whether prior relationships or characteristics of the spouses are productive of some of the consequences. To some extent, the latter is true. Several studies have shown that of very early marriages, from one third to one half, involve premarital pregnancy.[5] Both the divorce rate and the rating of dissatisfaction with the marriage are related to premarital pregnancy. Christensen and Meissner found the divorce rate for premaritally pregnant brides about double that of brides who were not pregnant.[6] Although premarital pregnancy is not limited to early marriage, it is more prevalent and therefore a fraction of the higher divorce rate is attributable to premarital pregnancy.

Personal inadequacies among those marrying early have been cred-

---

[5]Lee G. Burchinal, "Trends and Prospects for Young Marriages in the United States," *Journal of Marriage and the Family,* **27** (May 1965), p. 248.
[6]Harold T. Christensen and Hanna H. Meissner, "Studies in Child Spacing: III—Premarital Pregnancy as a Factor in Divorce," *American Sociological Review,* **18** (Dec. 1953), p. 643.

ited by some as explaining part or all of the consequences of early marriage. Havighurst has stated the case for this analysis of early marriage: "It is more true to say that the people with the poorest chance of making a good marriage are more likely to marry early, than to say that early marriage causes failure in marriage. There is no evidence that these people would make better marriages if they waited to marry for three or four years beyond their present rather early age."[7]

Based on current evidence, which is not very satisfactory, some of the higher dissolution rate and negative affect in early marriage is associated with early age as an index of social maturation, some with premarital pregnancy and the personal characteristics of persons marrying early. However, marriage involves adult roles and youth who have a few more years experience in earning a living, deciding how to spend their income, and coming to terms with neighbors, police, landlords, and employers are more likely to have the competencies and motivation for playing the central roles in marriage. For example, the unemployment rate for eighteen-year-old men may be 15 per cent whereas at the same time it is only 5 per cent for men of twenty-five. Thus many who couldn't secure or retain a position at age eighteen, are able to do so a few years later.

The public, and here we include many students, frequently respond to divorce statistics or other indications of the consequences of early marriage by pointing to the differential rate of maturity from person to person. This response poses dual problems, one of which is, "What is maturity?" Because physical maturity can be assumed, the relevant aspect of maturity is the competency of the person for playing the roles attached to the positions of spouse and parent.[8]

It cannot be denied that people achieve a given level of role competency at different ages. Some are as competent at eighteen as others at thirty-five. If an absolute standard of competency were established, some would reach it by nineteen, some would never reach it. This, however, is the less important aspect of maturity. The boy of nineteen who may be able to support a family at a minimum level may by age twenty-five be able to provide comfort and security. The same is true of the developing competencies of a girl. She may reach a minimum level of competence by age seventeen, but will be much beyond that marginal point five years later. Because social and psychological maturity are not obvious, any adolescent who wishes to marry can conclude that he is mature and therefore capable of becoming an adequate spouse and parent.

[7]Robert J. Havighurst, Paul Hoover Bowman, Gordon P. Liddle, Charles V. Mathews, and James V. Pierce, *Growing Up in River City* (New York: John Wiley & Sons, 1962), p. 130.

[8]We are aware of recent literature reporting higher spontaneous abortion rates and stillbirths for children of very young marriages. However, we are not convinced that these are due to physiological immaturity.

232

Who Marries Younger?

The median age at marriage has declined in American society over the past fifty years, with more girls marrying at or before age eighteen, similarly more boys at twenty or younger. Still there is a great range in the ages at which Americans marry, with an appreciable number marrying at fifteen or younger whereas others take their vows at age seventy-five or older.[9]

EARLY HETEROSEXUAL INVOLVEMENT[10] Most studies of early marriage have included the dating history of the individuals. A preponderance of the studies has shown that a larger proportion of those marrying early began dating early, dated more frequently, and dated one person exclusively. It is hardly surprising that those who start first in interacting intimately with the other sex in terms of reciprocal sex relationships sooner arrive at the deepest emotional and physical relationship to the other sex—marriage.

Actually, the "going steady" relationship bears some similarities to marriage. It is a security system for the adolescent world, in which boy and girl are assured of a partner for school dances or other functions for which partners are necessary or desirable. It affords companionship, a contemporary with whom problems and experiences can be shared. It provides for greater emotional and physical expression, through permissible kissing, petting, and sometimes sexual intercourse. In these respects, it is a short step to marriage, and one that may be attractive in that it promises more complete satisfaction of these needs or legitimization of physical relationships that are already established. In American society, the modal pattern of courtship and marriage includes an extended period of increasing intimacy with the opposite sex, starting in early adolescence with group parties, infrequent and unconnected dates, "going steady" experiences, engagement, and marriage. The process typically involves a number of years, learning about the other sex and effective ways of interacting with it, reinforcement of these activities through need gratification, until a sufficient level of intimacy is reached for marriage to appear a reasonable possibility. Although it can happen in American society that a person marries without having considerable experience in dating and courtship, it is unusual. Therefore, to begin dating at thirteen and to go steady at fifteen predicts early marriage, whereas to delay the start of the process another four years predicts later marriage.

---

[9]U.S. Department of Health, Education and Welfare, "Facts on Aging," January, 1963, p. 7. In 1959, 3,410, including 124 for whom it was their first marriage, married at seventy-five or older.

[10]Much of the following discussion is drawn from a paper by Karen Winch Bartz and F. Ivan Nye, "Early Marriage: A Propositional Formulation," *Journal of Marriage and the Family,* **32** (May 1970), pp. 258–268.

PARENTAL ENCOURAGEMENT OF EARLY MARRIAGE The statement that parents encourage early marriage is heard with some frequency. Whether this assertion is true depends on whether it is taken literally, that parents encourage or coerce children into marrying earlier than they wish, or that parents encourage certain activities and interactions that are likely to result in early marriage. We have not seen any evidence that parents suggest to early teen-age adolescents that it would be desirable for them to get married, although this, like most possible family behavior, probably occurs occasionally. The literal statement is not true as the modal pattern. However, parents do encourage early dating and encourage social activities, dances especially, that require a date. How much pressure parents typically apply is not known but we were quite impressed by the instance in our small college town of the mother who wanted her nine-year-old daughter to start dating and bought her a pair of "falsies" to increase her sex appeal! An extreme case, undoubtedly.

To marry successfully is a very high value and even to be viewed as very desirable spouse potential is highly desirable. Parents want these experiences for their children, usually for the benefits to the child, but also as a status item for themselves. To have a child popular with the other sex is comparable to having one who is an outstanding scholar or a leader in school activities.

The encouragement of dances at a younger and younger age appears to be based on the assumption that the earlier one begins to interact with the members of the other sex, the better he will know them and the more successful and pleasant will be his relationships with them. What tends to happen, however, is that the relationships and social skills develop to a point at which sexual intercourse begins or at least is a primary objective, with early marriage the result. Attention becomes centered on the other sex rather than on schoolwork, hobbies, and other interests.

Current evidence suggests that it is not true that parents typically coerce or try to manipulate their children into early marriage, but an appreciable number encourage early dating and early social activities requiring dates, which, in turn, encourage steady dating. Early marriage is in part an unintended consequence of parental actions intended to increase their children's success in courtship and marriage.

RATIONAL DECISION: ESCAPE The idealized picture of the decision to marry is that two fall in love and on the basis of that condition marry. Although emotional involvement is central to American marriage, the decision is hedged in by considerations of one's own age and financial prospects and the age, race, religion, and other characteristics of the potential spouse. The emotional and the rational typically interact in the decision of whom and when to marry.

Escape has been an obvious explanation for very early marriage and

234

has received frequent attention from researchers.[11] Here it is useful to borrow a psychological concept, that of reinforcement. Attending high school imposes punctuality, dress prescribed within limits, restriction on movement and activities, and some stress in performance. If these efforts and deprivations are not rewarded, either immediately or strongly and predictably for the future, then marriage may afford one avenue of ridding oneself of unrewarded efforts and burdensome restrictions. This motivation may partially explain those *very* early marriages that we have termed *deviant marriage.* These middle adolescents have attained essentially full physical maturity and have some sexual needs, but are still under a pervasive set of parental and school restrictions. They sometimes feel that they are adults, that they can support themselves, and that they have enough education. The future may appear to them to be an interminable extension of an unrewarding present in which they play the roles of children.

For the precocious marriage (girls seventeen to eighteen, boys nineteen to twenty) the escape motivation appears unconvincing. Parental control has typically become less restrictive, and youth are out of high school (or nearly so) or in the more permissive environment of the college. Why rebel after restrictions are eased?

Escape seems a logical partial explanation for deviant but not for precocious marriage.[12] Case material sometimes contains this explanation and some support is offered by Havighurst: "Girls are more fortunate than boys in River City because a girl who finds the pathway to adulthood blocked in the school may easily find an alternative, marriage. . . . Of 67 girl dropouts, 52 married by the age of 18."[13]

Some of these girls dropped out because of marriage; others dropped out first, but married soon.

EARLY MARRIAGE AS A GOAL Marriage is a central objective for many girls. They view adult life as occurring within the framework of marriage and, in most instances, a family. Most have no plans for a career, for traveling extensively, or for other objectives that would conflict with a marriage. As soon as they have completed as much

---

[11]Supporting evidence for an escape motivation is provided by four researchers: Rachel Inselberg, "Marital Problems and Satisfactions in High School Marriages," *Journal of Home Economics,* **59** (Nov. 1961); Floyd M. Martinson, "Ego Deficiency as a Factor in Marriage," *American Sociological Review,* **21** (Apr. 1953); J. Joel Moss and Ruby Gingles, "The Relationship of Personality to the Incidence of Early Marriage," *Marriage and Family Living,* **21** (Nov. 1959); Samuel H. Lowrie, "Early Marriage: Premarital Pregnancy and Associated Factors," *Journal of Marriage and the Family,* **27** (Feb. 1965). Lack of support was found by Lee Burchinal, "Adolescent Role Deprivation and High School Age Marriages," *Marriage and Family Living,* **21** (Nov. 1959).

[12]Unfortunately, the escape motivation has usually been estimated retrospectively. Because an early marriage, especially one precipitated by premarital pregnancy, can cause a deterioration in relationships with parents, it appears crucial that the necessary data be collected well in advance of the marriage.

[13]Robert J. Havighurst et al., op. cit., p. 119.

formal education as their reference groups deem respectable, some are ready to marry, provided a prospect appears personally attractive and competent to play the roles attached to the positions of husband and father. They see no reason to delay marriage when these conditions are fulfilled even if they are only seventeen or eighteen at the time. Occasionally, elements of this goal attainment may be present in marriages of fifteen- or sixteen-year-old girls, usually in combination with lack of reinforcement of their activities in school or at home.

The concept of the precocious marriage serves well here. The girl who marries by choice (no premarital pregnancy) at age seventeen or eighteen is probably achieving a goal long held. In terms of a permanent marriage or one that she won't later regret, the action may still be premature, because divorce rates for girls of this age are three times as high as those marrying at age twenty-two or later. In sociological perspective she probably lacks the training, the experience, and perhaps some of the motivation for effective role-playing in marriage, and she is more likely to marry a young man similarly lacking in these abilities.

The marriage of very young men can hardly be explained in such terms. Marriage is an expectation for most—they will probably marry sometime because most men do, but it is not a goal toward which they direct their energies. Marriage at an early age has been considered something to be avoided because it means the acceptance of heavy responsibilities unnecessarily early and the preventing of the completion of education and training or the accumulation of resources to begin one's own business or to buy a car and furnish a home.

SOCIAL AND EMOTIONAL DEVIATION It is a seeming paradox that those who never marry are frequently described as social and psychological misfits, whereas the same explanation is offered for early marriage. Some support is provided by Havighurst for a relationship between antisocial and aggressive behavior and very early marriage.[14] If very early marriage is viewed as deviant social behavior, it is reasonable that it should be related to *other* deviant social behavior, as it is apparently. Very early marriage very frequently is precipitated by premarital pregnancy. As premarital intercourse is generally legally proscribed, there is little doubt that a relationship exists between proscribed social behavior and very early marriage. However, the antisocial behavior is of a rather special type; that is, sexual, or conflict with the school or with parents.

Whether emotional problems are likely to lead to early marriage is not clear, although there is some evidence of a relationship.[15] However, potential spouses with obvious emotional problems are likely to be

---

[14]Ibid., p. 120.
[15]Some support is provided by J. Joel Moss and Ruby Gingles, op. cit., pp. 372–377.

shunned. Such problems, too, are more frequently associated with introverted and withdrawn behavior, which would not be consistent with the extended period of dating that usually precedes marriage in American society. It may be that adolescents with unfulfilled emotional needs may be tempted to try to meet these within the more intense and exclusive bonds of marriage.

SOCIAL CLASS Boys and girls who marry young are likely to find their places in society on the lower socioeconomic levels (Table 9.2). Whereas half of the boys marrying at seventeen or eighteen were first employed in the lowest socioeconomic occupations or in the armed forces, only a quarter who married at thirty or later are in these low-paying positions. The occupations of the husbands of brides parallel these figures with twice as many of the husbands of brides seventeen to eighteen in lower occupations as those of brides marrying at twenty-three or older. Even these facts do not provide the complete picture, because the unemployment rate for young men of seventeen to twenty is always much higher than for those of twenty-five or older. It is of passing interest that farm managers marry at the oldest age of any occupational group.[16] Age at marriage also shows a substantial continuing relationship to the income of the husband, with men who married at an earlier age continuing to earn small incomes.[17]

Table 9.2
First Occupational Status Distributions by Percentage of Grooms by Ages of Brides and Grooms, Iowa, White Marriages, 1953–1957

Occupational Status of Grooms*	Ages of Brides				
	17 or under	18	19–22	23–29	30 or over
N	11,088	15,736	37,019	10,394	2,198
High	26.1	28.8	43.9	51.1	46.1
Middle	19.3	21.5	20.9	24.4	29.2
Low	42.8	36.4	23.9	18.6	22.6
Armed forces	11.8	13.3	11.3	5.9	2.1
	Ages of Grooms				
N	2,580	4,404	35,951	28,771	4,727
High	34.4	27.7	34.4	45.8	49.2
Middle	16.3	19.6	19.4	24.1	26.6
Low	40.2	38.7	30.2	24.6	22.3
Armed forces	9.1	14.0	16.0	5.5	1.9

*High-status occupations include professionals, managers, farm operators and owners, officials, and proprietors; middle-status occupations include clerks, salesmen, and operatives; and low-status occupations include domestics, farm laborers, and other laborers.
SOURCE: From Lee G. Burchinal, "Trends and Prospects for Young Marriages in the United States," *Journal of Marriage and the Family*, **27** (May 1965), p. 249. Reprinted by permission.

[16]Glick, op. cit., p. 118.
[17]Ibid.

If education is taken as an indicator of social class, the picture is more complex. Men with one to three years of high school education marry almost two years earlier than the median of all men, but the age at marriage for men with seven or fewer years of education is almost as high as it is for college graduates, and is higher than for men with one to three years of college education.[18] How can this curvilinear relationship between education and age at marriage be explained?

Any explanation of this relationship is tentative, and critical examination is in order. First, the median age at marriage for those with seven years or less education (in urban areas) was 25.8 and for college graduates 26.1, which is considerably beyond the age education is completed, even for most college graduates. These figures indicate that for boys, age at marriage is not merely a matter of waiting until they are out of the classroom.

For men with minimum education, steady, well-paid employment is rare. Their income may be no more than enough to provide for their own necessities. In this category of men are found large numbers of men who never marry. It presumably takes this untrained group of men longer to reach a point at which they might hope to be able to support a family or at which a girl might hope that they could.

The older age of marriage for college graduates can be explained in part as the deferment of marriage by some in order to complete their education, but also in part by the higher standard of living internalized by this category of youth. The group with one to three years of high school who marry three years earlier than either the little-educated or the college graduates is harder to explain. They drop out of school between the ages of fourteen and seventeen, so that school does not delay marriage as it does for some who graduate from college. They have a better education, somewhat better socialization in speech and dress, and better family connections than the minimum-education group, so that they can find employment sooner and a type better paid and with better prospects of stability. We propose, therefore, that this group of boys can sooner expect to be able to support a family than those with less than eighth-grade education and need not delay marriage to complete education as do some of the college graduates.

This analysis, although true, may not be adequate to explain the large differentials in age at marriage. The high school dropout may be low in deferred need gratification and more disposed to obtain the gratifications available through marriage as soon as possible.

Attention to this point has been focused on occupational and educational achievement by age of marriage. These are relevant to the social-class position of the new family. Is the low occupational status of

---

[18]Ibid., p. 116.

238

the early-marrying person simply the continuation in the lower social class of people who were born and socialized there? Havighurst's data show some relationship of parents' social-class position to age at marriage of their adolescent children; a larger proportion of lower-class girls marry early. Only the top quartile academically of the boys in this socioeconomic classification appear to marry later.[19]

The Age-at-Marriage Complex

We have noted a relationship between social class and early heterosexual involvement, with early marriage and family instability, negative affect, and low social-class placement as consequences. Can these be tied together in a system of meaningful propositions? In Figure 9.1 these relationships are diagramed.

The social-class origin of the individual is taken as the starting point, because this is where he is born and receives a socialization distinctive in terms of the values, goals, and expectations of his parents, neighbors, and peer group. The middle class provides a milieu in which education, hard work, creativity, and a high standard of living are both valued and expected. The lower class inculcates these values and expectations in its young to a lesser degree and provides fewer models of adults of high education or achievement. Children are more likely to

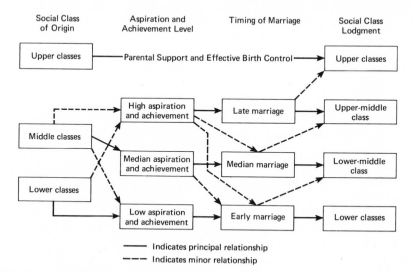

Figure 9.1. Interrelationship between Social Class, Aspiration and Achievement, and Early Marriage.

[19]Robert J. Havighurst et al., op. cit., p. 121.

239

incorporate the values and expectations of their milieu into their personalities. Middle-class children, therefore, are more likely to have higher aspirations and to be better equipped to compete in school. Some, however, will not compete successfully and will develop low aspirations. Some lower-class children will compete successfully and will be encouraged by parents, teachers, or others to aspire to a higher education and to higher occupations.

Because early marriage places obstacles in the path of higher education, adolescents with high aspirations and high achievement will tend to postpone involvement with the other sex or to keep it on a less intense level. However, some do not anticipate that emotional involvement will lead to early marriage or do not see early marriage as a disadvantage and will become emotionally involved.

Adolescents with low aspirations and achievement need not for long postpone intense heterosexual involvement because of its threat to higher education, because they do not expect to attend college. They may also seek compensating experiences in early marriage. More of them will become intensely involved at an early age. Low-achievement males, however, will be less attractive to girls as marriage partners, and some of both sexes will be too shy or too unsuccessful in attracting the other sex to become heavily emotionally involved early.

Although people who become emotionally involved with the other sex at an early age tend to move on into early marriage, either as a matter of choice or as a consequence of a pregnancy, not all serious emotional involvements lead to marriage; some of those early involved emotionally will delay marriage. The opposite occasionally occurs; some who begin to date late marry immediately and thus fall into the early-married classification, but late involvement and early marriage are virtually mutually exclusive.

Late marriage is associated with higher placement in social-class position, higher family stability, and a preponderance of positive affect. If late marriage is combined with high aspirations and high achievement, these families must find their location in the upper middle or lower upper class, especially if they are of middle-class origin with the manners and skills in social intercourse that the middle-class milieu can provide.

Middle-class youth with high aspirations and achievement who marry early are likely—because of premature entry into the labor force and earlier, heavier family responsibilities—to find social-class placement in the lower middle or upper lower class. Because of the lower occupational achievement of the husband, the frustrations of husbands in prematurely curtailing their education and training, and the inclusion of a higher proportion of forced marriages in this category, family stability is less and the negative affect more common than in the previous type.

240

Individuals with low aspirations and achievement who marry late are the most uncertain group with respect to social-class position. Some undoubtedly move into steady employment as semiskilled workers and as such are classified as upper lower class. Probably more will continue to be unskilled and intermittent workers. Their marriages are more stable than those of the fourth group because they typically have reached full adult status and responsibilities before marriage and have a smaller proportion of forced marriages.

The fourth group originate in the lower class, have low aspirations and achievement, and marry early. The families created can predictably be placed in the lower lower class, have low stability, and are more pervasively characterized by negative affect. These families begin with a set of liabilities and with no evident compensating assets.

AGE IN UPPER-CLASS MARRIAGE Little has been said about age at marriage in the upper class. This is partially because of the paucity of research on this segment of society and partially because the segment of society living on inherited wealth is small and comparatively uninfluential insofar as patterns of family living are concerned. The evidence available points to an older median age at marriage, at least in the Western world.

There are several reasons for delaying marriage in the upper class. The educational level of expectation is high—a college degree or its equivalent. Beyond this, a sophistication in manners, in knowledge of leisure sports, and in knowledge of the social world is expected. Strong parental control over marriage can and does veto early marriage. Provided the child marries within his social class and limits the size of his family, such issues as motivation to succeed or achievement in school and work are largely irrelevant, because the family income is inherited. However, the upper-class couple that bear a large family precipitate their children into the middle class, where, in general, they confront the same issues as do the children born of middle-class parents, although the children of upper-class parents have greater resources from their families of orientation as actual or potential backing.

CROSS-CULTURAL COMPARISONS Although the data are skimpy, it is clear that the United States is somewhat precocious in age of marriage in comparison with the rest of the industrialized Western world and Japan as well. It appears that the United States has the youngest median age at marriage of any industrialized society (Table 9.3). On the other hand, it appears that we have a later age at marriage than the whole Mohammedan world or India. Data for most preliterate societies are lacking.

It is an interesting, even fascinating, question why marriage comes earlier in American than in other industrialized societies. Because we have not been able to sort out the characteristics of societies and hold

241

Table 9.3
Average Age at First Marriage in Selected Countries*

Country	Sex	Before 1900	1900	1910	1920	1925	1930	1935	1940	1945	1950	1955	1959
Norway	M	28.2	27.8	27.9	27.6	28.1	28.7	29.1	29.3	29.2	29.3	28.2	
	F	26.4	25.9	25.7	25.4	25.6	25.9	26.3	26.4	26.4	26.4	25.2	
United States	M	26.0	25.0	25.0	24.0		24.0		24.0		23.7	23.2	22.3
	F	22.0	21.0	21.0	21.0		21.0		21.0		20.5	20.4	20.2
Sweden	M		28.0	28.0	29.0		29.0		29.0			28.2	
	F		26.0	26.0	26.0		26.0		26.0			25.1	
Finland	M	27.3	27.1	26.0	26.6		26.6		27.2	27.4	26.0	24.9	
	F	25.2	24.8	23.6	23.8		23.8		23.4	24.3	23.6	23.2	
England and Wales	M	25.8	26.6	27.2	27.9	27.5	27.4		27.5	26.8	27.2	26.6	
	F	24.4	25.1	25.6	25.8	25.6	25.5		25.4	24.6	24.5	24.2	

*Exact year of computation varies somewhat from nation to nation.
SOURCE: Adapted from William J. Goode, *World Revolution and Family Patterns* (London: The Free Press, Collier-Macmillan Limited, 1963), p. 47.

these constant, we can only list some differences between the United States and other industrial societies that might explain the earlier marriages.

First, American children enjoy more autonomy in relationship to their parents than children in any other industrialized society. Behind permissive practices stands an ideology that views the blocking or frustrating of children as not only unpleasant for the child, but potentially dangerous to his personality development. Although most parents do not desire early marriage for their children, when they are confronted with a decision by a child to marry, the parents are likely to defer to the child's wish.

Second, American society provides a seemingly unique combination of relative permissiveness toward premarital sexual intercourse (at least there is little chaperonage of adolescent dating) with a strong feeling that illegitimate children are a disgrace. A large number of children are conceived outside of marriage, but unlike in Sweden, where the pressure to conceal such a pregnancy by marriage is low, the first solution considered in America is a hasty, early marriage.

The relatively high income level in the United States, accented by ready consumer credit, enables the early establishment of households and in this way appears to be related to early marriage. The most rapid gain in early marriage in the United States occurred in the decade from 1940 to 1950, a decade of sharply increased prosperity. Caution in drawing conclusions is necessary, however, because some very prosperous industrialized societies, such as Sweden, have late median ages at marriage. Sweden also has one of the higher percentages of people who never marry.

American adolescents are inundated by sexual stimuli through movies, TV, books, magazines, and advertisements. Women's (and to a degree men's) dress is designed to maximize the secondary sexual characteristics of the person. Sexual attraction is often presented as the supreme value in novels and films, in that one throws away kingdoms, prior marriages, and anything else to marry the person who attracts him the most. That this emphasis and sexual stimulation results in a higher degree of preoccupation with sex and that some enter marriage earlier than they would otherwise does not seem unreasonable.

To sum up, we suggest that in the United States there is much stimulation of sexual needs and interests and little social control exercised over adolescents' sexual behavior; at the same time, pregnancy outside of marriage is considered a disgrace, the economic opportunity to establish a household early is maximized, and more autonomy from parents to marry is provided. Some or all of these factors are undoubtedly determinants of the early median age at marriage in the United States, but they probably do not exhaust the list of causes.

A Propositional Formulation[20] The relationships diagramed in Figure 9.1 and thus far informally discussed can be more formally summarized in a set of interrelated propositions. Because a number of other variables are always involved, all of these propositions are presented as probability statements.

1. Individuals from middle-class families are more likely than those from the lower social class to have high occupational aspirations and high achievement.
2. Adolescents with high occupational aspirations and high achievement are less likely to become emotionally involved with the other sex at an early age.
3. Those who become emotionally involved with the other sex at an early age are more likely to marry early.
4. Families created by an early marriage are more likely to find social-class location in the bottom half of the social-class hierarchy.
5. Families created by an early marriage are more likely to be unstable.
6. Families created by an early marriage are more likely to be characterized by a predominance of negative affect.

Some Cautions Figure 9.1 and the six propositions stated may seem to imply that both the determinants and the consequences of early marriage are readily explainable. The truth is that most of the correlations are low and that much of the variation in age at marriage is not yet accounted for. These propositions suggest other interesting relationships. For example, if middle social-class status is related to high achievement and motivation in adolescents and such achievement and motivation are related to late heterosexual involvement, then shouldn't middle-class status be related to late heterosexual involvement?

The answer appears to be no. One of the major values for middle-class parents is that their children be competent in heterosexual relationships so that they will enjoy their dating period, be able to marry, and have some choice of whom they will marry. It is assumed that early and frequent dating is likely to lead to the achievement of those goals; therefore there is a tendency for middle-class parents to push adolescents into dating, although they may fear premarital pregnancies and very early marriage.

One other special caution: we know very little about the stability of lower-class marriages that occur late. The lower class is characterized by high divorce and desertion rates, but older marriages tend to be more stable.

[20]For the complete formulation, see Bartz and Nye, op. cit., pp. 258–268.

Part III

Family Organization and Interaction

10

Changing Husband's, Wife's, and Parental Roles

Much has been written concerning changing feminine roles, little about changes in the roles men play. This could reflect the greater accessibility of women to researchers, but it seems rather to reflect much greater changes in female roles. Some may question whether it is possible to have changes in the roles of mothers and wives without these being accompanied by changes in those of fathers and husbands. However, it *is* possible, because the family is not a closed system. Tasks the mother has performed, such as the care of a preschool child, can be performed by other women in a nursery. The meal she formerly cooked at home can be prepared for her family in a restaurant. This is not to say that changes in females roles do not affect men's roles. They do, but they do not necessarily produce as large a change in the male roles, because some of the change is in interaction with organizations outside the family.

FUNCTIONS AND ROLES One of the landmarks in the conceptualization of family behavior was provided by Ogburn when he divided family tasks into seven categories: economic, protective, religious, recreational, educational, status-conferring, and affectional.[1] Current sociologists might agree that socialization would be a more appropriate term than education, and they might want to add another function (as we do), such as therapeutic, to recognize the family as a supporting agency against the frustrations and insecurity of activity in the competitive, impersonal world of the other institutions. Otherwise, this list of functions simplifies and makes intelligible the infinite variety of tasks that families perform. Ogburn detailed how the family was losing these

[1]William F. Ogburn and Clark Tibbitts, "The Family and Its Functions," *Recent Social Trends in the United States,* Report of the President's Research Committee on Social Trends (New York: McGraw-Hill Book Company, 1933), pp. 661–708.

functions (except affection) to the rapidly expanding economic, governmental, educational, religious, health, and recreational institutions and organizations. Whether the family is losing these functions or whether it is essentially that other institutions are providing additional services to individuals and to society has provided a topic for many classroom discussions and spirited arguments.[2]

Regardless of the specifics of Ogburn's thesis, it is true that a given set of tasks can be performed by different types of social organization. For example, in many preliterate societies the extended kin group, the clan, wages war and defends itself in the absence of a government in the sense that governments are organized in contemporary industrial societies. Therefore, the distribution of functions between the family and other institutions will differ from time to time. With increased industrialization, greater specialization occurs as it becomes more efficient for an organization to perform a limited number of operations and exchange the goods and services produced with those produced by other organizations. For example, the specialization in a university produces more adequate knowledge of various topics than if each professor tried to teach in every field.

Because family functions represent the tasks performed by the whole group, these tasks can be divided up among family members (segregated roles) or may be shared. For example, child socialization typically is shared by mothers and fathers, whereas housekeeping has typically been allocated entirely to the wife. Change in familial roles can stem from changes in the functions of the family or in reallocation of these functions among family members, or both.

CONCERN OVER CHANGING FAMILIAL ROLES Although Ogburn and many writers who have followed him have emphasized the loss of family roles, we are impressed by what we think is the emergence of several new roles. We agree with Parsons and others that the family is not disorganized, or about to disappear or to enter a long period of decline.[3] It is changing, like all other institutions in dynamic societies. It relinquishes some tasks to commercial and governmental organizations; it assumes new responsibilities as the need is felt and as the resources become available. Change in the family could not be arrested unless changes in the economic and other institutions also ceased.

Change *is* productive of problems during the transitional period. Kirkpatrick found that in a change in familial roles, each person wanted to receive the rewards and avoid the costs. For example, when a woman took paid employment, she wanted to keep the money she earned for her own use while expecting her husband to share her

[2]For a recent analysis, Clark E. Vincent, "Family Spongia: The Adaptive Function," *Journal of Marriage and the Family,* **28** (Feb. 1966), pp. 29–37.

[3]Talcott Parsons and Robert F. Bales, *Family, Socialization and Interaction Process* (Glencoe, Ill.: The Free Press, 1955), Chapter 1, pp. 3–34.

housekeeper role. He, in turn, wanted to share her earnings while expecting her to continue to perform all the tasks she had done prior to her employment.[4] However, such conflict and confusion seem to be a temporary phenomenon. Now that American society has experienced several decades of employed wives, it is rare to hear of a wife or a husband who takes such a position. Employed wives realize that the products of their labor should go to the support of the group, as do those of the husband. Husbands have come to realize that a wife cannot add eight hours of work outside the home and still perform all the tasks that she did before taking employment.

The more serious intellectual error, however, is to confuse what is with what should be, or even what is with what has always been. Rossi calls attention to the latter error with respect to wives in employment. This is not a new phenomenon. The *only* time in history in which being a housekeeper and caretaker of children was considered a full-time job has been in the past few decades.[5] Psychoanalytic theory has been especially erroneous in this respect, opposing employment for women or a decision to have no children as indications of some character problem. The confusion was in mistaking what *was,* prior to World War II, with what must or ought to be. Familial roles are in a continuous process of change. In a rapidly changing society this must be so.

Changes in Husband and Father Roles

Although attention has focused on female role changes and the problems attendant on them, there is evidence that men find their roles, at least in current American society, even more difficult to enact. They die on the average some seven years younger than women; they commit about five sixths of the crimes solved by police; they are a large majority of the alcoholics and drug addicts; and they are more likely to commit suicide. Hacker, who has written one of the few treatises on men's roles, singles out three special sources of male inadequacy in role-playing. These are (1) problems associated with the provider role—which have been aggravated in modern societies; (2) the ambiguity of role expectations for men, which leaves many in doubt concerning what is expected of them, and (3) difficulty in interpreting their roles in terms of the changing roles of their wives.[6] In our discussion of roles, we will utilize a concept more specific than masculinity or femininity,

---

[4]Clifford Kirkpatrick, *The Family as Institution and Process* (New York: The Ronald Press Company, 1963), Chapter 6, pp. 126–148.

[5]Alice Rossi, "Equality Between the Sexes: An Immodest Proposal," *Daedalus,* **93** (Spring 1964), pp. 607–652.

[6]Helen M. Hacker, "The New Burdens of Masculinity," *Marriage and Family Living,* **19** (Aug. 1957), pp. 227–233.

which could include an almost unlimited range of behavior, attitudes, and feelings.[7]

Changes in the Provider Role

Men have always enacted this role but the cultural milieu of industrial societies changes to a degree the nature of its enactment. In hunting and gathering societies and societies characterized by self-sufficient agriculture, unemployment is not a structural component of the society. In many industrial societies it is. In American society it has varied from about 4 per cent in the decade of the sixties, somewhat higher in the fifties, and 10 per cent or higher during the thirties. Therefore, some men have the problem of not being able to enact the provider role and many others can do so only intermittently, as their jobs last only a period of weeks or months. Most of those who are employed must perform to meet the criteria of others who evaluate them. If one fails to meet a standard or if it is believed another employee would do it more effectively, one may lose his opportunity to enact the provider role. (This differs greatly from the conditions surrounding the enactment of female roles). Finally, industrial societies provide visible measures of the degree of success men achieve in their role in the form of the size of income and the level of consumption they maintain.

Men whose wives are not employed have more complete responsibility for providing for their families than has been characteristic of most societies. The pioneer woman generally cultivated the garden and fed the livestock as well as processing the food products—such as canning, baking—and making clothing. In most families the wife has ceased performing these productive tasks and their cost is borne by the husband.

Furthermore, as Hacker points out, middle-class occupations require interpersonal skills and controls on behavior less characteristic of preindustrial societies. Men must maintain pleasant, cooperative relationships with fellow workers and especially with supervisors. They must fit their work to their employers' needs, not to their own inclinations.[8] Finally, men must undergo a lengthy period of education to prepare for induction into the higher occupations before being permitted to enact the provider role in those occupations.

These conditions suggest that the enactment of the provider role by the male in industrial societies is accompanied by considerable hazards. Agreement seems general, if not complete, that the provider is

---

[7]It is our belief that some of the confusion about masculinity and femininity is in the concepts themselves. They are both too broad and too vague to be of great value in the analysis of the family.

[8]Ibid., p. 232.

the key male role. Inadequacy is likely to be disastrous for the man personally and a major hazard to the stability and the adequate functioning of the families of which these men are a part. This problem is discussed in more detail in Chapter 17.

Industrial societies provide some "props" for the male in his provider role in the form of unemployment insurance, accident insurance, relief payments, and provisions for pensions or salary continuances in old age, but these afford only a fraction of the buying power of regular employment, and any of these that involve an element of charity are generally considered inadequate role performance by the husband.

Changes in the Socialization-of-Children Role

As is true of the provider role, fathers have always enacted a role in the socialization of children, but the cultural context in which it is played has changed. Most fathers are separated from their children most of the day, which limits their opportunities to supervise and indoctrinate children. Fathers are no longer the sources of occupational and religious knowledge for their children. Psychoanalytically oriented parent education has warned fathers against corporal punishment and prescribed warm and affectionate relationships and a large degree of permissiveness for children. The decomposition of the neighborhood and the extended family as agencies of social control deprive fathers of their aid in controlling children. Good transportation and an abundance of unused physical energy combined with permissiveness make it possible for adolescents to conduct their recreational life well away from parental view.

As a substitute for restrictiveness and the use of corporal punishment, parents have tried to communicate more effectively with children, to provide the rationale for parental and societal regulations, to obtain the voluntary cooperation of their children, and to use withdrawal of love when these fail.

Finally, advances in behavioral science have shown that personality is primarily the product of social experience, not of heredity, and there is a widespread practice of holding the parents accountable for the inadequacies and the antisocial behavior of their children. "There are no bad children, only neglectful parents" stated this philosophy in its extreme form. As a consequence, many middle-class parents have experienced chronic guilt feelings concerning their child-socialization role.

The father's socialization role, as well as his provider role, appears more hazardous in industrial society; however, he has, with some exceptions, been able to cease being the employer of his children. He has fewer children to socialize and several studies disclose a more

251

intimate, affectionate father-child relationship in the emerging small, urban family (Chapter 15).

Optional Roles for Fathers

Some familial roles are assigned to women, leaving the activity of the father on a permissive or voluntary basis. This is true of most child-care tasks such as feeding babies, changing diapers, and putting children to bed, as well as many tasks in the housekeeper role. Men may cook meals or clean the house, but unless their wives are incapacitated, these tasks are not obligatory for men. Therefore, men do not have these as prescribed roles.

Even in these activities there have been some changes because it appears that housekeeper tasks had been *proscribed* for men. To have had it known that one cooked meals or cleaned the house would have exposed the man to ridicule in the extended family and in the neighborhood. Therefore, it appears that the child-care and house-keeper activities have changed from being proscribed for men to being permitted. In a few limited categories of families, these roles may be prescribed for men—where the wife is incapacitated or the wife is employed and the husband is not, such as is often found in student marriages.

Emerging Male Familial Roles

Emerging roles must be treated as hypothetical, because insufficient data currently exists to establish them definitely. Likewise, they are likely to exist in one or some segments of the population. With these qualifications in mind, we propose that three male familial roles are in the process of being recognized: sexual, therapeutic, and recreational.[9]

Sexual intercourse roles are discussed in detail in Chapter 13, so will receive only brief attention here. Recent literature has stressed the sexual potential and needs of women, their capacity to enjoy sexual intercourse and to achieve orgasms, which, in turn, provide an affectional and physical response to the man that increases his pleasure.[10] Because the pleasure of the wife is an end in itself and indirectly increases the husband's pleasure, then it follows that the husband has a duty to provide the stimulation, timing, and setting that are conducive to sexual response in his wife. Thus, in this respect, sex can be considered as work.[11]

---

[9] Very limited research with our college students supports existence of these roles for that segment of the population.

[10] Jessie Bernard, "The Fourth Revolution," *Journal of Social Issues* special issue on *The Sexual Renaissance in America,* **22** (Apr. 1966), pp. 76–78.

[11] Lionel S. Lewis and Dennis Brissett, "Sex as Work: A Study of Avocational Counseling," *Social Problems,* **15** (Summer 1967), pp. 8–18.

This conception of a sexual intercourse role for the husband is quite different from that of only a few decades past, in which sex was considered a masculine pleasure that the wife provided to the husband in return for his economic support. There was no prescription in the norms that the husband was duty-bound to provide sexual gratification for his wife. As Hacker and others have pointed out, this is a difficult role for the man because it calls for him to create emotional states in his wife that will result in her experiencing orgasm.[12]

It is suggested in Chapter 13 that the sexual intercourse role for husbands has emerged in the middle class and there is some evidence suggesting that it has not yet been generally accepted in the lower classes.

A second emerging role we have termed *therapeutic.* It is the personal problem-solving role, whether the problem be intellectual, ethical, or emotional. If the problem involves feeling unloved, the spouse can give affection; if intellectual, information or interpretation; if ethical, another view of the problem. The literature provides more discussion of this role for females, but there are indications that women may need therapeutic services as much as the husband.[13]

Bernard has referred to part of the therapeutic role as "stroking." She says, "One of the major functions of positive, expressive talk is to raise the status of the other, to give help, to reward; in ordinary human relations, it performs the stroking function. As infants need physical caressing or stroking in order to live and grow, even to survive, so also do adults need emotional or psychological stroking or caressing to remain normal."[14]

Another aspect of the therapeutic role is illustrated by Bernard in discussing a technique of Madame de Staël, a noted conversationalist. "Her most remarkable talent," her biographer tells us, "consisted not so much in communicating her own ideas as in inspiring and helping others to formulate theirs."[15] This aspect of the husband's role is to act as a "sounding board" for the spouse to help her clarify and evaluate her ideas related to the problem.

In short, although spouses are not trained, in a formal sense, as counselors, they have the opportunity and increasingly, we hypothesize, the duty to provide the therapeutic services that have come to be associated with the roles of a professional counselor. Like other family roles, some men perform it well, some fairly well, and some very poorly.

The increased choices available to women, the changing nature of

[12]Hacker, op. cit., p. 231.
[13]Robert O. Blood and Donald M. Wolfe, *Husbands and Wives* (New York: The Free Press, 1960), Chapter 7, "Understanding and Well-being," pp. 175–220.
[14]Jessie Bernard, *The Sex Game* (Englewood Cliffs, N.J.: Prentice-Hall, 1968), p. 137.
[15]Quoted in Bernard, ibid., p. 138.

253

their roles, the wide dispersion of kin, resulting in the relative unavailability of mother or sisters, increase the relative importance of the husband as a therapeutic resource. The emergence of this role is facilitated by the wife's paid employment, because this provides an additional set of common experiences for husbands and wives. Studies showing that communication is more frequent between middle-class couples as well as an ideology of companionship and sharing imply an earlier acceptance of this role in the middle than in the lower class.

The concept of a *recreational role* for husbands proposes that he has a duty to provide for the recreational needs of other family members. If such a role exists, then the husband is not free to pursue his own recreational interests only, but must make these compatible with those of the wife.

The existence of this role requires two assumptions: (1) that recreation is a legitimate and important activity for all members of the family and (2) that family members cannot find adequate and appropriate recreation without the participation of other family members. The first of these assumptions seems to require no support, but the second is the basis for lively debate.

The belief that families can most effectively engage in recreation together was popular in the decade of the fifties and early sixties. One woman's journal carried the subtitle "The Magazine of Togetherness."

Most recreation requires the expenditure of money and, until now, most families have not been able to afford separate recreation for all family members. This becomes less of a limiting factor as family income increases. Moreover, because recreation is considered pleasurable, it was believed that sharing it would strengthen affection among family members. Finally, separate recreation of spouses involving persons of the other sex has been believed to facilitate the development of emotional ties with the other sex that may threaten the marriage.

The ideal of recreation together results in many compromises and much frustration. Few women are enthusiastic about camping, fishing, and hunting. Many men, after adjusting to working with people on their jobs, would rather not have more of the same by entertaining in the evening, which the wife may require after spending her days housekeeping. Also, children usually have different recreational interests than their parents.

It appears that there may be more intrinsic contradictions in the recreation role than in any other. The family in which all share a genuine enthusiasm for the same recreation is probably part of a small minority. Recreation apart as individuals is financially possible for an increasing number of families but whether it is a threat to the continuation of the family group is not yet known. A statistical finding that "families that play together stay together" reveals little except that

254

these people have more similar recreational interests and *perhaps* like each other better. Would couples with unlike recreational interests decrease the likelihood of divorce by spending all their recreational time together? This is a good question that needs careful research to provide a valid answer.[16]

Why should this role emerge now? The apparent answer is that most people *now* do little physical work. They have energy, time, and an increasing amount of financial resources available for recreation. Sunday was a day of rest from hard labor. Now it and Saturday are days to go somewhere and do something. Recreation is seen not only as intrinsically valuable but therapeutic in that it relaxes the worker and prepares him to be more effective on the job. As such, it probably is achieving a higher priority in the family value system.

Changing Wife and Mother Roles

Women in advanced industrial societies have seen their provider tasks move away from them to the bakery, the cannery, the dry-cleaning establishment, and the clothing factory, and the processing of food to processing plants. Many of their child-care and child-socialization tasks have moved to the school, yet their housekeeping role is still in their house or apartment as, in most instances, is the care of the preschool child. That economic production is now spatially separated from the residence "tears women apart." If they are economically productive, they must compromise or improvise on their housekeeper, child-care, and child-socialization roles. The pressure is reduced when the youngest child enters school but it does not cease. Thus, many women have accepted two sets of roles, physically separated with resulting tensions and compromises. Others have elaborated the tasks that can be performed in their houses in an attempt to make them sufficiently meaningful to themselves and their husbands. It is this dilemma and society's response to it that is at the heart of the numerous and often heated discussions of women's roles. It is this "schizophrenia" that leads us to believe that changes in women's roles are even greater than those in men's.

The Lost Provider Role

It is now reasonably well established that women have had a provider role throughout the history of the race, losing it only briefly during the latter stages of the Industrial Revolution and now regaining

[16]Homans' proposition that people who interact more like each other better is obviously relevant, but it is not clear whether they like each other better because of the interaction or interact more because they like each other. See George C. Homans, *Social Behavior: Its Elementary Forms* (New York: Harcourt Brace Jovanovich), pp. 181–190.

it again. Viewed in this perspective, the atypical period is not the present, as women in increasing numbers take employment, but the recent past several decades in which they have not been providers. However, one important environmental aspect is different—the spatial distance between the locations of her roles.

How does society react to such stresses? Its first reaction was to "view it with alarm," a second to research its consequences for family members and family relationships,[17] and finally to begin to develop services that would reduce some of the tension. These include an increasing number of day-care centers both private and public, more restaurants and dry-cleaning establishments, more preprocessing of food so that it is ready to cook, and finally, professional housecleaning services for cleaning the house, washing the windows, and so on. Such businesses emerge both as the felt need for them grows and as employed wives have more money available with which to pay for them. Such services will increase in number and quality as even more married women enter the labor force. These services enable women who take employment to reduce their housekeeping and child-care roles, provide substitutes to enact these roles, in part, and enable women to reduce the "schizophrenia" between the house and the office.[18]

Changed Child-Care and Child-Socialization Roles

Researchers have concluded that since about 1920, child-training philosophies and practices (of the middle class, especially) have been affected by the advice of educators. Such advice at first emphasized rigid care schedules, and, in general, very restrictive practices. By 1940, these had been reversed to emphasize permissiveness and self-regulation. The era of the "child-centered family" had begun. By 1960 there was some evidence of a countermovement back toward moderate permissiveness (Chapter 15).

Perhaps more important than the specific strategies employed is the increased emphasis placed on these roles. Some of this emphasis stems from relatively recent behavioral science research, which shows the extreme malleability of the child and the dominant place of social experience in his socialization. (Earlier, parents had assumed that character, behavioral traits, and competencies were inherited.) Added to this is the extreme emphasis placed on the mother-child relationship by psychoanalytic theory. Many believe that mothers who prefer not to take employment further emphasize the crucial nature of this role in order to *justify* a career as a homemaker during a period in which many

[17]Much of this research is reported in F. Ivan Nye and Lois Wladis Hoffman, *The Employed Mother in America* (Chicago: Rand McNally & Co., 1963).
[18]M. K. Sanders, "The New American Female," *Harpers,* **231** (July 1965), pp. 37–43.

tasks were moving from the house to the school and the factory. One aspect of the "inflation" of the child-care and socialization roles was a major increase in the birthrate from 1946 to 1957. Bernard refers to this as the "motherhood mania," during which middle-class women tried to develop child-care and housekeeping roles into a significant and satisfying life career. One explanation attributes this to the influence of psychoanalytic theory, which asserted that women could find significance and satisfaction only in child-bearing and -rearing.[19]

As already discussed, the child-socialization role has increased in absolute difficulty because of the loss of the extended family and the neighborhood as effective agents of social control. Also, the urban environment offers less space for physical activity and more opportunities for deviant behavior.

Moreover, mothers who rear children by themselves face one potential problem less frequently encountered by fathers—loss of physical control of adolescent children. Few daughters can challenge their fathers physically; few sons will dominate their fathers physically; but most adolescent boys are larger and stronger than their mothers. One mother of a fifteen-year-old boy said, "He's bigger and stronger than I am, and I don't know when he is going to decide to beat me up."

Finally, legal agencies have in recent years provided less support for parents. Social-work theory, heavily dependent on psychoanalytic theory, has tended to assume that the fault for child delinquencies lies with the parents and have given sanction and support to rebellious adolescents. Absence of the extended family, the virtual disappearance of the neighborhood as a unit for social control, and the unavailability of community support have increased the difficulty of adequately enacting the socialization role.

Changes in the Housekeeper Role

Housekeeper and child-care and socialization roles have located the woman in the family house or apartment; the employee role has drawn her to the office and factory. The process of shifting the tasks in the housekeeper role to special organizations is a gradual but ever-continuing one. The past two decades have seen most of the food processing shifted from the kitchen to the factory. No longer do carrots come in ten-pound bags, complete with dirt, tops, and hairy roots. They have been trimmed, washed and scrubbed, ready for the pot. Clothing manufacturing, canning, baking, and dry-cleaning departed to specialized agencies some time ago. Here and there a housewife "counterattacks" with home baking, canning, and making her own or her

---

[19]Jessie Bernard, "The Status of Women in Modern Patterns of Culture," in *Marriage and the Family*, ed. by Jeffrey Hadden and Marie Borgatta (Itaska, Ill.: F. E. Peacock, 1969), p. 182.

children's clothing, but these are akin to sweeping back the ocean with a broom. Although rearguard skirmishes persist, the larger issues have been decided. Some wives devote as much time as ever to housekeeping, but they need not in order to achieve the same level of cleanliness achieved by their mothers. Each year more housekeeping tasks in a larger proportion of families migrate from the family to other specialized agencies. The crowded restaurants and the success of housecleaning companies dramatize the process.

The migration of housekeeping tasks is slowed by the lack of day-care facilities for preschool children. If the wife must stay in the house to tend children, she can perform several housekeeping tasks during the day. If adequate day-care facilities become available, the attenuation of the housekeeper role is likely to increase.

This is not to depreciate the housekeeper role. It is still important for most wives and their families, but it will become less critical each year.

Changes in Women's Sexual Role

Women have always had a responsibility to be sexually available to their husbands. This has been a major part of their exchange for the economic support of a man for them and their children. However, with the advent of a sexual role for husbands, an element is added to that of wives. Wives must not only be available frequently, but they must *enjoy* participation; that is they should receive pleasure from foreplay and intercourse, because this (1) stimulates the husband and increases his pleasure directly and (2) provides evidence for him that he is enacting his sexual role well. Finally, with pleasure valued for itself, wives come to feel a duty to enjoy sex. The middle-class wife can reward her husband by giving evidence of enjoying sex or punish him by communicating indifference or distaste. (Chapter 13).

Emergent Familial Roles for Women

Reference has been made to two emergent roles for women: therapeutic and recreational. The therapeutic role for women appears to be clearly recognized, at least in the middle class. Women should listen to their husbands' frustrations, serve as a "sounding board" for their novel ideas, build them up when they are discouraged, and reassure them when they feel insecure. In fact, some wives give this role as a reason for not taking employment. Whether this is indeed their principal reason, or whether they don't wish to take paid employment for other reasons, is not obvious. It is not currently clear whether lower-class couples see the therapeutic role for themselves.

The nature of emergent female roles in family recreation is less clear. Recreation is now considered an important family activity. Foote wrote as early as 1954,"Family living in the residential suburb has come to

258

consist almost entirely of play." He explains what might seem an extreme statement by continuing, "Popular recognition of this *fait accompli* is only partial because of ambiguities in distinguishing work from play. The do-it-yourself movement, for example, is a pleasant simulation of work; it is amateur, unpaid and usually far from efficient, however skillful and productive."[20]

Research evidence of the importance of pair recreation has been furnished by Blood and Wolfe. "In Detroit, 48 per cent of wives choose companionship in doing things together with the husband as the most valuable aspect of marriage. This far outstrips the other four aspects—love, understanding, standard of living, and the chance to have children. Love is a poor second, with only 27 per cent of first choices."[21] Although companionship in doing things with the husband is not a precise definition of joint recreation, their data suggest that such joint recreation is important to most wives. Also relevant to the present discussion was Blood and Wolfe's finding that recreation ranked second as a subject for disagreements between husband and wife.[22]

The above suggests that recreation is highly valued activity and that it is one in which there is a lack of consensus concerning the roles of husband and wife. Husbands probably place a lower value on joint husband-wife recreation because other forms of recreation are more readily available to them than to their wives.

Emphasis on similar recreational interests does not seem to be a crucial basis for arriving at a decision to marry. A possible reason for this lack of concern with different recreational interests is that at this stage the euphoria of romance and sexual stimulation result in couples' concluding that recreation "consists" of being together.

At present, it can only be stated with some confidence that recreation is a highly valued activity and that for wives, at least, joint recreation with their husbands is especially valued. Couples are pursuing recreational interests partly together, partly individually, largely but not entirely through one-sex groups such as bridge clubs, bowling leagues, and so on. If joint recreation is a necessity for the continuation of marriage, then large and frequent compromises are necessary; if not, then spouses will increasingly pursue individual recreational interests. Finally, if wives value joint recreation more than do their husbands, then they will make more of the compromises. One older woman, when her skill and enthusiasm for fishing drew complimentary notice,

---

[20]Nelson Foote, "Family Living as Play," revision of a paper read before the National Council on Family Relations, Oakland, Calif., July 1954.

[21]Robert O. Blood and Donald M. Wolfe, *Husbands and Wives* (New York: The Free Press, Paperback Edition, 1965), p. 150.

[22]Ibid., p. 241.

explained, "I found I had either to take up fishing or find a new husband, so I took up fishing."

Social Class and Emergent Roles

Several emergent roles have been offered as hypotheses—sexual for husbands and therapeutic and recreational for both husbands and wives. Most of the indications of these emergent roles are from middle-class families. There also is some research evidence indicating a relative absence of such role-playing in the lower class. Komarovsky found that in blue-collar marriages, discussion of problems between husband and wife are rare. Instead they consult with siblings, parents, or even unrelated persons of their own sex rather than with their spouse.[23] Likewise, with the sexual intercourse role for the husband, Rainwater found that a minority (37 per cent) of lower-lower-class men mentioned the desirability of sexual gratification for the wife, whereas 85 per cent of Protestant and 46 per cent of Catholic middle- and upper-lower-class husbands did so. An even larger difference was shown among husbands who mentioned a specific disinterest in whether the wife experienced sexual gratification: 39 per cent of the lower-lower class compared to only 3 per cent of the higher-class Protestants and 11 per cent of higher-class Catholics.[24] Rainwater's data also show that the sexual intercourse role for the husband seems to be emerging earlier in Protestant than in Catholic families.

The Interchangeability of Familial Roles

If one examines the bases for the division of labor (roles) between men and women, he sees two bases for it: (1) Women average less in physical strength than men, and especially is this true during the latter months of pregnancy, and (2) women provide the milk that has been required by small babies down through the ages. Thus, it was less efficient for women to hunt, make war, or do work requiring the heaviest physical labor, and it was efficient for them to care for the young infants that they nourished.

Technical advances have diminished the significance of these differences. Machines have made it possible for women to occupy almost any job or profession and presumably to discharge the duties as

[23]Mirra Komarovsky, *Blue Collar Marriage* (New York: Random House, 1962), Chapters 5, 6, and 7, pp. 112–177.

[24]Lee Rainwater, *Family Design* (Chicago: Aldine Publishing Company, 1965), p. 104. Rainwater's sample of lower-lower-class couples was too small to analyze by religion.

effectively as men. At the same time, the development of adequate formulas to replace the mother's milk makes it possible for a man to feed and care for babies. As a result, family roles can be enacted in three different ways: (1) the segregation of some roles, such as child care and housekeeping, to the woman, provider to the man, and child socialization shared; (2) the sharing of all tasks, with the woman sharing in providing and the husband in housekeeping and child care, and (3) interchangeability or substitutability of role players, in which one parent may enact a role or some task within it for a time, then the other carries it for a time. All three are possible and all have their adherents in a technologically advanced society.

Those who strongly defend a highly segregated family-role pattern still see some biological tie to the roles each sex has occupied in the past—that there is some inborn "need" for women to bear and care for children and for men to provide the material sustenance for the family. Because this assumes a tie between the role and the biological nature of men and women, they fear that women will cease to be feminine if they hold responsible positions or men masculine if they discharge housekeeping tasks. Finally, there is concern whether a blurring of familial roles will reduce sexual interest.

Shared Familial Roles

The second pattern involves sharing responsibility for some familial roles. For example, the wife's contributing to family income by taking paid employment, the husband's performing some of the housekeeper and child-care tasks. This pattern has received much support from some educators who see in it both a democratic family pattern and one characterized by the intimacy of sharing tasks. Rainwater has presented data that show more pleasure in sexual intercourse between spouses who share family tasks and a higher proportion who are satisfied with their spouse.[25] Other proponents see role-sharing as the only equalitarian family pattern. They feel that each spouse should share in the tasks of each role—in its stresses, boredom, challenges, and rewards. This pattern, if carried out fully, would place equal responsibility on the spouses for earning income, child-care and socialization, and housekeeping tasks.

Although it seems possible to share all roles in this manner, spouses sometimes try to practice it with respect to some, but not all, roles. Thus, in the Soviet Union, women are encouraged to take full-time employment—sharing the provider role—but still are expected to discharge the housekeeper role without participation by the husband.[26]

---

[25]Ibid., pp. 61–117.
[26]David R. Mace, "The Employed Mother in the USSR," *Marriage and Family Living*, **23** (Nov. 1961), pp. 325–330.

In American society, wives who do not share the provider role may still expect their husbands to "do their share" of caring for the baby, assisting in the kitchen, or cleaning the house.

Bott has found a relationship between the degree of role segregation between spouses and the closeness of their relationships with relatives outside the conjugal family: "Those families that had a high degree of segregation in the role relationship of husband and wife had a close-knit network; many of their friends, neighbors, and relatives knew one another. Families that had a relatively joint role-relationship between husband and wife had a loose-knit network; few of their relatives, neighbors and friends knew one another."[27] Bott offers two explanations for her findings. First, if spouses are in close interaction with a network of friends and relatives (who are, in turn, in interaction with each other), this provides an effective reference group that can and does exert pressure on its members to follow traditional role definitions. These role definitions follow a segregated pattern with some things being "women's work," others the responsibility of men alone. Infrequent interaction with a less integrated network of people does not provide such social control. Second, Botts suggests that frequent, intimate interaction with kin and friends outside the conjugal group provides some of the services and some of the emotional needs of spouses so that they are less dependent on each other and interact less intensively with each other. Whether these are the only explanations or not, joint or shared role patterns and loose kin-friend networks are characteristic of mobile, industrial societies and appear likely to become increasingly characteristic of such societies.

Substitutable Roles
Substitution in familial roles has always occurred in emergencies. During severe economic depressions, men lose their jobs and the wife earns the family income, as she usually does if she is widowed or divorced. During the illness or absence of the wife, the husband enacts the housekeeping and child-care roles. Such substitutions, however, are accomplished with considerable difficulty, partly because one is socialized for some but not other familial roles. Rossi argues for complete socialization for both sexes ". . . if boys and girls took child care, nursing, cooking, shop and craft classes together, they would have an equal opportunity to acquire comparable skills and pave the way for true parental substitutability as adults. They should be learning something of how to complement each other, not just how to compete with each other."[28] She proposes that if each sex possessed some com-

[27]Elizabeth Bott, *Family and Social Network* (London: Tavistock Publications Limited, 1957), p. 59.
[28]Rossi, op. cit., p. 645.

petency in all roles the crises of death, divorce, separation, or illness would be less traumatic, because each could function with some adequacy in the roles customarily enacted by the spouse.

Substitutability has special relevance to a society that now forbids discrimination against women in employment or in training leading to employment. Unless present trends toward economic differentiation are entirely reversed, an ever-increasing proportion of wives will participate in the economic support of the family, while husbands reciprocate by sharing housekeeping and child-care duties. In a growing proportion of families the wife will be the principal provider and the husband may take principal responsibility for housekeeping tasks. However, it seems likely that both would share both sets of roles unless one is severely incapacitated. This role reversal is likely to be minimized, however, by the migration of housekeeping and child-care tasks to specialized agencies external to the family (Chapter 24).

Role Conflict

A rapidly changing society can be expected to be characterized by role conflict as individuals and groups experiment with new patterns of behavior. Conflict enters at two points: (1) variations in definition of appropriate behavior in the enactment of a given role, *intrarole conflict,* and (2) conflicts between the responsibilities of two roles, *interrole conflict.*

Intrarole Conflict

Let us first review intrarole conflict—consisting of a different perceptions of appropriate behavior within a role. There appear to be two principal reasons for it. First, roles are defined by subgroups within a society as well as by the society as a whole (Chapter 1). Thus, the Catholic Church can proscribe most means of birth control in the sexual role whereas the remainder of American society approves their use. Therefore, when Catholics, Protestants, and Jews intermarry they usually find that they are defining some of their familial roles differently. Second, although roles prescribe that duties must be performed, they do not specify how they should be performed. For example, parents must socialize their children but they may do so with strict discipline or a permissive pattern, with corporal punishment or through love-oriented techniques. Consequently, there are many possibilities for conflicting perceptions of the appropriate enactment of a given role. Finally, it is relevant that individuals endeavor to minimize their costs and maximize their rewards in human interaction. Therefore, ambiguities are likely to be interpreted by each so as to delegate the tiring, boring, or frustrating tasks to the spouse and to maximize pleasant, stimulating, and rewarding activities for oneself.

Interrole Conflict

Two general bases for interrole conflict will be briefly explored: (1) normative prescriptions of responsibilities for one position that conflict with those prescribed for another and (2) patterns of role enactment by individuals that produce role conflict.

An example of the first is found in the conflict of the responsibilities of the provider with those of a mother with preschool children. The job requires her presence in the office, the child requires her presence in her house. The conflict must, of course, be resolved by a substitute caretaker: a day-care center, a neighbor, or a relative. Societies generally do not assign contradictory roles to any class of persons. The provider role is not (yet, at least) prescribed to mothers of young children. If they become employees, they take both the initiative for doing so and the responsibility of obtaining child care while they are at work.

In periods of crisis in a society or during very rapid change, a society sometimes does assign contradictory roles to classes of individuals. For example, in World War II, young fathers were drafted. Basic armed-forces pay rates were insufficient for supporting a family. Family allowances and an inexpensive insurance were provided to help these fathers meet their provider roles, but nothing could be done to enable them to discharge their child-socialization roles. Currently, American society faces a dilemma in assigning the provider role to widowed and divorced mothers of young children.[29] If the father is dead, unavailable, or inadequate, who should provide for the children? In earlier days, the extended family would have done so, but it has scattered and the modern nuclear family is ill equipped to house and care for a second family. Initially, society's reaction was governmental aid to dependent children—the state, in effect, assuming the role of provider. However, the state provides unwillingly and only at a subsistence level. To rid itself of the provider role, the federal government has recently legislated vocational training for women who are heads of families and the subsidizing of day care for the children of mothers supported by governmental aid to the families of dependent children, provided the mother can and will take employment. The future of the provider role for families headed by females is not clear, but it appears likely that the mother will be encouraged to assume the provider role with some

[29]Erdman Palmore, Gertrude L. Stanley, and Robert H. Cormier, *Widows with Children Under Social Security,* U.S. Department of Health, Education, and Welfare, Social Security Administration, Office of Research and Statistics, Research Report No. 16 (Washington, D.C.: U.S. Government Printing Office, 1966).

subsidization by the society. In Sweden this model has been developed but with stringent provisions for contributions of absent fathers as well as by the mother.[30] If this direction of change continues, women who are heads of families will enact the provider role.

A second major source of interrole conflict stems from unusual role enactment by individuals. For example, most offices, factories, and businesses currently operate in the United States on an eight-hour day and a five-day week. The employee role preempts these hours. If a wife asks her husband to come home to help her with child care or household tasks during that period, she creates role conflict for him. In effect, time committed to that role would be withheld from it. The reverse seems to be true although less obvious. If a husband's work day is from 8:00 A.M. to 5:00 P.M. it is assumed that after 5:00 P.M. he is available for child-socialization and recreational roles. The man who stays at or returns to the office in the evening is removing time from those roles to add it to the provider role. Such statements must be qualified somewhat in that some occupations lend themselves less well to fixed, limited hours. However, interrole conflict most frequently seems to be attributable to unusual enactment of one role that, in effect, then infringes on the time or resources normatively available to another role. Even so, role enactment may be more effective if it can include an element of flexibility so that the person can occasionally respond to some unusual requirement of a role even though it causes temporary confusion or neglect in another role.

Some Patterns in Role-Playing

We have examined seven familial roles: provider, housekeeper, sexual intercourse, therapeutic, recreation, child care, and child socialization. There are many differences in how they are perceived and in the motivation and the ability of family members to enact them. Too, they vary by family life cycle in that there are no child-care and socialization roles until there are children and little remains of these after children marry and establish their own families.

Kirkpatrick has described a number of distinctive constellations of feminine role-playing that emphasize some roles while largely ignoring others. In the following discussion we have elaborated somewhat on his formulation and have employed the concept *pattern* in place of *path.*[31]

---

[30] Alva Myrdal, *Nation and Family* (Cambridge: MIT Press, Paperback Edition, 1968), Chapter 18, "The Incomplete Family," pp. 327–338.
[31] For his original formulation , see Kirkpatrick, op cit., pp. 448–458.

Maternity-Homemaking Pattern

This pattern is the nearest to the continuation of the role enactment of families of earlier phases in the industrialization of the society. It implies a large family, personal care and socialization of children, the processing of food in the home rather than in the factory, and personal cleaning of the home. It is even more specific in what it *excludes* for the wife, that is, gainful employment. Role segregation is characteristic of this pattern, with the husband accepting the entire responsibility for providing for the family and the wife taking complete responsibility for the housekeeping and child-care roles. This pattern has been established long enough to acquire the reinforcement of tradition.

Companion Pattern

In this pattern the wife eliminates or minimizes maternal and economic productivity roles. Rather, it might be said that she stresses sexual, recreational, and therapeutic ones, devoting her time to personal attractiveness and centering her life about the interests and activities of her husband. She is available to participate in his recreational activities and to provide diversion and/or emotional support of compensatory or therapeutic types. From an economic point of view she is a "parasite," but her part in her husband's affectional and recreational life and in supplying therapy for his frustrations and insecurity may result in his valuing this pattern of role-playing by his wife.

Career Pattern

This is the opposite of the traditional maternity-homemaking pattern. It typically involves none or, at most, one or two children. Children are planned so as to interfere as little as possible with a career. Child supervision and care are shared with day-care facilities and baby sitters. Care of the house, clothing, and food preparation are shared as fully as possible with specialized businesses and/or nonfamily employees. The husband and children are likely to share some of the household tasks that noncareer wives perform.

Family-Plus-Partial-Career Pattern[32]

In the family-plus-partial-career pattern, priority is given to childbearing, child care, and housekeeping responsibilities in the home. However, in this pattern more of the housekeeping responsibilities are delegated to nonfamily agencies. When such agencies are inadequate or

---

[32]This represents a fusion of Kirkpatrick's fifth and sixth types, ibid., pp. 454–460. Kirkpatrick distinguishes two types on the basis of small or large families. We are disposed to think that family-plus-job would be a more precise identification of this pattern, because it usually lacks the full commitment that a career requires.

unavailable, the wife curtails or temporarily relinquishes her paid employment. Employment emphasizes addition to family income rather than a career. The wife's primary responsibility is to her child-care and housekeeper roles within the family, but she does not consider it necessary to perform all these tasks personally, only to see that they are adequately performed.

In terms of our role analysis, Kirkpatrick's *maternity-homemaking pattern* stresses housekeeper, child-care, and child-socialization roles. By emphasizing these, and not entering paid employment, these women avoid the "schizophrenia" of needing to be in their house and in an office at the same time, but they face eroding roles as housekeeper tasks move outside the home and as their children leave for school and, later, marriage.

The *companion pattern* stresses recreational, therapeutic, and sexual roles at the expense of the others, whereas the *career pattern* minimizes housekeeper, child-care, and child-socialization roles. It is not now clear how career wives enact their sexual and therapeutic roles. Research here would be welcome. The recreational role seems to be little affected except for formal entertaining, which is curtailed.[33]

Male Familial Role Patterns

No attempt to specify male familial role patterns comparable to Kirkpatrick's has been made and, indeed, there appears to be less diversity.[34] Many women now have a choice to enter or not to enter paid employment. No such legitimate choice exists for men, although a few voices have been heard asserting that work should be voluntary. Men have the provider role and it dominates their family responsibilities. However, considerable variation exists in how they enact the role, from working only enough to provide subsistence living to devoting virtually all their time and attention to this role. In a society that has attempted to limit the work week to forty hours, about 5 per cent of men "moonlight" by obtaining an additional part-time position. Such preoccupation with the provider role has sometimes resulted in the neglect of child-socialization and recreational and even sexual roles. However, it results in added income in which all family members share, so protests against it have not been general or insistent.

Research is yet to explain such "overcommitment" to the provider role, but several tentative explanations have been advanced. At lower-income levels, some men place a high value on having more luxuries than their primary salary or wage can provide. Also, in industrial

[33]Nye and Hoffman, op. cit., Chapter 25, "The Recreation and Community" pp. 363–371.

[34]One relevant discussion of paternal role behavior is provided by Leonard Benson, *Fatherhood: A Sociological Perspective* (New York: Random House, 1968).

societies, a man's worth is estimated largely from his income or the level of living it supports. To "succeed" is often interpreted in terms of how much one earns. The second job is instrumental to these goals. Another part of this group find their house and spouse relatively unattractive and prefer to spend more time away from them. This group of husbands is not limited to any class. Finally, in some executive and professional positions, the job itself furnishes rewards—intellectual challenge, high status, and power—so that a man is willing to invest a very large amount of his time in it even though he likes his home and has no special need for the added income.

Besides the provider role, the principal role choice for men seems to be in whether they will share in the tasks of the housekeeper and the child-care roles. These have been allocated to the wife, but it has become acceptable behavior for men to feed and change babies, and to do marketing and cooking. Whether this is also true for housecleaning and mending clothes is not clear. These seem to be the last tasks to stay specifically in the feminine domain. The picture of the husband in an apron with a dustpan in his hands is likely to suggest the ultimate in male subjugation and degredation!

The Future of Role Changes

The forecasting of social behavior is always hazardous and with that caution in mind, we offer three predictions: (1) the continued development of specialized organizations, mostly commercial but perhaps some governmental, that will perform an ever-increasing proportion of the tasks in the housekeeper, child-care, and child-socialization roles; (2) the gradual evolvement of a provider role for married women in which they will come to be expected to work in paid employment most if not all of their adult lives; and (3) a greater and greater sharing of all familial roles with an accompanying interchangeability of role enactment by spouses. These predictions will be discussed in more detail in the final chapter of the book.

11
The Employed Mother and Her Family

The latter half of the twentieth century has witnessed the emergence of a new role for the mother, that of provider. Her entry into this role has not been an easy or painless one. It has been denounced by politicians, civic leaders, nonemployed women, and psychiatrists. Many, if not most, employed mothers themselves have been ambivalent and sometimes felt guilty concerning enacting a new role that competes so strongly at points with the responsibilities for child or household care traditionally assigned to them.

THE CULTURAL SETTING The provider role for women who have minor children has been considered a recent development, but this is only partially true. Anthropologists' reports show that women typically secure part of the goods that their families require. However, in preliterate societies, mothers usually take their children to the place the mother works or the extended family provides convenient supervision by grandparents, aunts, or older siblings. Even in modern Western societies, employment of mothers outside the home has a long history. Such labor manned the early factories until labor legislation made the cheap labor of women and children unavailable or less attractive. Klein shows clearly that in blue-collar occupations, the mother has never been fully "emancipated" from the factory job.[1]

Even so, the cultural setting has changed rapidly in the past fifty years. The rapid development of labor-saving equipment in industry and the growth of clerical and sales occupations and of educational and health institutions have created many occupations that can be performed as well by women as by men. Employers prefer an intelligent and well-educated woman to an incompetent man. This preference has

[1]Viola Klein, *Britain's Married Women Workers* (London: Routledge & Kegan Paul; New York: Humanities Press, 1965), Chapter 1, pp. 1–20.

269

resulted in the necessary conditions for the employment of larger numbers of women—that is, the demand for their labor.

At the same time, service establishments such as laundries, cleaning establishments, bakeries, canning establishments, and restaurants have been taking over more of the tasks that had been much of the economic contribution of the wife. In turn, each of these services has provided more employment for women and has placed an added strain on the husband's income. Effective contraception has brought smaller families, with the child-bearing period limited to a few years.

Many women have felt underemployed and undercompensated for economic activities in the home. One highly trained women said, "Certainly, I can earn about six cents an hour baking bread or canning, but I can earn ten dollars an hour conducting research." Finally, certain ideological beliefs in the equality of the sexes and the right of each person to make his maximum contribution to society have produced a relatively favorable social milieu for the married women who find the prospect of earning a salary attractive.

Trends in Paid Employment of Mothers[2]

It is important that one not confuse the increase in the occupancy of the provider role by women in general with occupancy by women who are mothers. If one looks at the former for a twenty-nine year period (1940–1969), he observes only a moderate increase in the employment of women (26 to 43 per cent)—interesting perhaps but probably nothing about which to become excited. However, the change in the proportion of wives employed (husbands present) more than doubled proportionately in the same years from 15 to 40 per cent, and if one looks at the data for married women (husbands present) who were mothers *with children* aged six to eighteen, the percentage in paid employment increased from an estimated 9 per cent in 1940 to 52 per cent in 1970, a gain of over 500 per cent, based on the earlier figure (Table 11.1). So, the change is less in the proportion of women in paid employment than in the proportion of women who are simultaneously occupying the roles encompassed in the mother position and those of the provider or paid employee—a combination of roles until recently considered to be incompatible.

The rapid increase in the proportion of mothers in employment holds also for those with children under six years of age. In 1948, it was

---

[2]Trend data reported here are taken from F. Ivan Nye and Lois Wladis Hoffman, *The Employed Mother in America* (Chicago: Rand McNally & Co., 1963), Chapter 1, unless otherwise indicated, pp. 3–17.

270

Table 11.1
Women in the Labor Force, 1940–1970

Marital Status	Employed Women							
	1940	1944	1948	1952	1955	1958	1960	1970
	Number (Millions)							
Single	6.7	7.5	5.9	5.5	5.1	5.4	5.4	7.0
married, living with husband	4.2[1]	6.2	7.6	9.2	10.4	11.8	12.3	18.4
No children under 18	2.7		4.4	5.0	5.2	5.7	5.7	8.2
Children 6–17 only		[2]	1.9	2.5	3.2	3.7	4.1	6.3
	1.5[1]							
Children 0–5		[2]	1.2	1.7	2.0	2.4	2.5	4.0
Widowed, divorced, living apart	2.9	4.7	3.7	4.1	4.6	4.8	4.9	4.5
All women	13.9	18.5	17.2	18.8	20.1	22.0	22.6	31.5
	Per Cent							
Single	48.1	58.6	51.1	50.0	46.6	45.4	44.1	53.0
Married, living with husband	14.7	21.7	22.0	25.3	27.7	30.2	30.5	42.6
No children under 18			28.4	30.9	32.7	38.8	34.7	42.2
Children 6–17 only			26.0	31.1	34.7	37.6	39.0	52.0
	8.6[1]	[2]						
Children 0–5			10.7	13.9	16.0	18.2	18.6	32.0
Widowed, divorced, living apart	35.4	42.0	38.3	38.8	38.5	40.8	40.0	36.2
All women	25.7	35.0	31.0	32.7	33.4	35.0	34.8	42.6

[1]Estimated.
[2]No information available.
SOURCES: Nye and Hoffman, op. cit., and *Statistical Abstract of the United States,* 1971, pp. 212–13.

11 per cent, in 1970 it was 32 per cent,[3] a gain of 300 per cent in 22 years. This is a larger gain proportionately for mothers of preschool children than for mothers of school-age children only, who gained from 26 to 51 per cent during the same twenty-two-year period. Thus, women with preschool children (husbands present) are only 60 per cent as likely to be providers for their families as are those whose children are of school age, but the trend since 1948 is for these women

[3]*Statistical Abstract of the United States,* 1971, pp. 212–213.

to enter the labor force at an even more rapid rate proportionately than those with older children only.

SINGLE WOMEN IN PROVIDER ROLES One category of women has changed little in the labor force, that is, never-married women. In 1940 there were 6.7 million of them, by 1970 there were only 7.0 million. As the reader may know, the marriage rate increased greatly during that period and there was a smaller proportion of women of employable age who were not married in 1970. Even of those who had remained single, a smaller proportion were employed, reflecting the smaller proportion of *younger* never-married women.

Greater proportions of widowed, divorced, and separated women have always been found in paid employment for obvious economic reasons. This proportion changed little from 1940 to 1970. Even a generation ago there was essential consensus that women who were heads of families should be allowed to gain paid employment if they possessed the necessary skills. For example, in 1970, of women living with husbands, 43 per cent were in the labor force, but of those separated, 54 per cent, and of those divorced, 72 per cent were working.[4] Of women living with husbands, most can choose whether or not to become providers; most of those without a husband cannot.

TYPES OF POSITIONS The kind of job as well as the proportion of wife-mothers employed has changed tremendously in the past six decades. In 1900, 19 per cent of all employed women were farm laborers or owners and managers; in 1971 it was 2 per cent. Then, only 4 per cent of women worked as clerks and in kindred occupations; in 1971, 34 per cent did so. Other jobs more common now than then include sales workers, service workers, and professional, technical, and kindred workers. Private household workers decreased greatly from 29 to 6 per cent (Table 11.2).[5]

It is significant, with respect to the place of women in the occupational structure of the society, that the proportion of women employed in professions has not increased greatly since 1900 and not at all since 1930. The assertion that men have careers but women have jobs gains some support from these figures. The failure to enter the professions in larger proportions, also casts some doubt on the expectation that women will, in the forseeable future, develop occupational equality with men, although there are current developments in legal equality, in contraceptives, and in attitudes toward large families that could eventually change this. These developments will be discussed in other chapters.

---

[4]Ibid., p. 8.
[5]Ibid., p. 13.

Table 11.2
Occupations of the Employed Female Population for the United States, 1900–1971

	Women Working							
Occupation	*1900*	*1910*	*1920*	*1930*	*1940*	*1950*	*1960*	*1971*
					Per Cent			
Professional, technical, and kindred workers	8.1	9.7	11.6	13.4	12.7	12.2	13.3	14.8
Farmers and farm managers	5.8	3.7	3.2	2.4	1.2	0.7	0.4	*
Managers, officials, and proprietors, exc. farm	1.4	2.0	2.2	2.7	3.2	4.3	4.6	4.9
Clerical and kindred workers	4.0	9.2	18.6	20.8	21.4	27.4	30.0	34.0
Sales workers	4.3	5.1	6.2	6.8	7.3	8.6	7.2	7.2
Craftsmen, foremen, and kindred workers	1.4	1.4	1.2	1.0	1.1	1.5	0.9	1.3
Operatives and kindred workers	23.8	22.9	20.2	17.4	19.5	19.9	16.1	12.9
Private household workers	28.7	24.0	15.7	17.8	18.1	8.8	9.8	22.3†
Service workers, exc. private household	6.7	8.4	8.1	9.7	11.3	12.6	15.4	
Farm laborers and foremen	13.1	12.0	10.3	5.9	2.7	2.9	2.0	1.7
Laborers, exc. farm and mine	2.6	1.4	2.3	1.5	1.1	.8	0.3	0.8
Total	99.9	99.9	100.0	100.0	100.0	99.9	100.0	99.9

*Data not available.
†In this enumeration, private household is combined with service workers. The total proportion in the two categories declined by about 10 per cent for the period 1960–1971.
SOURCES: Nye and Hoffman, op. cit., and *Statistical Abstract of the United States, 1971*, p. 222.

Social Characteristics of Mothers Who Accept the Provider Role

AGE OF CHILDREN Mothers with children below school age are much less likely to be employed. Proportionately only 60 per cent as many are providers as those all of whose children are six or older.

NUMBER OF CHILDREN It will come as no surprise that the smaller the family the more likely is the mother to be employed. In a large study conducted by Nye, mothers with only one child were overrepresented in paid employment by over 100 per cent and mothers with two children were also employed disproportionately. Those with three children were in the labor force in proportion to their numbers, whereas mothers with four or more children were employed in appreciably smaller numbers than their proportion in the general population.

The influence of the age of the youngest child and the number of children on whether the mother becomes a provider may be even greater than the data would suggest, because large families are more frequently found in the lowest income categories, where presumably the need for the income of the mother is the greatest. However, the education of the mother is also correlated with the size of the family and employment is more easily obtained by educated women. These two factors, then, tend to cancel each other and we are left with a considerable negative association between family size and paid employment. This association is most readily explainable in terms of the greater responsibilities of the mother as a housekeeper and a supervisor of her children. Her community responsibilities may also be greater, as well as demands on her time for recreational participation. Social pressure against her finding paid employment is also greater. This could be stated as a proposition: *The larger the number of children living at home, the less likely is the wife to be in paid employment.*

EDUCATION AND THE PROVIDER ROLE To the best of current knowledge, employed mothers of earlier periods were likely to be poorly educated. This fact is inferred because the most poorly educated men were the most likely to be unemployed, necessitating the employment of their wives. The jobs available to women in earlier days—household labor and agricultural work—required little or no education. Whether the implication is correct or not, the fact is that employed mothers currently average more education than mothers not employed. Disproportionately few mothers with less than eight years of schooling are employed. The disappearance of unskilled jobs has left the uneducated women with few employment opportunities. One wrote on her research questionnaire, "I'd like to have a job, but I don't know how to do anything." All studies show that a disproportionate number of mothers who have taken graduate work are employed. This could be stated as a proposition: *The more education completed by a married woman, the more likely is she to be employed full time.*

INCOME Most married women with employed husbands, when asked why they are working, reply that they have to for financial reasons. A more complete answer would be that unless they work they cannot have the level of living and security that they have with two incomes.

274

Table 11.3
Labor Force Participation Rates and Per Cent Distribution of Mothers (Husband Present), by Income of Husband in 1966 and Age of Children, March, 1967 (Mothers 16 years of age and over)

Income of Husband	Per Cent of Mothers in Labor Force with Children—			Per Cent Distribution of Mothers in Labor Force with Children—		
	Under 18 Years	6–17 Years Only	Under 6 Years*	Under 18 Years	6–17 Years Only	Under 6 Years*
Total..........................	35.3	45.0	26.5	8,750,000	5,269,000	3,481,000
				100.0	100.0	100.0
Under $1,000................	44.3	52.3	35.3	2.6	2.8	2.4
$1,000 to $1,999...........	38.5	45.9	31.4	3.1	3.0	3.3
$2,000 to $2,999...........	39.5	50.8	31.3	4.9	4.4	5.7
$3,000 to $4,999...........	41.9	52.0	34.5	18.3	15.9	22.0
$5,000 to $6,999...........	39.4	50.0	31.6	28.1	25.1	32.6
$7,000 to $9,999...........	33.8	46.9	21.9	27.7	30.4	23.6
$10,000 and over...........	25.4	32.9	15.7	15.2	18.4	10.4

*Also may have older children.
SOURCE: U.S. Department of Labor, Bureau of Labor Statistics, Special Labor Force Report No. 94.

The issue, however, is not a simple one. The highest proportion of employed wives is found at the lowest income level but the proportion does not decline substantially until the husband's income exceeds the median level $7,000 to $10,000 in 1967 (Table 11.3).

The highest proportion of wives employed (1967) was of those with husbands earning less than $1,000, but the proportion is virtually as high for those earning $5,000 to $7,000. Stated another way, the median income of husbands whose wives were *not* in the labor force was about $900 greater than those whose wives were in paid employment.

If there are no children under eighteen, there is no consistent relationship between the income of the husband and the likelihood that his wife will be employed. One is about as likely to find the wife of a man earning over $10,000 employed as of one earning $2,000. When children are in the home, the income of the husband does make a difference. After it reaches $7,000 the mother is less likely to be employed, but the decline is not great until above $10,000 if there are no children present below the age of six years.

It is apparent that several variables are interacting. One of these is needs: economic, status, intellectual, and social. Low- or no-income families need income for food, rent, clothing, medical care, and so on. This has been termed chronic economic need. Some 25 per cent of employed mothers are the sole support of their families—perhaps another 10 per cent are the principal support. Beyond this chronic need are the felt needs of family members for the optional goods, services, and experiences of an affluent society: not just living, but "gracious living." There is no limit to the income that is useful in the pursuit of the good life. It has been reported that many families receiving incomes of over $100,000 per year live a somewhat precarious existence, as income is not always equal to expenditures. Granted that this is true, the proportion of wives in the provider role declines sharply as the husbands' incomes approach the upper 10 per cent of incomes. For one thing, the wife's income is likely to add a smaller fraction to his as his income increases. Also, increases in income, although desired at any income level, appear to provide less motivation as incomes become higher. The difference between an income of $5,000 and one of $8,000 may be a very important one to a family, but the difference between $25,000 and $28,000 is likely to mean much less.

However, even if both chronic need and the desire for the good life are considered, it would seem likely that the wife would be most likely to be employed at the lowest income level, whereas the fact is that is not especially the case. The answer lies in the employer's needs. In general, *he* wants a trained and capable woman. Such women are more likely to be married to trained and capable men—men who are regularly employed and earning above the lowest levels. These women are likely to have positions available to them. If they do not have small children and if their husbands are not in the highest income brackets, the prospect often is attractive. .

AGE It is paradoxical that the highest proportion of mothers are providers at a time when they have the most children at home, between the ages of thirty-five and forty-four. Of course, this is not a time when many preschool children are at home. Their presence is a strongly retarding influence. Employment levels are high for women from age twenty to fifty-five. Why there is a decrease beyond fifty-five is not obvious. Surveys have shown that employers express a preference in employing women between the ages of twenty-one and forty-five. However, many women voluntarily leave the labor force after age forty-five. With children grown and financial responsibilities lightened, it may be that those women who have never enjoyed paid employment take the opportunity to leave it. At any rate, the common-sense notion that after children are grown is the time when women typically reenter the labor force is incorrect. Apparently, they have fewer motivations to do so and employers are less eager to employ them.

RACE There has never been a time in American society in which the Negro mother was not in the labor force; during the slavery period, the Reconstruction, or the contemporary period. The high rate of unemployment and the intermittent employment for Negro men have resulted in a larger proportion of Negro women functioning as heads of households. When the Negro father is employed, he typically earns a fraction of the amount paid white employees. For Negro families to share in the luxuries as well as the necessities of life it is more likely that two wage earners will be required.

These higher unemployment rates and the low stipends paid employed Negro men are reflected in the higher employment rates of Negro women. Sixty-one per cent of all nonwhite women with children six to seventeen were employed in 1971 compared with 51 per cent of white women. For those with children under the age of six, the proportion employed was 47 per cent for Negroes, 29 per cent for whites.[6]

A Theory of Work Commitment

Sobol, an economist, developed a theory of work commitment that integrates some of the social variables that have been discussed. Three concepts are employed to explain why a wife is likely to be in paid

---

[6]U.S. Department of Labor, *1969 Handbook on Women Workers,* Women's Bureau Bulletin 294, U.S. Government Printing Office, Washington, 1969, p. 42.

employment. The first concept is of *enabling conditions,* which make it relatively easy for a wife to perform her intrafamilial roles, such as housekeeper and socializer of children, while also performing the duties of a paid employee. These enabling conditions include having no children or at least none of preschool age. If preschool-age children are present, good day-care facilities are necessary. A permissive or supportive attitude on the part of the husband would also be necessary.

The second category of conditions are called *facilitating conditions,* those that make the woman attractive as an employee. These include advanced education, previous work experience, location in an urban area or another area in which employing industries are located. The third set are *precipitating conditions,* those that lead a woman to want to become employed. Sobol asked each woman her principal reason for taking employment and classified the answers as follows: chronic or temporary financial problems, 40 per cent; need to acquire assets, 37 per cent; felt need for accomplishment, 12 per cent; need to occupy time and meet people, 7 per cent; and need to work in a family business, 3 per cent. Sobol found that an even larger proportion of the younger wives planned to work than the proportion who were currently working.[7]

SUMMARY OF TRENDS Although women are continuing to enter the Labor Force at only a moderately increasing pace, from 26 per cent in 1940 to 43 per cent in 1971, the entry of married women with children under eighteen into employment has increased at a dramatic rate of over 500 per cent in that 31-year period. In 1971 more than half of the mothers with children between the ages of six and seventeen were employed at any given time. The proportion was 60 per cent as great for mothers with children under the age of six, but the rate of increase was larger for the mothers of younger children. The women employed in the highest proportions are the better-educated women married to employed men. These figures, added to the fact that this phenomenon has taken place during three decades of unprecedented prosperity, suggest that the *increase* is explained by women's being *drawn* into employment rather than forced into it.

Issues and Problems

After World War II when it became evident that the employed mother was a permanent and major aspect of family life, a number of serious social and personal problems were attributed to her new role as provider. Of these, perhaps none was a more serious or persistent

[7]Marion G. Sobol, "Commitment to Work," Chapter 3 in Nye and Hoffman, op. cit.

charge than that the increase of juvenile delinquency was caused by the increasing proportion of mothers in paid employment. Data collected by the Federal Bureau of Investigation indicated increases in juvenile delinquency of 6 to 10 per cent per year. With somewhat larger increases in the proportion of mothers employed, it is not surprising that the increases in delinquency were attributed to the demanding duties of her role as a provider.

Several associated facts may have made the employed mother an attractive explanation for increased delinquency. First, the employed mother made a major change in family patterns and such changes are automatically suspect, as most people confuse what has been with what ought to be. Second, employed mothers challenge the status of nonemployed mothers. For many years their household roles been eroding, because of smaller families and the fact that more food processing and clothing manufacture take place outside the family. Nonemployed mothers may react as much to this challenge to their status as to the undesirable effects on children or family stability. Also, men who face women's competition for their jobs and husbands who find their employed wives increasingly independent have reacted to the employed wife.

Another question posed with respect to the mother as a provider was that of her effect on family stability—or more precisely, on the divorce rate. Divorce had been on the increase (with minor fluctuations) since the first systematic records were accumulated late in the nineteenth century. During the decade of 1950–1960 it stood at just under one marriage in four and in 1970, one in three. Too high, many felt.

The broad issue encompasses several more specific ones, including the notion that the provider role of the wife is a psychological threat to her husband, which, in turn, assumes that husbands need to feel superior to and more powerful than their wives and children. Also raised is the question of whether occupying a provider role encourages masculine personality traits in the wife and leads her to become an aggressive and dominating person. Finally, and more obviously insofar as the general public is concerned, the question is raised of whether the employed mother necessarily neglects her roles as housekeeper, supervisor of children, recreational participant, and sexual partner to her husband.

If the physical demands of the role of housekeeper, supervisor of children, and recreational participant demand the full time and physical energy of the wife-mother, then it would follow that adding the demands of full-time employment overtaxes the time and the physical strength of the women. In generations past, when both housework and most paid employment involved more physical effort than is the case now, there was considerable evidence that the provider role provided a

279

hazard to the physical health of mothers.[8] However, it is not evident whether this continues to be true in an era in which the physical demands of both the home and the job typically are declining rapidly.

Impact on Other Family Roles[9]

It is apparent that women in ever-increasing numbers are electing to combine paid employment with their intrafamilial housekeeping, recreational, socialization, and child-care roles. The time has now arrived when more than half of all mothers with children aged six to seventeen (none under six) are in paid employment at any given time.

The important question then is not whether mothers should work while children are at home—because they are going to do so—but what effects their working has on their familial roles, and, ultimately on the lives of family members. This very broad question cannot be answered as completely as sociologists would like, yet the question has been the subject of both extensive and intensive research for several years and tentative answers can be provided.

Effects on Children

Because children are dependent on adults for fifteen or more years and because their immediate care has generally been assigned to the mother, the question most urgently asked is whether children are neglected when the mother leaves home for a full working day. This question can be considered in two ways: first, does the performance differ between children of employed mothers and those of nonemployed mothers? Specifically, do the children of employed mothers achieve less in school competition, do more of them become juvenile delinquents, do they have more mental health problems, and so on? The other assessment is in terms of the role behavior or attitudes of mothers and children: do the employed mothers and their children interact less, do the children perform more household tasks, do children confide less in working mothers, and so on? Both of these approaches have been researched by behavioral scientists.

School Performance

The results of studies of the performance of children have generally been reassuring to employed mothers, their families, and those sympathetic to them. In a large study by the senior author made in the state of

---

[8]Mabel A. Elliot and Francis E. Merrill, *Social Disorganization* (New York: Harper & Row, 1950), Chapter 11, "The Woman and Child in Industry," pp. 222–252.
[9]Data not otherwise identified are from Nye and Hoffman, op. cit., Chapters 4–14.

Washington in which several social variables were controlled, only small differences were found between the children of employed mothers and those not employed. Grades earned in school did not differ significantly, with the differences found in the sample actually favoring the children of the employed mothers. [10] In a study in a lower-class district of Detroit, Hoffman found that children of working mothers were less likely to perform well in academic work.[11] These findings permit two tentative conclusions: that performance doesn't differ in the middle class but does differ in the lower class.

Delinquency

Are sons of employed mothers more likely to be delinquent? Not much more likely, if at all. Again the social-class variable appears important. The senior author found in his middle-class families that a slightly smaller proportion of the sons of nonemployed mothers admitted delinquent behavior, but did not find this true in the lower-class sample.[12] Gold obtained similar results.[13] Glueck and Glueck in their research in a slum neighborhood found no differences in delinquent behavior of sons of mothers employed full time and those not employed.[14] Because the three researches are in agreement, it must be concluded that the boys of employed middle-class mothers are slightly more likely to be delinquent but that those of lower-class mothers are no more likely to be delinquent.

Why this should be so is not obvious to the authors. We offer the facts and invite the reader to formulate his own explanation. However, it should be emphasized that even in the middle class, the differences are slight and one *cannot* conclude that there is any appreciable rise in juvenile delinquency because of the employment of mothers.

How can this be so? Doesn't it matter whether the mother is in the home the whole day? Part of the answer lies in the fact that there are others to perform part of the child-care role. Most children of the age to perform delinquent acts are in school, where teachers and administrators perform the role of supervising the children. Working hours for the mother correspond quite closely with school hours. She is home evenings and weekends, as usually is her husband. Many agencies perform part of her role as housekeeper; and TV, movies, and peer groups provide considerable recreation for her children. In this milieu,

---

[10]Ibid., Chapter 10.

[11]Ibid., Chapter 6.

[12]Ibid., Chapter 10.

[13]M. A. Gold, *A Social Psychology of Delinquent Boys* (Ann Arbor, Mich.: Institute for Social Research, 1961).

[14]Sheldon and Eleanor Glueck, "Working Mothers and Delinquency," *Mental Hygiene,* **41** (July 1957), pp. 527–552.

the mother may take a full-time job without necessarily encountering serious problems in the performance of her other roles.

Mental Health

A lively controversy has raged concerning whether continuous contact during infancy with one mother figure is necessary for stable personality in children. If it is necessary, then the daily departure of the mother for employment outside the home while the child is young would cause personality damage. Perhaps the most articulate exponent of "maternal deprivation" has been Bowlby.[15] Research has not substantiated the hypothesis that there is any necessity for a child to be cared for by one woman. None of the current research found any measurable differences in symptoms of poor mental health in the children of employed and nonemployed mothers. The authors believe that it matters little who or how many people care for a child, provided it is given affection, stimulation, exercise, and adequate food and clothing. Of course if this is true, it still might follow that mothers are more likely to provide for those needs than are other women. The *quality* of the care of the child, whether by its mother or by someone else, appears to be the crucial variable.

Maternal Attitudes Toward Children

Does the employment of the mother affect her attitudes toward children? Nye employed an attitude-toward-children scale to obtain information on this point. Employed mothers were found to be notably less often made nervous or irritable by their children, to want more children than they had, and on the basis of total scores on the instrument, to be happier with their maternal roles than the nonemployed mothers.[16] This finding held true, however, only for mothers with four or less children. Hoffman found that the attitude of the mother toward her job was closely related to her attitudes and behavior toward her children. Those who enjoyed working were affectionate and companionable with their children.[17] In another study, Nye found that employed mothers were likely to be very close or somewhat distant from their adolescent children (adolescents' perception), whereas nonemployed mothers were more likely to be perceived as neither close affectionately nor distant.[18]

On the basis of somewhat less than complete evidence, the job often seems to act as a "safety valve" for the mother, reducing nervousness

[15]John Bowlby, *Child Care and the Growth of Love* (Geneva, Switzerland: World Health Organization, 1952).

[16]Nye and Hoffman, op. cit., Chapter 24.

[17]Ibid., Chapter 6.

[18]Ibid., Chapter 10.

and frustration, provided her employment is relatively free of such experiences.[19] For the mother who finds all her energy absorbed in caring for a large family or who dislikes her work, employment may create problems in the mother-child relationship.

Sharing Household Tasks

If the mother has a full-time job, it would seem reasonable that her husband and children share some of the housekeeping and other family duties. Both Hoffman and Douvan found that children of employed mothers were more likely to be given serious household responsibilities, especially children of lower-class families and children of mothers who did not enjoy their work outside the home. Nye found that husbands of middle-class working mothers were more likely to share household tasks, but that the children were not.[20] This reports contrasts to reports from the Soviet Union, where husbands are reported to feel no compunction in sharing in "women's tasks."[21] Douvan also reports that daughters of working mothers are more likely to have part-time paid jobs outside of the home. They appear to be more "work oriented" than those whose mothers are not in paid employment.[22]

It can be concluded that as American mothers occupy a provider role, other family members are likely to share some of the tasks she formerly performed alone. Will such responsibilities better prepare young girls for adult responsibilities? Are the household tasks that the husband shares therapeutic or do they only place an additional burden on him?

Parents as Models

Concern has been felt that mothers as providers confuse the role perceptions of children and increase the difficulty for the child in accepting the parent as a model. For boys this does not appear to be true in the middle-class part of the society. Douvan found that in this class, the sons of working mothers are as likely to choose their fathers as models as are those in families in which the mother is not employed.[23] Among boys in lower-class families, however, boys in families in which the mother is employed are less likely to choose their fathers as models. Douvan explains this by assuming that middle-class fathers are adequate providers (that is, that the mother works by choice), whereas

---

[19]Horace Gray, "The Trapped Housewife," *Marriage and Family Living,* **24** (May 1962), pp. 179–189.

[20]Nye and Hoffman, op. cit., Chapters 10 and 19.

[21]David Mace, "The Employed Mother in the U.S.S.R.," *Marriage and Family Living,* **23** (Nov. 1961), pp. 330–334.

[22]Elizabeth Douvan, "Employment and the Adolescent," in Nye and Hoffman, ibid., Chapter 11.

[23]Ibid., pp. 142–164.

283

lower-class mothers are forced into employment because of the inadequacy of the father. If this assumption is correct—and there is some evidence to support it[24]—then boys are less likely to choose their fathers because, in fact, they are inadequate providers. Because boys in middle-class families in which the mother is employed do choose their fathers as models, it appears that it is the performance of the father, rather than the employment status of the mother, that influences the choice.

Girls are *more* likely to choose an employed mother as a model at any class level. It appears that the employed mother is an attractive model for girls. Why this is true—whether such mothers are seen as having higher status, more authority, and autonomy in the family, whether they appear to lead more varied and interesting lives, or whether for other reasons—makes an intriguing question. However, most daughters seem to have little difficulty in accepting the provider role as a normal part of the life of the mother. It appears to be true that boys generally can accept their mother's employment also, provided their fathers are adequate providers and the mother is not forced into employment to meet the minimum needs of the family.

The Husband-Wife Relationship

Concern over the provider role of the mother with respect to husband-wife relationships has centered on three areas: the presumed neglect of the wife's other roles, especially care of the children and the house; the psychological threat to the husband as an adequate husband; and the threat to his position as the main locus of authority in the family. As a result of these problems it was thought that the stability of the family might be threatened.

The effects on children have already been reviewed. The results of the mother's employment seem generally not to be detrimental to her children. Employed mothers have generally been able to find competent substitutes for themselves and to satisfy the emotional needs of and maintain good relationships with their children. Furthermore, most mothers can move out of the labor force for periods of time when their families require their presence at home. However, there remain questions concerning how other roles might be affected.

[24]Some support for this assumption is provided by the fact that the children in working-class families with employed mothers are much more likely to mention financial problems as a principal problem. Also, current labor force data show that the median incomes of husbands of working wives are an average of $900 less per year than those of husbands of nonemployed women.

Recreation

It was assumed that the provider role would encroach especially on the mother's role as a recreational participant with her husband and children. It was assumed, perhaps unthinkingly, that recreational activities are viewed as relatively unimportant and would be sacrificed first.

One recreational activity—television viewing—is, indeed, sharply reduced, although employed mothers do not relinquish it completely. Another reduction is in the formal entertaining of other couples. Still another is in the amount of time spent by the mother in visiting in the neighborhood. It is significant for the study of the family that none of these reduced activities involve to any great extent other members of one's own family. Intrafamily recreation does not appear to be reduced, whether this involves games in the home, picnics, vacation trips, or visits to relatives. Nor are there appreciable differences in commercial recreation outside the home, such as movies, dancing, water sports, and other active sports. It appears that some nonfamilial recreation is curtailed sharply but not recreation with other family members, whether it takes place inside or outside the confines of the home. One is tempted to conclude that mothers as a whole have not regarded nonfamilial recreation very seriously and have placed a high priority on recreation that involves family interaction.[25]

Power and Authority

Studies have been made comparing the relative power in the family of employed and nonemployed mothers. Others have compared the power of the same mothers before and after employment.[26] In a rare instance of near-unanimity, social scientists agree that mothers who are providers exercise more influence in family decision-making. Perhaps this conclusion should not be surprising considering that the working mother plays an additional important role and that she has an additional alternative if the marital relationship should be entirely unsatisfactory to her.

The increase in the wife's power and authority brings the institution of the family closer to the goal of equality between husband and wife that is a widely verbalized value in American society and is increasingly discussed in other societies around the world. Whether either wives or husbands will like the emerging equality when its latent consequences become evident, one cannot be sure. The topic of power and authority will be explored more fully in Chapter 12.

[25]Nye and Hoffman, op. cit., Chapter 25, "Recreation and Community," pp. 363–371.
[26]David M. Heer, "Dominance and the Working Wife," Chapter 18, ibid., pp. 251–262.

Threat to Husband's Ego

The idea is frequently expressed that the husband will feel inadequate and hostile if his wife takes over part of the task of supporting the family. Such questions are difficult to research; however, some findings are relevant. Attitude studies have found fewer than the expected numbers of husbands opposed to the employment of their wives. In the Washington study, already alluded to, only 11 per cent of the husbands of employed mothers reported disapproval of their employment. Some husbands of nonworking wives reported that they would like their wives to enter paid employment.

Current information does not support the notion that husbands see the earnings of their wives as a threat to them. Part of this may be because most employed wives work in occupations inferior in status to those of their husbands and earn only a fraction of the salary. It may be that wives who earn more than their husbands may be a threat to their egos. If it is true, would the advantage of a wife's very large contribution to the family income compensate the husband for the insecurity feelings that it might produce?

Conflict

Frequent conflict is found in a larger proportion of marriages in which the mother is employed than in which she is not. Where measures of marital adjustment are employed, these combinations of behavior and attitudinal measures show conflict and negative affect more prevalent in marriages involving wives who are providers. This is true when such variables as social class, family size, the education of the wife, and previous marital status are controlled.[27]

Because several independent investigations have established that frequent conflict and dominant negative affect are found in more families with employed than nonemployed mothers, the intriguing question is why? Several hypotheses have been advanced. The first is *the selective factor hypothesis,* which states that conflict and negative affect between spouses lead to employment of the wife, rather than vice versa. One bit of evidence supports this hypothesis. Nye found that of the mothers not working who would like to be employed, a disproportionate share rated their marriages unsatisfactory.[28] Inferentially one other bit of evidence supports this hypothesis in that husbands of employed mothers average lower incomes than husbands of those not employed. Such lower earning power *might* be a cause of less satisfaction with the marriage.

Another type of selective factor hypothesis could be deduced from

---

[27]Nye and Hoffman, op. cit., Chapters 15, 19, 20.
[28]Nye and Hoffman, op. cit., Chapter 19.

Heer's findings that both employed mothers and their husbands tend to be higher in general dominance than spouses in marriages in which the wife is not employed.[29] Dominant wives married to dominant husbands probably produce more conflict than other combinations.

Second is the *increased freedom to voice opposition to the husband hypothesis,* which states that wives entirely dependent on their husbands hesitate to oppose their husbands' wishes or express their own displeasure. The woman who earns part of the family income is less likely to be so inhibited. Again, some inferential support is available. Heer and others have shown that mothers in the provider role do exercise more influence in family decisions.[30] Therefore it may be that the causes of conflict are no greater but that the freedom to make covert disagreement overt is increased.

Third, *the social change hypothesis* assumes that as social statuses change, confusion occurs and with it frustration and conflict. Kirkpatrick has formulated the proposition that as social definitions change, each participant tries to keep the privileges of the old definition and add those of the new, while trying to rid themselves of the old duties and to resist accepting new ones. Thus mothers who enter employment could be expected to try to keep personal control of their earnings, while persuading their husbands to perform some of the household tasks, whereas the husbands would expect to share their wives' earnings without sharing the household tasks.[31] Whether one accepts the Kirkpatrick thesis, which appears to be consistent with what is known about motivation, major and rapid social change does bring about a decrease in the predictability of behavior with consequent confusion and frustration.

The fourth is the *increased interaction hypothesis* suggested by a mother employed as a professor.[32] She suggests that one whole dimension of interaction is added to those that exist in other families, the dimension related to the mother's occupation. All other roles of the wife, husband, and children must be modified at points to fit the demands of the wife's provider role. Because of the mother's provider role, there is more content to family interaction and therefore added possibilities for disagreement, conflict, and negative affect.

All of these hypotheses offer reasonable explanations for the greater prevalence of husband-wife conflict in families in which the wife enacts a provider role, but none of them has sufficient evidence to be accepted as the principal explanation; nor has any been sufficiently

[29]Heer, ibid., pp. 251–262.
[30]Heer, op. cit.
[31]Clifford Kirkpatrick, *The Family as Process and Institution* (New York: The Ronald Press Company, 1955), Chapter 6, pp. 126–148.
[32]Professor Susanne Lloyd of Washington State University.

tested to enable one to discard it as a false explanation. Possibly, but not surely, each may provide a part of the explanation.

Finally, does employment of wives increase the divorce rate? This question cannot be answered with finality. A disproportionate number of employed mothers are divorcees; however, it is true that many, are employed *because* they are divorced and have no other source of adequate income. In the Washington project, employed and non-employed mothers were compared with respect to whether the marriage was a first marriage or a remarriage. Of those not employed, 12 per cent were in their second or subsequent marriage; of those employed full time, 13 per cent had been married more than once. A difference so small could be due to sampling error. This study does not answer the question adequately, but suggests that it is more likely that divorced women get jobs than that women get divorces because they have jobs.

Because there is more conflict in marriage when the wife is employed, shouldn't this conflict result in more divorce? Possibly, but current evidence does not suggest such a result. A small finding from the Washington study may be useful. Although mothers in the provider role reported more conflict and less happiness in their evaluation of their relationships to their spouses, they *didn't* report less satisfaction with the marriage. So what does the provider role offer the mother to compensate for more conflict with the spouse? More income; more security; a higher level of living; more power and authority in the family; and a whole set of relationships related to her work. These could compensate for somewhat more conflict with the spouse.

A later study by Orden and Bradburn sheds some additional light on the earlier studies. They emphasize that if the woman works from choice rather than because of financial duress, her freedom or choice (or autonomy) is increased, which increases her marital satisfaction. However, they found that adding the provider role typically adds to the tension level of both husband and wife; or, stated another way, if she enters employment voluntarily, it adds both satisfactions and tensions. If she enters it from duress, it adds tensions and decreases sociability and marital happiness.[33]

Effects on Wife-Mother

Second to interest in the effect on children, concern has been expressed about whether married women are physically and emotion-

---

[33]Susan R. Orden and Norman Bradburn, "Working Wives and Marital Happiness," *American Journal of Sociology*, **74** (Jan. 1969), pp. 392–407.

ally able to care for a home and a family and to satisfy the requirements of full-time employment. More specifically, does enactment of the provider role typically harm the physical or mental health of the woman?

Physical Health

It is evident that this question is complicated by selective factors. Only women in good health would *chose* to add full-time employment to their familial roles. Moreover, those who become seriously ill while employed are likely to leave their jobs. Even so, it is interesting that research has found that employed mothers in general have better health than those not employed. In one sense this answers the question—employed married women on the whole are a healthy group—but it leaves much unanswered. Does working typically *improve* maternal health? There is a hint that this is so in the findings that they are more likely to have a positive attitude toward their children. Some have also said that alternated office work and household chores are each restful because they provide different types of activities. Such fragments of support, however, are an insufficient basis for a conclusion that paid employment outside of the home improves the health of married women. However, the finding that they are physically more healthy as a category than the nonemployed strongly suggests that the notion that such employment is typically harmful to their physical health is incorrect.

Self-concepts

Feld has reported from a national study on the feelings mothers have toward themselves: "Employed mothers show more self-acceptance and fewer physical symptoms of distress; but, in contrast, they report more frequent doubts concerning their adequacy as mothers."[34] They are also more likely to feel that they have shortcomings as wives. Such feelings of anxiety and guilt have been sensed by many researchers studying employed mothers. It is interesting, however, that such mental states do not translate themselves into psychosomatic symptoms. Feld found slightly fewer such symptoms among employed mothers,[35] and Sharp and Nye found no differences between the employed and the nonemployed in this respect.[36] These facts would be consistent with two interpretations—that such anxiety and guilt feelings are not severe or persistent in the employed mother, or that in

[34]Sheila Feld, "Feelings of Adjustment," in Nye and Hoffman, op. cit., p. 340.
[35]Ibid.
[36]Lawrence Sharpe and F. Ivan Nye, "Maternal Mental Health," in Nye and Hoffman, op. cit., Chapter 21.

expressing such doubts and criticisms she is only giving a reply that she feels would be expected of an employed mother.

Satisfaction and Dissatisfactions

If it were possible to take every major aspect of married women's lives into account, would their lives be made more satisfying or less so to them as a consequence of their becoming providers? This is a difficult question to research. However, Nye obtained information relevant to it from some two thousand mothers in asking them to indicate their degree of satisfaction or dissatisfaction with seven aspects of their lives: their income, their house and furniture, their recreation, their daily work, their community as a place to live, their relationship to their children, and their relationship to their husbands. Employed mothers were better satisfied with their relationships to their children and with the community as a place to live. They did not differ significantly from nonemployed mothers with respect to feelings about income, house and furniture, recreation, or daily work. When scores were summed on the seven items, the employed mothers averaged higher satisfaction scores. This outcome still doesn't prove that being employed typically leads to more satisfaction in a woman's life, because one cannot be sure that the employed mothers would not have been better satisfied with their lives in any event, but the authors feel that it is some evidence that the additional role provides additional satisfactions. Another, more general, question would be: if the rewards do not exceed the punishments, why do women enter employment, and, having entered, remain there?

Provider Roles in Middle Age

If the "man (or woman) in the street" were asked, "When is the most favorable time for a mother to take paid employment?" probably most would say, "After her children leave home." Some researchers have investigated this answer—with surprising results. The findings concerning satisfactions to employed mothers reported above were for mothers with children under eighteen. When mothers were interviewed who had at least one married child, the opposite was found to be true. Differences in satisfactions in women aged forty-five to fifty-five favored those *not* employed. Even the questions that sought to determine these women's relationships to their sons-in-law and daughters-in-law revealed nothing favorable to the employed mothers of middle age.[37] Among younger women, employment was positively

[37]Nye and Hoffman, op. cit., pp. 327–329.

associated with life satisfactions; among older women, those not working were better satisfied than those who were—the opposite of common sense ideas about the favorable time for women to enter the labor force.

Why should such a reasonable-sounding proposition fail to be substantiated? One hypothesis is that the lesser-skilled and more poorly paid positions are held by most older employed women. They lack education and training that many of the younger women possess. An alternative hypothesis is that there is a reduction in physical energy and motivation in the later years. Some of the earlier financial objectives of the couple have been realized; others have been relinquished as unattainable or not worth the effort. Whether these are the reasons, present findings, plus employers' preferences for younger women, provide strong evidence against the popular belief that middle age is the ideal time for women to take on the provider role.

Summary

The reader is now aware that considerable research has been done with respect to mothers who become providers. What kinds of generalizations do they warrant? We shall consider these generalizations in the form of propositions.

There are no large differences between children of employed and nonemployed mothers. This is not to say that there are no differences at all. Several have already been discussed, but where differences have been found they are small.

Employed mothers tend to exercise more power in family decisions. The evidence is consistent in support of this proposition and includes both cross-sectional and before-and-after studies. The mother who is a provider commands financial resources that can purchase goods and services—the matters concerning which decisions are made. She is less dependent on her spouse financially and he is more dependent on her, as are the children. More wives in provider roles result in more equalitarian families and, also in more families in which the wife is the dominant spouse.

There tends to be more conflict between spouses in families in which the wife is a provider. Several independently conducted studies support this proposition. Because the studies are cross-sectional rather than "before-and-after," it is not certain that the higher conflict level is a consequence of the wife's occupancy of a provider role. However, most of the explanations advanced are based on the increased power of the wife or on role conflicts resulting from the wife's employment. Rather surprisingly, adequate information on whether the wife's em-

291

ployment results in more divorces is not available. Some relevant data suggest otherwise; for example, the employment of married women increased rapidly between 1950 and 1965 but the divorce rate has tended to remain at almost the same level during that period.

The health of employed women tends to be better than that of those not employed. A nationwide study found this proposition to be true both for illness presumed physical in origin and for that considered to be psychosomatic. It is most difficult to draw causal inferences because those in poor health are probably less likely to seek employment or to continue working if they become ill. The proposition is useful primarily as a refutation of the notion that becoming a provider is likely to be injurious to the health of the wife. Longitudinal research prior to and following employment will be necessary to determine whether employment is beneficial to women's health.

Mothers who are providers are more likely to experience guilt feelings concerning their roles as mothers. This concern about their adequacy in maternal roles comes through in most studies. American mothers have assumed that the direct and more or less continuous supervision of children was their responsibility. They realize that full-time employment is incompatible with this perception of responsibility for children. The knowledge that children have good care and supervision is not sufficient to prevent guilt feelings. This feeling of guilt may change as the mother's perception is changed to one of responsibility that children receive good care and supervision, rather than that the mother must, herself, have her children under her hour-to-hour care.

Younger women tend to like the provider role better than older women. Contrary to common-sense beliefs, younger women combine the family roles with that of provider with more success than do older women, despite the heavier child-care responsibilities of younger women. It is not clear whether the success of younger women in this role is due to intrinsic characteristics of the young—greater energy and a greater need to acquire assets—or to societal factors, such as greater expectations among the young that mothers will be providers and the better positions open to younger women by virtue of more education. If the intrinsic characteristics are involved, then presumably young women will continue to play this multiplicity of roles with greater satisfaction to themselves. If the cultural factors provide the explanation, these will change, and the current differences between younger and older mothers may not hold in the future.

If age is held constant, *the fewer the household duties the woman must perform personally, the more likely she is to occupy a provider role.* Women with few children (especially no preschool children); women who can buy processed food, cleaning, laundry, and similar

292

services; women with capable mother substitutes available—all of these are more likely to be employed. The increased availability of good day-care facilities, household conveniences, service industries, and the current trend toward smaller families are likely to result in an interest in the provider role on the part of an increased proportion of women. Women with fewer household responsibilities, and those who can hire others to perform part of them, experience less role conflict.

The more marketable her skills, the more likely the wife will be employed. The more education the wife possesses the more likely she is to be employed, even though highly educated women are likely to be married to men with good incomes. Of course, such women are likely to be more highly motivated as well as better trained. Employers also value previous work experience highly, especially recent experience. Other characteristics being equal, younger women have more opportunities for employment than older ones.

Recreation and community participation are selectively affected. The provider role reduces both neighborhood visiting and formal entertaining but not intrafamily or commercial recreation. Participation in community leadership roles is reduced but not in membership or in attendance of functions.

A Look Ahead

It seems safe to project present trends and to anticipate a continuing proportion of married women in provider roles. Such participation provides broader and more varied experiences for women, and the increased income provides more security and more choices for both the wives and their husbands. The harmful consequences anticipated have not been substantiated. It is equally clear that commercial facilities, from restaurants to day-care centers, will continue to provide more available and more effective substitutes for the mother's services for performing some of her other roles. It is likely but not inevitable that public services will be expanded to assist the married woman who is a provider, especially in public support of day-care and in extension of the programs of schools to include after-school recreation and supervision services. If all these developments occur, the role conflicts of employed wives and mothers will decrease in the coming decades. Such solutions to current guilt feelings, plus more specialized agencies to perform some of the tasks of employed mothers are likely to increase the attractiveness of the provider role, which may lead to changes in the socialization of girls. If future parents cease to discourage girls' interest in entering the professions and executive positions in business, more women will obtain the necessary training and motivation for entering such occupations and for regarding them as careers rather than as only a means of supplementing their husbands' income.

293

12

Power and Authority in the Family

The division of power between spouses and between parents and children has fascinated students of the family and the lay public alike. In Western societies and, indeed, throughout the world, where societies are changing, the distribution of family power is shifting—and consistently from male prerogative toward an equalitarian pattern. Laws giving to husbands the control of the property and the earnings of wives have gradually been modified, and legislation protecting the employment and the earning rights of women have largely removed the institutional provisions for male domination.

What, then, is the present distribution of power between spouses and what can be expected in the future?

For more than half a century women have sought equality in the political, legal, and occupational areas, and the task is not completed. At the same time, another perception is expressed in the story of two husbands discussing the matter. One stated, "I'm in favor of equality between the sexes." The other replied, "So am I, but the women will never grant it to us!"

IDENTICAL, OR SEPARATE BUT EQUAL? Emerging democratic, humanistic ideologies appear to be inconsistent with the exploitation of one sex by the other, but in what ways are equal rewards to be achieved? The Feminist Movement was dedicated to identical roles for the sexes. Post-Feminist thinking, perhaps realizing that the same experiences have different meaning and value for the two sexes, has sought opportunity in experiences that are equally desirable but not necessarily identical. *Equal* does not mean *the same.* Thus, those who seek equality for women ask, for example, that they not be barred on the basis of their sex from positions for which they are qualified, whereas those who advocate sameness want women to do everything that men do just because men do it. The first group would object, for example, to a woman's losing a promotion to a man who was much less qualified in all respects. And the second group would insist that half of all government officials be women, whether or not they were qualified. These are the two extremes of opinion; there are degrees between them. However, equal implies equal responsibilities or giving up special privileges based on sex. This aspect of equality will be explored next.

RESPONSIBILITIES Men who complain about women's being "more than equal" to men most frequently have reference to the fact that women usually need not play the provider role. Although men usually have no choice in seeking and retaining employment, married women are usually under no compulsion to do so. The stresses of competition in gaining employment and in achieving advancement or the necessity of meeting the same work schedule day after day, regardless of feelings or interests, are burdens men bear. Men observe that women do not bear these burdens, or at least not in the same way. Men's responsibilities go considerably beyond this in their being responsible also for suitable housing, the safety of the family, and the behavior of children in extrafamilial interaction with the world. These responsibilities may become unbearably heavy during periods of high unemployment or in some occupations that include unusual insecurities, such as sales on a commission basis, professionals in private practice, and athletic coaches. However, where stress is not a great problem, the "tyranny of the clock" may be. Men must be on the job at 8:00 A.M., no matter how repugnant that fact may be to them.

Women's responsibilities may be equally difficult. One psychiatrist termed the mother with open-ended responsibilities for her children "The Trapped Housewife."[1] He refers to the twenty-four-hour-per-day responsibility of the wife for her children. If she is aware of recent findings showing that personality is a social product, with the parent-child relationship especially important, she bears the added heavy burden of responsibility without the knowledge to deal with it adequately. Women, too, have the routine of preparing meals, house care, and laundry, although their time schedule is more flexible than that of the provider role.

Can it be said that male or female tasks place a heavier burden on the husband or wife? The provider role is a heavy and confining one for the male. The household care and supervision and development of children bear as heavily on the wife. Of course, one can say, "Well, I know a wife who does hardly anything at all. She has no children. They eat out all the time and have an apartment that requires almost no care." True, and it can be matched by the case of a wheat rancher who does

---

[1] Horace Gray, "The Trapped Housewife," *Marriage and Family Living,* **24** (May 1963), pp. 179–183. See also, Mirra Komarovsky, *Women in the Modern World: Their Education and Dilemmas* (Boston: Little, Brown and Company, 1953).

his principal work in a few months and has much of the year free to do as he pleases. These are the unusual cases, however, and establish nothing except that there is great variability in the number of responsibilities that individual men and women carry. It is easy to establish that men carry the heavy load as providers and in relating the family to the external environment and that women carry most of the burden within the boundaries of the home. That each is more impressed with his own burdens seems to be part of the perceptive pattern of human beings. That they should cite cases of individual families that support the argument that their sex is more heavily burdened is good debating strategy, but does not advance scientific knowledge. That processed food, ready-made clothing, and having fewer children to care for have lightened women's work can be established. Similar arguments can be advanced that men work a shorter day and a shorter week and that most receive vacations.

For both men and women, physical labor has declined, but for both, emotional stress has increased. Most men's occupations involve interaction with people (rather than with things or animals), which is more anxiety-producing. Woman's tasks are being redefined as personality development, child supervision, and the happiness and well-being of her husband, which can be anxiety-producing.

So long as children are cared for *within* the home and most family income is earned outside of it, there is little possibility of the two sexes' playing identical roles, but this has been ignored by those who think of equality only in terms of identical duties. For example, some wives have assumed that men should "do their share" of housework and baby care. Their husbands are washing dishes, changing diapers, and shopping for groceries. This occurs in families in which the wife is not gainfully employed as well as in those in which she is.

However, some husbands see no reason why their wives should not be gainfully employed (as men are), but also no reason why they (the husbands) should assume any of the household responsibilities.

The confusion of equality with the notion of identical experience produces controversy. Yet, is there any way that complete equality can be achieved except through identical experience? Is there no common currency with which different kinds of responsibilities can be weighed to determine whether one or the other sex carries the heavier burden? We shall return to these questions in the final section of this chapter.

Institutionalized Power—Authority

The distribution of power may be specified either legally or by custom (or both) or it may be left to each group to allocate power among its members. Generally speaking, when responsibility is allocated to a position, authority with respect to the operations that discharge the responsibility is also allocated to that position. However, power can also be institutionalized in the hands of dominant groups in a society, whether these are men or children, or a racial or ethnic category, without respect to responsibility.

If in the past in the non-Communist Western world the norms have prescribed that the husband is the head of the household, how does it happen that in so many instances the wife makes most of the major decisions? A set of responsibilities is allocated to the position of husband or wife. Power is necessary to the fulfillment of these responsibilities. The allocation to the husband of financial responsibility for his family also permits him to allocate his earnings as necessary. This implies, or sometimes specifies, that the wife must utilize his earnings effectively by preparing the food for meals and caring for household equipment. But this responsibility limits the husband's power by requiring that he give priority to the subsistence needs of his family. He is not free to spend all of his earnings on the horses! These allocations and limitations of power may be enforced, in part, by specialized government agencies, or entirely by informal social pressure and sanctions, including those from within his own family.

However, such societal norms do not forbid a wife from trying to influence any decisions that, by the norms of the society, are assigned to the husband. Some wives are so successful in influencing their husbands that, in fact, husbands abdicate to their wives the decisions they would be expected to make. The wife, in colloquial language, "wears the pants in the family." In such cases the responsibility for the support and protection of the family is separated from the power to discharge responsibility. In the instance of an ineffective husband and a capable and aggressive wife, she may accept the responsibility as well as the power to make decisions so that a complete role reversal occurs. This is likely to occur with increasing frequency as women compete on more equal terms in the labor market.

Viewed another way, the norms convey a general, diffuse set of expectations of what husbands and wives will do. Only a few of these are set down precisely as laws with formal sanctions to enforce them, even in differentiated societies. Where laws are involved, such as requiring that minor children be provided food and shelter, legal agencies are not concerned whether that support comes from the husband or the wife. However, if it were not forthcoming, the husband, if physically able and mentally competent, would bear the first responsibility. Thus, the financial responsibility for dependent children is assumed to be the responsibility of the husband, but the necessary condition is that support of the children be provided. If the wife or a

297

grandparent is able and willing to provide it, society does not intervene. However, a complete role reversal is a source of surprise and disapproval on the part of extended kin, friends, neighbors, and even business associates, and such marriages survive with difficulty. It might be said that society is concerned that the functions of the family *be* performed; parents, peer groups including kin, friends, and neighbors are concerned with *how* they are performed.

FROM INSTITUTIONALIZED PATRIARCHY TO WHAT? Few topics have attracted more discussion than the comparison of the patriarchal and the democratic family. Much of this discussion has stemmed from the Burgess thesis that the family in the Western world, and perhaps worldwide, is evolving from an institution composed of a set of rigidly, normatively defined positions and roles to one in which affection holds the group together and behavior is improvised on the basis of the needs of family members.[2]

Burgess and his colleagues seemed to assume that institutionalized families were necessarily patriarchal. By implication this assumption suggests that families not highly institutionalized are, or tend to be, democratic. This may have been true in the Western family systems toward the middle part of the twentieth century. As it happened, the emerging equalitarian family was noninstitutional in the sense that it provided alternative behavior for family members that was different from that of the previous generation.

However, there is no necessary relationship between the institutionalization of the family—that is, the specificity and rigidity of its positions and roles—and its patriarchal or other content. There is no reason why equalitarianism cannot be institutionalized, and Dyer and Urban have suggested that this is taking place.[3] In like vein, the terms *patriarchal* and *traditional* have been used interchangeably, but again the correspondence of these terms seems to be little more than an accident. It may be that by the late seventies students will be referring to the equalitarian, child-centered family as the "traditional" family! It is more precise, then, to refer to a father-dominated family as "patriarchal" than "institutional" or "traditional."

IS THE FAMILY ALWAYS AN INSTITUTION? It should be noted also, perhaps as an appropriate issue for debate, that the family in any society is *always* an institution and that it always has a set of positions—husband, wife, child, and sometimes others—whose duties, privileges, and responsibilities are defined. There is always variation in the perception of these duties and some dissent from majority points of

[2]Ernest W. Burgess, Harvey J. Locke, and Mary Margaret Thomes, *The Family, from Institution to Companionship* (New York: American Book Company, 1963).

[3]William C. Dyer and Dick Urban, "The Institutionalization of Family Norms," *Marriage and Family Living*, **20** (Feb. 1958), pp. 53–59.

view. During periods of rapid social change, such as this one, alternative roles may be relatively acceptable as is now true of the provider role for married women. However, even during periods of rapid social change there is a core of beliefs concerning the responsibilities of family members that are shared by most people in the society and that the society enforces by legal sanction, social pressure, or both. Authority patterns, as well as other characteristics of the family institution, continue to be defined by norms. These patterns have become more equalitarian, but are no less or more institutionalized for that reason.

PATRIARCHAL AND AUTHORITARIAN Earlier, a distinction was made between institutional and patriarchal family patterns in that equalitarian as well as patriarchal norms can be institutionalized. Authoritarian families have been found to be patriarchal, but, in principle, they need not be. Authority could be vested in the women of the family, forming a matriarchal family organization. If one is referring to a family structure in which the males are dominant, the more precise term is *patriarchal,* which includes the notion of authority, but specifies it as exercised by men. It is necessary to note that in the world view of the family, it frequently is not the father, but the *grandfather,* who wields most of the authority in the patriarchal family.

DEMOCRATIC AND EQUALITARIAN The concept of democracy has been borrowed from the study of governmental institutions. It is doubtful that this concept is appropriate to the analysis of the family. For example, if the assumption that everyone has an equal vote in making decisions is applied to husband and wife, any difference of opinion would result in a tie. The more general notion of democracy, that everyone participates in government, *is* applicable to the family. However, the concept *democratic* seems unnecessarily diffuse in its general context and inappropriate in some of its specific applications. The concept *equalitarian* appears more appropriate for the family, provided it is applied only to the husband-wife relationship. Equalitarian *may* be equated with identical roles (except child-bearing), but *need not* be. For example, a house in town and a farm in the country may have equal value without being alike in any specific attribute. The concept need only refer to the equal value of husband, wife, and children. It includes equal rights of family members without assuming equal or identical responsibility or power in *any given* activity.

PERMISSIVENESS AND AUTONOMY The permissive family has sometimes been equated with the democratic or equalitarian family. However, it has usually had special reference to parent-child relationships in which parents have allowed the child to do as he pleased without reserving the same rights to themselves. In effect, it usually has reduced *their* autonomy because they had to be available to serve the whims of their children. Recently a young father was observed spending hours

299

following his child about to prevent him from being injured. It didn't occur to the father to take his child where *he* wanted to go. This and alternative child-rearing philosophies are explored in more detail in Chapter 15.

Autonomy involves the right of the individual to make decisions about his own behavior in matters that are of concern primarily to himself. For a child, this might mean that he could choose what he wanted to eat, provided it contained the elements necessary to health. If he becomes ill, it is of concern to and imposes additional duties on others. For spouses, it may include their own choice of clothing and a choice of participating or not participating in couple or family recreation.

The "permissive family" lodges much power in the child, inasmuch as parents must orient and reorient their activities about the child's activities. The child may or may not be able to issue commands to his parents, but he may achieve the same effects by expressing his wishes concerning what he wants to do or by simply doing it.

The family that gives a great deal of individual autonomy (autonomic type) not only for children but for spouses, reduces sharply the "supply" of power because there are fewer joint activities. The degree of autonomy can vary from limited decisions, such as how one wishes to perform an individual task like studying, to extreme cases reported in disorganized families in which every member prepared his own meals without reference to the meal schedules of other family members. The amount of autonomy that can be tolerated by the group, in this instance the family, is discussed in Chapter 17. However, the principle can be established that the more autonomic the family, the less power there is to be divided among family members.

SUBCULTURAL INSTITUTIONALIZATION OF POWER In a complex society, such as that of the United States, encompassing a number of subcultures, it would not be surprising to find that in each subculture power is differently allocated among family members. The Catholic and Mormon churches allocate more responsibility and authority to the husband-father than do the major Protestant churches. The same has been thought to be true of farm families, immigrant families, and those characterized by less-educated parents. More specifically, it has been assumed that changes toward the equalitarian family have progressed farther in the Protestant, urban, middle-class, and more highly educated strata of the population. Blood and Wolfe tested these beliefs. In each instance their findings were opposite to the differential institutionalization propositions.[4] Rural husbands, at least in the fringe area around Detroit, had less power than urban husbands; and in rural

---

[4]Robert O. Blood, Jr., and Donald M. Wolfe, *Husbands and Wives, The Dynamics of Family Living* (Glencoe, Ill.: The Free Press, 1960), Chapter 2.

300

families that had migrated into Detroit, the migrant husbands had less power than those reared in the city. Catholic and Protestant husbands exercised the same amount of power, with those Catholic fathers active in church events exercising *less* power than the inactive Catholic husbands. Husbands with little education averaged less power than those with advanced education. Likewise, low-income husbands exercised less power than highly educated husbands. Finally, husbands in immigrant groups exercised less power than those who had been more completely acculturated.

These consistent findings contradict the belief that American subcultures differ in any important way from the power-related behavior of other American spouses. Because differential subcultural institutionalization is inadequate to explain the differential distribution of power between spouses, Blood and Wolfe suggest that this distribution follows *pragmatic power*.[5] This and other theories of power are discussed in the following sections.

Theories of Family Power[6]

The distribution of power has been the focus of theoretical interest of several family sociologists. An early scholar, Waller, offered the "principle of least interest." Although Waller developed this principle to explain courtship interaction, it is useful in explaining power in marriage. The person with the least interest in maintaining a marriage can exercise the most power in disputed decisions because he (she) has less to lose if the marriage is terminated.[7]

Blood and Wolfe developed a theory specific to husband-wife interaction with the proposition that the basis for determining the distribution of power from family to family is the comparative contribution of resources by the husband and the wife. The most recent statement of the proposition is, "Insofar as marital power is measured in terms of decisions governing transactions between the family and the external system, the comparative participation of the husband and the wife in the external system will determine the balance of power."[8] In general, it is their position that power parallels resources, economic or otherwise, contributed by each spouse to the marriage.

Heer proposed a third theory, utilizing some ideas of Waller's and

---

[5]Ibid.

[6]We have drawn heavily from David M. Heer, "The Measurement and Bases of Family Power: An Overview," *Marriage and Family Living*, **25** (May 1963), pp. 133–140.

[7]Willard Waller, *The Family, A Dynamic Interpretation*, rev. by Reuben Hill (New York: The Dryden Press, 1951), pp. 190–192.

[8]Robert O. Blood, Jr., "The Measurement and Bases of Family Power: A Rejoinder, *Marriage and Family Living*, **25** (Nov. 1963), pp. 475–477. See also, Robert O. Blood, Jr., and Donald M. Wolfe, op. cit.

some of Blood and Wolfe's, that is, that power is proportional to the desirability of subsequent roles if the marriage were dissolved. If the wife's earning power would be low as a single woman, her power in the marriage would be low. If her prospects for remarriage to another man of high desirability is unlikely, her power would be low. If the husband's earning power is low, his power is less than if he earns a high income. Heer proposes five bases of power within the family, including the following: "(1) external social control, (2) the prior internalization of norms, (3) discrepancy between actual return and return expected under an alternative to the existing marriage or family, (4) relative competence, and (5) relative involvement."[9] These will be examined.

SOCIAL CONTROL AND INTERNALIZATION OF NORMS The distribution of power as well as other social organization is part of the social heritage that transforms the human animal into the human being. What men and women can and can't do is taught to the child almost as inevitably as speech itself. If the children learn and accept these definitions without question the definitions are internalized and thereafter need not be externally enforced. Indeed, the children become agents in enforcing these definitions where other people are concerned. Allusion has already been made to means of social control by which the norms are enforced by societal action through a legal structure and/or by negative actions by reference groups, including kin. The anticipation of such coercive action is often as effective as the sanctions themselves. For example, if decisions concerning the husband's occupation are defined as a prerogative of the husband, his children learn this by word and example. If a wife makes her husband's occupational decisions, the couple will receive unfavorable notice from kin, friends, and colleagues.

Both the internalization of norms and the social controls by which they are enforced are specific aspects of the institutionalization of power already discussed.[10]

COMPETENCE AND INVOLVEMENT Competence and involvement will be discussed later under the heading "Syncratic and Autonomic Decision-Making" as *presumed competence* and *primary interest.* However, primary interest is discussed only in terms of the proportion of time allocated to an activity by each spouse. Heer adds that some matters are important for other reasons.[11] For example, the color of the

---

[9]Heer, op. cit., p. 139.

[10]French and Raven have employed the term *legitimate power* for what society allocates to social positions. John R. P. French, Jr., and Bertram Raven, "The Bases of Social Power," in *Group Dynamics: Research and Theory,* 2nd ed., ed. by D. Cartwright and A. Zander (Elmsford, N.Y.: Row, Peterson and Company, 1960), pp. 607–633.

[11]Heer, op. cit.

family automobile may be important to the wife and not to the husband. In that contingency, she would exercise more influence than her husband. Involvement and primary interest can be employed interchangeably in decision-making.

Discrepancy Between Actual Return and Return Expected Under an Alternative to the Existing Marriage or Family Heer suggests that the husband's contribution is comprised of his economic contribution, his personal attractiveness, and the quality of his interaction with his wife and children. The wife's contribution consists of her personal attractiveness and her performance of her various roles as mother to her children, homemaker, hostess, sex partner, and companion.

It is inferred that the wife with a husband who earns a small or irregular income, who is not personally attractive, and who is not pleasant in his interaction with her or their children is unlikely to accept many of her husband's decisions with which she seriously disagrees. If she is an attractive woman she may think she could do better with another man. Of course, if she is an unattractive, inefficient woman, she may feel that she would be unlikely to fare better in another marriage; however, she still might find single life comparatively attractive. The man (or woman) married to a person who would be rated higher than himself in the marriage market would be likely to defer to his spouse and be cautious in pressing issues that might threaten the marriage. Blood and Wolfe disagree: they reject the idea that most spouses consider the possibility of divorce and the type of person they might remarry.[12] We shall present some evidence under the heading "Family Life Cycle" that casts doubt on possible remarriage as a power variable.

Another alternative is a partial withdrawal from marital interaction in which one partner is willing and able to find rewards in activities outside of the marriage. Such alternative sources of rewards may enable that spouse to bargain more effectively in disputed decisions.

Whether spouses frequently think in terms of alternatives to their marriage—divorce and possibly remarriage—as Heer believes, is an interesting question. Others disagree. If spouses do think of these alternatives, a rational appraisal of the partner's assets and contributions compared to their own would be an excellent basis for allocating power with respect to disputed matters. If they do not think specifically about alternatives beyond divorce, some such calculative mechanisms seem to be operating, as will be evident in the discussion of pragmatic power.

[12]Blood, "The Measurement and Bases of Family Power: A Rejoinder," op. cit.

Pragmatic Power

When differences in the power of spouses are examined by the personal characteristics of the spouses, it is clear that power corresponds to differences in competence in role-playing, rather than in ideological differences. For example, it has been assumed that Catholic husbands exercise more power because the Church has stressed the responsibility of the husband as head of the family. The research evidence does not support this belief. Neither was the anticipated greater power of rural husbands, of husbands of low income or education, or of immigrant husbands supported from the research data. What has been shown to be associated with power is competence in economic and related matters in conjunction with the responsibilities one carries. This interplay of the competencies of the husband and the wife Blood and Wolfe call *pragmatic power,* which is the opposite of institutionalized power.[13]

INCOME OF HUSBAND As the income of the husband increases, his power with respect to his wife increases. At one time it was conjectured that husbands in the lowest socioeconomic classes exercised more authority because of their willingness to intimidate their wives physically. Because research has found much evidence to disprove this, it appears that such physical intimidation is less frequent than had been supposed. Divorce and desertion offer relatively easy escape for women physically mistreated. Also, the law forbids such physical mistreatment, and the spreading ideology of individual rights mitigates against such physical coercion.

It should be noted also that the divorce rate *decreases* as the income of the husband increases. Blood and Wolfe observed a steady and considerable gain in the power of the husband as his income increases. A highly satisfactory performance in the provider role results in more power for the husband and less likelihood that his marriage will end in divorce. The gain in power for the husband is based on his income alone and not on total family income: if the wife contributes through her employment, the power of the husband declines.

INCOME OF THE WIFE Several independent studies have shown that the power of gainfully employed wives is greater than that of wives not employed. A study by Heer employed a before-after design that showed that the power of the same women increased after they became gainfully employed.[14] This study lends additional support to the theories already mentioned. The employed wife has less to lose if the

[13]Blood and Wolfe, *Husbands and Wives, The Dynamics of Family Living,* op. cit., p. 29.

[14]David M. Heer, "Dominance and the Working Wife," *Social Forces,* **36** (May 1958), pp. 341–347.

marriage is broken because she has an income; the man has more to lose because he would lose income in addition to her services in the home and as a companion.

Wives who have been employed for a period of several years exercise even greater power. The average power score of husbands whose wives aren't employed (Blood and Wolfe scale) is 5.80; if the wife has been employed under one year, the score is 5.65; and the score is only 4.29 for husbands with wives employed ten or more years. This change in power scores suggests that the shift in power to the wife is greater the longer the wife is employed. Although the husband's power is higher the more hours he works, even unemployed husbands whose wives aren't employed have more power than husbands who work overtime and have employed wives.[15]

THE BLACK FAMILY The power structure varies markedly in the black families, with the husband averaging less power in each category than does the white husband. More than twice the proportion of the black families in the American sample are female- rather than male-dominated (44 per cent compared to 19 per cent). Part of the disparity is related to the heavier concentration of blacks in the lower class, but the disparity persists when social class is held constant. However, this disparity reflects not so much a smaller proportion of dominant black husbands as fewer equalitarian black families. The modal (most numerous) power relationship in white families is equalitarian whereas it is wife-dominated in black families.[16]

FAMILY LIFE CYCLE Blood and Wolfe and others have found a marked relationship between stages in the family life cycle and the distribution of power. The power of the husband is medium in the first stage of marriage before the birth of children. It increases with the birth of the first child and with the birth of each additional child. The wife's power is least when she has the most small children. Her power gradually increases as each child enters school and increases further when the last child leaves home. Finally, it increases again after the couple reach retirement age. It seems clear that as the number of dependents increases, the wife's bargaining power decreases, but it begins to increase as the feasibility of her entering employment increases, with fewer or no preschool children at home. Finally, this report shows it to be greatest after the retirement of the husband (although not much dependence can be placed on findings based on nine respondents).

If one follows the age of the wife instead of the cycle, the picture that emerges is a little different. It shows the husband's power increasing again after age sixty. Because some husbands are retired and some are

[15]Blood and Wolfe, op. cit., pp. 40–41.
[16]Ibid., pp. 35–36.

not, the husband's power after sixty-five apparently depends upon whether or not he is retired.

The other alternative for a wife is remarriage. It is not clear, however, that this possibility enters into the "bargaining" process. For example, the chances of remarriage are extremely high for the divorcee of thirty, and they decline steadily thereafter; however, her power increases during this period when her probability of remarrying declines. The probability that she will remarry is highest at a time when she is most likely to have preschool children. (Of course, the reason for the very high remarriage rate may *be* because she has preschool children to support.) The fact remains that the remarriage rate is *negatively* related to the power of the wife. However, possible remarriage may appear unattractive to a woman with several young children. It does seem probable that the degree of financial dependency of the wife, affected by the number and age of her children, *is* taken into account.

The power of the wife declines again after age fifty-five, until the husband's retirement. Here, two or more causes may be intertwined. The proportion of wives gainfully employed declines after fifty-five, so fewer have an income of their own. Also, the sex ratio becomes increasingly unfavorable for women. Men die some seven years younger than women, and because women marry men an average of three years older than themselves, the ratio of unmarried men becomes very unfavorable to remarriage for older women. The weight of evidence suggests, however, that employment status is the principal variable involved.

To sum up, the wife's power declines with the birth of each additional child, then increases as her children enter school. It further increases after the children have left home. After age fifty-five, it declines, provided her husband continues to be employed. If he retires, his power declines and hers increases.

POWER AND TASK PERFORMANCE Power has been treated in family context as influence in making decisions, most of which affect both spouses. It was observed earlier that the day has passed, at least for the family in the Western world, when the husband directs the wife in how she shall perform her duties; that is, such behavior is nonnormative. Evidence supporting this belief is available from Blood and Wolfe. They found that the spouse who exercised the most influence in making decisions was also more likely *to perform* some household tasks.[17] They take this as evidence of the noncoercive aspect of family task performance. Of course, family members do disagree on who will perform boring or unpleasant tasks. It may be that the choice for the more competent spouse is to perform the task or to see it go undone. For

[17]Ibid., Chapter 3.

306

example, the bills can pile up on the desk until one person finally pays them.

This theory allows still another partial explanation of family power. The more efficient spouse has the time, energy, and motivation to address himself to making family decisions and performing family tasks. The theory is consistent with variations in the family life cycle that provide heavy additional duties for mothers of young children, but it does not seem to be entirely consistent with the greater power of the employed wife. She does average more education and may be more efficient than the average nonemployed woman, but her time is largely preempted by her job, so that less time is available for tasks associated with making decisions.

This suggests that two propositions can explain much of the actual distribution of power:

1. The larger the number of and the younger the children, the greater the power of the husband.
2. The greater the economic contribution of the husband in comparison with that of the wife, the greater the power of the husband.

It helps to illuminate the nature of family power by adding a third proposition:

3. The greater the power of a spouse, the greater the number of marginal household tasks performed by that spouse. (By marginal, we mean those sometimes performed by one sex, sometimes by the other)

Power and Patterns of Decision-Making

Power presupposes a distinct superordinate-subordinate relationship in which the person in authority can legitimately require actions of the one in a subordinate position. For this reason, the concept probably is inappropriate for the description of husband-wife relations in the United States and is becoming outdated elsewhere. It *is* still appropriate in describing some parent-child relationships. This does not mean that one sex may not be in a more dominant position even though the era in which men are expected to give orders to their wives is passing. Many family enterprises require the joint activity of spouses. For example, once the house is selected both spouses ordinarily live in it, both ride in the family automobile, both use the same furniture, and both attempt to discipline their children. The spouse who makes the decisions about these and other joint activities *indirectly* exercises

307

considerable control over the other spouse, as well as enjoying personal autonomy.

SYNCRATIC AND AUTONOMIC DECISION-MAKING Couples can attempt to confer on all matters that are more than routine decisions (syncratic pattern) or can decide that decisions in one area are essentially the concern of the husband, whereas those in another area ought to be made by the wife (autonomic pattern).[18] Such decisions may be made on the basis of *primary interest* or *presumed competence.* Often the two coincide. The wife will decide what kitchen utensils to buy because they will be utilized almost entirely by her and because presumably she is competent to decide what equipment she needs. The husband is likely to decide when the car should be serviced or repaired. In these instances the decisions affect the other spouse little, if at all. Some spouses carry the autonomic (autonomous) pattern considerably further. The husband will decide what make of automobile to buy and the body style as well with little or no consultation with his wife. The wife may select the living-room furniture in like manner. One or the other may decide how the child is to be disciplined. In each case the results of the decision also involve the other spouse. Probably a majority of American spouses consult together at length on such matters, and the decision is usually a joint one.

There is one important limitation on the criterion of primary interest. If the decision involves a major expenditure, even for kitchen equipment, it becomes a value decision because the financial resources invested for one purpose are unavailable for another. Autonomic decisions, then, are more likely to involve minor decisions, as well as those in which only one spouse appears to have a major interest and greater competence.

Finally, couples differ markedly on how many enterprises they share. In some, most activities are shared. Herbst calls these "syncratic" families. In others, individuals largely pursue their own interests, sharing only a minimum of common activities. These are termed "autonomic" families.[19] For example, families who engage in all their recreational activities together are syncratic. Each spouse obviously has a greater common investment in syncratic activities and is less likely to want to delegate the decision-making to his spouse. In contrast, if each spouse attends movies by himself, one has little reason to try to influence the other's choice of movie.

Research has reported that syncratic or joint decision-making is more

---

[18]We take the terms from P. G. Herbst, "Family Living—Patterns of Interaction," in *Social Structure in a City,* ed. by O. A. Oeser and S. B. Hammond (London: Routledge and Kegan Paul, 1954), Chapter 12.
[19]Ibid.

308

common than the autonomic.[20] However, the joint pattern is associated in the public mind with democracy and intimate husband-wife relations, both socially desirable in current American society. Therefore, there may be a tendency to overreport shared decisions. The autonomic pattern has been associated with authoritarianism, although there is not necessarily a connection. If each spouse makes as many and as crucial decisions as the other, it is an equalitarian pattern, even if few joint decisions are made.

Which pattern satisfies more needs of the spouses and produces the least frustration and conflict? Probably a combination, with the proportion of each varying from one type of family to another and from one individual family to another. Some joint decision-making is virtually necessary in the purchase of costly items and services because these absorb financial resources, and in decisions on matters that demand major amounts of time and energy of both spouses, such as what type of housing to buy or rent. The limitation on joint decision-making is that the process absorbs time and energy and may result in arguments and quarrels. Further, if the matter is one that affects one person primarily (such as kitchen utensils), one spouse would appear to dominate the other if each spouse exercises 50-per-cent influence in an area in which one contributes only 5 per cent of the time spent on those activities. Perhaps an efficiency formula could be devised that would combine two propositions: (1) the greater the total time spent by one spouse in the utilization of the goods or services, the greater the share of decision-making allotted to that spouse, and (2) the larger the cost of an item or service, the more nearly equal the share of each spouse in the decision-making process. We suspect that most American families do, in fact, follow these propositions, with variations as already discussed and with different weighting of the two propositions.

TRENDS IN DECISION-MAKING There is no doubt that the wife's share in decision-making concerning the allocation of financial resources and relationships to the extrafamilial environment has increased. Her earnings in gainful employment plus even her *potential* to earn an income increase her power. Both the developing equalitarian ideology and the high value placed on companionship in marriage rationalize the trend.

Blood and Wolfe constructed a composite measure of spousal power comprised of the following eight items:

1. What job the husband should take.
2. What car to get.
3. Whether or not to buy life insurance.

[20]Blood and Wolfe, op. cit., Chapter 2.

4. Where to go on vacation.
5. What house or apartment to take.
6. Whether or not the wife should go to work or quit work.
7. What doctor to have when someone is sick.
8. How much money the family can afford to spend per week on food.

Employing these items, they judged about one quarter of the families to be female dominated, one quarter male dominated, and half equalitarian.[21]

Whether there is an increase in the husband's power in intrafamilial matters is less clear. Husbands appear to be taking an increasingly active role in all aspects of the socialization of their children. Seeming to contradict this trend is the literature characterizing the father as one who spends all of his time at the office or commuting and who sees his children infrequently.[22] There are families in which the latter pattern exists, but only a small proportion of the men in the United States spend two hours or more on commuter trains. Even the small proportion who do so is likely to decrease as modern expressways permit the office worker to travel much faster to the suburbs. Blood and Wolfe's findings are that the power of husbands in suburban families is greater than of those in the central city. This holds even when social class is held constant.[23] This empirical evidence seems sufficient to contradict the image of the suburban matriarchy and the "fatherless" suburban family.

On the basis of present knowledge, the power of wives is increasing in areas formerly largely controlled by their husbands. It is probable, but not certain, that husbands typically are exercising more power in intrafamily areas formerly the domain of women.

Evaluations of Family Power

There is no doubt that some men feel that the trend toward equality has gone too far. They usually cite one or two families in which the wife is clearly the dominant member of the family. However, the developing norm is equality, not female domination. In a sense, the examples cited are deviant cases that illustrate no general principle.

DO MEN NEED TO BE DOMINANT? Some writers think that men need to be dominant. Some women, likewise, think so. Usually, these are women who like a protected, passive role pattern and have no desire to

[21]Ibid.
[22]Burgess, Locke, and Thomes, op. cit., p. 71.
[23]Blood and Wolfe, op. cit.

compete with men or other women in the job market. The rationale they express is that men need to be the dominant creatures in the family in order to reinforce their egos for maximum competition in the business and professional world. As we have remarked in Chapter 10, this should be treated as a hypothesis rather than a proven proposition. It is a rationale not only for male dominance in the family, but for the passive, noncompetitive companion role that some women have chosen to enact. Whether or not the hypothesis is true, there appears to be no societal objection to male dominance, provided it is benevolent and provided it is mutually agreeable to husband and wife. We know of no evidence, however, that establishes that this pattern of relationship between men and women has any intrinsic merits beyond those related to the expectations of some adults based on their own socialization.

Will men feel deprived of the privileges of controlling female behavior? Some will, just as the white population of the South feels deprived as the status of the black improves,[24] but as Hacker has said, it will be only a temporary deprivation. When the society socializes children with no reference to male superiority, there will be no feeling of deprivation. Of course, for this change in socialization to occur, women's training for professions, their commitment to careers, and their performance in professional and executive positions must equal that of men. The image will have to correspond to the reality.

DO WOMEN NEED TO BE DEPENDENT? Do women have a cluster of needs related to dependence on men? To be happy and emotionally secure do they need to be protected, be shielded from complex decisions, lead a passive existence, be responsive emotionally to husband and children, but with no separate identities of their own? Much Freudian-inspired literature states this explicitly or implicitly.[25] Friedan provides an explosive "no."[26] There appears to be no evidence that there is any biological basis for women to play a dependent role. Single women live longer than married women and their mental illness and suicide rates are lower. The large group of women who have moved into gainful employment compare favorably by most indices with those staying in a more dependent role pattern.

HOW MANY ROLE REVERSALS? This generation of men and women will face one additional fact, that, in a considerable proportion of families, women will become the principal providers and will have all the experience of dealing with other social organizations that have long been the domain of men. Some timid and noncompetitive men will

[24]Helen Hacker, "New Burdens of Masculinity," *Marriage and Family Living,* **19** (Aug. 1957), pp. 227–233.

[25]For example, Ferdinand Lundberg and Marynia Farnham, *Modern Woman, The Lost Sex* (New York: Harper & Row, 1947).

[26]Betty Friedan, *The Feminine Mystique* (New York: Dell Publishing Company, 1963).

become housekeepers and supervisors of children. The question is not whether this will happen—it is happening already. The question is how these reversals of responsibilities and power will be evaluated by kin, friends, and colleagues, and what the effects will be on the personalities and role performances of the individuals involved.

Although the reversal in the provider role will result in greater power for those women, the ideology of equality and worth of individuals may moderate the unequal division of power as it currently does to protect, to a degree, the rights of women. In addition, the lingering patriarchal notions may even further dampen the swing of power to those women who are the principal providers.

Another limitation on the reversal of roles is the trend for house-keeper and child-care roles to be assumed by more specialized non-family agencies and for both husband and wife to work. Therefore, the man who becomes a full-time "homemaker" may continue to be an unusual role-player.

Certainly full careers for women, careers that may often surpass those of their husbands, will swing the distribution of power to them, but how drastically cannot be estimated. Such change will require the additional redefinition of roles with a transitional period of confusion. The new norms concerning power will come nearer to equality between the sexes in fact as well as ideology.

EVALUATION BY MEN AND WOMEN The question of deciding when an equalitarian division of power and responsibility has been reached between the sexes is difficult because of the impracticality of the two sexes enacting identical roles. One can obtain some common currency, however, by asking members of each sex whether they had ever wished they were of the other sex. In a poll of University of Minnesota students almost no boys had ever wished they had been born girls, but nearly half of the girls said they had at some time wished they were boys.[27] What can explain this large a difference?

It has been shown that women have some advantages. They can be gainfully employed or not. Even if they are employed they need not compete as strongly as do men. They live much longer. Only a fraction compared to men commit suicide. Their social deviation from their roles seems less than that of men. The point that women frequently volunteer when discussing social roles is their lack of freedom and initiative in many areas of life. They cannot take an overt role in dating or courtship; they must stimulate men to perform the sex act rather than performing it themselves. In social relations with men they are largely limited to reacting to men's actions rather than being free to

[27]Clifford Kirkpatrick, *The Family as Process and Institution*, 2nd ed. (New York: The Ronald Press Company, 1963), p. 157.

pick and choose among the whole population of men. They have not been permitted to fight the wars. There had been a strong resistance to their becoming astronauts, engineers, and foreign correspondents. Men can "ride the rails" on railroads or penetrate into so-called dangerous areas of cities—activities that have been largely closed to women.

The dominant roles that society still usually reserves for women are those attached to their residences—child care, food preparation, and care of clothing and the house. These roles have been much more confining than men's occupations, which require or permit them to travel considerably. Women do not feel that they have achieved full equality with men. We suggest that lack of autonomy may have accounted for the perceived difference.

Power and Marital Satisfaction

Blood and Wolfe, Rainwater, and, more recently, Centers and Raven related the family power structure to marital satisfaction. All found equalitarian power structures associated with being well satisfied with marriage. In their study, Centers and Raven found the proportion of persons "very satisfied" with the marriage to be husband dominant, 73 per cent; syncratic, 70 per cent; autonomic, 79 per cent; and wife dominant, 20 per cent.[28] The very low proportion of spouses who consider their wife-dominant marriages "very satisfactory" provide the most marked difference in relationship to power—a finding that is congruent with Blood and Wolfe's conclusions.[29] That the autonomic pattern is satisfactory to the largest proportion of couples is a new finding, being opposite to the Rainwater research which reported the syncratic pattern more closely related to satisfaction with the marriage.[30] Further research may be required to resolve this question. However, both are equalitarian patterns, one requiring more interaction, the other more autonomy. Finally, the husband-dominant pattern still seems to be acceptable to a large proportion of couples.

[28]Richard Centers and Bertram H. Raven, "Conjugal Power Structure: a Re-Examination," *American Sociological Review,* **36** (Apr. 1971), pp. 274–275.

[29]Blood and Wolfe, op. cit., p. 45.

[30]Lee Rainwater, *Family Design* (Chicago: Aldine Publishing Company, 1965), Chapter 3.

13

Sexual Roles in Marriage

The sexual attraction of men and women, resulting sexual intercourse, and the conception and birth of children provide the basis for the family institution; namely, the care and training of children. The lack of periodicity in the sexual receptivity of women provides a continued attraction for the male. The satisfaction of some of his sexual needs provides a basis for the continuing association of the father with the mother and children. The need of the mother for food during pregnancy and the long period of the dependency of her children, in turn, provide added motivation for the human female to be receptive to the sexual advances of the male. Without this continued attraction and receptivity, the human family as a continuous association between an adult male and female and their dependent children could hardly have come into existence.[1]

SEX AS MOTIVATION FOR MARRIAGE Contemporary sociologists view the satisfaction of sex needs by marriage as one of the reasons for the existence of the family. Ogburn did not specifically identify it as one of his list of functions of the family, evidently feeling that the affectional function included it.[2] Current sociologists usually list "sex-partner to the husband" as a role of wives. It is doubtful that any scholar of the family would be unaware of the function of the family both in meeting sex needs of spouses and in preventing these needs being met outside of the family where provision for the care and training of the child is less adequate.

In contemporary American society it is easy to equate interest in becoming married with interest in unrestricted sexual intercourse, but

[1]Margaret Mead, *Male and Female, A Study of the Sexes in a Changing World* (New York: William Morrow & Co., Apollo Edition, 1967), Chapter 10, "Potency and Receptivity."

[2]William F. Ogburn and Clark Tibbitts, *Recent Social Trends in the United States* (New York: McGraw-Hill Book Company, 1933).

just how critical is sex as a motivation for marriage? Both Terman and his associates[3] and Burgess and Wallin[4] asked large samples of urban middle-class couples their feelings about sex prior to their marriage. In each investigation most men anticipated sex in marriage with interest and anticipation or eagerness. The proportions were 87 per cent in the earlier study, 90 per cent in the latter. A majority of women also felt favorable anticipation toward the sexual experience of marriage; two thirds of Terman's and three fourths of Burgess and Wallin's female responses were favorable. However, over a fourth of the women in the latter and one third of the women in the earlier study viewed sex in marriage with disgust, aversion, or indifference. It must be concluded, therefore, that most young Americans viewed the sexual experiences in marriage positively, but that a small minority of men and an appreciable minority of women did not. Because freedom of choice is the norm in deciding whether or not to marry, a large number of Americans, especially women, have married with no interest in or a negative attitude toward sex. It should be remembered, however, that these studies are twenty to thirty years old. It may be that a smaller proportion of young women today have indifferent or negative attitudes toward sex.

In some other societies with more permissive sexual norms, such as those of the Trobriand Islands, Samoa, and at least to a degree Sweden, young unmarried people can and do engage in considerable sexual intercourse prior to marriage. It would be easy to conclude that marriage in these societies is entirely for nonsexual reasons, but this probably is not true. Mead has noted that the two former societies produce almost no illegitimate children, which she attributes to the fact that intercourse occurs only at the periods of increased sexual interest of women, just prior to and following menstruation, when women are infertile.[5] She also notes that it is only the more skillful lovers among the men who find such sexual favors. Some of the young men, then, apparently have none of their sexual needs met outside of marriage, and others only part of theirs. Perhaps the sexual needs of the most attractive girls are adequately met, but the less attractive and/or more timid girls might fare little better than their counterparts among the men. Therefore, it is doubtful that sexual desires can be ruled out even in those societies as motivation for marriage, although perhaps status and other social needs play as large a part in some societies as sexual interests.

The sexual interests and needs of boys are known to most girls of

[3]Lewis M. Terman et al., *Psychological Factors in Marital Happiness* (New York: McGraw-Hill Book Company, 1938), p. 248.

[4]Ernest W. Burgess and Paul Wallin, *Engagement and Marriage* (Philadelphia: J. B. Lippincott Co., 1953), p. 660.

[5]Mead, op. cit., p. 202.

315

marriageable age in the societies in which a period of dating precedes marriage. Women can stimulate men's interests by stimulating their sexual interests, and can maintain interest by continuing to stimulate these needs without satisfying them. Such techniques are employed both to continue men's interests in dating or to create a desire for marriage on the part of men.

Although percentages aren't available in motivational categories, it is possible to conclude that most, although not all, men have strong positive interests in sex prior to marriage and that this interest provides a major part of their motivation to marry. The same studies indicate that both sexes can marry without sexual motivation and that a considerable proportion of American women have done so. Neither of the above studies, nor the Kinsey research, nor any others provide a random sample of American sexual behavior, and even less is known about the attitudes of adolescents in other societies, so it is necessary to be contented with quite general statements. The same is, of course, true of trends in attitudes toward sex in marriage. Sociologists believe that girls are being presented with a more attractive picture of sex than their mothers were, and, therefore, probably the proportion with negative attitudes prior to marriage is decreasing. There is considerable clinical evidence indicating that a major proportion of the grandmothers of today's youth experienced sex as a necessary evil and did not hesitate to communicate this to their daughters. However, Freudian theory presented sex as both important and potentially edifying to both sexes. Fragmentary evidence from Kinsey, which indicated an increase in orgasm rate for women, suggested that sexual experience in marriage had become more gratifying for women.[6] This, as well as the Freudian ideas, have apparently led to an increasing pleasant anticipation by women of sex in marriage.

One point might be added: not only did a larger proportion of men have a positive attitude toward sex, but in the Burgess-Wallin data a much larger proportion indicated "eager longing" for sexual experiences, 13.2 per cent of men compared to 5.5 per cent of the women. It can be concluded that a very important function of sex in marriage has been to provide inducements for the young of both sexes to enter into a permanent relationship that provides an effective social group for the care and socialization of children. The part of sex in maintaining the stability of the marriage will be examined later.

SEX AS AN INTRINSIC VALUE Most young men possess rather strong positive sexual urges. Evidence from Samoa and the Trobriands suggests that this is true for unmarried girls in some cultural contexts, on the basis of periodicity. Although it is true that many young girls in

---

[6]Alfred C. Kinsey, Wardell B. Pomeroy, Clyde E. Martin, and Paul H. Gebhard, *Sexual Behavior in the Human Female* (Philadelphia: W. B. Saunders Company, 1953), p. 380.

316

American society voluntarily have sexual intercourse, it is less evident that they do this because they have positive sexual needs. Curiosity, a wish to please their companion, or sex as a means to some other end, such as marriage, are other motivations. Although the positive sex impulses of young girls in American society are not clear, it is evident that such needs develop in most women after sexual experience in marriage. Widowed and divorced women have sexual needs that they can identify without difficulty. Remarriage, then, provides for positive sex needs of formerly married women, as it does for men, both single and previously married. The satisfaction of these needs in marriage can be viewed in two contexts: the prevention of their being satisfied outside of marriage, with attendant social problems, or more adequate provision for such needs within marriage.

Sex in predominantly Christian societies continues to be colored by early Christian pronouncements against it as sinful and the notions that somehow mankind would be purer and more desirable without the taint of sex. These pronouncements recognized that intercourse was necessary for procreation and further that sexual impulses in young men were so strong that these could not generally be suppressed. Therefore, it became one of the duties of wives to provide for the expression of these sexual needs in their husbands. Therefore, marriage provided for the expression of undesirable but necessary sexual be-havior within a legal context in which the husband bore partial responsibility for the children produced. These notions about the sinful nature of sexuality undoubtedly contributed to frigidity in women and their negative attitudes toward sex. Desirable wives were identified as those with no interest in or experience with sexual intercourse, and virtuous feminine behavior in marriage was identified with lack of sexual responsiveness in marriage.

Another aspect of the sexual function of marriage is its superior provision for meeting sexual needs. As already mentioned, even the most permissive societies apparently meet only some of the sexual needs of some of its unmarried members. Marriage, with cohabitation, provides legal and convenient sexual access between spouses. More-over, in proscribing competition from other than the spouse(s) it provides a sexual monopoly of a partner for each spouse. Further, it provides an extended period for learning the needs and responses of the other. Research has shown that for about half of newly married couples, a period of from months to years is required for learning and accommodation.[7] Probably such learning is more important for the sex needs of the wife, because orgasm doesn't necessarily accompany sexual intercourse for women.

---

[7] Judson T. Landis "Length of Time Required to Achieve Adjustment in Marriage," *American Sociological Review,* **11** (Dec. 1946), pp. 666–677.

Recently, a third perception of sex has emerged. It has been recognized that sex can be a highly pleasurable and rewarding experience for both men and women. The continued improvement and dissemination of birth control information is moving advanced societies to a place where sex can be separated from procreation. The implications of this development have not yet been fully explored. However, Foote has pointed the direction in his article "Sex as Play." He says, in part:

The attraction of sex makes it the favorite form of play for millions of Americans. Why do not our thinkers go on from there to contemplate the kind of social life which might result from formal recognition of this fact, rather than implicitly or explicitly reverting to the prejudice that sex as play is bound to be sinful or at best amoral? Is it because to grant its status as play is felt to legitimize its pursuits without restraint? If so, the thinkers do not understand the nature of play.[8]

This view of sex as fun has not been accepted generally, but current and future generations will face it. This view can, however, be fitted into the ideology of sex within marriage without great difficulty. In fact, the "companion" role complex in wives' behavior includes the notion of the wife as an alluring and stimulating sex companion of the husband. Foote suggests that intercourse itself may become an art; that is, the whole process of stimulation and communication that includes intercourse. That this process is already well started will be evident later in the review of the husband's sense of obligation in trying to ensure that his wife experiences an orgasm whenever they have intercourse.

Sex and Marital Stability In the previous section, what the family does for sex has been explored. The question is, what does sex do for one facet of the family—its stability? It has been seen that where individuals have been polled, sex provides major motivation for both men and women to enter marriage. For women, initial interest is developed into a more positive need after a number of years of sexual experience in marriage. Premarital anticipation of the desirability of sexual experience would lead one to anticipate that sexual intercourse would play an important part in holding spouses together. This is not always true, however, especially for the wife, as the following case illustrates: "I expected to perform sex in marriage, but both before and since, I'm willing to admit it is a much overrated activity. Now and then, perhaps it's better. I am fortunate, I guess, because my husband has never been demanding about it, before marriage or since." [9]

---

[8]Nelson N. Foote, "Sex as Play", *Social Problems*, 1 (Apr. 1954), pp. 159–163.

[9]John F. Cuber with Peggy B. Harroff, *The Significant Americans, A Study of Sexual Behavior Among the Affluent* (New York: Appleton-Century-Crofts, 1965), p. 52.

In other cases, sexual life appears actually to mitigate against the unity of the marriage, as this case illustrates: "I do not feel I've achieved a good sex adjustment. I have orgasm sometimes. I am by no means warm and do not particularly enjoy it and am just as glad not to be bothered by it. There seems to be something bestial about it. I would prefer marriage without it."[10]

That sex life may mitigate against stability in a sizable minority of families is indicated by Landis. In his sample of parents of college students, one eighth of the couples agreed that their sex life had never been satisfactory to them. Another eighth disagreed in their evaluation (that is, their sex life was satisfactory to one but not the other).[11] Landis as well as other researchers found a considerable relationship between spouses' attitudes toward their sex life and their attitudes toward their marriage.

Most of the neutral or negative statements concerning sex per se come from women. It might be supposed, quite reasonably, that sex in marriage would be a greater source of dissatisfaction among women than among men. Evidence supports the opposite conclusion. Figure 13.1 shows that there is a larger proportion of husbands than wives who express lack of satisfaction with sex life. If low scores below 29 are combined, 39 per cent of husbands fall in this broader category of dissatisfaction with sexual experience. Similar findings were reported by Terman. Thirty per cent of the husbands registered three or more sexual complaints against the spouse compared to 7.5 per cent of wives to make that many complaints. It appears that it was chiefly women who rejected sexual intercourse per se. These women did not neces-

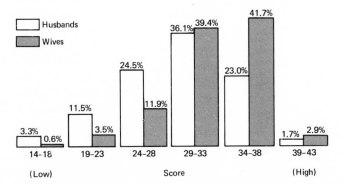

Figure 13.1. Sexual satisfaction scores of 601 husbands and 629 wives. [From Ernest W. Burgess and Paul Wallin, *Engagement and Marriage* (Philadelphia: J.B. Lippincott Company, 1953) p. 674. Reprinted by permission.]

[10]Burgess and Wallin, op. cit., p. 686.
[11]Landis, op. cit., pp. 666–667.

319

sarily identify such rejection with the personality or behavior of their husbands. They would not have been interested in changing husbands to find sexual gratification. They rejected sexual intercourse as a gratifying or meaningful experience, but this rejection does not always mean that the wife was unhappy with her sexual experience. If her husband did not press for intercourse, she might consider herself fortunate.

Husbands evaluated their sex life differently. Rarely did they reject sexual intercourse per se, but a considerable proportion were dissatisfied with their own sex experience, especially its frequency. There was close association between husbands' dissatisfaction with their sexual life and their dissatisfaction with the marriage. In contrast, there was little association between unsatisfactory sex life and dissatisfaction with the marriage for women. The opposite was true among couples who were highly satisfied with their sex life. Almost all the wives rated their marriage successful, but for men there was little relationship between a highly satisfactory sex life and a high degree of satisfaction with the marriage. For men, sexual satisfaction tended to be a necessary but not a sufficient condition for marital satisfaction; for women it predicted marital satisfaction but was not necessarily its cause.

A majority of both husbands and wives considered their sex lives satisfying and regarded it as an important part of their lives. As such, it contributed to marital stability.

SEX FOR REPRODUCTION Little need be said about the reproductive function of sex, yet it cannot be ignored entirely. Humorists have a good deal to say about the high birth rate in rural areas that have little organized recreation or in northern areas where winter nights are long. These areas may, in fact, have high birth rates, but for other reasons. Studies of attitudes of young people have shown that most express a desire for families of two or three children. It takes infrequent sexual exposures to produce this many children within a fertile period of over twenty years, which is available to most couples. The related notion that couples who have large families are more passionate is also untrue—at least the fact of having several children is not evidence of more sexual intercourse. Large families are the result of a deliberate decision to have many children, of ignorance of or the unavailability of contraceptive devices, or of carelessness in their use.

Intercourse is necessary for the conception of children unless artificial insemination is utilized, but it would be a rare couple that had sexual intercourse only for this purpose. Most intercourse is for the pleasure of one or both spouses.

SEX AS THERAPY Intercourse has frequently been described as intimate communication. In marriage, at least, this is true, and couples soon learn to understand through it what the spouse is feeling toward them. Emotion is communicated through the concentration of blood in the genital organs, which increases the tension and warmth of the organs; through warmth in the lips, communicated through kissing; and through the rate of breathing and other physical reactions. In marital sex, only the positive emotions such as affection, admiration, gratitude, and excitement can produce these physical changes. The fact that the spouse seeks this close, intimate contact may be interpreted as something of a compliment.

Sex can, therefore, communicate the positive emotions of one spouse for the other in a way that is more effective than most verbal communication. To the knowledgeable spouse, it is likely to be even more convincing than verbal communication because it can hardly be faked. Occasionally people, including spouses, say things they don't mean, but one cannot will the concentration of blood in the genital organs. The spouse who states ardent emotions and then delivers a "luke-warm" kiss is unlikely to be convincing.

Although sex has the possibilities of communicating affection in a more convincing and gratifying way than alternate communication, it does not always do so. It communicates to the understanding spouse the emotion present in the other spouse or the lack of it. Women can engage in intercourse without positive emotions and even with some negative ones. The idea of sex, itself, may be attractive to young men without any particular emotional involvement. Therefore, sex can take place with little emotion. This seems to account for much of its dissatisfaction to some young couples, especially wives, who feel that there is nothing to it. There *is* nothing very positive in their feelings to communicate. Sex cannot communicate affect when none is present.

The therapeutic potential of sex lies in this powerful, potentially gratifying, nonverbal communication. It can transmit love, sympathy, and admiration of one spouse for the other in a convincing manner. The spouse feeling frustrated or insecure may feel reassured as well as relaxed from this sexual experience. Although therapy is thought of as needed primarily in relation to a spouse's interaction with the extrafamilial world, couples also report that intercourse can heal friction and provide reassurance to spouses who have experienced some disagreements between themselves. It puts these in perspective as unimportant in comparison with the emotional bond between them.

Of course, like any communication, it can communicate hostility and indifference as well as positive emotions. It is unlikely to do this through the sex act itself, because negative emotions tend to prevent intercourse, but if one spouse makes an advance, its rejection through lack of response communicates lack of emotion or hostility as efficiently as acceptance can communicate positive emotions. Sex has high therapeutic potential, but obviously it cannot be prescribed like a pill

321

for depression, frustration, or insecurity. If there is affection and concern for the spouse, this positive involvement can be expressed effectively through sex.

Issues and Controversies

Some issues involving sex have the earmarks of social problems in that a large proportion of spouses find themselves involved in behavior that is unsatisfactory. Others are unresolved intellectual questions that divide scholars concerning the causes or consequences of sexual behavior.

ARE THE LESSER SEXUAL INTERESTS OF WOMEN PHYSIOLOGICALLY OR CULTURALLY BASED? Almost all research studies have found that men on the average desire sexual intercourse more often than women. This is a social problem in that it is a major source of dissatisfaction of men with marriage.

These general statements may obscure the amount of variation in sexual interest and capacity within the sexes. Although as an aggregate men have expressed a desire for more frequent sex, an appreciable proportion of married women desire intercourse more frequently than their husbands. Burgess and Wallin in their previously cited work found that some 18 per cent of the wives in their sample were experiencing appreciably *less intercourse* than they desired. Terman's data place the figure slightly higher. These data may be summarized as follows:[12]

	Wives (Per Cent)	Husbands (Per Cent)
Too frequent intercourse	24	3
Just the right amount	53	54
Too little intercourse	22	44

It should be noted that although some wives experienced more intercourse than they desired, this proportion is much less than that of the husbands who experienced less than they desired. Intercourse more frequently follows the wife's than the husband's preference.

A more recent study by Bell of women, all of whom had college degrees and had been married less than ten years, provided a slightly different set of data:

[12]Terman et. al., op. cit., p. 281.

	Wives
Too frequent intercourse	6%
About right	69%
Too infrequent intercourse	25%

This more recent study discloses fewer wives who have more intercourse than they desire and more who have it about as frequently as they desire it. It must be pointed out that the Bell sample is from the upper middle class. To the writers' knowledge this is the only study to show wives to be more passionate than husbands.[13]

Some of our own unpublished data bear on the issue. We asked a random sample of 210 parents of children in the third grade the question, "In your family who desires sexual intercourse more frequently, the wife or the husband?" In most families both agreed that the husband had stronger sexual desires.

	Husband's Response	Wife's Response
Husband much more frequently	36.7%	33.8%
Husband somewhat more frequently	41.0	37.1
Husband and wife exactly same	13.0	19.5
Wife somewhat more frequently	6.7	6.2
Wife much more frequently	1.4	1.0
No response	1.5	2.4

Our data (1972) support the early studies by Terman and Burgess. In fact, they suggest that the differences in sexual interests between husbands and wives may have become greater rather than less in the past 35 years.

The intellectual problem is whether the differences in interests are physiological and therefore inevitable or whether they are due to differential conditioning of boys and girls and differential normative definitions of the roles of husbands and wives. It is clear that these differences exist before marriage. The Burgess and Wallin study cited earlier showed that a substantial proportion of girls have approached marriage without anticipations that sex will be edifying and gratifying. However, this shows only that at about twenty years of age a larger proportion of men than women are interested in sex.

Most societies indoctrinate children with the undesirability of sexual intercourse between unmarried people. In America, from which most

[13]Robert Bell, "Some Factors Related to the Sexual Satisfaction of the College Educated Wife," *Family Life Coordinator*, **13** (Apr. 1964), p. 44.

of the sexual research comes, the indoctrination of girls is much more thorough and negative than for men. In restraining sexual interests and participation of girls, parents have not always distinguished between experience that is "bad" out of wedlock from what is "bad" per se. "A fate worse than death" was a phrase used not so long ago for a girl who lost her virginity without marriage. The phrase was never used to describe the loss of male virginity! Dating and courtship in American society have consisted to a considerable extent of attempts of boys to have sexual intercourse and the attempts of girls to terminate physical involvement short of that point. Such sexual intercourse for girls has been associated with unwanted pregnancy, loss of reputation and bargaining power, and awkward and self-centered techniques on the part of male partners.

The lack of sexual interest on the part of women is probably related to the fact that initiative has generally rested with the male. He must achieve an erection, which does not happen without positive interest. If the wife feels an interest in intercourse, she cannot initiate it directly. She must arouse interest in her husband so that he will follow through. Because women have been socialized to a passive, even negative, part in intercourse and because there remain some traces of the ideology that good women are uninterested in sex, considerable obstacles are in the path of women's initiating intercourse as a result of their own wishes for it. The interest of wives in intercourse might be much greater if they had equal control of *its timing.* When they are interested their husbands may not be at all. This unpredictability, among other things, prevents wives from taking contraceptive precautions with such devices as diaphragms before retiring. It means, too, that their greater inclination, which is somewhat periodic—prior to or following menstruation—usually is not entirely satisfied. The position in intercourse, certainly a cultural element, may not be irrelevant. The husband's body above the wife's, dominant in American society, restricts her choice of movement as needed in intercourse.

Thus far, this discussion shows that there is much cultural conditioning and definition that in many societies dampens the sexual interest and activity of women. Bernard expresses a strong cultural point of view when she terms this conditioning the "sexualization" or "desexualization" of the female body.[14] If the differences are cultural rather than biological, the issue might be decided by the discovery of a society in which women are clearly the more passionate sex. Hints that this is the case come from anthropological literature, but the evidence appears to be anecdotal. Whether it is generally true that in some

---

[14]Jessie Bernard, "The Fourth Revolution," in Ira Reiss (ed.), *The Sexual Renaissance in America,* a special issue of *The Journal of Social Issues,* **22** (Apr. 1966), pp. 76–88.

societies women are, as a sex, more interested in intercourse and more ready to participate in it would be a significant research problem.

Research presents evidence of a greater *capacity* of women than of men; namely, the finding that women frequently experience multiple orgasms during a single period of sexual stimulation. This capacity in the female is greater than in the male after age twenty.[15] A more recent study reports multiple female orgasms routinely, whereas this is not the case for males.[16] In folklore, this has its parallels in stories of the honeymoon in which the sexual interests and responsiveness of the bride place a heavy strain on the capacity of the groom. Actually, research on intercourse immediately following marriage indicates that that level of sexual demand by the bride is unusual. However, it appears from information regarding multiple orgasm that the female has a greater physiological potential for response than the male. If this is true, this potential is not consistently realized by a majority of women in sexual experience.

Is SEXUAL SATISFACTION CAUSE OR EFFECT? All studies of the sexual relationship and the degree of satisfaction with the marriage have shown a substantial correlation; that is, a tendency to evaluate both positively or both negatively. The unresolved question is which caused the other? Generally speaking, physiologically oriented scholars have assumed that the causes of satisfactory or unsatisfactory sexual adjustment were to be found in the size or the development of the genitals or the glandular functioning of the spouses. Sociologists usually have taken the position that one's sexual behavior is the product of socialization, social interaction, and values. Therefore, the experiences the person has had with his spouse and with the extrafamilial groups is likely to affect his sexual behavior and his attitudes toward it. Terman, in his longitudinal study of gifted children, found that he could predict divorce better from a marital happiness score than from sexual adjustment scores, and that if he added the sexual adjustment to the happiness scores, the accuracy of the prediction was not increased.[17]

Burgess and Wallin, in pursuing this question, found that dissatisfaction with sexual intercourse predicted dissatisfaction with the marriage for the husbands but not for the wives. A high sex-satisfaction score for either spouse made it possible to predict with some accuracy that that spouse would be highly satisfied with the marriage. Husbands who have intermediate sex scores are more likely to be well satisfied with their marriages, but the wife's evaluation of the marriage cannot be

[15]Kinsey et. al., op. cit., p. 718.

[16]William H. Masters and Virginia Johnson, *Human Sexual Response* (Boston: Little, Brown and Company, 1966), pp. 131.

[17]Unpublished manuscript by Lewis M. Terman, quoted in Burgess and Wallin, op. cit., p. 689.

325

predicted if she has an intermediate sex score (Table 13.1). Thus, it appears that the degree of sexual satisfaction predicts a husband's evaluation of his marriage, but for the wife it does not.[18] When the procedure is reversed, it is found that happiness scores predict dissatisfaction with sexual life for men but not for women. The opposite is found for high happiness scores; they efficiently predict a highly satisfactory sex life for the woman, but not for the man. To sum up, happiness scores predict sexual scores better for women in the happier marriages, better for men among the unhappily married.

More recent research shows that if one takes the proportion of sexual experiences *which result in orgasm for the wife,* the relationship between sexual experience and marital satisfaction is more impressive. Very few "very happy" wives have orgasms less than 10 per cent of their sexual experiences. Such associations do not demonstrate causality, but do show that the two conditions of sexual fulfillment and happiness in the marriage tend to be found together.

These analyses, although provocative, do not answer the question whether sexual gratification in marriage is primarily cause or effect. It remained for two of Burgess and Wallin's students, utilizing the Burgess-Wallin longitudinal data, to provide an additional test of the causal hypothesis. The first sexual and happiness scores were obtained after five years of marriage, the second after fifteen. The research question was "Will early sexual adjustment predict later marital happiness better than early happiness will predict later sexual satisfac-

Table 13.1

Female Orgasm Rate and Marital Happiness in Intact Marriages

Per Cent of Coitus Resulting in Orgasm	Marital Happiness Rating						
	1 Very Happy	1–2	2 Moderately Happy	2–3	3 Moderately Unhappy	3–4	4 Very Unhappy
	Per Cent						
0	4.4	3.2	9.0	16.1	15.8	*	19.0
1–9	3.6	9.5	4.5	12.9	8.8	*	19.0
10–39	6.5	20.6	11.3	3.2	10.5	*	9.5
40–59	9.5	12.7	17.1	12.9	15.8	*	4.8
60–89	16.5	17.5	17.1	16.1	14.0	*	9.5
90–100	59.4	36.5	41.0	38.7	35.1	*	38.1
Cases	587	63	222	31	57	4	21

*Too few to calculate
SOURCE: Paul H. Gebhard, "Factors in Marital Orgasm," *Journal of Social Issues,* 22 (April 1966), p. 90. Reprinted by permission.

[18]The correlation for husbands is .49. It is not given for wives, but obviously is considerably less.

tion?" Their analysis indicated that *each is equally effective* in predicting the other ten years later.[19]

Sexual Roles in Marriage

The emergence of recognized sexual roles is recent and is an indication of the increasing value placed on sexual experience. Although sexual needs, especially of the male, have always been recognized, sexual intercourse has been devalued. It was something that required attention, but the less said the better. It was viewed as an isolated phenomenon rather than one that could affect the whole husband-wife relationship and/or the stability of the family and the mental health of family members. Also, it was regarded as male gratification, with pleasures to the wife incidental, if any. Many women regarded it as "something one has to put up with." It was considered a biological phenomenon that could be and was satisfied by the wife's being more or less sexually accessible to the husband. With this low evaluation and a set of biological assumptions, it is not surprising that the sexual behavior seemed hardly complex enough or significant enough to be viewed as a role.

Recent literature, however, put intercourse in a highly strategic place in the development of personality and assigned it a central place in mental health problems. Thus, it took on new importance for both sexes. Each was seen as having important sexual needs and each sex was seen as important to the other, not in a passive sense of being a necessary participant, but one who by the *way* he or she participated became vital to the sexual needs of the other. The orgasm became the measurement unit of female sexual gratification. Intercourse in which the female experienced orgasm was considered an achievement, an experience in which she was not to become a failure. Only recently has it been recognized that women frequently experience considerable pleasure in intercourse that does not result in orgasm.

At first, variations in female response were explained in terms of a woman's being highly sexed or less so as a biological characteristic, but evidence was soon accumulated that placed heavy emphasis on her emotional feelings toward her husband and on his techniques for "arousing" her sexual interests and potential. This view of the husband as a manipulator of his wife's sexual potential led to a vast "how to do it" literature on sexual techniques for husbands.

The recognition that there is a *quality* as well as a quantity of sexual experience for the husband has been slower in developing. Emphasis

[19]Robert A. Dentler and Peter Pineo, "Sexual Adjustment, Marital Adjustment, and Personal Growth of Husbands: A Panel Analysis," *Marriage and Family Living*, **22** (Feb. 1960), pp. 45–48.

on orgasm may have obscured this recognition, in that men almost always experience an orgasm during sexual intercourse. Orgasm can usually be accomplished by the male with no more than passive cooperation from the female. However, orgasms vary from trivial experiences to emotional experiences of great intensity. The response or lack of it from the wife can make the difference between what has been termed "relief" (as though sexual needs were some type of minor irritant) to a high level of physical-emotional gratification. That intercourse *can* be a most effective way of communicating affection between spouses is being recognized. Therefore, it has a potential for reinforcing affection, for reassurance and security-giving that go beyond the physical gratification of the moment. With the diffusion of these beliefs in the greater potential of men for sexual experience has emerged a more complex role for the wife that goes beyond accessibility on request by the husband.

The matter may become quite complex. Both sexes recognize that intercourse can be gratifying for the wife. The husband recognizes that her sexual gratification depends on her feeling toward him and his techniques as a lover. Because female sexual interests depend on other matters, too, such as whether she is distracted by concern about one of the children, she will not always achieve an orgasm, whatever he does. If the wife fails to reach orgasm, the husband may feel guilty or inadequate, or both. This reduces his pleasure in the sexual act. Therefore, the wife feels a sense of obligation to reach an orgasm, or sometimes to feign one, so that her husband won't feel guilty about her lack of gratification. If the husband interprets her lack of response as lack of affection, he may feel rejected, also. Sex has become "dangerous business," even in marriage! Hacker has described this as one of "The New Burdens of Masculinity."[20]

For most couples the sexual role is hardly so complex and not a serious problem; however, both the increasing value placed on sexual experience and the recognition that its quality varies with the social-psychological interaction between spouses has led sociologists to list it as a marital role. It first emerged as a role of the wife—sex partner to the husband—presumably in response to the greater value placed on sex by men than by women, but as the value on female sexual gratification increases, increasing attention is given to the variations in men's knowledge and techniques as variables in the sexual gratification of their wives.[21]

[20]Helen Hacker, "The New Burdens of Masculinity," *Marriage and Family Living,* **19** (Aug. 1957), pp. 227–233.

[21]Lionel S. Lewis and Dennis Brissett, "Sex as Work: A Study of Avocational Counseling," *Social Problems,* **15** (Summer 1967), pp. 8–18.

Types of Marital Sex

It has been implied that heterosexual intercourse within marriage varies considerably in intensity and meaning. It is desirable to make these differences explicit before we proceed to variations in sexual roles. We shall attempt to describe three types of marital sex that frequently, but not inevitably, occur in sequence.

Sex to those who have not yet experienced it is regarded with a combination of curiosity and excitement. It is regarded as an important experience, and one that is usually, but not always, pleasurable. If the person is unmarried, sex is an uncertain experience in which there is considerable excitement "in the chase." It also involves an element of danger: of discovery, a possible unwanted pregnancy, and changes in the relationship between two people that develops in the sex act and colors the relationship thereafter. This type we term *novelty sex.* The attraction is in *the idea* of the act, rather than in the act itself—the fact that it is a new experience, a new relationship, and often one involving danger. The novelty is greatest in the first sexual experience of the individual, but an element of it is involved in the first intercourse with additional persons, even if one or both have had intercourse before. Less novelty remains even in a second experience with the same person. The author of the improbable-sounding title of an article in a sex magazine, "The Best Sex Is with a Stranger," was referring to this element in sex. Its importance sociologically is in the confusion of this type of sexual experience with the entire range of sexual experiences. Couples either before marriage or after frequently feel let down in that sex means nothing after one or a few nights together. The thrill and curiosity associated with the novelty of the experience is gone and nothing else has taken its place. At this stage couples may break the relationship before marriage, feeling they would receive little gratification from sex if they married each other. Married couples in the early stages of marriage feel disillusioned because sex has so little to give them when they expected so much.

The second type we will term *individually oriented* sex. There is a continuing sexual drive in the healthy young male. Prior to sexual intercourse it may have been gratified by orgasms stimulated by fantasy in dreams or in masturbation. Marriage provides a convenient and socially acceptable means of sexual stimulation leading to orgasm. Many discussions of sexual intercourse term this *relief from tension.* It is easy to misinterpret the phenomenon in this context, because usually the tension is created by intercourse or by the foreplay that the husband has initiated before intercourse. It is more accurate to think of the orgasm as a gratifying experience for the male as is, to a greater or lesser degree, the part of intercourse that precedes the orgasm, also. Orgasm

329

can be achieved by the male without any response on the part of the female.

The comparable gratification for wives is the orgasm. It offers an intense and pleasurable experience for the woman regardless of the husband's experience. If it is not experienced before the husband's orgasm, it is sometimes stimulated by manual manipulation by the husband. The orgasm for each is a separate event; therefore the term *individually oriented.*

This type of sexual gratification is frequently accompanied by conflict. There are some costs involved for women in intercourse. These include time and energy, in some instances, in taking specific precautions against pregnancy and douching afterwards. If she cannot utilize birth control, a danger of pregnancy is an additional cost. If the *only* result is an orgasm for the husband, most wives will prefer the experience at rare intervals, or as some have stated, marriage would be more attractive to them *without* intercourse.

The task of ensuring an orgasm for the wife may be equally taxing on the husband. Most husbands find it difficult to continue intercourse after they have experienced an orgasm. To manipulate the female genitals with the hands until orgasm occurs may be distasteful to the husband.

Individually oriented intercourse is gratifying to a degree to one or both spouses, but the intensity of the experience may be slight and the experience may be distasteful to one or the other, more often the wife. Where husbands are highly dominant in the family, this type of intercourse may take place frequently and lead many wives to feel that sex is a cross that wives must bear.

The third type, we suggest, is based on mutuality and interstimulation. It occurs only when both spouses desire it. The stimulation of the wife results in initial lubrication of the vagina so that initial intercourse is easy and pleasant. The arousal of each partner becomes a stimulus for further arousal of the other until orgasm results. This we term *mutual stimulation intercourse.* Both partners are likely to reach orgasm at about the same time, because the arousal of one stimulates the other. The concurrent arousal is conducive to the continued exchange of caresses and verbal expressions of affection. Besides providing gratification for both spouses, this type of intercourse differs from the others in that it produces more pleasure in the period prior to orgasm and a more *intense* orgasmic experience.

This third type of sex involves restraint and control—restraint in that it can occur only when both partners actively want intercourse; control in that each partner must control arousal to approximately that of the other. It is most likely to occur between couples who feel strong

330

affection for each other. In these marriages an indication of sexual interest by one spouse frequently stimulates interest in the other. This type of sexual activity is more likely to develop after some years of marriage because it requires restraints and controls not usually characteristic of early sexual experience. Also, couples are likely to develop this pattern after a period of trial and error alternating with the other patterns. Many couples never achieve this third level, and those that do don't always play their roles successfully.

LEARNING SEXUAL ROLES Some disagreement exists on the degree of complexity of sexual roles. Naismith quotes with approval the following passages from an earlier work of Dickinson's:[22]

Given affection and eagerness, here is a tapered cylindrical passage, elastic and *lubricated,* receiving an organ with a tapered point and tender cover in a quickening rhythm inciting to mutual ecstasy. . . . Nothing would appear less complicated for two persons who have never been indoctrinated with *shames* or *repulsion* and are free from *fears of conception, infection,* or *detection.* With the anatomical normalities that are usual, happy accord thus hangs on *preamble* and *timing,* on *gentleness* and *consideration* and a certain amount of *information* about each other's anatomy. (Italics ours.)

If Dickinson has listed the requirements for effective sexual role-playing, and it appears to be at least a good beginning, how many spouses find themselves well prepared and married to another who has none or few of the liabilities cited or implied? Apparently a bit more than half, to judge from their statements that their sexual experience was satisfactory from the beginning. Another 22 per cent of Landis's couples reported that it took from one month to twenty years to achieve sexual experience that was satisfactory to them. One eighth of the couples agreed they had *never* resolved their problems and for another one eighth only one of the spouses said that his sexual experience was satisfactory. A larger proportion of the sample reported that this part of their marriage was more unsatisfactory to them than any other.[23] In addition, it is not known how adequate the sexual life of some couples might be who reported "no problems." Studies quoted earlier indicated from one fourth to one third of the wives had no expectations that sex in marriage would be a pleasant experience.

Sexual roles are among the more difficult of family roles, although some couples encounter no major difficulties, at least as they view it. It appears, however, from the cited research that many learn through

---

[22]Robert L. Dickinson, in *Successful Marriage,* ed. by Morris Fishbein and Ernest W. Burgess (Garden City, N.Y.: Doubleday and Company, 1955). Quoted in Grace Naismith, *Private and Personal* (New York: Van Ries Press, 1966), pp. 6–7.

[23]Landis, op. cit., pp. 666–677.

some type of trial-and-error process because some 22 per cent of the total number reported initial difficulties that were resolved over a period of months or years.

As the socialization of the American is reviewed with respect to sexual roles, it is not surprising that spouses lack both concepts and skills for the role of sexual partner. To complicate the matter for many, sexual intercourse is "doing what comes naturally," and it is true that few couples will fail to achieve a sexual union that will result in an orgasm for the husband. Also, few couples have major difficulty in conceiving children. However, most Americans have come to expect more than this from their sexual life, and as couples have expected to receive more gratification, better understood sexual roles have become necessary, just as some other societies, such as Samoa, have held higher standards and have had better defined sexual roles to achieve them.

The training of the child in intercourse roles is opposite to that in other areas of behavior. Knowledge is kept from him, adult sexual behavior is secretive, and published material is kept from him, to the extent that this is possible. Sex education has been limited to reproductive information, which includes nothing about intercourse except that the sperm come from the penis and are deposited in the vagina, and so on. In addition to the vacuum of information provided, the subject is so permeated with emotion among adults that the child cannot seek information in the manner he would on other topics.[24] Of course, this cultural pattern has its function: to prevent intercourse before marriage. A society will hardly provide lessons in the techniques of accomplishing something that is prohibited!

The sexual information that is available to adolescents is mostly dysfunctional. In the movies, the hero is seen as doing everything he can to violate the sexual norms, often with success. This theme is occasionally provided variation by a heroine who violates all the norms and attempts to seduce the hero. At times, sex is portrayed as something approaching rape. These philosophies and techniques, although they sell movie tickets, are in the main dysfunctional to learning sexual roles appropriate to intercourse in marriage.

The extended dating period provides stimulation and opportunity for sexual intercourse before marriage. Such dating is colored by male attempts to seduce females and female titillation of male sexual needs to prolong male interests and, if the male seems eligible, to secure an opportunity to marry him. Again, the dating process is largely dysfunctional in that the male objectives are entirely self-centered and the

---

[24]Eleanore B. Luckey, "Helping Children Grow up Sexually," *Children*, **14** (July–Aug. 1967), pp. 13–15. See also, Gordon Shipman, "The Psychodynamics of Sex Education," *The Family Coordinator*, **17** (Jan. 1968) pp. 3–12.

female responses are manipulative and develop in females a negative pattern of sexual response.

A small minority of engaged persons find their way to a substantial literature on the sociology, psychology, and physiology of sex. More pick up a paperback in a drugstore or sample the "smorgasbord" of articles that is offered by the slick and pulp magazines. The latter varies in quality from articles written by the most knowledgeable social scientists and counselors to sexual quacks who know nothing except how to attract attention. This content is mainly technique-centered: "How to bring your partner to a boil." Technique, whether it is technically correct, is of little utility in sexual roles. Those who write it assume a human being is a thing, not the highly complex, evaluating, goal-oriented organism that he is. Highly educated youth probably practice some discrimination in the material they read dealing with sex and as a consequence have more accurate and relevant information than the less well educated.

Premarital counseling just prior to marriage is increasing. Doctors are often consulted because of their physiological knowledge, ministers because of the moral aspects of sex. Prior to the current decade neither profession was prepared to deal with the social psychology of sexual intercourse. Currently both professions are adding training in the social and psychological aspects of sex in the curricula of their professional schools. Professional organizations of the medical specialties are providing intensive postgraduate training for practicing physicians, especially on topics related to sex. The past quality of the information as well as the amount of exposure to it has usually been inadequate as sexual role training. Like the quality of printed material, the quality of premarital sex counseling varies from that given by highly trained and competent professional counselors to that given by quacks with nothing except their personal experience and values.

Besides a certain amount of information that some secure, a majority of couples are engaged for a period of months before marriage. This is a period during which each has made a commitment to the other. It offers an opportunity for a reorientation toward sex. The task in terms of sexual roles is to change from an ego-centered sexual concept to one that takes full account of the feelings and needs of the other. This probably occurs in some instances, but in how many cannot be estimated.

In summary, it cannot be said that much socialization conducive to effective sexual role-playing is available in American or most other societies. It is probably true that most adults don't have much to offer youth. A whole body of humor has grown up about the inadequacy of parents on the subject, as illustrated by the story of the father who was pressured by his wife into taking their adolescent son aside for a

333

discussion of the facts of life. The father returned some time later looking a bit stunned. "Did you have your talk?" his wife asked. "Yes," he replied, "and I learned quite a bit!" Aside from some professional literature and a few competent marriage counselors who are consulted by a minority of adolescents, probably the most useful socialization that some youth receive is a respect and concern for the rights of other people.

SPECIAL TASKS IN HUSBAND AND WIFE ROLES For those who view sexual intercourse in a broader perspective than the gratification of the biological urges of husbands, husbands' central task has been delineated as providing for the sexual stimulation and gratification of their wives. Often, this has been measured in terms of the proportion of times the wives experience orgasm. While orgasm is the climax of sexual experience, recent views have modified its importance. Many women have indicated that they received a great deal of pleasure from their intercourse on occasions when they did not reach orgasm. Some who infrequently experience orgasm state that they find the experience pleasurable in its psychological aspects—that is, the feeling of intimacy and sharing of feelings of affection—as well as in the physical pleasure in intercourse itself.[25] It may depend somewhat on the objective of wives. If it is only or primarily to experience the excitement of an orgasm, then intercourse that does not include it is frustrating. If they value as much or more the feeling of closeness, intimacy, and love, they enjoy the experience whether or not it culminates in orgasm. These two correspond to the *individually oriented* and *mutual-stimulation* sex discussed earlier.

Whether concern is focused on the female orgasm or not, the task of husbands remains that of playing the male role so that the female finds pleasure in the act. Women, in general, have desired intercourse less frequently than men and an appreciable number have not desired it at all.

Some of the behavior patterns believed to increase feminine pleasure in the sex act have been widely discussed, such as a long period of foreplay to arouse the emotions of the wife. The task of timing sexual intercourse to the interests and mood of the wife involves two rather different ideas of sexuality—one that female interest in it is essentially biological, the other that it is psychological. If the biological thesis is accepted, then the initial attitudes and moods of the wife are not important. The husband who has the requisite anatomological information caresses the appropriate body areas until the wife is physically aroused, not unlike a musician tuning an instrument. However, a psychological perspective sees female sexuality as controlled by atti-

[25]Burgess and Wallin, op. cit., Chapter 20.

tudes and feelings toward her husband at that particular period of time and absence of other distracting ideas. This perspective sees physical caresses, per se, as hardly relevant. However, to the extent that they communicate the idea of affection and attraction from the husband, they are likely to affect the mental set of the wife. Effective role-playing therefore has been discussed as (1) essentially physical stimulation of the wife leading to her arousal before intercourse or (2) the timing of sexual advances by the husband to correspond with her positive attitude toward him and her social environment, or to change a neutral mental set to a positive one by communicating affection for and attraction to her.

A crucial task in the sexual role of wives appears to be in providing more sexual experience for husbands. For example, over 50 per cent of the wives in Terman's study who had been married an average of eleven years preferred intercourse four or fewer times per month, and of the wives in the Burgess-Wallin study who had been married five or less years 25 per cent preferred four or fewer experiences per month. Apparently, the major source of male complaint concerning their wives was their sexual unavailability.[26] Where there is a difference in the sexual desires of spouses, these are more often resolved in favor of the wife. Terman's research shows that 42 per cent of the husbands in his sample had intercourse less frequently than they desired, but only 16 per cent of the wives had intercourse *more* frequently than they wished. It should be noted, however, that this is a matter of resolving differences in favor of the spouse who does not wish intercourse, rather than in favor of women. Almost 20 per cent of the wives indicated a desire for more sex, but less than 3 per cent of the husbands reported in engaging in intercourse more frequently than they wished.[27]

Rainwater has presented data supporting the position that the interests of the husband have more influence than those of the wife. He finds that among couples in which the wife is uninterested or negative toward intercourse, 39 per cent of the couples have intercourse at least twice weekly.[28] However, 61 per cent have it less frequently. Many men would prefer intercourse daily. Our reaction, then, to those data is that they don't address the question directly because the frequency that husbands wished intercourse is not given. It is our opinion, however, that men who are "strongly interested" in intercourse would want to experience it twice weekly or more. Therefore, probably less than 39 per cent, perhaps a much lower proportion than that, were having intercourse at their preferred frequency. The Rainwater data do not

[26]Ibid.

[27]Terman, op. cit., p. 281.

[28]Lee Rainwater, *Family Design: Marital Sexuality, Family Size, and Contraception* (Chicago: Aldine Publishing Company, 1965), p. 102.

335

seem to contradict the proposition that the less interested spouse is likely to have more influence on the decision whether or not the couple has intercourse at a given time. (The interested reader is referred to the Terman, Rainwater, and Kinsey reports for additional detail.) Still, the major problem for husbands has been the infrequent interest of wives in sex.

This problem is not a simple one if viewed within the context of mutually stimulated intercourse. It implies that wives would have to find means of increasing their own pleasure in intercourse if they are to be competent in playing a sex partner's role. We shall mention two possibilities without attempting to elaborate each.

First, the type of contraceptive is relevant. If the wife must get up to put a diaphragm in place this involves some inconvenience and may change the mood of one or both spouses toward intercourse. The oral contraceptive or the inner-uterine device avoid this. Second, women socialized against sex in childhood and adolescence find it difficult or may see it as inappropriate to communicate sexual interest to their spouses. Such communication problems probably will decrease as a result of less negative conditioning of girls with respect to sex.

Variables in Sexual Partner Roles

When and how frequently married couples have intercourse is a matter that they decide. However, that decision is affected by some of their own characteristics, such as age, and by norms of some of the aggregates of which they are members, such as their religious denomination or social class.

AGE The relationship between age and frequency of sexual intercourse is linear; in general, the older the persons or couples the less frequent the intercourse. The median (Kinsey sample) for wives twenty years old or younger was 2.8 times per week, decreasing to 2.2 times by thirty, to 1.5 by forty, 1.0 at fifty, and .6 by age sixty (Figure 13.2). Even the decrease between ages twenty and twenty-five is considerable. The range of frequency in his sample was from none to twenty-eight times per week. In addition to the general decline in sexual activity, it is noteworthy that intercourse does not end with the menopause. In incidence it is almost as high for women fifty to fifty-five as for those forty-five to fifty, although the decline is considerable from forty to forty-five. However, 20 per cent of the couples had ceased sexual intercourse by the time the wife was fifty-five.[29] Intercourse has no upper age limit, but its frequency diminishes, and a larger proportion of couples become inactive as they grow older.

[29]Kinsey et al., op. cit., p. 348.

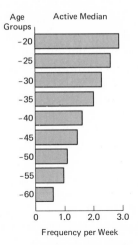

Figure 13.2. Active median: experience in marital coitus, by age. [Adapted from Alfred C. Kinsey, Wardell B. Pomeroy, Clyde E. Martin, and Paul H. Gebhard, *Sexual Behavior in the Human Female* (Philadelphia: W.B. Saunders Company, 1953) p. 350. Reprinted by permission.]

The basic capability to perform the sexual act does not disappear with age, but many physical changes occur. The upper limit for conception has been placed at about fifty for women, although this may change with the prescription of hormones for women. The fear of pregnancy is removed in later years. Probably more significant are changes in the genital organs and in the physiological reactions to orgasm. The lining of the vagina decreases in thickness and loses its folds. The size of the vagina decreases somewhat and the time for it to become lubricated increases. Some of the physiological changes during intercourse and orgasm are lost.[30] None of these changes prevent intercourse, but suggest that more stimuli are required to ready older couples to participate. The decreased tonality in the genital organs suggests, too, that the emotional experience is less intense. The proportion of sexual experiences resulting in orgasm decreases after fifty for women.

It should be noted that preferred frequency of intercourse also declines with advancing age at a rate similar to the decreasing incidence of intercourse (Figure 13.2). Although husbands' preferences decline sharply from thirty to sixty, the average is still about three times monthly. The wive's preferences show two irregularities. Woman forty-five to fifty desire almost as frequent intercourse as those thirty-five to forty. After age fifty-five, the average preferred by wives is less than once per month. It should be noted that these women were over fifty-five years of age thirty years ago. It does not *necessarily* follow that

---

[30]Masters and Johnson, op. cit., Chapters 15 and 16.

women in their early years of marriage today will place such a low value on intercourse in their older years.

The impact of age is different on the frequency of female orgasms. Fifteen per cent of the wives did not reach orgasm until they had been married more than a year. Another 10 per cent never experienced orgasm. At no age do women always reach orgasm during intercourse. The proportion of experiences resulting in orgasm steadily increases until the twentieth year of marriage or age forty of the wife, gradually declining thereafter. Orgasm, unlike coitus, seems to depend in part on sexual experience over a period of time. Social maturity or more adequate role-playing may also play a part, because the proportion of wives who experience it the first year increases with the age of the woman at marriage—from 66 per cent of those married before twenty, to 78 per cent who married between twenty-one and thirty, and 83 per cent for those who married after thirty.[31]

Why does intercourse decline so greatly with age and for increasing proportions of couples cease entirely? Kinsey and associates have attributed this decline to the declining physical capacity and interest of the husband.[32] It is our belief that there is more support for an explanation that takes the capacities and wishes of both sexes into account. First, it should be noted that the decline in frequency begins with the twenty- to twenty-five-year-old group, which has a considerably lower frequency than have those under twenty. The decline is greater from twenty to forty (that is, from 2.8 to 1.5 times per week) than from forty to sixty (1.5 to .6). Decline in physical capacity of either sex does not seem an especially convincing argument, especially that decline that occurs before age thirty. There is a decline of affection between spouses that occurs steadily between the early and the middle years of marriage[33] and in the evaluation that each marital partner has of the personality of the other.[34] Because sexual interests are affectionally stimulated, this decline is probably reflected in less frequent desire for intercourse. Visual stimuli become weaker as the aging body loses some of its appeal. Finally, the Masters and Johnson research alluded to earlier suggests lessening physical capabilities for intense excitement in orgasm. With the advent of hormones for women to replace those lost at menopause, some of the physiological changes that reduce capabilities for sexual excitation in intercourse may be delayed and motivation for more frequent intercourse in the later years may be

---

[31]Kinsey et al., op. cit., p. 382.

[32]Ibid., p. 354.

[33]Peter Pineo, "Disenchantment in the Later Years of Marriage," *Marriage and Family Living,* **23** (Feb. 1961), pp. 3–12.

[34]Eleanore B. Luckey, "Number of Years Married as Related to Personality Perception and Marital Satisfaction," *Journal of Marriage and the Family,* **28** (Feb. 1966), pp. 44–49.

increased to the extent that physiological change is involved. However, no prescription has been invented that restores middle-age marriage to the affectional level of the early years.

In addition to age, strictly speaking, the family life cycle may have some independent effect on sex life. The advent of the first child interrupts routines and pair activities. It and subsequent children provide for some of the affectional needs of spouses, especially of wives. This could account for some of the decline in marital coitus in the twenty to thirty age category, except that *no increase* in sexual activity follows the maturation and departure of the children from the home.

SOCIAL CLASS The frequency of intercourse appears to be unrelated to educational level, according to the Kinsey data.[35] The notion that the lower social classes are more virile or less inhibited or have fewer other pleasures and, as a consequence, have intercourse with considerably more frequency fails to receive research support. Neither do there appear to be differences in incidence by the occupation of the husband.[36]

Although incidence rates vary little, if at all, by social class, the *type* of sexual experience in intercourse does vary considerably. The proportion of women who achieve orgasm during marital intercourse increases with each increase in educational level of the wife. Likewise, wives from white-collar homes are more likely to experience orgasm than those from laboring occupations.

The differences in sexual gratification appear to be even more class-related. Eighty-six per cent of middle-class wives expressed a positive feeling toward marital intercourse compared with 69 per cent of those in the upper-lower class and 46 per cent in the lower-lower class (Table 13.2).[37] Examination of Table 13.2 suggests that the

Table 13.2
Wife's Gratification in Sexual Relations

		Very Positive	Positive	Slightly Negative	Rejecting
Middle class	(58)	50%	36%	11%	3%
Upper-lower class	(68)	53	16	27	4
Lower-lower class	(69)	20	26	34	20

SOURCE: Reprinted from Lee Rainwater, *Family Design* (Chicago: Aldine Publishing Company, 1965), p. 64; copyright © Social Research, Inc., 1965. Reprinted by permission of the author and Aldine-Atherton, Inc.

[35]Kinsey et al., op. cit., p. 354.
[36]Ibid., p. 356.
[37]Rainwater, op. cit., p. 64.

339

patterns of sexual response of the middle class are more similar to those of the upper-lower classes than are those of the latter to those of the lower-lower class. This suggests the influence of role performance in other areas. The lower-lower-class male is especially deficient in playing the provider role. The lack of pleasure of the lower-lower-class wife may be in part a reflection of her attitude toward him, in which she views him as a failure because of his failure to provide an adequate economic basis for the family.

Middle- and upper-lower-class males also show more interest in marital intercourse than do lower-lower-class males, white or black.[38] Because lower-lower-class males have marital intercourse as frequently, the difference in interest must stem from the comparative lack of interest and response on the part of lower-lower-class wives and/or the sexual techniques of the husbands. These data refute the ideas that sex is more enjoyable or that it preoccupies the lower-lower class.

Some specific evidence is available to show concern of the husband for the sexual gratification of his wife. This was volunteered by 85 per cent of the Protestant and 46 per cent of the Catholic middle- and upper-lower-class husbands in the Rainwater sample compared with only 37 per cent in the lower-lower class. Evidence of lack of any concern was evinced in the case of 3 per cent of the Protestant and 11 per cent of Catholic middle and upper-lower class, compared to 39 per cent of husbands in the lower class.[39] Either a large proportion of lower-lower-class husbands may be unaware that women can receive pleasure from intercourse, have given up in efforts to provide gratification, or are unconcerned whether or not the wife receives pleasure from intercourse.

The empirical data fit well the concepts of individual-oriented and mutual-stimulation intercourse. In the lower-lower class, sexual enjoyment is experienced only or primarily on the part of the husbands, and a large proportion of the husbands express no concern for the gratification of their wives. In the upper-lower class and especially in the middle class, there is considerable evidence of mutuality. Most husbands are concerned for the enjoyment of their wives, and both more wives and more husbands enjoy sex.

RACE Much has been written on the virility and sexuality of the American black in comparison with his white counterpart. Comparative studies of marital sexual behavior of the two races are rare. However, Rainwater found some evidence to support the notion. He found larger proportions of upper-lower-class blacks "highly interested" than whites of the same class. The same was true in the

---

[38]Ibid., p. 67.
[39]Ibid., p. 104.

340

lower-lower class. The upper-lower-class black was also more likely to be highly interested than the middle-class white. The order of interest from highest to lowest is[40]

Upper-lower-class black men	87 per cent
Middle-class white men	78 per cent
Upper-lower-class white men	69 per cent
Lower-lower-class black men	56 per cent
Lower-lower-class white men	35 per cent

The greater interest of black men apparently is not shared by their wives. Their degree of enjoyment is about the same as for white women. However, blacks are more likely to mention sexual life as one activity tending to keep women married. Clearly, research on marital sexual activity of blacks is inadequate, and the need for research is indicated.

RELIGION Neither Kinsey nor Rainwater found differences in the incidence of marital sex of Protestants and Catholics, but each found other differences. Members of Kinsey's devout Catholic sample tended to take longer to achieve their first orgasm after marriage, and at all ages, a smaller proportion of intercourse resulted in orgasm for devout Catholic wives. Also, a larger proportion never achieved orgasm.[41]

Rainwater found that fewer Catholic husbands expressed the view that sexual intercourse should be gratifying to the wife. The proportions for Protestants was 85 per cent compared to 46 per cent for Catholic husbands. A seemingly contrary finding in the same study was that Catholic husbands were more likely to view sex as socioemotional closeness rather than psychophysical relief and pleasure only.[42] The two findings, however, probably are compatible. It apparently hasn't occurred to many Catholic men that intercourse is an activity that can or should be gratifying to the wife. Even this limited research indicates that the meaning and outcome of intercourse, although not its incidence, is affected by Catholic and Protestant ideology. It would be interesting to know how fundamentalist religious ideology affects marital sex life.

EXTRAMARITAL SEXUAL RELATIONS Few types of behavior are better concealed than extramarital sexual intercourse. Kinsey attempted to measure it, and reported that about one fourth of married women[43] and one half of married men[44] at some time during their marriage have

[40]Ibid., p. 67.
[41]Kinsey et al., op. cit., pp. 381–382.
[42]Rainwater, op. cit., pp. 104, 111.
[43]Kinsey et al., op. cit., p. 181.
[44]Alfred C. Kinsey et al., *Sexual Behavior in the Human Male* (Philadelphia: W. B. Saunders Company, 1948), p. 587.

341

extramarital intercourse. How accurate these figures may be cannot be determined. His volunteer samples lead one to think that the figures are too high, but because some of his respondents may have hidden this particular behavior, it could also be too low. Certainly, the figures were higher than most believed prior to his research. Complicating the matter further is the fact that some couples permanently separated are still legally married, and that others may be separated for years prior to a divorce. Technically, any intercourse they have during these years is extramarital. About all that can be said is that it occurs in an appreciable number of instances among married women, and among a larger proportion of married men.

A number of theories have been advanced to explain extramarital sexual experience. These are speculative. Psychiatrists have frequently advanced the explanation that it is evidence of fears of inferiority: inability to perform the sexual act or the fear that one is unattractive to the other sex. However, any theory based on the special psychological characteristics of the men involved is difficult to maintain because apparently about half of the male population is involved.

A more sociological explanation is that boys are socialized to take sexual initiative toward the other sex. At marriage, the norms proscribe sexual advances to women other than the spouse, but the resocialization of men at marriage is not entirely effective. Other women continue to appear attractive, and social control to prevent husbands from following some of these sexual interests is not very effective in a mobile, urban society.

The understanding of extramarital sexual behavior is increased by a recognition that its meaning and content vary greatly. Intercourse with a prostitute is apparently primarily for novelty and ordinarily involves no selectivity on her part or any continued relationship. A second type is based on a pickup relationship for a single evening or two. Because it is essentially noncommercial, the pickup involves some attraction on the part of both partners. The experience is one estimated by the two involved as likely to be pleasant and worthwhile in itself. Its primary element is novelty, but it includes some elements of response. In most instances, it involves no continuing relationship nor very deep, intense emotional commitment. Finally, there is extramarital intercourse that is an integral element in a continuing extramarital affair with a history and, often, a future. This type may eventually disrupt a marriage, or two, if both are married, and result in a new marriage or marriages.

One interesting, very specialized variation is that of wife- (or husband-) trading clubs. These are organized for the purpose of obtaining extramarital sexual experience for its own sake, with no emotional or legal commitments. These are very secret groups, of course, because members want to maintain their marriages and their reputations.

The sociology of extramarital sexual relationships is yet to be developed, but one aspect of it has received attention; that is, with whom it should not occur. Zetterberg proposes that a new set of "social incest" criteria are being developed that discourage extramarital relationships that are most likely to be disruptive of marriages and occupational or friendship ties. He suggests that included in the "incest" category are secretaries where men are employed, spouses of fellow employees and neighbors, and all women in the city in which the individual lives.[45]

Cuber offers an interesting classification of extramarital relationships. The first class is, in effect, a substitute marriage. It comes into being as a result of some chronic deficiency in the marriage that leaves one or more important needs of one spouse unmet. This type of extramarital relationship frequently lasts for years and in many respects resembles other marriages. In societies permitting polygamy, it would be a second marriage. In a monogamous society it differs in two important respects: it is usually kept secret and it is illegal. Children, if any, are illegitimate.

The second type occurs in the context of a long-term separation of marital partners because of military service, travel connected with earning a living, or other circumstances usually beyond the control of the couple. Because sexual and other marital relationships with the spouse are impossible, one or both spouses may form temporary extramarital relationships with another person. In most respects this arrangement resembles the first, but it is assumed that it will terminate with the return of the spouse.

The third type involves what Cuber calls "the true Bohemians." "These are people who simply do not accept the monogamous commitment with respect to their personal lives, although they still feel committed to and fulfilled in marriage and parenthood."[46] These engage in brief extramarital sexual experiences without any expectation or desire that they will lead to a long-term relationship.

Cuber, on the basis of limited research data, challenges the assumption that extramarital sexual relationships are detrimental to those involved. However, so little has been scientifically established that perhaps the soundest position is to reject premature conjectures of causes and consequences, keeping in mind that extramarital in-

---

[45]Hans Zetterberg, "The Secret Ranking," *Journal of Marriage and the Family,* **28** (May 1966), pp. 134–143.

[46]John F. Cuber, "Adultery: Reality Versus Stereotype," in *Extra-Marital Relations,* ed. by Gerhard Neubeck (Englewood Cliffs, N.J.: Prentice-Hall, 1969), p. 193.

tercourse is a phenomenon with as diverse motivations and behavior (and consequences) as premarital or marital intercourse. Research is possible on extramarital intercourse, but the problems of interviewee cooperation are formidable.

Needed Information on Marital Sex

Earlier, two general problems were discussed that have received much attention but have not been satisfactorily resolved: whether the lesser sexual interests of women are due to biological or cultural factors and whether attitudes toward sex experiences affect attitudes toward other areas of the marriage, or whether the latter are the determining variable in producing satisfying or unsatisfying sexual relations. As marital sexual behavior in various contexts has been discussed, other questions have emerged that also merit research.

The decline of sexual activity with advancing age has been noted. Some authorities have attributed this to the declining sexual capacity of the male but there is also evidence of declining interest and a decline in the speed and intensity of the female response. It is not clear whether this decline in sexual incidence, which starts *before* the age of twenty-five, is due more to physiological changes, to decline in the affectional relationships between the spouses, or to a decline in other stimuli provided by the spouses for each other.

There are considerable differences in the attitudes and sexual responses of women by social class. Is this primarily because of the differences in sexual philosophies and techniques of husbands by social class, in the generalized attitudes that wives have toward their husbands by class, or in the different expectations wives hold of the possibility of sex being gratifying to them?

There is limited evidence that membership in significant subcultural groups, such as religious and racial, have considerable differential impact on attitudes and values placed on sex and probably on behavior, also, but studies employing adequate samples of these groups are too few to allow firm conclusions.

Finally, there are two closely related problems. A study of marital sexual behavior and attitudes is needed that employs an adequate national probability sample to supply statistical sexual norms. Kinsey attempted this (to his credit), but in our judgment his samples are not adequate to provide a description of sexual behavior in which full confidence can be placed. It would also be of maximum usefulness to have a picture of changes in sexual behavior that are occurring from decade to decade so that these can be related to other changes in the society, such as the entry of women into paid employment. This would require repeated national surveys of sexual behavior, employing probability samples and utilizing the same items each time.[47]

A host of more limited studies would also improve our understanding of marital sex, such as the effect of the wife's enacting the provider role or the effect of the number of children in the home on spousal sexual behavior, or whether the frequency of intercourse in childless families shows the same pattern of decrease with age as that of families with children.

The past few decades have shed considerable light on marital sexual behavior, but even more remains to be learned.

---

[47]We are aware of the data of Kinsey et al. on changing sexual behavior, but some of it is based on recall of as much as forty years. Some incongruities are apparent, also, such as a decline of sexual incidence by about 40 per cent in the sixteen-to-twenty-year category of wives from those born prior to 1900 to those born between 1900 and 1910 then more thereafter. Therefore, it is our belief that these data add nothing to our knowledge except perhaps to show the need for adequate trend data on these matters, and for this reason we have not presented them here. The interested reader can find them in Kinsey et al., *Sexual Behavior in the Human Female,* op. cit., pp. 356–358, 380, 397.

14

Family Size and Fertility Control

There has been so much discussion of the "population explosion" and of "standing room only" on the planet, that it is easy to lose perspective on how the size of the nuclear family has changed and what it may be like in the future. In historical perspective there can be no doubt of both the direction and the magnitude of the change. It is toward smaller families, and the change has been impressive. We see in Figure 14.1 that the birthrate declined from over 50 per 1,000 population in 1820 to 17 in 1970, a reduction of two thirds, or, put another way, American women on the average are bearing only about one third as many children as their great-great-grandmothers in 1820. The same changes

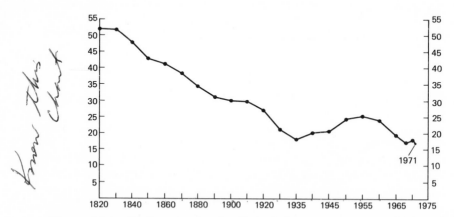

Figure 14.1. Birth rates in the United States, 1820–1971. [Adapted from Ronald Freedman, Pascal K. Whelpton and Arthur A. Campbell, *Fertility Planning, Sterility, and Population Growth,* New York: McGraw-Hill, 1959; *Statistical Abstract of the United States,* Bureau of the Census, 1971 and Vital Statistics Report 20, #11, Public Health Service, January, 1972.]

are occurring in Great Britain, where women married in the period 1862–1869 averaged 6.5 births whereas those married in 1925 had borne only 2.2 by 1946.[1] In the United States, even the changes since 1910 have been impressive. In that year, of women aged forty-five to forty-nine, 46 per cent had borne more than 4 children, compared to only 14 per cent of that age group in 1955.

If it is true that the trends in family size have been toward smaller families, why the alarmist literature on a population explosion? There are several reasons. From 1935 to 1957 there was a reversal of the trend toward smaller families (see Figure 14.1). These increases came at a time when the death rates continued to fall so that total population increased rapidly during this period. These large increases came at a time, also, when the society was aware of the problems of a large population, traffic congestion, smog, pollution, and pressure on recreational resources. For the first time many Americans ceased to view population increases with pride and satisfaction and to think of them as a source of social problems. By the early sixties, the United States had received the first bill for larger families in the form of the necessity for a tremendous expansion in public school facilities and teachers. Individual families also felt the cost in food, clothing, medical care, and education costs, present and anticipated.

The increases in family size in the United States were paralleled by similar ones in most of Western Europe, but were accompanied by a more dramatic population increase in Latin America, Africa, and South Asia. These areas did not experience increases in birth rate, but rather dramatic decreases in the death rate, due to better sanitation, drugs, and medical services. Prior to World War II, a family in which ten children were born might see three survive to adulthood. More recently, of the same number, eight or nine would live to adult status. Thus, unless the birth rate declines, some of these areas such as Latin America face the prospect of the population's doubling in a few decades. Because the production of food and other necessities does not increase at this rate, much of the world faces the possibility of malnutrition and starvation.[2]

Finally, for reasons not entirely clear, the higher birth rate from 1947 to 1957 was viewed as a permanent change in fertility. However, beginning in 1957, the trend back toward a lower birth rate resumed, and by 1971 the decline in the fertility rate was a full one third below that of 1957 (Figure 14.2). Demographers have viewed this new

[1]Ronald Freedman, Pascal K. Whelpton, and Arthur A. Campbell, *Fertility Planning, Sterility, and Population Growth* (New York: McGraw-Hill Book Company, 1959), p. 3.
[2]William and Paul Paddock, *Famine—1975!* (Boston: Little, Brown and Company, 1967).

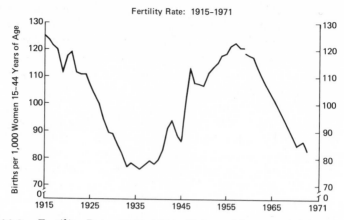

Figure 14.2. Fertility Rate: 1915–1971. [Adapted from Monthly Vital Statistics Reports 14, #5 (July, 1965), 19, #13 (September, 1971) and 20, #11 (January, 1972)]

downturn in the birth rate with caution, noting that it could be caused by temporary factors. They note that many women over twenty-five have already borne three children and (therefore) are having fewer children, whereas the newly married seem to be delaying having children longer than formerly. Presumably these will have children later. The reader will note that the fertility rate is still higher in 1971 than in 1935, whereas the birth rate is lower. This is because the proportion of women of childbearing age in the population was higher in 1971 than in 1935. In the seventies and eighties the children born in the 1947 to 1962 period will reach childbearing age, which will increase the proportion of people of childbearing age in the population. At present, however, *both* older and younger women are having fewer children. One can see in Table 14.1 that the birth rate has declined substantially since 1957 for women in every age category. It is ap-

Table 14.1
Birth Rates by Age of Mother: United States, 1940–1968

Year	Rate Per 1,000 Women						
	15–19	20–24	25–29	30–34	35–39	40–44	45–49
1940	54	136	123	83	46	16	2
1947	79	210	176	112	59	17	1
1957	96	261	199	119	60	16	1
1964	73	220	179	104	50	14	1
1967	68	174	143	79	39	11	1
1968	66	167	140	75	36	10	1

SOURCE: Statistical Abstracts of the United States, Bureau of the Census, 1970, p. 48.

parent, therefore, that the long-term trends toward smaller families has resumed. Let us look at the social changes that seem to play a part in the shift to fewer children.

The Society of Smaller Families

Why are women bearing, on the average, only about one third the number of children borne by their great-great-grandmothers? Two answers will come readily to mind: (1) they want fewer children, and (2) they have better control over their fertility. Let us examine the first reason.

CHILDREN AS ECONOMIC ASSETS In contemporary urban America it is difficult to imagine a child as an economic producer, yet throughout history his economic contributions have been essential to the family. He has been an economic asset to his parents in two principal ways: as a helper while a child and as a provider for his parents' needs after they became too feeble to work. The latter role has been especially significant. Social Security and other governmental and private programs for the economic support of the aged are of very recent origin. Through the ages, it has been the responsibility of children to support and care for their aged parents. Few events were more catastrophic than to have no children and especially to have no sons, because in most societies the care of parents was the responsibility of the son and his wife. In a sense, to have many sons was like having many retirement systems! It is not surprising, then, that the status of the wife was dependent to a considerable extent on her ability to bear children, especially sons. Given this function, parents were not only willing to have children, but considered it almost a matter of survival to do so. Because the death rate among children has been high until recently, not only children, but several children were highly valued. By their birth, one ensured his old age as well as it was possible to do at that time.[3]

There is some doubt whether children ever were economic assets by virtue of their role as workers on family farms and other family enterprises. Some have considered them economic assets because of this contribution. Typically, farm-reared children are of some help by age seven and probably boys earned a surplus over their keep during adolescence, provided they were not enrolled in school. We doubt,

---

[3]Incidentally, the success of programs of family limitation in the developing countries will be dependent in part on social legislation to provide for the elderly. Until there is an alternative to care by one's children in old age, parents in those societies will insist on conceiving many children. Children continue to be a more important asset in the rural sector of society with its paucity of alternative provisions for care of the aged than in urban areas.

however, that children are typically an asset over the entire period of their minority because of their labor, although such labor does contribute to their keep and reduces the net cost of rearing children. Two social changes have reduced the value of children's labor drastically: movement of families to the city and compulsory school attendance. The majority of children in contemporary American urban society make no appreciable contribution to family income, although this is not true of some urban societies. Even less do today's urban parents expect their children to support and care for them in their old age. With relatively few exceptions, urban children, and especially American children, with their prolonged period of enrollment in the educational system, have ceased to make the important economic contributions to their families that were characteristic of the childhood of their grandparents.

CHILDREN AS ECONOMIC LIABILITIES We have seen that children have lost their roles as providers for their families. At the same time their care and education has become increasingly costly. Udry stated in 1965[4] that the average family furnished an outlay of $20,000 in rearing a child to adult status. Another way to view the economic cost is that it approximates the total salary of the family for three years. Thus, a family with an income of $2,000 would spend an average of $6,000 on each child, whereas one with $15,000 would spend $45,000 on each child. With inflation, rising incomes, increased expectation, and an increase in the average time spent enrolled in educational institutions, the absolute amount will increase. Sussman and Burchinal have shown that parents continue appreciable financial support of their children even after they have reached adulthood and married.[5]

Expensive to rear as most urban children are, the figures cited indicate only part of the cost. Campbell points out that children also usually prevent the mother from taking employment at least until they are in school.[6] Even at poverty levels, he estimates that this costs an average of $2,000 annually.[7] For middle-class women it would be much more.

Finally, in societies in which education is supported by taxation, each additional child costs the community a large sum through support of the school system. In 1971, the average cost to the community to educate a child through high school graduation (state of Washington

[4]J. Richard Udry, *The Social Context of Marriage* (Philadelphia, J. B. Lippincott Co., 1966), p. 443.

[5]Marvin B. Sussman and Lee Burchinal, "Parental Aid to Married Children: Implications for Family Functioning," *Marriage and Family Living,* **24** (Nov. 1962), pp. 320–332.

[6]Arthur A. Campbell, "The Role of Family Planning in the Reduction of Poverty," *Journal of Marriage and the Family,* **30** (May 1968), p. 244.

[7]Ibid., p. 242

350

average) was $8,916. At this rate, the education of a family of six would cost the community more than $50,000.[8]

CHILDREN AS SOCIAL ASSETS AND LIABILITIES It is quite clear that one or more children are wanted by most couples. Not only do couples confirm this verbally but if they have no natural births, many adopt children and a few utilize artificial insemination. Why people want children is less clear. Most studies have focused on how many children are desired or on the desired spacing of births, rather than on why children are wanted. However, some reasons can be mentioned with a degree of confidence. Most babies are cute, dependent, and affectionate. They are at the same time open in feelings and behavior and intriguing as they take on the more complex mental processes and behavior patterns of more fully socialized persons. Children can provide a set of relationships with parents that cannot be duplicated between adults. Finally, because the care and rearing of children is the principal reason for the institution of the family, children validate the status of wife. With children, the status of wife becomes an occupation. Without the roles of child care and socialization of children, there is some doubt that the care of the house and the preparation of food constitutes an occupation for the wife.[9]

However, despite evidence of the continued attractiveness of parental status, there are stresses in addition to the economic ones already discussed. The child-care role typically ties the mother very closely to the family abode. Psychiatrists see an appreciable number of young mothers who find close confinement during the children's preschool years more than they can bear. Grey discussed this phenomenon under the title, "The Trapped Housewife."[10]

Are these stresses related to social change? Apparently. The urban environment with its heavy traffic, railroads, docks, and other potential dangers to the child requires closer supervision of the child. Also, the separation of the nuclear from the extended family has eliminated convenient mother substitutes so that many mothers can leave their abodes only infrequently. Finally, and presumably more important, come the new responsibilities of the child-care and socialization roles. These stem from the widespread realization that the personality that a child develops is the product of his social experiences, not, as some of our ancestors assumed, the product of an irresponsible heredity. If his

---

[8]Records of the Pullman Public Schools, Pullman, Washington, 1971.

[9]Hoffman and Wyatt have suggested that this was a major motivation for the larger families during the 1947–1957 period. Lois Hoffman and Frederick Wyatt, "Social Change and Motivations for Having Larger Families: Some Theoretical Considerations," in Marriage and the Family, ed. by Jeffrey K. Hadden and Marie Borgatta (Itasca, Ill.: F. E. Peacock, 1969).

[10]Horace Grey, "The Trapped Housewife," Marriage and Family Living, 24 (May 1962), pp. 179–183.

351

character was simply inherited from some uncle or grandfather, this sharply limited the responsibility of the parent. Parents were expected to feed, clothe, and discipline their children and provide an opportunity for them to obtain an education. But if the child failed to perform acceptably, the parent could not be held responsible—some quirk of inadequate heredity was blamed. No longer is this true. The middle class and increasingly other elements in society are holding the parent responsible not only for his own parental role-playing, but for the attitudes, values, and behavior of his children.

Parental ability to meet such expectations is limited and made difficult for two principal reasons. First, other groups shape the child, especially the school and the neighborhood. These cannot be controlled by the parent. Second, knowledge of child-rearing has been limited, with untested theories utilized in the absence of confirmed theory. Finally, normative expectations for the child have expanded, so that it is no longer enough to rear a conforming, self-supporting individual. He must also be productive and innovative and must be a happy, secure, and outgoing person. These are much greater expectations than those facing our grandfathers. Moreover, scientific knowledge, even if adequately disseminated, is not at a point in its development at which it can provide a precise formula for producing conforming, productive, happy, and secure individuals.

Relevant, too, is the fact that many parents are producing "hippie"-type children. In terms of social exchange, what does the parent receive for his commitment of time and the equivalent of his total income for three years? Whether or not any young parent thinks he might produce a child with these characteristics, the existence and high visibility of this type of young person may have an impact on the societal image of the nature of human progeny and may lead some young couples to approach parenthood cautiously.

Rennie found that having children of any number was related to a lower level of marital satisfaction. She reports, "People currently rearing children were more likely to be dissatisfied with their marriages than people who had never had children or whose children had left home, regardless of race, age or income level."[11] Because she employed a large random sample of parents, this finding must be taken seriously. It may mean that rearing children in contemporary American society has become an unprofitable enterprise psychologically and sociologically as well as economically.

Finally, there is the reward or punishment of social approval or disapproval. Are mothers of large families regarded with approval as making a fine contribution to the society or even as "heroes," as at

---

[11]Karen S. Rennie, "Correlates of Dissatisfaction in Marriage," *Journal of Marriage and the Family*, **32** (Feb. 1970), p. 66.

times they have been designated in the Soviet Union, or are they regarded with disapproval as inept or irresponsible types who contribute to the population problem and to the higher tax rate necessary to educate them? We shall have to be frankly speculative on this point in the absence of research, but we deem the matter worth brief exploration.

Societal attitudes toward population growth is the central issue. It didn't just happen that the USSR decided to reward the production of large families. It faced the menace of attack by Nazi Germany. Men were needed both to be soldiers and to create the heavy industry to provide the sinews of war. In the United States, during most of its history, an underpopulated continent has provided opportunities for an expanding population, and to have a rapidly increasing population seemed socially desirable. By contrast, during the Depression of the thirties, many parents could not support their children, so that the arrival of children was regarded with, at best, mixed feelings. This depression period produced a birth rate so low as to anticipate a stationary or declining population throughout the Western world.

With the advent of greater prosperity following World War II large families became "stylish" again and the young mother with four or five young children was greeted with approval. By the sixties, American society was paying the bill for these large families in overcrowded cities, pressure on recreational facilities, and burgeoning taxation to support public schools and colleges. The mother of many children was no longer regarded with unmixed admiration, but in some circles was seen as a selfish or careless person who was taking more than her share of space in a crowded world. Although generalized approval or disapproval of large families on the part of the public can hardly be decisive in the decision to have children, it probably has some influence. People enjoy the approval of the general public even though they may be less responsive to it than to the attitudes of their own families and more intimate reference groups.

Effectiveness of Family Planning

We hypothesized that child-rearing has become to many burdensome psychologically because of the heavy responsibility placed on parents to produce happy and productive as well as conforming children. As a consequence, positive motivations for conceiving large families have declined. However, it should be clear that couples require no positive motivations whatever to produce large families. The sexual needs of couples result in intercourse of sufficient frequency to produce large families unless birth control, abortion, or infanticide is practiced.

How many conceptions would result for an average couple if no

353

effort were made to control conception? This is something like asking what man would be like if he grew up with no interaction with other people. However, some estimates have been made by students of fertility. Taylor has stated: "Data show that assuming no contraception, about half the women who have given birth will have conceived within three months of the first post-partum menstrual period, four-fifths within one year."[12] If the data on which this statement is made are adequate, women who are fecund would average bearing a child about every year and a half. When such women marry at an average of age twenty, their families would average twelve or so children, and considering multiple births, families of 20 would not be rare. The fact that families of even twelve are rare indicates that most couples make some attempt to control their fertility. The folk notions that large families indicate passionateness or virility in the spouses is without any foundation. Copulation at an average frequency would typically produce, in the absence of sterility, families of ten to fifteen children, provided no birth control was employed. Likewise, the notion of some that the low birth rate in large cities is due to low fecundity is sociologically naïve. As we shall note later, those segments of city populations not regularly practicing birth control have large families.

Like innumerable interesting social facts, the history of the practice of contraception is lost for lack of adequate surveys of earlier periods. Nonliterate societies have utilized a variety of techniques with varying degrees of success. Actually, the decline in birth rates shown in Figures 14.1 and 14.2 is indicative of the combination of the efficiency of contraceptives available and the determination of couples to employ them to limit family size. Data from Great Britain indicate that the use of contraceptives increased from only 15 per cent of the couples married before 1910, to 40 per cent married from 1910 to 1920, to 58 per cent married between 1920 and 1924, to 66 per cent of those married from 1935 to 1939.[13] Higher rates were found in the United States during a more recent period. Employing a probability sample from the entire country, Freedman et al. found that in 1959, 70 per cent had employed some method of family limitation and that over 94 per cent of fecund couples (those currently able to bear children) had employed or expected to employ some method of family limitation.

It has been noted that unless some biological abnormality is present,

[12]Howard C. Taylor, Jr., "A Family Planning Program Related to Maternity Service," *American Journal of Obstetrics and Gynecology,* **9** (July 1966), pp. 726–731, quoted in Lynn Landman, "United States, Underdeveloped Land in Family Planning," *Journal of Marriage and the Family,* **30** (May 1968), p. 197. Another study reported the average time required for conception at only 2.3 months. See Christopher Tietze et al., "Time Required for Conception in 1727 Planned Pregnancies," *Fertility and Sterility,* **1** (July 1950), p. 338–346.

[13]Freedman, Whelpton, and Campbell, op. cit., p. 6.

there need be no positive motivation to have children. Unless the couple takes precautions against having children, they are likely to have them soon and often. It has also been noted that there are increasingly strong reasons for family limitation. Paralleling these increased interests in spacing and limiting the number of children, contraception has become an increasingly effective and convenient means of family limitation. Presumably the increased market for contraceptives has provided the incentive to invent and market the newer mechanical and chemical devices.

Of the several techniques commonly employed, it is possible to distinguish three general types: those utilized by the male or requiring his cooperative action, those requiring manipulation by the female of her genitals prior to or immediately following intercourse, and the oral contraceptives taken as pills at regular intervals.

In the first group are the condom used by the male, the rhythm method requiring abstinence during the period the female is fecund, and coitus interruptus or withdrawal of the penis before orgasm. The three have in common that all interfere with sexual gratification, all require specific cooperation of the male and, perhaps for these reasons, they have low efficiency as contraceptives. It is the female who has the greater immediate interest in family limitation, and devices that depend on male initiative or on cooperative behavior by both partners are relatively inefficient. In addition, irregularities in the female menstrual cycle add an additional hazard to the rhythm method.

In the group depending on manipulation of the female genitals prior to or following intercourse are the diaphragm, the intrauterine device, douching, and suppositories. Of these, the diaphragm and the intrauterine device are regarded as effective if utilized properly. Although the intrauterine device prevents conception of the egg, it is not known exactly why it does so.[14] Its use is limited primarily by the concern of many women that it is dangerous to their health, although such fear is believed groundless. The diaphragm requires examination by a physician and instruction in its proper use. It must be inserted before intercourse and for maximum effectiveness requires the use of a contraceptive jelly. The douche and the suppositories are considered relatively ineffective.

The diaphragm and the intrauterine device have proved quite effective in families in which they have been regularly utilized. They require rational action by the woman prior to intercourse and involve techniques not obvious to the woman. Therefore, they have been

---

[14]For a discussion of the various theories advanced to explain the function of the intrauterine device, see Christopher Tietze, "Spirals, Loops and Rings Tested as Contraceptives," *Medical World News* (Nov. 8, 1963.).

355

utilized mainly by the well-educated woman in the middle and upper classes. This knowledge of reproductive organs, a rational outlook involved in family planning, and a willingness to handle her genitals are lacking among many poorly educated women.

Another limitation of the diaphragm is that it requires an interruption in the foreplay to intercourse while the woman inserts it. This lessens the pleasure of intercourse or even prevents it if the woman doesn't want to make the effort to obtain and insert it; in some instances couples gamble on conception by having intercourse without it.

By contrast, the oral contraceptive requires no active participation on the part of the male or any manipulation of the genitals by the female or internal examination by a medical doctor. It requires no special effort just prior to or following intercourse. If taken regularly it is extremely reliable. Current data suggest that newly married couples are obtaining efficient contraception from the beginning, whereas effectiveness in the use of other methods frequently has been attained only after one or more accidental conceptions.

The ultimate contraceptive device is the sterilization operation, which terminates the reproductive capacity of the couple. A national survey found that 9 per cent of the couples of childbearing age had terminated fecundity in this way. Of these, in about 90 per cent of the cases, the operation had been performed on the wife.[15] The reason given for performing the operation on the wife is that in the event of a separation the children usually are placed in the wife's custody and the husband might wish to have children by his next wife. An unstated reason may be that if the wife becomes pregnant after the husband is sterilized, considerable doubt would be placed on the paternity of the child.

Finally, new oral contraceptive pills are reported in development that can, from a single pill, produce infertility for extended periods. Also, one that may be taken after intercourse is being tested. These pills are likely to provide effective contraception in nonmarital sexual intercourse as well as more efficient control of fertility within marriage. Because few if any pregnancies are desired from nonmarital intercourse, these pills can be expected to reduce greatly the number of illegitimate births.

ABORTION AS BIRTH CONTROL Abortion has been employed in most societies as a means of child spacing and for the limitation of family size. Where legal and sufficiently inexpensive, it is an effective means. Among the industrial nations, Japan has achieved a zero population growth by this means.

Prior to the reform of the abortion laws beginning in 1967, it was

---

[15]Ronald Freedman, Pascal Whelpton and Arthur Campbell, *Family Planning, Sterility and Population Growth* (New York: McGraw-Hill Book Company, 1959), p. 26.

estimated that 1,000,000 illegal abortions were performed in the United States or about one for every three live births.[16] By 1972, more than a dozen states had liberalized their laws to permit abortions to protect the mental as well as physical health of the mother. Four states—New York, Hawaii, Alaska, and Washington—leave the decision to the mother and her doctor, provided the interruption of the pregnancy is in the early weeks of the pregnancy. All of these states have residence requirements except New York.[17] Further, recent court decisions have cast considerable doubt on the authority of legislatures to decide whether a pregnancy shall go to full term.[18] Currently, it is freely predicted that all restrictive abortion laws will be repealed or ruled unconstitutional.[19]

Although it is not certain that all abortion laws will, in fact, be repealed or invalidated, the prospect is sufficiently likely to merit a brief estimate of its probable effects. Early data from New York state are suggestive.

During the first six months that New York's new abortion law was in effect an estimated 69,000 abortions were performed in New York City's municipal, voluntary, and proprietary hospitals, and several special abortion clinics. This means that for every live birth in New York City, there is one abortion. Approximately half the abortions done in New York City are done for patients who admit to being out of state.[20]

If the above estimates are correct, about 25 per cent of the pregnancies in New York City were being terminated by legal abortions.

If criminal laws relating to abortion are removed, it can be expected that almost all pregnancies of unmarried girls will be terminated by abortion rather than resulting in forced marriages or illegitimate births. The same appears likely for most unwanted pregnancies of married women unless abortion is prevented by religious or other moral convictions. The elimination of most unwanted pregnancies could lower the birth rate by an estimated 450,000 births yearly.[21] Whether the effects might be even greater and result in an entirely stabilized (zero-growth) population cannot be forecast with any degree of confidence.

[16]Leslie Aldridge Westoff and Charles F. Westoff, *From Now to Zero* (Boston: Little, Brown and Company, 1968), p. 117.

[17]U.S. Department of Labor, Women's Bureau, "Abortion Laws" (WB70-237, June, 1970).

[18]Ibid.

[19]Edmund W. Overstreet, "Logistic Problems of Legal Abortion," *American Journal of Public Health,* **61** (March 1971), p. 498.

[20]Association for the Study of Abortion, "New York Report," **5** (Fall 1970–Winter 1971), p. 1.

[21]Pascal K. Whelpton, Arthur A. Campbell, and John E. Patterson, *Fertility and Family Planning in the United States* (Princeton: Princeton University Press, 1966), p. 44.

Social Distribution of Children

To the uninitiated, having none, a few, or many children is purely a decision of the husband and wife, or in a few instances of one or the other. But if this is the case, why do the middle class have few children, the lower class many, the cities small families, the farms large ones, the Negroes many, Caucasions fewer, Catholics more, Protestants fewer? The sociological answer is that these aggregates have subcultures that place greater or lesser value on childbearing and that offer more or less knowledge and access to means of birth control. Let us look briefly at each of these subcultures of fertility.

SOCIAL CLASS AND CHILDREN One sociologist with a flair for catching reader interest titled his book on contraception and fertility *And the Poor Get Children*.[22] In so doing he emphasized one of the best documented of social facts—that the middle and upper classes are generally successful in controlling their fertility whereas the lower class is not.

Of the several indicators of social class, education of the wife is one of the more closely related to family size. In Table 14.2 it is clear that as education increases, the average size of the family becomes smaller. This is true for each increment in education. When college education is compared with eighth-grade education or less, the less educated women have families that are about double in size of those with a college degree.

Income shows a similar although less dramatic relationship than for the education of the mother. According to data assembled from the census the fertility rate for the "poor" and "near poor" (intact urban families of four or more with income less than $4,158) is tremendously higher than for the "not poor" (Table 14.3).

Table 14.2
Children Ever Born to Women Ever Married, by Education of Wife, 1969

Education of wife	Women 15–44 years old* Children ever born per 1000 women	Women 45–59 years old* Children ever born per 1000 women
Less than 8 years	3,398	3,523
8 years	3,206	2,827
High school 1–3 years	2,944	2,744
High school 4 years	2,286	2,298
College 1–3 years	2,116	2,378
College 4 years or more	1,790	1,996

*Note: The women in the older age category 45–59 were in their childbearing age some thirty years prior to the period for those aged 15–44.
SOURCE: *Statistical Abstract of the United States, 1971*, p. 51.

[22]Lee Rainwater (Chicago: Quadrangle Books, 1960).

358

Table 14.3
Children Ever Born per 1,000 Wives Twenty-five to Forty-four Years Old, by Age, Race and Family Income, 1969

	White		Black	
Family income	25–34 years old	35–44 years old	25–34 years old	35–44 years old
Under $3,000	2,812	3,536	3,931	4,221
$3,000 to 3,999	2,843	3,532	3,654	4,680
4,000 to 4,999	2,590	3,479	3,406	4,473
5,000 to 7,499	2,553	3,166	3,017	3,870
7,500 to 9,999	2,426	3,014	2,745	3,636
10,000 to 14,999	2,218	2,954	2,011	2,780
15,000 and over	2,047	2,865	(B)	(B)

B: Base less than 75,000

SOURCE: *Population Characteristics,* Bureau of the Census, Series P-20, *203* (July 1970), p. 15.

Campbell reports that the nonpoor have about the number of children that are desired by all social classes; therefore the difference between the birth rates of the poor and the nonpoor represents excess or undesired children. He estimates that these undesired births numbered about 450,000 births in 1966 or about 12 per cent of all births in the United States that year.

Following the previous discussion, two questions need to be asked concerning social class: first, is there a higher positive value on large families among lower-class parents, or, second, are the differences in family size explained by the greater competence of the middle and upper classes in preventing conception?

A very simple explanation would be that low-income couples have more children than middle- and upper-income families because they *want* more. However, national surveys do not support this explanation. Whelpton and associates reported that three was the average number of children desired in all social classes and racial aggregates.[23] Actually, the mean desired by Caucasian women was 3.3 whereas for Negroes, more of whom are classified as lower class, the mean number desired was 2.9.

Among couples in which the wife had an eighth-grade education or less and the husband earned $4,000 per year or less, 39 per cent of the couples stated that they had *more* children than they wanted.[24] Because couples are reluctant to say that they didn't want the children they have, the proportion in this category is presumably considerably higher than 39 per cent.

[23]Whelpton, Campbell, and Patterson, op. cit., p. 44.
[24]Ibid., p. 248.

In a later study, wives were asked to state an ideal size of family for a high-income family and for a low-income family. They gave 4.8 as an ideal size for high-income families compared to 2.2 for low-income families.[25] These data offer impressive evidence against the idea that lower-class couples typically desire large families.

If there are no differences by social class in desired family size, then the difference must be due to differences in effectiveness in controlling family size. Sociologists who have studied the matter in detail find several relevant class differences that may for convenience be listed as propositions.

1. Lower-class women as an aggregate have less knowledge of the physiology of reproduction.
2. Lower-class women as an aggregate have less knowledge of contraceptive devices than middle-class women.
3. Lower-class women as an aggregate are less likely to believe that they can plan their lives and control their fate.
4. Lower-class women as an aggregate have more aversion to employing contraceptive devices that require the manipulation of their genitals.
5. Lower-class women as an aggregate are less likely to take an active-positive attitude toward sexual intercourse and are more likely to see their part as passive acquiescence.
6. Lower-class women as an aggregate are more likely to be fearful of the harmful effects of contraceptive devices such as the intrauterine device and the diaphragm, which must be placed within their bodies.
7. Lower-class women as an aggregate are more likely to wait until they have had as many or more children than they want before they begin attempts at birth control.
8. The cost of contraceptives is more likely to be a deterrent in the use of contraceptives by lower-class women.[26]

A combination of these propositions plus less cooperation from and communication with the husband appears to account for the inadequacy of birth control by lower-class couples.

If, for a moment, we return to the concept of subculture, we see the social-class subcultures as characterized by the same attitudes on preferred family size—in all social classes. However, in the middle and upper classes there has been a widespread diffusion of knowledge of contraceptives, a more rational philosophy of life embodying a con-

[25]Ibid., p. 35.
[26]Rainwater, op. cit.,

fidence in one's ability to control his own destiny, less repugnance in handling one's own genitals, better communication with and cooperation from husbands, more positive interest in sexual intercourse, and more financial resources with which to pay for medical examinations and contraceptive supplies. It should be noted, however, that all these conditions relate to differential effectiveness in practicing birth control rather than to differences in preferred family size. With the advent of more simple and convenient contraceptives, such as the oral pill, especially if its availability is subsidized for the poor, this class difference may decline and eventually disappear.

ILLEGITIMATE BIRTHS A special case of differential birth rate by social classes is provided by estimates of the proportion of illegitimate births among the poor and near poor and the nonpoor. Campbell estimates that about 16 per cent of the births in the former category are illegitimate compared to 2 per cent in the latter.[27] Why this should be so is not entirely clear, because such fragmentary evidence as the Kinsey studies shows no higher incidence of nonmarital intercourse among lower-class women. Several differences in avoiding conception and dealing with it after it occurs may explain the class differences. Middle- and upper-class women may, in a larger proportion of cases, delay intercourse until they are engaged so that the pregnancy occurs after marriage or if prior to it, can conveniently be legitimized by marriage. They are more likely to have an accurate knowledge of safe periods during the menstrual cycle. If an abortion is desired, they have more financial resources with which to obtain it. Finally, women in the lowest income groups who have intercourse outside of marriage may have it more frequently. Whereas most middle-class men have some attractiveness as husbands because of their competence as providers, many lower-class men do not. An unemployed man, if considered as a possible husband, may be rejected as another mouth for the woman to feed. Faced with the choice of bearing an illegitimate child or marrying its unemployed father, some women will choose the former as the more "profitable" course of action of the two.

In general, the reasons for a higher illegitimate birth rate among the poor are similar to those producing differential birth rates by income among those married. The situation is further complicated by the inability of many poor men to play the provider role adequately, which contributes to the conclusion on the part of some unmarried pregnant women that they would rather bear an illegitimate child than marry its father.

Occasionally the simplistic explanation is advanced that poor women have illegitimate children because they like it that way or because it is profitable to rear children on relief. An increasing volume

[27]Campbell, op. cit., p. 238.

of research on lower-class families has failed to find *any* support for such ideas. In almost every instance a nonmarital pregnancy constitutes a crisis for the woman—of whatever class.[28]

RACE AND FAMILY SIZE Because a larger proportion of blacks are poor and have less education, it would be expected that they would have more than their share of large families, which is the case. This has been true for as far back historically as records have been kept. Although fertility rates for the two races almost coincided in 1947, the baby boom of the fifties produced a larger increase for blacks than for whites and, although it began to decline after 1957, the fertility rate (number of children born per year per 1000 women aged fifteen to forty-four) was still 115 for blacks in 1968 compared to 82 for whites.[29]

However, it appears that blacks have no special preference for large families. Reference to Table 14.3 shows that in the "not poor" category of intact families with incomes of $4,150 or more, the fertility rate is *lower* for blacks than for whites. Blacks with good education and income limit their families as effectively, or even more so, than do whites. Among women with one or more years of college training who had about completed their families (aged thirty-five to forty-four years), black women had had an average of 2.3 children, whereas white women had had an average of 2.6 children.

It is among the poor and the near-poor that the black birth rate is high. Reference to Table 14.3 shows that the preliminary estimate of black fertility in these lower-income categories was 195.2 compared to 152.2 for the poor and near-poor whites. Again the differences cannot be explained by the number of children desired, because blacks prefer somewhat *smaller* families than whites. In terms of the overall black birth rate, the socioeconomic factor cannot be overemphasized. Whereas only about 40 per cent of white children were in the poor and near poor categories, almost 66 per cent of black children were in poor and near-poor families.[30]

Because blacks have an average preference for a *smaller* family than whites and because they actually average considerably larger families, the excess fertility or proportion of children that weren't wanted is greater for them than for nonblacks. From Table 14.4 it is clear that blacks before marriage want about 25 per cent smaller families than nonblacks. After a decade of marriage and the birth of an average of 2.7 children, they have raised their preferred number, but it still is considerably below the average preferred by nonblacks. However,

[28]See especially Lee Rainwater, "The Lower Class Family Crucible of Identity," *Daedalus,* **95** (Winter 1966), pp. 172–216.

[29]U.S. Bureau of the Census, "The Social and Economic Status of Negroes in the United States, 1970," Current Population Reports, P-23, No. 38 (July 1971), p. 113.

[30]Campbell, op. cit., p. 244.

362

Table 14.4
Average Number of Children Wanted, Number Born, and Number Expected

| | Number Wanted | | | |
Race	Just Before Marriage	At Interview	Births at Interview	No. Expected
White	3.2	3.3	2.3	3.1
Nonwhite	2.4	2.9	2.7	3.6

SOURCE: Adapted from Pascal K. Whelpton, Arthur A. Campbell, and John E. Patterson, *Fertility and Family Planning in the United States* (Princeton: Princeton University Press, 1966), pp. 44, 46.

although whites expect to have about the number they want, blacks expect to have about 30 per cent more children than they want.

From these facts, two conclusions are justified: blacks prefer smaller families than nonblacks but the birth control techniques that they are employing are not sufficiently effective to enable them to control their fertility to the number of children that they want. One other implication also seems clear, that when effective birth control is generally available to lower-income women, the birth rate in this sector will decline appreciably. In this respect it is illuminating to look at Table 14.4.

RURAL-URBAN FAMILY SIZE That families in rural areas are on the average larger than those in cities might well be stated as a sociological law. These differences in the United States are large and consistent, and they appear to hold equally in other societies, including those currently emerging from agrarian and hunting economies. Since 1800, urban families have averaged between 56 and 72 per cent of the size of rural families, with interestingly enough, the greatest difference occurring in 1940 and the least differences in 1950.[31] This difference resulted from more efficiency in birth control in urban areas during the Great Depression, and also from a larger increase in birth rates in the city once the "baby boom" started after World War II. The birth rate increased in rural areas also after World War II but less than in the cities.

The average size of completed families was about 50 per cent larger for rural than for urban families.

The reasons for the larger rural families may be evident from the earlier discussion of the reasons for the long-term trend toward smaller families. Social Security and private life insurance for retirement developed earlier and more adequately in urban areas, freeing parents from dependency on their children in old age. The labor of children on farms has continued to have some value and to offset partially the

[31]William Petersen, *Population* (New York: The Macmillan Company, 1961), p. 217.

financial costs of child-rearing. The psychological costs of parenthood are generally less, because children require less close supervision and mothers have fewer alternative uses of their time outside the home. Finally, the effective contraceptive techniques are less generally utilized in the rural areas. Data from a national sample reveal that 82 per cent of Protestant couples of childbearing age in large cities were employing contraception whereas only 65 per cent of Protestant farm couples of similar ages were utilizing contraceptive techniques. A similar difference was found between city and farm Catholics with 61 per cent of city but only 45 per cent of farm Catholic couples practicing contraception.[32]

In explaining the larger average farm family, we believe it useful to introduce the idea of an intensity variable in family planning. For most couples (except the few with sterility problems) there is no problem in conceiving as many children as or more children than they desire. Therefore, wanting children in a positive sense is usually irrelevant to family size. Instead, it is the intensity of determination to *restrict* family size plus the efficiency of the contraceptive devices that determines family size. For some of the reasons given, farm couples regard large families with less negative concern than do their urban counterparts. Therefore, they are less effective in the practice of birth control.

RELIGIOUS INFLUENCES The teachings of the Catholic Church encourage large families and currently prohibit all types of birth control except abstinence. Most other religions do not consider birth control to be a religious issue. It will become apparent that the Catholic teachings have some influence on the behavior of Catholic couples. For example, fewer Catholic couples (32 per cent) began contraception before the birth of the first child than did Protestants (52 per cent) or Jews (83 per cent).[33] However, as couples have children and with the advancing age of the wife, the differences in birth control become less. By age thirty-nine, among fecund couples (those who can readily conceive) 85 per cent of the Catholic women were practicing birth control compared to 93 per cent of Protestant wives.[34] This means that Catholic wives are much more likely to wait until they have had some children before beginning birth control, but that about seven of eight have begun some type of family limitation well before the close of the fecund period. Catholics are much more likely to utilize the rhythm method, which is generally accepted by their church, than are Protestants, but in the above-mentioned national survey (1955) 30 per cent had utilized some

[32]Freedman et al., op. cit., p. 150.
[33]Ibid., p. 110.
[34]Ibid., p. 106.

method condemned by their church. A later survey (1965) placed this figure at 53 per cent.[35]

As might be expected, the more active Catholic Church members are more likely to conform entirely to doctrine. However, inactive members are less likely to utilize methods other than rhythm than are Protestants, so the socialization of Catholics seems to exercise appreciable influence, even among those who are inactive in church participation.[36] Among mixed Protestant-Catholic marriages, the birth control practices more often correspond to the religion of the wife than those of the husband. The notion that the strong position of the Catholics on birth control results in Protestant women's changing their birth control behavior is incorrect, although Catholic husbands seem to influence Protestant wives more than Protestant husbands influence their Catholic wives. However, it is generally true that it is the wife whose preferences are followed.[37]

Catholic wives on the average have wanted slightly larger families than Protestants (3.5 compared to 3.1), but they tend to reduce these wishes after they have had and begun to rear some children. The same wives after fifteen years of marriage had reduced the average of desired children to 3.1. By contrast, Protestant wives desired an average of 2.9 children at the time of marriage and still preferred that number after fifteen years of marriage. This resocialization of Catholic attitudes concerning family size is illustrated by the following case:[38]

At the time of her marriage, this young Catholic mother wanted six children but after the first was born she decided that four would be enough because she and her husband began to realize "how much they cost." After the birth of her third child, she and her husband decided not to have anymore "because we decided it cost too much and we couldn't give more than three all we wanted them to have."

This was a couple with an above-average income.

Although Catholics have expressed a preference for slightly larger families on the average and expect to have more children, the national survey quoted found that those aged thirty-five to thirty-nine had actually had the same average number of children (2.6) as Protestants. The Catholic wives expected to add an average of .5 children to this

---

[35]Charles Westoff and Norman Ryder, "Methods of Fertility Control Used in the United States: 1955–65" in *Family and Fertility,* ed. by William T. Liu (Notre Dame, Ind.: University of Notre Dame Press, 1967), p. 167.

[36]Raymond H. Potvin, Charles F. Westoff, and Norman R. Ryder, "Factors Affecting Catholic Wives' Conformity to Their Church Magisterium's Position on Birth Control," *Journal of Marriage and the Family,* **30** (May 1968), p. 271.

[37]Freedman et al., op. cit., p. 105.

[38]Ibid., p. 280.

365

total, whereas the Protestants expected only an average of .2 more. Whether these expectations will prove accurate is impossible to forecast accurately, but the birth rate is very low beyond the thirty-five to thirty-nine age period, so we would anticipate slightly if any more births among the Catholic than the Protestant wives.

It seems clear that Catholic ideology and values embrace the ideal of large families. These lead to preparental wishes for large families and to verbalized expectations of more children "sometime," but the costs—financial, social, and psychological—of rearing large families in an urban society are about the same for Catholics as for Protestants. This is not to say that Catholic doctrine has no influence. More Catholic women postpone the beginning of birth control, utilize the rhythm method only, and verbalize desires and plans for large families. Moreover, the Catholic population is concentrated in urban areas where child-rearing has more costs than in rural areas. If Catholic doctrine on birth control did not exist, the fertility of these families would be less because of their urban concentration. If Catholic and Protestant birth rates are compared within a residential category, such as farm, small town, or metropolitan area, the Catholic rate is a little higher, that is, from 5 to 15 per cent higher.

Impact on Family Relationships

Because effective birth control enables many couples to decide the number of children they will rear and gives them some control over the spacing of children, the question is raised, what difference will family planning make in the socialization of children, in appropriate role-playing by children, in relationships among family members, and in the other goals that spouses wish to achieve? These questions have occasionally evoked the interest of sociologists for some decades and have produced some related research by psychologists and physicians.

Part of the question—effects on the achievement of nonfamilial goals—may be answered in a summary fashion. Children are an expensive investment in money and parental time, especially that of the mother. Earlier it was noted that, on the average, a child may be expected to cost parents the equivalent of the total income of the family for three years. Although no one has attempted to estimate the amount of the mother's time that must be committed to the child, it might well equal three years of her life.

It is clear, therefore, that the decision to conceive another child must be a decision to forego other goals, whether these be material wants, travel, further education, and so on. Although any particular goal may be postponed rather than foregone forever, the postponement of one

366

goal also further postpones other goals of somewhat lower priority. This is not to argue against having large families, only to place the decision within the perspective of a choice in the allocation of money and time. The decision of family size is a value judgment that is reserved to the decision of each couple.

Effects on Affect and Role-Playing

The analysis of the effect of family size on family relationships encounters the usual problems of causal relationships. The reader is cautioned not to accept all differences between large and small families as *due to* differences in family size. As we have seen, couples who have large families are more likely to have fewer years of education, to be poorer, to live in or be from rural areas, or to be Catholic. Also, in a few instances, causal relationships may be reversed; that is, one may be poor partly because he has several children, especially if they came close together while the couple was young.[39] With these cautions in mind, we summarize a recent paper that reviews the relationship between family size and authority patterns, affect, and stress in playing parental roles.[40]

FAMILY SIZE AND AFFECT AMONG MEMBERS By affect, we mean the feelings that people have about other persons or things. In this instance, we shall review the evidence of positive and negative affect in large and small families. The evidence from several studies is consistent that there is, on the average, somewhat more positive affect among family members in small than in large families. Some of this evidence is shown in Figure 14.3. The lower line employs a measure of the perception adolescents have of their parents' interest in and affection for them. The upper line shows mothers' attitudes toward their roles as mothers, from which it is inferred that if they like their maternal roles, they like their children. Other data concerning adolescents' affection for their parents and of spouses for each other show a slight relationship indicating more positive affect in smaller families. There is no support in any of the studies (even from J. H. S. Bossard, who advocated large families[41]) for the idea that large families are more affectionate than small ones.

SIZE AND AUTHORITARIANISM Large families tend to be more author-

[39]Ronald Freedman and Lolagene Coombs, "Childspacing and Family Economic Position," *American Sociological Review,* **31** (Oct. 1966), pp. 631–648.

[40]F. Ivan Nye, John Carlson, and Gerald Garrett, "Family Size, Interaction, Affect, and Stress," *Journal of Marriage and the Family,* **32** (May 1970), pp. 216–226.

[41]J. H. S. Bossard and Eleanor Boll, *The Large Family System* (Philadelphia: University of Pennsylvania Press), 1956.

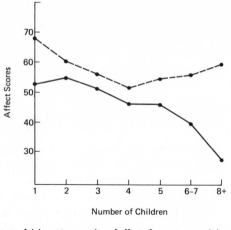

Number of Children

—— Adolescent perception of affect of parents toward them
--- Mothers' responses (attitude toward her parental role)

Figure 14.3. Parental Affect Toward Children. [From F. Ivan Nye, John Carlson, and Gerald Garrett, "Family Size, Interaction, Affect, and Stress," *Journal of Marriage and the Family,* **32** (May, 1970), p. 217. Reprinted by permission.]

itarian than small ones. This is not only true of families, but of groups in general: the larger the group, the more formal is the structure required, the less interplay there is between leaders and followers, and the greater the proportion of decisions that are made by those in leadership positions. Bossard and Boll have presented the explanation that parents with several children have less time to interact with each and, of a necessity, tend to issue orders and to enforce them, if necessary, by corporal punishment.[42] Not only do parents tend to be more authoritarian with children, but there is some evidence that one or the other is more likely to be dominant in relation to his (her) spouse. This is more likely to be the father, provided social class is held constant (that is, families are compared with other families within their own social class).

Some of the evidence with respect to punishment is shown in Figure 14.4. Large families are more likely to employ corporal punishment, whereas more small than large ones employ discussion and reasoning strategies. The reasons appear self-evident in that discussion and reasoning strategies require much more time and the parents of large families can allocate less time to each child.

One interesting exception to this proposition was found in a recent study: when control over boys and girls was analyzed separately, the

[42]Bossard and Boll, op. cit., pp. 126–147.

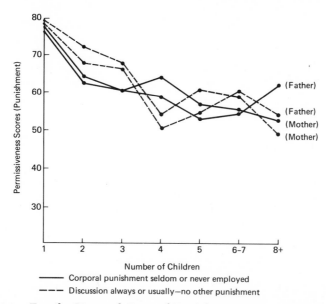

Figure 14.4. Family Size and Type of Punishment. [From F. Ivan Nye, John Carlson, and Gerald Garrett, "Family Size, Interaction, Affect, and Stress," *Journal of Marriage and the Family,* **32** (May, 1970), p. 222. Reprinted by permission.]

closer controls in large families were found to be imposed on girls rather than boys. Boys in large families (six or more) were found to be controlled *less strictly* than those in smaller families, but girls were found to be more closely restricted in large than in small families.[43] This is the only exception that has come to our attention to the relationship between family size and authoritarianism.

FAMILY SIZE AND STRESS ON PARENTS In what (if any) ways do large families affect the personal feelings and functioning of the parents? Few researchers have addressed the issue directly, but fragmentary evidence suggest that some additional stress is experienced by many parents of large families. Higher incidence of mental illness has been reported.[44] Several reports have shown higher alcoholism rates among fathers of large families.[45] Some of our own data are shown in Figure 14.5. The measures of psychological functioning of the mother—psychosomatic symptoms and the indicators of her disposition—provide no support for the stress hypothesis. Mothers of as many as eight children average no more symptoms than those with one to three

[43]Nye, Carlson, and Garrett, op. cit., p. 221.

[44]E. D. M. Todd and M. B. Edin, "Puerperal Depression," *The Lancet,* **2** (Dec. 12, 1964), pp. 1264–1266.

[45]Bossard and Boll, op. cit., p. 108.

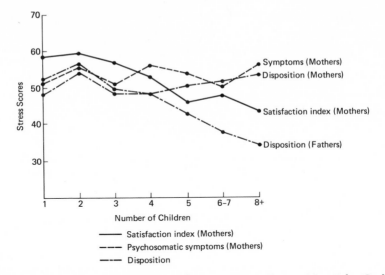

Figure 14.5. Family Size and Parental Stress. [From F. Ivan Nye, John Carlson, and Gerald Garrett, "Family Size, Interaction, Affect, and Stress," *Journal of Marriage and the Family,* **32** (May, 1970), p. 223. Reprinted by permission.]

children. However, her "satisfaction index," which is composed of her self-evaluation of her satisfaction with her husband, children, house, income, daily work, and community, shows a marked decline with increased family size. This provides some evidence of a more negative perception of their lives among women who have large families. This is in contrast to the relationship shown in Figure 14.3, which shows her evaluation of her role as mother. This suggests that there are other effects of large families on the lives of mothers that are included in the satisfaction index and that are not reflected in their attitudes toward the maternal role itself.

The lone measure of stress on fathers in Figure 14.5 provides additional evidence that the effects of large families may be greater than had been thought.[46]

Social Competence of Children

There is much mythology concerning "desirable" family size insofar as the development and functioning of children is concerned. Most of this falls into two sets of beliefs: (1) only children are lonely and are

[46]For a more detailed discussion of this section, see Nye, Carlson, and Garrett, op. cit., pp. 222–223.

handicapped in social development by lack of a sibling with whom to interact, and (2) the "best" size of family for the development of the child is somewhat larger than average, say, three to five. Bossard lent some respectability to these notions with his essays on family size.[47] The data, however, show this is not true, insofar as relationships among family members is concerned.

Bonney researched the popularity among schoolmates of children from different families of different sizes and concluded "the figures on 'only' children are very consistent in showing the greater social success of the 'only' child." Children with one or two siblings were found to occupy an intermediate position, with those having three or four siblings still lower in popularity ratings.[48]

From the several studies discussed, we see no basis for assuming that large families are "good" families in any general sense. On the contrary, there is considerable evidence that the small family of two children or even one is better adapted to the urban milieu than are large families. This is not to say that some couples will not be pleased to have large families. Some parents for religious reasons, for role reasons (to make their parental roles meaningful), or for relationship reasons (liking for associating with children—and eventually grandchildren) will want and have large families and, in most instances, perhaps, will enjoy having large families. However, the mythology that large families are "good" families in the sense that they produce generally socially desired outcomes finds no research support whatever. This mythology may have had validity in the earlier, less differentiated epochs of society, although we cannot be certain this was the case. It has no validity today.

Summary

The long-term trends in family size are toward smaller families. This downward trend, temporarily reversed from 1940 to 1957, resumed in the latter year and is continuing toward smaller families. Among the reasons believed to account for the trend is the disappearance of any economic or material need for children, that is, to care for one in his old age. The economic costs of child-rearing have increased, with the labor of most children reaching a point where it has no value. It is hypothesized that the social and psychological costs of child-rearing have also increased, as alternative uses of maternal time have developed and

[47]Bossard and Boll, op. cit., p. 320.
[48]Merl E. Bonney, "Relationship Between Social Success, Family Size, Socio-Economic Background, and Intelligence Among Children in Grades III to V," *Sociometry,* **7** (Feb. 1944), pp. 28–33.

371

as parents have come to be held responsible for the productiveness and happiness of their children as well as their conformity.

Accompanying the loss of the economic value of children and the increased costs of rearing them are more efficient techniques of birth control, available first to the middle class but now spreading to other aggregates, which allow an increased number of parents to procreate only the number of children they desire.

The research on the effects of family size on affect, family relationships, stress in parental role-playing, and child behavior discloses *no* support for the mythology that "large families are good families." To the contrary, it provides some evidence that the small family of two children may, in a differentiated urban society, be in more instances productive of the affect and relationships most widely valued in American society. This tentative conclusion not withstanding, the range of family size preferred by individual couples will surely continue to extend from no children to a dozen or even more.

15

The Socialization of Children

In this chapter we shall seek a perspective on the responsibilities of the family for transforming a newborn infant into an adequately functioning adult. It is a process and responsibility that is shared with the extended family, the community, the religious organization, the peer group, and—in differentiated societies—with the school and sometimes with agencies of government.

Socialization can be defined in different ways, depending on the frame of reference of the discipline involved.[1] Sociologists, who focus on role-playing, find definitions such as Clausen's are useful: "Socialization consists of those patterns of action or aspects of action which inculcate in individuals the skills (including knowledge), motives and attitudes necessary for the performance of present or anticipated roles."[2]

In the following pages we shall look at the objectives and philosophies of parents in socializing children, and the strategies and tactics they employ. Changes in both objectives and tactics will be reviewed and hypotheses presented concerning changes in socialization that have occurred in the recent past.

The perceptive reader will be aware that current knowledge leaves many questions unanswered or only tentatively answered. Sociologists have come late to the scientific study of childhood. Currently, there is no subdiscipline of "child sociology" to compare with child psycholo-

---

[1] Other disciplines may be interested in other dimensions of socialization. For example, psychologists might want to define it as the process of personality development. See Edward Z. Dager, "Socialization and Personality Development in the Child," in *Handbook of Marriage and the Family,* ed. by Harold T. Christensen (Chicago: Rand McNally & Co., 1964), pp. 740–781.

[2] John A. Clausen et al., *Socialization and Society* (Boston; Little, Brown and Company, 1968).

373

gy or the discipline of child development. Nonetheless, sociologists have powerful conceptual tools that may be utilized to organize much of the knowledge now available about children and stimulate research on socialization from a sociological perspective.

In focusing on the socialization role of parents, we must not overlook another role, that of child care. Care that maintains and protects the child in its early years is necessary to survival, and binding responsibilities have been placed on parents to discharge this role adequately. We shall note briefly how society provides for the child-care function when parents can't or won't discharge it.

Socialization for What Roles?

In a changing society, it may be obvious that familial roles will change. True, some seem to be present regardless of the type of society—socialization of children is a good example—but others may emerge, others may disappear. Some are appropriate to children, others to spouses and parents. As was noted in Chapter 10 recreational, therapeutic, and, for men, sexual intercourse roles seem to be emergent in current American society. Many authors discuss male and female roles, which is legitimate, because men and women do have different sets of normatively defined responsibilities. However, we feel that the roles defined by sex involve such a broad range of behavior that they are of little use. For example, a girl of eight and her mother are both female but the differences in their roles probably exceed their similarities. Therefore, we shall focus on socialization at two different levels: socialization for the adult roles that men and women play, and the childhood roles of children still living with their parents.

Socialization for Adult Roles

Parents have more or less definite beliefs concerning the roles their children will play as adults, and likewise they have beliefs concerning the experiences, training, attitudes, and values that are conducive to the ability and willingness of children to enact these roles adequately in adult life. It requires no crystal-ball-gazing for a parent to anticipate that a son will have to become a provider, at least for himself, and that a girl will have to become a housekeeper, at least for herself. Likewise it is extremely likely that the boy will also become a provider for a wife and children and have responsibilities for socializing his children, just as it is likely that a girl will be required to keep house for a husband and children, to care for children, to share their socialization with a husband, and to provide for the sexual needs of a husband. Kohn's recent research shows that fathers value personality traits in their sons that they have found useful in their own occupational experience.

374

Thus, middle-class fathers value creativity, self-control, and respon-sibility, whereas lower-class fathers value obedience and conformity more highly.[3] The most perceptive parents may also foresee ther-apeutic roles for both sons and daughters and for sons, a sexual role when they marry. Therefore, we see the socialization role of the parents as one in which they almost continuously look toward the future adult their child will become, at the same time being concerned with his present enactment of childhood roles.

The Roles of Children

The conceptualization of children's roles has failed to emerge as an explicit formulation. Of course it has been implicit whenever one discusses duties of children, but even such discussions have been largely limited to children in farm families or in the less differentiated societies.

Urban American society has failed to indicate in any specific way its positive expectations of children. Nonetheless, it is our belief that there *are* normatively defined roles for children; these will be listed and discussed briefly. The reader should know that such specification is new and tentative, and therefore critical examination of childrens' roles may be especially appropriate. Likewise, they may be normatively defined in some social classes but not in others.

The Student Role

In a literate society it is necessary for the child to learn to read and write, and as production, distribution, and governmental functions become more complex, knowledge of more complex and specialized subjects becomes necessary and, therefore, continuation of that school-ing over a longer period of time becomes more crucial.

In literate societies (but not in nonliterate ones) the child enacts a student role. In it, he has the responsibility to attend school, to devote appropriate time to study and practice, and to restrict his activities so that he does not interfere with the training of other students. Some sociologists are now referring to the student role as an occupation because it involves a definite set of duties and a highly structured time schedule. "Students of the sociology of occupations generally regard study as work, and much school work is oriented to occupations. Thus, the role of the student may reasonably be regarded as an occupational role in its own right".[4]

---

[3]Melvin Kohn, *Social Class and Conformity* (Homewood, Ill.: Dorsey Press, 1969).
[4]Walter L. Slocum, *Occupational Careers* (Chicago: Aldine Publishing Company, 1966), p. 146.

It is noteworthy that the definition of the student role varies by society, by social class, and by individual family. Most states in the United States require enough years in school to assure literacy, middle-class parents pressure children to at least graduate from high school, whereas some individual families hold to a standard of a college degree or even graduate work.

Peer-Group Role

Children are expected to interact with the peer group both in and out of school. The solitary child is viewed with concern if not alarm. It is believed that interpersonal skills develop from use and that to become adequate, children must interact. Also, the belief is widespread (although not necessarily accurate) that early contact with the other sex provides some knowledge and training needed in courtship activity and marital roles.

The child is expected to play with and engage in other group activity with the peer group. He is expected to learn to compete, as appropriate, and to restrain hostile activity that might result in his expulsion from the group. The prescriptions for the child in the peer-group role may consist more of the way children should behave in the peer group than the level of participation they must maintain in it.

A peer-group role may not be prescribed in less differentiated societies that require less interpersonal skills in adult role-playing. The role seems also related to the belief that one enjoys oneself more in groups than by himself. As we shall discuss later, in contemporary American society one "has a duty to be joyful."[5]

The Housekeeper Role

Do children have definite household duties the nonperformance of which brings sanctions? The answer appears to be a definite "yes" for caring for one's own bedroom. Boys or girls are expected to hang up clothes, keep some order among the equipment in the room, and perhaps sweep or dust. For girls, the duties may extend to helping in the preparation of food and in the cleaning operations following the meal; for boys, mowing the lawn and related outdoor tasks.

The Courtship Role

It is expected that adolescents will begin participating in mixed-sex groups early and dating at least in middle and late adolescence. This is considered both preparation for the selection of a spouse and the

---

[5]Martha Wolfenstein, "Fun Morality: An Analysis of Recent American Child-Training Literature," in *Childhood in Contemporary Cultures,* ed. by Margaret Mead and Martha Wolfenstein (Chicago: University of Chicago Press, 1963), Chapter 10.

enactment of marital roles and "fun" in itself. The adolescent who does not initiate interaction with the other sex is viewed with concern and finds himself manipulated and pressured to participate in heterosexual groups early and individual dating later in adolescence.

Sibling Roles
Siblings are expected to assist each other in playing student and peer-group roles by exchanging information, providing contacts, and, for the older, protecting the younger. They are expected to provide recreation for each other when peer-group associates are not available.

Nonrole Activity of Children
It should be clear that much activity of children is not part of any role. Children play with parents but are not obligated to do so. Individual recreation, such as TV watching or recreational reading, is not part of role behavior. Parents rarely pressure children to engage in these activities; in fact, they may attempt to discourage these, because preoccupation with these activities prevents the child from discharging his duties in his several roles.

Proscriptions in Children's Activities
The "don't's" in parental socialization may refer to discouraging nonrole activity, such as individual recreation that prevents the enactment of required roles, or proscriptions may refer to behavior that interferes with the activity of others, in or outside the family. Thus, excessive noise or rough play that might destroy equipment are proscribed. Stealing, physical injury to peer-group members, or slanderous verbalization that prevents the legitimate activity of others are proscribed.

Relationship of Child to Adult Roles
The proper enactment of child roles is preparation for adult roles. The child who performs the student role effectively and continues in it until he graduates from college is obtaining much of the knowledge and many of the skills that he will need in adult roles, especially that of provider. Typically, he also has developed a set of work habits and a capacity for deferred gratification that will render him effective in his provider and other roles.

The same may be said, in general, for the peer-group role, that it facilitates social skills and accustoms one to considering the needs and deferring to the legitimate activities of others. Of course this is not true for antisocial gangs. The housekeeping and courtship roles have obvious counterparts in adult roles. However, the adequate enactment of these roles has immediate utility in the family, as well as a training

377

function for adult roles. For example, the housekeeper role has immediate usefulness in reducing the tasks of the mother. Both the peer-group and the courtship roles are thought to be "fun" as well as functional to long-range goals, and competent enactment of the student role provides status both to the child and to his parents.

Child Roles: Duties to Oneself

It is a curious (and perhaps significant) characteristic of childhood roles in the United States that the duties involved are largely to oneself: primarily the development of adequate knowledge and skills to enact adult roles competently. The immediate rewards go mostly to the child, not his parents, in that the activity is fun or will make him happy. There are exceptions to this in that competency in the student or peer-group roles may enhance the prestige of the parent or the competent enactment of the housekeeper role may appreciably lighten the work of the mother.

What may prove significant in this situation is that it would appear that children exchange nothing with the parents—that is, children are a tremendous cost to parents but provide no rewards or only trivial and unpredictable ones. The fact that parents continue to have children, although smaller families than formerly, suggests that there is something rewarding about having children. Rheingold suggests that there are some things in providing for the care of children that "seem to be reinforcing in their own right."[6] She suggests that to give comfort or pleasure is pleasurable to the one who makes comfort and pleasure available to the other. In more general terms, Homans terms this type of reward a "profit in altruism."[7] Perhaps a more productive hypothesis is that small children give affection and gratitude to the parent in exchange for the things parents provide to them and that these rewards are valuable to parents. Nonetheless, couples in contemporary society may well ask whether these rewards equal the costs of parenthood.

It may be that part of the explanation for the continuation of parenthood lies in its normative definition—that couples ought to have children. There is sufficient evidence that some religious organizations take this position and this is likely to be true of societies that view themselves as underpopulated or who feel that they need more children to man their armies. Such normative definitions, however, are likely to decline in a society that sees itself as experiencing a "population explosion" threatening to its future. Furthermore, wars of survival

---

[6]Harriet L. Rheingold, "The Social and Socializing Infant," in *Handbook of Socialization Theory and Research,* ed. by David A. Goslin (Chicago: Rand McNally & Co., 1969), p. 785.

[7]George C. Homans, *Social Behavior: Its Elementary Forms* (New York: Harcourt Brace Jovanovich, 1961), p. 79.

378

in the future are likely to be fought with rockets rather than rifles, so that industrial development is more relevant to national defense than a high birth rate.

Although most childhood duties are primary preparation for adult roles and therefore the children are the *principal* beneficiaries, such preparation avoids potential costs to parents and society. Children who reach adulthood without the ability or willingness to enact adult roles usually become a burden to their parents, to society, or to both. In a certain sense, therefore, adequate preparation for adult roles *is* an obligation owed by children both to their parents and to society.

Changes in Values and Objectives in Child Socialization

Sociologists must discuss changes in the family with caution, unless they involve something that has been regularly counted in the Census or similar sources, such as family size or income. Beyond these, he has little precise data on families of past eras. With such caution in mind, what seem to be the principal changes in adult and child roles?

One of the more obvious changes has been in the care of aged persons by their children. Until adequate retirement and pension systems, recently supplemented by Medicare, became available, people too old to support themselves were generally dependent on their children. This is no longer generally true, although in special circumstances it still is. The change in childhood socialization takes cognizance of the fact that the child no longer need be socialized with a sense of duty to care for his parents (in highly differentiated societies), because such care becomes unlikely to be required of him.

Concomitantly, the need for the child's contribution to current economic production has almost disappeared. Therefore, socialization no longer need be focused on duty (except to one's own long-term preparation for adult roles). Rather, childhood can be devoted to play and fun—and many attempts have been made (unsuccessfully) to convince the child and his teacher that school is also fun!

Wolfenstein documents this change in values from a duty-oriented to a fun-oriented socialization by analyzing the advice to mothers given in the *Infant Care* bulletin of the Children's Bureau from 1914 to 1951. In the latter issues, she points out that fun is not only allowable but it is mandatory:

. . . It is now not adequate for the mother to perform efficiently the necessary routines for her baby; she must also see that these are fun for both of them. . . . In the earlier period the mother's character was one of strong moral

379

devotion. There were frequent references to her "self control," "wisdom," "strength," "persistence," and "unlimited patience." The mothers who read these bulletins might either take pride in having such virtues or feel called upon to aspire to them. . . .

In the most recent period, parenthood becomes a major source of enjoyment *for both parents* [italics ours] [the father having come much more into the picture than he was earlier]. The parents are promised that having children will keep them together, keep them young, and give them fun and happiness. As we have seen, enjoyment, fun and play now permeate all activities of the child. "Babies—and usually their mothers—enjoy breast feeding; nursing brings 'joy and happiness' to the mother." "You ought to enjoy your child." When a mother is told that most mothers enjoy nursing, she may wonder what is wrong with her in case she does not. Her self-evaluation can no longer be based entirely on whether she is doing right and necessary things but becomes involved with nuances of feelings which are not under voluntary control.[8]

Some problems created by a duty to enjoy and love children will be discussed later in this chapter.

Taken together, it appears two major transitions have been made in the objectives of socialization. In earlier eras in which the family functioned nearer to the subsistence level, the child was socialized to be economically productive while still a child. He might milk the cow, weed crops, and assist his father in a variety of tasks, as did the daughter the mother. Further, he was inculcated with a strong sense of duty toward caring for parents when they were no longer self-supporting. More recently, economic production has been removed from the duties of children as has the eventual care and support of parents. Childhood has come to be thought of as a time for play and fun. Further, this type of childhood has been assumed to be effective in producing a happy, outgoing, productive adult.

Actually, there is one major contradiction in the present milieu of the child—school. Parents, and sometimes teachers, take the position that school is fun (if not play), but this is generally inconsistent with the facts. Rather, school is the one major work aspect of childhood in differentiated, noncommunist societies, and its scope is extending upward through adolescence as well as to more days in the school year. Also, more pressure is placed on children to excel in school and to obtain far more training than merely the requirements for literacy. We propose the thesis that the *school role is becoming the new work role for children.* If this is a viable concept, then perceptions of childhood in the United States have passed through three rather different conceptions: (1) The child as an economic producer, assisting the father or mother. This was also considered relevant and effective training for

[8]Wolfenstein, op. cit., pp. 173–174.

adult roles. (2) Childhood as a period of play and fun with no work or very minimal work. Again, this "happy" childhood was viewed as building a personality structure that would result in a happy, affectionate, and productive adult. (3) A definition, not yet clear or complete, of childhood centered about the school role, with the child obtaining information, training, and a set of work habits that would prepare him for maximum productivity in adult life. Perhaps implicit in this last definition is that adults who are effective in their roles are likely to be emotionally stable and happy, rather than productive because they are happy and emotionally stable.

Parental Strategies in Child-Rearing

At any given time, in a complex society, a variety of child-rearing practices will be employed; however, one is likely to be relatively dominant at a given time, and perhaps another a few years later or earlier. This is especially true in societies characterized by rational decision-making rather than tradition alone. The basis for decision-making keeps changing as new theories and facts about child-rearing become available.

Authoritarian Pattern

Although facts concerning child-rearing a hundred or more years ago are fragmentary, the "fragments" are consistent in providing a picture of strict authority of parents over children. This authority was fully backed by legal and religious sanctions, even to the point of allowing a rebellious child to be put to death.[9] Mogey refers to the power of the husband over his family in the eighteenth century as "unlimited."[10] Such extreme use of parental authority was presumably rare, but there is little doubt that parents in the Western world, and especially fathers, exercised relatively strict control over children, although this is not true of all less differentiated societies.[11]

The "strategy" of child-rearing in this era was to require unquestioning obedience of the child and to utilize such punishment as might be required to obtain obedience. Such phrases as "Never mind why, do as I say!" and "Don't talk back to me!" were common phrases in parental vocabularies. Such maxims as "Spare the rod and spoil the child"

[9]William F. Kenkel, *The Family in Perspective* (New York: Appleton-Century-Crofts, 1966), p. 168.

[10]J. M. Mogey, "A Century of Declining Parental Authority," *Marriage and Family Living*, 19 (Aug. 1957), p. 235.

[11]Ellsworth Faris, *Discipline Without Punishment* (Salt Lake City: University of Utah Press, 1952).

indicated that obedience was valued for itself as well as a means for obtaining the desired compliance of the child. Such a statement strongly implied that such obedience to authority could be obtained only by corporal punishment.

It is sometimes difficult to visualize such different techniques of child discipline as were dominant in colonial times in the United States. Earle describes some of these:

Birch rods were tauntingly sold in London streets with a cry "Buy my fine Jemmies." . . . A crowning insult was charging the cost of the birch rod on the schoolboy's bills; and in some cases making the boy pay for the birch out of his scant spending money.

Birch trees were plentiful in America . . . and whippings, too.[12]

Frequent corporal punishment was characteristic of punishment in the family, in school, and even for offences against the community—that is, public floggings. Such punishment was also provided by the schoolteacher. The socialization strategy was parental orders enforced by corporal and other punishment in which the community and school provided strong support for the parent. Doubtless parents often explained the rationale for their commands, especially to older children, but such explanations were not deemed essential to the socialization process.

Ogburn and Nimkoff from fragmentary colonial sources provide some notion of child-care philosophies of that period.

The manners of children we are told, were formal; and parents were addressed as "esteemed parent" or "honored sir and madam." In a little book of etiquette which was circulated among the colonists, instruction in the proper behavior of children at the table runs as follows:

Never sit down at the table til' asked, and after the blessing. Ask for nothing; tarry til' it be offered thee. Speak not . . .

They provide a picture of a family that might be termed "parent-centered" in contrast to the child-centered family of recent years.[13]

The intriguing and important question to the sociologists is *why* this pattern, dominant during the early stages of industrial development in the Western world, was later to be replaced by another set of strategies? The question cannot be answered with certainty but some hypotheses will be offered. Families were under considerable pressure economically, both from the relatively unproductive economic technology and

---

[12]Alice Morse Earle, *A Social History of the American Family* (New York: Macmillan, 1904). Quoted in William F. Ogburn and Meyer F. Nimkoff, *Technology and the Changing Family* (Cambridge, Mass.: Riverside Press, 1955), pp. 200–201.
[13]Ibid.

382

from a value system centered on upward social mobility. The labor of the child was valuable to improve or even maintain the economic position of the family. The father, in fact, was the employer of his children. Because he did not pay wages to his children, he had to maintain strict discipline to obtain the amount of labor desired from them.[14]

Another characteristic of the family of the pioneer and early industrial period that may have explanatory power was its size. Families of eight to twelve children were not uncommon. Bossard and Boll have elucidated the problems of maintaining order and efficiency in families of that size.[15] Parents do not have the time or energy for long parent-to-child chats with that many children. Nor do they have the time and energy to cope with the disorder that generally accompanies permissive child-rearing practices.[16] More of this later. Besides being work centered and authoritarian, these practices possessed a strong puritanical content. Parents frequently told their children that masturbation would result in insanity, and special precautions were advocated to prevent the child's handling its genitals.[17] Strict discipline, generally enforced by corporal punishment, was believed to be a necessity.

Another characteristic of the societies that spawned the authoritarian family was their relatively slow rate of social change. Parents could prescribe appropriate behavior on the basis of their own experience. Later the rate of social change increased so greatly that parents had difficulty in anticipating the social world in which their children will live.

Besides their authoritarian child-rearing practices, these families have been characterized by some other interesting labels, including *traditional.* They were traditional as representing a point of departure from which we view present changes in the family. They were also traditional in the sense that they viewed family norms as *intrinsic* or right without regard for consequences, whereas the emergent types of family norms are based on instrumental considerations—on expert opinion that one type of family practice will produce a better personality type or some other desirable outcome (whether or not that belief is well founded).

These families were also relatively highly "integrated," in that a large proportion of the family member's time was spent in interaction with

[14]It is interesting that many societies have obtained work from children without corporal punishment. Whether they have obtained *as much* labor from children as in the Western world is not obvious.

[15]J. H. S. Bossard and E. S. Boll, *The Large Family System* (Philadelphia: University of Pennsylvania Press, 1956), Chapter 7.

[16]Robert O Blood, Jr., "Consequences of Permissiveness for Parents of Young Children," *Marriage and Family Living,* **15** (Aug. 1953), pp. 209–212.

[17]Wolfenstein, op. cit., p. 169.

other family members. Specifically, they worked together a great deal and the family produced a relatively large proportion of the goods and services that it consumed. More of the child's socialization occurred within the family than was the case later.

Along with being integrated, this type of family was "group centered" in that individual members subordinated their own interests, needs, and careers to the necessities of the group. Thus, children might be kept out of school to work to provide necessary family income or a daughter might have given up marriage if her parents were incapacitated and needed her care. All members were considered to be responsible for all others. This premise necessitated socialization with a heavy emphasis on duty and responsibility to the family collectively and to other members individually.

Permissive Child-Centered Pattern

In the decades of 1940 to 1960 and still continuing with perhaps some modifications, there has been major change from strict practices to permissive and child-centered patterns.[18] In discussing this, Bronfenbrenner lists the following:

1. Greater permissiveness toward the child's spontaneous desire.
2. Freer expression of affection.
3. Increased reliance on "psychological" techniques of discipline versus direct methods such as physical punishment, scolding, or threats.[19]

The change toward permissiveness is illustrated by Stender from the types of advice offered mothers by writers in popular women's magazines between 1890 and 1948. These are shown in Table 15.1. They show a trend toward permissiveness advice as early as 1930. The upper portion of the table shows the strategies employed to guide character and personality development, the lower for scheduling feeding of the infant.[20]

It is difficult to trace the inception of a philosophy, but permissiveness and the child-centered pattern seem to have emerged from certain tenets of psychoanalytic theory, finding statement in Spock's *Baby*

---

[18]Urie Bronfenbrenner, "Socialization and Social Class Through Time and Space" in *Readings in Social Psychology,* ed. by Eleanor E. Maccoby, T. M. Newcomb and E. L. Hartley (New York: Holt, Rinehart and Winston, 1958), pp. 400–425.

[19]Urie Bronfenbrenner, "The Changing American Child—A Speculative Analysis," *Merrill-Palmer Quarterly,* **7** (Apr. 1961), p. 74.

[20]For mothers who followed this advice, predominantly in the middle class, the earliest period was one of moderate permissiveness, changing to high restrictiveness from 1910 to 1920 and thereafter becoming steadily more permissive until the end of the survey.

384

Table 15.1
Percentage of Methods Recommended for Two Aspects of Child Training as
They Appeared in Three Women's Magazines Analyzed in 10-Year Intervals
for 1890–1948

	1890	1900	1910	1920	1930	1940	1948
	%	%	%	%	%	%	%
I. Guiding Character or Personality Development							
Discipline (reward and/or punish)	18	14	34	34	38	28	2
Provide a good home influence	61	53	30	12	14	5	3
Ignore undesirable behavior	12	5	9	0	12	18	4
Look for cause and plan accordingly	0	0	0	1	14	48	84
Invoke divine aid	15	20	15	0	0	0	0
Feed properly	0	0	0	50	0	0	0
Miscellaneous	4	5	12	3	21	2	8
II. Infant Disciplines							
Tightly schedule, cry it out	0	22	77	100	75	33	0
Loosely schedule	100	78	23	0	0	0	0
Self-regulate, "mother"	0	0	0	0	25	66	100

SOURCE: Celia B. Stendler, "Sixty Years of Child Training Practices," *Journal of Pediatrics,* **36** (Jan.–June 1950), p. 126. Reprinted by permission.

and Child Care[21] and in some issues of the Children's Bureau publication, *Infant Care.*[22] The crucial relevant assertions that have been advanced are that the first five years of the child's life determine his values and behavior thereafter and that most adult personality and behavioral problems are caused by an unhappy childhood and especially an unhappy relationship between parent and child. Added as a type of superstructure to these beliefs is the assumption that even small frustrations of the child's wishes or any type of corporal punishment

[21]Benjamin Spock, rev. ed. (New York: Pocket Books, 1957). A recent report states that 20.5 million copies of this publication have been sold.
[22]*Infant Care,* Childrens Bureau, Department of Health, Education and Welfare, Washington, D.C.

are interpreted as parental rejection and likely to inflict permanent damage on the personality. A companion belief is that if the child develops without frustrations in a loving relationship with its parents, it will become a conforming, productive, and affectionate person.

Such theories have been reviewed in some detail by Lindesmith and Strauss. They write:

A point of view which looms very large in these writings [culture and personality originating in psychoanalytic theory] is the one that emphasizes the predominant character forming efficacy of the infant disciplines: bowel and bladder training, nursing, weaning, mothering restraint of motion, punishment, amount and kinds of frustration, and so on. Thus, M. B. LaBarre virtually ascribes the main features of Japanese personality to the rigid bowel training of infants.

W. H. Sewell was most instrumental in discrediting the assertion that the specific infant-training practices stressed in psychoanalytic literature determine later personality development of the individual.[23] Lindesmith and Strauss, after reviewing the evidence, conclude that such practices have not been shown to affect adult personality. Quoting H. Orlansky, they wrote

(a) Various writers attribute different and contradictory effects to the same or similar childhood experiences; (b) the alleged influences of given infant disciplines or types of experience on personality have not been proven; (c) the method of "proving" that early infancy is of primary importance is shot through with . . . unsupported assumptions; (d) postinfantile childhood experiences are probably of more vital importance in shaping personality than the prelingual (infancy) ones.[24]

The failure to establish empirical links between infant training practices and later personality development does not necessarily mean, however, that other types of childhood experiences do not have a significant effect on personality development. Studies by Piaget and his followers have stressed the importance of environmental stimulation and freedom to explore one's environment as elements in cognitive growth.[25] Other investigators have asserted the dire consequences of maternal deprivation, maternal rejection, and lack of parental warmth

---

[23]William H. Sewell, "Infant Training and the Personality of the Child," *The American Journal of Sociology,* **58** (Sept. 1952), pp. 150–159.

[24]Alfred R. Lindesmith and Anselm L. Strauss, "A Critique of Culture-Personality Writing," *American Sociological Review,* **15** (Oct. 1950), pp. 587–600.

[25]See John H. Flavell, *The Developmental Psychology of Jean Piaget* (Princeton, N.J.: Van Nostrand Reinhold Co., 1963).

and security for the development of such personality characteristics in the child as self-esteem, empathy, interpersonal competence, psychological stability, and conscience.[26] It is uncertain, however, how lasting is the effect of these early childhood experiences.

Social Class and Permissiveness

Early studies of childhood training practices reported the lower social class to be more permissive.[27] Later studies contradicted this, finding middle-class parents more permissive. These contradictions led to a review by Bronfenbrenner of sixteen studies bearing on the matter. He concluded that from about 1930 to 1945 middle-class mothers employed more strict discipline but thereafter became increasingly permissive. Lower-class mothers, exposed less to "expert" opinion, were more consistent over the period but tended toward increased permissiveness in the latter period. His survey shows (research appears unanimous on this) that lower-class parents are more likely to utilize physical punishment, whereas middle-class mothers utilize discussion and love withdrawal. The latter methods are reported more effective in producing the desired behavior in the child.[28]

One alternative explanation has been advanced: that the greater permissiveness of the lower class in the earlier studies was neglect rather than permissiveness. Lower class parents become very restrictive when the child does something which inconveniences the parent. There is considerable evidence of neglect in studies of the lower-lower class but little in the upper lower class, where parents generally are reported as conscientious.

Problems in Permissive Socialization

How does it work out in practice to permit children to do as they wish? Blood compared the experiences of parents who reared their children by permissive practices with those employing restrictive practices. He reports,

---

[26] A comprehensive review of research on the consequences of human deprivation has been published by the U.S. Department of Health, Education and Welfare: *Perspectives on Human Deprivation: Biological, Psychological, and Sociological,* National Institute of Child Health and Human Development, U.S. Dept. of Health, Education, and Welfare, 1968. See also Alfred R. Lindesmith and Anselm L. Strauss, "A Critique of Culture-Personality Writing," *American Sociological Review,* 15 (Oct. 1950), pp. 587–600.

[27] Davis and Havighurst, op. cit., pp. 698–710.

[28] Urie Bronfenbrenner, "Socialization and Social Class Through Time and Space," op. cit., pp. 400–425. For a more recent study which attempts to assess the influence of socioeconomic status on maternal childrearing practices and to evaluate changes in maternal behaviors and socialization techniques, see: Elinor Waters and Vaughn J. Crandall, "Social Class and Observed Maternal Behavior from 1940 to 1960," *Child Development,* 35 (1964), pp. 1021–1032.

Permissive parents found their lives more disrupted by their children's behavior. More of their activities were disturbed by the children's noisiness, while privacy for any purpose between dawn and bedtime was more difficult to achieve.

When asked what types of damage occurred to their living room furnishings, permissive parents likewise reported more trouble on that score. . . . permissive parents almost automatically incurred more cluttered living rooms.

These parents *expected* damage to furniture. To minimize it, they

are especially apt to take steps to render their living rooms "invulnerable." Rather than expecting the child to adapt himself to the fragility of the room, such parents adapt the room to the boisterousness of the child.

Although this group of parents experienced many inconveniences, most believed permissiveness to be worthwhile in that they believed it would produce happier and more productive children and, later, adults. However, parents of older children were less permissive than those of younger ones, either reflecting higher expectations by the parent for appropriate social behavior by the child or the greater potential of older children for damage from uncontrolled play. The unhappiest parents were those who were employing permissive practices but who lacked a rationale for doing so—who had heard they should be permissive but didn't know why such practices were thought to be desirable.[29]

Permissiveness seems to have some other undesirable effects. Sears, Maccoby, and Levin report that permissiveness toward the aggressive behavior of the child increases its expression.

Permissiveness does increase the amount of aggression in the home, however, and it is worth considering what it does to the child himself. An angry child is not usually a happy child, nor is he one who receives affection and willing companionship from others. He is a source of discomfort to family and peers, and probably receives some retaliation. He upsets his siblings, raises the level of frustration imposed on his parents, and inevitably has an increase, to some extent, of his own aggression—anxiety.[30]

There are still other reasons for questioning whether a high degree of permissiveness provides effective socialization either for the enactment of children's roles or as training for adult roles. All role-playing involves patterned interaction with other members of a group, whether the group is the family, a class with its teacher in school, or the business or professional group in which one earns a wage or salary. The child must be taught both expected and prohibited behavior (as well as

[29]Blood, op. cit., pp. 209–211.
[30]Robert R. Sears, Eleanor E. Maccoby, and Harry Levin, *Patterns of Child Rearing* (Evanston, Ill.: Row, Peterson and Company, 1957), p. 268.

what is permitted or optional). Such learning is expedited by rewards for appropriate behavior and sanctions for disapproved behavior. The child in a highly permissive environment is likely to remain an unsocialized child who will find it difficult to function in the nonpermissive peer group or later in an equally nonpermissive work group. The unsocialized child is likely to be the unhappy child because he is likely to be rejected because he disrupts group activities as he tries to reach his own goals directly, heedless of the "rules of the game."[31]

Trend Away from Permissiveness

Has there been a swing away from extreme permissiveness? The answer is difficult because no general measure of permissiveness is available from the past or available from the present. However, there are a few indicators of less permissiveness. Spock, perhaps the most widely read adviser on child care, wrote in 1957: "If the parent can determine in which respects she may be too permissive and can firm up her discipline, she may, if she is on the right track, be delighted to find that her child becomes not only better behaved, but much happier."[32] This is a mild, much-qualified endorsement for more discipline. In effect, it says only that it is possible that more discipline may achieve better results than less or no discipline. It seems likely that the trend toward permissiveness has run its course, and that a mild reversal toward less permissiveness *may* have begun, but the evidence for a firm conclusion at this time is insufficient.

Some Theories of Socialization

Because socialization is an extremely broad topic, which is inspiring a considerable and rapidly growing literature, the present treatment of its theory must be brief and therefore oversimplified. It draws primarily from Brim[33] and Maccoby.[34] For a more detailed treatment the reader is referred to them.

[31] A number of psychologists have pointed to the unfavorable consequences of a lack of parental control for the development of a stable personality: cf. S. Coopersmith for its effect on the child's self-esteem (*The Antecedents of Self-Esteem,* [San Francisco: W. H. Freeman and Co., 1967]); and for its relationship to child schizophrenia see W. Goldfarb, "The Mutual Impact of Mother and Child in Childhood Schizophrenia," *American Journal of Orthopsychiatry,* **31** (Oct. 1961), pp. 738–747; and H. L. Lennard et al., "Interaction in Families with a Schizophrenic Child," *Archives of General Psychiatry,* **12** (Feb. 1965), pp. 166–183.

[32] Spock, op. cit., p. 326.

[33] Orville G. Brim, Jr., "Personality Development as Role Learning," in *Personality Development in Children,* ed. by Ira Iscoe and Harold W. Stevenson (Austin: University of Texas Press, 1960), pp. 127–161.

[34] Eleanor E. Maccoby, "The Choice of Variables in the Study of Socialization," in *Marriage and the Family,* ed. by Robert F. Winch, Robert McGinnis, and Herbert R. Barringer (New York: Holt, Rinehart and Winston, 1962), pp. 228–244.

In psychology, two major theories, psychoanalytic and learning theory, have offered competing explanations of socialization. These are now receiving an infusion of sociological theory, which both complicates and illuminates them. The psychological theories will be reviewed first, followed by a look at the sociological approach.

Maccoby, after warning that the following is necessarily an oversimplification, distinguishes between psychoanalytic and learning theory as follows:[35]

I believe it would be reasonably accurate to say that a learning theorist would regard socialization as a learning process in which certain actions of the child are selected out, by virtue of reinforcement, others tried and dropped because they are in some way punished or nonreinforced. The parents have a primary role in administering the rewards and punishments for the child's actions, although they do not necessarily do this deliberately and consciously as a teaching effort. And, of course, there are other sources of reward and punishment than the parents' reactions which will help to determine what behavior the child retains.

The psychoanalytic approach, on the other hand, would emphasize not the detailed learning of specific actions on the basis of their outcome but the providing of conditions which will motivate the child to take on spontaneously the socialized behavior the parents want him to have. The terms introjection, internalization, learning through role playing, and identification have been used in this connection; they all refer to the child's tendency to copy, to take on as his own, the behavior, attitudes, and values of the significant people in his life, even when the socializing agents have not said "that's a good boy" or given him a piece of candy for performing these acts or holding these values.

These theoretical positions are not in conflict at all points because the approval of a warm parent can serve as a reinforcement for appropriate behavior by the child. However, for those holding the psychoanalytic position, the acceptance and approval of the parent appears to be both a necessary and a sufficient reinforcement for the behavior of their children. Learning theory recognizes a variety of kinds of rewards (not excluding food) from a variety of persons. Because money is exchangeable for such a broad class of goods and services, it has been termed a "general reinforcer."

The learning-theory position has been reinforced by research in operant conditioning, an *operant* being anything that induces a repetition of behavior. For example, O'Leary and others obtained drastic modification in children's behavior in school by introducing a system by which teachers rated the behavior of students. These ratings were exchangeable for reinforcers such as candy and comic books:

---

[35]Ibid., p. 234.

"with the introduction of the token reinforcement program, a dramatic, abrupt reduction in deviant behavior occurred."[36]

More support for the learning position is provided by Bing in her finding that the intellectual development of the child is more closely related to the *amount* of interaction between parent and child rather than the *kind* of interaction.[37] However, Maccoby acknowledges some importance in the emotional relationship in that children tend to avoid cold, hostile parents while staying within interaction range of warm ones. The issues between psychoanalytic and learning theory have not been resolved. However, in our brief review, we find learning theory as a more general and more readily testable theory, and therefore prefer it when the two theories conflict.

Socialization as Role Playing

The legacy of Mead, Cooley, and James[38] represents perhaps the major sociological contribution to socialization.[39] The process of becoming human involved, for these social psychologists, the development of a self. And this is accomplished, they maintained, through the individual's participation in social interaction. The distinguishing characteristic of the self (from other social objects) is that it is a reflexive phenomenon—it is both subject and object within the same entity. James distinguished between these two phases of the self: the "I" and the "me," the self as knower and the self as known. One evaluates oneself from the standpoint or perspective of others. In coining the concept "looking-glass self," Cooley emphasized the reflective nature of the self, i.e., one's self-reference is determined by his imagination of how he appears in the minds of others. Mead, in referring to the human being as having a self, simply meant that such an organism is able to act socially toward himself, just as toward others. He may praise or blame himself; he may be ashamed of himself. In short, the human being can become the object of his own actions.

The mechanism that enables the individual to view himself as an object is that of role-taking. According to Mead, it is only by "taking the

[36]K. Daniel O'Leary, Michael B. Evans, Richard A. Sandargas, and Wesley C. Becker, "Behavior Modifications of an Adjustment Class: A Token Reinforcement Program," *Journal of Applied Behavior Analysis,* **92** (Spring 1969), pp. 3–15.

[37]Quoted in Maccoby, op. cit., p. 233.

[38]For examples of their work in this area see G. H. Mead, *"Mind, Self, and Society: From the Standpoint of a Social Behaviorist,* edited by Charles W. Morris (Chicago: University of Chicago Press, 1934); C. H. Cooley, *Human Nature and the Social Order* (Glencoe, Ill.: The Free Press, 1956, originally published in 1902); William James, *Principles of Psychology* (New York: Henry Holt, 1892).

[39]We are indebted to Viktor Gecas for the following discussion of the historical development of socialization concepts.

role of the other" that the individual acquires a platform for getting outside himself and thus for viewing himself. (This whole process is made possible by and involves symbolic communication. It is through the use of language that the child acquires not only the meanings and values of his group, but also transcends his individual perspective to that of others.)

Mead discussed the emergence of the self as a process of learning, internalizing, and organizing roles. The child passes through two main stages in this socialization process, the "play" stage and the "game" stage. In the play stage the child takes on a number of different roles. He *plays at* being a cowboy, a spaceman, a soldier, and so on, often talking to himself while playing at being two or more people in an interaction. By actually acting out different roles, the child develops the ability to (mentally) take the roles of others.

The role-taking in the play stage, however, is simple and limited. It involves only brief fragments of behavior and there is no organization or integration of the separate roles. In the game stage the various roles become *organized.* The distinctive experience of the game stage is that the child is placed in the position of having to take a number of roles simultaneously. In a game such as football, a player must be able to put himself in the position of every one of the other players on the field in order to anticipate their responses and to be able to perform his own role. He begins to grasp the fact that the roles of others are intertwined and that his own role has a specific place in this organization. What is more, the child in the game stage learns to abstract the various roles into a generalized role or, in Mead's terms, a "generalized other." This concept of the generalized other applies to the organized roles of participants within a defined situation. The individual, then, evaluates his own role performance from the standpoint of the generalized other. Objectively, the generalized other represents the group or society in abstract, evident in such expressions as "What will *people* think?" or "What will *they* say?" Subjectively, it is manifest in the individual's conscience or standards of conduct. To the extent that a person's generalized other is stable and consistent, there is stability and consistency in his behavior.[40]

From the sociological perspective on socialization, the importance of role-taking and role-playing cannot be overstressed. Sociologists view most behavior as occurring within the framework of roles. They can and do demonstrate that a given person displays different behavior

---

[40]Mead's concept of the generalized other has found contemporary expression in such ideas as H. S. Sullivan's "significant other" (*The Interpersonal Theory of Psychiatry* [New York: W. W. Norton & Company, 1953]), and T. Shibutani's "reference group" (*Society and Personality* [Englewood Cliffs, N.J.: Prentice-Hall, 1961]).

depending on the role he is enacting at the time. Roles provide structure for behavior, investing it with significance in terms of a set of expectations and providing an increased degree of predictability. Brim has extended the application of the concept to personality itself. That is, one does not simply display different segments of the self as he enacts different roles, but the self *is* a collection of role perceptions and role performances of the person: "the learned repertoire of roles is the personality. There is nothing else. There is no 'core' personality underneath the behavior and feelings: there is no 'central,' monolithic self which lies beneath its central *manifestations.*"[41] There is no such things as a "warm," "aggressive," or "dependent" person. The "dramaturgical" school of symbolic interaction in sociology, represented by Irving Goffman, Gregory Stone, and Anselm Strauss among others, holds a similar view of the self. They maintain that selves are "masks" that the role-player wears—they change with the role he is playing and the audience before whom he is performing. This is not to say, however, even from this perspective, that there is no unity or continuity to the self. The roles one plays are not completely independent of one another. Usually there is some degree of role integration giving a certain amount of organization to the self. Brim illustrates this position by showing that such presumed psychological traits as dominance or dependency are role specific; that is, a man may act dominantly in the office but be dominated in the family or vice versa. Maccoby lends qualified support to this position by reporting research indicating no *relationship* in dependency between boys tested at different times during their formative years. "The children who were dependent at age three or four were not the same individuals who emerged as dependent in adulthood."[42]

Socialization through role-learning illuminates, in that it specifies the behavior that is appropriate at a given time and place. The teacher who acts the same in a classroom as at a cocktail party would either be fired as a teacher or be a colossal bore at the party. Socialization, to be effective, must be specific to roles. Brim has proposed that whether a person effectively enacts roles depends not on motivation alone but also on knowledge of the content of appropriate behavior in a role and the abilities to enact the role.[43] Socialization involves motivation, knowledge, and abilities for role enactment.

The sociological approach to personality does not preempt the whole socialization process. Learning theory is needed to explain why some people are willing to expend more effort than others to obtain the

---

[41]Brim, op. cit., p. 141.

[42]Maccoby, op. cit., p. 242. This implies that the early years are less significant as predictors of adult behavior of people than was formerly believed.

[43]Brim, op. cit., pp. 143–147.

knowledge required for role-playing or why some more than others are highly motivated to expend the effort to enact a role well.

Collective Care of Infants

Most children are reared and in their early years socialized by parents within a family structure. Although this is customary, is it essential? There is a strong tendency for societies to assume that because some societal task has been discharged by a given type of social organization there is something essential in that social organization or in some of the social relationships that it usually provides. Such a traditional approach seems to be even more characteristic of thinking about the family than about other social systems. Limited evidence on this issue is now available both within America and from reports on other societies.

The more extensive programs in collective infant care have been developed in socialist societies. Meers and Marans, in reporting on these programs, caution that these countries have certain goals in child socialization that are not shared in individualistic, capitalistic societies, namely, to develop cooperative behavior in children.[44] The reader should keep this facet in mind in reviewing these programs of infant care.

USSR—The Children's Collectives

In 1956 the Soviet Union launched a program to create "the new Soviet Union man," and instituted a program to shift a major part of child care from the family to day nurseries. The program includes children three months to seven years. *Day care* comprises 85 per cent of the extrafamilial care and consists of from five to ten hours of care daily. *Boarding care,* which is next in frequency, includes care of the child five days each week, the return of the child to its parents on weekends. *Residential care* involves the total care of the child and is used only in the absence of alternatives. "In 1964, it was reported that over seven million children, representing almost 10 per cent of the Soviet population of preschool and school age children, were being raised in facilities."[45] (Ten per cent is the combined total for the three types.) The plan calls for a steady expansion of day care until it includes all children in the USSR.

---

[44]Dale R. Meers and Allen E. Marans, "Group Care of Infants in Other Countries," in *Early Child Care,* ed. by Caroline A. Chandler, Reginald S. Lourie, and Ann DeHuff Peters (New York: Atherton Press, 1968), pp. 237–282. The following discussion is based on Meers and Marans.

[45]Ibid., p. 240.

The plan for young children is for each seven or eight babies to have a nurse and her assistant. For older children, the groups are combined to number about twice that size. In some nurseries the ratio is nearer twelve for the younger and twice that many for the older children. The program specifies that children shall receive adequate exercise and stimulation. At least equally stressed are the emotional needs of the child.

Accompanying the description of every task of the nurse or "nyanya" is the instruction to be happy, tender, gentle, and encouraging. Nowhere is there mention of stern measures to be taken, no negative responses, no punishment. The role of the worker in the child-care facility is to set an example for the behavior of her charges, to take a positive approach to the learning of appropriate skills at each stage of development. A positive emotional state is seen as important for the physical well-being of the child, as well as providing a better atmosphere for learning. . . . When a child cries or is unhappy, it is seen as a failure of the upbringer.[46]

Defective children are recognized early because of close medical supervision and are given specialized treatment and care.

Infant Care in Israel

Approximately 4 per cent of the population of Israel live on collective farms or kibbutzim. There children are cared for and trained primarily by nurses and teachers. Babies and older children live in quarters apart from their parents, but visit their parents and spend much time after working hours in their parents' quarters. Even during the first year, babies are usually housed apart from parents, although mothers do much of the feeding and caring for babies during the first year. (Actually, each kibbutz develops its own rules and practices, so there is considerable variation from one to another.) Both parents are employed full time, with some women specializing in the care of babies and children. However, parents take a warm interest in the care and personality development of their children and spend much time with them. The theory appears to be to leave the more difficult problems of care and discipline to the nurses, while the parents, freed of such problems, could develop closer affectively colored relationships with their children.

Because the kibbutzim have produced adults who have been reared entirely by nurses and teachers, there is considerable interest in the outcome in terms of the types of personalities produced and in their adult role-playing. Some observers think that they have disproportionate personality problems, but the evidence is neither complete nor

[46]Ibid., p. 245.

compelling. Ninty per cent of those reared in kibbutzim elect, on completion of their term of national service, to return to the kibbutz to live and rear their own children.

Rabkin and Rabkin have made the most specific statements about the personality of adults reared in the kibbutzim, based both on previous studies and on their own data. Some of the recent studies show the intellectual development of those raised in the kibbutzim to be superior to the United States and Israeli children reared in families. Drawing on these and their own data, they conclude, ". . . we can sum up the kibbutznik: he is a healthy, intelligent, generous, somewhat shy but warm human being, rooted in his community and in the larger Israeli society. He shows no signs of the emotional disturbance we would expect from a violation of our ideal mother-child relationship." Besides this conclusion, they offer the interesting speculation, "The kibbutznik has a deep sense of belonging to his kibbutz and his country. The privatization of our family life may counter this belongingness. We may find that if we expose our children to meaningful group experiences in early life, we will give them a sense of integration in something beyond their family, enabling them to identify with the community and the nation."[47]

French Day Care for Children of Working Mothers

For over fifty years, the Paris Administration of Public Assistance has operated day-care centers (crèches) for children aged two months to three years. These centers are open from 7 A.M. to 7 P.M. Nursing assistants—caretakers—are women who have completed the American equivalent of junior high school, at about age fourteen, plus two years of additional vocational training. "In general, they appear warm and gentle with babies and obviously skilled in techniques of feeding, bathing, and initiating games and songs with the older children."[48] The ratio of babies to each nursing assistant is from six to ten.

Evaluation of Group Care

The programs in France and in Communist East Europe are fulfilling their purpose—to release mothers for productive labor. Those in the USSR and Israel have, in addition, the objective of providing a more favorable milieu for the socialization of children. Whether this is being achieved cannot be determined. Neither is it now possible to determine whether there are typical adverse consequences from group care. The Rabkin and Rabkin research strongly supports the position that group care plus some interaction with parents is as effective in socialization

[47]Leslie Y. and Karen Rabkin, "Children of the Kibbutz," *Psychology Today,* 3 (Sept. 1969), p. 46.
[48]Ibid., pp. 271–272.

396

as is care entirely in private families. Moreover, there are waiting lists of parents who wish to place their children in such care, so it can be predicted that such care will be expanded. Because the kibbutzim have existed for over sixty years and the French centers for over fifty years, it would seem that if group care of this type has some pronounced effect on personality or adult role-playing, such consequences should be obvious. In all of these group-care programs children have parents and, in all but the kibbutzim, children spend only the weekdays in the day-care centers. Their socialization differs greatly from those reared in orphanages.

Socialization by One Parent

The great majority of children live with both biological parents, but recent figures show almost eight million living with the mother only, another seven tenths of a million with the father only.[49] In addition, large numbers of children spend their days in day-care centers or in the care of persons other than their mothers.

Maternal Deprivation

A considerable amount of literature has developed about whether there is some unique relationship between the baby and its mother, either biological or mother-substitute. The proponents of the mother-child relationship argue that the child must become accustomed to the care of one person during its earliest years, whereas those opposing maintain that it is the quality of the care rather than who provides it that is important. Thus, there are two issues that frequently become confused. First, babies require consistent services—not only for food, warmth, and cleanliness, but for exercise, stimulation, and entertainment. Early studies of children in orphanages and hospitals in which the children received food, warmth, and cleanliness, but little exercise, stimulation, and entertainment revealed that these babies had slower rates of development and higher rates of personality disturbances than those reared in families.[50] Yarrow notes, however, that in these institutional settings it is not just the absence of a loving mother but often a total environment for the child that is inferior. However, he notes that there probably are some intrinsic problems in having one "caretaker"

---

[49]U.S. Bureau of the Census, *Current Population Reports,* Series P-20, No. 225, "Marital Status and Living Arrangements: March 1971," U.S. Government Printing Office, Washington, D.C., 1971, p. 20.

[50]Leon J. Yarrow, "Separation from Parents During Early Childhood," in *Review of Child Development Research,* ed. by Martin L. and Lois Wladis Hoffman (New York: Russell Sage Foundation, 1964), pp. 95–103. For an extensive review of studies on separation from mother, the reader is referred to Yarrow.

397

for several children in that this caretaker is less familiar with the individual needs of children and is more likely to follow the same routines for all of the children in his care.

One matter is hardly an issue. Babies and small children require intensive care, supervision, and training. Severe retardation, psychosis, serious injury to health, and even life itself are at stake. Mothers usually, but not always, provide such care. Infanticide, abandonment of children, neglect and cruelty of mothers toward their children occur with some frequency. Such abuse is of sufficient frequency and severity to require laws to protect children from abuse by parents. The Illinois law (1965) is introduced by these words,

An infant is brutally beaten by a parent who can't stand a child who cries . . . a terrified child, too young to speak is treated for multiple burns obviously inflicted with a lighted cigaret . . . youngsters are chained to beds in a dark room without food or water.

Because these situations defy comprehension, we don't like to think about them. But we must think of them, for they happen almost every day.[51]

Zalba has distinguished between neglect and abuse: ". . . while neglect may be a form of cruelty, it is more often caused or exaggerated by extreme poverty or ignorance."[52] Data on the total number or proportion of abused children is not at hand, but Paulson and Drake review a survey of 662 such cases reported in newspapers in 1962.[53] Over half of these involved were children under the age of four years. More than a fourth of the children were fatally injured.[54] The assumption that care of a child by its biological parents assures good care is not always correct.

Care may also be provided by substitute mothers or by professional caretakers. Such care may be excellent or poor depending on the adequacy in numbers and training of the caretakers and the financial resources available to the institution.

Whether day-by-day care of the child *by one person* during the period up to three years is crucial is less clear. Although this position has been taken by some, it is challenged by a variety of facts, including the long-range experiment in the kibbutzim. Caldwell, after reviewing experimental studies of "multiple mothering," in which children were cared for by several caretakers, concluded, "At this juncture it is not

---

[51]Cyril H. Winking, "The Abused Child Law," *Department of Children and Family Services* (Springfield, Ill.: State Office Building, 1965).

[52]Serapio Richard Zalba, "The Abused Child: 1. A Survey of the Problem," *Social Work,* **11** (Jan. 1966), pp. 3–16. Quoted in Morris J. Paulson and Phillip Blake, "The Physically Abused Child: A Focus on Prevention," *Child Welfare,* **48** (Feb. 1969), p. 88.

[53]"Bibliography on the Battered Child, Clearinghouse for Research in Child Life," *Children's Bureau* (Washington, D.C.: U.S. Department of Health, Education, and Welfare, 1963).

[54]Paulson and Blake, op. cit., p. 89.

possible to reach definite conclusions about the effects of intensity of maternal contact during infancy outside of situations that might be regarded as grossly depriving."[55] Mead, after a review of anthropological literature, concludes,

At present, the specific biological situation of the continuing relationship of the child to its biological mother and its need for care by human beings are being hopelessly confused in the growing insistence that child and biological mother, or mother surrogate, must never be separated, that all separation even for a few days is inevitably damaging, and that if long enough it does irreversible damage. This, as Hilde Bruch . . . has cogently pointed out, is a new and subtle form of antifeminism in which men—under the guise of exalting the importance of maternity—are tying women more tightly to their children than has been thought necessary since the invention of bottle feeding and baby carriages. Actually, anthropological evidence gives no support at present to the value of such an accentuation of the tie between mother and child . . . . On the contrary, cross-cultural studies suggest that adjustment is most facilitated if the child is cared for by many warm, friendly people.[56]

Paternal Deprivation

Some four million children in 1960 were being reared in homes without a father or a father substitute present. The lack of a father is associated with some problems of child care and perhaps of child socialization. The more obvious deficit is economic—in the provider role, which in father-absent homes usually must be enacted in whole or in part by someone other than the father. That economic deprivation is prevalent is shown by Chilman in that in 1960, 81 per cent of families with children that were headed by a woman were classified as "poor," whereas this was true of only 38 per cent of families with a male head.[57] If a child has no father he is likely to be a member of a poor family.

Is it equally true that the child's socialization for child and adult roles may suffer equally? Much concern has been expressed concerning the development of masculine identification and the learning of appropriate masculine behavior.[58] Bell, in summing up the psychological and sociological research, concluded,

in the process of examining all the studies that have related the variable of fatherlessness to possible impact on children, . . . in general I find the studies are unable to say with any conclusiveness that the father's presence in the

[55]Betty M. Caldwell, "The Effects of Infant Care" in Hoffman and Hoffman, op. cit., p. 62.
[56]Margaret Mead, "Some Theoretical Considerations on the Problem of Mother-Child Separation," American Journal of Orthopsychiatry, 24 (July 1954), p. 477.
[57]Catherine Chilman, Growing Up Poor (Washington, D.C.: U.S. Department of Health, Education, and Welfare, 1966).
[58]Benson has reviewed these studies in some detail. Leonard Benson, Fatherhood, A Sociological Perspective (New York: Random House, 1968), Chapter 10, "Fatherlessness."

home is of critical importance to the behavior and/or adjustment of his children. I find that studies by psychologists suggest that fatherlessness causes problems for children, while studies by sociologists do not suggest this.[59]

Herzog and Sudia, after reviewing four hundred studies, say,

Existing data do not permit a decisive answer to the questions about the effects on children of fatherlessness. As Maccoby remarked about a small group of father-absence studies, "the issue must remain open for further evidence." We can add that, on the basis of what we have found so far, we would not expect adequate evidence to indicate dramatic differences stemming from fatherlessness, per se.[60]

It is not obvious why studies of the masculinity of boys in father-present and father-absent families fail to agree. It may be that the psychological studies are more influenced by psychoanalytic theory, which views imitation as the primary socialization process. The alternative, learning theory, implies that one learns (or repeats) behavior that is rewarded (reinforced) and that plenty of role models are ordinarily available. That is, if a boy is ten years old it is appropriate for him to act like a ten-year-old boy, not a thirty-year-old man. He can obtain a sufficient number of cues from other boys of the same or a slightly older age.

The same is true when he enters an occupation or becomes a husband or father. He learns from those enacting the role and from his own experience, retaining the behavior that is reinforced, dropping that which is not reinforced or is negatively sanctioned.

Some sociologists, including the senior author, have acted on the assumption that the research issues for child socialization are not whether there are advantages in two-parent over one-parent families, but whether there are advantages in retaining a deserting father or maintaining a marriage characterized by chronic conflict between the father and the mother. His research[61] and that of Landis[62] provide evidence that child socialization is more effective in father-absent families or families with a step-parent than in those intact families in which conflict is chronic.

Finally, what of father-present families in which the father provides an inappropriate male model? If the father as a model has an influence on the son's socialization, that influence would seem to be *dys-*

[59]Robert R. Bell, in a review of *Fatherhood, A Sociological Perspective,* in *Journal of Marriage and the Family,* **31** (May 1969), p. 408.

[60]Elizabeth Herzog and Cecelia E. Sudia, "Fatherless Homes, a Review of Research," *Children,* **15** (Sept.–Oct. 1968), p. 181.

[61]Ivan Nye, "Adjustment of Children in Broken and Unhappy, Unbroken Homes," *Marriage and Family Living,* **19** (Nov. 1957), pp. 356–361.

[62]Judson T. Landis, "A Comparison of Children from Divorced and Nondivorced Unhappy Marriages," *The Family Life Coordinator,* **11** (July 1962), pp. 61–65.

functional if the child sees the adult male as a "drunk," as cruel to his wife and children, and/or as economically dependent. This issue is discussed in more detail in Chapter 17, "The Malfunctioning Family."

Finally, assuming comparable competence, it presumably is easier for two parents to care for and socialize children than for one to do so, and it seems reasonable to anticipate that two would be more effective in achieving the task.

The studies cited lead to three tentative generalizations concerning father absence:

1. Father-absent families are more likely to be economically deprived.
2. Socialization of children is probably easier and more effective in father-absent than in father-present families where there is chronic conflict between husband and wife. This is probably especially true of families in which the father provides an inappropriate model for boys.
3. Whether the absence of the father results in a lack of masculine identity and role behavior remains an open question.

A Position on Child Socialization

Much has been written on child socialization but relatively few general conclusions have been arrived at that have received broad consensus from behavioral scientists. From some of the research, theory, and essays on the subject, we shall advance a number of informal propositions. Because much of the needed research is yet to be conducted, some of these propositions may have to be revised at a future date. Therefore, the reader is invited to examine the following proposals critically.

The Nature of the Child Socialization Role

There is a wide range of parental child-socialization practices that produce adults who enact their roles adequately. To illustrate, the beginning of the century was a period of intermediate permissiveness. This was followed by a period of restrictive, repressive child-rearing, followed, in turn, by a period of extreme permissiveness. Now the trend seems to be moving back again toward an intermediate point. Children have come through all these environments to become productive adults. Likewise, the small conjugal family, the large extended family, and the communal child-rearing agencies, as in the kibbutzim, have all produced effective adults.

Therefore, *the range* of adequate, permissible child-socialization practices is broad. A comparison with the range of provider roles may

401

be helpful. Fathers must provide for the economic needs of their families, but mechanics, policemen, teachers, and farmers *all* rear children who become productive adults. In a similar vein, there are many strategies of child-rearing that are effective. Children must have their biological needs met, be protected, and obtain the necessary information required to enact childhood and adult roles. *How* this is done seems less important.

The Place of Expertise in Child Socialization

Theories of child socialization with supporting research have proved inadequate for constructing blueprints for parents. It is little short of ridiculous to review first the swing to extreme restrictiveness, then extreme permissiveness, and now perhaps back to the starting point. The result has often been confusion, with unnecessary conflict between the philosophies of the generations. The quest for the "best" child-rearing practices has proved illusive.

As Bruch has written, "The educated young mother, the one who spends most time in reading and listening to information on child care, is all too often overwhelmed and frightened by the responsibilities that are held up before her and consequently has many more problems in raising her children."[63]

One special problem has been to attempt to develop prescriptions for child-rearing from untested or erroneous theories. Again Bruch says,

Even more serious are the errors that are committed in the name of psychoanalytic theories. Many experts who deal in parent education have only a dim or distorted knowledge of psychoanalysis, though they quote it frequently and cling tenaciously to theories that they have misunderstood or that have been abandoned as incorrect. . . . What is overlooked is that psychoanalytic observations are made on sick people. Devereau points out "People are in analysis precisely because they, themselves, constrict and distort, rather than sublimate, individualize, and adapt their aggressive impulses."[64]

More recently, LeMasters has elaborated the problems that unrealistic expectations of experts have created for parents. The tendency of social scientists to hold parents totally accountable for the behavior of their children has led many parents to feel inadequate and guilty even though they have labored hard in their roles as parents.[65]

All this does not imply that there is no role for the expert, only that it

---

[63]Hilde Bruch, "Parent Education or the Illusion of Omnipotence," *American Journal of Orthopsychiatry,* **24** (July 1954), p. 724. See also, L. Kanner, *In Defence of Mothers: How to Bring up Children in Spite of the More Zealous Psychologists* (Springfield, Ill.: Charles C. Thomas, 1941).

[64]Ibid., p. 725.

[65]E. E. LeMasters, *Parents in Modern America* (Homewood, Ill.: Dorsey Press, 1970), Chapter 1.

is a more modest one of communicating relevant facts and suggestive theory—material that is frequently very useful to parents but that does not provide the basis for a blueprint that all parents should follow. Because each child is somewhat different and each parent somewhat different, prescriptions that instruct the parent in how to rear his child are inappropriate and will be even when the behavioral sciences are mature.

Child-Rearing Practices

Of current theories, we believe that those based on reinforcement theory have considerable promise. Very briefly, parental strategy is based on rewarding desired behavior and not rewarding undesired behavior. Becker has observed that much of the child-rearing of recent decades was exactly the opposite of this—acceptable behavior brought no response from the parent but inadequate or antisocial behavior brought parental attention, sympathy, reassurance of worth, and desired objects or experiences.[66] Reinforcement theory stresses rewarding desired behavior rather than punishment of undesired behavior, although the latter is not ruled out. Punishment is relatively ineffective because much antisocial behavior is undetected. Also, frequent punishment results in the child's attempting to avoid the parent, therefore reducing the parent's effectiveness as a positive socialization agent.

Socialization for Child and Adult Roles

Goals of socialization must be relevant to the stage of development of a society. In an urbanized, differentiated society, effective adult role-playing (for men) requires increasing knowledge, including the knowledge of how and where to obtain knowledge. Likewise, economic and social activity is likely to occur in groups so that the child requires socialization for effective participation in groups. However, differentiated societies provide a great variety of occupational roles and not all individuals must be highly trained and extensively socialized in group life.

Because adult roles are dominantly work roles of one type or another, child socialization that develops favorable attitudes and experience relevant to work are likely to further socialization for adult roles. The student role and the housekeeper role in childhood are relevant. Both are more realistically conceptualized as work rather than fun, and adequate rewards as reinforcement are needed as well as, perhaps, sanctions for nonperformance. Extreme permissiveness and an absence of work in childhood provide noncontinuous socialization for children—that is, "childhood is play, adulthood is work." This noncon-

---

[66] Wesley C. Becker, personal conversation with the senior author.

tinuity may result in a youth's electing to remain a child both psychologically and sociologically, and refusing to accept adult roles, or, at least, it may result in a traumatic transition into adulthood, without some of the basic attitudes and habits useful for competition in occupational roles.

Limits of Parental Responsibility

Parents have primary, ordinarily complete, responsibility for child care—feeding, clothing, and protecting children—the exceptions being the incapacity of the parents to discharge their obligations or unusual needs of a child, such as one mentally retarded, which may justify institutional care. However, their responsibilities for socialization are more limited. As societies become more differentiated, more groups and agencies share in the socialization of children—the school, the peer group, the church, sometimes the police or a social worker, and later, the economic organization in which he works or, if unemployment is high, fails to find work. Although the family is probably still the most crucial agency of socialization, all these others play a part and share the responsibility for the effectiveness of the person in adult roles. Finally, the child influences parental behavior toward him by manipulating his parents, even in infancy. Rheingold says,

The infant modulates, tempers, regulates, and refines the caretaker's activities. He produces delicate shades and nuances in these operations to suit his own needs of the moment. By such responses as fretting, sounds of impatience or satisfaction, by facial expression of pleasure, contentment, or alertness he produces elaborations here and dampening there.[67]

Of course the older child and the adolescent manipulate parents on a much more sophisticated scale.

Many an educated parent of the past two or three decades has been unnecessarily anxious in his child-care and socialization roles. Research has failed to support the idea that this or that particular piece of parental behavior affects the personality or the adult role-playing of the child. Whether the parent feeds on demand or on schedule, breastfeeds or bottle-feeds, toilet-trains or does not—all appear unimportant. What *is* essential is that the child receive adequate, nourishing food; that he be comfortable, and clean; and that he receive exercise, stimulation, and recreation. He needs protection, knowledge, and a reasonable development of skills in the socialization process, too, but there are many groups and agencies that participate in this process and that must share the responsibility for the outcome of the socialization process.

[67]Harriet L. Rheingold, op. cit., p. 785.

16

The Family and the Kinship System

Wherever and whenever marriages occur, bonds are established that link together not only a husband and a wife but also members of two previously unrelated autonomous nuclear families into patterned networks of relationships that constitute what is known as a *kinship system,* that is, "a structured system of relationships, in which individuals are bound to one another by complex interlocking and ramifying ties."[1] The kinship system involves both *affinal* (in-law) ties, created through the marital bond, and *consanguineous* (blood) relations established by birth.

In American society, relatives (technically referred to as *kindred*) are incorporated into a *bilateral* kinship system, in which the descent of both parents is given similar recognition and at birth offspring become affiliated equally with the relatives of the father and the mother.[2] By way of contrast, this bilateral structure may be compared with the more prevalent *unilineal* kinship system, in which individuals are normally affiliated with relatives of a single parent only—that is, they trace their descent either through the father, which establishes a *patrilineal* kinship system, or through the mother, which establishes a *matrilineal* kinship system.[3]

[1]George Peter Murdock, *Social Structure* (New York: The Macmillan Company, 1949), Chapter 6, "Analysis of Kinship," pp. 91–112.

[2]For a sophisticated statement on the classical structure of American kinship, see Talcott Parsons, "The Kinship System in Contemporary United States," *American Anthropologist,* **45** (Jan.–March 1943), pp. 22–28.

[3]Although kinship systems are universal cultural phenomena, they take a variety of forms, many of which we have not mentioned. For those interested in more elaborate and detailed conceptual distinctions concerning kinship systems, we suggest, as a start, Murdock, op. cit.; also his "The Kindred," *American Anthropologist,* **66** (Feb. 1964), pp. 129–132; Ernest C. Schusky, *Manual for Kinship Analysis: Studies in Anthropological Method* (New York: Holt, Rinehart and Winston, 1965); and William Davenport, "Nonunilinear Descent and Descent Groups," *American Anthropologist,* **61** (Aug. 1959), pp. 557–572.

In this chapter, we shall concentrate on the contemporary bilateral American system. There has been considerable professional controversy in recent years over the role of the extended family in advanced and highly differentiated societies such as our own. The argument centers around a series of questions concerning whether extensive kinship ties can persist in metropolitan industrial societies. We shall, begin, therefore, with an examination of the history and theoretical issues involved in that controversy as well as the research that has been undertaken in attempts to resolve it.

Urbanization and Kinship

For some time sociologists assumed that life in an urban and industrialized setting tends to pull families apart because of the diverse contacts, especially those in secondary groups to which family members have access. This assumption holds that people become so highly individualized in the city environment that they have little time to spend with family members; that in urban settings intrafamilial and interfamilial activities are drastically curtailed. As Wirth phrased it, "The family as a unit of social life is emancipated from the larger kinship group characteristic of the country and the individual members pursue their own diverging interests in their vocational, educational, religious, recreational, and political life."[4]

In recent years, however, a number of investigations have provided evidence that casts considerable doubt on the assumptions just stated and that at the same time lends substantiation to the opposite viewpoint—namely, that the family, and in particular the extended family, is viable in urban societies. These studies have generally indicated that some type of extended kinship system is operating for most urban families, although there is considerable variation in the patterns or modes of interaction both within and between social classes.

This "rediscovery"[5] of the kin group represents an interesting and important as well as instructive aspect of family sociology. It is our purpose in this chapter, therefore, to trace in some detail this rather dramatic shift in emphasis by sociologists toward urbanization and kinship, to examine current research on the extended family in the

[4]Louis Wirth, "Urbanism as a Way of Life," *American Journal of Sociology,* **44** (July 1938), pp. 1–24.

[5]Our use of the term *rediscovery* must be qualified. Extended kin relationships of the type to be discussed in this chapter "may or may not always have existed in urban, industrial America. It is possible that they always did exist but were overlooked by sociologists concentrating on the study of the nuclear family. It may also be that a revival of extended kinship relationships has taken place in recent decades. The question as to whether or not the nuclear family was ever more completely isolated from kin cannot now be resolved"; in Hyman Rodman (ed.), *Marriage, Family, and Society* (New York: Random House, 1965), pp. 204–210.

United States, and to examine the implications of that research for families.

Changing Conceptualizations of Urban Kinship: A Theoretical Overview[6]

Before about the mid-twentieth century a commonplace observation in sociological and anthropological literature was that the extended family did not play a very significant role in industrialized and urbanized societies. Indeed, it was "sometimes stated, almost as an axiom, that the urban milieu results in the extreme attrition of kin relations."[7] It has been observed that many of the leading and early sociological theorists, as well as more contemporary social theorists, rather consistently stressed the social isolation of the urban nuclear family. Their conclusions were based in part upon their observations of the consequences of a general principle, that "social differentiation in complex societies requires of its members a readiness to move, to move to where there are needs for workers and where there are opportunities for better jobs."[8] We shall have more to say later in the chapter regarding the consequences of geographical mobility on kinship ties. Here we simply note that the effects of a nuclear family's mobility on its relations to the kin group were typically depicted as disintegrative, particularly in the move from the country to the city. Locke's early statement, that "wherever mobility has been relatively easy and extensive the large family pattern of grandparents, the marriage family, uncles, aunts, in-laws, and other near relatives has disappeared,"[9] is illustrative of this position.

This particular hypothesis concerning the disintegration of family relationships is but one of a number of related hypotheses that collectively and in their simplest form hold that urban settings are strongholds of secondary groups and inimical to primary groups other than the nuclear family. In Wirth's well-known phrase: "Distinctive features

[6]Some of the material for this section is drawn from the junior author's doctoral dissertation and related published articles. See Felix M. Berardo, "Internal Migrants and Extended Family Relations: A Study of Newcomer Adaptation," unpublished Ph.D. dissertation, Florida State University, Tallahassee, 1965; "Kinship Interaction and Migrant Adaptation in an Aerospace-Related Community," *Journal of Marriage and the Family,* **28** (Aug. 1966), pp. 296–304; "Kinship Interaction and Communications Among Space-Age Migrants," *Journal of Marriage and the Family,* **29** (Aug. 1967), pp. 541–554.

[7]Scott Greer, "Urbanism Reconsidered: A Comparative Study of Local Areas in a Metropolis," *American Sociological Review,* **21** (Feb. 1956), pp. 20–25.

[8]Marvin B. Sussman and Lee Burchinal, "Kin Family Network: Unheralded Structure in Current Conceptualizations of Family Functioning," *Marriage and Family Living,* **24** (Aug. 1962), pp. 231–240.

[9]Harvey J. Locke, "Mobility and Family Disorganization," *American Sociological Review,* **15** (Aug. 1940), pp. 489–494.

407

of the urban mode of life have often been described sociologically as consisting of the substitution of secondary for primary contacts, the weakening of bonds of kinship, and the declining social significance of the family, the disappearance of the neighborhood, and the undermining of the traditional basis of social solidarity."[10] In this context the contemporary urban elementary family of husband, wife, and dependent children is said to stand in isolation, and relations with other kin are not considered to be of significant consequence, whereas in rural areas extended family ties are depicted as strong and pervasive.[11]

Sussman has commented on the literature that espouses the rather traditional point of view we have been describing. He notes that in the latter perspective a

neolocal nuclear family system, one in which nuclear families live by themselves independent from their families of orientation, is thought to be particularly well adapted to the needs of the American economy for a fluid and mobile labor market. It is also suggested that differences in occupational status of family members can best be accepted if such individuals live some distance from one another. Support for these theories is found in the high residential mobility of Americans; one in five families make a move during a given year and presumably these families are nuclear ones.[12]

Sussman goes on to note that Freudian analysts, students of ethnic relations, and social-stratification theorists have all posited similar viewpoints emphasizing the functionality of the isolation of nuclear-related families from one another. These theorists adhere to the position that the demands associated with occupational and geographical mobility have brought about a family pattern in urban areas consisting of relatively isolated units that operate without much support from the kinship system.

Beginning in the second half of the twentieth century, however, the position of these theorists was increasingly called into question by a number of investigations of extended-family relations in different areas of the United States.[13] Moreover, research on family life in other countries has raised a similar question. Thus, extended kin apparently play a significant role in the lives of the contemporary French-

---

[10]Ibid.

[11]William H. Key, "Rural—Urban Differences and the Family," *Sociological Quarterly,* 2 (Jan. 1961), pp. 49–56. Key cites several studies that have posited this thesis. "The assertion in many cases, and the inference in others, is that the extended family is most important in rural areas and that the nuclear or conjugal family stands as a relatively independent unit in urban localities."

[12]Marvin B. Sussman, "The Isolated Nuclear Family: Fact or Fiction?" *Social Problems,* 6 (Spring 1959), pp. 333–340.

[13]The relevant research has been aptly brought together in Sussman and Burchinal, op. cit.; and Marvin B. Sussman, "Relationships of Adult Children with Their Parents in the United States," in *Social Structure and the Family: Generational Relations,* ed. by Ethel Shanas and Gordon F. Streib (Englewood Cliffs, N.J.: Prentice-Hall, 1965), pp. 62–92.

Canadian family, both in its rural and its urban forms.[14] Certain British sociologists and anthropologists have uncovered empirical evidence of kin relations in a series of studies concerning families residing in East London.[15] Current investigations of modern Japanese society likewise indicate that family units other than the isolated family are compatible with urban industrialization.[16] Finally, in his analysis of changes in family structure in sub-Saharan Africa, Arabic Islam, the West, China, Japan, and India, Goode concluded that "no matter what index is used, the family in the most industrialized nations has not taken on the supposed characteristics of the isolated nuclear family system. The extended kin network continues to function and to include a wide range of kin who share with one another, see one another frequently, and know each other." Further, "the frequency of social participation between the average modern nuclear family and its relatives may not have been reduced at all."[17] In this connection, certain contemporary anthropological theorists have gone as far as to suggest that any type of kinship structure is compatible with urban society.[18]

The latter viewpoints are, of course, at variance with the traditional model of the isolated nuclear family previously discussed. The major points of difference between these two viewpoints are neatly caught in a statement by Axelrod concerning the broad perspective of the relationship of urbanization to group membership:

The more traditional view emphasizes the impersonality of relationships in the urban community, the wide importance of formal and secondary group association, and the decline of the kinship group [whereas] the newer view, while admitting this, gives informal group contacts a more important place. The traditional view sees the family and the extended kin group as playing a much more circumscribed role, the second emphasizes the changed role of the family.[19]

[14]Philippe Garique, *La Vue Familiale des Canadiens Français* (Montreal: Presses Universitaires, 1962).

[15]Raymond S. Firth (ed.), *Two Studies of Kinship in London,* London School of Economics, *Monographs on Social Anthropology,* No. 15 (London: Atlone Press, 1956); Peter Townsend, *The Family Life of Old People: An Inquiry in East London* (London: Routledge and Paul Kegan, 1957); Michael Young and Peter Willmott, *Family and Kinship in East London* (Glencoe, Ill.: The Free Press, 1957).

[16]Iwao Ishine and John Burnett, "The Japanese Labor Boss System," Research in Japanese Social Relations, Interim Technical Report No. 3 (Columbus: Ohio State University, 1952).

[17]William J. Goode, *World Revolution and Family Patterns* (Glencoe, Ill.: The Free Press, 1963), p. 75.

[18]John Bennett and Leo Despres, "Kinship and Instrumental Activities: A Theoretical Inquiry," *American Anthropologist,* 52 (Apr. 1960), pp. 254–267.

[19]Morris Axelrod, "Urban Structure and Social Participation," *American Sociological Review,* 21 (Feb. 1956), pp. 13–18. For a more recent and more detailed elaboration of these divergent viewpoints, see Bernard Farber (ed.), *Kinship and Family Organization* (New York: John Wiley & Sons, 1966), in his introduction to Chapter 4, "Family and Kinship in Contemporary Society," pp. 117–122.

CURRENT CONCEPTUALIZATIONS OF URBANIZATION AND KINSHIP The "newer view" has led to reexamination of the position of the social isolation of the urban family and to new conceptualizations of family patterns. Some of these conceptualizations may be briefly mentioned here. Jaco and Belknap, for example, have posited the emergence of what they term a *fringe family* in the peripheral areas of metropolitan districts, whose structure and functions are somewhat different from the traditional urban and rural types, but in which the kinship system may be assuming a more prominent role as the basis for social status. The latter considerations lead them to ask a series of questions, such as: "Is the strengthening of kinship in this sense making the family as important as occupation in determining status in the urban community? If occupation is still maintaining major importance as a status-basis in the fringe, is the kinship system becoming more important in maintaining occupational lines?"[20]

Some sociologists began to speak of a resurgence of the *urban familism* within the metropolis itself. Haller, for example, observed that

today's urbanites are largely in the second or third generation of residence in the city. It takes only a few generations . . . to link the individual tightly into a web of kinship. By now, a large proportion of the residents of large urban centers doubtless have many such links to others in the same city, and these carry with them a complex set of mutual obligations. . . . A great many people . . . find pleasure in fulfilling these obligations. Could it be that the job—once so central to the urbanite's whole being—serves now as an economic support for an enjoyable extended family life? In a word, is there an emergent urban familism?[21]

Sociologists have conducted studies in various parts of the country in attempts to decide the question of whether familism actually exists in the city and, if so, to determine its extent and assess its consequences. We shall examine some of the research findings later in the chapter.

Further efforts to conceptualize modern urban kinship systems are apparent in the work of Litwak,[22] who argues that the nuclear family does not *necessarily* break away from an extended family system. Rather, the family participates in a *modified extended family system*. Whereas the traditional or "classical" extended family system was

---

[20]E. Gartly Jaco and Ivan Belknap, "Is a New Family Form Emerging in the Urban Fringe?" *American Sociological Review,* **18** (Oct. 1953), pp. 551–557.

[21]A. O. Haller, "The Urban Family," *American Journal of Sociology,* **66** (Feb. 1961), pp. 621–622.

[22]Eugene Litwak, "Occupational Mobility and Extended Family Cohesion," *American Sociological Review,* **25** (Feb. 1960), pp. 9–21; "Geographical Mobility and Extended Family Cohesion," *American Sociological Review,* **25** (June 1960), pp. 385–394.

characterized by geographic propinquity, occupational nepotism, and strict authority relations, the modified extended family system encourages geographical and occupational mobility but at the same time maintains communication and identification among its members and continues to encourage mutual aid. Although *kinship orientation* among relatives is maintained, the actual coalescence, that is, drawing together or uniting of the kin group in terms of proximity and greater emphasis on physical contacts, often takes place only after the individual members (husbands) have reached their peak in occupational careers and earning capacity. This latter notion is a provocative hypothesis that, although given some support by Litwak's data, needs more extensive testing before its complications can be adequately explored. Reiss, for example, had pointed out that "the cumulative effect of years of mobility is a wider dispersal of kin in the later family cycle phases. This assumes, of course, that the mobility of individuals is random with reference to the residence of extended kin. There is no information to indicate that this is not the case. Apparently, as the years go on, kin tend to live farther apart geographically."[23] Nevertheless, this notion does raise some interesting questions. For example, which of two kin groups—the husband's or the wife's—will a person eventually attempt to reunite with? As we shall see later there are some cogent reasons for expecting that such coalescence will tend to follow the female line, at least in American society.

Finally, Sussman's related proposal of a *kin family network* is still further evidence of attempts to conceptualize contemporary family patterns.

The kin family network is composed of nuclear families bound together by affectional ties and choice. Unrequired for the maintenance of the network are geographical propinquity, neolocal residence, occupational nepotism, interventions in occupational and social mobility efforts or a rigid hierarchal authority structure. Members and nuclear families of the network volunteer to help rather than to direct activities. They perform supportive rather than coercive roles.[24]

In summary, it may be said that current family theory and research interests have shifted not only to the general structure of the American kinship system, but also to the manner in which it is handled in particular cases; that is to say, the variations in pattern of kin contact. It is within the context of this preliminary background statement on the

[23]Paul J. Reiss, "The Extended Kinship System: Correlates of and Attitudes on Frequency of Interaction," *Marriage and Family Living,* **24** (Nov. 1962), pp. 333–339.

[24]Marvin B. Sussman and Lee Burchinal, "Parental Aid to Married Children: Implications for Family Functions," *Marriage and Family Living,* **24** (Nov. 1962), pp. 320–332.

411

reconceptualization of urban kinship that the following examination of contemporary American extended family relations should be placed. We will begin with the initial studies that demonstrated the existence of extended family ties in modern urban society and move from there to studies of how and under what conditions these ties function and to the social correlates of varying types of kinship extension.

Empirical Evidence of Urban Kinship

THE CONNECTICUT STUDY In the early fifties Dotson conducted intensive interviews with fifty *working-class families* in New Haven, Connecticut, concerning their formal and informal social participation. His findings revealed that although the members of these families did not participate to any important extent in formal association, such as lodges and women's clubs, most of them did have an active social life within the kin group; "in at least 15 of the 50 families, leisure time activities of the husbands and wives were completely dominated by the kin group. In another 28 families, regular visiting patterns with relatives constituted a major, although not exclusive, form of social activity."[25] This study suggests that the presence of a high degree of kinship interaction tends to preclude other types of formal social participation. As a matter of fact, about two fifths of the husbands and wives had no intimate friends outside of their own families. The Connecticut study provided some early evidence that the role of informal social participation, especially within the family and kin groups, had, perhaps, been underestimated by previous investigators of modern city life.

THE LOS ANGELES STUDY Additional evidence was provided by Greer in a study of urban neighborhood participation in two Los Angeles census tracts characterized as "high" and "low" urbanized areas. When a sample of over three hundred housewives in these areas were queried concerning the participation of the adult family members in various formal and informal groups and activities, it was found that "the most important single kind of social relationships for both samples is kinship visiting. A large majority of both samples visit their kin at least once a week."[26] These and related findings led Greer to suggest that kin relations in America might be growing in importance because of the diminished reliance placed upon neighborhoods and local community contacts.

THE DETROIT STUDY At about the same time, an investigation of the urban social participation of Detroit residents was uncovering similar evidence of kin relations. Again, an analysis of visiting patterns revealed that

[25]Floyd Dotson, "Pattern of Voluntary Associations Among Working Class People," *American Sociological Review,* **16** (Oct. 1951), pp. 687–693.
[26]Greer, op. cit., p. 22.

more people get together frequently with their relatives outside the immediate family than they do with friends, neighbors, and co-workers. About half of the population report that they see these relatives about once a month or more often. This is in sharp contrast to the stereotype which pictures the city dweller as devoid of kinship relations.[27]

These findings are perhaps the more significant in view of the knowledge that a large percentage of the residents of Detroit are migrants from other cities and from areas around the nation.

THE SAN FRANCISCO STUDY Finally, Bell and Boat found further support for the findings in the other studies cited through their research on the nature and extent of informal relations in San Francisco. They compared male residents of four different types of neighborhoods with respect to the amount of socialization with neighbors, relatives, friends and co-workers; the nature of their informal contacts; the sources of their friendships; and the extent of their personal relations in formal associations. "Perhaps the most striking aspect of the findings," they commented, "is the importance of kin-groups as a source of informal relations in each of these neighborhoods."[28] Thus it was clear that the kin members were more likely to provide intimate social contacts than neighbors or co-workers in each neighborhood. The San Francisco results, therefore, corroborate Axelrod's comment that: "The extended family may have lost its function as an economic producing unit in the city, but relatives and friends continue to be an important source of companionship and mutual support."[29]

To sum up, data from research conducted in various parts of the United States have amply demonstrated the widespread persistence of urban kinship. This has led one of the leading contemporary scholars in this area to urge family sociologists to pursue other important facets of the kinship system:

The evidence of the viability of an existing kinship structure carrying on extensive activities among kin is so convincing that we find it unnecessary to continue further descriptive work in order to establish the existence of the kin network in modern urban society. The far more important task is to determine

[27] Axelrod, op. cit., 13–18. The rank order of the comparative importance of the types of informal groups was reported as (1) relatives, (2) friends, (3) neighbors, and (4) co-workers. This pattern did not hold, however, for a small group in the sample characterized by exceptionally high status, high income, or some college education. Within each of these three categories, friends replaced relatives in the rank order. But even among the exceptional groups, from 50 to 75 per cent get together with relatives frequently. Other samples periodically derived from the Detroit Area Study (DAS) have exhibited similar frequencies of kinship contacts.

[28] Wendell Bell and Marion D. Boat, "Urban Neighborhoods and Informal Social Relations," *American Journal of Sociology*, **62** (Jan. 1957), pp. 391–398.

[29] Axelrod, op. cit., pp. 13–18.

the meaning and significance of kin network activities for the members of the system and to discover how the functions of the kin system affect the workings of other social systems in the society.[30]

In this connection, we want to look now at some of the functions performed by kin groups in modern society other than those of social activity and companionship.

Urban Kinship and Family Welfare Norms: The Helping Hand

The persistence of the kinship system in modern society is partially explained by the fact that its membership has continued to function as a primary agent in promoting the welfare of family members through a variety of mutually supportive activities. For example, the kindred:

1. Sanction adherence to traditional ceremonies and rituals by gifts and congratulatory rewards.
2. Provide sponsorship for economic activities for members.
3. Promote the economic welfare of members through the performance of special favors.
4. Provide sources of aid and personal services as well as sympathy in times of crisis.

As Farber has observed, inasmuch as "these activities cannot easily be relegated in any institutionalized way to another recognizable group, many sociologists regard the persistence of the kindred as a reflection of its operation as a unit influencing the personal destiny of its members."[31]

In a series of interviews concerning family continuity and help patterns among intergenerational families, sociologists have uncovered networks of kin assistance and involvement. "The lifelines of the network are help and services exchanged among members of nuclear families related by blood and affinal ties. Help, service, and social interaction characterize the activities of this interdependent kin family system identified as the kin family network."[32] For example, in a Connecticut sample of white, middle-class Protestant families, nearly

---

[30] Sussman, "Relationships of Adult Children with Their Parents in the United States," op. cit., pp. 62–92. For students interested in the subject of urbanization and kinship ties, this chapter provides an excellent starting point. It is especially to be recommended for its extensive review of available literature and its elaborate statement of varied theoretical stances with respect to sociological explanations of extended family relations.

[31] Farber, op. cit., Introduction to Chapter 4, "Family and Kinship in Contemporary Society," pp. 117–122.

[32] Sussman and Burchinal, "Parental Aid to Married Children: Implications for Family Functioning," op. cit., pp. 320–332. This is by far the most extensive and up-to-date review and summary on the topic.

414

80 per cent of the parents had established a pattern of providing aid and services to their married children's families, and in 70 per cent of the cases the parents felt that the recipients would suffer a loss of status if the aid were not continued. This assistance pattern, moreover, appeared in both working-class and middle-class households.

In this same connection, the San Francisco study discussed earlier also queried the persons interviewed as to whom they would call upon to take care of them if they were ill: 77 per cent of the low-income and 84 per cent of the high-income groups reported they would count on extended family aid in cases of sickness lasting a month or longer. The rank order of importance in this connection was (1) relatives, (2) friends, (3) co-workers, and (4) neighbors.

Many other instances and types of kinship assistance involving patterns of mutual aid have been discovered by family sociologists in recent years. The findings of various investigations in this area have been aptly summarized by Sussman and Burchinal,[33] as follows:

1. Help patterns take many forms, including the exchange of services, gifts, advice, and financial assistance. Financial aid patterns may be direct as in the case of young married couples . . . or indirect and subtle. . . .

2. Such help patterns are probably more widespread in the middle and working class families and are more integral a feature of family behavior. Very few families included in available studies reported neither giving nor receiving aid from relatives. . . .

3. The exchange of aid among families flows in several directions, from parents to children and vice-versa, among siblings, and less frequently, from more distant relatives. However, financial assistance generally appears to flow from parents to children.

4. While there may be a difference in the absolute amount of financial aid received by families of middle and working class status, there are insignificant differences in the proportion of families in these two strata who report receiving, giving, or exchanging economic assistance in some form.

5. Financial aid is received most commonly during the early years of married life. Parents are probably more likely to support financially "approved" than "disapproved" ones, such as elopements, interfaith and interracial marriages. Support can be disguised in the forms of substantial sums of money or valuable gifts at Christmas, anniversaries or birthdays. High rates of parental support are probably associated with marriages of children while they are still in a dependency status; ones among high school or college students are examples. Many other forms of assistance, in addition to direct and indirect economic exchanges, take place between

[33]Sussman and Burchinal, "Kin Family Network: Unheralded Structure in Current Conceptualizations of Family Functioning," op. cit., pp. 231–240. The reader is cautioned that the majority of the studies from which these findings are derived involved white, upper-middle-class, Protestant, and college student populations and, therefore, their general applicability to other populations in our society is limited.

415

members of the kin network, such as babysitting, performing household duties, providing a place to live, etc.

Moreover, it is worth noting that the vast majority of these acts of filial and kin responsibility are carried out voluntarily or on the basis of a sense of affection and of an ethical obligation, rather than because of a compulsion to do so emanating from the legal system.[34] We shall examine the notion of "filial responsibility" and its implications for family structure in greater detail in Chapter 22.

The pattern of assistance between married college students and their initial family of orientation represents a particularly interesting facet of contemporary kinship exchange systems, inasmuch as the married student population has shown a continuous growth over the past several decades. Currently, it has been estimated that approximately one fourth of all college undergraduates in the United States are married and, at the graduate level, the figure is even higher. A substantial proportion of these couples, as we have noted, are being subsidized, either directly or indirectly, through various forms of assistance provided by parents. It has been suggested that the overwhelming evidence of such subsidization represents a clear contradiction to one of the major assumptions associated with a bureaucratic ideology, namely, the belief in financial autonomy for young nuclear families:

The pattern and direction of financial aid calls into question the current belief that couples adhere to the norm of financial autonomy immediately after marriage. Among generationally linked nuclear families, the aid pattern is so persistent in its direction that the notion of the financial autonomy norm must be considered more of an ideal construct than an actual condition found extensively in society. . . . It appears that the ideological stance of the young couple is to maintain an image of autonomy, and perhaps in a meaningful way, to avoid such aid if at all possible, but nevertheless not to reject such aid when it appears to assist in the achievement of economic stability and a level of living in consonance with the young couple's aspirations.[35]

Thus, the married college husband may reject a direct offer of support money from his parents or in-laws, but is more likely to accept a gift of furniture, a much needed typewriter, or clothes for the children, particularly if such items are coincidentally offered on a day of special occasion, such as a birthday, a Christmas holiday, or a wedding anniversary.

---

[34]Research supporting this statement may be found in Sussman, "Relationships of Adult Children with Their Parents in the United States," op. cit., p. 70, footnote 26.

[35]Ibid., pp. 78–79. (An earlier and more extensive statement concerning the autonomy norm may be found in Sussman and Burchinal, "Parental Aid to Married Children," op. cit.) pp. 320–332.

416

Geographic Mobility and the Extended Family

As noted earlier in the chapter, early sociological theorists took the position (1) that limited opportunities for today's highly specialized occupations force the head of the family and his dependents to be spacially mobile, and (2) as a consequence of the nuclear family's mobility, that an extended family system could not be developed or maintained in an industrialized and urbanized society in which bureaucratic norms predominated. The consequences of geographical mobility for family structure, therefore, have been an intergral part of the general theory of the isolated nuclear family. Until recently, however, there has been very little systematic research evidence concerning the relationship of kinship groupings to migrant status and behavior patterns.[36] In view of the high degree of physical movement evident in our society today, such investigations become important to understanding not only social organization in general but family organization in particular.

Increased urbanization and industrialization in the United States have been accompanied by unprecedented migration and an accelerated rate of household formation.[37] Indeed, data from the national census suggest that we have become an uprooted population and one of rather impermanent residence. Approximately one fifth of our citizens change addresses in any given year, and this amounts to nearly 40 million people. Studies indicate that less than four out of ten people were born in the area where they currently reside. Moreover, six out of ten persons aged thirty have moved from their place of birth. In terms of spatial distance, one family head out of five is now living over one thousand miles from where he was born; 5 million families move from one state to another each year.[38] Certainly the following observation, made by de Tocqueville more than a century ago, would appear all the more applicable to America today:

In the United States, a man builds a house in which to spend his old age, and he sells it before the roof is on; he plants a garden and rents it just as the trees are coming into bearing; he brings a field into tillage and leaves other men to gather the crops; he embraces a profession and gives it up; he settles in a place, which he soon afterwards leaves to carry on his changeable longings elsewhere.[39]

[36]Ted T. Jitodai, "Migration and Kinship Contacts," *Pacific Sociological Review,* 6 (Fall 1963), pp. 49–55.

[37]Peter H. Rossi, *Why Families Move* (Glencoe, Ill.: The Free Press, 1955).

[38]U.S. Bureau of the Census, *Current Population Reports,* Series P-20, No. 156, (Dec. 9, 1966), "Mobility of the Population of the United States: March, 1965 to March, 1966," U.S. Government Printing Office, Washington, D.C. Due to a continual growth in the population as a whole, increasingly greater numbers of people are experiencing geographical mobility.

[39]Alexis de Tocqueville, *Democracy in America,* Vol. 2. (New York: The Century Co., 1898), p. 164.

It is also worth mentioning, in this connection, that rather significant differences in mobility patterns exist between members of various socioeconomic strata, with a resultant differential impact on extended family ties. There is, for example, considerable evidence from any number of migration studies to support the hypothesis that white professional, managerial, and technical groups are more likely than manual workers to move greater distances,[40] and consequently, are more apt to be without relatives in the immediate community of residence.[41] Differences between high-status and low-status groups in terms of the distances they have moved largely reflect the occupational demands of a complex industrialized and bureaucratic society for highly trained personnel. Rose has noted the processes involved here, remarking that

generally speaking, lower-class people find many more intervening opportunities in a given distance than upper-class people do. Relatively specialized persons and others who seek the better paying jobs must move a greater distance to find them, while those who are less specialized—whose remuneration is lower on the average—can find their "opportunities" close by. Similarly, when employers seek employees to fill specialized (including managerial) positions, they must look farther afield and move them a greater distance, than when they seek workers to fill relatively unspecialized positions.[42]

People with specialized skills, such as professional workers and managers, typically have greater levels of educational attainment and, as we shall see shortly, generally have a lower intensity of interfamilial ties than less educated individuals. The extended family systems that have been examined by sociologists are to a considerable degree class-linked. Hollingshead's description of the so-called established upper-class family is illustrative in this connection:

The established upper-class family is basically an extended kin group, solidified by lineage and a heritage of common experience in a communal setting. A complicated network of consanguinial and affinal ties unites nuclear families of orientation and procreation into an in-group that rallies when its position is threatened. . . . Each nuclear family usually maintains a separate household, but it does not conceive of itself as a unit apart from the larger kin group. . . .

[40]Arnold M. Rose, "Distance of Migration and Socio-Economic Status of Migrants," *American Sociological Review,* **23** (Aug. 1958), pp. 420–423.

[41]Litwak, op. cit., pp. 9–21.

[42]Rose, op. cit., p. 423. However, migrant Negroes who are of the lowest socioeconomic status represent an exception because they often travel unusually long distances in migrating from the South to northern areas. Moreover, they are more likely than whites to migrate to distant locations because friends or relatives had previously established a residence there.

418

An important factor in the extended established family's ability to maintain its position through several generations is its economic security.[43]

Hollingshead notes that in the established upper-class family the degree of kinship solidarity in conjunction with intraclass marriages results in a relatively high order of stability. This may be contrasted with the "new upper-class family" that has achieved its position primarily through economic success in the current generation.

The new family is very unstable in comparison with the established family. It lacks the security of accepted position at the top of the local status system. . . . The stabilizing influence exerted on the deviant individual by an extended family group, as well as friends, is absent. (Many upwardly mobile families break with their kin groups as part of the price they pay for their mobility.) Then, too, the new family is composed of adults who are self-directing, full of initiative, believe in the freedom of the individual, and rely upon themselves rather than the kin group.[44]

Again a high rate of geographical mobility is a concomitant factor here, often being a prerequisite to successful occupational achievement. Heads of families who are now in the upper middle class are frequently people who left their home communities as young adults to attend a college or university. After completing their formal education they generally took jobs in some community other than the one in which they were trained and oftentimes other than their home town. Indeed, the probabilities are high that they either relocated or were transferred from one community to another as they moved up in their occupational careers.[45]

To summarize, during the early years of matrimony the husband assumes increasing and time-consuming responsibilities, such as raising a family and pursuing a career. He is busy with occupational achievement, and this frequently involves geographical movement. His focus of attention, therefore, is likely to be diverted for a time away from extended family ties, and his obligation to maintain them may be overshadowed by more pressing considerations.

Geographic Mobility and Kin Sentiment

An important aspect of the theory of a modified extended family system is the assumption that kinship orientation or identification can

[43]August B. Hollingshead, "Class Differences in Family Stability," *The Annals,* **272** (Nov. 1950), pp. 39–46.

[44]Ibid., pp. 42–43.

[45]Ibid. One of the most popular and widely read contemporary analyses of this process is William H. Whyte, Jr., *The Organization Man* (New York: Doubleday and Company, 1956). (Originally published by Simon and Schuster.)

419

be maintained despite geographical mobility. Indeed, there is now considerable evidence to support this contention. For example, in his own New York sample, Litwak found that "those individuals more closely identified with the extended family also are more likely to leave the city and presumably their nearby relatives," but that "once having moved away from them they are likely to retain their family identity."[46] Reiss's evidence in his Boston sample showed a strong desire for relatives to live closer than they did and, in addition, over half of the families interviewed wanted more kin contact. Moreover, nine out of ten felt that they had an *obligation* to keep in touch with relatives, and cited time, cost, and distance as major reasons for not satisfactorialy fulfilling this obligation.[47] A majority of newcomer families to urban communities in North Carolina indicated a strong interest in seeing their parents more often. In fact, a frequent source of community dissatisfaction among these families was that relatives and friends were not near enough. Specifically, the most satisfied families were more likely to have parents residing either in the community or in the surrounding area, to visit them frequently, and to express feelings of closeness to both their mothers and their fathers.[48] Similarly, new-comer families to Florida communities expressed a strong desire to see their relatives, particularly members of the family of origin, more often.[49] As shown in Table 16.1, the desire for increased kin contact is most acute for opportunities to visit those relatives living beyond the borders of the state. A substantial proportion of those families with relatives within the state, however, also desired increased interaction with those relatives.

Clearly then, families on the move do retain a strong orientation toward the kindred. Emotional bonds between extended family members, cultivated through long periods of socialization and intimate interaction, are not easily extinguished by mere physical separation of member units. Moreover, research has consistently shown that a large proportion of mobile families communicate (via letters, telephone calls, telegrams, birthday cards, and so on) with their kin groups.[50]

[46]Litwak, "Geographical Mobility and Extended Family Cohesion," op. cit., p. 389.

[47]Reiss, "The Extended Kinship System," op. cit., p. 339. There was, however, strong disapproval of common residence with kin. Migrant families desired their relatives to live closer, but "not too close."

[48]John Gulick and Charles E. Bowerman, "Adaptation of Newcomers in the Piedmont Industrial Crescent," Urban Studies Program, Institute for Research in Social Science (Chapel Hill: University of North Carolina, 1961, mimeographed). Also, John Gulick, Charles E. Bowerman, and Kurt W. Back, "Newcomer Enculturation in the City: Attitudes and Participation," in *Urban Growth Dynamics,* ed. by F. S. Chapin and S. F. Weiss (New York: John Wiley & Sons, Inc., 1961), pp. 315–358.

[49]Berardo, "Kinship Interaction and Communication Among Space-Age Migrants," op. cit., pp. 541–554.

[50]Ibid.

Table 16.1
Desire to See Kin by Residence and Relationship of Kin*

Desire to See Kin	Relationship of Kin				
	Parents %	Brothers %	Sisters %	Kinfolk† %	In-laws‡ %
Kin Living in Florida					
More often	42.7	46.2	42.1	39.1	27.3
About the same	53.2	52.2	56.4	57.7	65.6
Less often	4.1	1.6	1.5	3.2	7.1
Total	100.0	100.0	100.0	100.0	100.0
	(335)	(247)	(273)	(379)	(410)
Kin Living outside of Florida					
More often	78.2	81.0	81.5	62.5	64.4
About the same	20.0	18.2	17.4	35.5	32.7
Less often	1.8	.8	1.1	2.0	2.9
Total	100.0	100.0	100.0	100.0	100.0
	(444)	(614)	(609)	(980)	(859)

*All percentages have been tabulated on the basis of the total number of respondents having the specified relative living in or outside of Florida.
†Includes first cousins, uncles, aunts, and grandparents.
‡Restricted to the parents, brothers, and sisters of spouse.
SOURCE: Felix M. Berardo, "Kinship Interaction and Communications Among Space-Age Migrants," *Journal of Marriage and the Family,* **29** (Aug. 1967), p. 551. Reprinted by permission.

Such communicative networks function to sustain kinship orientation between member units scattered over wide areas of the continent. Litwak's notion, that "extended family relations can be maintained over great geographical distances because modern advances in communicative techniques have minimized the socially disruptive effects of geographic distance," appears to be well founded.

Determinants of Kin Interaction Under Conditions of High Mobility

What, then, do we know about the consequences of geographic mobility on patterns of kin interaction? In a society characterized by a high level of internal migration, what factors are associated with the maintenance of satisfactory ties with the kindred? What variables exert the greatest influence in determining current patterns of extended family relations, and does their relative importance increase or diminish at various stages of the family life cycle? Now that it has been shown that such relations can be maintained in contemporary society, what is the nature and extent of these relations? Does the availability of relatives influence the direction of migration, or do individuals prefer to locate where there is the best economic opportunity? What are the sentiments of family members concerning their separation from the kindred? The various sections to follow will take up these and related questions in order to specify more concretely the relationship between migration and extended family relations.

A. LOCATION OF RESIDENCE We have noted earlier that residential mobility, particularly among upwardly mobile and high-status groups, generally diminishes the ready availability of kin and thereby produces a noticeable reduction in extended family face-to-face contact. A number of studies have shown this to be the case, at least in the initial period of migration.

1. Availability of Relatives. That residential mobility leads to a widespread dispersion of the kin group is evident from Litwak's observations of a sample of urban families residing in Buffalo, New York, and Berardo's examination of kindred relations among newcomer families migrating to contiguous locales of east-central Florida. Both studies found that a significantly larger proportion of the professional, managerial, and technical persons than other occupational groups had no relatives residing in the immediate community. Berardo, for example, reports that two thirds of the migrants to the Cape Kennedy region did not have any relatives living in the city proper, and over two fifths were without relatives in the surrounding area of the state. Of the most recent newcomers, nearly 70 per cent had no available relatives in the immediate community.[51]

2. Reduction in Kinship Interaction. Both the Litwak and Berardo studies confirmed that geographical mobility is accompanied by a considerable reduction in the intensity of interfamilial contacts, particularly among recent newcomers. For example, in the New York group, over half of the people with relatives residing in the city received one or more family visits a week, whereas only 4 per cent of those without relatives in the city received visits of any kind this often. Reiss's analysis of the frequency of interaction between 161 white middle-class families residing in the metropolitan Boston area and their extended kin provided additional confirmation of the inverse relationship between spatial distance and frequency of kin visitation. Both the degree of relationship to kin and the location of residence of kin accounted for a large proportion of the variation in the amount of contact with relatives, with the residential variable having the closest relationship to frequency of interaction.[52]

B. LENGTH OF RESIDENCE What happens to relations with relatives

[51]Felix M. Berardo, "Internal Migrants and Extended Family Relations: A Study of Newcomer Adaptation," op. cit., pp. 89–91; also, "Kinship Interaction and Migrant Adaptation in an Aerospace-Related Community," op. cit., pp. 296–304.

[52]Reiss, "The Extended Kinship System: Correlates of and Attitudes on Frequency of Interaction," op. cit., p. 336. Similar findings regarding the degree of relationship to kin and location of kin have been reported by Berardo, "Kinship Interaction and Communication Among Space-Age Migrants," op. cit., pp. 541–554.

422

following the initial period of migration, when families have settled down in their new location and have lived there for some time? There is strong evidence that the extent of kinship contact is directly related to length of residence in the community of destination. Jitodai, for instance, found that during the early phase of migration white-collar workers who had relocated in the Detroit area had lower rates of contact than natives, but it increased substantially over a period of time and eventually these initial differences between the two groups were eliminated.[53] There is some indirect support here, it would appear, for the hypothesis discussed earlier and advanced by Litwak regarding the eventual consolidation of the kin group. In any event, the notion that families eventually overcome an initial disadvantage with respect to kinship contacts as a result of their moving would seem to be well founded. In fact, more recent evidence suggests this holds true regardless of the age of the couples involved.[54]

1. Regional and Rural-Urban Background. In the developing and understanding of the relationship between geographical mobility and extended family cohesion it is important to know not only *where people have moved to* but also *where they have migrated from.* The area in which a person is born and has spent most of his early adulthood may have some influence on the pattern of his relationships with relatives in subsequent years when he has married, has begun raising a family of his own, and has moved to another area. It is generally supposed, for example, that people from the South, particularly those from the rural areas, exhibit relatively strong familistic values in comparison to persons reared in other regions, and that these values tend to carry over into the urban setting. Killian's study of 150 rural, white southern migrants to Chicago is illustrative here.[55] Kinship and community ties continued to be the dominant type of interpersonal relationships among these migrants. The rural and small-town pattern of visiting was maintained in the new urban setting through frequent visits "back home," which took place in good as well as poor economic circumstances. "The Southern community of origin continued to be home and its norms were still praised as the best even when they could not be followed. Yet [few] actually returned to the South to stay; instead, irregular going back and forth, regulated largely by employment opportunities in Chicago, was the pattern."[56] In essence the northern settlement area was regarded as an extension of the southern

[53]Jitodai, op. cit., pp. 51–53. Blue-collar natives, on the other hand, did differ significantly from blue-collar migrants in this respect.

[54]Berardo, "Kinship Interaction and Migrant Adaptation in an Aerospace-Related Community," op. cit., pp. 296–304.

[55]Lewis M. Killian, "Southern White Laborers in Chicago's West Side," unpublished Ph. D. dissertation, University of Chicago, 1949.

[56]Lewis M. Killian, "The Adjustment of Southern White Migrants to Northern Urban Norms," *Social Forces*, 32 (Oct. 1953), pp. 66–69.

home. As a result, the children tended to grow up viewing Chicago as a temporary location rather than their "home town."

Killian's study demonstrated the influence of both regional and rural background on subsequent patterns of kin visitation in an urban setting. Our previous discussion, however, suggests that the impact of these factors will be altered through continued residence in the new locale. Indeed, there is some evidence to this effect from the Detroit study mentioned earlier. There, the increase in the rate of kin contacts among urban migrants "eliminated or reversed any consistent pattern of socio-economic and rural-urban differences after the initial period of residence."[57] Moreover, among those who had relatives within the area, southern migrants did not differ in any consistent manner from others with respect to frequency of contact with relatives. "No regional patterns of differences in contact rates are found for either the urban or rural migrants of both sexes."[58]

Kinship Determinants of Patterns of Mobility

Up to this point we have been treating mobility in typical sociological fashion, that is, as an independent variable in relation to certain types of human behavior. Thus, we have emphasized the relation between occupational mobility and geographical mobility in terms of their combined influence on extended family ties. However, sociologists have also found it both necessary and instructive to reverse this procedure and to treat "familism" or "kin interaction" as the independent variable. The general question then becomes, "How do extended family ties affect patterns of mobility?" We turn to various areas of inquiry suggested by that question now.

LOCATION OF KIN AND GEOGRAPHICAL MOBILITY Implicit in the previous discussion is a long-established sociological generalization that labor tends to flow in the direction of greater economic opportunity. Although this notion of economic opportunity is well founded, it needs modification or at least some qualification in view of the recent findings that kin ties have more significance in the lives of today's families than previously believed. For example, the location of effective or intimate kin[59] apparently exerts considerable influence on the destination, choice, and directional patterns of migrant families. More specifically, persons in search of new jobs often locate where their relatives

---

[57]Jitodai, op. cit., p. 53.

[58]Ibid.

[59]Refers to relatives who are actively involved in an individual's kinship system as opposed to nominal kin, who constitute the remaining group of relatives tied to the person by birth or marriage, but of whom he has no intimate knowledge. Similar conceptual distinctions may be found in the family literature, see Firth (ed.) *Two Studies of Kinship in London,* op. cit.; Lorraine Lancaster, "Some Conceptual Problems in the Study of Family Ties and Kin Ties in the British Isles," *British Journal of Sociology,* **21** (Dec. 1961), pp. 317–333, and other articles in this same issue.

are already established. Recent studies of the migration of families from the rural mountain areas of eastern Kentucky to the more urbanized and industrialized areas of Ohio and Indiana are illustrative here.[60] They show that members of the extended family tended to migrate to the same place and that families from old town neighborhoods now living in the new community were almost all related by kinship ties. The consistency of the directional pattern of migration appeared to be considerably influenced by kinship relations. "The kinship structure provides a highly pervasive line of communication between kinfolk in the home and the new community which channels information about available job opportunities and living standards directly and most meaningfully." Moreover, many of the families "encourage migration and provide 'havens of safety' in the community, as well as a socio-psychological 'cushion' for the migrant during the transitional phase."[61]

These findings closely parallel and confirm those reported in the Killian study, previously cited, of migrants from the lowlands of Tennessee and Kentucky who had moved to Chicago. He found that the anonymity and heterogeneity of the urban environment encouraged the development of a Southern "ethnic" or "hillbilly" area in that large metropolis. There was also a tendency for such areas to be divided into "clusters" of families who originated from the same town. "Newcomers from the South consistently tended to settle near relatives or friends who had migrated earlier. Often one of the important motives for migration itself was encouragement from earlier migrants."[62] The ties with the old community and kinship clusters within Chicago were strong factors in the residential location of newer migrants, who therefore constantly reinforced the development of ethnic southern clusters within the city. The process itself is not unlike that experienced by ethnic and racial immigrants to the United States who moved into the urban ghettos.

Finally, the pattern of migration among a group of southern mountain whites and Negroes to the Hough area of Cleveland is worth noting.[63] Although most of these families had lived in the area five

[60]James S. Brown, Harry K. Schwarzweller, and Joseph J. Mangalam, "Kentucky Mountain Migration and the Stem Family: An American Variation on a Theme by LePlay," *Rural Scoiology,* **28** (March 1963), pp. 48–69.

[61]Ibid.

[62]Killian, "The Adjustment of Southern White Migrants to Northern Urban Norms," op. cit., pp. 66–69.

[63]Marvin B. Sussman and R. Clyde White, *Hough Area: A Study of Social Life and Change* (Cleveland: Western Reserve University Press, 1959), especially pp. 7–9, 89–92. This study also revealed that many of the recently arrived families were closely related within a matrix of mutual assistance and activities. Relatives were sources for financial aid, second only to banks, and for assistance in times of personal trouble, second only to clergymen. Additional data on interfamily visitation and exchange of services, such as child care, also indicated an intricate matrix of interfamily activities.

years or less, 67 per cent of the whites and 86 per cent of the Negroes had relatives living in the Cleveland metropolitan district. Of these, 34 per cent of the whites and 60 per cent of the Negroes had relatives residing within the Hough area itself. Further, 11 per cent of the whites and 19 per cent of the Negroes had three or more families of relatives living within the Hough area. That the kindred is influential on the directional patterns of family movement is obvious.

The reader has no doubt noticed that the families we have been discussing in this section are rural white families from the South. The majority of research in this area has, indeed, been concentrated on these as well as migratory southern Negro families. Both groups represent lower- or working-class families. Among white middle-class families of higher status, the influence of the kinship system on the migration patterns of member families is apparently not nearly as strong or direct. Middle-class families generally have greater economic independence and autonomy and are not as reliant as lower-class families on the kinship group for assistance in moving into a new location.[64]

KINSHIP TIES AND UPWARD SOCIAL MOBILITY Explicit in the theory regarding the functionality of an isolated nuclear family system in an achievement-oriented industrial society is the assumption that extended family ties interfere with the upward social mobility of individual members and families. Successful upward mobility requires significant role changes suitable to a new status and rigid conformity to bureaucratic norms and values.[65] In this perspective, intense involvement with the kin groups, including strong adherence to their norms and values, their obligations and expectations, is viewed as a serious threat to career development and a major obstacle to high occupational accomplishment.

It will be recalled that Litwak posed a counterargument to this position with his notion of the *modified extended family system,* which, instead of impeding the mobility and occupational efficiency of its member units, actually supports them in such endeavors. (We shall take up the specific nature of this support shortly.) Litwak admits that families "on the way up" frequently encounter the dilemma of accommodating relationships with both co-workers and kin, and that each group often represents different class systems and sometimes opposite sets of attitudes and behavior. He observes, however, that the upwardly mobile family is able to resolve the dilemma partially by taking steps to avoid a "collision course" between the two groups, for example, by keeping their interaction with kin separate from that with associates and friends. The necessity for this type of segregation is no doubt

[64]Eldon D. Smith, "Migrating and Adjustment Experiences of Rural Migrant Workers," unpublished Ph.D. dissertation, University of Wisconsin, 1953.
[65]Whyte, op. cit.

426

dependent in part on the extent of the status disparity between the mobile couple's current position in the social structure and that of their immediate kinsmen. Thus, rising young couples whose social origins are from lower-class ethnic minorities are more apt to feel obligated to resolve the dilemma through the technique of segregated relationships than persons with higher socioeconomic backgrounds.

Leslie has suggested that the probability of upwardly mobile families encountering this dilemma may diminish considerably as time passes and as the couple continue to rise on the social scale.

The farther they climb and the more secure they become in their new status, the less need there may be to hide their parents, like skeletons in the closet. Moreover, with the increasing affluence of parents, the virtual completion of the process of assimilation of European immigrants, and with the leveling of tastes and styles occuring in the larger society, the gulf between parents and their upwardly mobile children may not be so wide as it once was. There even seems to be a spreading awareness among young middle-class people-on-the-rise that most of them have similar parental backgrounds and that they need not be ashamed of those backgrounds. To the degree to which this is true, there may even be some mingling of parents with the young couple's associates.[66]

In any event, the evidence to date shows that extended family relations are not incompatible with upward social mobility. Schwarzweller's study of people migrating from the southern Appalachian region to industrial centers in the North is a case in point. He found that a high degree of kinship interaction (as measured by frequency of visitation with parents) did *not* hold back the migrant's career attainment.[67] Schwarzweller also points to one of the major limitations of research in this area, namely, the use of cross-sectional designs in which relationships between variables are assessed at one point in time only. He suggests that although the findings support the hypothesis that in the early stages of a person's career occupational achievement is not hindered by kin relations, further studies of a longitudinal nature dealing with the husband's various stages in the work career are needed before the hypothesis can be completely rejected.

Geographical Mobility, Kinship Ties, and Newcomer Adaptation

Economic assistance patterns of the type we have been discussing in the preceding pages function primarily to assist upwardly mobile

[66]Gerald R. Leslie, *The Family in Social Context* (New York: Oxford University Press, 1967), pp. 335–337.

[67]Harry K. Schwarzweller, *Family Ties, Migration, and Transitional Adjustment of Young Men from Eastern Kentucky*, University of Kentucky Agricultural Experiment Station Bulletin 691 (May 1964). See also, "Parental Family Ties and Social Integration of Rural to Urban Migrants," *Journal of Marriage and the Family*, **26** (Nov. 1964), pp. 410–416.

families to achieve their occupational goals and at the same time provide them with goods and services felt to be essential to maintaining a middle-class status and style of life. The kin group and, in particular, the parents of young married couples are often in a position to offer a convenient helping hand toward the attainment of these objectives.

There are, however, other problems directly associated with geographical mobility in which the ability of the kindred to lend a helping hand may be considerably circumscribed. These problems have to do with developing the social relationships essential to a satisfactory accommodation to a new community. Mobility poses special problems or dilemmas for establishing interpersonal relationships and becoming socially integrated into strange surroundings. Newcomer families are, in a loose sense, marginal groups, inasmuch as they are temporarily out of tune with people in their old community as well as those in the new location. As strangers and oftentimes as transients they are frequently regarded with suspicion and antagonism. Whyte's comments concerning the experiences of the "organization man's" family illustrate the problem:

The newcomers can often sense the distaste. The transients may tell you about a wonderfully exceptional town they hit, but they are more likely to tell you of the town that proffered a cold shoulder. Sometimes they speak of outright antagonisms on the part of locals. If the community is one that has been expanding rapidly, the apprehension over the newcomers can get translated very quickly into such matters as zoning and club restrictions, and the little developments that encircle some towns from what is in effect a ring of animosities.[68]

Under such conditions, do the kindred have any bearing on the adjustment patterns of mobile families and their integration into the life of the community? It is to this general question and others related to it that the following section is devoted.

Before we begin, however, a note of caution is in order. The research evidence that deals with the relationship between kinship ties and newcomer adaptation is not easy to evaluate. Because of the differential characteristics of the various sample populations studied, meaningful comparisons are often difficult to make. Moreover, and perhaps as a result, some of the empirical evidence tends to be either contradictory or inconclusive in nature. Finally, it is necessary to say a word about the concept of *social integration* and related terms, such as *social*

[68]Whyte, op. cit., p. 302. See also the chapters by Lee G. Burchinal and Ward W. Bauder, Gordon E. Bivens, Helen Merrell Lynd, in Part IV, "Problems and Adjustments of Families Who Move," in the volume by the Iowa State University Center for Agricultural and Economic Development. *Family Mobility in Our Dynamic Society* (Ames, Iowa: Iowa State University Press, 1965), pp. 197–250.

adaptation. This concept has received varied and, not infrequently, ambiguous definitions in the sociological literature (in many cases, it is not defined at all). In order to minimize confusion, therefore, we shall use the term *social integration* here simply to denote the extent to which families identify with and become involved in the social life of the host community. We are not, by this definition, referring to the assistance kindred may provide in getting newly arrived relatives situated and settled in a new community. In the latter instance, members of the kindred may provide related newcomers with a general orientation on arrival, or help them locate housing and employment, and so on. We could view such activity as important and significant, but more psychologically supportive in nature rather than functionally effective for social integration.

Our question regarding the connection between extended family ties and the social integration of newcomer families has recently been explored by Schwarzweller, who tested the proposition that "close identification with the parental family, as manifested by frequent interaction with the family of origin, tends to 'hold back' the migrant from becoming socially integrated into the urban, industrial community."[69] Specifically, he hypothesized that less "familistic" newcomers to industrial centers in the Ohio valley would prove more adaptable to their new communities than those exhibiting a higher degree of familism. As it turned out, this was not the case at all. For example, the two groups did not significantly differ in the number of friends reported, church membership, and membership in secular organizations. Indeed,

the degree of familistic behavior did not make any difference in the extent of the migrant's involvement in either the informal or formal structure of the social situation, external to the kinship structure. It appears, therefore, that the less familistic migrants had "sloughed off" extended family ties without, as yet, substituting more diffuse associations (less familistic) characteristic of social integration in urban society.[70]

It is suggested, however, that one reason no difference between the two groups was uncovered might be the residential recency of the families studied and that the differences in social integration may manifest themselves at some later stage in the migrant's career.

[69]Schwarzweller, op. cit., Bulletin 691, p. 26.

[70]Ibid., p. 33. There were some trend patterns, however, that suggested that the most familistic migrants were more anomic and showed less residential stability than their less familistic counterparts. In this sense, "the more familistic migrants . . . tended to be tied into the societal structure to a lesser degree, in terms of their feelings about the new community as a place to live and their orientation to society as an abstract entity" (pp. 31–39).

Schwarzweller's main thesis, however, has received additional confirmation from a more recent analysis of the social integration of newcomers to the east-central region of Florida. These were white middle-class families whose social characteristics were totally different from the rural types studied by Schwarzweller. Again, the question posed was whether the community adaptation of in-migrant families was contingent upon their kinship ties and again the results were negative.

Whether the individual had little or frequent interaction with kin did not substantially affect his general satisfaction with the host community. Nor did frequency of kin contact make any difference with regard to the migrant's involvement in community organizations. Finally, a migrant's neighboring patterns were not influenced by extended family activity.[71]

In this instance, the attitude of newcomer families was primarily a function of their length of residence in the new locality. The availability of kin does not appear to be as influential a factor as duration of residence in the process of social integration.[72] As we noted earlier in the chapter, stability of residence has emerged as an important contributor to satisfactory integration into the social life of the urban community.

Concluding Remarks

In this chapter we have presented a rather detailed picture of kinship ties as they are found to exist in present-day American society. The evidence is overwhelming that extended family relations can be maintained in a modern and complex urbanized and industrialized

---

[71]Berardo, "Kinship Interaction and Migrant Adaptation in an Aerospace-Related Community," op. cit., p. 303. It should be noted, however, that in the previously cited North Carolina study, the most satisfied newcomer families were more likely to have parents residing either in the community or in the surrounding area, to visit them frequently, and to express feelings of closeness to their parents. See Gulick, Bowerman, and Back, op. cit., pp. 315–358.

[72]Both the Schwarzweller and Berardo findings are in general agreement with the results of an earlier investigation by Omari of rural Negro families moving to Beloit, Wisconsin. He utilized socioeconomic and community indexes of adjustment and found that the presence or absence of relatives did not seem to be significantly related to either index. Relatives provided considerable assistance in terms of helping newcomer relations to acquire a job or locate living quarters, but such aid did not seem indispensable to ultimate adjustment. Omari warns, however, that the importance of relatives may have been concealed, for "it is possible that since all migrants in Beloit have relatives, the effect of not having a relative is not revealed here. Or, that having one or two relatives only, give a migrant all the advantages that 10 or more relatives can offer." Thompson P. Omari, "Factors Associated with Urban Adjustment of Rural Southern Migrants," *Social Forces*, **35** (Oct. 1956), pp. 47–53.

social setting. As a consequence of our discussion, however, some may feel justified in drawing the conclusion that there is a high degree of *kinship solidarity*[73] that characterizes our nation. Such a conclusion, however, needs considerable qualification when compared to long-established anthropological knowledge concerning family systems in other societies around the world. In this connection, the following observations are worth bearing in mind.

1. In comparison to many other family systems, the American kinship system has not institutionalized a high level of solidarity among its related nuclear family units.[74] That is to say, it is not characterized by the interlocking and compelling network of complex rights and duties associated with extended family systems in highly kinship-oriented societies. By way of example, Bardis compared high school and college students in the United States with similar groups from a peasant area of the Peloponnesus in Greece in terms of their responses on his Familism Scale.[75] Certain of the statements on the sixteen-item scale referred to extended family orientations, including the following.

1. At least one married child should be expected to live in the parental homes.
2. The family should have the right to control the behavior of each of its members completely.
3. A person should always support his uncles or aunts or parents-in-law if they are in need.
4. The family should consult close relatives (uncles, aunts, first cousins) on its important decisions.
5. A person should always share his home with his uncles, aunts, first cousins, or parents-in-law if they are in need.

The Greek students scored significantly higher on these items and on the Familism Scale than their American counterparts—even those from

[73]Our definition of kinship solidarity is wider in scope than that used in most of the studies cited in the preceding pages. It is more in line with the definition posited by Marsh, who sees kinship solidarity as being "characterized by: (1) the number of people encompassed in a person's web of kin obligations and rights, (2) the extent of interdependence among nuclear families related by blood or marriage, and (3) the extent to which kin ties and obligations take precedence over non-kinship roles and relationships. In this definition, kinship solidarity is manifestly not limited to ties within the nuclear family." Robert M. Marsh, *Comparative Sociology* (New York: Harcourt Brace Javanovich, 1967), pp. 72–82.

[74]Ibid.

[75]Panos D. Bardis, "A Comparitive Study of Familism," *Rural Sociology,* **24** (Dec. 1959), pp. 362–371. See also, "Attitudes Toward the Family Among College Students and Their Parents," *Sociology and Social Research,* **63** (May–June, 1959), pp. 352–358.

a conservative Mennonite college in the Midwest, thus indicating a much higher level of kinship solidarity.

2. The number of persons encompassed in a person's web of kin obligations in the United States is comparatively small in relation to more extended-family-oriented societies. This is in part because of the impact of geographical mobility on our bilateral kinship system. Reiss has commented on this aspect of extended family relations.

American culture specifies a bilateral kinship system in which interaction and solidarity with kin is based upon degree of biological relationship. For this reason there is no social principle which systematically differentiates between kin of the same biological relationship. Geographic mobility, however, has the effect of creating kinship systems which do not have bilateral structures either with respect to interaction or with respect to solidarity. It is true that as a group American kinship systems are statistically bilateral since mobility has a random effect upon the distance of residence of specific kin. As a result of geographic mobility, however, kinship systems are not actually bilateral with the exception of those in which relatives of each degree of relationship live at approximately the same distance. Perhaps American kinship systems could be better referred to as ecologically structured.[76]

The facts of the matter are that research on extended family relations in the United States has consistently revealed that active patterns of kinship interaction are carried on between a relatively small and circumscribed group of relatives. In most instances, such interaction takes place primarily, and in many instances almost exclusively, between married offspring and members of their immediate family of orientation, particularly the parents-of-origin. The remainder of the kindred constitute what has been referred to as nominal relatives, who remain peripheral and often of relatively insignificant consequence.

Primitive societies provide a useful contrast here. There are comparatively few subgroups other than family and kinship units present in such societies, and interfamilial sentiments are spread over a much wider range of kinsmen than in our own. Consequently there is a strong sense of kinship solidarity. Moreover, extensive family relationships are not segmented by widely separated and often, as a result of geographical mobility, isolated residences as they are with us; "in most primitive societies each home spreads out into another and the households intermingle in a communal life and without privacy, or the desire for it."[77] The primitive situation permits a widespread diffusion of emotional and dependency elements among a large circle of relatives. In contrast, most families in America exhibit an intensive

[76]Reiss, "The Extended Kinship System," op. cit., p. 336.
[77]E. E. Evans-Pritchard, *The Position of Women in Primitive Societies and Other Essays in Social Anthropology* (New York: The Free Press, 1965), p. 49.

emotional concentration and dependency within the relatively circum-scribed group of the nuclear unit. These differences have important implications for family and kinship solidarity. For example, when death occurs in our nuclear family, the event is likely to be highly traumatic for the survivors and actually disruptive for the family. This is less likely to be the case among the primitives, where an aggregate of intimate kinsmen are able to provide social and psychological support for the survivors and act as a strong cushion against the shock of crisis.

3. Through the use of demographic data on family life cycles, Collver has pointed to still another reason why kinship solidarity is greater in less differentiated agrarian societies, such as India, than in more highly differentiated societies, such as the United States.[78] In America the family cycle may be viewed as a series of distinct stages:

1. A very short period from marriage to the first birth.
2. A short childbearing period.
3. A long period in which the children are growing up.
4. A short interval in which the children marry.
5. An extended phase in which the parents live on without any children in the home.
6. Several years of widowhood.

In contrast, the Indian family cycle is better characterized by a continuous flow through the various stages, with little to distinguish one stage from another. For example, the Indian husband, more often than his American counterpart, remains a member of his father's household; the Indian bride spends time at her family's home before and after the birth of her first child; because of the longer span of childbearing years, women not uncommonly become grandmothers while still bearing children of their own. Because the stages of the life cycle are less differentiated in the Indian family, the household tends to be a more extensive and more solitary unit, at any given time, than is the United States household. Thus,

in the United States, the married couple, assured of a long span of life together, can take on long-term responsibilities for starting a new household, rearing children and setting aside some provisions for their old age. In India, by contrast, the existence of the nuclear family is too precarious for it to be entrusted entirely with these important functions. The joint household alone has a good prospect for continuity. When two or more couples pool their resources and their labor they are better able to supply their minimum needs

[78] Andrew Collver, "The Family Cycle in India and the United States," *American Sociological Review,* **28** (Feb. 1963), pp. 86–96. The general notion being discussed here is borrowed from a more explicit statement by Marsh, op. cit., pp. 78–79.

than they could separately. When one adult dies others remain to care for the orphaned children. Aging parents deprived of their sons may still be adequately assisted by grandchildren or nephews living with them. Certainly the degree of independence enjoyed by the nuclear family in America would be out of the question in rural India.[79]

4. Except perhaps in the upper echelons of the class structure, the extended family system in America may be further characterized by the inability of its member units to enforce conformity to its norms effectively through powers of coercion. As we noted earlier, "members and nuclear families of the network volunteer to help rather than direct activities. They perform supportive rather than coercive roles."

The kinship system's limited capacity to sanction its membership effectively has been attributed to at least two major factors, namely, its unstable composition and the greater role of women than men in conducting its affairs.[80] In this connection Farber has made the following observations: (1) Because membership in our kinship system is based upon achieved rather than ascribed status, "members can withdraw voluntarily and the individual can change the membership of the group he accepts as kindred in order to meet his needs as critical situations arise. . . . The kindred is thus unstable as a collective enterprise because the individual can manipulate its membership and membership is voluntary."[81] (2) In the more kinship-oriented unilateral societies around the world, older males actively oversee the kinship system and at the same time dominate the economic and political spheres. Consequently, they can effectively constrain individuals attempting to deviate from extended family norms. In American society with its bilateral structure, however, women have assumed the responsibility for sustaining the kinship system but lack sufficient power and authority in the economic and political spheres. As a result, they have limited capacity to impose sanctions and control the actions of deviant members of the kindred.[82]

5. Finally, the low degree of kinship solidarity in the United States is evidenced by the fact that certain nonkinship roles and relationships frequently take precedence over kin ties and obligations.[83] In our society, there are relatively few rights and duties that extended kin can consistently expect of each other or demand one another to observe. Consequently, members do not hesitate to give priority to the demands of individuals and groups external to the kinship system.

[79]Collver, op. cit., p. 96.
[80]Bernard Farber, *Family: Organization and Interaction* (San Francisco: Chandler Publishing Co., 1964), pp. 212–214.
[81]Ibid.
[82]Ibid.
[83]Marsh, op. cit., p. 81.

434

Part IV

Family Reorganization
and Interaction

17

The Malfunctioning Family

All families have problems and make mistakes, and many, at some time, experience severe crises, intense conflict, and sometimes a divorce or desertion.[1] But most families, especially in the classes most familiar to college students, perform the essential functions of families well enough so that they do not constitute a problem for the society. There are, however, a substantial number that display *chronic malfunctioning* and must be supported, supervised, and sometimes constrained to perform their functions in a manner acceptable to society. Some of these function adequately for a time, requiring assistance and supervision for only limited periods, whereas a smaller number require such attention for the entire family life cycle.

Types of Malfunctioning

The idea of adequate functioning poses the question of *which* family functions are crucial to societal values and of *what level* of functioning is acceptable to society. Our general criteria of malfunctioning are chronic failure to provide sufficient food (including the vitamins and minerals needed for health), comfortable and appropriate clothing, housing that is physically comfortable and not overcrowded, the medical care necessary for good health, and education and the other socialization necessary to enable the child to enact adult roles successfully.

It is first necessary to distinguish between (1) individuals who perceive familial roles as normatively defined and who consistently

[1] Jetse Sprey, "The Family as a System in Conflict," *Journal of Marriage and the Family*, **31** (Nov. 1969), pp. 699–706.

437

strive to enact these roles but who are *unable* to do so because of limited opportunities or abilities, and, by contrast, (2) those who either do not perceive their familial roles normatively, or who make no attempt to enact them. Examples will aid in clarifying the distinction. In some occupations, such as migrant farm labor, the pay is so low and the employment opportunity so irregular that although the fathers understand that they should support their families and they work whenever the opportunity presents itself, and although the mothers usually work in the fields, also, they can't earn enough to provide adequate food, housing, clothing, and medical care for their families, or to permit them to keep their children in school. This might be called *submarginal functioning.* Thus, a family is malfunctioning in failing to provide for the minimum needs of its members.[2] In general this type of malfunctioning has produced minimal concern to the society. The families do the best that they can and require relatively little financial support from society. The long-range effects in the bad health and the illiteracy of the children are not immediately or dramatically apparent.

Contrasting with the submarginal role player and submarginal families are what might be termed the *non-role player* and the *disorganized family,* which result from the failure of parents to enact key roles. For example, any husband or father who consistently refuses employment or any who work but personally utilize all their own earnings, as may the alcoholic, the gambler, or the drug addict, fall into this category. These are the more obvious economically malfunctioning families, which are more likely to require continuous public assistance and not infrequently supervision and protection for some members of the family.

There is, of course, an interrelationship between the two types of malfunctioning families. High rates of unemployment, discrimination, and inadequate training and abilities increase the difficulties of adequately playing the role of provider, so it is not surprising that the slums, minorities who are discriminated against, and occupation groups with little opportunity for adequate and secure income are likely to produce more than their share of men alienated from their provider roles and of families disorganized as a consequence.

Examples of provider malfunctioning illustrate *submarginal* and

---

[2]Schorr has made the point that what is *submarginal* is redefined in each decade as a society becomes more affluent. There is no doubt that this is true. Not only does what is desirable increase, but so does what is necessary. Thirty years ago a sixth grade education would allow entry into most jobs; now double that amount of education is usually required. Likewise, the diet believed adequate in earlier decades is now known to be deficient in vitamins and minerals. We do not confuse wants—which are insatiable—with requirements for good health, physical comfort, and socialization that will enable the individual to play adult roles within normative boundaries. For a detailed discussion of poverty and remedial programs, see Alvin L. Schorr, *Poor Kids* (New York: Basic Books, 1966).

438

disorganized familes have been drawn from the worker role but malfunction is not limited to the economic sphere. The child-care, socialization, and house-care functions can also become the basis of malfunctioning families.

Family Roles and Family Functions

Primary responsibility for a given set of tasks is assigned to one or the other parent, but the nature of the family group is such that if one parent can't or doesn't perform a function, the other and/or the older children may do so. Therefore, the failure of the husband to provide for the family or of the wife to prepare the food doesn't mean that these functions aren't performed by the family, or, if there is only one parent, he or she, with help from the children, may perform all the roles of parents. To the extent that family functions are performed efficiently and the health, safety, and welfare of family members are safeguarded, such reversal of roles or the enactment of all roles by one parent does not, in itself, constitute a malfunctioning family because the necessary and vital functions of the family are being performed. However, the family as a group is organized with the expectation that it will contain at least two adults and a division of labor has been devised on this basis. If one member is essentially nonfunctioning it is doubly difficult for the other to perform both sets of tasks. The failure of one to perform expected tasks (unless excused by ill health or unavailability of employment) is likely to cause conflict within the family group as it suffers from lack of services, and some members experience added stress from attempting to play additional roles.

It is clear, then, that the failure of one family member to enact his roles does not *necessarily* produce a malfunctioning family but it deprives the family of one set of resources, is likely to result in fewer goods and services for the family, is likely to add duties to the other family members, and, unless rationalized by special circumstances, can be expected to generate conflict in family relations and strain on personality. Inadequate role-playing, therefore (whatever its cause), is the basis for family malfunctioning but such failure by one parent may not result in malfunction if other family members are able and willing to assume the responsibilities of that family member.

Provider Malfunction

The most obvious, most common, and probably the most basic family malfunction in Western capitalistic societies is in the provider role, which results in a frequent or continuing submarginal level of living.

439

Because the husband-father has the primary responsibility as provider, this type of malfunctioning family is caused by the inability or the unwillingness of the male to provide for the material needs of his family, *or* by the failure of the society to provide employment opportunities for all adult men, or both. However, the failure of the wife to control her fertility is also relevant, because each additional child adds burdens to the provider role.

Provider malfunctioning is a major and continuing aspect of lower-lower-class American family life. Four to 6 per cent unemployment has been typical of our society since World War II. Among Negroes and American Indians the rate has been double that or more. Also, it appears disproportionately higher for immigrants and second-generation immigrant stocks who have not yet learned the language and customs of the society.[3]

Whether this proportion of nonemployed is a result of societal inefficiency or of the characteristics of the unemployed has been vigorously argued. Those who support the latter view often contend that 4 per cent unemployed is an irreducible minimum, because some people are changing jobs and others are "unemployable." However, the relative lack of unemployment in Western Europe recently argues against this position, because there unemployment rates of less than 1 per cent are common and in West Germany there have been periods in which the jobs available numbered hundreds of thousands *more* than the number of workers available. It appears, therefore, that a pool of unemployed is *not* a necessity of capitalistic industrial societies, although for one to exist is common, and, in the United States, unemployment has been a chronic condition.

However, there is evidence that the socialization process may also be partly at fault, because unemployment is double or higher for Negroes and American Indians. Illiteracy, and lack of advanced education, lack of communication skills, and a defeatist attitude toward being able to secure and hold good positions produce adult men who are less attractive as employees. Prejudice against Negroes, American Indians, and foreigners increases this inadequate and negative socialization and makes it more difficult for men from these aggregates to obtain and retain employment. Even among Anglo-Saxon Americans, dependency tends to breed dependency or unemployment to breed unemployment. Studies of slums, for example, have disclosed families that have been economically dependent for three generations.[4]

More specifically, the children of dependent families are less likely

[3]Ludwig Geismar and Jane Krisberg, *The Forgotten Neighborhood* (Metuchen, N.J.: The Scarecrow Press, 1967).

[4]Ludwig Geismar and Michael A. LaSorte, *Understanding the Multi-Problem Family* (New York: The Association Press, 1964), p. 62.

440

to receive adequate education, good diets, and medical care; have fewer models of adult men who work regularly; and observe that unemployment and dependency are in the normal course of events. Such jobs as are available are likely to be poorly rewarded, temporary, and unstimulating. Once a pattern of unemployment and dependency is established, it socializes boys to become adults who are not well prepared to be efficient and dependable workers. As a consequence, many employers would rather utilize their regular employees overtime or purchase labor-saving equipment than employ young adults socialized in the slums.

A high concentration of provider malfunctioning was revealed in a 1969 survey that found that: (1) workers living in slum areas had unemployment rates two and a half times higher than the national average, (2) unemployment among teen-agers was especially severe: 30 per cent of slum youth were unemployed (in a year in which the national unemployment rate was only 3.6 per cent), (3) weekly earnings of less than $65 were reported by one of six full-time workers, (4) about one in five slum workers had been unemployed at some time in the past twelve months.[5]

SUBMARGINAL ECONOMIC FUNCTIONING As already noted, the less obvious malfunctioning family is the one in which family members accept normative definitions of their roles and enact them as well as their abilities and societal opportunities permit. The malfunctioning is usually not obvious in terms of day-to-day crises but exacts a toll in poor health, illiteracy, and consequent unemployment when the children attempt to join the adult labor force. Its families are recruited from several large overlapping aggregates of people; slum dwellers, Negroes, American Indians, and recent immigrants, and from families headed by women. These groups have in common that they are employed irregularly in poorly paid occupations. Even in some families in which the father is regularly and fully employed, he earns too little to support the large families that are characteristic of the poor. At a minimum wage of $1.60 per hour, a fully employed man would earn about $3,200 a year. If he has six children, eight in all in the family, the income per capita is $400. However, full employment is rare among unskilled workers. If he is employed half the time, his income is $1,600 a year, which is not uncommon among migrant labor families. As already noted, it has been necessary for children of migrant labor families to work in the fields to help earn the day-to-day support of the families, which results in illiteracy or semi-illiteracy in the next generation.

In the urban black community in which concentrations of families

---

[5]U.S. Department of Labor, Bureau of Labor Statistics, *News* (February 20, 1969), pp. 1–2.

headed by women are found in disproportionate numbers, this type of submarginal family is common. Most of the jobs held by lower-class unskilled women are not protected by the minimum wage laws. As a consequence, they may be working for as little as one half the minimum wage. In a recent year the average earnings for Negro families with female heads was $1,665.[6] Here the problem is not unemployment but not receiving a living wage. The problem is further increased by the working mother's needing to hire child-care services out of these submarginal earnings.[7]

The submarginal family has often been praised for its courage, its loyalty among family members, and its willingness to labor under adverse circumstances, and no doubt it deserves such praise. However, to glorify the submarginal family is to fail to understand it.[8] It meets its day-to-day economic responsibilities at the cost of foregoing adequate medical and dental care, of a diet lacking in proper balance, of overcrowding and lack of privacy in housing, and of the potential of its children through lack of education. By definition it is submarginal because it fails to provide adequate medical care, adequate diet, adequate housing and clothing, and an education adequate for competition in the adult job market.

Disorganized Economic Functioning

In contrast to the economically submarginal family, which appears at a casual glance not to be a problem family at all, there is no doubt about the malfunctioning economically *disorganized* family. In it, the provider function is not being adequately performed by anyone. No one is regularly employed, or, if one is, the earnings are not utilized to obtain and pay for the goods and services necessary to maintain the family. It occurs both as a malfunction in the economic institution of society, which fails to provide employment opportunity for all adult males, and in the socialization process, which fails to prepare some males to be productive in employment. Because no adult is playing the provider role, society must—for example, through aid to families of dependent children and public assistance.

[6]Catherine Chilman and Marvin B. Sussman (eds.), "Poverty in the United States in the Mid-Sixties," *Journal of Marriage and the Family,* **26** (Nov. 1964), p. 393.

[7]Billingsley differentiates within the lower lower class on the basis of the *working poor* and nonworking poor. These correspond approximately to our submarginal and non-role-playing in the provider role. Andrew Billingsley, *Black Families in White America* (Englewood Cliffs, N.J.: Prentice-Hall, 1968), p. 9.

[8]For an exposition of the capabilities and limitations of the poor, see Frank Riesman, "Low-Income Culture: The Strengths of the Poor," *Journal of Marriage and the Family,* **26** (Nov. 1964), pp. 417–421.

Economically disorganized families come disproportionately from the same categories as economically submarginal families—from minority groups that have been discriminated against in employment, from slum families, and from families headed by women. Again, there is much overlapping in these categories.

Causation of Economic Family Malfunctioning

In considering the *causes* of family malfunctioning, one does well to proceed with caution because causation is a complex matter. However, it appears clear that one cause is the economic organization of the society, and another is the socialization of individuals.

INSTITUTIONAL CONTRIBUTION TO MALFUNCTIONING As noted earlier, American society has been and currently is characterized by substantial unemployment; that is, there are usually 4 to 6 per cent of adult males classified as able to work who are looking for work and who have not found it. There is no national policy that places *effective* responsibility for providing employment to all adult males. If the unemployment rates rise high enough (and what is high enough is not clear), the federal government may, itself, become an employer and thereby act to reduce unemployment. However, the "normal" state of American society seems to be 4 per cent or more unemployment rather than full employment. Because other policies require that those without other means of support be given public assistance, it is tempting to conclude that some societies prefer to support adult men in idleness to providing them an opportunity to earn their own livings (and that of their families).

As noted earlier, another element is the management decision-making process. The most efficient workers are hired first. Remaining among the unemployed are the least educated,[9] including illiterates, the young, large numbers of minority groups, the alcoholics, some with emotional problems, some with minor criminal records, and others who for one reason or another are relatively unattractive as employees. In considering hiring from this pool, some employers decide instead to employ present employees overtime, even if premium pay is necessary. (Recent surveys show that more than 5 per cent of the employed work at two or more jobs.) Thus, some of the unemployed would be employed if their socialization were better. There is a sociopolitical

---

[9]The negative influence of a slum environment on school achievement is a complex one that cannot be explored here. The reader is referred to Martin Deutsch et al., *The Disadvantaged Child* (New York: Basic Books, 1967), especially Chapter 3, pp. 39–58.

443

issue here in that society permits some men to "moonlight" or work a substantial amount of overtime, while others have no employment.

INADEQUATE SOCIALIZATION AND ECONOMIC MALFUNCTIONING Why are some men unemployable or at some point why do they give up seeking employment? Homans's proposition that people tend to repeat activities *that in the past have rewarded them* is appropriate.[10] It is even more useful if it is reversed. Activities that are not rewarded are, after a period of time, discontinued. Homans points out that any kind of activity, seeking work included, involves costs: expenditure of energy and commitment of time. Such costs must result in rewards if the activity is to continue. Men who seek work without finding it or who find only temporary, badly paid employment, eventually stop trying. At some point welfare payments, although not intrinsically attractive, provide more rewards for less cost.

The socialization that produces adult men that employers prefer not to employ is a complex process. We have already noted that some of the unemployed are illiterate and some are of foreign origin and cannot communicate in English. To be able to read and write in English is a prerequisite for most employment. Many employers now also require high school graduation as a prerequisite to employment. Offenbacher has stated the problem in these terms:[11]

the issue is not whether the poor do or do not wish to become middle class. The real issue is that they must learn to read, be on time, dress appropriately, talk to employers, and generally offer the skills and personal characteristics which will enable them to find satisfactory employment.

Being black or Indian has been a major bar to employment. Apparently, employers have associated such minorities with illiteracy and inadequate motivation on the one hand, and prejudice of the public against being served by them as salesmen and service workers on the other. Recent action constraining employers against discrimination is ameliorating this situation in part.

Finally, socialization for employment includes considerably more than formal education or specialized training. It includes an instrumental value placed on work. Work must be viewed as highly productive of the objects and experiences desired. For male slum dwellers, work has often been poorly rewarded. Work socialization includes the idea of punctuality in arriving at work, regularity of appearance on the job, appropriate clothing for the tasks, the ability to communicate, the idea of accepting and following the direction of supervisors, and the inhibition of rivalry and hostile verbalizations and actions. To be

[10]George C. Homans, *Social Behavior: Its Elementary Forms* (New York: Harcourt Brace Jovanovich, 1961), p. 53.

[11]Deborah I. Offenbacher, "Cultures in Conflict: Home and School as Seen Through the Eyes of Lower Class Students," *The Urban Review*, 2 (May 1968), p. 8.

adequately socialized for work, a man must have observed men going to work regularly, must have seen them well rewarded for their efforts, and must have worked, himself, whether for pay or not. He must have acquired favorable attitudes toward work.

THE BLACK PROVIDER Although all that has been stated earlier applies to the black-American family, because of continued discrimination the malfunctioning in the provider role among black men has been especially prevalent. Moynihan has indicated a direct tie between employment discrimination against blacks and their roles as providers.[12] Rainwater has commented on the same phenomenon.[13]

If we are right that present Negro family patterns have been created as adaptations to a particular socioeconomic situation, it would make more sense to change that socioeconomic situation and then depend upon the people involved to make new adaptations as time goes on. If Negro providers have steady jobs and decent incomes, if Negro children have some realistic expectation of moving toward such a goal, if slum Negroes come to feel that they have the chance to affect their own futures and to receive respect from those about them, then (and only then) are the destructive patterns . . . likely to change. The change, though slow and uneven from individual to individual, will in a certain sense be automatic because it will represent an adaptation to changed socioeconomic circumstances which have direct and highly valued implications for the person.

Among the secondary effects of the lack of opportunity for Negro men has been a lack of feeling of responsibility by a sizable minority of lower-class men for support of women and children. In order to accept such responsibility they must have had their efforts rewarded and seen the efforts of others rewarded. Many young boys in the black community have observed the opposite experiences. Apparently, as a result of the inadequacy of a considerable proportion of black men as providers, lower-class black women have developed a somewhat different attitude toward marriage. If marriage means principally that a woman has to feed another person, why bother with it? "The girl . . . has good reason to be suspicious of the likelihood that men will be able to perform stably in the role of husband and provider; she is reluctant to be tied down by a man who will not prove to be worth it."[14] The *principal* contribution of men to a marriage is economic support.[15] If

[12]Daniel P. Moynihan, *The Negro Family: The Case for National Action* (unpublished).
[13]Lee Rainwater, "Crucible of Identity: The Negro Lower Class Family," *Daedalus,* **95** (Winter 1966), p. 208.
[14]Rainwater, op. cit., p. 188.
[15]Aldous finds that a man's position in the family depends on whether he has a job of some kind. Its type and location are also important. Joan Aldous, "Occupational Characteristics and Males' Role Performance in the Family," *Journal of Marriage and the Family,* **31** (Nov. 1969), pp. 707–712. See also earlier studies: Mirra Komarovsky, *The Unemployed Man and His Family* (New York: The Dryden Press, 1940); R. C. Angell, *The Family Encounters the Depression* (New York: Charles Scribner's Sons, 1936).

this is unlikely to be forthcoming, why marry? Faced with this prospect, some Negro women prefer to have sexual relationships without marrying these partners and, even if a pregnancy results, the more "profitable" alternative may be to bear an illegitimate child than to marry a man who cannot consistently discharge the provider role.[16] Illegitimacy is relatively low among high-income Negro families.

The broad lines of the interplay between unemployment, family economic malfunctioning, and inadequate socialization seems reasonably clear. Long-term unemployment of husbands and fathers leads to dependency on welfare or the earnings of the mother. In either event, the disorganization of the family and of the personality of the father is likely to occur. Boys growing up in slums, especially those additionally handicapped by racial or ethnic discrimination, are less likely to receive the type of socialization that fits them for productive jobs or careers. This inadequate socialization, in turn, reduces their opportunity for well-paid, steady employment. This dilemma is portrayed schematically in Figure 17.1. In Figure 17.1, chronic unemployment is seen as causing changes in both family structure and functioning, and as directly affecting health and socialization. Family structure and interaction patterns, in turn, add to problems in health and socialization. Finally, the latter have an adverse effect on opportunities for employment.

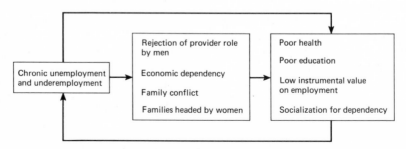

Figure 17.1 Chronic Unemployment, Family Structure and Functioning and Socialization Outcomes.

THE INSTITUTIONALIZATION OF WELFARE RECIPIENTS If unemployment of several per cent of the adult men is a permanent characteristic of a society *and* if public support for those who are destitute is a recognized obligation of the society, then should "being on relief" be accorded recognition as a respectable status? Should there be "careers" as welfare recipients and should the roles of adult men be reorganized

---

[16]We define *profit* here as Homans uses the term, as the greatest profit to the individual making the decision. In some instances, such as pregnancy outside of marriage, it may be that neither alternative is attractive but one is less unattractive than the other.

without the provider role? One interesting example of this recently came to the writers' attention. A father of nine children, usually on relief, conceptualized his status as a "career father," devoting most of his time to supervising and playing with his children. He rationalized that in helping to rear nine children he was making an adequate contribution to society!

Although the institutionalization (including legitimization) of welfare recipient status in a society is possible, current American thinking is predominantly negative. During the Johnson Administration the President touched a responsive cord by advocating better education and retraining programs, which would transform "tax consumers into taxpayers." In January, 1964, he asked for an "unconditional war on poverty," and proposed programs "to enable every individual to build his earning power to full capacity," and "to assure all citizens of decent living standards regardless of economic reverses or the vicissitudes of human life and health."[17] Perhaps this position received additional support from the knowledge that continuous unemployment is disorganizing to adult men in a society that expects adult men to be employed. From the criterion of either the well-functioning family or the well-functioning male personality, guaranteed employment appears to be preferable to guaranteed income.

THE ISSUE OF RETAINING UNEMPLOYED FATHERS IN THE FAMILY The original Aid to Dependent Children legislation made support of children contingent on the absence of an employable father in the home. As a consequence it was asserted that fathers deserted their families so that their wives and children would be eligible for such assistance. This assertion suggested that, unwittingly, the federal government was engaged in breaking up families. Subsequent amendments removed the criterion of no employable male and later acts were legislated as Aid to Families of Dependent Children. To what extent the earlier provisions actually encouraged desertion is not known, but these provisions and the later revisions of the Act focused attention on the consequences, positive and negative, of having a chronically unemployed father in the home.

Recent psychological writing has placed considerable emphasis on the importance of an adult male model as part of the socialization of boys.[18] It seems clear that a boy's socialization is considerably advanced by having an appropriate model in the home to demonstrate that men go to work each morning, dress appropriately, and make

[17]*Economic Report of the President. Transmitted to the Congress, January, 1964* (Washington, D.C.: U.S. Government Printing Office, 1964), pp. 14–15.

[18]Henry Borow, "Development of Occupational Motives and Roles," in *Review of Child Development Research,* Vol. 2, ed. by Martin L. and Lois Wladis Hoffman (New York: Russell Sage Foundation, 1966), pp. 373–422.

provision for the care and safety of their families.[19] Such a model can also supply verbal information on male adult behavior and the rationale for it. Finally, the enactment of the provider role by the husband is crucial to the economic functioning of the family. The issue, however, is not whether a fully employed, well-functioning father is a good thing to have about the home, but whether a chronically unemployed father, who doesn't go to work, who cannot tell a boy how the adult work role functions, who is unlikely to dress appropriately, who in many instances is an alcoholic and/or has mental problems, and who, in some instances, has a criminal record is a useful socializing agent and an appropriate male model. Will the boy learn appropriate male behavior from him?

Considerable clinical evidence records that families that have been extremely disorganized have registered considerable improvement after an alcoholic and/or criminal father has been removed through desertion or divorce. Welfare funds are no longer diverted to the father's interests and the mother is able to feed, clothe, and supervise her children with more success. In effect, the state substitutes for the father in the provider role and the mother carries out the maternal roles traditionally assigned to her. The proponents of keeping the disorganized father in the family insist that boys, at least, need a male model in the home, and some will add that girls, too, need to learn how to interact with adult males. The issue, however, is whether the above type of father provides an appropriate model.

Clearly, a small minority of fathers are *liabilities* to their wives and children. Perhaps 95 per cent of fathers, possibly even more, play generally helpful and constructive roles in their families, providing not only better economic functioning, but affection, supervision for children, and protection. Taking these fathers as models, some have, not surprisingly, reached sweeping conclusions—that *all* families are better off having the father in the family than for an unemployed, alcoholic, and abusive father to desert or be divorced or separated from the wife and children. The position favoring retention of such fathers may also be influenced by the expectation that fathers financially support their families. If it is accepted that some fathers shouldn't live with their families, society tacitly accepts the financial responsibility for these families, but, again, this minority of fathers do *not* support their families, in any event, and are likely to divert welfare funds to their own use.

The *long-term* solution seems to us to be to provide employment *for all adult men* and encourage and support the socialization of boys so that they can be competent as providers when they become adults.

[19]For a review of research on the effects of father absence on various aspects of sex-role development, see Henry B. Biller, "Father Absence and the Personality of the Male Child," *Developmental Psychology*, 2 (Mar. 1970), pp. 181–201.

Other Malfunctioning Roles

Although chronic provider malfunctioning is probably more common and certainly more obvious than other family malfunctioning, it is clear that other types exist with serious results for individuals and society. These include malfunctioning in child care, child socialization, housekeeper, and sexual roles. It should become clear, also, that provider malfunctioning multiplies and in some instances may be the principal cause of malfunctioning in other roles. In each instance a distinction should be made between *submarginal role-playing* and *non-role-playing* and between *submarginal families* and *disorganized families.*

CHILD CARE The child-care role includes feeding the child regularly with an adequate diet, clothing it comfortably and appropriately, and protecting it from physical injury or traumatic experiences.

The most obvious instances of submarginal child care are among female-headed families in which the mother must take paid employment to meet the economic needs of the family but, because of minimal wages, cannot afford day-care services. Children are sometimes turned loose on the street or in the care of older children who are incapable of providing adequate care. The diet, medical care, and clothing of such children are likely to be inadequate, as a direct result of submarginal economic functioning. The same is likely to be true for children of migrant laborers. Another type of submarginal role-playing is provided by the grossly ignorant parent who gives a baby alcoholic beverages or tobacco, or who provides an inadequate diet because of ignorance of nutritional needs.

Non-role-playing exists when one or both parents do not accept normative responsibilities for child care. It may take the form of neglect—failure to feed or clothe children—or cruelty and abuse. In either event, it requires the intervention of outside agencies. These are likely to admonish parents, to threaten them with legal action, and, finally, if the condition is not corrected, to remove the child from the family. Chilman has listed a number of dysfunctional child-rearing practices (Table 17.1). Although these practices are not limited to the very poor, they are more frequently found among the very poor.

CHILD SOCIALIZATION Reference has been made to socialization of boys for occupational roles, with the indication that the chronically unemployed father presents an inappropriate model for his sons. We have also noted the tendency of some slum-reared boys to drop out of school, thereby failing to obtain the education necessary for successful competition in the job market. Some of the dropping out of school is due to a low instrumental value placed on education, some to the infrequency of reward reinforcement *in* school, some to the expense of attending high school and foregoing other uses of time during that

449

Table 17.1

Child-Rearing and Family Life Patterns More Characteristic of the Very Poor Compared with Patterns Associated with Successful Adaptation to Middle-Class Society

Patterns Reported to Be Characteristic of the Very Poor	*Patterns Conducive to Adaptation to Middle-Class Society*
1. Inconsistent, harsh, physical punishment.	1. Mild, firm, consistent discipline.
2. Fatalistic, personalistic attitudes, magical thinking.	2. Rational, evidence-oriented, objective attitudes.
3. Orientation in the present.	3. Future orientation, goal commitment.
4. Authoritarian, rigid family structure; strict definition of male and female roles.	4. Democratic, equalitarian, flexible family structure.
5. "Keep out of trouble," alienated, distrustful approach to society outside family; constricted experiences.	5. Self-confident, positive trustful approach to new experiences; wealth of experiences.
6. Limited verbal communication; relative absence of subtlety and abstract concepts, a physical-action style.	6. Extensive verbal communication; values placed on complexity, abstractions.
7. Human behavior seen as unpredictable and judged in terms of its immediate impact.	7. Human behavior seen as having many causes and being developmental in nature.
8. Low self-esteem, little belief in one's own coping capacity; passive attitude.	8. High self-esteem, belief in one's own coping capacity; an active attitude.
9. Distrust of opposite sex, exploitive attitude; ignorance of physiology of reproductive system and of contraceptives.	9. Acceptance of sex, positive sex expression within marriage by both husband and wife valued as part of total marital relationship; understanding of physiology of reproductive system, effective use of contraceptives.
10. Tendency not to differentiate clearly one child from another.	10. Each child seen as a separate individual and valued for his uniqueness.
11. Lack of consistent nurturance with abrupt and early granting of independence.	11. Consistent nurturant support with gradual training for independence.
12. Rates of marital conflict high; high rates of family breakdown.	12. Harmonious marriage; both husband and wife present.
13. Parents have low levels of educational achievement.	13. Parents have achieved educational and occupational success.

SOURCE: Catherine S. Chilman, "Poor Families and Their Patterns of Child Care: Some Implications for Service Programs," in *Early Child Care,* ed. by Laura L. Dittman (New York: Atherton Press, 1968), p. 221. Reprinted by permission.

period. Recent research has shown that part of the inadequate socialization has been the product of differential treatment and low expectations for slum children on the part of teachers.[20]

Our distinction between submarginal and disorganized families is that the parents in the former understand the socialization children need if they are to become functioning adults and accept their responsibilities to try to provide it, whereas the parents in the latter ignore their children except when their behavior frustrates the parents or the parents are threatened by outside agencies. In extreme instances, the parent may consciously socialize the child for criminal behavior. The socialization of children of non-role-playing parents is toward day-to-day survival, learning from parents, older children, police, and social workers. If the child is old enough, such socialization may serve immediate needs, but lead eventually to a sentence to a correctional institution or to adult dependency. Socialization toward criminal careers, either by parents or by others because of parental neglect, provides a basis for legal action against the parent, and, if uncorrected, leads to removal of the child from the family.

THE HOUSEKEEPER ROLE Society has been slow to take cognizance of malfunctioning in the housekeeper role, but currently society is doing so by noting that failure in this role results in inadequate child care. The recognition of "homemaker services" as a social-service specialty is a recognition both that housekeeping functions are essential to the welfare of family members *and* that some women are failing to enact this role adequately. Failure may be due to ignorance of the norms, incapacity, or failure to accept the responsibilities of the role. Submarginal performance is attributable to ignorance and incapacity, non-role-performance to ignorance of the norm or "refusal" of its requirements.

Provider malfunctioning obviously affects the housekeeper role because it limits the resources available in the household. Further compounding of problems in the housekeeping role is provided by high prices charged to slum families and lack of skill by lower-class families in maximizing their purchasing power. These families are less conscious of the high interest rates on installment purchases and the danger of overuse of credit. The number and growth of small loan firms are testimonial to the extent of ineffective income management, principally but not exclusively, in low-income families.

FERTILITY CONTROL Until relatively recently, American society has

---

[20]Robert Rosenthal and Lenore F. Jacobson, "Teacher Expectations for the Disadvantaged," *Scientific American,* **218** (Apr. 1968), pp. 19–24. In this study students whose teachers were told that they (the students) were exceptionally bright achieved much more during the year than did students of equal ability whose teachers were told that they (the students) were subnormal.

451

been slow to prescribe in sexual and fertility matters. However, recently it has taken note that the uncontrolled fertility of lower-lower-class women usually results in babies who will have to be supported by AFDC or other welfare programs. As a consequence, both the federal and some state governments have started limited family-planning services to women who wish to utilize them. Here the traditional thinking that procreation is of private concern only has come into conflict with the public commitment to provide essential services to children. To date, no political entity has directly penalized parents for having large families, although some units do so indirectly by limiting the amount of welfare funds that are paid to a family regardless of its size.

Male and Female Malfunctioning

Submarginal and non-role-playing have been observed in the performance of all the functions of the family but those involving men seem to be at the same time more frequent and more crucial. In disorganized families, it seems most often the problem is traceable to male role-playing, whereas any stability that is present for meeting needs is usually contributed by the mother.[21]

It is illuminating to compare this disparity between the functioning of the sexes in the lower-lower-class with that of the sexes in the middle class. In the latter, both sexes generally function adequately in terms of normative expectations. If anything, it is the middle-class male who is more fully engaged in his roles than many middle-class women (except those with small children or in paid employment) with relatively minor responsibilities.[22] Unemployment is rare because the middle-class male has advanced education and training and has internalized instrumental values and attitudes toward work that enable him to be an efficient and productive employee. Indeed, a small proportion of middle-class husbands are "overengaged" in the provider role, in that they have a second or third job or frequently work overtime. The middle-class husband who is unemployed for an extended period is likely to become downwardly mobile into the lower-lower-class, because middle-class status is based on occupational performance.

Returning again to the lower-lower-class, there are no barriers for wives' playing their traditional roles as housekeepers and in care and supervision of children. The only barriers beyond their own actions are those of fathers who fail to enact the provider role. Lower-class women,

---

[21]Moynihan, op. cit., pp. 30–37.
[22]Helen Hacker, "New Burdens of Masculinity," *Journal of Marriage and the Family,* **19** (Aug. 1957), pp. 227–233.

however, are generally not held responsible for the incapacities of their husbands. Thus, they can generally play their roles acceptably. *Advanced* training and education (or even a knowledge of English) are not necessities for housekeeper and child-care roles.

In contrast, the provider role is not similarly free of obstacles. A husband may be willing to work and may look for employment but not find it. As long as the economic structure needs only part of the adult manpower available, there are, in effect, institutional barriers to provider role-playing by lower-lower-class husbands.

Thus far in this chapter attention has been directed to the aggregate of families that are chronically malfunctioning. It is essential to draw a distinction between families that have problems and occasional crises—this would include all families—and those that as a general characteristic of their functioning fail to meet the minimum needs of family members.

In summary, based on our general criteria, malfunctioning families are those that chronically fail to provide sufficient food with the vitamins and minerals needed for health, comfortable and appropriate clothing, housing that is not overcrowded, the medical care necessary for good health, and the education and other socialization necessary to enable the child to enact adult roles successfully. Family malfunctioning is caused by failure in the enactment of family roles, but the failure of one family member may be compensated for by the extra efforts of other members of the family. Thus, many families in which there is only one parent, or in which one parent cannot play his roles, are still effective family groups that meet at least the minimum needs of family members.

Family malfunctioning may be attributed to the characteristics of the unsuccessful role player or, especially in the case of the provider role, it may be attributed to malfunctioning in the economic institution of the society, which fails to provide opportunity for employment for an appreciable proportion of its adult men. In minority groups family malfunctioning may be partially attributed to discrimination in employment against men in the minority populations. However, chronic unemployment in one generation adversely affects the socialization of the next, so that the children of the slums taken as an aggregate are less well able to compete for employment when they become adults.

A distinction has been made between *submarginal role-playing,* in which family members accept the responsibilities in their roles and attempt to meet them, and *non-role-playing,* in which the family members do not perceive their roles normatively or else, having accurately perceived them, ignore or refuse the responsibilities. Submarginal role-playing leads to *submarginal families,* which may not be generally perceived as a problem but that eventually exact a high cost in poor health, poor education, unemployment, mental health prob-

453

Table 17.2
Social Welfare Measures as a Percentage of Gross National Product, United
States and 13 Western European Nations: 1958–1960

Country	Per Cent	Country	Per Cent
West Germany	17.0	Sweden	12.6
Luxembourg	16.8	United Kingdom	11.1
Austria	14.8	Denmark	11.1
Italy	14.7	Norway	10.9
Belgium	14.4	Switzerland	10.2
France	14.0	Ireland	8.9
Netherlands	12.9	United States	7.0

SOURCE: James C. Vadakin, *Children, Poverty, and Family Allowances* (New York: Basic Books, 1968), p. 138. Reprinted by permission.

lems, and a disproportionate number of people who give up in attempting to play normative roles and become non-role-players.

Role rejection leads to *disorganized families,* which, if the role rejection is in the provider role, require welfare support; if the role rejection is in child care or socialization, the intervention of social agencies becomes necessary to protect the health, safety, and socialization of the children.

Family malfunctioning may occur in any area of family life but is most frequent and obvious in the provider role, presumably because of the nature of an economy that requires an employer willing to hire *as well as* a man willing to work. No such block is encountered in playing the other family roles, except as they may be limited by the malfunctioning in the provider role.

To date, American society has failed to develop comprehensive programs aimed at preventing family malfunctioning. Rather, it has provided public assistance to alleviate some of the consequences of unemployment and aid to dependent children to provide subsistence in fatherless homes. It may come as a surprise to some that the United States has lagged behind most modern European societies in the proportion of its income devoted to social welfare (Table 17.2). Recently, new proposals have been advanced to meet problems of economic malfunctioning. These will be briefly presented in the following section.

Proposed Programs Relevant to Family Malfunctioning

Public awareness of the stresses generated among family members and family stability by the unavailability of steady, adequate employment has led to a number of proposals for providing income to all families. Generally, these have not included strong support for full employment, which is the institutional change essentially proposed in the preceding discussion. Rather, these proposals have taken the form of systematic payment of public funds to families either as *guaranteed income* or as *child allowance* systems. A brief review of these proposals follows.

Guaranteed Minimum Income

A variety of specific proposals has been developed and offered to guarantee a minimum income to every individual and family in the United States—some proposals quite similar, others quite different. They all, however, generally involve the use of the federal tax system as a means of redistributing income and ensuring that no person or family would fall below a specified income level.[23]

Some proposals include the device of a "negative income tax," which essentially involves a reverse income-tax procedure—based on extending income-tax rates below zero to negative levels—whereby persons earning incomes below a specified amount would, upon filing their income tax forms, receive a supplementary stipend from the federal government to make up the difference. The goal here is to narrow the gap between the poor family's earned income and the income it actually needs to remain above the poverty level. Other proposals favor establishing a minimum income standard and then providing that minimum to all citizens, rich and poor, as a matter of public policy. Under such a program, the usual public assistance criteria of eligibility based on need would be irrelevant; the stipend would be given regardless of the amount of income a family or an individual had earned on their own during the year. The latter proposal, therefore, differs from the negative income-tax proposal in two significant aspects: (1) It is universal in application (and therefore more expensive) and would be available to all citizens, whereas the negative income-tax proposal would be confined exclusively to people with earnings below some specified amount while a positive tax would still be required of those whose incomes are above this amount. (2) It requires no justification in terms of need, whereas proposals involving a negative income tax usually require some type of demonstration of need for eligibility.

Obviously, guaranteed minimum income proposals, regardless of the specifics, have stimulated much controversy and debate among people both in and out of the government. Such proposals run counter to the American value system emphasizing individual self-reliance, which has linked a man's income to his economic productivity. The proposals

---

[23]For analyses of these proposals, see Christopher Green, "Guaranteed Income Plans—Which One Is Best?" *Trans-action,* 5 (Jan.–Feb. 1968), pp. 49–53; James Tobin, "Do We Want Children's Allowances?" *The New Republic* (Nov. 25, 1967), pp. 16–18.

have many critics, and charges of "creeping socialism" and loss of work incentive, as well as substitute proposals for guaranteeing full employment or merely extending existing public assistance programs, are frequently voiced. Nevertheless, support for some type of guaranteed minimum income program is growing, and many believe that some such income maintenance program will be adopted in the not-too-distant future.[24]

One criticism of the guaranteed minimum income is that it substitutes the government for the father in the crucial provider role. Enactment of this role has been the principal contribution of husbands to their wives and families. It has occupied most of their time. In a sense a government payment for the earnings of the husband substitutes the earnings of *other* husbands for that of the man receiving the guaranteed income. It can be argued that, in the long term, this would destroy the exchange of services that is the basis for marriage and would lead to personality deterioration among men. By contrast, full employment would go far to providing a stable basis for marriage, particularly in the lower-lower-class, and would be supportive of adequate personality functioning in men in this class.

Family Allowances

Contemporary discussions and debates over the various income maintenance proposals have been paralleled by a resurgent interest in family allowances, sometimes referred to as children's allowances. A family allowance program involves systematic payments by the national government to families with minor children; the amount of the payment being determined in accordance with the number of children.[25] With the exception of the United States, nearly all of the industrialized nations of the world have established some form of family or children's allowances (Table 17.3). In some countries, family allowances are limited to larger families only, whereas in others a fixed stipend is provided each child in families large and small. Some

---

[24]One such proponent, Robert Theobald, has argued that such a program is essential for both short-run and long-run reasons. In the short-run, it is required because an ever-growing number of people—blue-collar, white-collar, middle-management and professional—cannot compete with machines. In the absence of the guaranteed income the number of people in hopeless, extreme poverty will increase. In the long-run, we will require justification for the distribution of resources which is not based on job-holding, because this is the only way we can break the present necessity to ensure that supply and demand remain in balance—a necessity which is compatible with continued development of the individual and continued survival of the world.
Robert Theobald, "The Goal of Full Unemployment," *The New Republic* (March 11, 1967), pp. 15–18.

[25]James C. Vadakin, *Family Allowances* (Miami: University of Miami, 1958). The following discussion is guided in large part by that work. See also, Scott Briar, "Why Children's Allowances," *Social Work*, **14** (Jan. 1969), pp. 5–12.

Table 17.3

Percentage of National Income Devoted to Family
Allowance Payments for Selected Nations, 1961

Nations	Family Allowance Payments as Percentage of National Income
Belgium	3.12
Canada	1.83
France	4.76
German Federal Republic (West Germany)	0.39
Italy	2.57
Netherlands	1.54
Sweden	1.30
United Kingdom	0.64
USSR	0.32
USA (AFDC Program)	0.29

SOURCE: David M. Heer and Judith G. Bryden, "Family Allowances and
Population Policy in the U.S.S.R.," *Journal of Marriage and the Family*, **28**
(Nov. 1966), p. 517. Reprinted by permission.

countries initially adopted such programs on the assumption that they
would lead to a desired growth in population through increased birth
rates. Still others initiated family allowances in a serious effort to
provide a more equitable distribution of income for families with
children. Many countries, such as Canada, adopted such a program
over two and a half decades ago.[26] Although similar proposals have
been periodically advanced in the United States, they have never been
adopted.

Family allowance systems are frequently proposed or established in
recognition of the fact that the economic burdens of rearing children
are among the basic causes of poverty and its associated ills.[27] That an
inverse relationship exists between family size and family income has
been well documented; larger families definitely tend to be in the
lower-income categories.[28] Despite the fact that family income has been
steadily rising throughout the past decade, the relatively greater
concentration of children in low-income families continues to persist.[29] Additional children mean greater expenditures, and with each

[26]Bernice Madison, "Canadian Family Allowances and Their Major Social Implications," *Journal of Marriage and the Family*, **26** (May 1964), pp. 134–141.
[27]Alva Myrdal, *Nation and the Family* (New York: Harper & Row, 1941), p. 66.
[28]Vadakin, op. cit., p. 14.
[29]*Poverty in the United States*, Committee on Education and Labor, House of
Representatives, 88th Congress, Second Session (Washington, D.C.: U.S. Government
Printing Office, Apr. 1964); Chilman and Sussman, op. cit., pp. 391–398.

successive child the family income must be further stretched to meet the needs of individual family members. There is a good deal of evidence that as a family's size increases, its comsumption standards decrease. "If consumption standards of large families are to bear an equitable relation to the general population, it is obvious that for many millions of families the earnings of the breadwinners must be supplemented."[30]

Part of the problem derives from the wage structure in modern industrial society, which is geared to and rewards *individual* productivity without considerations of family needs and responsibilities.

Thus, a single man with no family responsibilities and a married man with a large family to support, both doing identical work, receive the same amount in wages if they work for the same period (time wages) or produce the same output (piece wages). Regardless of the vast differences in their needs, both workers are rewarded equally since their respective economic contributions are equal. Quite clearly then, the modern labor market is based on the concept of an *industrial* rather than a *social* wage.[31]

It has long been argued that adherence to a wage system that is based strictly on the product of a man's labor without due consideration for the size of his family prevents the adoption and practical implementation of a family allowance program or a national minimum for families of every size.[32]

The arguments posed in opposition to a system of family allowances are essentially the same as those raised in connection with guaranteed minimum income programs. They most frequently center around questions of cost, the effect on the birth rate, and the impact on work incentives. That the cost of such a program would be substantial cannot be denied. It has been estimated that a family allowance program in the United States similar to those in operation in Canada and in the Scandinavian countries would cost $9 billion, or slightly more than 1 per cent of the gross national product.[33] On the other hand, it is a small cost in comparison to the $50 billion estimated combined cost of our present complicated and multiwelfare system, only a small portion of which ever reaches the poor. Some have argued that the United States

[30]Charles I. Schottland, "Government Economic Programs and Family Life," *Journal of Marriage and the Family,* **29** (Feb. 1967), p. 121.

[31]Vadakin, op. cit., p. 4.

[32]Myrdal, op. cit., p. 76.

[33]"The Case for a Family Allowance," *New York Times Magazine* (Feb. 5, 1967). Estimated cost based on payments of $8 a month for all children under six years of age, and $12 a month for children between six and seventeen years of age. However, as Briar has shown these costs could be materially reduced if they are subject to income tax. Briar, ibid.

458

has no need for a family allowance, inasmuch as the same result is accomplished through the federal income-tax exemptions for children. As Vadakin has demonstrated, however, such arguments are not borne out with respect to providing for *large, low-income families*.[34] Income-tax deductions are not an effective method for subsidizing children in low-income families, although the subsidy to high-income families is substantial. Low-income families have paid a minimum rate of 14 per cent on taxable income, so that a deduction of $600 provides an additional $84 a year. For a family in the highest income bracket, the rate has been 65 per cent on taxable income. Such families receive an additional $390 for the deduction. Intended or not, the tax deduction procedure subsidizes the rich much more than the poor.

Family allowances provide an equitable means for redistributing income to those families that bear the burden of rearing a large proportion of the nation's population. Such allowances could be *substituted* for the present income deduction for children.

Although some countries initially adopted family allowance systems on the assumption that they would lead to a desired population growth through an increased birth rate, they have generally been quite ineffective as a device for accomplishing this goal.[35] A recent analysis of the relationship between income maintenance programs and the birth rate in the United States and elsewhere found no conclusive evidence that the former materially affected the latter.

A rigorous scientific demonstration has not been provided that income maintenance will lead to a higher birth rate or that it will not. A new income maintenance program would in all probability lead some people, including some people who are poor, to have additional children. But this effect would probably be trivial in relation to concurrent developments and not discernible in subsequent population figures.[36]

Moreover, the argument that family allowances will simply make large families larger is not borne out by the evidence at hand.[37]

One of the strongest allegations made concerning the effects of family allowances is that they will adversely influence worker incentives, but here the evidence is somewhat less conclusive. In France, family allowances apparently have adversely affected the incentive of workers. France has a high level of family allowance payments and not infrequently a worker is able to obtain as much in allowances as he

[34]Vadakin, op. cit., pp. 16–64.
[35]Ibid., p. 120; Madison, op. cit., pp. 139–140.
[36]Alvin Schorr, "Income Maintenance and the Birth Rate," *Social Security Bulletin,* **28** (Dec. 1965), pp. 22–30.
[37]Madison, op. cit., pp. 134–141.

would in wages. However, the cause-effect relationship here is not altogether clear because of other forces present in French society that could also account for the loss in incentives, including very low wages, housing shortages, and generally adverse economic and political conditions.[38] The situation in Canada, however, where wages are relatively higher and the economic and political situation more stable, represents a contrasting picture. Madison, in analyzing Canada's experience with family allowances, draws the following conclusions, all of which are contrary to what had been prophesied by early opponents of the program:

allowances have not generated nation disunity or antagonism between Catholics and Protestants; they have not impaired Dominion-provincial relations; they have not depressed wages since they have not entered into wage negotiations and have exerted no influence on employment policies; so far, they have not proven to be an excessive fiscal commitment; their cost has not barred the obtaining of tax funds for other social welfare purposes; the program has not deteriorated into a relief measure; they have not provided incentive to the production of large families among the economically unproductive and chronically dependent sections of the population and among Catholics; overpayments have not been numerous or large, and fraud has been minuscule, and a giant peacetime bureaucracy has not resulted.[39]

Such positive evidence is perhaps all the more relevant when one considers the physical as well as cultural proximity and economic similarity of Canada to the United States. There is little question that Canadian allowances have provided an effective method of improving child welfare and family life.

Although there are a variety of arguments pro and con regarding the implementation and consequences of family allowances, the fact remains that the idea is becoming increasingly popular. The major revolution in civil rights that characterized the sixties in America created mounting pressure for major social and economic reform to eliminate the current inequities in the distribution of income.

Family allowances or increased income transfers to take account of family size can have a stabilizing and beneficial effect not only on families but on the economy. Such measures are more likely to stimulate consumption than comparable income transfers to the aged; they would undoubtedly increase home ownership and improve housing conditions, but, most important, they would recognize the importance of the individual child in a large family rather than penalize the child in terms of his share of family income.[40]

---

[38]Vadakin, op. cit., pp. 134–135.
[39]Madison, op. cit., pp. 140–141; see also, Vadakin, op. cit., pp. 136–137.
[40]Schottland, op. cit., p. 122.

Perhaps what is really at stake here is recognition of the unique institutional role the family plays in society. One sociologist has suggested that as America strives toward achieving the Great Society, its War on Poverty should be accompanied by a War on Family Disorganization.

Full Employment as an Alternative

The alternative to guaranteed income plans is guaranteed employment for those able to work plus adequate pensions for the disabled, the elderly, and others who are incapacitated. Until minimum wages are much higher than at present the alternative plan could also require a system of child allowances to provide adequate incomes for low-income families with many children. Guaranteed employment would probably require that the federal government be prepared to provide employment if and when the private sector does not do so. It is a practicable alternative—several European countries have had almost no unemployed since World War II and one major society, the Federal Republic of Germany (West Germany), has actually had more jobs than workers available during most of that period.

As we have already noted, the difference between employed and chronically unemployed fathers is a crucial one for family relationships and personality integration, the stability of the family, and the socialization of children.[41] It is a political as well as an intellectual issue and one that will continue to be debated by students of society.

[41]Rodman provides strong support for this position. Hyman Rodman, "Family and Social Pathology in the Ghetto," *Science,* **161** (Aug. 1968), pp. 756–762. See also, Aldous, op. cit.; Komarovsky, op. cit.; and Angell, op. cit.

18

Divorce and Desertion

This chapter takes a cautious look at the complexities of the American divorce system, to scrutinize the historical trend of our divorce rates, the social characteristics of the divorced population (including separations and desertions), the consequences of marital breakups for the spouses and the children, and then come to some conclusions as to whether or not divorce in this country poses a threat toward undermining the stability of our family system and our social structure. In order to view the American situation in a more realistic light, it is necessary to place it within the context of a cross-cultural perspective and compare its circumstances with the experience of other societies around the world, both large and small.

Cross-cultural Perspective on Divorce

Two decades ago Murdock attempted to place the divorce situation in contemporary United States in a cross-cultural perspective by comparing family stability in forty non-European (essentially small and preliterate) societies in Asia, Africa, Oceania, North America, and South America.[1] He found that (1) in all the societies (except one) there were institutionalized procedures for terminating a marriage, and (2) in three fourths of these societies, both sexes had equal rights to initiate divorce (interestingly enough, in 10 per cent of the societies, women possessed superior rights). More important, however, was the finding that in 60 per cent of the sample the divorce rate was higher than in the United States. On the basis of these findings, Murdock concludes that: "Despite the widespread alarm about increasing 'family disorganiza-

[1]George P. Murdock, "Family Stability in Non-European Cultures," *The Annals of the American Academy of Political and Social Science,* **272** (Nov. 1950), pp. 195–201. See also John J. Honigmann, "A Comparative Analysis of Divorce," *Marriage and Family Living,* **15** (Feb. 1953), pp. 37–43.

tion' in our own society, the comparative evidence makes it clear that we still remain within the limits which human experience has shown that societies can tolerate with safety."[2]

The greater divorce incidence of these simpler societies does not mean, of course, that marital instability is condoned. Almost none place a positive value on divorce, and nearly all employ a variety of devices to preserve the stability of the marital relationship (bride price, parental influence and support, incest taboos, prohibitions against adultery, and so on). Moreover, the higher divorce rate in these societies has not undermined the family *system* nor has it appreciably effected other types of social disorganization. In fact, family sociologists are in general agreement that there is no necessary relationship between the instability of family *units* and the instability of family *systems* or societal disorganization. For example:

It is likely that high divorce rates have been common in Arab countries for many generations, as they are now, but there is no evidence that this has been until recently a changing family system. That is, the Arab family system creates—and, within limits, copes with—the problems of a high divorce rate and its essential structure remains unchanged.

Moreover:

it is evident that if the rates of occurrence of major family happenings, such as the percentage eventually marrying, percentage married at certain ages, divorce rates, fertility patterns and so on, are changing, then it may be that the family system is also changing and that at least some parts of it are dissolving or undergoing disorganization. On the other hand, some of these changes may actually reduce the rates of occurrence of some phenomena classically called "disorganization," such as divorce, separation, illegitimacy or desertion. Thus, for example, the rate of desertion has been dropping in the United States. In Latin American countries in process of industrialization, with all its predictable *anomie,* the rate of illegitimacy has been dropping. Japan's family system has been undergoing great changes over the past generation and thus by definition certain parts of it must have been "dissolving," but the divorce rate has steadily dropped. Finally, even though the old family patterns may be dissolving, they may be replaced by new ones which control as determinately as the old.[3]

Udry has suggested that America's divorce rates probably could be twice to three times what they currently are without serious repercus-

[2]Murdock, op. cit., p. 197.

[3]William J. Goode, "Marital Satisfaction and Instability: A Cross-Cultural Class Analysis of Divorce Rates," *International Social Science Journal,* **14** (1962), pp. 507–526. Reprinted in Reinhard Bendix and Seymour M. Lipset (eds.), *Class, Status, and Power,* 2nd ed. (New York: The Free Press, 1966), pp. 377–387.

Table 18.1

Divorces per 1000 Marriages in Selected Countries, 1890–1965.*

Country	Year							
	1890	1900	1910	1920	1930	1940	1950	1965
U.S.	55.6	75.3	87.4	133.3	173.9	165.3	231.7	258 (1965)
Germany		17.6	29.9	40.7	72.4	125.7	145.8	112 (1965)
England & Wales				8.0	11.1	16.5	86.1	91 (1965)
Australia		13.6	12.4	20.4	41.2	41.6	97.3	91
France	24.3	26.1	46.3	49.4	68.6	80.3	106.9	101 (1965)
Sweden		12.9	18.4	30.5	50.6	65.1	147.7	168 (1966)
Iran						194	211	173 (1960)
Egypt					269 (1935)	273	273	216 (1963)
Japan	335	184	131	100	98	76	100	81 (1965)
Algeria	370 (1897)	352	288	396	286	292	†	54 (1963)

*All figures calculated from governmental sources and from *Demographic Yearbook,* 19th issue (New York: United Nations, 1967).

†1950 Algerian figures are not used, because in that year over 200,000 marriages from previous years were registered civilly, for the first time, thus reducing the true level of divorce rates. How much this underregistration in previous years inflated the divorce rate is not known. Decennial years are used in the table, but in a few cases the true year is one year off. The 1963 figure may be very inaccurate.
  A better measure of divorce frequency is the number of divorces per 1,000 existing marriages, but the latter figure is not often available. The above rate compares marriages in a given year, with divorces occurring to marriages from previous years. However, changes from one year to another, or differences among countries, may be seen just as clearly by this procedure.

SOURCE: William J. Goode, "Family Disorganization," in *Contemporary Social Problems,* ed. by Robert K. Merton and Robert A. Nisbet, © 1961, 1966, 1971, by Harcourt Brace Jovanovich Inc., and reproduced with their permission.

sions. In fact, he does not think it unreasonable to hold that under our present social structure with its high remarriage rate that a strong family system could be maintained even if all first marriages were terminated through divorce.[4]

The charge that the United States has the world's highest divorce rate today is valid only when it is compared with the current rates of the larger and more modern nations. But this has been the case for only a relatively short period of time. As can be seen in Table 18.1, in the past the divorce rates in many modern nations well surpassed that of the

[4]J. Richard Udry, *The Social Context of Marriage* (Philadelphia: J. B. Lippincott Co., 1966), p. 527.

464

United States. It should be noted that, with the exceptions of Japan and Algeria, the divorce rate for all the other countries listed in Table 18.1 has steadily risen since 1890. These data also clearly reveal that there is considerable variation in divorce rates from one society to another as well as within the same society over time. Thus, for example, in 1890 the Japanese divorce rate was more than six times as high as the United States rate. Now the situation is reversed, with the United States' rate nearly three times that of Japan. The time perspective, therefore, is very important when one is making comparative analyses of family systems.

Table 18.2
Common Legal Grounds for Divorce, United States, 1967

Grounds	Number of States
Adultery	50*
Desertion	47*
Cruelty	45
Felony and conviction of imprisonment	45*
Alcoholism	41
Impotency	32
Nonsupport	30
Insanity	29
Separation or absence	25*
Pregnancy at marriage	13
Drug addiction	12
Incompatibility	4

*And the District of Columbia
SOURCE: U.S. Department of Labor, Women's Bureau.

Grounds for Divorce

There is a wide variation among the countries of the world as well as within a single nation concerning grounds for divorce. In some nations, such as Spain, divorce in the usual sense is simply not allowed. In others, for example India and Japan, divorce may be obtained by mutual consent of the spouses. In the Soviet Union grounds for divorce are not enumerated in the law but a marriage can be dissolved, "when the court, having examined all the relevant circumstances, concludes that the application for dissolution of the marriage has been made for carefully considered reasons and that family relations cannot be restored."[5] In some areas, such as Iran and the British Solomon Islands Protectorate, a man may divorce his wife simply by pronouncing *"talak."* Burmese husbands can divorce their wives if they are "like a master or enemy." In Cambodia, if a wife deserts the conjugal home for one night without legitimate reason, this is grounds for divorce.

It is well known that in the United States, the grounds for divorce

[5]"Dissolution of Marriage, Annulments of Marriage and Judicial Separation," United Nations E/CN.6/415/Add.2, Table 1 and note 5 (Feb. 1965).

vary considerably among the states. Overall, there are at least forty different grounds for obtaining a divorce in our nation. In Kentucky alone divorces can be granted on the basis of any one of twenty different grounds. The most common legal grounds are represented in Table 18.2. We shall discuss the nature of these grounds and their relation to divorce actions later in the chapter. It should be noted that approximately 60 per cent of all divorces in America are granted on grounds of physical or mental cruelty, and about one third are granted on grounds of desertion. These are followed by adultery, which accounts for less than 2 per cent of all divorces in the United States. There is considerable variation from one state to another.

Divorce Rates in the United States

For more than a century the United States government has been officially collecting and publishing tabulations on the incidence of divorce. The divorce rate may be computed in several different ways, some giving a more accurate picture than others. Regardless of the method used, however, the results essentially lead to the same conclusion, namely, that the long-term trend in American divorce rates has been upward. That this upward trend is not simply a reflection of our increasing population is demonstrated by the figures presented in Table 18.3. For example, during the period 1900–1930, the population increased by 62 per cent but the number of divorces increased by 251 per cent. Again, during the period 1930–1960, the population showed a 47 per cent increase, whereas the number of divorces climbed by 101 per cent.

Fluctuations in Divorce Rates: Effects of Wars and Depressions

Although the long-term divorce trend has generally been upward, it is worth noting that the rate has fluctuated at different periods in our history, especially during periods of war and economic depression. The trend of the divorce rate since it was first computed in 1867 showed a long-term increase that reached a record peak in 1946. During this approximately eighty-year period, the rate increased from .3 to 4.3 per 1,000 population. The trend was accelerated by wars and reversed by economic depressions. If we look again at Table 18.3, we can see that the rate initially declined from the slight post-World War I peak, then began again to assume its upward trend until interrupted by the Great Depression of the thirties. Then it began to climb again, almost doubling during World War II and the immediate postwar years, going from 2.2 in 1941 to 4.3 in 1946. It declined rapidly thereafter, returning to the pre-World War II figure of 2.2 in 1957. It remained at approxi-

466

Table 18.3
United States Divorce Rates, 1860–1970

Year	Population (Thousands)	Number of Divorces	Divorces per 1,000 Population	Divorces per 1,000 Married Females
1860	31,443	7,380	1.2	1.2
1870	39,818	10,962	1.5	1.5
1880	50,156	19,663	2.2	2.2
1890	62,948	33,461	3.0	3.0
1900	76,094	55,751	.7	4.0
1910	92,407	83,045	.9	4.7
1920	106,466	170,505	1.6	8.0
1925	115,832	175,449	1.5	7.2
1926	117,339	184,678	1.6	7.5
1927	119,038	196,292	1.6	7.8
1928	120,501	200,176	1.7	7.8
1929	121,770	205,876	1.7	8.0
1930	123,077	195,961	1.6	7.5
1931	124,040	188,003	1.5	7.1
1932	124,840	164,241	1.3	6.1
1933	125,579	160,920	1.3	6.1
1934	126,374	204,000	1.6	7.5
1935	127,250	218,000	1.7	7.8
1940	132,457	264,000	2.0	8.8
1941	133,669	293,000	2.2	9.4
1942	134,617	321,000	2.4	10.1
1943	135,107	359,000	2.6	11.0
1944	133,915	400,000	2.9	12.0
1945	133,434	469,341	3.5	14.4
1946	140,686	610,000	4.3	17.9
1947	144,073	483,000	3.4	13.6
1948	146,730	408,000	2.8	11.2
1949	149,304	397,000	2.7	10.6
1950	151,861	385,144	2.6	10.3
1955	165,069	364,450	2.3	9.3
1960	179,992	393,000	2.2	9.2
1961	183,057	414,000	2.3	9.6
1962	185,890	413,000	2.2	9.4
1963	188,658	428,000	2.3	9.6
1964	191,372	450,000	2.4	10.0
1965	193,813	481,000	2.5	10.6
1970	203,185	715,000	3.5	13.5

SOURCES: U.S. Bureau of the Census, *Statistical Abstract of the United States: 1967,* 88th ed. (Washington, D.C., 1967); *Divorce Statistics Analysis: United States—1963,* National Center for Health Statistics, Series 21, No. 3 (Oct. 1967); U.S. Bureau of the Census, *Historical Statistics of the United States, Colonial Times to 1957* (Washington, D.C., 1960); Paul H. Jacobson, *American Marriage and Divorce* (New York: Rinehart and Company, 1959); issues of *Monthly Vital Statistics Reports.*

Figure 18.1. Divorce Rates: United States, 1920–1968. [From *Monthly Vital Statistics,* "Divorce Statistics, 1968," **19** (January 26, 1971), p. 1.]

mately this level until 1963, but since then it appears to have resumed an upward trend once again. The national divorce total of 534,000 for 1967 was the highest annual number recorded since the World War II peak of 610,000, and in 1970 it exceed that figure, reaching 715,000.[6] The current divorce rate of 3.5 per 1,000 population is the highest national divorce rate since 1947. It is quite possible that the rate of divorce will continue to climb and eventually reach the 4.3 peak of 1946.

That the divorce rate becomes accelerated during wartime periods and declines during economic depressions is a well-recognized pattern (Figure 18.1). Wartime conditions frequently lead to hasty marriages, long separations between spouses and their families, opportunities for extramarital involvements, and so forth, any one of which may eventually lead to divorce. Moreover, research has shown that many couples simply are unable to reestablish and sustain their marriages under the heavy strains of postwar adjustments.[7] In the case of economic depressions, the tax on financial resources during such periods makes the costs of divorce extra prohibitive to many people. During times of economic hardship, couples who have become alienated may postpone divorce because the alternatives at the moment are unattractive.

Duration of Marriage to Divorce

Another indicator of a society's marital stability that is of sociological interest is the length of time that couples remain married, in the present

---

[6]U.S. Department of Health, Education, and Welfare, Public Health Service, "Annual Summary for the United States, 1970," *Monthly Vital Statistics,* **19** (Sept. 21, 1971), p. 9.
[7]Reuben Hill, *Families Under Stress* (New York: Harper & Row, 1949), pp. 252–257.

context, the period that elapses between the wedding and the day when the divorce decree (or annulment) is granted. Actually, the duration of marriage to divorce is composed of three distinct phases: (1) The time between marriage and final separation, that is, when the couple cease to share the same household. Couples may have parted company long before the granting of the divorce decree. This period is of greatest importance to the study of family disruption because its conclusion marks the end of the only period when the family is functioning as a complete social unit. (2) The time between separation and the filing of a petition for a divorce decree. The duration of this period depends in part on the decision of the parties involved to initiate divorce proceedings and partly on state laws, which specify the time that must elapse in order for a certain legal ground for divorce to arise, for example, desertion, voluntary separation, or insanity. Consequently, this period may last anywhere from a few weeks to several years.[8] (3) The time between the filing of a petition and the granting of the divorce decree. The duration of this period is determined almost exclusively by state law. All of these periods have different characteristics and their length is caused by different factors, all of which affect the duration of marriage to divorce decree.[9]

Sociological analyses of marital disruptions have rather consistently revealed that the majority of all divorces occur in the very early years of marriage. The *highest percentage of divorce decrees* are granted within the first three to four years of marriage, with the incidence declining steadily each year thereafter.[10] The generalization that emerges here is that the probability of divorce decreases as length of marriage increases. Drawing on what we learned about the stability of early marriages in Chapter 9, we may extend the generalization to read: the older the age at first marriage and the longer the duration of marriage, the lower the probability of divorce. Although some couples divorce even after thirty or more years of marriage, their total number is relatively small in comparison to the frequency of marital disruption occurring at earlier stages of the marriage cycle. The *median* or average duration of time from marriage to the actual granting of the divorce

[8]Thomas P. Monahan, "When Married Couples Part: Statistical Trends and Relationships in Divorce," *American Sociological Review,* **27** (Oct. 1962), pp. 625–633.

[9]Unfortunately, the complete and current nationwide statistics on the duration of marriage to separation and on the duration of separation to divorce are not available.

[10]Paul H. Jacobson, "Differentials in Divorce by Duration of Marriage and Size of Family," *American Sociological Review,* **15** (Apr. 1950), pp. 235–244; William M. Kephart, "The Duration of Marriage," *American Sociological Review,* **19** (June 1954), pp. 287–295; Thomas P. Monahan, "When Couples Part: Statistical Trends and Relationships in Divorce," op. cit., pp. 625–633. The year for which the modal number of divorces are granted varies among the states. For example, in one analysis of sixteen states, the modal year of duration was one year in thirteen states, two years in five states, three years in one state, four years in one state, six years in one state, and one state had no single modal year of duration. *Divorce Statistics Analysis: United States—1963,* op. cit., p. 25.

decree is roughly seven and one half years, although it must be emphasized that this figure varies considerably from city to city and state to state.

Contemporary sociologists are in agreement that separation dates provide a much more accurate and meaningful picture of the period at which true marital disruption takes place than divorce dates. Indeed, it is well recognized that couples who eventually divorce were often alienated long before their actual separation took place. Nevertheless, separation dates most clearly reflect the point at which one or both of the spouses have decided to dissolve the marriage. The *maximum percentage of separations* also occurs in the early stages of marriage, but with the greatest number taking place within the first year or two, with the incidence declining with each subsequent year.[11] The *median* duration of time from marriage to separation, as compared to divorce, is approximately five years. Moreover, as Monahan has observed:

Duration of marriage to *separation* varies from area to area, from time to time, and from one population class to another. It has been found that couples have longer durations of marriage to separation when they are in their first marriage, have children, are in higher socio-economic occupational groups, generally, and live in less metropolitan but middle-sized population areas. The grounds chosen for divorce and the legal structure are also related to duration, and it is likely that race, educational achievement, premarital pregnancy, and other elements also bear a relationship to this measure of marriage duration.[12]

Finally, as we noted at the beginning of this section, the time interval between separation and divorce depends both on the decisions of the couples to initiate official divorce proceedings and on the applicability of the laws of the state in which the divorce is to be obtained. Consequently, the duration from separation to divorce also shows much variation among the different states.

The important point to be emphasized here is what the duration of marriage to separation data reveal, namely, that the first year or so of marriage is really the crucial period for establishing the basis of a stable marital relationship. It is during this initial period that the couple must learn to enact a whole set of new marital roles and to achieve sufficient competence in them so that the material, social, and emotional needs of each are met, at least at a tolerable level. For many younger couples, this is their first attempt at adult role-playing—at earning an independent living, at managing a house or an apartment, and at establishing a workable set of relationships with the community. If one or both of the couple fail to understand the responsibilities of marital roles, or are unwilling and/or unable to enact them effectively, the

[11]Kephart, op. cit., p. 290; Monahan, op. cit., p. 630.
[12]Ibid., p. 633.

470

marriage is never established as a functioning entity, even though they may live together continuously or intermittently for weeks or months and the divorce may not occur until the second year or even later. Most of the separations of the first year or even two are probably of this type. Some of the marital roles never become active in a functioning sense. These very early divorces, in a sense, were less the breakup of a marriage than the failure of two people to bring the marriage into being as an effective functioning entity in the first place.

Regional and Rural-Urban Divorce Differentials

For several decades now the census data have consistently revealed a regional divorce differential in the United States, with the divorce rate tending to increase from east to west. Typically, the divorce rate is *lowest* in the Northeast, followed in turn by the north-central region, the southern region, and lastly the western region. The rate for the West is about four times as high as that for the Northeast.[13]

Sociologists have not been able to explain these regional variations completely, although several factors have been advanced to account for them.[14] It has been speculated that the "frontier" tradition of the West promotes and supports a more relaxed if not a more tolerant attitude toward divorce than the tradition found in the more conservative areas of the East. Higher rates of migratory divorces in the West no doubt partly account for these regional differences. Until very recently, some of the eastern seaboard states have had such restrictive divorce laws that persons found it easier to move to other regions of the country to obtain their decrees. The fact that the West has been registering the greatest net gains in population from internal migration for many years may also contribute to its higher rate. People who are geographically mobile, one suspects, are more adventuresome in outlook and less conformist. Mobility releases them from the restraints of their home community. It also increases their likelihood of entering a mixed marriage, which carries a greater divorce risk potential. In addition, there is a greater concentration of young adults—the persons with the greatest probability of divorce—among the western population. Further, the ethnic, racial, and religious composition of a region will also influence the divorce rates. Thus, the higher concentration of the Catholic population in the Northeast helps to account for the lower divorce rates in that general region.[15] Finally, the fact that states in the western and southern regions of America generally have higher *mar-*

---

[13]*Monthly Vital Statistics Report,* **16** (Sept. 27, 1967), National Center for Health Statistics, Washington, D.C., p. 3.

[14]Henry Pang and Sue Marie Hanson, "Highest Divorce Rates in the Western States," *Sociology and Social Research,* **52** (Jan. 1968), pp. 228–236.

[15]Paul C. Glick, "Marriage Instability: Variations by Size of Place and Region," *The Milbank Memorial Fund Quarterly,* **41** (Jan. 1963), pp. 43–55.

riage rates than other regions further raises the probability that they will also have greater divorce rates.

Rural-urban divorce differentials, which show a greater likelihood of divorce in the cities, have similarly been regularly observed over the years. There are many conditions of urban life that increase the probability of a higher divorce rate. The anonymity and impersonality of social relationships in the city release people from former community controls over their behavior. Under such conditions, less stigma is apt to be felt over divorce by the city dweller. Urban life has a liberating effect on women, allowing them to obtain jobs and achieve greater economic independence, and therefore they are less inclined to maintain an unhappy marriage. Moreover, many people migrate to the cities following their separation from their spouses or after their divorce.[16]

Racial Variations in Divorce

Perhaps no other area more clearly reveals the limitations of current national divorce statistics than that pertaining to race. These statistics lack the necessary detail essential for making sound generalizations about white versus nonwhite divorce differentials. For example, statistics from the 1970 national decennial census indicate that a greater percentage of Negroes than whites are either separated or divorced. However, the figures reported reflect the marital status of the population *only at the time of the census enumeration* and, therefore, give no indication of what proportion of the races have been previously divorced and remarried. The National Vital Statistics Division also publishes information on divorce rates, based upon reports it receives from some twenty-odd states who participate in the Divorce Registration Area (DRA). Many of the state reports, however, are incomplete and frequently fail to designate race.

The most reliable national data to date—because it includes both previous and current marital status—comes from a 1957 sample survey of 22,000 households conducted by the Bureau of the Census.[17] Analysis of these data clearly shows that a greater percentage of Negro males (19.8 per cent) and females (19.9 per cent) were divorced than white males (14.1 per cent) and females (16.7 per cent).[18]

Socioeconomic Status and Divorce

It seems that prior to the forties the notion that divorce was most prevalent among the upper socioeconomic groups in American society

[16]William F. Ogburn and Meyer F. Nimkoff, *Technology and the Changing Family* (Boston: Houghton Mifflin Company, 1955), Chapter 10, "More Disruption."

[17]National Office of Vital Statistics, *Special Reports*, **45** (1957), p. 298.

[18]Adequate and reliable national divorce rates for mixed white-nonwhite are unavailable. Estimates of Negro-white marriages over the years indicate that less than one half of 1 per cent of all divorces involve a white-nonwhite couple.

was rather widely accepted, even by some sociologists.[19] Because desertion was more frequent among the lower socioeconomic strata, it was assumed (incorrectly) that that their divorce rate was lower. As precise data became available, however, they showed that this notion was false and that, in fact, just the opposite was true. That an inverse relationship exists between socioeconomic status and marital instability has now been well documented by several researchers. Whether socioeconomic status is measured by occupation, income, education, or some combination of these, the results generally remain the same— as people move up the socioeconomic structure, a corresponding *decline* in the divorce rate will be observed. The highest divorce and separation rates occur in the lower socioeconomic groups in our society.

An analysis of the broad but standard census occupational categories by Hillman reveals the general *pattern* of divorce rates that has been substantiated by subsequent studies, with only slight variations (Table 18.4). She found the greatest proportion of divorces occurred at the bottom of the occupational scale among private household and service workers, as well as laborers, and then steadily declined as people moved up in the occupational hierarchy. Thus, for example, Table 18.4 shows that the divorce rates among private household workers is nearly *three times* that of managers, officials, and proprietors. Farm owners and managers, generally viewed by sociologists as rather distinct groups, have the lowest divorce rate, whereas farm laborers, in contrast,

Table 18.4
Percentage of Males Divorced, by Occupation, United States, 1950

Occupational Grouping	*Divorce per 1,000 of Those Ever Married*
Professional, technical, and kindred workers	18.49
Managers, officials, and proprietors exc. farm	16.59
Sales workers	24.22
Clerical and kindred workers	25.70
Craftsmen, foremen, and kindred workers	24.15
Operatives and kindred workers	26.18
Service workers exc. private household	42.35
Private household workers	47.24
Laborers exc. farm and mine	32.80
Farmers and farm managers	7.86
Farm laborers and foreman	40.76

SOURCE: Karen G. Hillman, "Marital Instability and Its Relation to Education, Income, and Occupation: An Analysis Based on Census Data," in Robert F. Winch, Robert McGinnis, and Herbert R. Barringer (eds.), *Selected Studies in Marriage and the Family* (New York: Holt, Rinehart and Winston, 1962), pp. 603–608.

[19]Terman's statement that "it is well known that more divorces occur in the higher classes" is representative of this earlier view. Lewis M. Terman, *Psychological Factors in Marital Happiness* (New York: McGraw-Hill Book Company, 1938), p. 167.

fall into the high divorce group as was the case with other laborers.

Hillman's findings have generally been confirmed by subsequent analyses of the 1960 decennial census data by both Bernard (focusing on men in the forty-five to fifty-four age bracket) and Udry (focusing on men in the twenty-five to thirty-four age bracket).[20] Moreover, small-scale sociological investigations of the relationship between occupational levels and marital instability have consistently demonstrated that divorce is more characteristic of the lower than the upper socio-economic strata. Kephart's analysis of nearly 1,500 Philadelphia divorce records, Goode's study of 425 Detroit area divorcees, and Monahan's analysis of 4,500 Iowa divorce records all support the thesis of an inverse correlation between frequency of divorce and socio-economic level.[21] Kephart's finding that "the upper occupational levels are underrepresented, the middle occupational groups 'hold their own,' and the lower occupational levels are overrepresented in divorce actions," generally summarizes the statistical evidence in this area thus far. Indeed, the cross-cultural evidence suggests that marital instability is more characteristic of the lower strata than the upper in most modern nations in the West.[22]

SEX AND RACIAL DIFFERENCES Some of the above studies also utilized income and education as indicators of socioeconomic status, and they have generally confirmed the inverse relationship found between occupational level and divorce. When these studies are analyzed separately by sex and race, however, some modification of the original generalization of an inverse relationship between socioeconomic status and divorce occurs. Studies by Hillman, Goode, and Monahan all report varying patterns of divorce by educational level among non-white males and among females of both races.[23] However, the relation-

---

[20]Jessie Bernard, "Marital Stability and Patterns of Status Variables," *Journal of Marriage and the Family,* **28** (Nov. 1966), pp. 421–439; J. Richard Udry, "Marital Instability by Race, Sex, Education, and Occupation Using 1960 Census Data," *American Journal of Sociology,* **72** (Sept. 1966), pp. 203–209; "Marital Instability by Race and Income Based on 1960 Census Data," *American Journal of Sociology,* **72** (May 1967), pp. 673–674.

[21]William M. Kephart, "Occupational Level and Marital Disruption," *American Sociological Review,* **20** (Aug. 1955), pp. 456–465; William J. Goode, *After Divorce* (Glencoe, Ill.: The Free Press, 1956); Thomas P. Monahan, "Divorce by Occupational Level," *Marriage and Family Living,* **17** (Nov. 1955), pp. 322–324.

[22]William J. Goode, op. cit., pp. 507–526. Goode presents some data to indicate that at an earlier period in their history, some Western countries were characterized by higher divorce rates among the upper strata. He argues that only when the legal divorce procedures were sufficiently liberalized and divorce made economically feasible for all did the lower stratum rates begin to surpass those of the upper strata and reflect the greater difficulties of lower-class family life.

[23]Hillman, op. cit., pp. 603–608; William J. Goode, "Family Disorganization," in *Contemporary Social Problems,* ed. by Robert K. Merton and Robert A. Nisbet (New York: Harcourt Brace Jovanovich, 1966), pp. 509–514; Thomas P. Monahan, "Educational Achievement and Family Stability," *The Journal of Social Psychology,* **55** (Dec. 1961), pp. 253–263.

ship between education and divorce rates is obviously affected by age, a variable that these studies all failed to control for.

Udry's analysis of the 1960 census data clearly supports the general inverse relationship between educational level and marital disruption; for both sexes and races, the higher the educational level the lower the divorce and separation rate. The only exception occurred among females with graduate training, who showed higher rates of marital disruption than their white and nonwhite male counterparts.[24] His analysis of the income data also strongly supports the noted relationship between income and marital instability—the lower the income the higher the rate of divorce and separation, with the ratio of white to nonwhite marital disruption widening with increasing income.[25]

The initial generalization, that the highest divorce and separation rates are most prevalent in the lower socioeconomic groups in our society, seems firmly established. The greater marital disruption in the lower-class levels, however, cannot be attributed solely to the factors of occupation, education, and income. As Bernard has shown, even when these variables are held constant between the universe of whites and nonwhites, "a wide gap in marital stability remains between the two worlds."[26] Such persistent differentials in marital instability no doubt reflect the greater sociological, sociopsychological, and cultural stresses and difficulties generally associated with conditions of life in the lower class.

Children in Divorce
Among the more striking social trends in recent decades are those reflecting a long-term growth in both the proportion of divorced couples with minor children and the total number of children affected by divorce. For example, in the mid-twenties slightly more than a third of all divorce actions in the United States involved minor children, but by the mid-fifties the figure was approaching one half, and in the mid-sixties the proportion had risen to include well over three fifths of all divorcing couples.[27] Thus, there has been a rapid decline of the proportion of childless divorced couples and, in fact, they have comprised less than one half of all divorces annually for more than a decade.

---

[24]Udry, "Marital Instability by Race, Sex, Education, and Occupation Using 1960 Census Data," op. cit., p. 207. This exception aside, ℓ comparison of nonwhites and whites of the same sex indicated that nonwhite rates of disruption were consistently from one and a half to more than twice the rates for whites of the same educational level.

[25]Udry, "Marital Instability by Race and Income Based on 1960 Census Data," op. cit., pp. 673–674.

[26]Bernard, op. cit., p. 437.

[27]*Vital Statistics of the United States, 1960*, III, Sec. 3, 4, 7, pp. 3–11 to 3–14, National Vital Statistics Division, HEW, Washington, D.C.; *Monthly Vital Statistics Report*, 16 (Sept. 27, 1967), National Center for Health Statistics, Washington, D.C., p. 2.

Table 18.5
Estimated Number of Children Involved in Divorces and Annulments: United States, 1953–1969

Year	Estimated Number of Children Involved	Average Number of Children Per Decree
1953	330,000	.85
1954	341,000	.90
1955	347,000	.92
1956	361,000	.95
1957	379,000	.99
1958	398,000	1.08
1959	468,000	1.18
1960	463,000	1.18
1961	516,000	1.25
1962	532,000	1.29
1963	562,000	1.31
1964	613,000	1.36
1965	630,000	1.32
1966	669,000	1.34
1967	701,000	1.34
1968	784,000	1.34
1969	840,000	1.31

SOURCE: Public Health Service, *Monthly Vital Statistics Report,* "Divorce Statistics, 1969," **20** (July 22, 1971), p. 3.

The substantial increase in the total number of children affected by divorce is equally impressive (Table 18.5). For example, in 1948 it was estimated that 322,000 youngsters were involved in parental divorces. A decade later, the yearly figure had climbed to 398,000, and by 1964 the number of children affected had grown to 634,000. To put this in somewhat more dramatic terms, in the single decade encompassed by the period 1953–1963, the number of divorce decrees granted annually increased by approximately 10 per cent, but the number of children involved in divorces increased by almost 77 per cent! Moreover, the average number of children per decree, as well as the ratio of children per divorce decrees with children, have both steadily risen during this same period.

The supposition that having children would help prevent divorce, which was rather widely accepted in American folklore and by many social scientists, has been challenged on a number of grounds for some time.[28] Moreover, it is quite clear from the evidence presented in the previous paragraphs that the presence of children no longer—if it ever did—constitutes a sufficient deterrent to divorce.

[28]Thomas P. Monahan, "Is Childlessness Related to Family Stability?" *American Sociological Review,* **20** (Aug. 1955), pp. 446–456.

Migrant Divorces

All states within the United States have enacted laws that require a specific period of continuous residence before a person may legally file for a divorce. This requirement is apparently designed to discourage or prevent an individual from "shopping around" in another state for an easy jurisdiction in which to initiate a divorce action. Because the residential requirements vary among states, however, and because there is considerable variation in divorce laws as well as court procedures from state to state, interstate migration for the sole purpose of obtaining a divorce has long existed in the United States.[29]

Indeed, a handful of states with rather lenient divorce laws and court procedures, as well as unusually short residence requirements, have gained national notoriety as "divorce mills." In such areas, a person is able to move in for the minimum period needed to establish bona fide legal resident status, and then depart as soon as the divorce decree is granted. According to Elliott, the

urge to commercialize divorce in America seems to have stemmed from activities of a New York lawyer who recognized the possibilities of exploiting the relatively lenient grounds for divorce in Nevada on behalf of New York clients who were either too embarrassed or too honest to press charges of adultery against an estranged mate. Consequently he advertised the opportunities for securing a respectable divorce after a short residence in Nevada.[30]

Other states, anxious to obtain some of the profits from this rather "lucrative business" have enacted similar provisions. Currently six states—Alabama, Arkansas, Florida, Idaho, Nevada, and Wyoming—have short residence requirements. For the especially affluent, Puerto Rico, the Virgin Islands, and Haiti (the latter requiring merely a one day visit) provide alternative migratory divorce meccas.

Although migratory divorces typically are granted to the plaintiff with virtually little or no attempt to ascertain the facts of the case, problems do arise. Under the so-called full faith and credit clause of the Constitution, the Supreme Court has ruled that a marriage or divorce

[29]Paul H. Jacobson, *American Marriage and Divorce* (New York: Rinehart and Company, Inc., 1959), p. 103. Migratory divorces need to be distinguished from divorces of migrants, that is, of people who migrate and obtain a decree in their new place of *permanent* residence, and from divorces obtained outside the *county* of usual residence of the person but within his permanent state of residence. Neither of these are considered as migratory divorces as the term is employed here.

[30]Mabel A. Elliott, "Divorce Legislation and Family Instability," *The Annals of the American Academy of Political and Social Science,* **272** (Nov. 1950), pp. 134–147. In 1966, however, New York liberalized its previously rigid code, which allowed divorce only on the grounds of adultery. The new code broadened the earlier provision by classifying sodomy and a homosexual act by either spouse as adultery, and added four new grounds, including "cruel and inhuman treatment."

477

performed in one state must be given full legal recognition in all other states. Many states, however, raise questions from time to time about the validity of the plaintiff's residence in these states and frequently refuse to accept such divorces as valid when test cases are made.[31] In the state of Alabama, for example, action was taken by state authorities and the Bar Association against unconstitutional granting of migratory divorces in that state. As a result, the number of divorces granted in Alabama declined nearly 28 per cent between 1960 and 1963, and the annual divorce rate declined from 5.3 to 3.7.[32]

Although most migratory divorce actions are not challenged, simply because both the parties involved desire a termination of the marriage, occasionally a spouse will contest a divorce obtained in another state by the estranged marital partner (Mexican divorces are especially vulnerable to such challenges). The Supreme Court has ruled that such contests may be legally entertained by the relevant state courts, and the majority of such contests are in fact resolved at the state level. Unfortunately, the outcome of such cases is not always predictable.

The full faith and credit clause, the varying residence requirements, and the opinions and reversals of the Supreme Court have combined to make the status of migratory divorces an uncertain one. . . . Alimony, children, property settlements, continued change of residence, and other factors tend to complicate matters. And since one case is seldom *exactly* like another, lawyers admit that they are not always certain how a particular suit will be decided.[33]

What this all means is that until the situation becomes further clarified many divorces obtained through interstate migration are on tentative if not shaky grounds because they are potentially subject to challenge and subsequent reversal or nullification.

The uncertainty surrounding migratory divorces has evolved in large part from the laxity of the courts in enforcing their own residence requirements and the activity of some people seeking divorce in taking advantage of this fact. Although it is not possible, for a variety of reasons, to estimate precisely the total number of migratory divorces that occur, there is general agreement that their numerical importance is relatively small. Jacobson estimated that migratory divorces probably account for no more than 3 to 5 per cent of the total number of divorces granted annually, and more recent estimates generally support this estimate.[34]

[31]Morris Ploscowe, *The Truth About Divorce* (New York: Hawthorn Books, Inc., 1955), pp. 151–161.

[32]*Divorce Statistics Analysis: United States–1963*, op. cit., pp. 9–10.

[33]William M. Kephart, *The Family, Society, and the Individual*, 2nd ed. (Boston: Houghton Mifflin Company, 1966), p. 562.

[34]Jacobson, op. cit., p. 109; *Divorce Statistics Analysis: United States—1963*, op. cit., p. 9.

Divorce as Legislation and Process: The American System

Divorce litigation in the United States is predicated on the so-called adversary system of law, which essentially requires that in any legal suit there must be an innocent party (plaintiff) and a guilty party (defendant). Thus, in order for a couple to have their marriage dissolved officially, one spouse—usually the wife—must assume the plaintiff's role and bring legal suit against the other, who is accused of committing an offense(s) that, in the particular state where the charge is filed, legally constitutes grounds for a divorce. Under the adversary system of law a divorce action is supposed to be a legal contest between two parties. The married couple involved, therefore, are legally forbidden from mutually agreeing to the divorce beforehand. Should any such form of collusion on the part of the couple come to the attention of the court, it is bound by law to deny them a divorce.

The facts of the matter are, however, that in a majority of the divorce cases, the spouses have in one way or another essentially agreed to terminate the marriage through divorce long before the court hearing ever takes place. Moreover, their attorneys have often suggested that a "convenient" ground be used to avoid embarrassment or legal difficulties that would complicate and prolong the divorce action. The settlement arrangements are worked out in advance and then recommended to the court, which in turn usually does not question them except in a very perfunctory manner. In essence, the court, the attorneys, the couple, and sometimes even the witnesses themselves are all involved in what actually amounts to a circumvention of the theory of contest required by the adversary system of law. It has been estimated that "less than 10 per cent of all divorces are *really* contested."[35] Although spousal defendants in divorce actions are notified of the upcoming hearing, only a minority ever actually attend. On the basis of the evidence presented in court by the "innocent" spouse, the "guilt" of the absent partner is assumed and the divorce granted.

One might be tempted to conclude from this discussion that dissolving a marriage is a relatively uncomplicated and painless event, but nothing could be further from the truth. For the vast majority of couples the process of divorce remains a highly upsetting if not emotionally traumatic experience. It must be remembered that in most instances the decision to break up the marriage has not been made lightly and has been preceded by a period of spousal conflict, unhappiness, and some degree of personal disorganization. In the majority of cases, "the process of divorce conflict is a relatively slow one, in which the

[35]William M. Kephart, *The Family, Society, and the Individual,* op. cit., p. 554.

bitterness of the interaction serves gradually to estrange the partners from one another. They are 'being divorced' for months before the decree."[36] Throughout the process, the husband and wife have experienced a number of emotional and sometimes physical "bouts" before reaching the point of "agreeing," often reluctantly, that a divorce may be the only satisfactory solution to their problems. Not infrequently the marital hostilities are continued even after attorneys have been retained to initiate the legal machinery necessary to bring the marriage to an end. As their attorneys begin the preliminary negotiations over the various strategies to be taken in court as well as the postdivorce arrangements, one or both spouses may attempt to "get even" by taking a recalcitrant position on decisions regarding custody and support of the children, division of property, alimony payments, and so on, or by refusing to "go along" with the contrived charges to be placed before the court as a basis for the divorce action. By the time the arrangements have finally been hammered out, it is not unusual for the husband and wife involved to be more at odds with one another than ever before, and both may have become rather hostile toward the attorneys, the legal system, and society in general. As Leslie has noted:

Before the negotiations are completed, what may have started out as an attempt by both partners to reach an equitable solution often has degenerated into bitter conflict. Virtually all authorities in the field are agreed that much of the vindictiveness which has traditionally been associated with divorce in the United States is traceable to the hostilities that are engendered by the divorce process itself.[37]

In sum, the legal process of divorce as it currently exists directly influences the nature of interaction between the spouses in a manner that often further accentuates prior antagonisms.

REFORMING THE DIVORCE PROCESS In view of the preceding discussion, it is worth noting that in recent years divorce laws and the applicability of the adversary concept to divorce actions have been increasingly challenged in the United States.[38] From a sociological perspective, the apparent discrepancy between rules of law regarding

---

[36]William J. Goode, *After Divorce* (New York: The Free Press, 1956), p. 185. Later published in paperback under the title, *Women in Divorce.*

[37]Gerald R. Leslie, *The Family in Social Context* (New York: Oxford University Press, 1967), p. 608. For a more detailed and expanded discussion of the divorce process and divorce legislation, see Kephart, *The Family, Society, and the Individual,* op. cit., Chapters 20–22, and "Legal and Procedural Aspects of Marriage and Divorce," in *Handbook of Marriage and the Family,* ed. by Harold T. Christensen (Chicago: Rand McNally & Co., 1964), pp. 944–968.

[38]Monrad G. Paulsen, "For a Reform of the Divorce Laws," *New York Times Magazine* (May 13, 1962), pp. 22–41; "The Sorry State of Divorce Law," *Time* (Feb. 11, 1966), pp. 26–27.

480

divorce contests and actual court practices represents a "large-scale patterned evasion" of dominant legal norms.[39] It reflects an obvious disparity between public mores and legal regulations. Such widespread contravention of normative systems is not, of course, confined to the area of divorce. It has been noted by sociologists to occur in many different contexts of American life and history, such as the high consumption of alcoholic beverages during Prohibition. These disparities represent circumstances in which a gap exists between the desires of a significant proportion of the public and the ideals incorporated into the legal system. The development of a more liberal philosophy and attitude toward divorce in the United States, which seek expression in contemporary divorce proceedings, runs counter to established legal regulations. However, "marriage and family law that runs counter to popular beliefs and well established behavior tends in the long run to be modified, formally abolished, or tacitly ignored. Nevertheless, such adjustments are usually slow, and many divergencies between law and practice typically exist at any given time."[40]

Legal institutions are ordinarily very conservative in nature and, therefore, change slowly under the impact of growing social pressures. Consequently, a basic cultural lag has existed in our divorce laws because of the traditional conception of the divorce action as punitive litigation involving a guilty and an innocent party that requires that one spouse bring accusations against the other in terms of recognized legal causes. Thus, as noted earlier, the court proceedings are almost always a ritualistic farce because of pretrial collusion between the spouses and because false or fictitious reasons are given for the divorce action. "This discrepancy between the law of the books and the law in action, which we find in so many states, has, through its tolerance or promotion of collusive practices and perjury, developed into a serious threat to the morals of the bar and the respect for law among the public."[41]

Several solutions have been suggested over the years that, if implemented by legal and public support, would seem to offer a rational means of attuning the laws to the inescapable reality that a major portion of divorces are desired by both parties. Although extensive review and discussion of these suggested legal reforms need not be entered into here, it is perhaps worth noting one of the most recent recommendations offered by the Task Force on Family Law and Policy,

[39]Robin M. Williams, Jr., *American Society,* 2nd rev. ed. (New York: Alfred A. Knopf, 1967), pp. 372–396. Williams, like many others, notes that through actual practices of the courts the law, in effect, is coming to permit divorce by mutual consent.

[40]Ibid., p. 48.

[41]Max Rheinstein, "Trends in Marriage and Divorce Law of Western Countries," *Law and Contemporary Problems,* **18** (Winter 1953), p. 19. See also: Max Rheinstein, *Marriage Stability, Divorce, and the Law* (Chicago: The University of Chicago Press, 1972).

481

a specially appointed group of lay and professional persons charged with the responsibility of studying divorce and related family problems.[42] The Task Force suggested that there are three basic principles that should guide any revision of state divorce laws.

1. Where it is contemplated that a marriage is to be broken, there should be a sufficient time lapse before a divorce is granted, regardless of the cause of the break-up, to permit the respective parties to reconsider, seek counseling if they wish, and perhaps change their mind.
2. Marriage is basically a private relationship which should not be manipulated by government in the absence of an overriding public interest.
3. The concept that there must be a guilty party to any divorce is unrealistic and unnecessarily creates hostility between the parties, which is often detrimental to their children.

Under the Task Force proposal, a one-year voluntary separation would be required to enable the husband and wife to reconsider their decision to dissolve the marriage (North Carolina, Ohio, and District of Columbia laws currently incorporate this procedure). The only fact that would need to be established would be the period of time of separation.[43] There would be no requirement in the law that fault be established, nor that the personal difficulties between the parties be laid before the court. The availability of these grounds for divorce would have the virtue of not requiring that a marriage be opened up to public exposure. If the grounds for divorce that require a showing of fault and assume a "guilty" party were eliminated, the doctrines of condonation (a spouse who has forgiven the other spouse's wrongdoing is precluded from obtaining a divorce on that basis) and recrimination (a countercharge by the defendant in a divorce action of wrongdoing by the plaintiff as a defense against the divorce) would both become obsolete.

Whether the states will be receptive to the Task Force proposal remains to be seen. Few, if any, sociologists would be in favor of complete freedom to divorce and total relaxation of the law. Rather, they would be inclined to agree with Lichtenberger's contention that a major function of law is not to prevent divorce or to render it less frequent, but to regularize the procedure through which divorces are obtained, by codification of approved practices, in the interest of

---

[42]U.S. Department of Labor, *Report of the Task Force on Family Law and Policy,* Citizens Advisory Council on the Status of Women, Washington, D.C., (April, 1968), pp. 34–38.

[43]Also recommended is that the law recognizes that where one party deserts, but the other party wishes to continue the marriage, the deserted party may obtain a divorce after a period of six months; the deserting party after eighteen months. This would essentially make desertion a nonfault basis for divorce.

conformity and social solidarity.[44] In line with this position is the so-called conciliatory or therapeutic approach to divorce that has emerged in recent years. Such an approach attempts to remove the litigious procedure of accusation and guilt from the courtroom and substitute in its place a therapeutic procedure of family welfare. The court, in conjunction with experts in the field of family relations, considers not just the question of guilt and injury but the personal and collective welfare of all family members as well. The court attempts to promote in a positive fashion society's interest in family stability, at the same time protecting the rights and privileges of individual family members.[45] Besides the welfare of family members, society has a collective interest in family stability in that following many divorces, insufficient financial support is available to the children so that the wife and children must be supported from public funds.

Indications of Divorce Reform

We noted earlier that the legal system has responded slowly to changing public sentiments regarding marital and family relationships. Nevertheless, widespread dissatisfaction with our current divorce laws has led some states to institute recent reforms more in line with contemporary attitudes regarding marital dissolution. The trend is moving in the direction of laws that, in effect, would allow divorce by mutual consent rather than requiring the necessity of a punitive adversary procedure. Thus, about two fifths of our states now recognize some specified period of "separation without cohabitation" as sufficient grounds for divorce. The most significant changes have occurred in California and Florida. In the early seventies, both these states implemented what are essentially "no fault" divorce laws. In California, for example, a couple may now simply file for divorce because of "irreconcilable differences." The court, on the basis of evidence presented at a hearing, determines whether the irreconcilable differences are present and, if so, it issues a judgment for the marriage to be dissolved. In both Florida and California, the new laws also reflect a more equalitarian view with respect to child support and alimony. Now, *either* spouse can be required to pay alimony, and the court can require either or both to contribute to the support of minor children. The extent to which the courts will *in fact* implement this equalitarian attitude toward alimony and child support will be of considerable interest to both the married and the nonmarried in the years to come!

---

[44]J. B. Lichtenberger, "Divorce Legislation," *The Annals of the American Academy of Political and Social Science,* **160** (March 1932), pp. 116–123.

[45]For a detailed discussion of this approach, see Kephart, *The Family, Society, and the Individual,* op. cit., pp. 627–633.

Desertion

Any analysis of family disruption would be incomplete without some discussion of another major and prevalent form of marital termination, namely, desertion. Sociological analyses of desertion are somewhat hampered by the fact that the exact number of couples involved in such cases is unknown because, unlike divorce, such actions often do not become a matter of legal record. Obviously, a spouse who deserts is still legally married and therefore is prohibited from remarrying until a such time as a divorce is obtained. It is not unusual, however, for a deserting partner to migrate to another state and subsequently file suit for a divorce in that state. In some such cases the desertion itself may never be recorded. Statistics on recorded desertions, which provide only a partial picture, come primarily from Aid to Dependent Children (ADC) files, from applications to local courts to secure support payments from absent husbands, and from divorce records in which desertion has been entered as the ground for divorce. Further difficulties are encountered by the lack of a clear definition of desertion itself. The Bureau of the Census uses the term *marital separations,* and defines this so as to include those "couples with legal separations, those living apart with intentions of obtaining a divorce, and other persons permanently or temporarily estranged from their spouses because of marital discord." Within this broader context some sociologists have estimated that the total number of such separated couples runs into the millions.[46]

Although there are many instances of wives deserting their husbands and families, in the overwhelming majority of recorded cases it is the husband who is the runaway spouse. Sociologists writing in the fifties estimated the number of deserting husbands at about 100,000 annually.[47] This was a conservative estimate at best and no doubt the total *number* is considerably higher today. It should be noted here that many husbands who abandon their families exhibit a recidivist pattern, that is, they flee from the home but then later return for a period—sometimes voluntarily and sometimes under pressure—and then absent themselves again. The exact rate of this type of recidivism is, of course, not known.

More precise information on the social characteristics associated

---

[46]Kephart, *The Family, Society, and the Individual,* op. cit., p. 591, also cites an unpublished mimeographed report by Thomas P. Monahan, *Families in Conflict,* Philadelphia Municipal Court, 1955, in which it is estimated that three out of every one hundred married couples are *truly* separated and another large group of families live together in a state of intermittent or permanent marital conflict. The combined figure for both groups is estimated to be about 10 per cent of all existing families.

[47]Ray E. Baber, *Marriage and the Family* (McGraw-Hill Book Company, 1953), pp. 493–494.

with desertion has been developed by Kephart and Monahan through a series of independent as well as cooperative analyses of data obtained in Philadelphia.[48] Their findings, which in many ways show a striking parallel to those regarding divorce, may be summarized as follows. (1) When desertion rates are analyzed by occupational level, they follow a pattern very similar to that observed in the case of divorce. In general, rates are lowest among professional groups and then steadily increase as one moves down the occupational ladder. Philadelphia court records show, for example, that the proportion of desertions among professionals and proprietors was about 3 and 9 per cent, respectively, compared to 22 per cent among the skilled and 37 per cent of the semiskilled workers.[49] (2) Comparison by race shows that Negroes are clearly overrepresented in desertion cases whereas whites are under-represented. Thus, in the Philadelphia study Negroes constituted only 17 per cent of the total married male population but accounted for 40 per cent of the desertions.[50] Some writers have argued that this Negro-white differential is essentially a reflection of the unstable Negro family system, which had its roots in slavery. Although there may be some truth to this, it is perhaps more the case that the high desertion rates among *contemporary* Negroes is a reflection of their position in the occupational structure. Negroes are heavily concentrated in the lower occupational classes, and Kephart's analysis indicates that as they improve occupationally their desertion rates are reduced to a considerable degree.[51] (3) Compared to other major religious groups, Catholics have the highest desertion rate. The Philadelphia data show, for example, that "in the white desertion and non-support cases which came to court, the Catholic group, with reference to their proportion in the population, is overrepresented by nearly 40 per cent. On the other hand, the Jewish group is underrepresented to somewhat the same degree. The white Protestant class is about 25 per cent under-represented."[52] The greater Catholic desertion rate is partially accounted for by church proscriptions regarding outright divorce. Moreover, Catholics are disproportionately represented among the lower

[48]William M. Kephart and Thomas P. Monahan, "Desertion and Divorce in Philadelphia," *American Sociological Review,* 17 (Dec. 1952), pp. 719–727; "Divorce and Desertion by Religious and Mixed Religious Groups," *American Journal of Sociology,* 59 (March 1954), pp. 454–465; William M. Kephart, "Drinking and Marital Disruption," *Quarterly Journal of Studies on Alcohol,* 15 (March 1954), pp. 63–73; "Occupational Level and Marital Disruption," *American Sociological Review,* 20 (Aug. 1955), pp. 456–465; Thomas P. Monahan, "Is Childlessness Related to Family Stability?" op. cit., pp. 446–456.

[49]Kephart, "Occupational Level and Marital Disruption," op. cit., p. 462.

[50]Ibid., pp. 461–462.

[51]Ibid.

[52]Monahan and Kephart, "Divorce and Desertion by Religious and Mixed Religious Groups," op. cit., p. 462.

485

occupational groups, where both divorce and desertion reach their highest levels. (4) Compared to divorce cases, desertions are much more likely to involve minor children. This may be because of several factors. For instance, forced by the economic urgency of the situation, deserted mothers come to the attention of official agencies and courts much sooner than in the case of a childless wife whose husband has abandoned her. Moreover, marriages that have been disrupted by desertion tend to be of longer duration than those terminated through divorce, thereby increasing the probability of children's being present in the deserted household.[53]

Husbands who attempt to escape the economic burdens and responsibilities of growing families are of particular concern to the community and the state. Unless or until the wayward husband can be located, such families must be supported out of public funds. At one time, a father could desert his wife and family without much fear that he would be tracked down and forced to meet his familial obligations. This was especially true in those instances in which the husband had fled to another state. In the past, "because of a general apathy and reluctance of civil authorities (primarily) to prosecute fugitive husbands, few extraditions—which are costly and complicated processes, as well—were ever accomplished."[54] Eventually, however, as legislators increasingly recognized the tremendous financial drain placed upon public funds to support abandoned families, the states worked out agreements that have made it more difficult for a man to escape his family responsibilities. Through reciprocal support legislation, a court order for support issued in the home state will now be recognized and enforced in any other state where the deserting husband happens to be located. One obvious advantage of such interstate legislation is that extradition becomes unnecessary to enforcement of the support order; payment can be extracted from the husband regardless of where he resides.

Although this system of mutual enforcement of family support has considerably improved upon the situation of the past, it has by no means eliminated the possibility that deserting husbands will avoid their financial responsibilities. In one study, court orders for support were placed on only about half of the husbands during a given year.[55] Moreover, authorities "remain reluctant to confront a man with his marital responsibilities and to energetically insist that he support the wife and children he has abandoned, or suffer imprisonment."[56] This

---

[53]Monahan, "Is Childlessness Related to Family Stability?" op. cit., pp. 446–456.
[54]Thomas P. Monahan, "Family Fugitives," *Marriage and Family Living*, **20** (May 1958), pp. 146–152.
[55]Ibid., p. 149.
[56]Ibid., p. 150.

reluctance to bring criminal proceedings against such men arises out of fear that such action would only further alienate them from their families and in the process make reconciliation efforts all the more difficult. Moreover, it is recognized that jailing the husband actually compounds the immediate problem of financial support because it effectively prevents him from earning an income. Most contemporary social workers and domestic court authorities would probably agree with Steigman's statement: "One should not resort to arresting a deserting husband, even when the arrest is not motivated by vindictiveness, if alternative means are available for working out problems of financial support."[57]

Although desertion accounts for one of the most serious types of broken families, surprisingly little research has been undertaken concerning the major consequences of this kind of marital disruption and the various role adjustments it requires on the part of the families involved. Although such consequences and adjustments are in many ways similar to those involved in divorce, in other ways they are different.[58] The deserted wife, for example, is in the highly frustrating position of having a legal husband but one who is not physically available, and she may be in this position for a considerable period of time. Legally, she cannot remarry until a divorce is obtained or her husband dies. Women who have been deserted experience varying degrees of role ambiguity emanating from vague and contradictory normative expectations concerning appropriate behavior. The manner in which they resolve this ambiguous social situation represents an important area for empirical inquiry.

SEPARATION There are two rather different types of separation: those that have been legally adjudicated and legally recognized and those that have not. The former differ from divorce only in that the couple are not free to remarry. A property settlement and arrangements for the care of children are included in the legal separation. In most instances, this arrangement is made by couples who find divorce difficult for religious reasons.

Among those informally separated, two subclasses can be distinguished: desertion, in which one or the other takes unilateral action by simply leaving the household and usually the community. The other subclass follows a mutual agreement to live separately, each maintaining his own residence. This differs from legal separation in that the couple are free at any time to resume living together if they wish.

---

[57]Joseph E. Steigman, "The Deserted Family," *Social Casework*, **38** (March 1957), pp. 167–171.

[58]For an elaboration of these differences, see Kephart, *The Family, Society, and the Individual,* op. cit., pp. 595–599. See also Samuel H. Lerner, "Effects of Desertion on Family Life," *Social Casework*, **35** (Jan. 1954), pp. 3–8.

Presumably, separations by mutual agreement involve property, child support, and other arrangements that are more satisfactory to both spouses than those taken unilaterally by one spouse.[59]

What happens to the wives, husbands, and children following a divorce? What types of partial and reconstructed families develop to replace the former family? What new roles must be learned and old ones unlearned? In Chapter 20 we shall explore these sequels to divorce.

[59]In some ways, separation, particularly the informal type, creates greater difficulties and stresses for the spouses and children than divorce. See, for example, Rose DeWolf, *The Bonds of Acrimony* (Philadelphia: J. B. Lippincott Co., 1970).

19

On the Causes of Divorce

We have seen in the past chapter that the long-range trend of divorce has been upward. Sociologists have advanced several reasons that merit thoughtful evaluation.

The Trend Toward Higher Divorce Rates

INCREASED INDEPENDENCE OF INDIVIDUALS By now, the student is sufficiently familiar with the idea of declining family functions. It might be more stimulating to view the individual as more liberated from such complete dependence on a particular group. The family once did "everything"; therefore, a person was extremely dependent on the family. True, this resulted in a low divorce rate, but it provided few options for individuals caught in a group that could not meet their needs.

With the continuing differentiation and mechanization of society, the individual can now meet his clothing needs at a department store, can rent a furnished apartment rather than being compelled to build a house, can obtain food precooked or in a restaurant, and so on. Thus, the individual is no longer at the mercy of a marriage or family relationship that locks him into a frustrated or unproductive life. True, marital dissolution has its costs, also, which will be reviewed later.

In one sense, the individual is more dependent on his fellows than ever before, because he creates a smaller proportion of the goods and services that he requires, but he can obtain more of them from sources other than the family, so he is less bound to it.

AFFLUENCE AND PERMISSIVE ATTITUDES Professional and lay people alike have commented on the greater social acceptability of divorce and have given a more accepting attitude as a cause of the rise in divorce

489

rates. The present task is not to question the more permissive attitudes but to ask why they have occurred. Our thesis is that attitudes are more permissive because the consequences of divorce are typically less catastrophic. Still, divorce is intrinsically expensive, at least in independent nuclear families. After the dissolution of the marriage, the husband must purchase food preparation, the care of a house or an apartment, the care of clothing, and, in seeking female companionship, must purchase recreation. Two cannot live nearly as cheaply apart as together, and a remarriage of the husband further adds to total expenses. In a society with higher incomes, in which many women can earn a salary, it is possible to dissolve a marriage and yet have all family members provided for above a subsistence level. Also, an affluent society provides a type of "divorce insurance" through its public welfare programs, in which the society collectively assumes some of the costs of divorce.

The question is sometimes raised whether public welfare programs do not increase marital dissolution because they enable mothers to support themselves without a husband. It is undoubtedly true in some instances that such programs enable a couple (or the women only) to terminate a bad marriage. However, these programs should not be viewed as some type of separate cause of divorce. They are a strategic arrangement by which a society that places a high value on individual welfare and individual needs and a relatively permissive attitude toward divorce provides some amelioration of the consequences of divorce among the lowest income groups. There would be little point in accusing a program of causing divorce unless the society is ready to take a more restrictive attitude toward divorce and to value group stability over individual needs. It is probably true, also, that few couples, when deciding on a divorce, recognize the extra financial costs entailed and anticipate that the wife and the children will require welfare assistance. Attitudes toward divorce are more tolerant than a generation ago, but this is neither mysterious or inexplicable—the society and its capacities and capabilities have changed so that more divorces can be tolerated and more autonomy can be granted individuals.

It is frequently asserted that adults today expect more from marriage and from their occupations and interests outside of marriage. This seems to be true and for the same reason: more individualism and more opportunity to pursue individual interests are possible in an affluent, differentiated society. In a society functioning at a subsistence level, the primary concern must be focused on survival, but in an affluent society there are optional resources, some of which can be invested in greater autonomy for its members.

490

It follows that if attitudes are more permissive toward divorce, its costs become less; that is, divorces are less vigorously opposed by extended family, friends, and associates and the penalties imposed on the divorced become less. The perception that divorce is followed by less severe consequences tends in itself to reduce opposition to divorce.

Finally, one can ask whether or not sociology itself has not played a part in producing a more tolerant attitude toward divorce. Researchers have studied the effects on children and have found that children of divorced parents have, in more instances, fared better than those from intact families in which there is chronic conflict. This proposition will be discussed in more detail in the following chapter. Likewise, researchers find that most younger divorced persons remarry soon, so that a divorce usually does not limit the individual to single life. How influential have these findings been to date?

In a word, then, the more permissive attitude toward divorce apparently stems from a more affluent society that can absorb the extra costs of divorce without necessarily neglecting other economic needs.

INTRINSIC TO INSTRUMENTAL PERSPECTIVE Dissolution may be viewed either as an evil (intrinsically bad) or as a negative or a positive step, depending on its consequences (instrumental). American society appears to have been making the transition from viewing it as an evil to treating each case more or less separately.

This change is illustrated by a study of novels published between 1858 and 1937 in which divorce was the central theme: there was a definite change from concern over the fact of divorce, to the effects of divorce on children, to the question of alimony, and later to the problem of postdivorce adjustment. Because consequences follow the action, they cannot form the basis for a decision. The anticipated consequences for the wife, the husband, the children, and for the extended family or ADC, which may, following the dissolution, have to support the mother and children, become the basis for the approval or disapproval of a proposed divorce.

The change from intrinsic valuation to instrumental valuation of divorce tends to refocus attention on the problems associated with divorce, and action is directed toward the amelioration of such consequences rather than the opposition of divorce *in toto.* Also, as the following chapter will show, research and clinical findings disclose that much of the family pathology is present before a divorce, not caused by it. Such evidence focuses attention on the prevention of family pathology instead of total opposition to measures that are taken in response to malfunctioning.

491

Perspectives on Divorce

SOCIAL AND PSYCHOLOGICAL PERSPECTIVE The social and psychological perspective on divorce has, not surprisingly, differed considerably. Psychologists look for inadequate or confused personalities as the source of marital difficulties. Mudd presented this perspective several years ago in a conference on divorce:

It is often contended that the most prevalent reason for divorce is the lack of maturity of one or both partners. If both partners are, emotionally speaking, children, spoiled and stunted in development, can social case work aid them in growing? . . . If any of us, lay or professional, should see two ten-year-old children biting, scratching, and beating each other, would we leave them to batter each other until they voluntarily asked someone to help them stop? No, of course we would not! Then why should case work or any other arm of society remove its assistance from the thousands of "ten-year-olds" who are destroying each other in marriage, cruelly, painfully, and often unwittingly?[1]

Personal inadequacy seems to be the basic assumption of the psychological perspective. To prevent or to ameliorate marital stress, attention is focused on these inadequacies.

Psychoanalytic writing provides a major variant in psychological perspective. It views marital problems as arising from personality malformation dating from early experience in the family. Waller and Hill described this perspective as follows:

A psychoanalytic interpretation of divorce would lead us to think of it as arising from factors deeply ingrained in the personalities of the participants, deposited there from early experiences in their own parental families. Thus, a man may have been reared in such a way as to make him dependent upon women, so that he cannot find happiness except in leaning upon a strong female character. If he chances to marry a dependent, feminine type of woman, there ensues a relentless struggle over the question who shall be leaned upon by whom, and divorce is the probable outcome. Or it may occur that one selects a certain type of person as a love object because of supposed characteristics which it is to be presumed that one needs in a marriage partner, but one finds after marriage that the person lacks these characteristics. Even if one has not been deceived in his choice, it may happen, largely because of ambivalences, that the sort of person whom one can love is not the sort that one can live with happily, and divorce ensues. Or perhaps one marries a mother substitute, and the woman indeed plays out this role, but it turns out after all that this is not a sufficient basis for the erotic life of marriage. Or a man has a peculiar split in his love attitudes; he can love ideally only a woman who satisfies his need for a mother substitute, but he is sexually incapable except with a woman of a

---

[1]Law School, University of Chicago, *Conference on Divorce,* Conference Series Number 9 (Feb. 1952), pp. 68–69.

492

different type; unless he can reunite his love attitudes, he is likely to face divorce. Various other sorts of pathological love choices create their own particular problems.[2]

Sociological perspective differs from these points of view at several points while being compatible at others. It views behavior in the special perspective of marital and parental roles. The relevant and crucial behavior of the spouses is in their provider, child-care, child-socialization, housekeeper, and other roles. Sociologists see the normative content of these roles as gradually changing and evolving, and they see the family norms in constant interaction with the norms in the economic and political institutions. Sociological perspective, then, views family behavior in the distinctive roles of the family in the larger setting of the society. This view allows the sociologist to interpret changes in the dissolution rate over time and between social classes and in other meaningful milieu of the society. Sociological perspective, we feel, is more adequate for explaining changes in the divorce rate, which rise at the end of wars and during prosperous periods and decline following the postwar peaks and during depressions. The relatively high rate of success in the remarriage of persons who have been divorced seems better explained by sociological perspective, as does the higher divorce rate in the lower class and in heterogeneous marriages. Again, the marriage that has functioned adequately for twenty years and then ends when the youngest child leaves home is unnecessarily difficult to explain by psychological concepts.

At one major point the two perspectives coalesce. Competent role-playing is central to adequate marriage and family life. Immaturity may well be described as the inability or unwillingness of young men and women to enact provider or child-care roles. Likewise, malformation of personality as described by the psychoanalysts may prevent adequate role enactment in marriage. To the extent that this is true, the two perspectives touch. Because this is a text on the sociology of the family, the psychological perspective will not be pursued here. The reader is referred to our earlier book[3] and to Hess and Handel[4] and to Flugel[5] for examples and discussion of the psychological framework applied to the family.

[2]Willard Waller and Reuben Hill, *The Family* (New York: The Dryden Press, 1952), p. 509.

[3]F. Ivan Nye and Felix M. Berardo, *Emerging Conceptual Frameworks in Family Analysis* (New York: The Macmillan Company, 1966), Chapters 7 and 8.

[4]Robert D. Hess and Gerald Handel, *Family Worlds, A Psychological Approach to Family Life* (Chicago: The University of Chicago Press, 1959). See also Gerald Handel (ed.), *The Psychosocial Interior of the Family* (Chicago: Aldine Publishing Company, 1967).

[5]John C. Flugel, *The Psycho-Analytical Study of the Family* (London: Hogarth Press, 1921).

493

MALE-FEMALE PERSPECTIVE Is divorce generally attributable to husbands or wives? This question is discussed in most treatises on the family, but often the assumption is made that the initiative is usually from the husband. The fact that some three fourths of divorce actions are filed by women is explained by the chivalric attitude of the male.

These assumptions *may* be true but we believe the evidence is weak and contradictory. In the first place, the proportion of the divorce actions that are filed by women has increased over the past two decades. Is chivalry really experiencing a revival? Further, Goode found that 63 per cent of the divorced women queried said that they had been the first to raise the question of divorce. Why, then, are men so ready to accept the responsibility for divorce? We will explore briefly some of the apparent assumptions and indicate why they seem to be ill-founded.

Marriage has been considered a more desired status for women than for men. If this is true, then isn't it reasonable that more marriages are broken by male than by female initiative? Possibly, if a broken marriage meant a permanent return to single status, but this isn't true because the great majority of both sexes remarry.[6] The woman who takes the initiative in divorce is not necessarily rejecting marriage, only a husband. The fact that family roles play a more central place in women's than in men's lives does not mean that women are more content to live in a family group that deprives and frustrates them. It can be argued that they would be more eager to escape a bad marriage. Almost all men physically depart from their homes and families when they go to work, but many women do not. It appears that marriage means more to the woman's life—more gratifying if it is good, more frustrating if it is mediocre.

Another assumption is that husbands encounter more unattached women in the course of their daily lives, whereas wives are more restricted in their contacts. Thus, men have more opportunities to become attached to other women. Although the opportunities are more frequent, husbands generally are not seeking other attachments that would complicate their lives and perhaps lead to a divorce, to a loss of home and family, and to remarriage and even more complex responsibilities. Men have more contact with single members of the opposite sex but they prefer to keep these from emotional levels that would lead to serious triangle situations.

If women bring most of the divorce actions, do men provide most of the legal grounds for divorce? Apparently so. It has been true that the central place of the provider role in the malfunctioning family and the

---

[6]Of those divorced between 1934 and 1943, about 85 per cent had remarried by 1948. Paul Glick, "First Marriages and Remarriages," *American Sociological Review,* **14** (Dec. 1949), p. 733.

provider role in *industrial societies* is assigned to men. (This isn't necessarily true in nonindustrial societies.) As noted earlier, the provider role is a difficult one in a free enterprise economy in that it requires that some employer be available to offer employment. Family problems due to inadequate provider functioning are attributed to the husband. Because of the relevance of strength, physical cruelty is usually a complaint against the husband rather than the wife. Conviction and incarceration for criminal behavior is primarily due to male behavior. Adultery, also, is a more common act among husbands than wives.

It is evident that most of the grounds for divorce in American society focus on male behavior. In agrarian societies, childlessness has been an important ground for divorce but children are less crucial in industrial societies. Other female offences against the marriage, such as being a poor cook, a poor disciplinarian, or an unresponsive sexual partner do not appear as legal grounds for divorce. These may be distressing to the husband but they are not regarded as threatening to society and therefore do not appear as legal grounds for divorce. Moreover, husbands have more means of neutralizing the disliked behavior of their wives or compensating for inadequacies in their marriages. A husband's work takes him away from home as a normal event, providing other activity and a group of associates. Many travel, spending considerable time away from home. Bars and cocktail lounges are utilized more by husbands than wives, and even for meeting sexual needs alternatives are more available to the husband.

Finally, it is useful to look at categories of families that have high dissolution rates. Conspicuous are the high rates in the lower social class and among blacks. It is not evident why a higher proportion of lower-class and Negro men should seek divorce, but there is a strong rationale for female initiative: large proportions of these men cannot and do not enact the provider role satisfactorily.

We have presented a thesis that initiative for divorce probably comes more frequently from the wife than the husband. We have shown that legal grounds for divorce encompass mostly male behavior, that males have more alternative means of meeting needs without a divorce, and that in obtaining a divorce, most women do not give up marriage—only a particular marital partner. In this thesis we take issue with many writers.

Permanent Availability

The facts on divorce rates, trends, and the prevalence of remarriage in American society have led sociologists to conceptualize marriage in somewhat untraditional thought. The term *sequential marriage* or

495

sequential monogamy has been employed. However, because a majority of marriages have been permanent, this term is likely to be misleading because it describes, at most, a minority.

Farber has developed a related concept, that of *permanent availability.*[7] Of it, he writes:

each individual, at least theoretically, is permanently available as a potential mate to all other cross-sex individuals. An important point here is that being married does not restrict an individual with respect to his future potentiality as a mate in later marriages.[8]

The family group takes the form of a voluntary association in which a person continues membership as long as his personal commitment to the other family members exceeds his commitments elsewhere.[9]

neither time nor prior marriage, including current married status, reduces availability of the individual as a mate.[10]

Contemporary American marriage is viewed by Farber as a voluntary matter for each individual with no especial interest in the matter either by the extended family or by society. Kin have no interest because the young adult establishes an independent family and is not regarded as a resource to his kinship group. Permanent availability implies that "all members of a society face a constant pressure to be highly competent in interpersonal relations if they wish to maintain their current marriage and remain in a favorable competitive position in the perennial marriage market."[11]

To the extent that individuals see themselves as permanently available through divorce for remarriage to new partners, divorce is encouraged. The theory implies that divorce can be explained by the greater attractions of new spouses. It implies that one is expected to better his lot in society by moving on to more attractive marital partners in somewhat the same way one would move to a new position that offered a higher salary or better working conditions. It assumes that the norm of permanent marriage has been replaced by the norm of permanent availability.

To the extent that the concept of permanent availability corresponds to the real world, it is useful in describing a high and increasing divorce rate. Indeed, if it corresponded entirely to reality, we should be hard pressed to explain the two thirds or so of all marriages that last for a lifetime.

---

[7]The present discussion of Farber's model is concerned only with the aspects relevant to divorce. For a complete discussion, see Bernard Farber, *Family: Organization and Interaction* (San Francisco: Chandler Publishing Co., 1964).

[8]Ibid., p. 109.

[9]Ibid., p. 110.

[10]Ibid., p. 112.

[11]Ibid., p. 478.

It is our feeling that a small number of people subscribe to the principle of permanent availability as described. However, the norm of permanent marriage still stands, in the sense that it is the preferred and expected pattern of marriage of a large majority. A stigma, albeit a lessening one, is attached to divorce. A divorce still calls forth negative reactions and is seen as regrettable, if no worse. However, the norm of permanent marriage is relatively weak, as numerous exceptions or loopholes provide adequate justification for many couples. Sanctions grow weaker but do not disappear. Kin and society still have an interest in marital stability, partly because a divorce may result in some of the provider or child-care roles being shifted to kin or tax-supported agencies. Although the concept of permanent availability is a stimulating one, we shall make it clear that we view marital dissolution as primarily a failure of spouses to attain an expected level of role enactment rather than the positive attraction of alternate spouses. We don't accept the idea that couples typically marry provisionally, until a better prospect comes into view.　*good !*

Levels of Involvement

In viewing causes of marital dissolution it is useful to devote some attention to the nature of the relationship that is being dissolved. Some divorces occur after only a few days, others after a few years, and still others after most of the adult life of the couples.

THE ABORTED MARRIAGE A casual look at the divorce statistics would lead one to think that the critical period in marriage is the second or third year because divorce rates are highest then. However, there is a considerable period of delay between the time a couple decides to divorce, the filing of the divorce suit, and the granting of the decree. Monahan found this period to average 3.2 years.[12] He states that it is in the *first* year that the largest number of couples decide that their marriage is a mistake.

In this type of marriage, the couple never establish a marriage as a going concern. In some cases the couple hasn't established a normal sexual relationship, in some the husband has been unemployed or for other reasons has not provided an economic basis for the couple, many have not established their own household, and others have found in the responsibilities and limitations of marriage a life quite different from their stereotype of it.

In viewing this variety of reasons for the nonestablishment of a general marital relationship, we may distinguish two more general

[12]Thomas Monahan, "When Married Couples Part: Statistical Trends and Relationships in Divorce," *American Sociological Review,* **27** (Oct. 1962), pp. 625–634.

types. In the first are couples one or both of which are not ready to enact the adult work roles normative to marriage. This may be for lack of training, lack of experience in work roles, or lack of adequate perception of adult roles. These are the special problems of young marriages but are not limited to young marriages. The other type of abortive marriage stems from an immediate realization that one has married someone with whom he does not wish to spend his life. The reason may be primarily an inadequate acquaintance with the other or what we might think of as inadequate motivation. For example, the woman just wanted to get married, not necessarily to this one man, or the man had an especially strong desire for sexual intercourse without a more general attraction to the woman. Finally, we may distinguish a third type of short marriage that is deviant even in its objectives, that is, a planned short-term marriage to legitimize a sexual adventure. These have been termed weekend marriages, which may take place Friday evening with divorce action filed Monday! They may be mutually agreed upon or may be in the plans of only one of the couple. A middle-aged divorcee described her second marriage as follows: "We got married and went on a honeymoon up to Canada. When we got back he said he didn't want to set up housekeeping. 'Suppose you keep the diamond engagement ring I gave you and we'll call it square.' I said o.k., and that was the end of it."

Our thesis is that a sizable minority of marital dissolutions involve these abortive marriages—marriages that, although the couple have legally married, have not resulted in the establishment of a set of functioning relationships and in the couple's enacting the family roles that are necessary for a permanent marriage. Although legally the marriage has existed, socially and psychologically it has never been fully established. The dissolution of these marriages tends to have minimal consequences for the individuals involved and for society, except in instances in which children are conceived. In the latter case, if the marriage is aborted because of unreadiness for adult role-playing, the wife and child are likely to have to be supported by public assistance or by the wife's parents.

MEDIOCRELY FUNCTIONING FAMILIES In contrast to the abortive marriage, in which spouses fail to enact familial roles even at marginal level, the mediocrely functioning marriage achieves at least this much. The man is generally employed and the wife makes a commitment to keeping the house orderly, the food prepared, and the children cared for. A sexual relationship is established. Life can be lived in this group milieu. Some couples live this way for a lifetime. However, the material level of living is not very high, the house is not very attractive, the children bring minimal satisfactions, the food is not very good, and the sexual life is devoid of much excitement or gratification. As a consequence, there is not much positive affect among family members and

498

quarreling and negative affect may be common. This type of family may continue indefinitely but it is vulnerable. Boredom, with an unrewarding life and a preference to return to single status, may disrupt this type of marriage.

A divorce in this type of marriage may have minimal emotional effects because the marriage has not been characterized by intense positive affect, but socially it often creates problems because it usually involves minor children and the husband's earnings are unlikely to be sufficient to support two households. Wife and children may have to be supported through public assistance or may have to live at a submarginal economic level. If the husband continues to support them, he may be unable to remarry. One or both spouses may be relieved to be free of the compulsory associations of the marriage but may find that the extra expense of living apart places great strain on their limited resources.

INTERRUPTED FUNCTIONING MARRIAGES In a third category, we place marriages that once functioned well and were characterized by strong positive affect. These are marriages that at one time were satisfying to both spouses. They may end in dissolution in several ways. A strong attachment may develop for someone outside the marriage. Because both spouses are effective role players they may be intrinsically attractive to unattached persons. Two examples have recently come to our attention in which the husband became sexually involved with a young, unattached woman, fathered an illegitimate child, and then felt obligated to divorce his wife and marry the girl. In other instances the role-playing of one spouse, which has been notably effective, becomes inadequate; for example, the husband becomes an alcoholic or the woman stops devoting attention to her appearance.

It is these interrupted functioning marriages that cause deep traumas such as have been described by Waller[13] and Kirkpatrick.[14] Because these divorces usually occur later in marriage than the others, children are sometimes grown and less affected and wife and children are unlikely to require welfare or kin support. Even so, if the wife has been out of the labor force for a decade or more the divorce may bring a considerable reduction in her level of living.

We have tried to show that marriages vary greatly by the type of relationships that exist between the spouses and the length of time the marriage spans. The *aborted* marriages can almost be called nonmarriages, because they never fully existed in a sociological sense. The *minimum* functioning marriages have never functioned entirely adequately and, therefore, have never developed the deepest emotional

---

[13]Willard Waller, *The Old Love and the New* (Carbondale and Edwardsville: Southern Illinois Press, republished in 1967).

[14]Clifford Kirkpatrick, *The Family as Process and Institution* (New York: The Ronald Press Company, 1955), Chapter 22, "Deciding About Divorce," pp. 604–634.

ties. However, their dissolution after a period of years often leaves personal problems in unmet sexual needs and in difficult financial problems. Finally, *interrupted functioning* marriages frequently, although not always, create for one or both spouses traumas that have been described by Waller, Kirkpatrick, and others.

A Partial Theory of Marital Dissolution

We have seen that industrialization has created a society so differentiated in its structure that the single person can live in it with a reasonable degree of comfort. The single woman can provide for herself and be protected by a special agency, the police. The single man can have his clothing cared for, his food prepared, and a variety of commercial recreation provided. Further, the single, including the divorced and widowed, have large numbers of persons of like status with whom they can associate and from whom they can find spouses. Finally, welfare programs have been devised to meet the minimum needs of some hardship cases involving women and children. This type of society provides an alternative to unsatisfactory marriages as do the consanguineous family systems of some preliterate societies. Finally, the evolution toward a differentiated society is continuing. The limitations on the status of the unmarried are likely to become still less in the future. Finally, Farber has proposed that in this type of society, the decision to marry does not carry a final commitment for life; that is, adults are permanently available for remarriage.

These changes provide insight into the growth of the divorce rate but tell us very little about why some marriages dissolve whereas most do not. As we have noted, the psychologists view this question through a framework of personal inadequacy and maladaptive childhood experience. Although the sociologists need not argue the invalidity of personal abilities and motivation, he sees them more clearly in the behavior of individuals in the specific context of their enactment of family roles. For example, it is indirectly relevant for a father to be industrious but it is directly relevant that he provide well for his family. Although the correlation between being industrious and being an able provider is high, it is by no means perfect. For example, one father of three young children was not working at all. He had patented a successful invention and was providing well for his family but presumably would have scored "indolent" on a psychological measure.

Sociological research and theory-building, then, have occurred within the framework of role-playing, reference groups, and of social characteristics relevant to the roles, norms, and values of the family. Within this general framework, there has been a voluminous amount of research and speculation on the causes of marital dissolution. From this large and growing body of reports and sociological thinking, we have abstracted some theoretical ideas about divorce,[15] some of which are included in the following discussion.

Marital dissolution may be defined rather simply as the dissolving of a socially recognized marital arrangement. It includes divorce, desertion, and permanent, voluntary separation. It does *not* include anything concerning marital satisfaction, levels of communication between spouses, or effectiveness of role-playing.

ROLE PERFORMANCE AND EXCHANGE IN DIVORCE Reference has been made to the necessity for minimum levels of family role performance if a marriage is to be established initially and to continue. Allusion has also been made to the fact that divorce rates are low where role performance is relatively high (low divorce rates in higher income families). The word *relatively* should be stressed for, as Cutright emphasizes, divorce rates are relatively lower in the higher income levels of any society, regardless of the absolute amount of income that is earned.[16] Glick and Norton document this proposition dramatically with annual census data from the entire United States. In Figure 19.1 (from their work) it can be seen that the divorce rate is three times as high in the lowest compared to the highest income category.[17]

These observations can be placed within a more systematic frame of reference in which a marriage is viewed as an exchange of services and cooperative activities within a normative framework. The general theory to be utilized is that of Thibaut and Kelley.[18] The key concepts are *rewards, costs,* and *profits.* These are general terms that refer to objects, activities, or feelings that are rewarding or costly to a person. For example, a feeling of frustration or insecurity is a *cost* in this theoretical scheme. A *comparison level* is what a person feels he should receive in his exchanges with his spouse. A *comparison level for alternatives* as employed here is a comparison of the profits in another relationship with those in the one in which he is now engaged.

In marriage, the rewards that each spouse furnishes to the other are encompassed in their role performances. For example, the husband

[15]Adapted from two papers by F. Ivan Nye, Lynn White, and James Frideres, "A Partial Theory of Family Stability," read before the National Council on Family Relations, Minneapolis, 1966, and "A Preliminary Theory of Marital Dissolution," read before the American Sociological Association, Boston, 1968.

[16]Philipps Cutright, "Income and Family Events: Marital Stability," *Journal of Marriage and the Family,* **33** (May 1971), pp. 291–307. Apropos of this point, average income is higher in the United States than in Japan or Western European nations but so, also, is its divorce rate. Income is currently (1972) increasing in the United States but so, also, is the divorce rate. It is the *relatively* high income within a society that is related to a low divorce rate.

[17]Paul C. Glick and Arthur J. Norton, "Frequency, Duration and Probability of Marriage and Divorce," *Journal of Marriage and the Family,* **33** (May 1971), p. 314.

[18]John W. Thibaut and Harold H. Kelley, *The Social Psychology of Groups* (New York: John Wiley & Sons, 1959).

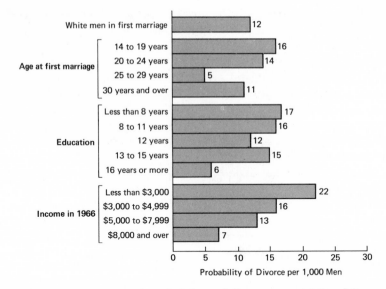

Figure 19.1. Average annual probability of divorce per 1,000 white men in their first marriage less than 5 years by selected characteristics: 1960–1966. [From Paul C. Glick and Arthur J. Norton, "Frequency, Duration, and Probability of Marriage and Divorce," *Journal of Marriage and the Family,* **33** (May 1971), p. 314. Reprinted by permission.]

rewards the wife by performing the provider role and thereby furnishing the material objects and services needed by the family. The wife rewards the husband by performing the housekeeper role, preparing food, caring for his clothing, and cleaning the habitation. Through the norms, each has an expectation of what the other should do or what he *ought* to receive from his spouse in exchange for the services he provides. The norms defining the appropriate role performance are established by the society but may be modified by the social class or by the ethnic or other subcultural group with which the couple identify themselves. Finally, the expectation is modified for each person by his perception of what others like himself receive. Insofar as he receives from his spouse what he *ought* to receive, he is satisfied with the marriage. It must be remembered that all the family roles are involved, not just one or two. A man may be satisfied with his wife as a housekeeper but dissatisfied with her as a sexual or recreational partner.

It must be added that the level of costs in the marriage are perhaps equally relevant. A woman's decision to seek a divorce may be influenced by her being beaten by her husband, or a wife may put excessive pressure on her husband to earn a high income, or either may be unwilling to allow the other any autonomy to pursue individual interests. These costs, as well as the rewards furnished by the role-

502

playing of the spouse, enter into the comparison level that leads to a conclusion that one is getting what he deserves or more or less than that.

Ordinarily, if a spouse feels that his marital situation is at or above his comparison level, he will not initiate or be interested in a divorce. If both spouses view the marriage in this way, the marriage is likely to be considered a happy one and is unlikely to be terminated by divorce, separation, or desertion.

However, it is possible that a marriage in which each spouse views the marriage as satisfactory may be broken by interaction with a third party. This third person may provide an even more profitable exchange with one spouse (or may appear to promise one). In this event, the *comparison level for alternatives* is higher than the profit in the marriage and the marriage may be broken. The qualification *may* is necessary because there are a variety of costs involved in divorce and these may be so high that the alternative marriage would not be profitable when the total costs of the divorce are taken into account.

This general theory may also account for the occasional happy marriage that is disrupted following a sexual affair of the husband with an unmarried girl. If she becomes pregnant, the husband may decide it is his duty to divorce his wife to protect his mistress. In this instance guilt over causing the pregnancy increases the costs of the original marriage until the remarriage appears more "profitable," even though otherwise he would prefer the original marriage.

Finally, value congruence or conflict should be brought into the discussion. If spouses have about the same values, they can reward themselves as they reward their spouse. If both like to travel, the husband can reward his wife with a vacation journey while enjoying it himself. If he dislikes travel, the same activity in rewarding his wife becomes costly to him. Thus compromises in which the couple follow her interests one week and his another are costly and have relatively low profits, because one is rewarded only every second week and the activity of the alternative week is costly.

In this application of sociopsychological theory to marital stability, role performance is a key concept. Without a minimal level, the marriage may not become a functioning reality. If all roles are performed at a level that leads the spouse to feel that he is receiving what he should (or more) in marriage, he will be satisfied and unlikely to initiate a divorce. However, if a third person intrudes, offering a higher profit in an alternative marriage, he may seek a divorce if its costs do not appear prohibitively high. Finally, marriages of couples with similar values provide higher profits in marriage and therefore have a higher probability of stability than those in which there are major value conflicts.

20

Sequel to Divorce

In 1971 an estimated 768,000 marriages ended legally in divorce or annulment. Actually, most had ended months or years earlier when one or the other of the couple moved out of their common abode. Then what? Just as life doesn't begin with marriage, it obviously doesn't end with divorce. What happens to husbands, wives, and children and how do their familial roles change with the dissolution of the family?

Living Arrangements

Currently, about three in five divorces involve children. Of those that do not, the husband and wife revert to a type of single status, although there is no normative expectation that they will return to live with their parents. Women are likely to move into apartments; men do the same or enter boarding establishments.

For families with children, a greater variety of arrangements occur. The custody of the children is usually awarded to the mother. The arrangement followed by most who are financially solvent is for the wife to remain in the family abode with the husband seeking new quarters. If finances do not permit this arrangement, mother and children may move to less expensive housing or move in with the mother's parents. Census data for 1971 disclosed some 716,000 children, with no fathers present, living with their mothers in their grandparents' homes.[1] The mothers and their children in this arrangement are classified by the census as "secondary families."

STAYING WITH RELATIVES In some instances in which the parent can't or won't maintain a separate residence, the child is left with

[1]U.S. Census of Population, *Marital Status and Living Arrangements* Series P-20, #225 (Nov. 1971), p. 19.

504

grandparents, an aunt, an uncle, or other relatives. Smith refers to this as intermediate care,[2] assuming that it will last only until the parent makes other arrangements. In fact, this is usually true, but some children following divorce are reared to adulthood by some other relative. In other instances, the child is left for a time with relatives, then picked up by the parent for a time, then returned to that relative or another one, depending on the success of remarriage or the success of the parent in financing and arranging for day care or a housekeeper.

Smith comments negatively on the grandmothers as substitute mothers, noting their general tendency to spoil the child:

Grandparents, particularly grandmothers, tend to exercise a baneful influence over their grandchildren. In reading records, one finds a refrain like the following repeated over and over again: "The children had been sent to their grandparents' home. There they had been utterly spoiled, permitted to have their own way in everything." This holds true even in so-called normal situations; but, when a step-relationship enters the picture, the detrimental influence usually becomes manifold.[3]

It should be noted however, that it is usually the children of the less effective parents who are left with relatives. Some of the detrimental effects credited to grandparents might be more validly credited to the parents. There is doubt, also, about the attitudes of grandparents toward becoming, in effect, parents again. Smith notes that with younger age at marriage, there are millions of grandparents between the ages of forty-five and sixty-five whose children have left home, leaving them with little to do and an eagerness to reenter a meaningful role. However, Stone, in an empirical study, found that couples over sixty-five who were rearing grandchildren were more likely to express dissatisfaction with their lives.[4] It may be that the two positions are not contradictory because Smith refers to the forty-five to sixty-five aggregate, whereas Stone's study population was over sixty-five. It might be that even the younger grandparents would not care to have complete responsibility for children once they had experience with it.

The number of children living with grandparents is large, over three fourths of a million in 1971—with about another 150,000 living with aunts, uncles, and other relatives.[5]

CHILDREN IN ONE-PARENT FAMILIES Most children following a divorce will live for a time with one parent, then with a step-parent,

[2]William C. Smith, *The Stepchild* (Chicago: University of Chicago Press, 1953), Chapter 15, pp. 134–141.
[3]Ibid., pp. 136–137.
[4]Carol L. Stone and Walter L. Slocum, *Thurston County's Older People*, Washington Agricultural Experiment Station's Bulletin 573 (May 1957), Washington State University, Pullman.
[5]Census of Population, op. cit., p. 19.

because most of the divorced remarry—almost half within two years[6]—and, as we have seen, some of the children will have lived for a time with other relatives. Eventually over five sixths of the divorced will remarry. For the young divorced, the remarriage rate is much higher.

Families in which children are living with one parent we term *partial families* to distinguish them from the normative model with two parents. The *partial family* of mother and children has become a major type in American society. In 1971, 8,714,000 children under 18 were listed as living with the mother only, which was 12 per cent of all children under 18, or viewed another way, one child in 8 was living with his mother only.[7]

The number of partial families headed by fathers is much smaller, yet in absolute numbers it is considerable, about 764,000 in 1971. This is about one-eleventh the number living with the mother.

If the partial families headed by mothers and fathers are combined, we find that about 13 per cent of all children under 18 were living with one parent only—ten of eleven of these with the mother. If the number who are living with relatives other than a parent are added, over 9 million were living with one parent or a relative, or almost one child in seven.

TRANSITIONAL AND PERMANENT ARRANGEMENTS How do people live after a divorce? For children there are usually two sequential arrangements. Preceding the divorce decree and for a few years following, they live with one parent, usually the mother, or a grandparent or other relative. Following this period, the parent remarries, and the child lives with a parent and a step-parent. In about two thirds of the cases this will be his mother and a step-father.[8] Because over six sevenths of divorced persons remarry, most children of a divorced couple will live with a step-parent during some part of their childhood, except for the one in six divorces that occur after children have left home. Because the remarriage rate is high for the young divorced, almost all very young children of divorces will live for a time with a step-parent. In a minority of cases, because the *redivorce* rate is about one in three, living with a step-parent will be followed by another divorce and living again with one parent, usually the mother, or another relative.

FAMILY OF ORIENTATION AND THE DIVORCED In societies with consanguine families, the husband would return to his parents, the wife and children to hers. Although this happens with some frequency in American society, Goode points out that the norms do not define it as a

---

[6]Paul H. Jacobson, *American Marriage and Divorce* (New York: Rinehart, 1959), pp. 69–70.

[7]U.S. Census of Population, op. cit., p. 19.

[8]Smith, op. cit., p. 197.

duty either for the grandparents to reabsorb their divorced adult children or for the latter to return to the parental home. The decision is made on the basis of personal sentiments, rather than duty.[9]

This phenomenon can be placed in a broader societal perspective; namely, that children, whatever their marital status, are expected to move out of the parental home as soon as they reach adult status. The single may continue to board at home, but this is based on personal sentiments. Parents have no duty to provide an abode for their adult children nor children to continue to live at home. In many instances marriage provides the occasion for leaving the parental abode, but many have already moved out and, if marriage is delayed, the expectation is that the young adult will find his own housing. It is less that there is no duty for parents to reabsorb the divorced, but more that there is no normative expectation that the young adults will continue to live at home indefinitely.

For a moment, let us explore *why* this norm is characteristic of current American society. Employment is by individuals, not family groups. The young adult is usually of no assistance in the family enterprise because there are few family enterprises, unlike the case in many preliterate societies, in which the family is the chief unit of production. Therefore, there is no need for the unmarried adult to live at home. More likely his employment will make it more convenient for him to live elsewhere. For him to live at home creates an inefficient group. It restricts his autonomy, because in most matters the parents will make the family decisions. It compromises the autonomy of parents because they must take his needs into account. All have less privacy than if he moved into his own quarters. Therefore, in a differentiated society, adult children are likely to live away from their parents' abode whether or not they are married.

Two conditions may lead the divorced woman to return to the parental family: inability to find or keep employment that will support her and her children or the presence of small children with no adequate provision for day care. Such return, however, reduces the autonomy of all involved and is viewed as a comparatively unattractive alternative.

Role Behavior in Partial Families

THE PROVIDER ROLE IN PARTIAL FAMILIES One of the major costs of divorce is in the relative inefficiency of the postdivorce economic arrangements. For the ex-husband these costs flow both from the necessity of paying rent on an additional house, apartment, or room (a

[9]William J. Goode, *After Divorce* (Glencoe, Ill.: The Free Press, 1956), pp. 12–15.

considerable cost in itself) and in the loss of the wife's services. She can no longer market, cook, launder and repair clothing, and clean and order his living quarters. He may attempt to perform these services himself but men are not socialized to these tasks and most lack both the skills and the attitudes required for adequate performance of these duties. More often he will purchase these services by living in a boarding establishment or by eating in restaurants. The purchase of such services is expensive. Both the divorced husband and wife are likely, also, to consume more commercial recreation to substitute for the companionship of the spouse. The economic result of divorce, then, is to add substantial expenses to the family without any compensating economies or added income. If the ex-husband remarries, he obtains the services that he lost from his former wife but at the cost of maintaining a second family.

Because divorce and desertion are most common at the lower income levels, and because monetary problems often precede a divorce, the added expenses most frequently must be borne by families whose resources are already severely strained. This added stress leads to several alternative courses of action.

The first effect on the provider role is to necessitate finding an added source of income for the wife or to reduce expenses. "On the average in 1962, the mother raising her children alone had the same number to look after as the mother sharing responsibility with a husband, although she usually had about 40 per cent as much income to do it on."[10] As noted earlier, one way to reduce expenses is for the wife and children to move in with her parents, or for the wife to leave the children with a relative. In effect, this adds income from the grandparent or another relative in that the needs for food and shelter of the mother and children are largely met by others than the mother or her ex-husband. Added income may be obtained from several other sources. One of these is for the ex-wife to take paid employment. The proportion of young divorcees in paid employment is twice as high as for young married women.[11] This is true for women with preschool as well as older children. Thus, the ex-wife's paid emloyment seems to be the most common source of added income for the partial family.

For those divorced women with several small children and with little education or training to offer an employer, public assistance may be the only practical immediate source of added income.

Finally, the mother can increase her income by remarriage. Unless

[10] *Poverty in the United States,* Committee on Education and Labor, House of Representatives, 88th Congress, Second Session (Washington, D.C.: Government Printing Office, Apr. 1964).

[11] F. Ivan Nye and Lois Wladis Hoffman, *The Employed Mother in America* (Chicago: Rand McNally & Co., 1963), p. 15.

508

the new groom brings children to the reconstituted family or is paying child support to children of a former marriage, the income of the reconstituted family may be greater than before divorce, because remarriage does not release the ex-husband from his obligations to pay support for his children. It appears, therefore, that if the ex-husband honors his obligations, the wife, if remarried to a provider of average provider competence, may fare well, but if she does not remarry and especially if her ex-spouse reneges on his obligation, hers is an extremely disadvantageous position. As Chilman has said of families headed by women: "They represent only one-twelfth of all families with children, but make up more than a fourth of all who are classified as poor."[12]

Divorce, if children are involved, places an especially heavy obligation on men—one that they sometimes cannot or will not assume. As already noted, costs are always increased with a divorce involving children, because either he must pay support to his ex-wife or, in rarer instances, care for their children himself, which will require payments for day-care services, housekeeper services, laundry and drycleaning services, and so on. If the children stay with the mother, the father must rent quarters for himself and perform or hire the housekeeper services that wives ordinarily perform. If he remarries, he must support the new family plus the children of the previous marriage. Of course, occasionally these obligations cancel each other, as in the legendary neighborhood in which most of the couples were remarried. Child support checks flowed about in a circle from the husband of one reconstituted family to the wife of another.

The provider role of divorced men is complicated by the fact that disproportionately they are lower-class males, and therefore have small incomes and large families. Indeed, financial problems are most frequently cited as the cause of divorce. In these instances inadequate income is stretched farther to try to support two residences and, often, two families. This creates a situation in which the ex-husband cannot discharge the added responsibilities of the provider role. This results in two patterns, both dysfunctional. In one of these, a divorce occurs and a court awards child support to the children in the custody of the wife. The husband finds that he cannot pay his own expenses in maintaining a separate residence and pay the prescribed child support, so he reneges on the support and the wife must find her entire income elsewhere, as already discussed. The other course is desertion of the family without a divorce. Besides the financial cost of the divorce action, the father may know that he cannot pay the amount of child

[12]Catherine Chilman and Marvin Sussman (eds.), "Poverty in the United States in the Mid-Sixties," *Journal of Marriage and the Family*, **26** (Nov. 1964), p. 393.

support (and possibly alimony) that a court would be likely to require. If so, a legal divorce is a financial impossibility. Such instances presumably account for part of the higher desertion rate among the lower class. This description is of a conscientious husband who would prefer to meet his obligations. Of course, not all fit this description.

In summary, divorce places unusually severe stresses on the provider role. Often, a family income inadequate to support one household must be split between two. Even in higher income brackets, families usually live up to their incomes, so that all family members are faced with a reduction in their level of living. Wives react to inadequate income by taking paid employment, doubling up with relatives, obtaining public assistance, and/or remarrying. Ex-husbands reduce their level of living and pay support or renege or desert without a divorce. Thus, the financial cost of divorce is less in paying for the divorce decree than in creating an inefficient arrangement that requires two residences and prevents the usual exchange of services between wife and husband.

CHILD CARE AND SOCIALIZATION IN PARTIAL FAMILIES Child care, provisions for the child's physical needs and protection, and socialization, that is, training him to act appropriately as a child and preparing him for adult roles, seem to be the *raison d'etre* for the family. Marriage permits the mother to care for small children while the father provides for some of her needs and theirs.

Divorce disrupts this division of labor. If small children remain with the mother, it is difficult for her to take paid employment. If she does, it is difficult for her to hire day-care services and have enough remaining to support her family. If the children go with their father, it is even more difficult because he usually must hire both day-care and cooking services, care of clothing and house care, as well. Furthermore, "solo" fathers or family-dominant fathers are not very effective as socializing agents.[13] It is the mothers who are the conservatives, who revere the societal norms, who nourish appropriate role performance, and who most effectively discourage deviant behavior.

Much, although not all, of the neglect of children—lack of proper feeding, supervision, and protection of small children—comes from lower-class families headed by women who are working to support their families but whose earnings are little if any more than the amount that would be required to pay for adequate child-care services or by mothers who cannot afford to pay a babysitter when they leave the home for recreation.

The absence of a father in a family, whether by divorce or death,

---

[13]Judson T. Landis, "A Re-examination of the Role of the Father as an Index of Family Integration," *Marriage and Family Living*, **24** (May 1962), pp. 122–128.

poses a difficult and urgent issue for differentiated societies character-ized by nuclear families. Who should play the provider role for these families? We have seen that even if the ex-husband is alive, in a large share of cases his earning are insufficient, and in the case of death, insurance and/or Social Security is usually insufficient. American society has temporized on the issue, providing aid to dependent children, but providing it at a submarginal standard. In effect, this society seems to be saying: "We will support life in these families but nothing more."

Sociologically, the question may be stated: Do the roles of child care, socialization, and housekeeping constitute an adequate occupation for a woman who has no husband for whom she may render these and other services? Certainly she does less than the married woman with an equal number of children. As one young mother of two remarked, "Oh, it's not the children who take the time, it's my husband. I'm always getting ready to do something for him or with him." For the woman with a husband and children, the norms define the child-care and housekeeping role complex as an adequate occupation, worthy of recognition, and constituting an appropriate exchange of services with the husband for his economic support. But what of the ex-wife or the widow who performs only part of these services? Is rearing children a full-time occupation and, if so, is society ready to support these women at an income level at which they and their children can have good diets, attractive homes, automobiles, average educations, and recrea-tion comparable with that of intact families? If so, additional interest-ing speculation follows. Would many women who now have unap-preciative and unattractive husbands decide that they'd prefer not to have such husbands and enact only the maternal roles? Would this choice, in turn, reduce the bargaining power of such husbands and force them to become more considerate and cooperative spouses?

Currently, it seems American society has *not* accepted the maternal role as a sufficient contribution to society, and, in effect, by providing a submarginal level of subsistence for partial families, it tries to motivate them to become self-supporting. However, it has not yet provided the institutions that are necessary for the solo parent to function efficiently and to share in the rewards of the society.

Two institutional changes appear necessary before solo parents can be self-supporting and share equally in the rewards of the society. First, adequate day-care facilities must be available, probably gratis to the solo parent, because he or she often has only part of an income and usually a modest one. Second, public support of further education and job training will be necessary for many women who dropped out of school early to start families. A small additional facility, perhaps, but probably not unimportant, would be special housing centers that

511

provide for the evening care of children, at least occasionally. Solo parents have more rather than fewer recreational needs than do married parents.

We feel that this issue has been dodged and compromised rather than faced in American society. It affects millions of children and solo parents and its consideration can hardly be delayed longer. In effect, American society is neither providing a legitimate and rewarding status for solo mothers *as mothers* nor is it providing the supporting institutions that would make it possible for them to be providers without neglecting their children. If it did either, this society would increase the effectiveness of solo parents of both sexes and, among other results, would reduce the pressure on the formerly married to remarry just to meet pressing needs for a division of labor that would provide child care on one hand and economic support on the other.

THE SOCIALIZATION ROLE AND DEVIANT BEHAVIOR The question is commonly asked: What are the effects of divorce on children? As we have noted earlier, this type of question probably indicates a basic confusion about divorce, or at least its answer is usually confusing. The asker probably wants to know how children in families in which there has been a divorce differ from those in intact families. The answer, equally confusing, has been to compare children from broken families to those from legally intact families.

As was noted earlier, two different components enter into the experience of people who have been through a divorce. First, there was a period during which the marriage was not performing some of its functions in a manner satisfactory to one or both spouses. This may have been a period of many years dating even from the wedding or of only a few days. In most marriages, it was a period of months or years. This period included a range of unmet needs including financial need, sexual need, inadequate care and socialization of children, and inadequate therapeutic and recreational role-playing. In most instances this period involved arguments, quarrels, hostility, suspicion, and dislike. Such behavior and feelings are also found in families that remain permanently intact, but their proportion is much lower than in those families that are finally dissolved by divorce.

The other experience broken families have is the divorce process, itself. This process begins at the time the parents finally separate, continues through the divorce proceedings, and then continues into the postdivorce period as long as either of the parents is identified as "divorced."

One can identify roughly three types of families: (1) those in which the level of conflict is low, the affect balance is positive, and there is no divorce; (2) those with high conflict and negative affect balance in which a divorce never occurs; and (3) those in which a divorce occurs.

The better question, therefore, is to ask how the behavior of children (or their feelings) differ among these three types of families: well-functioning marriages with positive affect, malfunctioning marriages with negative affect but no divorce, and malfunctioning marriages with negative affect and divorce.

Now, the original question of what the effects of divorce are on children can again be considered. It appears evident that the nearest approximation can be obtained from a comparison not of children in intact homes with those in broken homes, but of those in families with high conflict and negative affect with those who have experienced a divorce. Actually, even this procedure is not completely satisfactory because from the latter group one must accept those experiences that *follow* divorce—living with a solo parent or with a parent and a step-parent.

Studies of children's statements about their experiences and feelings during and after a divorce leave no doubt that it is intrinsically an unpleasant experience. It involves uncertainty about future living, redefinition of one's relationships to both parents, explanations to friends, and for an extended period, the special status of living in a divorced family. These, in themselves, are inconvenient and embarrassing experiences, often accompanied by uncertainty and sometimes anxiety. Divorce is often compared to surgery—it is a rare person who enjoys a visit to a hospital or the convalescence after surgery.

However, the divorce process also sometimes produces very distinct feelings of relief on the part of the children of parents engaged in chronic conflict. As Landis found, in a considerable proportion of instances, the children anticipated that a divorce would come sometime and were glad to have it occur.[14] Goode,[15] Bernard,[16] and others reported similar reactions. For some children the relief from conflict and hostility is great. However, it was also found that the divorce came as an unhappy surprise to many children. Parents had been able to hide their conflict from their children. For these children the experience was traumatic.

The experience of divorce, therefore, can be placed within the context of exchange theory. Some children lose very little in terms of the social interaction of their parents because conflict between their parents has created tense, uncomfortable family relationships. The termination of this conflict is a relief. Other children, who have had a comfortable, pleasant existence with congenial relationships with both

[14]Judson T. Landis, "The Trauma of Children When Parents Divorce," *Marriage and Family Living*, 22 (Feb. 1960), pp. 7–13.

[15]Goode, op. cit., pp. 12–15.

[16]Jessie Bernard, *Remarriage: A Study of Marriage* (New York: The Dryden Press, 1956).

513

parents, lose a great deal. One can say with no more than a slight overstatement that divorce is therapeutic for the first group of children, traumatic for the second group.

Unfortunately, most of the empirical research on children from broken homes employs only a dichotomy between unbroken and broken home. This research, with an almost monotonous regularity, discloses more deviant behavior of one or another type in the broken-home category. For example, Smith reviews numerous studies that show that there are a disproportionate number of children from broken homes in various types of institutional custody, reformatories, "training schools," and the like.[17] As already noted, this kind of research tells little if anything about the effects of divorce itself. What *is* more relevant is the comparison of children in intact families characterized by high levels of conflict and negative affect with those who have been through a divorce. There is no question about breaking smoothly functioning families with high positive affect. The question that *is* frequently asked is whether a malfunctioning family should be kept intact either because it, even so, is judged more effective than a partial or reconstituted family or because the divorce process is, in itself, traumatic. This distinction was made by Nye[18] and Landis.[19]

Although Nye anticipated little difference between the behavior and feelings of children in unbroken homes characterized by high conflict and negative affect and those who had experienced a divorce and, in most instances, were living with a step-parent, the data disclosed a different picture (Table 20.1). Differences were found in delinquent behavior, psychosomatic symptoms, sensitivity about appearance (lack of self-confidence), and in several relationships with parents. All of the differences indicate less deviant behavior, less stress and strain on personality, and more positive affect toward parents in the children from divorced or separated families than from the intact families in chronic conflict. Landis's research, although involving different behavioral indicators, disclosed a similar type of difference favorable to the children of divorced parents.

Table 20.1 shows that children from intact, effectively functioning families produced the fewest behavioral and affective problems; partial and reconstituted families were intermediate; and the most frequent deviant behavior and affect problems were in the intact families characterized by conflict.

If one looks at the behavior and feelings of children as indicators of

[17]Smith, op. cit., pp. 189–202.

[18]F. Ivan Nye, "Child Adjustment in Broken and Unhappy Unbroken Homes," *Marriage and Family Living*, **19** (Nov. 1957), pp. 356–361.

[19]Judson T. Landis, "A Comparison of Children from Divorced and Nondivorced Unhappy Marriages," *Family Life Coordinator*, **11** (July 1962), pp. 61–65.

514

the role-playing of parents, the preceding comments permit several summary statements. First, such role-playing *is* relevant to the role-playing and affective states of children. Second, marriages characterized by low conflict and positive affect produce the least deviant behavior and negative affect in children. Third, more parents in partial and reconstituted families perform parental roles effectively than do parents in intact marriages characterized by high conflict and negative affect. Fourth, children feel relief in a divorce that removes them from a highly conflicted family but they feel distress or even trauma from those in which they were unaware of any conflict or negative affect between their parents. Fifth, there is at least temporary distress for children during any divorce process and some discomfort in being identified as a member of a unit created by divorce. Such distress does not, in most instances, permanently damage the role-enactment capacity of the child.

Earlier it was believed that the development of younger children was affected more adversely by divorce than that of older children. Evidence continues to accumulate to the contrary: babies and small children seem to have little if any recollection of the original parent and regard the stepparent as their father or mother. The stepparent, likewise, is more likely to regard the child as his own and enact his parental roles as he would with his own biological child.[20]

THE ROLE MODEL ISSUE A considerable number of scholars, more oriented to psychology than sociology, believe that young children need to have both an adult man and an adult woman in the household to serve as adult models.[21] In a sense this is an explanation for the greater proportion of deviants in the broken-home category; that is, the reason Johnny is a problem to his teacher or the police is that he does not have an adult role model. Others feel that there are better explanations for the greater behavioral and affective problems among the children from broken homes. Some of the data in Table 20.1 are germane to the issue because they permit the comparison of children living with only the mother (solo mother) to those living with both parents in conflicted families. These data show substantially less delinquency and physical sensitivity for the children in the solo mother homes; also, their relations to their mothers are consistently characterized by more positive affect. Only in church attendance is the comparison substantially favorable to the conflicted unbroken home, and that difference is small enough so that it may be due to chance.

Thomes recently addressed the issue by comparing the self-concepts

[20]Smith, op. cit., Chapter 8, pp. 79–86.
[21]For a review, see Leon J. Yarrow, "Separation from Parents During Early Childhood" in *Review of Child Development Research,* Vol. 1, ed. by Martin L. and Lois Wladis Hoffman (New York: The Russell Sage Foundation, 1964).

515

Table 20.1
The Percentage of Adolescents from Broken and Unhappy Unbroken Homes Who Fall into "Poorest Adjustment" Categories*

Criteria of Adjustment	Happy Unbroken %	Unhappy Unbroken %	All Broken %	Divorced & Separated %	All Other Broken %	Solo† Mothers %
Psychosomatic illness	26	50**	33	31	38	43
Physical sensitivity	27	50***	30	31	28	31
Delinquency	23	48*	36	39	29	33
Acceptance of parent (M)	31	42	35	35	33	17
Acceptance of parent (F)	20	55*‡	41	37	50	
Acceptance of child (M)	31	55*‡	42	44	39	27
Acceptance of child (F)	27	69**	42	40	49	
Discipline (M)	28	45*‡	31	30	35	20
Discipline (F)	21	46*‡	31	30	35	
Freedom and responsibility (M)	20	33	29	25	37	21
Freedom and responsibility (F)	24	41	32	28	41	
Money (M)	22	37	30	29	30	21
Money (F)	22	46	37	35	44	
Value agreement (M)	23	47**	25	26	23	17
Value agreement (F)	21	53***	33	34	29	
Appearance (M)	30	48*‡	34	31	40	35
Appearance (F)	26	59**	27	26	32	

	(N=112)	(N=158)	(N=115)	(N=43)	(N=40)	Solo[†]
Mutual recreation (M)	24	39	33	34	33	21
Mutual recreation (F)	24	52	42	42	44	
Occupation (F only)	19	47**	25	26	21	48
Information and advice (M)	42	44	43	41	48	
Information and advice (F)	26	56	48	46	56	28
Disposition (M)	30	57**	34	36	29	
Disposition (F)	29	75**	38	37	39	
Parental interaction	18	100	36	36	38	
School grades (D and F)	7	7	12	13	7	8
School teams (None)	77	81	85	84	88	81
Church attendance (Never)	9	10	15	16	14	18
Delinquent companions	52	60	52	53	50	60

*Percentages are based on the proportion from that category falling into the poorest adjustment *tercile* of the whole sample except in the cases of physical sensitivity, school teams, and delinquent companionship. In those the adjustment distribution was dichotomized.

+"Solo" mothers is not an exclusive category. They are included in both the separated and divorced and "all other broken" categories.

‡Difference significant at 5 per cent level between Unhappy Unbroken and All Broken.

**Difference significant at 1 per cent level between Unhappy Unbroken and All Broken.

SOURCE: F. Ivan Nye, "Child Adjustment in Broken and in Unhappy Unbroken Homes," *Marriage and Family Living,* **19** (Nov. 1957), p. 359. Reprinted by permission.

of children in father-absent homes with a sample of children from the same (lower) class whose father was at home. She states:

The results of all three instruments were that there were no significant differences between children from father-absent homes and children from mother-father homes. This certainly suggests that there were no gross differences between the groups of children in the conscious perception of certain aspects of the self.[22]

The issue might be restated thus: Is the socialization of the male child advanced if he has *any* type of man around the house, even if he doesn't work, abuses his wife and children, and is drunk a considerable part of the time? Probably most sociologists would say no. The mother can do better by herself. On the other hand, the evidence is overwhelming that the most effective family, as a general model, is the one with two parents, both of whom are enacting their roles competently.

HOUSEHOLD-CARE ROLES OF THE DIVORCED What happens to the care of the clothing, the house, and furniture and the preparation of food after the divorce? Mundane matters, perhaps, but essential to life's continuation. Like everything else about divorce, these tasks are done inefficiently. Two abodes to care for—two sets of meals to prepare and serve. There is no satisfactory arrangement for the divorced couple with children. The mother must work if she is to have an income that keeps her family above the subsistence level. The result is that in a typical week she enacts the provider, child-care, child-socialization, and housekeeper roles and has little time left for recreation.

For men, the dilemma is to be able to afford to hire the services once performed by their wives. Few men can support their children and have enough left to buy their meals, laundry service, drycleaning, house care, and recreation. Not many men have the energy left after a day's work—or the skills—and the positive attitudes to perform these tasks for themselves. The divorced man paying child support is likely to be badly housed, badly fed, and badly clothed and to have little for recreation.

The divorced couple without children face none of these problems. The woman can work and care for an apartment while the man can afford to hire such services as he needs.

SEXUAL AND THERAPEUTIC FUNCTIONS IN PARTIAL FAMILIES How are sexual and therapeutic needs met by the divorced? Except for autosexual outlets, these needs must be met by another person. Although each of these needs can be met in a variety of ways, divorce provides no normative arrangement for either need. In some ways the situation of the divorced is similar to that of the never-married adult, yet unlike it

[22]Mary Margaret Thomes, "Children with Absent Fathers," *Journal of Marriage and the Family,* **30** (Feb. 1968), pp. 89–96.

in two respects. Often the never-married have not completely severed interaction with their parents. More of the single feel free to take a problem to a parent for reactions and support. Marriage discourages such intimate interaction with parents and provides a more readily available therapist in the spouse. If the parent is to serve again in that capacity, the relationship in most instances must be reestablished after divorce. Ministers, counselors, and psychiatrists, as well as friends, may provide such therapeutic services to the extent that these people are available. The divorced person without a confidant other than the spouse who is not willing or able to use the services of a professional counselor may have no one with whom to share his most difficult problems. It might be added that the divorced person is likely to be faced with *more* complex problems than the single person and, therefore, may have more urgent need for therapeutic services.

The sexual needs of the divorced person differ from those of the single person in that the divorced person has had a legitimate outlet for a period of time. Clinical evidence indicates that the sexual needs of divorced and widowed women are considerably stronger than usually expressed by young women prior to marriage. Most single men seek sexual intercourse before marriage and after divorce, too. There are, of course, no normative provisions to meet these needs. Both sexes on occasion indulge in intercourse outside of marriage but few find arrangements that consistently meet their sexual needs. Divorced women face the same strong sanctions against intercourse as never-married women—possible pregnancy, venereal disease, and an unfavorable reputation. For men there is the prostitute or perhaps occasional gratification with a dating partner. Sexual gratification remains as much an unsolved problem for the divorced person as for the single person, but probably involves more intense needs for young divorced people because they have had the experience of the gratification of sexual needs.

DIVORCE AND STRESS ON SPOUSES The stresses on the divorced couple have received less attention here than the possible effects on children, but it should follow from the difficulties in role-playing of the divorced—in the provider, child-care and child-socialization, and household-care roles and the interruption of sexual, therapeutic, and recreational roles—that the spouses would feel stress also. Goode found that divorced women with children indicated major stresses, reporting increased problems in the following areas: difficulty in sleeping, 62 per cent; poorer health, 67 per cent; loneliness, 67 per cent; low work efficiency, 43 per cent; memory problems, 32 per cent; increased smoking, 30 per cent; increased drinking, 16 per cent.[23] The greatest evidences of stress occurred at the time of actual separation.

[23]Goode, op. cit., p. 186.

These increases in stress, however, appeared to be a temporary phenomenon, as few indicated greater problems at the time of the interview some months after the divorce.

The divorced of both sexes have higher death and suicide rates than the married. The same is true, however, for the widowed.[24] Further, poor mental health may be a *cause* of a divorce as well as a consequence and may be one reason for not remarrying, and, therefore, adds another person to the death rate in the divorced category. Conclusions, therefore, should be drawn cautiously.

CONCLUSION The role-playing of the divorced with children has been shown to involve intrinsic inefficiencies. The complementary arrangement in family structure in which the male assumes primary responsibility for the provider roles, the female for child care, socialization, and household care, is broken by the divorce. The more numerous the minor children in a marriage, the less efficient the family functioning following divorce. These inefficiencies contribute to the high rate of remarriage of the divorced. Despite inconveniences, embarrassment, and uncertainty during the postdivorce period, children who have gone through a divorce appear to function better than those still in families characterized by high conflict and negative affect. The divorced with no children revert essentially to the status of the single adult with only a slight stigma from the divorce status. However, they, like those with children, lose arrangements for meeting sexual, therapeutic, and recreational needs.

Remarriage

Folk wisdom had it that a divorce ended marriage for a person, that few would dare or care to remarry after an unsuccessful experience. Systematic record-keeping has shown that the opposite is true. Over half marry before the third year and over six sevenths within fifteen years.[25] Of those who *do* remarry, two thirds marry within two years, three fourths within three.[26] The probability that the divorced will remarry is much greater than for the widowed: "at age 40, the divorced woman has 65 chances in 100 of remarriage, the widowed woman, 29, and the single woman only 16."[27] It is clear, therefore, that most

[24]Howard E. Freeman and Wyatt C. Jones, *Social Problems: Causes and Consequences* (Chicago: Rand McNally, 1969), p. 519. Felix M. Berardo, "Widowhood Status in the U.S.: A Neglected Aspect of the Family Life Cycle," *The Family Life Coordinator,* 17 (July 1968), pp. 191–203.

[25]Bernard, op. cit., p. 57.

[26]Glick, op. cit., p. 139.

[27]Bernard, op. cit., p. 57. It should be noted that "chance of remarriage" is an inappropriate concept. Many who do not remarry have one or more opportunities.

divorced people remarry and do so within what appears to be a short period of time. It should be remembered, however, that these people are of mature status eligible to marry. If one took a single population of girls aged nineteen or boys twenty-one, he would find a very high proportion marrying within three years, also.

REMARRIAGE AS A CAUSE OF DIVORCE Some sociologists, viewing the early remarriage of the divorced, have assumed that many of the courtships that resulted in these remarriages must have predated the dissolution of the original marriage and therefore were the precipitating cause for the divorce. This is true in some instances, as case histories indicate that one spouse fell in love with another person and asked for the divorce, or his spouse reacted to his affair by filing for divorce. However, the proportion of divorces caused by a triangle (or rectangle) probably is smaller than the early remarriage figures suggest. There is a relatively long period between the final break in the marriage—when one spouse moves out—and the granting of the divorce. Goode found from Michigan data that the average time from the decision to divorce to filing for divorce was 3.2 months and from filing to decree was 8.3 months.[28] The median time between separation and divorce is much greater in some other states, being reported as about 5 years in Philadelphia and in Washington, D.C. Preliminary national data give this interval as 3.2 years.[29] This is more than the median time between the divorce decree and remarriage, or, stated another way, the median time between the final separation and remarriage is about 6 years, although it is only 2.7 years from divorce to remarriage. Even the person who remarries a year after the divorce has probably been separated four years from his spouse before remarriage, which is hardly precipitous action. Goode found, also, that couples in which the wife was in love with another man prior to the divorce moved *more* slowly toward divorce than was true of marriages in which this was not the case. The same was true if the husband was involved with another woman. This suggests (perhaps subject to further evidence) that it is not emotional involvement in a triangle that usually produces precipitous divorces but that divorce comes sooner when both are generally disenchanted with the marriage.[30]

It might be noted, too, that not all affairs that disrupt marriages result in remarriage to the third party. The event may lead the offended spouse to file for divorce, although the interest of the other spouse in the third party is minor. Even triangles involving serious emotional involvement may encounter problems or affective changes that prevent

[28]Goode, op. cit., p. 137.
[29]Thomas P. Monahan, "When Married Couples Part: Statistical Trends and Relationships in Divorce," *American Sociological Review*, 27 (Oct. 1962), p. 625–633.
[30]Goode, op. cit., p. 141.

a remarriage to the third person. Consequently, it appears that although some of the emotional attractions in remarriage have caused the divorce, the proportion might easily be overestimated.

REMARRIAGE OF WIDOWS AND DIVORCEES CONTRASTED The higher remarriage rates of divorcees than of widows has intrigued sociologists. Even when age is held constant (as in the quotation from Bernard), the divorcee of forty is twice as likely to remarry as the widow and four times as likely as the single woman. Folk wisdom would have had it that the divorced are disillusioned with marriage, happy to be free, and therefore unlikely to remarry. Although most divorcees remarry and many soon after the decree, this is less true of widows. Explanations for the difference include feelings of loyalty to the deceased spouse and disapproval by children and friends. In terms of parental roles, their situation is similar. Widowers have no child support to pay to their wives, but they do have the children to care for. Most widows with minor children can collect Social Security payments until the children are eighteen, whereas divorcees may expect child support from their ex-spouses.

Their situations do differ in some respects. The status of widow commands respect and support from relatives and the public. By contrast, the status of divorcee is regarded with disapproval and even distrust. This status can be replaced with the more honored one of being remarried. The status of widow appears to be more honored and supported than that of being remarried, whereas the status of being divorced is regarded with much less approval than remarriage.

It has already been shown that final separation precedes divorce by an average of three years. The divorced woman of forty is likely to have been free to begin dating again when she was thirty-seven. By custom, widowed women are expected to wait for a year before recommencing dating, so in effect, there may be as much as four years' difference on the average between the time the two populations begin dating and courtship looking toward remarriage. In a limited number of divorces, interest in a third person was the reason for the divorce and remarriage to that person follows the divorce. This would not be true for widows.

Finally, the widowed may be less attractive remarriage prospects financially. The widow is likely to have children but no child-support payments. The widower is likely to have children, whereas the divorced man usually does not. A widow marrying a widower is likely to be caring for at least two sets of children. The divorced woman marrying a widower is likely to be in the same situation.

OTHER VARIABLES IN REMARRIAGE Men with high incomes remarry rapidly, whereas those with low incomes do not. Of 1,000 widowers or divorced men in 1949, 491 of those in the highest income levels had remarried by 1952, compared to only 59 per 1,000 in the lowest income category.[31] This suggests both that remarriage may be too expensive for low-income men (a majority of whom have children to support) and that such men may be unattractive to women because of their limited capacity as providers. Two widows in the forty-year-old category were heard to comment on this point on separate occasions, "There isn't one eligible unmarried man in this town" (both lived in towns of about 15,000 population). There were scores of unmarried, divorced and widowed men in these towns but most were in the minimum income categories, earning less than the widows who made the statement.

Children have been considered a handicap in remarriage but recent data challenge that assumption. Women with three or more children do marry less frequently but apparently because they are older. With age standardized, there is little difference. Actually, women with one or two children are less likely to remarry than those with more or those with none. Although little should be made of differences of the magnitude shown in Figure 20.1, it might be noted that even one child introduces the uncertainties and complications of a stepfather relationship. One or two children provide some companionship for the mother without the heavier financial problems of caring for more. Thus, she would face the same complexities in a remarriage as the mother of a larger family but with less to gain financially from the relationship. This may explain the differences from the mother's point of view but what of the man's wishes? Does the mother of several children of

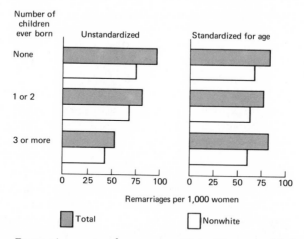

Figure 20.1. Remarriage rates for women 15 to 54 years old, by number of children ever born and color: 1948 to 1950. [From Paul C. Glick, *American Families* (New York: John Wiley & Sons, Inc., 1957) p. 138.]

[31]Glick, op. cit., p. 135.

necessity settle for a man of less earning power or of other unattractiveness? In terms of exchange theory, we would hypothesize that this is the case.

Remarriage Roles

Although perhaps as many as one in four of American marriages are remarriages, it is generally unclear how the behavior of the remarried parent should differ from that of original parents. Perhaps this is less surprising than it seems at first glance, because in almost all respects the remarried spouses and stepparents have the same sets of responsibilities as original spouses and parents. Yet, behavior, attitudes, and even normative prescriptions differ.

PROVIDER IN REMARRIAGE Currently about 60 per cent of divorces involve children. Of widows and widowers, it is estimated that some 75 to 80 per cent of those who remarry have children.[32] Therefore, most marriages of two people formerly married involve children and even in marriages involving only one remarried person the majority involve children.

For remarriages without previous children or alimony, the provider role is identical with that in an original marriage, but if minor children exist from one or more previous marriages, a variety of obligations appear. The first type of remarriage includes a divorced woman and a single man. Her children are entitled to financial support from their biological father. In this type, the couple begin with a ready-made family but one that is partially subsidized. The remarriage of the mother does not change the responsibility of the biological father for the support of his children. Thus, if the second husband is as able a provider as the first, the family should be better supported than during the original marriage. It should be noted, however, that the second husband also has responsibilities for the support of his wife's children, if for any reason the support of the biological father is inadequate.[33]

In the second type, a divorced man with children in his own custody marries a woman without children. No support is owed to his family nor does he owe any to others. His provider role is identical with that of a father in an original marriage. In similar circumstances is a single man who marries a divorced woman whose ex-husband has reneged on his support payments or one who married a widow with children. Although he did not father the children, he has responsibility as a provider for one family.

---

[32]Bernard, op. cit., p. 11.
[33]Adele Stuart Meriam, *The Stepfather in the Family* (Chicago: University of Chicago Press, 1940), pp. 36–43.

A third type is composed of a divorced man with children not in his custody who is remarried to a divorcee with children in her custody. In this type he *pays* out child support to his ex-wife, while his wife *receives* child support from her ex-husband. As long as both ex-husbands honor their commitments, income and outgo cancel, leaving provider responsibilities similar to the second type, that is, with responsibility for one set of children.

In a fourth type, a divorced man with children not in his custody marries a woman without children. He supports his second wife and pays child support to his ex-wife. His expenses are larger than those of unbroken families because it is inefficient to support two households.

Fifth, a divorced man with children not in his custody marries a woman with children—a widow or a divorcee without child support from her ex-husband. He must support two households and two sets of children plus one wife. This exerts maximum stress on a man as provider. In all these examples, the provider role is likely to be further increased by children from the new marriage.

Although the provider role in remarriage is basically similar to that of original marriages, it is clear that it usually is not identical and that usually it is heavier because of the intrinsic costs in maintaining family members in two abodes. If all the men involved were to meet their provider role fully the burden would be much heavier on them than in original marriages. However, many can't or don't, with the result noted earlier—that families headed by women contribute very disproportionately to the population below the poverty level.

CHILD SOCIALIZATION AND CONTROL It is in child socialization and control that the most confusion arises in remarriage roles. For example, one new stepfather of girls aged seven and nine said, "I'll never lay a hand on them." He felt disciplining them was not his duty or privilege. Children often similarly feel that only their biological father should discipline them. Because he isn't present, socialization and social control in these families is likely to be less effective. In other reconstituted families, especially if the children are small, the stepparent assumes that his role is identical to that of the biological parent and his assumption of the role is accepted by his stepchildren. It has been recounted that sometimes a prospective stepfather partially assumes this role during his courtship of the mother. In such instances, apparently, this responsibility is not without attractions for the stepparent.

The assumption of the socialization role is complicated if the biological father is furnishing child support. It seems that a stepfather not supporting a child has less basis for disciplining him. Viewed in this light, to take disciplinary action appears to be a privilege. However, the stepfather, if the child lives with him, not the biological

525

father, is responsible for the child's actions.[34] Therefore, the assumption of socialization functions by the stepparent seems consistent with his responsibilities and most likely to produce an adequately socialized adult.

If there are two or three sets of children—two by previous marriages plus children from the remarriage, the issue of favoritism frequently arises. Parent-child interaction in urban societies has difficult aspects within original families—conflict is normal—but with stepparent status these problems can be attributed to differential behavior or motives on the part of the stepparent or the child.[35]

Despite confusion in the perception and enactment of parental roles by stepparents, they seem on the whole to be more effective than in the original, conflicted families or in the partial families headed by one parent only. Goode concludes: "We found that almost all mothers worried about the effects of the divorce on their children, but that almost all remarried mothers subsequently thought that their children's lives had improved after the divorce."[36]

Bernard found that most stepparents exhibited an affectionate attitude toward their stepchildren. (Table 20.2). It differed little whether the stepparent was divorced or widowed. About 33 per cent were neither affectionate or rejecting. Only about 5 per cent were definitely rejecting in their attitudes toward their stepchildren.

OTHER FAMILIAL ROLES The household care, sexual, therapeutic, and

Table 20.2
Reported Attitudes of Men and Women Toward Children Acquired Through Marriage

	Affectionate	Neither Affectionate nor Rejecting	Rejecting
Divorced men (207)	64.3%	30.9%	4.8%
Widowed men (204)	64.2	30.9	4.9
Divorced women (260)	55.8	37.4	6.8
Widowed women (199)	59.8	35.7	4.5
Wives of divorced men (429)	51.3	41.0	7.7
Wives of widowed men (419)	60.1	35.1	4.8
Husbands of divorced women (466)	64.6	31.3	4.1
Husbands of widowed women (320)	67.2	28.8	4.0

SOURCE: Adapted from Jessie Bernard, *Remarriage: A Study of Marriage* (New York: The Dryden Press, 1956), p. 222.

[34]Ibid., Chapter 4, pp. 36–52.
[35]See Bernard, op. cit.; Meriam, op. cit.; and Smith, op. cit.
[36]Goode, op. cit., p. 329.

recreational roles apparently are little if any different in remarriages. Certainly, normatively they are no different. However, enactment and evaluation may be affected by the prior experience and personal competence and standards of the former spouse. The remarried spouse may judge himself fortunate or unfortunate in terms of this comparison. Some observers have also viewed the ex-spouse as a continuing rival to the new spouse. This type of triangle has formed the basis for numerous novels and movies. If such rivalry exists, it usually disappears with the remarriage of the ex-spouse.

Permanence and Affect in Reconstituted Families

How permanent are second marriages? If the divorced are intrinsically people who cannot live in the close set of relationships or who lack ability to discharge familial roles, no second marriage of two divorced people should survive. However, if divorce is more often caused by the wrong choice of a spouse, then people should profit from the experience and make more appropriate choices the second time. Because divorce is especially frequent among very young marriages, the older remarriages might be expected to be more stable.

Data are not available to provide a precise figure on the redivorce rate, but Monahan's study of redivorce in Iowa shows it about double that of original marriages.[37]

REASONS FOR HIGHER REDIVORCE RATES Original marriages include a population not found among the divorced, namely an aggregate of people who for some reason, most often religious, will not divorce under any circumstances. The size of this aggregate, however, is not known. All of the divorced have demonstrated that if a marriage is sufficiently repugnant they will resort to divorce.

There are other relevant differences in the two populations. Because divorce rates are higher among the low-income and less skilled occupations, the remarried have less competence in the crucial provider role and probably less in the child-care and socialization roles. Certainly this is true of the sexual role (Chapter 13). The divorced, therefore, have a disproportionate share of people with less competence in enacting the various family roles. Therefore, they have a higher probability of redivorce, not because they have been divorced but because more of them have limited competences for enacting marital roles.

---

[37]Thomas Monahan, "The Duration of Marriage to Divorce: Second Marriages and Migratory Types," *Marriage and Family Living,* **21** (May 1959), pp. 134–138.

Finally there are some reasons that *do* have something to do with the divorce, itself. Frequently more stress is placed on the provider role because the divorced husband must support two residences, and not infrequently, two sets of children. Also, the child-socialization role is complicated by confusion concerning appropriate role-enactment by the stepparent. Finally, stigma associated with divorce is probably a hinderance to identification with the reconstituted family. In short, the average reconstituted family begins with less resources, more stress on its capabilities, and stigma attached to the divorced status.

AFFECT IN REMARRIAGES It is evident (Table 20.2) that in most reconstituted marriages, the affective relationship between parents and stepchildren is affectionate or at least not rejecting. In the husband-wife affective relationship, remarriages are characterized by about the same combinations of positive and negative affect as are original marriages. Some differences, however, may be worth noting. Apparently more remarriages occur for "practical" reasons—a divorced or widowed woman with children and inadequate financial support may marry a man to whom she is not especially attracted. One young divorcee with small children said, "Well, I looked over several and Jim seemed to be the steadiest worker and to have the fewest expensive habits." Likewise, a man widowed or deserted has urgent need for a housekeeper. Although such motivations for remarriage do not preclude relationships of strong positive affect, such feelings are not necessarily present. Such "practical" criteria also enter into original marriages, but the presence of children in partial families provides an additional utilitarian motivation for remarriage.

Remarriages have some advantages. Couples average some ten years older, and, with other characteristics held constant, older marriages tend to be more stable and more satisfactory to the spouses. Also, the remarried have a more adequate perception of the requirements and limitations of group living. A woman evaluates her husband's performance against a standard. If that standard is perfection, few husbands will be equal to it. This lack of perfection can be illustrated by the comments of many divorcees concerning the sexual advances they received from the husbands in couples they had known for years. They were shocked to find that a large proportion of these husabnds were not monogamous. If they had thought, as apparently they did, that all husbands were faithful to their wives, then they would feel their own husband was different if they observed some interest in some other woman on his part. On the average, probably the remarried know a little more about the modal patterns of role enactment by spouses.

The remarried know, too, that being single again has more problems and fewer gratifications than they may have thought before divorce. The loneliness, lack of sexual experience, and inadequate therapeutic and recreational outlets lead to more appreciation of these gratifications in the remarriage. It may be concluded that although remarriages differ in some respects from original ones, and the redivorce rate is higher, the affect in those that survive is about equal to that in original marriages.

EVALUATION OF DIVORCE Divorce has usually been deplored, but we believe that it is marital and family malfunctioning, not divorce, that produces most of the consequences that societies would prefer to avoid. Although the divorce process creates some inefficiencies in the provider role and some confusion and ineffectiveness in the child-socialization role and some embarrassment, uncertainty, and tensions in the family members, it also seems to be adequately substantiated that both children and adults function more effectively in partial and reconstituted families than they do in conflicted intact families characterized by negative affect. Stated another way, the consequences of divorce are less dysfunctional than the continuance of high levels of conflict and negative affect in intact families. Action, therefore, to be valid, would be focused on programs that render more efficient the process of matching future spouses and that create societal conditions conducive to effective family role-playing. Some of these conditions were discussed in Chapter 17.

Currently, American social structure makes little provision for partial families. It is estimated that the divorced who remarry live in partial families for an average of 5.9 years, 3.2 between separation and divorce and 2.7 afterward. The widowed who remarry live in partial families for an average of 3.5 years. Those who don't remarry, of course, live in them until their death.

In a society that is geared to intact, two-parent families, the partial family often experiences stresses and even privation. For example, we have seen that female-headed families constitute a fourth of all families living in poverty. Only through the subsistence programs of Aid to Dependent Children and other public welfare programs has society taken action to restructure society in terms of the needs of the partial family. Bohannan and Huckleberry, in taking note of this, have called for "back-up institutions" for the family. By this, they mean institutions that can take over the responsibilities of a social unit that cannot meet its prescribed duties.[38] To a very limited extent government agencies perform this function through ADC, foster care, and other welfare programs, but at a subsistence level. What is required if partial families are to function at or near the level of intact families are adequate day-care services gratis for partial families and educational and training programs for women who are to function as the providers for their families. These are minimum requirements for first-class citizenship for members of partial families.

[38]Paul Bohannan and Karan Huckleberry, "Institutions of Divorce, Family, and the Law," *Law and Society Review,* **1** (June 1967), pp. 81–102.

Part V
The Postparental Family

21

The Middle-aged Family

The rapid and accelerated period of social change that has characterized American society from the late nineteenth century to the present
has been accompanied by significant modifications in family structure
and organization, with rather important implications for middle-aged
and old-age families. Research concerning the consequences of these
changes has led to a reexamination and revision of several earlier
positions and misconceptions regarding family relations in the second
half of the life cycle.

In this chapter we want to examine some of these misconceptions
against the backdrop of current empirical findings on the family life of
mature American parents. Before doing so, however, it is necessary to
consider briefly certain social and demographic shifts that have re-
shaped our family structure and organization over the past several
decades. In this connection, it will be useful to begin with what family
sociologists refer to as the family life cycle.

The Family Life Cycle

The concept of *family life cycle,* sometimes termed *family career,*
has been utilized by sociologists and others to describe and analyze the
changes in family structure and organization that occur through time.[1]
In general, families are depicted as progressively moving through a
number of stages, or phases, commencing with a basic nucleus of the
newly married couple, *expanding* with the birth and maturation of

[1]Rural sociologists are usually credited with being among the first to apply the
life-cycle concept to the family. See Pitirim A. Sorokin, Carle C. Zimmerman, and C. J.
Galpin, *A Systematic Source Book in Rural Sociology* (Minneapolis: University of
Minnesota Press, 2, 1931).

children, then *contracting* with their marriage and departure from the home, and finally terminating with the death of the parents. (Actually, the family as such never really dissolves because the married offspring ensure intergenerational continuity, during which the cycle is repeated over and over again.)

Throughout the family life cycle, its members as well as the family as a whole perform certain *developmental* tasks essential to its survival, growth, and continuity. Duvall,[2] who defined a family developmental task as "a growth responsibility that arises at a certain stage in the life of a family, successful achievement of which leads to satisfaction, and success with later tasks, while failure leads to unhappiness in the family, disapproval in society, and difficulties with later family developmental tasks," has listed eight basic tasks for American families:

1. Physical maintenance—providing shelter, food, clothing, health care, etc.
2. Allocation of resources—meeting family needs and costs, apportioning material goods, facilities, space, authority, respect, affection, etc.
3. Division of labor—deciding who does what, assigning responsibility for procuring income, managing the household, caring for family members, and other specific tasks.
4. Socialization of members—guiding the internalization of increasingly mature and acceptable patterns of controlling elimination, food intake, sexual drives, aggression, etc.
5. Reproduction, recruitment, and release of family members—bearing or adopting children and rearing them for release at maturity, incorporating new members by marriage, and establishing policies for inclusion of others: in-laws, relatives, stepparents, guests, family friends, etc.
6. Maintenance of order—providing means of communication, establishing types and intensity of interaction, patterns of affection, and sexual expression—by administering sanctions ensuring conformity to group norms.
7. Placement of members in the larger society—fitting into the community, relating to church, school, organizational life, political and economic systems, and protecting family members from undesirable outside influences.
8. Maintenance of motivation and morale—rewarding members for achievements, satisfying individual needs for acceptance, encouragement and affection, meeting personal and family crises, refining a philosophy of life and sense of family loyalty (through rituals, festivals, etc.).

Developmental tasks confront all families, regardless of social class, as they pass through various phases of the life cycle, and they are implemented through the roles assumed by family members in the course of interacting with each other and with members of the larger society. Successful achievement of family tasks at one stage of the life

[2]Evelyn M. Duvall, *Family Development,* 3rd ed. (Philadelphia: J. B. Lippincott Co., 1967), Chapter 2.

534

cycle makes for a smooth transition to the next stage. "If a developmental task is not satisfactorily accomplished at its appointed time, it may not be achieved as well later, and its failure may be reflected not only in itself, but in the incomplete fulfillment of related aspects of development."[3]

There are a number of theoretical and practical problems associated with delineating a clearly defined sequence of family life-cycle stages, and establishing the essential developmental tasks, which are valid for all families. Although we shall not attempt to explore these problems of family cycle analyses, it should be noted that in addition to the two broad divisions of expansion and contraction mentioned earlier, various other schemes have been devised that seek to spell out in greater detail the variations in family patterns over the life cycle.[4] Through the years scholars have elaborated the simple two-stage cycle into four, seven, eight, and even twenty-four cycles in their efforts to study, evaluate, and predict family development.[5] Rowe, for example, has recently traced the trend in these efforts to define the various stages, and the composite he developed is illustrated in Table 21.1. In recent years, researchers utilizing the so-called developmental approach to studying the family have provided some rather sophisticated refinements of the family life-cycle concept.[6] As a frame of reference, the life-cycle approach is useful in an attempt to understand the changing patterns of family living through the years.

Changes in the Family Life Cycle

We turn now to certain shifts in the composition and structure of American society that are closely related to alterations occurring in the family. Although the implications of these broad societal changes for

[3]Ibid., p. 33.

[4]For some early attempts, see E. L. Kirkpatrick et al., "The Life-Cycle of the Family in Relation to its Standard of Living," Research Bulletin No. 121 (Madison, Wis.: Agricultural Experiment Station, University of Wisconsin, 1934); Howard F. Bigelow, "Money and Marriage," Chapter 17, in Marriage and the Family, ed. by Howard Becker and Reuben Hill (Boston: D. C. Heath, 1942), pp. 382–386.

[5]Corollary efforts by Glick to standardize and quantify the stages of the life cycle are particularly outstanding. See Paul C. Glick, "The Family Cycle," American Sociological Review, 12 (Apr. 1947), pp. 164–174; "The Life-Cycle of the Family," Marriage and Family Living, 17 (Feb. 1955), pp. 3–9.

[6]Reuben Hill and Donald A. Hansen, "The Identification of Conceptual Frameworks Utilized in Family Study," Marriage and Family Living, 22 (Nov. 1960), pp. 299–311; Roy H. Rodgers, "Improvements in the Construction and Analysis of Family Cycle Categories," Western Michigan University Press, 1962; also his "Toward a Theory of Family Development," Journal of Marriage and the Family, 26 (Aug. 1964), pp. 262–270; Francis A. Magrabi and William H. Marshall, "Family Development Tasks: A Research Model," Journal of Marriage and the Family, 27 (Nov. 1965), pp. 454–458.

Table 21.1
Delineations of Stages in the Family Life Cycle

Family Cycle Stage	Sorokin, Zimmerman, and Galpin (1931)	National Conference on Family Life (1948)	Duvall (1957, p. 8)	Feldman* (1961, p. 6)	Rodgers (1962, pp. 64–65)
I	Starting married couple	Couple without children	Couple without children	Early marriage (childless)	Childless couple
II	Couple with one or more children	Oldest child less than 30 months	Oldest child less than 30 months	Oldest child an infant	All children less than 36 months
III		Oldest child from $2^{1}/_{2}$ to 5	Oldest child from $2^{1}/_{2}$ to 6	Oldest child at preschool age	Preschool family with (a) oldest 3–6 and youngest under 3; (b) all children 3–6
IV		Oldest child from 5 to 12	Oldest child from 6 to 13	All children school age	School-age family with (a) infants, (b) preschoolers, (c) all children 6–13
V		Oldest child from 13 to 19	Oldest child from 13 to 20	Oldest child a teen-ager, all others in school	Teen-age family with (a) infants, (b) preschoolers, (c) school-agers, (d) all children 13–20
VI	[III] One or more self-supporting children	When first child leaves till last is gone	When first child leaves till last is gone	One or more children at home and one or more out of the home	Young adult family with (a) infants, (b) preschoolers, (c) school-agers, (d) teen-agers, (e) all children over 20

VII	(IV) Couple getting old with all children out	Later years	Empty nest to retirement	All children out of home	Launching family with (a) infants, (b) preschoolers, (c) school-agers, (d) teen-agers, (e) youngest child over 20
VIII				Elderly couple	When all children have been launched until retirement
IX			Retirement to death of one or both spouses		Retirement until death of one spouse
X					Death of first spouse to death of the survivor

*Feldman enumerates Stages IX, X, and XI to classify childless families to correspond to families with children in the stages of childbearing, child-rearing, empty nest, and old age (Stages II to VIII).

SOURCE: George P. Rowe, "The Developmental Conceptual Framework," in *Emerging Conceptual Frameworks in Family Analysis*, ed. by F. Ivan Nye and Felix M. Berardo (New York: The Macmillan Company, 1966), pp. 198–222. Reprinted by permission of the author and publisher. The table was adapted from Pitirim Sorokin, Carle C. Zimmerman, and C. J. Galpin, *A Systematic Source Book in Rural Sociology*, Vcl 2 (Minneapolis: University of Minnesota Press, 1931); Evelyn M. Duvall and Reuben Hill, Co-Chairmen, *Report of the Committee on the Dynamics of Family Interaction* (Washington, D.C.: National Council on Family Life, May 1948, mimeographed material). Evelyn M. Duvall, *Family Development* (Philadelphia: J. B. Lippincott Co., 1957); Harold A. Feldman, *A Report of Research in Progress in the Development of Husband-Wife Relationships* (Ithaca, N.Y.: Cornell University, January 30, 1961, mimeographed); Roy H. Rodgers, *Improvements in the Construction and Analysis of Family Life Cycle Categories* (Kalamazoo, Mich.: Western Michigan University, 1962).

the family are far-reaching, they often go unnoticed or unappreciated by younger people, whose perspective is short-ranged and oriented to the here and now, and whose focus of attention and energy is primarily devoted to matters of love, courtship, and mate selection.

INCREASED LONGEVITY The tremendous changes effected through the application of modern science and technology to the fields of public health, nutrition, education, and medical care represent some of the outstanding achievements of the twentieth century. Their impact, in terms of increased longevity, has been phenomenal. Men and women today can typically look forward to a period of survivorship that far surpasses that of any previous generation in the history of mankind. The average life expectancy has risen from less than fifty years at the turn of the century to seventy or more years in the second half of the twentieth century.

The consequences of this increased life span are reflected in national statistics. Census estimates for 1970 report about 20.1 million people aged sixty-five or over in the United States, or about 9.9 per cent of the total population. There are, in addition, 18.5 million people aged fifty-five to sixty-four, or about 9.1 per cent of the total. Together, these two groups, which roughly correspond to what family sociologists generally refer to as middle-aged and old-age families, constitute over 18 per cent of our entire population. Both groups have *doubled* proportionately since 1900, and the number of people in these older age groups have shown a sixfold increase. People sixty-five and over, moreover, have shown a 50 per cent increase since 1950.[7] By 1980, the number of people fifty-five to sixty-five and sixty-five and over is expected to climb to 21 and 23 million, respectively, or 44 million people fifty-five years old or older.

THE EXPANDED FAMILY LIFE CYCLE Increased longevity has, in effect, extended the family life cycle. Tibbitts, a nationally known gerontologist and student of the family, has aptly noted this change, commenting:

In earlier, short-lived, low energy, subsistence societies, essentially three stages comprised the average life, which probably rarely extended beyond four or five decades. These were a short period of childhood and preparation and a period of active adulthood, followed, for those not suddenly cut-off, by a period of old age. A few may have experienced a stage akin to what we now regard as middle-age or later maturity. We now recognize [however] that we have literally opened the life-cycle and inserted the stages of middle age and later

---

[7]U.S. Bureau of the Census, *Estimates of the Population of the United States, by Age, Color, and Sex* (Washington, D.C.: Current Population Reports, Series P-25, No. 352, Nov. 1966); U.S. Department of Health, Education, and Welfare, Administration on Aging, *Facts About Older Americans* (May 1966), Washington, D.C.

maturity. The period of preparation is longer. Early adulthood—the period of establishment—is followed by the new periods of middle and later maturity, and, eventually, by old age.[8]

The consequences of increased longevity are perhaps more clearly illustrated by the information presented in Table 21.2, which depicts the changes that have occurred in the family life cycle from 1890 to the present and projects the additional changes that are likely to take place by 1980. It can be seen that the modern family is in many respects quite different in character from the family of yesteryear, as reflected by the following changes:[9]

1. Men and women marry at younger ages.
2. The childbearing period is shorter.
3. The empty nest, characterized by the marriage of the last child, comes sooner.
4. More men and women complete their life span as individuals and as a married pair.
5. There is a longer period together as a couple after the children have grown (the typical family in 1890 had no such period).
6. Each family member has a larger number of older living relatives now than formerly.

Table 21.2
Median Age of Husband and Wife at Selected Stages of the Life Cycle of the Family for the United States: 1890–1980

Stage	1890	1940	1950	1960	1980
Median age of wife at:					
First marriage	22.0	21.5	20.1	20.2	19.5–20.4
Birth of last child	31.9	27.1	26.1	25.8	27–28
Marriage of last child	55.3	50.0	47.6	47.1	48–49
Death of one spouse	53.3	60.9	61.4	63.6	64–66
Median age of husband at:					
First marriage	26.1	24.3	22.8	22.3	22–23
Birth of last child	36.0	29.9	28.8	27.9	29–30
Marriage of last child	59.4	52.8	50.3	49.2	51–52
Death of one spouse	57.4	63.6	64.1	65.7	68–69

SOURCE: Paul C. Glick, David M. Heer, and John C. Beresford, "Social Change and Family Structure: Trends and Prospects," paper delivered Dec. 29, 1959, to the American Association for the Advancement of Science, as reproduced in Evelyn M. Duvall, *Family Development* (Philadelphia: J. B. Lippincott Co., 1967), p. 23. Reprinted by permission.

[8]Clark Tibbitts, *Middle-Aged and Older People in American Society,* U.S. Department of Health, Education, and Welfare, Administration on Aging, OA No. 227 (1965), Washington, D.C. (pamphlet).
[9]Evelyn M. Duvall, op. cit., p. 22.

Thus, a few generations ago men were marrying at older ages, typically in their mid-twenties, and frequently died *before* their youngest child had matured, married, and left the household. Similarly, women were marrying a few years later than they are now and, because of the shorter life span and the early demise of the husband, were frequently widowed while their children were still adolescents. Today, in the typical American family, which is smaller in size than any of its predecessors and in which children are more closely spaced, the last child will reach adulthood, marry, and leave the home while the parents are alive and in their late forties or early fifties.[10] The following *post-parental period* may be defined as two stages: (1) the period between the so-called launching of the last child and the beginning of the husband's retirement at age sixty-five, which will last on the average about 13.5 years, and (2) the age of retirement, from which it will be another 16 years or so before the death of the last surviving spouse.

The expansion of the family life cycle brought about through increased longevity has created a rather extensive intergenerational overlap, thereby increasing the probabilities of prolonged interaction between kin of different generations. Thus, becoming a grandparent at age forty-five is not at all uncommon today, and a woman can look forward to being a "grandmother for twenty or thirty years, and thus recapitulate vicariously every phase of her grandchildren's development."[11]

The new and extended periods of middle and old age, however, have also been characterized by changing relationships between the husband and the wife, between married children and their parents. It is to the second half of the life-cycle and the family and intergenerational relationships that accompany it that the remainder of this chapter will be devoted.

Definitional Problems Regarding Middle and Old Age

From a scientific standpoint, the terms *middle age* and *old age* are rather vague and ambiguous. Social scientists have, in fact, encountered numerous difficulties in attempting to develop a clear-cut and consistent conception of aging. Simple *chronological* definitions, for example, are highly unreliable and frequently misleading. A case in point would be the occurrence of *physiological* aging in a chronologically young person. Similarly, there are many chronologically old

---

[10]Paul C. Glick and Robert Parke, Jr., "New Approaches in Studying the Life-Cycle of the Family, *Demography,* **2** (1965), pp. 187–202; "Prospective Changes in Marriage and the Family," *Journal of Marriage and the Family,* **29** (May 1967), pp. 249–256.

[11]Nelson N. Foote, "New Roles for Men and Women," *Marriage and Family Living,* **23** (Nov. 1961), pp. 325–329.

people who are physiologically energetic and active. Other criteria of aging run into similar problems. Thus, a person may be chronologically and physiologically old, but not regard himself as such. Instead, he may have a *psychological* conception of himself as being of middle age or younger, and act in accordance with that conception. For instance, in one study of older people, half of those between the ages of sixty-five and sixty-nine answered the question, "How old do you feel?" by replying "middle-aged" or even "young." Not until a group past eighty years was polled did all of them say that they felt "old," or "aged."[12] There is a high degree of consensus among gerontologists that "the clocks that seem to govern the life cycle of human physical systems may operate in ways at considerable variance from any sociopsychological timing mechanism."[13] The widespread occurrence of such discrepancies has impeded the development of a generally acceptable scientific classification of the aged and the aging process.

Moreover, evidence from the comparative sociology of the aged points to still other complicating factors, namely, the *cultural proscriptions* placed upon those in a given age category. Social anthropologists have long since discovered that many cultures define and view "old age" quite differently.

Old age has been said to begin quite early or rather late in life, and it may last a very long or a short time. By conventional norms, its coming may be resented and discounted or welcomed and treasured. It may be considered an idle and useless period in life or an active and fruitful one. It may bring promotions in position and homage or demotions in both. It may be expected to drag itself out in dull, tedious boredom or go by quickly with interest and zest. Thus, the onset of aging may be viewed as a curse on the one hand or as a challenge on the other. But most peoples meet it somewhere between these two extremes.[14]

The definitional problems engendered by chronological, physiological, psychological, and sociocultural influences have frustrated *descriptive* efforts to present a *static* picture of the latter half of the

[12]Robert J. Havighurst and Ruth Albrecht, *Older People* (New York: Longmans, Green, and Co., 1953), p. 9. See also Bernard S. Phillips, "Role Change, Subjective Age, and Adjustment: A Correlational Analysis," *Journal of Gerontology,* **16** (Oct. 1961), pp. 347–352.

[13]Bernard Kutner, "The Social Nature of Aging," *The Gerontologist,* **2** (March 1962), pp. 5–8.

[14]Leo W. Simmons, "Social Participation of the Aged in Different Cultures," *The Annals of the American Academy of Political and Social Sciences,* **279** (Jan. 1952), pp. 43–51; "Attitudes Toward Aging and the Aged: Primitive Societies," *Journal of Gerontology,* **1** (Jan. 1946), pp. 72–95; *The Role of the Aged in Primitive Societies* (New Haven: Yale University Press, 1945); "Aging in Primitive Societies: A Comparative Survey of Family Life and Relationships," *Law and Contemporary Problems,* **27** (Winter 1962), pp. 36–51.

541

life-cycle according to *discrete* stages. Thus, for example, we have defined the *aged* or *retired family* in this volume as encompassing families in which the head of the household has attained age sixty-five. This common lay definition of the aged is arbitrarily chosen for pedagogical purposes; there are other, equally valid conceptions of this stage of the family life cycle. The application of the term *aged* to the population sixty-five years and over developed with the passage of the Social Security Act of 1935 and subsequent amendments. This act, in effect, stabilized sixty-five as the moment of retirement because persons could qualify for some of its provisions only when they had reached their sixty-fifth birthday. In addition, the majority of employing companies or firms set their mandatory retirement requirements at age levels that approximately coincided with the time of eligibility for Social Security.

Gerontologists generally agree, however, that from an analytic point of view, it is more realistic to perceive aging as part of the *continuous developmental process* that spans the entire life cycle.[15] From this perspective, Kutner's concept of social aging as a process of redifferentiation and reintegration is perhaps most apropos.[16] By *redifferentiation* Kutner means

the necessity of a redefinition of the self and of relationships to others brought about by changes in physical vitality; changes in the social circumstances of living, such as widowhood and the departure of family and friends from the social orbit; changes in the conditions of life, such as relocation, retirement, reduced income, increased uncommitted free time and reduced status. The dynamic interplay between such changes and one's self-perception gradually defines a new series of roles which require the abandonment or modification of others.[17]

The corollary process of *reintegration* centers around stabilization and homeostasis.

When the individual establishes new roles and accepts the new functions, these roles and functions are then integrated into the self-system. Maladjustments and personality disintegration in old age may result from the unsuccessful attempt to integrate a new system of roles.[18]

As Kutner sees it, the process of redifferentiation and reintegration is

---

[15]Clark Tibbitts, "Origins, Scope and Fields of Social Gerontology," in *Handbook of Social Gerontology,* ed. by Tibbitts (Chicago: University of Chicago Press, 1960), pp. 3–26.

[16]Kutner, "The Social Nature of Aging," op. cit., pp. 5–8.

[17]Ibid., p. 6.

[18]Ibid., p. 7. Although Kutner ties his conception of redifferentiation and reintegration primarily to the assumption of retired status, the grandparent role, the widowhood role, the transition to a reduced standard of living, and the assumption of new older adult activities, we feel its applicability to those years immediately following the marriage of the last child is easily justified.

no different in nature from those continuing processes occurring during earlier growth and formative years. The concepts of redifferentiation and reintegration are very much related to the notion of *role flexibility* described by Havighurst, in that both emphasize the necessity for discarding earlier roles and learning new patterns of behavior appropriate to one's stage in the life cycle.[19]

Middle Age: Initial Phase of the Postparental Period

Despite the difficulties encountered by those seeking to establish a scientifically valid conception of middle age, sociologists have made some progress in illuminating various facets of the middle-aged family in their efforts to emphasize the growing significance of this phase of the life cycle. In the process, they have developed a variety of terms or phrases to describe the middle-aged family and to capture its essential characteristics. Thus, for example, Waller designated this period as the "launching stage" to signify the activity of parents in guiding their adult children into jobs, marriage, and independent living.[20] Many other sociologists employ the phrase "empty nest" to indicate the period following the "flight" of the children from the home and to emphasize the void created in the parents' lives as a result of their departure. Cavan prefers the term "postparental couple," which implies both the departure of the children from the home as well as the reduction of the family unit to the original dyad of husband and wife.[21] The *middle-aged family* represents the initial phase of the postparental period. It typically commences when the wife is in her late forties and the husband is in his early fifties. It lasts until the age of retirement, which marks the beginning of the second phase of the postparental period.[22]

Middle Age as a Crisis Experience

The presence of an extensive population of middle-aged, postparental families is, as we have remarked elsewhere, a distinctly twen-

---

[19]Robert J. Havighurst, "Flexibility and the Social Roles of the Retired," *American Journal of Sociology,* **59** (Jan. 1954), pp. 309–311.

[20]Willard Waller, *The Family: A Dynamic Interpretation,* rev. by Reuben Hill (New York: The Dryden Press, 1951), pp. 425–449.

[21]Ruth S. Cavan, *The American Family* (New York: Thomas Y. Crowell Company, 1953), p. 573.

[22]Some authors prefer to view the middle years as consisting of essentially two stages. The first stage would be that period during which the children are being launched toward independence. The second stage would start with the departure of the last child from the home and extend to the beginning of the husband's occupational retirement. In this chapter, we combine these and treat the middle years in terms of a single stage.

tieth-century phenomenon and one that has only recently and rather slowly gained the attention of scientific inquiry.[23] Much of the early descriptive literature on the subject was based upon casual observations and clinical evidence, and tended to characterize the middle years as rather disorganizing or a crisis period filled with potential conflict. Certainly it is a time when the situational and environmental contexts of the marriage are undergoing various changes simultaneously. The children are leaving home and this requires a reorientation of roles, particularly on the part of the mother. The father has in all likelihood reached the apex of his career development and earning power and is beginning to reconcile his achievements with his aspirations and look toward retirement. Evidences of physiological decline and other signs of aging are becoming more apparent, accompanied by their psychological and social concomitants.[24] It is during this period, for example, that women are experiencing the climacteric and encountering the reality of a diminishing sexual appeal. As a consequence of these and other factors mentioned, such as the declining parental role, patterns of marital interaction developed over long periods of cohabitation must now be realigned to adapt to the circumstances of middle age. Under certain circumstances, conflict may arise over one or both of the couple's inability to execute a successful accommodation.

The changing conditions of the middle years are reflected in part by the major marital problems reported by couples who have reached this important juncture in life. As seen in Table 21.3, these problems are of a comparatively different order and magnitude from those that predominate among younger marriages. The data, based on a study of over 25,000 cases recorded by marriage counselors in England and Wales over a three-year period, show that among the recently married, sexual adjustment, adapting to new living conditions, and dealing with the pressures of parental influence all emerge as major areas of difficulty. Among marriages of much longer duration, however, the significance of these factors has greatly diminished and difficulties arising from ill health, infidelity, and general incompatibility have become more salient. Thus, for example, the proportion of spouses reporting ill health as a "disturbing factor" in the marriage increases from 12 per cent among those married three years or less to 23 per cent among those married eighteen years or more. Again, whereas infidelity is a relatively minor issue among the recently married, the proportion of older spouses voicing this complaint is more than four times as great, the

[23] Arthur F. Gravatt, "Family Relations in Middle and Old Age: A Review," *Journal of Gerontology*, **8** (Apr. 1953), pp. 197–201.

[24] A. Joseph Brayshaw, "Middle-Aged Marriage: Idealism, Realism and the Search for Meaning," *Marriage and Family Living*, **24** (Nov. 1962), pp. 358–364.

544

Table 21.3
Types of Problems Reported to Marriage Counselors by
Husbands and Wives

Type of Problem Reported by Spouse	Couples Married 3 Years or Less	Couples Married 18 Years or More
Sex	40	15
Living Conditions	24	7
Parental Influence	22	9
Ill Health	14	29
Incompatibility	12	23
Infidelity	6	26
Income	3	6

SOURCE: Adapted from A. Joseph Brayshaw, "Middle-Aged Marriage: Idealism, Realism, and the Search for Meaning," *Marriage and Family Living,* **24** (Nov. 1962), pp. 358–364. Percentages, based on 25,000 cases, do not total 100% because some couples reported more than one type of disturbing factor in their marriages.

figures increasing from 6 to 26 per cent, respectively. (Caution must be exercised, however, in interpreting these findings because they are based on data derived from a select population, that is, only those persons who have sought marriage counseling. They cannot be easily generalized to the larger, nonclient married population.)

Conjugal Relations in Middle Age

For most middle-aged couples, the transition to postparental roles is partially anticipated and cushioned through earlier life situations and experiences that, in effect, prepare them for living without the immediate presence of their children. Deutscher has described a number of these "socializing opportunities" that most people encounter and that have the *potential* for facilitating the transition to postparental life.[25] These transitional learning experiences include such events as the departure of children for extended periods when they go off to college, enter military service, serve in a foreign country as a member of the Peace Corps, or leave to gain work experience, such as taking a summer job at a distant resort. Sometimes it is not the child who leaves but the parent. Typically the father is apt to be temporarily absent from the home, such as in the case of the traveling salesman, railroad

[25]Irwin Deutscher, "Socialization for Postparental Life," in *Human Behavior and Social Processes,* ed. by Arnold M. Rose (Boston: Houghton Mifflin Company, 1962), pp. 506–525. Deutscher uses the word *opportunity* advisedly, noting that: "Individuals react to the socialization process in different ways; on some it 'takes' and on others it doesn't. The simple fact that an individual is provided with a particular socializing experience does not necessarily result in his defining it as such or in his being socialized as a result of the experience" (p. 510).

545

workers, and the like. Such events no doubt can function to wean the parents away from the children and the children away from the parents, as well as assisting the latter in gradually adapting to post-parental family life.

It has been noted how much of the early descriptive literature on middle-aged persons tended to characterize this period as placing particularly severe strains on the individual and on the husband-wife relationship. Later empirical research, however, has generally failed to support this characterization. Although it is true that some couples do find postparental life rather disrupting, the majority apparently do not encounter any drastic adjustment problems. In one study, for example, a group of "quasi-postparental" parents, that is, persons with single children under eighteen years of age living at home, were compared with a group of "true postparental" parents, that is, those without any single children under eighteen years of age living at home, in terms of their degree of satisfaction with family income, housing and furniture, recreational activities, parent-child relationships, spousal relationships, daily work, and the community as a place to live. No significant differences in satisfaction in these various areas of living were evident between the two groups, suggesting that postparental life is as satisfying as earlier periods.[26]

For the majority of middle-aged couples, the postparental phase represents something of a euphoric stage in their lives, a time when they have been for the most part alleviated from the major social and economic burdens and responsibilities of parenthood. Consequently, it is often a period of new found freedom.[27] Thus, for example, in the case of the wife, the departure of children from the home means less cooking, mending, cleaning, and other physical tasks associated with the homemaking and housekeeping roles of the mother. In the case of the husband in his middle years, the fact that he no longer must worry about providing essential economic support for one or more children gives rise to a sense of relief long anticipated. For both husband and wife, there are accompanying feelings of real accomplishment and satisfaction over having successfully reared children to adulthood and launched them into an independent existence.

The exodus of children from the home invariably leads to certain modifications of the interaction and activity patterns of middle-aged couples. In one sense, the parents are in the same situation as before the

---

[26]Leland J. Axelson, "Personal Adjustment in the Postparental Period," *Marriage and Family Living*, **22** (Feb. 1960), pp. 66–68. Axelson did find, however, a significant increase in loneliness and a decrease in community activities on the part of women in the true postparental period.

[27]Irwin Deutscher, "The Quality of Postparental Life: Definition of the Situation," *Journal of Marriage and the Family*, **26** (Feb. 1964), pp. 52–59.

arrival of children. The family household has once again been reduced to the original marital dyad, and this recreates a form of earlier interdependence in that the spouses must now fend for themselves and rely heavily on one another for protection, comfort, and support. Spouses seem to become more aware or sensitive to the need to look after each other. A frequently reported consequence of all this is a heightened interpersonal relationship between the husband and wife. Sussman's investigation of New Haven, Connecticut, postparental couples is illustrative in this connection.[28] He found that with the children gone, most of the parents reported a gradual but marked increase in joint participation in a variety of activities, both within and outside of the home. They appeared to be drawn closer together into a form of renewed companionship reflected by the development of mutual undertakings, such as when entertaining friends, dining out together, or just going to the movies.

Some additional evidence from a related study of postparental couples in Cuyahoga County, Ohio, indicates that this intensification of interspousal activity is apt to be more characteristic of the middle than the lower class.[29] This is partly attributed to the differences in intergenerational continuity between the two groups. Middle-aged, lower-class spouses typically lived closer to their married children's families and spent more of their leisure time with them, which provided them with a certain degree of role continuity. The middle-class couples, on the other hand, had less extensive interaction with their married child's family and were less likely to be living in close proximity to them. Consequently, they experienced greater changes in social roles during the postparental phase and were more likely to spend their leisure time with nonfamilial persons. Moreover, "the higher social classes generally have internalized the value of a productive leisure, and with children no longer underfoot, they have the time and the money to pursue the pleasures of leisure."[30] The long-postponed vacation, the distant trip, and other ventures can now be undertaken with little, if any, parental concern and responsibility to stand in their way.

[28]Marvin B. Sussman, "Activity Patterns of Post-Parental Couples and Their Relationship to Family Continuity," *Marriage and Family Living*, **17** (Nov. 1955), pp. 338–341. The data also show that those parents exhibiting high family continuity, that is, who managed to maintain continuous relationships with their married child's family, were least likely to desire or seek new kinds of activities as a means of effecting a social adjustment to the void created by the departure of children.

[29]Marvin B. Sussman, "Intergenerational Family Relationships and Social Role Changes in Middle-Age," *Journal of Gerontology*, **15** (Jan. 1960), pp. 71–75

[30]Ibid., pp. 73–74. These greater changes in social roles on the part of middle-class couples do not necessarily lead to dissatisfaction. On the contrary, the small amount of research in this area indicates that, for example, the middle-class wife expresses greater satisfaction with this period of life than her lower- or working-class counterpart.

547

THE MIDDLE-AGED POSTPARENTAL WIFE There is some consensus among family researchers that, in terms of role changes observed among middle-aged couples, the postparental stage is a more crucial time of life for the wife.[31] During this phase of the family life cycle, most husbands continue to give the major portion of their time, attention, and energies to their occupation, from which they gain not only income but a strong sense of identity, usefulness, and satisfaction. Hence, husbands generally do not perceive this period as producing any drastic revisions in their family routines or as disrupting their primary role as household provider. The home-centered roles of the wife, on the other hand, undergo a more noticeable, though not necessarily severe, change at this turning point in life. The leave-taking of children essentially forces her to reorganize her daily routines with respect to housekeeping, meal planning, shopping, and so on. Moreover, their departure now leaves her with a considerable amount of surplus free time, often creating a need or a desire for new activities and outside contacts to substitute for former child-rearing chores.[32]

Although there are a number of alternatives available, many women attempt to meet this need by reentering the paid labor force, still others through increasing their participation in voluntary associations or community civic affairs. The extent to which such activities prove to be adequate substitutes for declining home-centered roles is not known. Some sociologists have voiced serious doubts in this regard. Note, for example, Foote's comment: "Hardly a day goes by but what the doorbell rings and some bored housewife demands money for a so-called philanthropy that offers her fund-raising as a way to improve her leisure. These angels of mercy with their raffle tickets and pledge cards hardly strike us as having found the solution to their problem."[33] He also has serious reservations about the feasibility of part-time work's adequately meeting the needs of these wives. Most of the part-time jobs currently available to women tend to be unskilled, poorly paid, and insecure; they simply do not provide the economic and intrinsic rewards of full-time work and, therefore, are more apt to lead to frustration. Moreover, middle-aged wives desiring full-time employment frequently discover they lack the necessary education or contemporary skills required to secure the types of jobs that would provide them with a sense of fulfillment. In general, middle age is a period in which women leave rather than enter the labor force, but of those who enter it, for some unknown proportion of middle-aged

---

[31]Evelyn M. Duvall, op. cit., p. 401.
[32]Sussman, "Activity Patterns of Post-Parental Couples . . . ," op. cit., p. 340, and "Intergenerational Family Relationships . . . ," op. cit., p. 74; Axelson, op. cit., p. 67.
[33]Nelson N. Foote, op. cit., pp. 326–329.

women, a return to paid employment (even part-time) or involvement in various types of community service is a successful solution to the problem of expanding what they consider to be a constricted and discontenting social life.[34]

The entry of a middle-aged woman into a position of paid employment has numerous implications with respect to her personal life and rather important consequences for the husband-wife relationship. She now must reorganize her daily routine into a more rigid schedule in order to synchronize the demands of employment with domestic responsibilities. Working outside of the home exposes her to a new array of persons and social groups who reflect a wide range of ages, experiences, and values. As she strives for status among these new associates, her own value system may undergo certain changes.

Work skills, efficiency, punctuality, concentration, impersonality, control of emotions, ability to maintain smooth secondary relationships, and acceptance of regimentation replace the homemaking skills, permissiveness of conduct and emotional expression, personal relationships, and independence of work arrangements of family life. Competitiveness directed toward promotion replaces family cooperativeness, and individualism is sharpened, for each worker must look out for herself, whereas in the family unity gives protection and security.[35]

The degree of satisfaction an older married woman will obtain from employment will vary, therefore, with the extent to which she successfully accommodates to the different value system of the occupational world. Such an accommodation, of course, will depend both on the nature of the work that she performs and on how strongly she identifies with it.

The employment of a middle-aged woman is also apt to bring about certain alterations in the husband-wife relationship. If her outside work consumes too much of her time and energy, it may interfere with her capacity to keep up with domestic duties. She may, therefore, bring pressure upon the husband to take on a greater share of the household tasks and, if he is reluctant or unwilling to do so, tension and conflict may ensue. Moreover, the wife's employment provides her with a regular source of income. The possession of a paycheck not only contributes a sense of independence, but it also improves a woman's power position vis-à-vis her husband and allows her to operate on a

[34]Arnold M. Rose, "Factors Associated with the Life Satisfaction of Middle-Class, Middle-Aged Persons," *Marriage and Family Living,* **17** (Feb. 1955), pp. 15–19. For a research report which presents a less optimistic picture, see: F. Ivan Nye and Lois Wladis Hoffman, *The Employed Mother in America* (Chicago: Rand McNally, 1963), pp. 327–329.

[35]Ruth S. Cavan, op. cit., pp. 576–577.

more equalitarian basis within the home with respect to task-sharing, planning, and decision-making.[36]

Generally speaking, however, the shifts in established patterns of husband-wife interactions created by older married women's obtaining outside employment are likely to result in tension or conflict in only a minority of marriages. In the first place, middle-aged wives do not ordinarily secure jobs that would put them in competitive roles with their husbands. That is, they are not involved in occupation *careers.* Consequently, they do not command a level of income and prestige comparable to that of their husbands. They usually think of their income as *supplemental to* that of the husband. Therefore, aside from the initial period of accommodation following the wife's employment, most aspects of the husband-wife relationship among *middle-aged couples* are not seriously disturbed.

Kinship Interaction in the Middle Years

We saw in Chapter 16 that the American kinship system is characterized by a complex network of social relations involving patterns of visitation and mutual exchanges of goods and services between members of the extended family. With respect to economic assistance, it was noted that the general pattern is for middle-aged parents to provide some sort of cash subsidy for their married children, particularly during the early years. As Sussman and Burchinal describe this for the middle class,

the flow of aid is from parents to children. As children become middle-aged the stream may be reversed, children now help their parents. Middle-class, middle-aged children may be giving subsidies to young married children and aged parents at the same time. A frequent pattern of aid is to turn to the needs of aging and often ailing parents after children have been aided in beginning their marriage and careers. This pattern is more a function of high income of parents and age of members of nuclear linked units than preference to help children over parents.[37]

The central supporting and sustaining role of the middle-aged parental generation in the kinship network is well illustrated by the data in Table 21.4, taken from a Minnesota study of mutual assistance patterns among three-generation families. The study focused on the

[36]Robert O. Blood, Jr., and Donald M. Wolfe, *Husbands and Wives* (New York: The Free Press, 1960), especially Chapters 2 and 3.

[37]Marvin B. Sussman and Lee Burchinal, "Parental Aid to Married Children: Implications for Family Functioning," *Marriage and Family Living,* **24** (Nov. 1962), pp. 320–332.

Table 21.4
Help Given and Received in Five Areas Among Three-Generation Families*

Generational Level	Economic		Emotional Gratification		Household Management		Child Care		Illness	
	Gave %	Received %	Gave %	Received %	Gave %	Received %	Gave %	Received %	Gave %	Received %
Grandparents	26	34	23	42	21	52	16	0	32	61
Parents	41	17	47	37	47	23	50	23	21	21
Married Children	34	49	31	21	33	25	34	78	47	18
Total %	100	100	100	100	100	100	100	100	100	100

*Some percentages do not add to 100 because of rounding.
SOURCE: Reuben Hill, "Decision Making and Family Life Cycle," in *Social Structure and the Family: Generational Relations*, ed. by Ethel Shanas and Gordon F. Streib (Englewood Cliffs, N.J.: Prentice-Hall, 1965), p. 125. Reprinted by permission.

amount of help given and received by each generation in five areas: economic, emotional gratification, household management, child care, and illness. It can be seen that in the first four areas the parental generation clearly gives substantially more help than it receives than either the married child or the grandparental generations. Even in the final area of illness they provide as much assistance as they receive. The married child generation is next most involved, giving more aid than it receives in three of the areas—emotional gratification, household management, and support during periods of illness. As might be expected of this generation, it is the recipient of much more economic and child-care assistance than it renders because of its greater needs in these areas. In contrast to the parental and married child generations, the grandparental generation receives substantially more help than it gives in all of the areas, with the exception of child care, which is not relevant to them. Hill interprets these differences in mutual assistance patterns among the three generations in terms of the ways families perceive their position and function in the kinship network:

In the beginning of the life-span the married child generation is apparently quite willing to receive various kinds of help and perceives itself more or less in equilibrium in its giving and receiving. It appears to benefit more from exchanges that are reciprocal than does the grandparent generation. The grandparents perceive themselves as both meager givers and high receivers, almost in a *dependency status,* whereas the parent generation, in contrast, is high in giving and modest in receiving, a *patron-type status.* Only the married child generation appears high both in giving and receiving, a status of high reciprocity and interdependence within its social network.[38]

We shall present a more detailed discussion of the grandparental generation in Chapter 22. At this point we merely take note of the fact that because of their high dependency status, they are in a rather vunerable position vis-à-vis the rest of the kin network. The parental generation, on the other hand, because of its more affluent position, is able to disperse assistance when called upon. Its needs are considerably less than either of the other two generations. Finally, research has shown that when such assistance is provided, it is more apt to come from the wife's parents than from the husband's parents, and that this is true for both working- and middle-class families.[39] The reason for this will be made apparent in the following section, where the relations between parents and their married children are examined in greater detail.

[38]Reuben Hill, "Decision Making and the Family Life Cycle," in *Social Structure and the Family: Generational Relations,* ed. by Ethel Shanas and Gordon F. Streib (Englewood Cliffs, N.J.: Prentice-Hall, 1965), pp. 113–139.
[39]Bert N. Adams, "Structural Factors Affecting Parental Aid to Married Children," *Journal of Marriage and the Family,* **26** (Aug. 1964), pp. 327–331.

The In-Law Relationship

In the previous section, as well as in Chapter 16, emphasis was placed on the key supportive functions performed by middle-aged parents as members of their respective kinship groups. There is, however, a more familiar and difficult aspect of their involvement in extended family relations that has significant implications and that should be examined, namely, their particular role as parents-in-law.

THE IN-LAW PROBLEM That the relationships between young married couples and their parents-in-laws are frequently a source of tension and conflict in the American family system is well known. The so-called in-law problem is a subject of popular interest, widely discussed and portrayed in the mass media as well as in popular novels. The obtrusive in-law is a familiar stereotype in our soap operas and figures prominently as the agitator of family troubles as described in letters that are written to the widely circulated "Dear Abby" newspaper column. In-law relations are a constant source of humor in our society, and mother-in-law jokes have long been standard stock-in-trade to comics and cartoonists alike. Moreover, sociological research has consistently demonstrated that in-law difficulties are a conspicuous aspect of American marriages. Duvall, for example, in a pilot study of several thousand married persons from various parts of the nation, found that approximately three fourths had one or more in-law problems.[40] It is important, therefore, to examine the nature of this special relationship in the United States and to analyze those facets of our cultural and familial systems that contribute to the development of in-law difficulties.

CULTURAL PATTERNING OF IN-LAW INTERACTION In many cultures around the world, especially those represented by the Far East, the specific nature of in-law relationships is defined and circumscribed by rather explicit institutional arrangements. In the traditional joint Hindu family of India, for example, when a young couple marries custom dictates that the daughter-in-law be brought into the husband's household in conformity with the patrilocal residential pattern. There she becomes the most subordinate member of the household with little influence and authority, and is obligated to give explicit obedience to her mother-in-law and to avoid the elder males. Until she bears children, especially sons, she cannot expect to improve her status in the household. Although there is evidence that this traditional pattern of family relations is changing under the impact of Western ideology,[41] nevertheless "the dominance of the elder woman of a household is still

[40]Evelyn M. Duvall, *In-Laws: Pro and Con* (New York: Association Press, 1954), pp. 187–188.

[41]William J. Goode, *World Revolution and Family Patterns* (New York: The Free Press, 1963), Chapter 5, "Changing Family Patterns in India," pp. 203–269.

common in the culture, a dominance that extends to all household matters and even to the daughter-in-law's relations with her husband and children. The mother of the eldest male in the family is in the position of authority."[42] An analogous pattern of family relationships is found in the classical form of the Chinese family. This family system, with its emphasis on the continuity of the male line, is organized on a patrilineal, patrilocal, and essentially patriarchal basis. Thus, following marriage the young bride is expected to join her husband's household and to give allegiance to her parents-in-law.

A married woman's duty is first and above all toward her parents-in-law, just as a married man's is primarily toward his parents. Even marriage itself is couched in terms of securing a daughter-in-law and making an addition to the household. A man who suppressed his wife because of his father and mother, and a woman who neglected her husband because of her parents-in-law, would be equally praised; a husband who failed to favor his parents, and a wife her parents-in-law, because of his or her spouse would be condemned.[43]

In this system, like that of the Hindu joint family, obligations to the kinship group take precedence over the marital relationship of the young couple. The new wife maintains a subservient position in the household, submitting to the authority of the parents-in-law. Only with the passage of time, and the birth and rearing of sons, will her prestige and power increase. Again, the classical Chinese family system has undergone change under the impact of westernization and the spread of Communist ideology.[44]

Nevertheless, both the Chinese and the Indian family systems illustrate the influence of cultural value systems in establishing a framework for structuring in-law relationships. In both instances, conjugal relations between young married couples are not ordinarily permitted to assume precedence over other kin obligations.[45] Cultural values assign much greater import to the solidarity of the larger, patrilineal kin group. Consequently, the prescribed patterns of authori-

[42]David G. Mandelbaum, "The Family in India," in *The Family: Its Function and Destiny,* ed. by Ruth N. Anshen (New York: Harper & Row, 1959), pp. 167–187.

[43]Francis L. K. Hsu, "The Family in China: The Classical Form," in Ruth N. Anshen, op. cit., pp. 123–145.

[44]Goode, op. cit., Chapter 6, pp. 270–320. See also Maurice Freedman, "The Family in China, Past and Present," *Pacific Affairs,* 34 (Winter 1961–1962), pp. 323–336; Morton N. Fried, "The Family in China: The Peoples Republic," in Anshen, op. cit., pp. 146–166.

[45]In many preliterate societies, of course, spousal obligations are completely dominated by involvement in the larger kin network. In such societies, kinship roles are inextricably bound up with the economic, political, and religious institutions. Extended family responsibilities have a comprehensive claim over the lives of the couples and demand their complete loyalty. Traditional kinship obligations permeate all aspects of their lives. Under such circumstances the possibility of the marital relationship's becoming preeminent is restricted.

ty, especially those that exist between the married pair and the parents-in-law, reflect this emphasis and are accordingly patterned to support it.

The structure of family relationships in the Western hemisphere, of course, provides a sharp contrast to the systems just described. Unlike the Asiatic system, in Western ideology the solidarity of the marital tie generally takes precedence over the claims of the extended family. This is particularly the case in middle-class American society, where the obligations of a husband and wife to each other and to their offspring supersede the demands of the kin network on their loyalty and attention.

If a man's occupation interferes with his marital responsibilities, prevailing values demand that the occupational role be changed to be consistent with marital obligations. Most Americans take seriously the Biblical injunction to leave their mothers and fathers at marriage and cleave unto their spouses. Thus, nuclear family ties completely eclipse all other kinship obligations and diminish their significance.[46]

The neolocal residential pattern that characterizes our society means that upon marriage young couples are normally expected to leave the homes of their respective families of orientation and establish an independent household. Underlying this system are two major presuppositions: (1) that newly married couples possess the economic and emotional maturity necessary for successful independent living, and (2) that their parents are prepared and willing to relinquish all influence and authority over their lives. In-law problems arise in the United States when the two generations fail to validate either or both of these assumptions.

IN-LAW PROBLEMS AND DURATION OF MARRIAGE There is good evidence that in-law difficulties are most prevalent in the early years of marriage, a period when the new couple and their parents are working out the realignment of family relationships and loyalties. Thomas, for example, studied some seven thousand Roman Catholic marriages that had been terminated by divorce and found that in-law relations were the single most frequently reported cause of marital breakup during the first year of marriage; in subsequent years other problems became more prominent.[47] Additional confirmation of this finding is provided in the more recent investigation by Blood and Wolfe of over nine hundred families in Detroit, Michigan, in which they found the greatest concentration of in-law disagreements occurring at the beginning stages of

[46]J. Richard Udry, *The Social Context of Marriage* (Philadelphia: J. B. Lippincott Co., 1966), p. 376.

[47]John L. Thomas, "Marital Failure and Duration," *Social Order,* **3** (Jan. 1953), pp. 24–29.

marriage; 15 per cent of the sample reported in-law disagreements during the honeymoon stage, with the percentage declining steadily throughout the remaining stages of the life cycle.[48]

There is a combination of both sociological and psychological factors that help explain why in-law difficulties are most acute at the youthful stages of marriage, among which perhaps the following are most common.

1. Some middle-aged parents experience considerable ambiguity when finally faced with having to relinquish the parental role completely. Having organized a major portion of their lives around the rearing of their children—directing, supervising, and making decisions for them—parents are reluctant to discontinue this role and to surrender the authority, influence, and control that goes with it. Because of a strong emotional attachment, they may have difficulty accepting the fact that their children are now mature adults who are ready and able to shoulder the responsibilities of marriage. The immature parent-in-law is not emotionally prepared to give up his adult child and to grant him independence and autonomy. Such parents frequently promote conflict and hostility by their continued attempts to prolong the parental role by intruding upon and dominating the lives of the young married couple.

2. In-law difficulties may be similarly generated by the inability of the adult married child to cut the apron strings and become independent of his or her parents. From infancy through childhood, the young person is physically and emotionally dependent upon his mother and father. He looks to them for guidance and assistance and quite naturally develops a close attachment to them. As the person moves toward physical adulthood, however, he is expected to become less reliant on the parents and to establish an emotional independence from them. Young adults entering marriage who have failed to complete this weaning process and who remain overly attached to and dependent upon their parents are apt to invite in-law meddling and interference. The young wife who continues to turn to her parents when problems arise, for example, may anger her partner, who perceives the activities of the parents as threatening or undermining his role as husband. Running home to mother, either physically or emotionally, inevitably leads to an intensification of hostility toward parents-in-law, whether they deserve it or not. The alienation is further compounded in those instances in which the parents maintain the view that the son-in-law or daughter-in-law is not a worthy match for their child.[49]

[48]Blood and Wolfe, op. cit., pp. 247–248.

[49]Willard Waller, *The Family: A Dynamic Interpretation,* rev. by Reuben Hill (New York: The Dryden Press, 1951), p. 290.

The probability of these kinds of in-law difficulties' occurring is apparently lessened by the age and maturity of the newly married couple. The Landises, for example, found that the amount of in-law difficulty is closely related to the age at which the young spouses were married. More specifically, their data reveal that among those wives who had married between ages seventeen and nineteen, only 45 per cent reported the quality of their in-law relationships as excellent, compared to 63 per cent of those marrying at twenty-four or older. Whereas only 7 per cent of the latter indicated a fair to poor in-law adjustment, 21 per cent of the younger group did so.[50] These findings would suggest that the majority of the couples who had married at older ages had acquired the emotional maturity and independence required to function adequately in adult roles. Older persons are more likely to have completed their education and obtained employment. By achieving economic self-sufficiency, they lessen the chances of remaining dependent upon their parents and parents-in-law and thereby have a greater chance of avoiding the types of friction encountered by less mature, less sufficient couples.

3. In-law friction is also more characteristic of the early stages of marriage because of the initial confrontation of conflicting family subcultures.[51] The new husband and wife were born and reared in two distinctive family subcultures, each with its own set of normative patterns or standards of behavior. Some of these norms will be mutually shared because the couple have been reared in a common culture. "However, the husband and wife through socialization and experience in non-shared social systems may be oriented to normative systems that may be conflicting or at least foreign to the new marriage partner."[52] At the beginning of a new marriage, both spouses are still strongly identified with their families of orientation. They continue to feel that they are, and are considered to be, important if not integral constituents of their parents' family system. Thus, in addition to the tension of adjusting to the personal idiosyncrasies that each partner brings to the marriage, they also experience some degree of internal and external pressures to conform to the norms, values, and traditions of their particular family of orientation.

In the process of working out an accommodation to these differing family cultures, disagreements among newlyweds and between them and their parents and parents-in-law may arise over the most seemingly

---

[50]Judson T. and Mary G. Landis, *Building a Successful Marriage* (Englewood Cliffs, N.J.: Prentice-Hall, 1963), p. 340. See also Judson T. Landis, "Adjustments After Marriage," *Marriage and Family Living,* **9** (May 1947), pp. 32–34.

[51]F. Ivan Nye and Evelyn MacDougal, "Do Families Have Subcultures?" *Sociology and Social Research,* **44** (May–June, 1960), pp. 311–316.

[52]William G. Dyer, "Analyzing Marital Adjustment Using Role Theory," *Marriage and Family Living,* **24** (Nov. 1962), pp. 371–375.

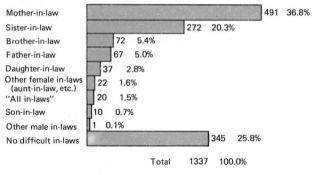

	Number	Per cent
Mother-in-law	491	36.8%
Sister-in-law	272	20.3%
Brother-in-law	72	5.4%
Father-in-law	67	5.0%
Daughter-in-law	37	2.8%
Other female in-laws (aunt-in-law, etc.)	22	1.6%
"All in-laws"	20	1.5%
Son-in-law	10	0.7%
Other male in-laws	1	0.1%
No difficult in-laws	345	25.8%
Total	1337	100.0%

Number and per cent of times mentioned

Figure 21.1. The in-law named most difficult by 1,337 persons. [From Evelyn M. Duvall, *In-Laws: Pro and Con* (New York: Association Press, 1954) p. 188.]

insignificant details of family life. "In the first months of marriage both parents unconsciously welcome decisions in favor of their own idiosyncrasies and breed little in-law tensions when their ways are snubbed. Even where parents are not actively involved in culture conflict, each parental family is a living demonstration to the child-in-law of a differing way of life and hence a challenge to his own."[53] With the passage of time, however, most couples effect some sort of conciliation between the conflicting demands emanating from members of the separate family subcultures, and in-law relationships settle down to a more harmonious pattern. If, on the other hand, members of either generation remain intractable, insisting that loyalty to family traditions be adhered to, then the difficulties may never be resolved and in-law conflict may continue indefinitely. Thus for example, in Landis's study of 409 happily married couples, it was found that about 10 per cent had not yet achieved satisfactory in-law relationships, even after twenty years of marriage.[54]

FEMALE INVOLVEMENT IN IN-LAW PROBLEMS Almost every major American study to date has shown that the majority of all in-law problems involve conflict between young wives and their mothers-in-law and sisters-in-law. More specifically, it is the mother-in-law relationship that is most troublesome. Duvall, who has conducted the most comprehensive investigation of in-law relationships to date, found that among 992 subjects in her sample who reported in-law difficulties nearly half named the mother-in-law relationship as being

[53]Robert O. Blood, *Marriage* (New York: The Free Press, 1962), p. 317.
[54]Judson T. Landis, "Length of Time Required to Achieve Adjustment in Marriage," *American Sociological Review,* **11** (Dec. 1946), pp. 666–677.

558

most difficult. Moreover, nine out of ten complaints about the mother-in-law were registered by wives.[55] As can be seen in Figure 21.1, husbands, male in-laws, and all other female in-laws, with the exception of the sister-in-law, are much less likely to be involved in in-law disputes. Other studies have confirmed this general pattern.[56] Most of the studies, it should be pointed out, involve predominantly middle-class families. Even among working-class families, however, this pattern seems to hold. Komarovsky's analysis of fifty-three working-class marriages showed that although husbands enjoyed relatively satisfactory affinal relations, one third of the wives were seriously dissatisfied with in-law relationships, especially with the mother-in-law.[57]

With little exception, then, it is primarily the women who are entangled in in-law difficulties, with the husband's mother emerging as the major target of criticism. Men apparently are able to maintain more harmonious ties with affinal kin. Husbands, for example, are less apt to dislike their mothers-in-law than wives are to dislike theirs, and even where strains do exist they are more likely to exercise restraint over any overt expression of hostility.[58] Poor in-law relations often emanate from the wife's attitudes and activities. Numerous studies have shown that females are generally more attached to and dependent upon their families of orientation than males. Stryker, however, in a study of 104 married persons living in university housing at Indiana University, found that poor husband-wife and husband-mother-in-law adjustment tended to occur as a result of the wife's attachment to her mother. Specifically,

when wives report dependence upon mother, husbands are less likely to be well-adjusted to their mothers-in-law than they are when wives are dominant or the dependency relationship is neutral . . . husbands are more likely to be well adjusted to their fathers-in-law when their wives report dependency upon their fathers. Wife's dependency upon mother does not appear to affect husband's adjustment to father-in-law; nor does her dependency upon father appear to affect his adjustment to mother-in-law.[59]

---

[55]Duvall, *In-Laws: Pro and Con,* op. cit., p. 187.

[56]Landis and Landis, op. cit., pp. 327–346; John L. Thomas, *The American Catholic Family* (Englewood Cliffs, N.J.: Prentice-Hall, 1956), p. 235; Paul Wallen, "Sex Differences in Attitudes to In-Laws—A Test of a Theory," *American Journal of Sociology,* **59** (March 1954), pp. 466–469.

[57]Mirra Komarovsky, *Blue-Collar Marriage* (New York: Random House, 1964), p. 259. However, further analysis of the data according to educational level revealed that husbands with less than a high-school education have as much difficulty with their mothers-in-law as their wives.

[58]Ibid.

[59]Sheldon Stryker, "The Adjustment of Married Offspring to Their Parents," *American Sociological Review,* **20** (Apr. 1955), pp. 149–154.

In Komarovsky's study of working-class marriages, cited earlier, the less educated husband's unsatisfactory relations with his mother-in-law were similarly associated with the wife's emotional dependence upon her mother.[60] In American society, where in-law relationships are essentially noninstitutionalized, the congeniality of the husband-mother-in-law tie is always tenuous, inasmuch as it is determined according to the changing nature of interpersonal attraction. In many societies around the world, the potential difficulty between the mother-in-law and the son-in-law is well recognized and in many instances elaborate rules of avoidance are instituted to prevent the development of problems.

In more than three-fifths of the world's societies, severe penalties follow upon the meeting of a man and his mother-in-law, and they shun each other accordingly. In northern Australia, a man who speaks to his mother-in-law must be put to death. In parts of the South Pacific, both parties would commit suicide. In Yucatan, men believe that to meet one's mother-in-law face to face would render a man sterile for life, so he may travel miles out of his way over dangerous territory to avoid being near her. Navaho men believe that they will go blind if they should see their mother-in-law, so she is not even allowed to attend the wedding.[61]

Patterns of strict avoidance are not, of course, common in our culture, and every son-in-law has relatively wide discretion in establishing a mode of conduct with respect to his in-law relationships.

In previous pages we have touched on many of the salient factors that help explain why most in-law problems are essentially female problems: the married daughter's continued attachment to and dependence upon her mother; the reluctance of mothers to surrender the active parental role gracefully or to replace the satisfactions of parenthood with some equally satisfying substitute activity; the inability to reconcile the norms of conflicting family subcultures as expressed through parental mothers and mothers-in-law as they attempt to exert influence on the new wife, and so on. Still other factors can be enumerated that have the potential for triggering in-law conflict, depending on the particular family situation. But there is a more general sociological explanation that helps account for in-law tensions between females and that seems applicable, regardless of the family situation. It has to do with the dominant role of females in the American kinship system.

[60]Komarovsky also found the husband-mother-in-law relationship to be unsatisfactory under other conditions, including (1) marriage to a better educated wife, (2) wife's hostility toward her mother, and (3) economic and social interdependence, including a joint household with in-laws.

[61]John M. Schlien, "Mother-In-Law: A Problem of Kinship Terminology," *ETC: A Review of General Semantics*, **19** (July 1962), pp. 161–171.

Sociological analyses of sex-role differentials concerning the types and extent of kinship interaction in the United States have consistently demonstrated that women play the predominant role in perpetuating kin ties in our society; they are the primary actors in sustaining contacts with various relatives. Much of the research cited in Chapter 16 substantiates the notion that women have a greater involvement in kinship groups and have generally assumed the function of representing the nuclear family in discharging various obligations to relatives.[62] It is they who most frequently write the letters and send the occasion cards and gifts, make the telephone calls, and provide various services for and visit with kinfolk. Moreover, the evidence is clear that females also tend to maintain closer relationships with their immediate family and kin than do males.

The central role of the woman in performing duties imposed by kinship apparently provides opportunities for her to show a preference for the maternal side of the family despite the normative pattern of treating maternal and paternal relatives equally. In those activities with relatives which are more clearly obligatory, a woman is able to express her preference for her own blood relatives, and in doing so increase their contact with her children.[63]

What this in fact means is that the majority of extended family interactions in the United States are organized around the mother-daughter relationship.[64] Such female domination of the kinship system no doubt considerably enhances the probabilities of women's becoming involved in a variety of situations conducive to the development of in-law difficulties.

In-law troubles are not, of course, an inevitable consequence of being married. In many instances, the married couple and the parents-in-law accommodate to each other with little or no difficulty. Moreover, contemporary couples, especially those in the middle class, have an effective option available to them for diminishing the extent of in-law friction—they can move. The high degree of geographical mobility characteristic of today's young middle-class couples creates spatial distance between generationally linked families and considerably

---

[62]Two recent major works that are not cited in Chapter 16 but that provide additional evidence and confirmation of the primary role of women in our kinship system are Bert N. Adams, *Kinship in an Urban Setting* (Chicago: Markham Publishing Company, 1968); Hope J. Leichter and William Mitchell, *Kinship and Casework* (New York: Russell Sage Foundation, 1967).

[63]Lee N. Robins and Moroda Tomanec, "Closeness to Blood Relatives Outside the Immediate Family," *Marriage and Family Living,* 24 (Nov. 1962), pp. 340–346.

[64]This apparently holds true for family relations in Britain. See Peter Willmott and Michael Young, *Family and Class in a London Suburb* (London: Routledge and Kegan Paul, 1960); Michael Young and Hildred Geertz, "Old Age in London and San Francisco: Some Families Compared," *British Journal of Sociology,* 12 (June 1961), pp. 124–141.

reduces physical contact between them. Under such circumstances, the potential development of in-law strain is effectively minimized and the ability of the couple to function independently is enhanced.

Finally, there are certain trends evident in American society that have the potential for diminishing the extent of in-law tensions and conflict. We noted in our discussion of changes in the family life cycle that as a result of younger age at marriage and the compression of childbearing into a shorter time span, couples are now able to complete their child-rearing function much earlier in life than was the case in the past. One consequence of this change is to reduce the generational gap between parents and their married offspring. Modern parents are perhaps in a better position to identify with their married offspring and to understand their outlook and problems than parents of a previous generation. They are, one might suggest, considerably more "in-law wise."

22

The Retired Family

In 1949, a provocative article entitled "Are the Aged Ex-Family?" appeared in a major journal and emphasized the lack of attention given to older families in sociological textbooks.[1] The charge was made that writers overwhelmingly concentrated on earlier phases of the life cycle to the neglect of later stages, and that the references to the aged that did appear reflected primarily personal observations and experiences. Actually, the textbooks reflected the paucity of systematic sociological knowledge on aging up to that time.

Since the mid-twentieth century, however, scientific interest in the aged has quickened with the emergence of the field of gerontology as a full-fledged discipline.[2] Interest in the study of aging families was partly brought about by the dramatic growth of our older population. In 1850 persons aged sixty-five and over constituted only 2.5 per cent of our population, whereas today the proportion is 10 per cent, that is, more than 20 million people. Consequently, a considerable amount of empirical research on the sociology of aging has been undertaken and systematic knowledge regarding older families has begun to accumulate. In the process, a number of earlier notions regarding family relations among the aged have slowly eroded under the scrutinizing light of scientific inquiry.

By the time most married couples are approaching the age of retirement, their children have already matured, married, and established independent households. Consequently, the *retirement family* typically is composed of simply the aged husband and his wife.

[1]Belle B. Beard, *Social Forces,* **27** (March 1949), pp. 274–279.
[2]Clark Tibbitts, "Origins, Scope, and Fields of Social Gerontology," in *Handbook of Social Gerontology,* ed. by Tibbitts (Chicago: University of Chicago Press, 1960), pp. 3–26.

Approximately two thirds of all aged persons are husband-wife couples living together, most of whom maintain their own households.

Conjugal Relations in Old Age: The Retirement Family

With the onset of retirement, the aged couple embark on still another phase of the family life cycle, one that frequently necessitates major readjustments in the conjugal relationship. Harmonious relations among elderly couples are often conditioned by events that precede retirement, not the least of which are the habitual patterns of marital interaction established in previous stages of the family cycle. Fried and Stern, for example, found that nearly all of the aged couples whom they interviewed, and who rated their marriages as satisfactory, had a previous history of good marital relations. Moreover, almost half of these marriages had become even more satisfactory as the partners aged. On the other hand, most of the older couples who rated their marriages as unsatisfactory "had been unsatisfactory more or less from the beginning, and approximately half deteriorated further as the partners advanced in years."[3] For some older couples, then, marital adjustment in later years is simply a reflection of the adjustment worked out earlier in life.

THE RETIRED HUSBAND AND MARITAL ADJUSTMENT Although a favorable marital adjustment among older couples is no doubt dependent in part upon many factors (physical, economic, emotional, and so on), nevertheless a successful accommodation to the retirement role on the part of the husband appears to be especially crucial.[4]

During most of his adult working life, the American husband engages in sharply differentiated roles from those of the wife. From a sociological point of view, he

has his primary roles and acquires his primary conceptions of himself in two institutional systems: the occupational, where he is a worker, and the familial, where he is husband and father. These two systems are sharply separated both geographically and temporally; life on the job is normally quite distinct from life in the household and involves different actors, different goals, and different status. Nonetheless, there is a profound interdependence and interpenetration of the two because the "success" of the male in his familial roles (husband, father) is defined, partially, in terms of his achievement in his occupational role (worker).[5]

[3]Edrita G. Fried and Karl Stern, "The Situation of the Aged Within the Family," *American Journal of Orthopsychiatry,* **18** (Jan. 1948), pp. 31–54.

[4]Ruth S. Cavan, "Self and Role Adjustment in Old Age," in *Human Behavior and Social Process,* ed. by Arnold M. Rose (Boston: Houghton Mifflin Company, 1962), pp. 526–535.

[5]Aaron Lipman, "Role Conceptions of Couples in Retirement," in *Social and Psychological Aspects of Aging,* ed. by Clark Tibbitts and Wilma Donahue (New York: Columbia University Press, 1962), pp. 475–485.

It is, then, primarily by virtue of his significance in the occupational sphere and in the attendant social roles of the family provider, that the husband manages to develop and sustain a satisfactory self-image and status in the home.

The primary role of the wife, on the other hand, lies mainly in her capacity to manage the internal and domestic affairs of the household. As Cavan has noted, this role has the most continuity in the life of the wife: "No matter what other role she fulfills, the homemaking role is basic. The mother role rises to a crest, declines, and disappears. Paid employment comes and goes. Homemaking as a role continues from the day after the wedding to the end of the marriage."[6] Thus, it is primarily by virtue of her significance in the household and the attendant social roles of wife, homemaker, and companion that the woman manages to develop and sustain an acceptable self-image and status in the home.

With the onset of retirement, however, these traditional sex-differentiated roles and the self-concepts that are derived from them frequently undergo various degrees of strain and alteration, especially in the case of males. Whereas many wives of retired families are able to continue satisfactorily their traditional role as homemakers, a similar pattern of role continuity is denied the husband; "the role of wage earner, which he had conceived as his primary role, is suddenly withdrawn; structurally he is isolated from the occupational system, and this shock often has grave effects upon his entire existence. If the married male is to adjust to retirement, he must necessarily redefine his social function and his familial role."[7]

Throughout most of his adult life the husband has been, sociologically speaking, the *instrumental leader*[8] of the family and, as such, has performed certain *instrumental roles* involving task-oriented activities related to being an effective provider for his wife and children. Because retirement drastically (and sometimes abruptly) curtails his status as the major breadwinner, however, questions arise as to what adaptations he makes to mollify the strain created by permanent severance from the occupational world and how they affect the marital relationship.

Some insights into this problem are provided by Lipman's study of a group of primarily upper-class socioeconomic retired couples residing in metropolitan Miami.[9] He found, among other things, that successful

---

[6]Ruth S. Cavan, *American Marriage* (New York: Thomas Y. Crowell Company, 1959), p. 337.

[7]Lipman, op. cit., p. 476. See also, in this connection, Cavan, "Self and Role Adjustment in Old Age," op. cit., pp. 526–535.

[8]The wife, on the other hand, functions as the expressive leader, performing expressive roles involving affectional and emotional supportive roles within the family. Morris M. Zelditch, Jr., "Role Differentiation in the Nuclear Family: A Comparative Study," in *Family, Socialization, and Interaction Process,* ed. by Talcott Parsons and Robert F. Bales (Glencoe, Ill.: The Free Press, 1955), pp. 307–352.

[9]Lipman, op. cit., pp. 475–485.

marital adjustment following retirement partly depends on the extent to which the husband replaces a self-conception functionally related to employment and the associated instrumental role of provider by developing a substitute *expressive role* in the home.

In retirement, since the man can no longer attain the work and achievement goals, striving for them and adherence to them is associated with poor adjustment. A feeling of usefulness and purposefulness is achieved by the male increasingly through assistance with household activities, and emphasizing expressive qualities such as giving of love, affection, and companionship to his wife. A new and meaningful functional role is thus created that aids in individual adjustment.[10]

Thus, the better-adjusted retired husbands in this sample were more apt to be willing to share household chores and responsibilities with their wives, such as assisting with the grocery shopping, helping with the housework, making breakfast, washing dishes, and so on. Moreover, they were more likely to agree that wives have a right to expect their husbands to share in household activities.

Other of Lipman's data led him to question the rather widespread assumption that women experience little or no role discontinuity following their husband's retirement, but simply retain their traditional role of housewife. He found that the husband's increased involvement in household activities and his emergent expressive orientation necessitates a reciprocal shift in the wife's domestic role and her self-image.

Since her husband's new activities have blurred the traditional distinction between the male and female roles, the woman can no longer view her major role primarily as good housekeeper and homemaker. Both men and women who had clearly and rigidly defined their preretirement role in a predominantly instrumental fashion that strongly differentiated husband's and wife's activities, now move toward a common area of identity in role activities—an area that emphasizes sharing and cooperation, where similar expressive qualities such as love, understanding, companionship, and compatibility become the most important things they can both give in marriage. These non-sex-differentiated supportive roles that demand expressive, rather than instrumental qualities, appear well adapted for the personality system of both the husband and wife in retirement.[11]

Thus, a successful transition to the retirement role is dependent on *both* the husband and the wife's making changes and accommodating changes in the other's behavior and self-conceptions. Often this is easier said than done. If, for example, the wife resents the husband's intrusion into the domestic affairs of the household and resists his

[10]Ibid., pp. 483–484.
[11]Ibid., pp. 484–485.

566

intrusion, tension in the marital relationship is likely to develop. Evidence from Kerckhoff's study of husband-wife expectations and reactions to retirement suggests that this type of role tension is more apt to occur among retirement families representing the lower occupational levels.[12] He found that compared to preretired and retired couples from upper and middle occupational levels, lower-level spouses were much more passive in anticipation of retirement and had fewer plans and expectations. They did not experience retirement as a particularly pleasant change in their lives and they tended to have much more negative reactions to it. With respect to this discussion, his data also show that

lower-level husbands and wives normatively rejected participation of the husband in normal household tasks more frequently than either of the other two groups. In spite of this, however, lower-level husbands actually participated in such tasks about as often as other husbands. The fact that they did this in the face of norms which preclude such behavior was undoubtedly one of the reasons for the conjugal role tension noted.[13]

Despite the potentiality for marital conflict that arises as a result of the husband's retirement and his subsequent involvement in household activities, most aged couples apparently manage a satisfactory accommodation to the situation with a minimum of disharmony in the conjugal relationship.[14] Some wives no doubt welcome the husband's assistance with domestic chores and are not irritated by his activity in the home, particularly if he takes on household tasks that are more in line with a male than a female role. In one study it was found

that the increased performance by the retired husband was not general for all tasks but displayed considerable selectivity. Household activities which are designated by the culture primarily as feminine in orientation (the family laundry, ironing, household dusting, and making the beds) remained almost exclusively the responsibility of the wife, while activities requiring greater mechanical skill or physical strength (moving and repairing furniture, repairing a faucet, and removing and burning trash) along with the administrative tasks (paying household bills) were shifted from the wife to the husband.[15]

---

[12]Alan C. Kerckhoff, "Husband-Wife Expectations and Reactions to Retirement," *Journal of Gerontology,* **19** (Jan. 1964), pp. 510–516. Additional evidence that persons from the lower income and occupational levels are least likely to plan for retirement may be found in William M. Smith, Jr., "Family Plans for Later Years," *Marriage and Family Living,* **16** (Feb. 1954), pp. 36–40.

[13]Kerckhoff, op. cit., pp. 510–516. Data from this study also provides further confirmation for the argument that husbands normally face a more difficult adjustment process upon retirement than wives.

[14]John A. Ballweg, "Resolution of Conjugal Role Adjustment After Retirement," *Journal of Marriage and the Family,* **29** (May 1967), pp. 277–281.

[15]Ibid., pp. 279–280.

Some women no doubt gain an increased sense of companionship from the husband's greater physical presence in the home and from sharing various household tasks with him. For many couples, the heightened realization of their greater dependency upon one another in old age tends to draw them closer together. There is, indeed, good reason to believe that for most married couples a combination of these and other positive factors operate simultaneously to stabilize the marital relationship eventually, once the aged parents have moved beyond the initial adjustment period immediately following retirement.[16]

Finally, it should be emphasized that retirement need not *necessarily* have a deleterious effect upon conjugal relations in old age. Many husbands, for example, experience considerable continuity in the father role as they move from preretirement to retirement. Thus, when a sample of adult children were asked a series of questions designed to assess their perception of the familial situation and their relationship with the father following retirement, the following responses were obtained; (1) over 70 per cent said the father's retirement had not created any serious difficulties; (2) 30 per cent felt retirement had brought their father closer to his immediate family, and 68 per cent reported no change at all in this respect; (3) 93 per cent felt the father had as much to say about family matters as he had had in the years preceding retirement; (4) 94 per cent testified that the father had not tended to interfere with their lives since his retirement; (5) 83 per cent said the fact that the father had retired had not affected the way in which family members got along with one another.[17] These responses indicate that there is considerable stability and harmony in family roles and relationships in retirement.

The Aged Family and the Alienation Myth

While American society was undergoing a rapid and major transition from an agrarian based society to a predominantly urban and industrialized nation, a conception of the aged emerged that stressed the involuntary structural isolation of older couples from their children and relatives, as well as associated feelings of neglect and boredom. Parsons has expressed this point of view as follows:

In various ways our society is oriented to values particularly appropriate to the younger age groups, so that there is a tendency for older people to be left out of it. The abruptness of retirement from occupational roles also contributes to the difficulty. But of primary concern at present is one implication of the structural isolation of the conjugal family. The obverse of the emancipation of children

---

[16]For a discussion of some of these factors, see Fried and Stern, op. cit., pp. 31–54.

[17]Gordon F. Streib, "Intergenerational Relations: Perspectives of the Two Generations on the Older Person," *Journal of Marriage and the Family,* **27** (Nov. 1965), pp. 469–474.

568

from their families of orientation upon their marriage and occupational independence is the gradual depletion of that family until the older couple is left alone. In our kinship system this situation is in strong contrast to that in systems in which membership in a kinship unit is continuous throughout the life-cycle. There, very frequently, it is the oldest members who are treated with the most respect and enjoy the greatest responsibility and authority, but with us there is no one left to respect them or for them to take responsibility for or have authority over.[18]

In this perspective, the labor demands of a bureaucratic society for a highly mobile nuclear family system, in which the young give priority and allegiance to the norms of occupational achievement, are said to isolate older people from their families. From this perspective a stereotypic picture developed that depicted the aged family as rejected, lonely, *and* a liability.[19] To a considerable extent, this stereotype continues to prevail today, not only through the popular mass media, but among scientific literary circles as well.

SOCIAL ISOLATION OF AGED PARENTS: THE SHATTERING OF A MYTH In recent decades, however, empirical evidence has accumulated that casts considerable doubt upon what Shanas has termed this "myth of alienation."[20] She cites, in addition to her own data from the United States, the World Health Organization report that summarizes research from various other countries, as follows:

Wherever careful studies have been carried out in the industrialized countries the lasting devotion of children for their parents has been amply demonstrated. The great majority of old people are in regular contact with their children, relatives, or friends. . . . Where distance permits, the generations continue to shoulder their traditional obligations, of elders toward their children, and the children to the aged.[21]

Thus, for example, in Shanas's own analysis of national census data on persons sixty-five years and older, she found that the majority of the noninstitutionalized aged in America who had children were in close

---

[18]Talcott Parsons, "The Social Structure of the Family," in *The Family: Its Function and Destiny,* rev. ed., ed. by Ruth N. Anshen (New York: Harper and Brothers, 1959), pp. 241–274. See also "The Aging in American Society," *Law and Contemporary Problems,* **27** (Spring 1962), pp. 22–35; "The Kinship System of the Contemporary United States," *American Anthropologist,* **45** (Jan.–March 1943), pp. 22–38; and "Age and Sex in the Social Structure of the United States," *American Sociological Review,* **7** (Oct. 1942), pp. 604–616.

[19]Beard, op. cit., pp. 274–279.

[20]Ethel Shanas, "The Unmarried Old Person in the United States: Living Arrangements and Care in Illness, Myth, and Fact," paper prepared for the International Social Science Research Seminar in Gerontology, Makaryd, Sweden, Aug. 1963.

[21]World Health Organization, *Mental Health Problems of the Aging and the Aged,* Technical Report, Series, No. 171 (Geneva: World Health Organization, 1959).

proximity to at least one of them and saw them often; only 15 per cent live more than a short ride from some child, about a third live with a child.[22] More than two thirds of all aged parents see their children at least weekly and when this is not possible they keep in touch either through letters or by telephone.[23] Cross-cultural comparisons (Table 22.1) reveal that in Britain and Denmark, as well as in the United States, regardless of social class, "old people who live apart from their children tend to have at least one child in the immediate vicinity. Between half and two-thirds of all old couples, irrespective of class, either share a household with a child or live within ten minutes distance from a child."[24] Such findings are impressive, to say the least, in light of the high geographical mobility, particularly of young families, which we have discussed earlier in this volume.

Shanas attributes the sources of this myth to the aged themselves— especially *childless* old people—and professional welfare workers. Childless old people evidently are more likely than other old people to believe that children neglect their aged parents, and professional workers deal mainly with the aged who are without families or who have, indeed, been alienated from their families. She argues that when aged families are alienated from their kin, such patterns were probably established much earlier in the family history. Others have similarly suggested "that the subjective factors, loneliness and boredom, are more usually symptoms of personal distress than of a family's neglect; that such symptoms in old age may stem from remote causes, from socialization in the early life of the persons, and from a lack of personal resources for self-determination and mastery."[25]

Contrary to the alienation theory, it appears that retired parents generally continue to support the norms and values characteristic of the American occupational and stratification system and encourage their adult children to adhere to them. Thus, Streib found that when older persons were asked to choose between social mobility for their children or having their children stay close to their parents, they felt very definitely that the children should follow the demands of greater career development.[26] Although the aged parents recognized that

[22]Ethel Shanas, "Living Arrangements of Older People in the United States," *The Gerontologist,* **1** (March 1961), pp. 27–29. See also Robert G. Brown, "Family Structure and Social Isolation of Older Persons," *Journal of Gerontology,* **15** (Apr. 1960), pp. 170–174.

[23]Alvin L. Schorr, *Filial Responsibility in the Modern American Family,* U.S. Department of Health, Education, and Welfare, Washington, D.C., 1960.

[24]Ethel Shanas, "Family Help Patterns and Social Class in Three Countries," *Journal of Marriage and the Family,* **29** (May 1967), pp. 257–266.

[25]Donald P. Kent, *Aging—Fact and Fancy,* U.S. Department of Health, Education, and Welfare, OA No. 224 (Washington, D.C.: U.S. Government Printing Office, 1965).

[26]Gordon F. Streib, "Family Patterns in Retirement," *Journal of Social Issues,* **14** (1958), pp. 46–60.

educational as well as occupational achievement frequently involves spatial separation from their children, they denied that such mobility caused their children to lose respect for them or to neglect them. Similarly, when Brown asked an aged sample in North Carolina if they thought their family or relatives neglected them, over 80 per cent responded with a definite "not at all."[27]

Indeed, both of these studies, particularly that of Streib, provide evidence that strongly suggests that *successful* upward mobility in most instances does not alienate offspring from their aged parents nor does it adversely affect intergenerational relationships. Indeed, when Streib compared the family relations of those children who had attained some degree of occupational achievement, he found "that where all the children have been more successful than their parents, they are more likely to keep in close touch with their parents and to form a close-knit family than those families in which the children have been less successful in getting ahead."[28]

Kinship Relations in Old Age: Filial Responsibility

The maxim that children should respect and support their elderly parents is one of the oldest and most deeply rooted precepts to evolve from our Judeo-Christian heritage. The injunction to "Honor thy father and mother" has passed down through the ages as part of the cultural mores to confront each new generation. As we noted earlier, however, the extension of the life cycle has created considerable intergenerational overlap, so that today the obligations of filial responsibility to the aged have become all the more a reality for greater numbers of families.

How is the contemporary generation meeting the demands of filial responsibility? It is true, as Dinkel stated in the forties, that

in the past, elders were fairly certain that come what might in the history of their personal relations with their offspring the latter would be willing to give assistance if it were necessary. Now, the children often take into consideration the nature of their personal relations with parents in order to come to a decision as to whether or not to help them. Parents, therefore, cannot be sure of obtaining support no matter how smooth their interaction with children happens to be at a particular time.[29]

Does Dinkel's finding that young adults of the World War II era were reluctant to support aged parents when there were various other

[27]Brown, op. cit., p. 171. There was some slight evidence for social isolation to be related to feelings of neglect among upper-status respondents, resulting perhaps from their higher expectations for close filial contact.

[28]Streib, "Family Patterns in Retirement," op. cit., pp. 413–414.

[29]Robert M. Dinkel, "Attitudes of Children Toward Supporting Aged Parents," *American Sociological Review,* 9 (Aug. 1944), pp. 71–83.

Table 22.1
Percentage Distribution: Proximity of Nearest Child of Persons Aged 65 and over by Social Class

Proximity of Nearest Child and County	White-collar			Working-class			Agricultural Workers		
	Men	Women	All Persons	Men	Women	All Persons	Men	Women	All Persons
Same household									
Denmark	16	17	17	17	16	16	31	31	31
Britain	27	43	36	42	45	44	*	*	49
United States	16	25	21	26	37	32	25	30	28
10 minutes or less distant									
Denmark	30	30	30	32	36	34	34	29	31
Britain	22	20	21	23	25	24	*	*	21
United States	31	33	32	34	31	33	34	37	36
11–30 minutes distant									
Denmark	22	23	23	26	26	26	18	21	19
Britain	18	14	16	16	15	16	*	*	14
United States	17	14	15	17	16	16	15	14	15
31–60 minutes distant									
Denmark	16	15	16	11	11	11	8	11	10
Britain	13	9	10	8	7	7	*	*	5
United States	11	9	9	7	4	5	13	6	8

One hour or more distant									
Denmark	16	14	15	14	11	13	9	8	8
Britain	20	14	17	11	8	9	*	*	11
United States	25	19	22	16	12	14	14	13	13
Total									
Denmark	100	100	100	100	100	100	100	100	100
Britain	100	100	100	100	100	*	*	*	100
United States	100	100	100	100	100	100	100	100	100
Number of cases†									
Denmark	330	368	698	376	430	806	252	243	495
Britain	198	266	464	547	773	1,320	48	37	85
United States	253	307	560	465	510	975	174	267	441

*Percentages are not computed when base is less than 50.

†The percentage of eligible respondents who answered this question is Denmark, total 99.4, men 99.5, women 99.4; Britain, total 97.8, men 98.3, women, 97.5; United States, total 98.2, men 99.0, women 97.6.

SOURCE: Ethel Shanas, "Family Help Patterns and Social Class in Three Countries," *Journal of Marriage and the Family*, **29** (May 1967), p. 263. Reprinted by permission.

institutional sources of aid available still hold for the contemporary generation?[30] What is the nature of intergenerational relationships between aged parents and their children in present-day America?

ECONOMIC SUPPORT If one defines filial responsibility *solely* in terms of financial assistance, then the argument that children no longer support their aged parents appears to be a valid one. Schorr, in an extensive review of current practices in filial responsibility estimated that the proportion of the aged receiving *cash* contributions from children with whom they are not residing does not exceed 10 per cent in any given year and is frequently less.[31] As we have noted in previous chapters, the flow of financial assistance is generally in the opposite direction, that is, from parents to children.

Viewing filial responsibility strictly on the basis of cash donations from adult children to aged parents obviously represents an extremely narrow and largely unrealistic conception of that responsibility. As we shall demonstrate shortly, when the concept is more properly expanded to include other economic and equally important (but perhaps less obvious) forms of assistance, as well as certain intangible social contributions, the picture regarding the performance of filial duties changes considerably to the extent that the argument posed in the preceding paragraph becomes invalid. First, however, we shall discuss two of the attitudes aged parents have toward accepting support from their children that need to be stressed.

1. Many aged parents categorically reject any form of economic support from their offspring. Among the various reasons they give for not wanting to accept financial assistance from their adult children are the following:[32]

1. The economic responsibility of the offspring should be toward their own families.
2. Economic support from one's children is humiliating and signifies relinquishment of parental authority.
3. The children did not ask to be brought into the world and cannot be expected to accept responsibility for their parents.
4. The older person considers the question of self-support in old age a challenge that he wants to meet without the aid of his children.

[30]Robert M. Dinkel, "Parental-Child Conflict in Minnesota Families," *American Sociological Review*, 8 (Aug. 1943), pp. 412–419.

[31]Schorr, op. cit. See also: "Filial Responsibility and the Aging, or Beyond Pluck and Luck," *Social Security Bulletin*, 25 (May 1962), pp. 3–9.

[32]Fried and Stern, op. cit., pp. 43–45. This study revealed that the most influential factor in determining the attitude of the aged toward accepting support from offspring was cultural background: "immigrants from eastern Europe, most of whom were brought up in the institutional type of family, tend more to expect support from their children than the subjects brought up in the Anglo-American environment."

5. The support of the older person is the responsibility of the government rather than of the offspring.

6. It used to be a moral obligation for children to support parents. Present-day standards no longer sustain this moral obligation and the old person feels he should be independent like the majority of old people.

The fact of the matter is that most older parents (like most middle-aged parents) are highly reluctant to accept any contributions from their children. This will be all the more so if they feel or suspect that taking such money will interfere in any way with the adult children's meeting their own needs and achieving their own goals and aspirations. As Schorr has commented, "an American parent is ambitious for his children and grandchildren, as they are for themselves. . . . Even when the parent is less ambitious for his children, he may prefer to do without such contributions and make some sacrifice in his standard of living so that he may keep his feeling of independence."[33]

The older parents' reluctance to accept financial assistance from their children is all the more interesting in view of their own economic situation. Although it is true that older persons generally need less income to live on than they did earlier in their lives (many will have paid for their homes, their children will have married and established their own independence, and so on), nevertheless the majority of the aged are existing on drastically reduced incomes.[34] For example, the median income for all families in the United States in 1970 was approximately $10,000, whereas the median for families headed by a person sixty-five years of age or over was only half that amount. Viewed another way, the median income for families headed by a person sixty-five years of age or over was less than half that of families with heads younger than sixty-five. Differences in income by sex further highlight the low economic status of the aged. Among women over sixty-five, more than one fifth have incomes of less than $1,000 per year, and over three fifths have annual incomes of less than $2,000. Under 10 per cent of all aged women report at least $5,000 in a single year. Among men over age sixty-five, about 4 per cent have incomes of less than $1,000, and nearly 23 per cent have annual incomes under $2,000. Only 30 per cent of all aged men reported incomes of at least $5,000.

2. Financial aid is only one aspect of filial responsibility and aged

[33]Schorr, "Filial Responsibility and the Aging, or Beyond Pluck and Luck," op. cit., p. 5.

[34]U.S. Bureau of the Census, *Current Population Reports,* Series P-60, No. 51, "Income of 1965 Families and Persons in the United States," (Washington, D.C.: U.S. Government Printing Office, January 12, 1967).

parents generally rate its importance *below* certain other considerations. Several studies, such as those conducted by Streib, reveal that there is (to use Streib's phrase) a "hierarchy of norms" regarding family assistance and that within the context of this hierarchy "older persons think that it is much more important for children to maintain affectional and social ties than to help them in a material way."[35] Similarly, Shanas's analysis of data based upon a nationwide sample of the aged led her to conclude that what older people wanted from their children was love and affection. Many older parents are reluctant to ask their children for financial assistance, fearing this would threaten the affectional relationship between the generations.[36] And in a more recent investigation, both the parents *and* their adult children (95 per cent of whom were living apart from the parents) were asked to respond to the following question: "Some people think that the major responsibility children have to their parents is financial; others feel that ties of affection are more important. How do *you* feel?"[37] Nearly two thirds of the parents responded that affection was more important than financial assistance, whereas two thirds of the children stated that *both* affection and financial aid were equally important.

Table 22.2
Comparison of the Exchange of Goods and Services Between Retired Parents and Their Adult Children

	Contact and Aid Given by Parents		Contact and Aid Given by Children	
	Reported By Parents	Reported By Children	Reported By Parents	Reported By Children
Visit frequently	74%	69%	74%	72%
Ask to visit often	74	78	74	81
Write often	53	39	53	29
Take care when ill	51	56	37	46
Give financial help	48	38	10	12
Live close	45	50	46	47
Give advice on business	37	33	20	31
Provide home	9	8	5	8
None of above	—	3	6	2
N =	291	291	291	291

SOURCE: Gordon F. Streib, "Intergenerational Relations: Perspectives of the Two Generations on the Older Parent," *Journal of Marriage and the Family,* **27** (Nov. 1965), pp. 469–476. Reprinted by permission.

[35]Streib, "Family Patterns in Retirement," op. cit.
[36]Ethel Shanas, *The Health of Older People* (Cambridge, Mass.: Harvard University Press, 1962), p. 141.
[37]Streib, "Intergenerational Relations: Perspectives of the Two Generations on the Older Parent," op. cit., p. 472.

576

Thus from the standpoint of the older generation, the maintenance of close affectional ties is of paramount importance. Parents are unwilling to jeopardize close family ties with their children by expecting financial assistance from them. The children, on the other hand, having broken some of their emotional ties with their parents and having established new ones within their own conjugal family, do not value so highly their affection relationships with their parents. There is, however, a sense of filial responsibility which is manifested by equating affection and financial obligations.[38]

It is clear that intergenerational social relationships and patterns of mutual exchange between retired couples and their offspring are varied and extensive (Table 22.2). Nevertheless, it is equally clear that material aid is well near the bottom of the list of priorities in parents' expectations of filial responsibilities. In the study we have been citing, 96 per cent of the adult children reported that their parents had neither asked for nor needed financial help and, conversely, 94 per cent of the parents said they had never asked for nor needed financial aid from their children.[39]

The Three-Generation Family: Sharing a Household
It was noted earlier that actual cash contribution from adult children to parents is not a common pattern among contemporary families, but vice versa. The giving of money, however, is only one form of economic assistance; there are other forms, including children's sharing a home with their aged parents. Various census data suggest that the proportion of aged parents with living children who share a household with one of those children ranges from one fourth to more than a third at any given moment. Moreover, even these proportions will vary depending on the social characteristics of any particular subgroup of the older population, including their residential location, their age, and their marital status. For example, the proportion of the aged sharing households is greater for women than for men, and substantially higher for widowed, divorced, and separated parents compared to married parents.[40]

Various studies have shown that it is much more typical for aged parents to move into the household of a married daughter than into that of a married son. Nimkoff, in discussing this pattern has remarked: "Apparently, if an aged parent has to be dependent, it is safer to be

---

[38]Ibid.

[39]Streib notes that these findings are different from those reported by Shanas, *The Health of Older People,* op. cit., p. 180. She found that 30 per cent of adult children with a living parent or parent-in-law were contributing to their financial support. He suggests that the discrepancy may be due to the affluence of his smaller sample, which did not represent a cross-section of the aged population.

[40]Arthur J. Robins, "Family Relations of the Aging in Three-Generation Households," in Tibbitts and Donahue, op. cit., pp. 464–474.

dependent on a daughter than a son. Or, to state it differently, since the woman usually sets the tone of the home and has the major responsibility for the management of the home, it is more satisfactory to be dependent on a daughter than on a daughter-in-law."[41] It appears, moreover, that in addition to performing a caretaker function for the old, women perform a number of other significant functions in providing aid for aged parents. Blenkner, for example, cites a study in New York City that shows that applications to a voluntary family agency are made predominantly by women in behalf of older persons.[42]

The figures cited earlier on three-generation living are rather enlightening in view of the fact that the overwhelming majority of the general population affirm the belief that it is much better for married offspring to maintain residences separate from their parents.[43] Thus, for example, Smith's analysis of data from two Pennsylvania cities show that when people were asked what they thought about older persons' living with relatives, only 14 per cent felt it was a good idea, whereas 50 per cent said it might work out sometimes, and 35 per cent of the respondents stated that they had no intentions of eventually living with their children.[44] Similarly, an Iowa study of older people revealed that an overwhelming majority were not at all eager to reside in the same household as their children and grandchildren, but preferred instead to live apart from the younger generations for as long as they were capable of doing so.[45] It appears, therefore, that most Americans are not in favor of three-generation living.

The question of whether elements of strain occur in three-generation households (that is, households containing a husband and wife and their dependent children, as well as grandparents) was investigated by Koller over a decade ago; he used a small sample of thirty families from Ohio and Virginia. He found that

the three-generation household was recognized by most of the informants as a hazardous type of family living in which the combined virtues of a diplomat,

[41]Meyer F. Nimkoff, "Changing Family Relationships of Older People in the United States During the Last Fifty Years," in *Social and Psychological Aspects of Aging*, ed. by Clark Tibbitts and Wilma Donahue (New York: Columbia University Press, 1962), pp. 405–414.

[42]Margaret Blenkner, "Social Work and Family Relationships in Later Life with Some Thoughts on Filial Maturity," in *Social Structure and the Family: Intergenerational Relations*, ed. by Ethel Shanas and Gordon T. Shreib (Englewood Cliffs, N.J.: Prentice-Hall, 1965), pp. 46–49.

[43]Schorr, "Filial Responsibility in the Modern Ameican Family," op. cit., pp. 5–18. Notes that anywhere from 50 to 95 per cent of the general population take the position that parents and children should maintain separate households.

[44]William M. Smith, Jr., "Family Plans for Later Years," *Marriage and Family Living*, **16** (Feb. 1954) pp. 36–40.

[45]The Research Committee on Social Gerontology, *Iowa Studies in Social Gerontology—A Research Proposal* (Iowa City: Institute of Gerontology, State University of Iowa, 1961), p. 51.

statesman, and saint are needed. The elders have had considerable authority in the past and they do not find it easy to relinquish power to their children. The husband and wife have just begun to live their lives independently and somewhat resent the intrusion of a threat to this newly found authority. The youngest generation, in turn, are baffled by the splitting of authority among their elders and their own desires to be "grown up."[46]

As in other studies, Koller found that the majority of three-generation families he studied were created by the wife's mother's moving into the home, and evidently conflict frequently developed between the two females over household routines, child-rearing, and other family matters.

Whether the three-generation family situation inevitably results in family strain and conflict remains an issue among professional gerontologists. For some time now family sociologists have been debating the pros and cons of this type of living arrangement. Schorr, for example, has challenged both the theoretical arguments and the empirical data emerging from American studies, which stress the negative or detrimental consequences of multiple family living. Noting that more sophisticated research in England has led to more positive conclusions, he argues that the American data only indicate that the three-generation household arrangement *may* but *not necessarily* cause problems leading to familial disharmony.[47] In defense of his position, Schorr cites an earlier statement by Burgess, to the effect that

Where both parents and children elect to live together, the arrangement may work out more or less satisfactorily. Where the wife is working, the mother-in-law often takes on the major charge of the household responsibilities. She may be happy to function as a babysitter. . . . Although there may be some disagreements, these tend to be minor, and both generations report the relationship as satisfying.[48]

In addition, Schorr further argues that

there can be no question that there are potential strains when parents and adult children live together. But potential strains are inherent in any living situation—in work, in rearing children, in marrying. If technical and popular literature confined themselves to the strains intrinsic to each of these activities, would we conclude that we should give them up?[49]

---

[46]Marvin R. Koller, "Studies of Three-Generation Households," *Marriage and Family Living,* **16** (Aug. 1954), pp. 205–206. Such tensions apparently do not have to be endured for any extended period of time. Koller found that three-generation family living was generally of short duration, most of them lasting no longer than five years, due to the death of the older parent(s).

[47]Schorr, "Filial Responsibility in the Modern American Family," op. cit., pp. 5–18.

[48]Ernest W. Burgess, "Family Living in the Later Decades," *The Annals of the American Academy of Political and Social Science,* **279** (Jan. 1952), pp. 111–112.

[49]Schorr, "Filial Responsibility in the Modern American Family," op. cit., pp. 5–18.

579

Some support for Schorr's contention emerges from Stone's interviews with aged people in the state of Washington, in which she concluded that elderly parents sharing living quarters with their adult children was a satisfactory arrangement *provided* such an arrangement came about voluntarily and through mutual agreement between the generations, rather than as a result of necessity or lack of a more suitable alternative.[50] In this study, the older parents residing with their adult children were more satisfied with their living arrangements, more permanently settled, and better adjusted than any of the other types of elderly groups interviewed.

Stone's analysis also points up another aspect of intergenerational living that sometimes goes unnoticed. In half of the three-generation households involved, the children actually were living *with* the parents rather than vice versa. That is to say, either the adult offspring had married and remained in the parental home, or they had had moved in with their parents-in-law. Such findings serve to remind us that three-generation households are not always created for the sole benefit of the aged parents and that "living together is frequently a situation in which *both* parties benefit, though a set of scales would tip one way or the other. And whatever the material balance, the receiver often renders services or repays with fondness, an important coin in itself."[51] It is perhaps because of this reciprocal nature of multiple family household relationships that many persons residing under such arrangements are able to work out satisfactory solutions to whatever problems arise.

In a related analysis, Stone examined the influence of three-generation living upon the youngest members of such households.[52] She did this by matching a sample of teenagers from three-generation families with a similar sample from two-generation families and then comparing the two groups in terms of a number of items designed to measure their individual activity and adjustment as well as their overall family interaction patterns. Her analysis failed to reveal any consistent differences between the three- and two-generation families with respect to their patterns of interaction. Neither was she able to discover any outstanding differences between the two groups of teen-agers with regard to their activity patterns. Stone suggests that the oft-made inferences concerning the detrimental consequences of three-generation living may be found to be erroneous in the light of

[50]Carol L. Stone, "Living Arrangements and Social Adjustment of the Aged," *Family Life Coordinator,* 6 (Sept. 1957), pp. 12–14.

[51]Schorr, "Filial Responsibility in the Modern American Family," op. cit., pp. 5–18.

[52]Carol L. Stone, "Three-Generation Influences on Teen-Agers' Conceptions of Family Culture Patterns and Parent-Child Relationships," *Marriage and Family Living,* 24 (Aug. 1962), pp. 287–288.

580

empirical research and that three-generation living need not be detrimental to family life or to teen-agers' personal adjustments.

Finally, in concluding this section, we repeat that gerontologists continue to take issue with those who view the evidence that most older people today are *not* residing in the home of adult children as reflecting a decline in the moral responsibility of the younger generation. The gerontologists challenge such a position on the basis of findings such as those we have been citing in this chapter. And as part of their argument, they seriously question some earlier notions regarding three-generation family living. For example, Kent, has observed:

There are few more cherished illusions than the position of the aged in the Golden Past. The three-generation family pictured as a farm idyl is common, yet all evidence indicates that at no time in any society was a three-generation family ever the common mode, and even less evidence that it was idyllic. Look at American history. The first settlers were largely people who left their parental generation in the Old Country. Their children in turn started the Westward Movement and left their parents in the east. This continued throughout the 17th, 18th, and the greater part of the 19th century. The stability of the three-generation family in America, if it existed at all, probably existed only in the very last part of the 19th century and the early part of the 20th. And there is no indication that the consideration of one for another that is essential to the ideal part of our picture has ever been present in greater quantity than now.[53]

Similarly, Tibbits has attacked the notion that the three-generation household was once the most predominant type in America and that within it virtually all of the aged could find refuge, as one of "the most persistent gerontological myths" of our times. He points out that in the eighteenth and nineteenth centuries life expectancy was considerably shorter than it is today and, therefore, "there were simply not enough older Americans to permit the three-generation family to be the common type even if older people had been distributed one per household."[54]

Nevertheless, many people continue to cling to the illusion of the three-generation family of the past. Sociologists and anthropologists have long since discovered, however, that old myths die hard, and apparently those surrounding family life in many instances die hardest of all.

Role Reversal in Old Age

A concept that has been widely utilized to characterize parent-child relations in old age, and a term that generally has negative connota-

[53]Kent, op. cit., pp. 17–18.
[54]Clark Tibbitts, *Middle-aged and Older People in American Society* (Washington, D.C.: U.S. Government Printing Office, 1965), pp. 25–26.

tions, is *role reversal.* For example, in a leading textbook in family sociology we are told that:

A reversal of roles is the most general characteristic of the relations between the aged and their children. It is closely related to the shift in power relationships which universally accompanies growth changes in the familial group. In a sense children are destined to become parents to their elders and parents are destined to become children to their offspring. The process may be slow or sudden, pleasant or painful, and roles may be conflicting or complementary. Certainly the process is not culturally regulated by formal ritual or even by consistent, well defined expectations.[55]

Similarly the psychiatric and social-work literature frequently treats role reversal as the logical outcome of the developmental process. This process has been rather dramatically described by one writer as follows:

As the years pass, the ravages of time shift the once clear distinction between the roles of the child and parent until these lines cross, so that they resemble nothing so much as fate's gigantic hourglass fallen on its side. Whereas the parent was once the dominant member in a parent-child relationship, he now clearly must occupy the subordinate and dependent position. Now there comes the time when the strength and the future be, not with the parent but with the by-this-time grown and even aging sons and daughters, so that those who in the morning of their life had been sheltered by the parent's protective arms must now assume the reverse role and learn to protect the protector and provide for the provider.[56]

There is little doubt that role reversals in old age do occur among *some* families and that in such instances conflicts often arise. The Glassers, for example, have explored the sociological aspects of conflicts between aged parents and their children through an examination of the case records of older clients requesting help from a Jewish family service agency in Detroit. Their analysis led them to suggest that many of the problems encountered by these elderly clients were role-reversal problems. They concluded that aged parents who are forced to seek various types of material assistance from their children in effect take on a dependency status similar to that of their children in an earlier period of the family history.[57]

[55]Clifford Kirkpatrick, *The Family: As Process and Institution,* 2nd ed. (New York: The Donald Criss Company, 1965), pp. 550–551.

[56]Arthur L. Rautman, "Role Reversal in Geriatrics," *Mental Hygiene,* 46 (Jan. 1962), pp. 116–120.

[57]Paul H. and Lois N. Glasser, "Role Reversal and Conflict Between Aged Parents and Their Children," *Marriage and Family Living,* 24 (Feb. 1962), pp. 46–51. The Glassers caution that their conclusions are not generalizable to other populations, because their sample was not representative of the aged, but consisted of a clinical group of Jewish applicants requesting assistance from a social agency.

582

For a number of reasons, however, it is difficult to assess the model of parent-child relations in old age that is based upon the concept of role reversal. For one thing, we do not have adequate data with respect to either the frequency with which such reversals occur nor, when they take place, what proportion actually lead to parent-child conflict. Moreover, it appears that much of the available research literature in which instances of role reversal are reported is based upon problem families. This clinical bias has led one critic to argue that role reversal is actually a *pathological* rather than a normal development in parent-child relations in later years.

Role-reversal may be a valuable concept in understanding the dynamics of the neurotic or immature but chronologically aging parent-child pair; it may serve the psychotherapist well in dealing with the senile or psychotic oldster; but as a model of normal behavior, as an ideal image by which to measure or toward which to direct client or patient behavior, it is inappropriate and a dead end. One may legitimately question whether the role-reversal concept is resorted to because it fits the facts, or because it fits the only theory the therapist has; for while it is true that the filial crisis marks childhood's end, the son or daughter does not thereby take on a parental role to his parent. He takes on the *filial* role, which involves being *depended on* and therefore being *dependable* insofar as his parent is concerned.[58]

Blenkner has taken the position that the mature adult usually manages to execute a positive, healthy resolution of the *filial crisis* (a developmental term whose meaning is analagous to that of role reversal) by

leaving behind the rebellion and emancipation of adolescence and early adulthood and turning again to the parent, no longer as a child, but as a mature adult with a new role and a different love seeing him for the first time as an individual with his own rights, needs, and limitations, and a life history that to a large extent made him the person he is long before his child existed. This is what the parent wants of his children; this is what society expects; this is what many Americans accomplish, with varying degrees of success, in their late forties and fifties. It is one of the ways in which they prepare themselves for their own old age, through identification with the parent, as in childhood they similarly prepared for adulthood."[59]

The nonclinical evidence, based upon larger and more representative samples of the aged population, would seem to support Blenkner's contention that intergenerational relationships in later years are *not* most commonly characterized by the phenomena of role reversal. For example, a study by Albrecht in which parent-child relationships were

[58]Blenkner, op. cit., pp. 57–58.
[59]Ibid.

583

analyzed from data gathered through interviews with a representative sample of aged parents residing in a midwestern community revealed that 85 per cent of these parents were performing roles characterized by either independence or responsibility, and only 15 per cent exhibited dependence, distance, or neglect.[60] She found that aged parents could generally be classified according to any one of four types: independent, responsible, dependent, and distant or lone parents. For our purposes, we may briefly contrast two of these types, the independent and the dependent.

Independent parents are persons who have allowed their children to become mature, independent adults while at the same time maintaining close social and affectional ties with them. They tend neither to dominate nor be dominated by their adult children. Most of these parents maintain separate households, although some live either next door or in the same house as their children. A few remarry and eventually effect a harmonious relationship between their offspring and their new spouse. Independent parents are characterized by an open pride in their children, by being able to accept advice and assistance from them without feeling threatened, and by a feeling of basic love and security in their relationships with their children. They take pleasure in interacting with members of the second generation, exhibit a sincere liking for them, and make some effort to maintain interests that promote common bonds. At the same time they have nonfamilial interests and activities that help maintain their own selfhood.[61]

Dependent parents, by way of contrast, manifest considerable role reversal in relationship to their children. They constituted, however, only 6 per cent of Albrecht's entire sample and tended to be among the eldest subjects. Because of their advanced ages, many of them are troubled by various illnesses and many were widowed. They frequently confine their activities to the home, and social participation outside the home is either absent or severely restricted. As a group, the dependent parents frequently require economic assistance, physical care, and/or constant attention from their children. There is an increasing reliance upon the children for such things as preparing meals, doing the housework, and the like.

Albrecht's results, as well as findings from numerous other sociological studies of the aged, strongly suggest that role reversal in the

[60]Ruth Albrecht, "Relationships of Older Parents With Their Children," *Marriage and Family Living,* **26** (Feb. 1964), pp. 32–35.

[61]Ibid., pp. 32–33. That the independent parent type is the most predominant type among aged parents has been corroborated by other studies of the aged. See, for example, Carol L. Stone and Walter L. Slocum, *Thurston County's Older People,* Washington Agricultural Experimental Stations Bulletin 573 (May 1957), Institute of Agricultural Sciences, State College of Washington (now Research Center, College of Agriculture, Washington State University).

parent-child relationship occurs among a minority of aged families. Moreover, it appears that such reversals, when they do occur, are most likely to take place in those cases in which the older parent has become physically disabled, or has reached a stage of senility, or has in some way lost the capacity to maintain his or her independence. Certainly most parents and their children neither seek nor welcome such reversals. For one thing, the parental role is a very rewarding one, consequently most people do not easily relinquish it. Secondly, adult children never really become parents to their parents, except in the very limited sense of providing various types of assistance and support. They do not, for example, rear parents through an extensive socialization process. In short, the role reversal model is rather sterile in terms of adequately conceptualizing the development of parent-child relations in later years among a normal population, although it may describe a situation characteristic of certain problem families that are encountered in a clinical setting.

The Role of Grandparenthood

In previous sections we have concentrated primarily on the interaction between middle-aged married couples and their older parents. We now want to turn our attention to another important aspect of intergenerational family relationships and consider the relationships between middle-aged and old parents and their grandchildren.

The long-term rise in average life expectancy and the consequent expansion of the latter half of the family life cycle has resulted in a substantial proliferation of surviving three-generation (or more) families in the United States. Increased life expectancy, in conjunction with the other changes in family structure and composition that we have discussed in Chapter 21—such as the earlier age at marriage, a shorter child-rearing period, and fewer children—have exposed more middle-aged and older couples to the role of grandparenthood than at any other period in history.

Strange as it may seem, however, the sociology and social gerontology of the grandparenthood role has remained a relatively undeveloped area from the point of view of empirical investigations. Most of the evidence we do have regarding grandparenthood is apparently derived from broader sociological studies of the aged.[62] Psychological

---

[62]Bernice L. Neugarten and Karol K. Weinstein, "The Changing American Grandparent," *Journal of Marriage and the Family,* **26** (May 1964), pp. 199–204. For students interested in pursuing an interest in grandparenthood, this article contains references to much of the pertinent literature.

interest in the phenomena of grandparenthood has also been minimal.[63]

Cross-cultural analyses by anthropologists have provided some insight into the role of grandparents. One of the better-known studies is the research by Apple, in which ethnographic data from seventy-five societies were compared to determine the influence of differential patterns of family authority on the social relationships between grandparents and their grandchildren. She found that in societies in which grandparents retain considerable household authority (by virtue of their economic power and/or because the aged are traditionally respected and given prestige) the relationships between the grandparents and the grandchildren are typically *not* of "friendly equality," but rather formal and authoritarian. Conversely, in societies in which the grandparent's generation retains little or no authority over the parental generation following the birth of grandchildren, the interaction between the grandparents and the grandchildren is typically friendly and warm, and characterized by an equalitarian or indulgent relationship. On the basis of these findings, Apple enunciates as a general principle that friendly relations between grandparents and grandchildren will occur where the family structure dissociates the grandparents from exercising family authority.[64]

Although the grandparental role has not been extensively or systematically studied in the United States, the available evidence suggests that the principle just stated is generally applicable to intergenerational relationships in our own society. Although American grandparents engage in a companionable and indulgent relationship with their grandchildren, their role is usually devoid of any direct responsibility and authority.[65] Albrecht, for example, found that grandparents had no coveted responsibility for grandchildren. Instead, they adhered to a hands-off policy, whereby it was understood that the authority and the responsibility for rearing and supervising grandchildren reside solely with their parents and that grandparents were not expected to interfere except in unusual circumstances. "Grandparents can give direct aid or take full responsibility for third generation members only if the children are orphaned, or the parents are absolutely unable to care for

---

[63]Alvin I. Goldfarb, "Psychodynamics and the Three-Generation Family," in Shanas and Streib, op. cit., pp. 10–45.

[64]Dorian Apple, "The Social Structure of Grandparenthood," *American Anthropologist,* **58** (Aug. 1956), pp. 656–663.

[65]Sue G. Updegraff, "Changing Role of the Grandmother," *Journal of Home Economics,* **60** (March 1968), pp. 177–180. This study found some evidence that the role of the grandmother in modern society is shifting toward increased indulgence and child care without a concomitant increase in authority. The data show that grandmothers of three different generations all exhibited low authority patterns with respect to their grandchildren.

586

them."[66] Nevertheless, the majority of American grandparents evidently derive pleasure and pride and an emotional satisfaction from interacting with their grandchildren.[67]

STYLE OF GRANDPARENTHOOD At a more specific level, however, there apparently is considerable variability from one family to another regarding the actual enactment of the grandparental role. An illustration of this variability is provided by Neugarten and Weinstein, who conducted interviews with seventy sets of middle-class grandparents (forty-six maternal, twenty-four paternal) residing within the metropolitan Chicago area. Through an inductive analysis of their data, the researchers were able to differentiate five major styles of grandparenthood.[68] Their descriptions of these are reproduced below, with the most frequently occurring style appearing first.

1. The *Formal* are those who follow what they regard as the proper and prescribed role for grandparents. Although they like to provide special treats and indulgences for the grandchild, and although they may occasionally take on a minor service such as babysitting, they maintain clearly demarcated lines between parenting and grandparenting, and they leave parenting strictly to the parent. They maintain a constant interest in the grandchild but are careful not to offer advice on childrearing.
2. The *Fun Seeker* is the grandparent whose relation to the grandchild is characterized by informality and playfulness. He joins the child in specific activities for the specific purpose of having fun, somewhat as if he were the child's playmate. Grandchildren are viewed as a source of leisure activity, as an item of "consumption" rather than "production," or as a source of self-indulgence. The relationship is one in which authority lines—either with the grandchild or with the parent—are irrelevant. The emphasis here is on mutuality of satisfaction rather than on providing treats for the grandchild. Mutuality imposes a latent demand that both parties derive fun from the relationship.
3. The *Distant Figure* is the grandparent who emerges from the shadows on holidays and on special ritual occasions such as Christmas and birthdays. Contact with the grandchild is fleeting and infrequent, a fact which distinguishes this style from the *Formal.* This grandparent is benevolent in stance but essentially distant and remote from the child's life, a somewhat intermittent St. Nicholas.
4. The *Surrogate Parent* occurs only, as might have been anticipated, for grandmothers in this group. It comes about by initiation on the part of the younger generation, that is, when the young mother works and the grandmother assumes the actual caretaking responsibility for the child.
5. The *Reservoir of Family Wisdom* represents a distinctly authoritarian

---

[66]Ruth Albrecht, "The Parental Responsibilities of Grandparents," *Marriage and Family Living,* **16** (Aug. 1954), pp. 201–204.

[67]Ibid., p. 201, and Neugarten and Weinstein, op. cit., pp. 200–201.

[68]Ibid., pp. 203–204.

patri-centered relationship in which the grandparent—in rare occasions on which it occurs in this sample, it is the grandfather—is the dispenser of special skills or resources. Lines of authority are distinct, and the young parents maintain and emphasize their subordinate positions, sometimes with and sometimes without resentment.

Approximately 32 per cent of all the grandparents in this study adopted the formal style, 26 per cent the fun-seeking style, 24 per cent the distant-figure style, 7 per cent the parent-surrogate style, and 4 per cent the reservoir-of-family-wisdom style.[69]

Neugarten and Weinstein also found that the Fun-Seeking and the Distant-Figure grandparental styles were significantly more characteristic of *middle-aged* grandparents, whereas the formal style was more likely to be adopted by *older* grandparents. These differences were true for both grandmothers and grandfathers.

GRANDMOTHERHOOD AND GRANDFATHERHOOD There are some apparent and distinct differences between the sexes in our culture with respect to the anticipation of and/or preparation for and reactions to the grandparental role. Moreover, the magnitude of these differences varies according to whether this role is achieved relatively early in the life cycle or in later years.

Both psychological and sociological data suggest that women are much more likely than men to undergo *anticipatory socialization* with respect to the grandparental role. This involves, among other things, periodically visualizing themselves as grandmother *prior* to the actual birth of grandchildren and often before their adult children are even married. Through the process of anticipatory socialization, mothers are able to rehearse the grandparental role by developing a grandmother self-image.[70] Typically this image is positive in nature and one that most women desire to give eventual expression to upon the arrival of grandchildren. Among some mothers, however, the grandparental role is perceived and experienced with mixed sentiments and anxiety.[71] Thus, a forty-two-year-old mother who perceives herself as youthful and attractive may view grandmotherhood as a threat to this self-image and therefore resent the new role or in some instances attempt to ignore or reject it entirely.

The more common reaction among middle-aged mothers, however, is probably a combination of joy, excitement, and pride. Persons achieving grandparental status in our culture usually gain additional respect

---

[69] About 7 per cent of the cases could not be classified because there is insufficient data.

[70] Ruth S. Cavan, "Self and Role in Adjustment During Old Age," op. cit., pp. 526–536.

[71] For some of the psychological conflicts encountered in assuming the role of grandmother see Helene Deutsch, *The Psychology of Women,* Vol. 2 (New York: Grune and Stratton, 1945), pp. 483–487.

and prestige in the eyes of other members of society. Moreover, as Leslie has noted

> grandmotherhood often is a major part of the middle-aged woman's solution to the loss of her children through marriage. As grandmother, she acquires a new sense of importance and usefulness. Moreover, she experiences again most of the joys of parenthood without having to cope with the exacting demands. Entering her children's homes as a visitor and/or baby-sitter, she can indulge herself and her grandchildren; when her energy or her patience wane, she has simply to leave and go to her own quiet home.[72]

The grandmotherly pattern established in middle age is easily carried over and maintained in old age unless the physical disabilities that often accompany the advanced years intrude to prevent its continuation.

Middle-aged fathers who find themselves grandfathers are less likely to be concerned about their new role. For most men the middle years represent the period when they are reaching the apex of their occupational careers and economic success. They are still primarily identified with and engaged in the work role. Consequently, intense male involvement in the grandfatherly role typically is postponed until the years following retirement. It is only at this later date that grandparental activities are apt to become a major focus of attention for men.

It has been suggested that in contemporary American society a general cultural definition of the elderly grandfather role has emerged that is essentially maternal in nature.[73] Unlike his counterpart in the patriarchal family of the past, the modern grandfather does not function as a primary source of authority for his grandchildren and, except under unusual circumstances, he is neither expected nor permitted to act as their financial provider. Instead, he assumes a slightly masculinized grandmother role involving such maternal tasks as feeding the grandchildren and babysitting for them, taking them for [carriage] rides, and so on. To make a successful accommodation to this new role, the grandfather must develop an orientation that differs considerably from the masculine instrumental role he has performed most of his adult life. Some make the transition smoothly, others do so with some difficulty because the maternal quality of the behavior required is either repugnant or embarrassing to them. The culture provides assistance

---

[72]Gerald R. Leslie, *The Family in Social Context* (New York: Oxford University Press, 1967), pp. 684–686.

[73]Cavan, "Self and Role in Adjustment in Old Age," op. cit., pp. 534–535. Neugarten and Weinstein, op. cit., on the other hand, argue that the grandparental types currently emerging in the United States, such as the fun-seeker and distant-figure types described in previous pages, are neither maternal nor paternal, but rather neuter in gender, because they involve little of the nurturance inherent in the role described by Cavan.

here by attaching status and respect to the grandfather role. Men occupying this position are generally the recipients of verbal compliments and praise from other members of society. The American grandfather is encouraged and permitted to engage in a quasi-maternal relationship with his grandchildren without discomfort or embarrassment.

Increasing numbers of Americans are moving into the grandparental role. Because this role typically entails a minimum of obligations and responsibilities, most persons find that its enactment allows a variety of opportunities for personal gratification and self-enhancement. Moreover, the grandparent functions to provide continuity in family interaction, and this function in itself gives persons who fulfill this role a valued position in American society.

23

Death and the Widowed Family

Ultimately all marriages are dissolved through the inevitable death of one or both members of the marital dyad. Perhaps because of widespread publicity created through the mass media, the general public is often led to the conclusion that the vast majority of broken families occur as a result of divorce, desertion, or separation. The fact is, however, that in any given year considerably more families are disrupted by the death of a spouse (usually the husband) than by any other cause. In recent decades, for example, approximately twice as many marriages have been terminated by death as by divorce, and this ratio increases substantially in the later stages of the marriage-family life-cycle.[1]

The death of the marital partner, therefore, is obviously the most prevalent form of family dissolution. It requires the development of alternative patterns of behavior if the survivors are to maintain satisfactory relations within the family, with the kin group, and with the community, and if they are to sustain personal equilibrium. From a sociological viewpoint, the period of widowhood (or widowerhood) necessitates some type of reintegration of roles suitable to a new status. The incident of death precipitates a reorganization of the family as a social system. Roles must be reassigned, status positions shifted, and values reoriented. For reasons to be noted shortly, families have been found to exhibit considerable diversity in their attempts to accomplish such transitions. Indeed, several decades ago Eliot, a pioneer in the

[1]More precisely, "in the early years of marriage, death constitutes a much smaller hazard to the continuity of family life than does divorce [and] it is not until duration 13 years that death exceeds divorce as a cause of marital disruption. Beyond that year of marriage, death takes an increasing toll and the frequency of divorce continues to decline." Paul H. Jacobson, *American Marriage and Divorce* (New York: Rinehart and Company, Inc., 1959), p. 147.

scientific study of the bereaved family, noted at least seven ways in which families might be affected by and react to death:[2]

1. The role of a family member exists in relation to the configuration and functioning of the family as a unit. A death tends to disturb this unity. The shifting of the roles of the various members under bereavement represents a reshaping of the configuration.
2. The consensus of the family in respect to these roles, i.e., in respect to its own pattern, may result; or, family conflicts may develop as a sequence to incompatible conceptions of the role of certain members under the new conditions.
3. Such conflicts or jealousies, or the lack of a common personal or domestic object or symbol of affectional attachment (conditioning stimuli) may result in a decreased family solidarity.
4. Acceptance of new interpersonal responsibilities may increase family solidarity.
5. Removal of authority, of habit-stimuli, of home, or of support may lead to a revision of family folkways.
6. Maturity of children who lose their parents may lead to individualism or turning to their own families.
7. The will, or personality, of the deceased, acting psychologically, as a dynamic complex in each member's memory, and reinforced by consensus, may activate the behavior of the entire family.

It should be noted that each of these changes refers to the reactions of the family *as a total unit.* A large portion of the scientific research on death, however, has tended to concentrate on *individual* responses to this crisis. As a consequence, our knowledge of the sociological features of the bereaved *family* is not as extensive as that concerning the personal adjustment processes of individual survivors.[3]

Regardless of whether reactions to death and bereavement are analyzed on the psychological (individual) or sociological (group) level, it should be noted that generalizations in this area are rather difficult to develop. This difficulty derives largely from the fact that the loss of a spouse or other family member is an incident that evokes a wide panorama of thoughts and behavioral patterns on the part of the surviving members, depending on a number of interrelated factors.[4] For example, a family in which the father was killed in battle while fighting for his country as a member of the military responds to his death quite

[2]Thomas D. Eliot, "The Bereaved Family," *The Annals of the American Academy of Political and Social Science,* **160** (March 1932), pp. 184–190.
[3]Felix M. Berardo, "Widowhood Status in the United States: Perspective on a Neglected Aspect of the Family Life-Cycle," *The Family Coordinator,* **17** (July 1968), pp. 191–203.
[4]Willard Waller, *The Family: A Dynamic Interpretation* (New York: The Cordon Press, 1938), Chapter 19, p. 492.

differently from the family in which the husband has chosen to annihilate himself by suicide or was the victim of a painful accident or an incurable disease. Again, the passing of an aged mother whose children have married and left the parental home triggers reactions unlike those brought about by the death of the very young wife whose children have not achieved adulthood. And so on. Thus, the definition of the crisis situation and its potentially disruptive consequences for the family have been found to be contingent upon a number of related circumstances. Family adaptability and integration, the affectional relations among family members, good marital adjustment, companionable parent-child relationships, a family-council type of control in decision-making, the social participation of the wife, and previous successful experiences with crisis have been confirmed by research as being positively associated with adjustment to subsequent crises.[5]

Recognizing the potential variation with respect to individual responses to death and bereavement, we shall limit the following discussion to some of the more common or recurring types of survivor reactions observed.

Psychological Reactions to Bereavement

Individual bereavement typically involves a sequence of fairly recognizable psychological processes (Table 23.1). Inasmuch as the death of a loved one is a highly traumatic event, initial reactions commonly take the form of temporary incapacitation. The survivor is stunned and frequently overwhelmed by the shock of death and may be rendered momentarily incapable of adjusting to the crisis situation. Customarily, relatives and friends are expected to intercede to offer condolences and to provide needed support and assurance. Sociologically, the "group imposes its imperatives upon the bereaved person, demanding a certain decorum, prescribing some forms of behavior and tabooing others. There is sometimes an impulse to give up the struggle, perhaps to seek to join the other in death, but society demands gently but inescapably that one continue to live."[6] A feeling of numbness is likely to be experienced, with the result that the survivor is only vaguely aware of the events taking place around him. The bereaved proceed through the wake, the funeral, or other rites in a dazed state of mind. The entire situation may seem unreal and the bereaved often show a certain reluctance to accept the harsh finality that the departed is gone forever.

For some the emotional burden of acute sorrow becomes unbearable

---

[5]Reuben Hill, "Social Stresses on the Family," *Social Casework,* **39** (Jan. 1958), pp. 139–150.

[6]Waller, op. cit., p. 499.

Table 23.1
Stages of Adjustment and Types of Responses to Bereavement*

I. THE IMMEDIATE STAGE	II. THE POST-IMMEDIATE STAGE	III. THE TRANSITIONAL STAGE	IV. THE REPATTERNING STAGE
Types of response	1. This stage usually lasts from the end of the immediate response to the death to the end of the funeral activities (when "everything is over" and "everyone has gone home").	1. This is the transitional stage between the time of first adjustments which make the suffering bearable and the period when acceptable adjustive patterns become established and integrated into the total life pattern.	1. This stage of behavior comes when the bereaved spouse reaches a period in adjustment to bereavement when he has already passed through a "trial and error" transitional stage and finds it necessary to resume "normal" life again.
1. Stoic	2. This is a period of temporary adjustment during which behavior is strongly influenced by culturally patterned controls.	2. This period is distinguished by "trial and error" behavior: there are experimental attempts by the bereaved person to arrive at some pattern of stabilized behavior....	2. This is a stage during which the bereaved person arrives at the formation of a more definite pattern of behavior about which there appears to be more permanence and stability than was characteristic of the adjustments in any of the earlier stages; a new life organization has apparently been developed.
a) An absence of weeping or any other type of violent, active emotion.	3. It is a period when actuality forcefully makes itself known and yet the bereaved person still fights against accepting actuality....	3. Interpersonal interaction, if it appears, comes to have a greater relative influence upon behavior because, although culturally patterned controls are still important, they are relatively less so.	*Types of Response*
b) The prevalence of a considerable amount of self-control: the ability to meet the immediate situation without the assistance of others.	4. During this period, person-to-person interaction has its first important influence upon the behavior of the bereaved spouse.	*Types of Response*	1. Projective
c) A minimum of speaking: the bereaved person did not speak but only at times when it was necessary.	*Types of Response*	1. Alternating	a) A tremendous emphasis upon interest in, attention to, and/or al-
2. Dazed	1. Acquiescent	a) Periods of extreme activity and "doing" al-	
a) Weeping was of short duration.	a) A "normal" reaction to the situation.		
b) A dazed, benumbed type of behavior marked almost all of the immediate response. "Normal" reactions to the environment were at a minimum; the bereaved person seemed to be in a state of insensibility as			

indicated by his lack of mental feeling or emotion.

  c) There was considerable behavior activity but it was distinguished by its undirected, random characteristics.

3. Collapse

  a) An immediate mental and physical collapse: complete exhaustion and loss of self-control. There was an evident inability to do anything: an apparent paralyzing action over voluntary muscles and all rational conduct.

  b) There was a minimum of weeping and it was a quiet sobbing, not a loud or violent crying.

  c) While this state of collapse lasted there was a minimum of speech.

4. Lachrymose

  a) Immediate weeping which was violent and steady, interspersed by short periods of comparative quiet.

  b) No apparent lack of energy or awareness of

    (1) A recognition of the facts as they actually existed; partial acceptance of them.

    (2) A realistic approach to and compliance with cultural regulations for the death situation: the assumption of a "normal part."

    (3) An air of seeming to adjust to the situation "as smoothly as possible."

  b) No overdependency upon or "leaning upon"; others; rather an apparent complete control of self and concentration upon the duties at hand.

2. Excited

  a) An almost continuous activity marked by an extraordinary degree of excitement.

    (1) An active leadership in making plans and arrangements.

ternating with periods of depression. . . .

  b) The alternation of the activity-depression periods is frequent: often they occur several times a day, sometimes less frequently.

  c) As time passes, periods of activity become longer, periods of depression shorter and less frequent.

2. Enforced-collaborative

  a) The first few days following completion of the funeral activities are marked by extreme dejection, a lack of speech, and considerable inactivity.

    (1) Gradually there is a return to the necessary duties, but great effort is required: responses to children, if any, and other persons are "forced."

    (2) A silent dejection, rather than weep-

affection for another person or other persons stands out as the predominant characteristic of behavior.

. . .

  b) The bereaved person is sometimes conscious of the fact that he is substituting relationships with others for the relationships which he formerly had with the deceased spouse.

2. Participative

  a) The outstanding characteristic of the bereaved spouse's behavior is his emphasis upon participation in activities. . . .

  b) The bereaved person is at times conscious of the fact that his emphasis upon activity is a form of adjustment to the bereavement which he has developed.

3. Identification

  a) Predominant in the behavior of the bereaved spouse is his

Table 23.1 *(Cont.)*

596

what had occurred and what was happening. The drain of energy was, of course, concentrated upon weeping.

  (2) An extremely alert, active response to rituals and ceremonies.

 b) A seeming thorough pride in much of this activity.

 c) An air of self-control which appeared artificial and "overdone."

3. Protestive

 a) Numerous periods of violent weeping interspersed with accusations of self, others, circumstances, and fate.

 b) The assumption of only a minimum role in the making of plans and arrangements.

 c) Loud weeping and outcries often occuring in response to the rituals and ceremonies.

 d) The absence of serious attempts to assume and maintain self-control.

4. Detached

ing, is predominant.

 b) Inability to sleep and eat is characteristic, especially during the first few days and nights following the funeral.

 c) After the first few days, attempts to assume a readjusted routine and to make necessary readjustments to others are more easily and successfully made but the effort still remains difficult.

 d) As the days pass, work, daily routine, and group demands allow less and less time for depression, and the bereaved person gradually becomes more "normally" active and cheerful.

3. Attention-seeking

 a) There are frequent attempts to secure at-

definite and conscious assumption or attempted assumption of the role of the deceased: in the family, in other small groups, and even sometimes in the community.

 b) Combined with this chief characteristic of behavior is emphasis upon activity—"doing something." In this respect it is somewhat similar to the participative response, but the outstanding emphasis upon identification is not found in the latter.

4. Memory-Phantasy

 a) Outstanding in the behavior of the bereaved spouse is the great amount of time given to mental imagery. This takes the form of daydreams, "bereavement dreams," and "memory-work" . . .

 b) The bereaved spouse

a) Long periods of apparent insensibility and detachment: an appearance of unconcerned calm.

b) The assuming of almost no active role in making plans and arrangements: active behavior is usually directed at least important things.

c) A response to customs and rituals which seemed almost automatic—an appearance of being "carried along" by these elements of the death complex.

d) Almost no weeping nor any other type of violent behavior.

5. Despondent

a) An almost continuous state of "low spirits" and gloom marked by an appearance of extreme despair and despondency: almost no weeping but definite dejection and a desire to be left alone.

b) A lack of energy

tention: signs of mourning are emphasized, the desire of "telling troubles" to others is evident, and similar attempts to secure attention are made.

b) Frequent weeping and despondency are evident, especially during the first few days following the funeral activities.

c) There are attempted overemphasized affectional attachments and much "sharing of fate" with children and/or near-by relatives and friends.

d) The proffered help of others is usually refused and often resented, especially during the first few days after the funeral activities.

e) With the passing of time, emphasis upon this attention-seeking type of behavior becomes relatively less predominant.

accepts part in the necessary activities of life but does not emphasize them as does he who makes the participative response. Projection and identification, if it can be said there is either, are not outstanding elements in his behavior.

5. Repressive-Seclusive

a) Chiefly characteristic of the behavior of the bereaved spouse is his attempt to hold himself aloof from the "normal" contacts and activities of daily life: he leads a secluded, solitary existence insofar as he can.

b) Outstanding about his behavior also is the bereaved spouse's concentration upon preserving mementos in order to retain the suffering aspect of adjustment to bereavement.

c) A third important aspect of his behavior is

Table 23.1 *(Cont.)*

throughout the entire period. c) Nonactive, despondent responses to rituals and ceremonies: a dejected compliance with a minimum of efforts exerted, marked by an appearance of inattention and concentration upon self.	the bereaved person's resistance to attempts of others to help in his adjustment: nothing is accepted willingly which will divert attention from the deceased.

*SOURCE: Thomas D. Eliot, "_____ of the Shadow of Death," *The Annals of the American Academy of Political and Social Science*, 229 (September 1943), pp. 87–99. Adapted from David Martin Fulcomer, "The Adjustive Behavior of Some Recently Bereaved Spouses: A Psycho-Sociological Study," Unpublished Ph.D. Dissertation, Northwestern University, 1942. (Reprinted by permission from authors and publishers).

and they may feel compelled to resort to escape mechanisms, such as fainting or excessive drinking. Others may breathe an inner sigh of relief, perhaps because a bitter or disharmonious marital relationship has finally been dissolved or because a loved one has at last been freed from pain and suffering. Still others persist in denying the actuality of what has occurred. Thus:

A very common reaction when a family has been notified that a serviceman has been killed in action is to find reasons for refusing to believe the news. In one case the serviceman had been drowned. The mother had been officially notified by the War Department that he was killed, another serviceman had identified the body, and it had been brought home to Chicago for burial. Because the mother had not been allowed to see the body, however, she did not believe it was her son. She had seen a picture of some soldiers in the Near East and was convinced that one was her son. It was impossible to explain to her that if he were alive he would write, and she is still convinced that he will come home after the war is over.[7]

In many instances it is only when the deceased is finally buried that disbelief fades and the reality of the circumstances emerges to be eventually accepted.

Death dramatically terminates habitual familial relationships, but mental acceptance of the finality of this interruption usually comes about rather slowly. Habitual responses built up through a period of intimate interaction and interdependence in family living are not quickly nor easily extinguished. Whenever such responses are actually blocked, as they are in the case of death, the mental processes act to continue them. Thus, family members find themselves periodically engaging in imaginary behavior with the deceased.[8] Past images of interactions with the departed member are mentally recreated, reenacted, and reexamined. There is a tendency to recall the positive attributes of the deceased and to minimize or even repress the negative characteristics. This process of emphasizing the more favorable qualities of an individual through selective memory eventually results in a highly idealized and therefore distorted conception of the dead. As we shall note later, such idealization may become a problem when the survivor spouse attempts to establish new heterosexual relationships or seeks to remarry.

---

[7]Thomas D. Eliot, "_____ of the Shadow of Death," *The Annals of the American Academy of Political and Social Science,* **229** (Sept. 1943), pp. 94–95.

[8]The conflict that evolves from the difficulty of accepting the death of a person to whom one has been intimately attached often finds expression in a series of *hallucinatory dreams* about the deceased. For a detailed discussion of this phenomenon, see Waller, op. cit., pp. 496–505.

The Surviving Marital Partner

Annual census data for the United States indicate that there are more than eleven million widows and widowers among our population today (not counting those currently married persons who were once surviving partners but have since remarried). The widowed female in particular has outnumbered her male counterpart by a continually widening margin. This can be seen by the distributions in Table 23.2, which indicates that although the number of widowers has remained essentially constant since 1930, female survivors have substantially increased during this period. More specifically, in 1940 there were twice as many widows as there were widowers. During the following decade widows increased by nearly 25 per cent while the number of widowers rose by only 3 per cent. By 1960 widows outnumbered widowers by more than three and one half to one, and this discrepancy has increased to a current ratio of more than four to one. In 1970, there were well over 9 million female survivors in the nation and their total number will continue to rise.

There are three major factors that are responsible for and contribute to the growing excess of widows in the United States, namely: (1) mortality among females is lower than among males and, therefore, larger numbers of women survive to advanced years; (2) wives are typically younger than their husbands and, consequently, even with sex differences in mortality have a greater probability of outliving their husbands; and (3) among the widowed, remarriage rates are considerably lower for women than for men.[9] In the following sections we want to examine these factors in greater detail.

Probabilities of Widowhood

The chances that a wife will outlive her husband are, of course, partly dependent on the disparity in their ages at marriage, with the probability of the wife's being the survivor increasing with the number of years that she is younger than her spouse. Thus, where the couple are the same age, the changes that the wife will outlive her husband are slightly more than 60 in 100, but they rise to 70 in 100 when she is five years his junior and to 80 in 100 if he is her senior by ten years. Only in those instances where the wife is at least six years older than her husband is it probable that she will die before he does.[10] Because, in line with American custom, the typical bride is younger that her groom, most women outlive their husbands. Over two thirds of the men in our

[9]Other major factors that help account for the excess of widows are the effects of war casualties, depressions, and disease pandemics. Jacobson, op. cit., pp. 24–27.

[10]Paul H. Jacobson, "The Changing Role of Mortality in American Family Life," *Lex et Scientia,* **3** (Apr.–June 1966), pp. 117–124.

Table 23.2
Number of Widowers and Widows, United States,
1890–1965, Fourteen Years and Older

Year	Widowers	Widows
1890	815,000	2,155,000
1900	1,178,000	2,718,000
1910	1,471,000	3,176,000
1920	1,758,000	3,918,000
1930	2,025,000	4,734,000
1940	2,144,000	5,700,000
1950	2,296,000	6,967,000
1960	2,112,000	8,064,000
1970	2,103,000	9,625,000

SOURCE: U.S. Bureau of the Census, *Statistical Abstract of the United States: 1970* (Washington, D.C.: Government Printing Office).

society marry women younger than themselves. Consequently, marriage customs, operating within the context of differences in mortality that favor females, make the process of family dissolution one that in the end leaves disproportionately larger numbers of women unattached.[11]

Widowhood as a Problem of the Aged Family

From a statistical standpoint, widowhood is largely a problem of the aged woman. As a result of the decrease in mortality prior to midlife, widowhood has for the most part been postponed to the latter stages of the family life cycle. Around the beginning of the twentieth century, approximately one in twenty-five persons was sixty-five years of age or older, as compared to about one in eleven today. Because the gains in longevity have been more rapid for females than for males, the growing proportion of elders in the total population is accentuating the problem of surviving spouses. Thus, at mid-century more than 50 per cent of the widows were sixty-five years old and older and approximately 9 per cent were under age forty-five. But in 1965, more than 60 per cent of the survivor wives in the United States were sixty-five years of age or older and only 5 per cent were under age forty-five.[12] This noticeable trend

[11]The female's greater chances for survivorship are dramatically illustrated by an examination of census data during the last several decades. Among all marriages broken by death during the last decade of the nineteenth century, the wife was the surviving spouse in less than 56 per cent of the cases. In 1930 the proportion had increased to 60 per cent and currently has passed the 70 per cent mark. Ibid., p. 122.

[12]Moreover, as a consequence of her longevity, the modern American widow can look forward to many more years of survival than her counterpart at the turn of the century. See Metropolitan Life Insurance Company, "Widows and Widowhood," *Statistical Bulletin,* **47** (May 1966), pp. 3–6; "The American Widow," *Statistical Bulletin,* **43** (Nov. 1962), pp. 1–4.

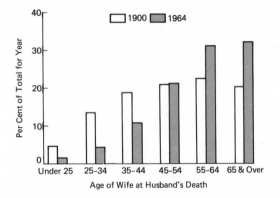

Figure 23.1. Age distribution of new widows, United States, 1900–1964. Percentages are estimated and include allowances for death of husbands in Armed Forces overseas during 1964. [From Paul H. Jacobson, "The Changing Role of Mortality in American Family Life," *Lex et Scientia,* **3** (April-June 1966), p. 121. Reprinted by permission.]

toward a postponement of widowhood until later stages in the life cycle is illustrated in Figure 23.1. There it can be seen that during the period 1900–1964, the number of women widowed at ages under thirty-five decreased from 18 to about $5^{1}/_{2}$ per cent, whereas the proportion losing their husbands at age sixty-five and over rose from 20 to 32 per cent. Moreover, the median age at which wives entered survivorship status rose from fifty-one years to fifty-nine years during this same period.

Husband Survivorship More Difficult[13]

In making the transition from married to widowed status, the bereaved are confronted with a variety of personal and familial problems. That they are not always successful in making the necessary adaptations is reflected in the findings that, when compared to married persons, the widowed rather consistently show higher rates of mortality, mental disorders, and suicide. This is especially relevant to aged families, who experience more disruption through the death of the wife or husband than younger age groups.

The aged person in our society generally finds it necessary to make certain economic and social accommodations in order to sustain a pattern of daily living that is acceptable to his self-concept. For the aged married this process is eased by a variety of conditions, including the benefits of mutual planning and sharing, reciprocal socioemotional support, and the psychosocial buttress of a long and continuous period

[13]This section draws heavily from Felix M. Berardo, "Survivorship and Social Isolation: The Case of the Aged Widower," *The Family Coordinator,* **19** (Jan. 1970), pp. 11–25.

of intimate paired interaction. For the aged widowed, however, the requirements for satisfactory living are confounded by the absence of a significant role partner. The sociopsychological supports essential to the maintenance of a balanced existence are often diminished and, in some instances, almost totally absent.

Research evidence suggests that for a variety of reasons survivorship adaptation may be more difficult for the older husband. In comparative terms the role of the wife remains relatively unchanged upon the death of her spouse. That is, she continues to perform her household tasks, such as cleaning and cooking, in much the same manner as when her husband was alive. Indeed, such tasks often may "constitute a very important variety of meaningful activity and ability to maintain certain standards of good housekeeping often represents a challenge and a test of the degree to which the older woman is avoiding "getting old."[14] Consequently, a large proportion of aged widows can maintain separate quarters and are capable of taking care of themselves. Moreover, the older widow is more likely than the widower to be welcomed into the home of her married children and find a useful place there.

In the case of the aged widower, however, the loss of his wife produces marked changes in his pattern of living.

A lifetime of close association with a woman whose complementary activities form the basis of a home now requires the most basic revision for which the widower may be wholly unprepared. If the wife was the homemaker-housekeeper, all those things upon which he depended and could anticipate in the management and upkeep of their mutual affairs devolve wholly upon him. The economy of convergent interests, the mutual resolution of each other's basic needs, the reciprocity of activities establishing well-ordered roles which are a bulwark of marriage are supplanted by a solitary and often disjointed independence. The vinculum that is marriage is disengaged by death and the widower may find himself incapable of remaking his life into an integrated whole.[15]

Spousal loss, then, creates certain practical problems for the older surviving husband. Faced with the daily necessities of maintaining a household, he is more likely than the surviving wife to need someone to prepare his meals, to do the cleaning, and to provide him with other types of general care.

In addition to the practical necessity of becoming proficient in domestic roles, the widower must find an adequate substitute for the

[14]Wayne E. Thompson and Gordon F. Streib, "Meaningful Activity in a Family Context," in *Aging and Leisure: A Perspective Into the Meaningful Use of Time,* ed. by Robert W. Kleemier (New York: Oxford University Press, 1961), pp. 177–211.

[15]Bernard Kutner, David Fanshel, Alice M. Togo, and Thomas S. Langner, *Five-Hundred over Sixty* (New York: Russell Sage Foundation, 1956), p. 63.

603

intimacy of that primary relationship once provided by his wife, and this is not easily accomplished. For many, remarriage would provide a partial solution, but courtship opportunities for older persons are extremely limited. Even if the husband is successful in locating a potential second mate, he will still have to overcome obstacles induced by a cultural bias in American society that often frowns upon such unions. Indeed, the older widower contemplating remarriage often finds

a barrier has been erected between what he wishes to do and what society expects him to do. His friends, his children and the community at large rise up and condemn his remarriage. He is regarded as "too old for that." The wagging fingers, the knowing smiles, the raised eyebrows and the cruel tongues are set in motion. Marriage is for the young in age, not the young in heart.[16]

It has been argued that such informal social sanctions often effectively curtail the number of older marriages and, in fact, force many elderly couples to marry in secret. Apparently, many such couples who marry in spite of family and community pressure do so by crossing state lines in order to avoid public opinion and public censure.[17] (We shall take up this problem of remarriage among the widowed in greater detail in a later section of this chapter.)

Finally, the retired widower's problems of adjustment are further compounded by the loss of his occupational role. For most of his adult life his work has been a principle source of his identity and self-conception. Retirement severs that identity, often in an abrupt fashion, and removes the husband from meaningful contact with friends and co-workers. The combined retiree-widower status places him in a position of structural isolation, leading to reduced communication and interaction with significant others. In general, American culture provides little in the way of guidelines concerning steps that must be taken if he is to reorganize his life successfully and avoid succumbing to the process of alienation.

For a variety of reasons then, including those already discussed, the aged widower often finds himself in a position of social isolation. Thus, in one study that compared the critical problems confronting an aged married and widowed sample, the aged widowers emerged as the most isolated subjects.[18] This was especially true among those who were

[16]Walter McKain, *Retirement Marriage,* Storrs Agricultural Experiment Station Monograph 3, University of Connecticut, 1969, p. 6.

[17]Ibid., pp. 6–7. McKain, for example, notes that in Connecticut in nearly one out of every five marriages involving older persons, one or both parties come from another state.

[18]Felix M. Berardo, *Social Adaptation to Widowhood Among a Rural-Urban Aged Population,* Washington Agricultural Experiment Station Bulletin 689, College of Agriculture, Washington State University, Pullman (Dec. 1967), especially pp. 28–29.

older, relatively uneducated, and residing in a rural environment. Another factor that led to social isolation was poor health, which sometimes caused a widower to be confined to his home and consequently limited his social contacts. In addition, it was noted that, in comparison with other marital statuses, widowers were least likely (1) to be living with children, (2) to have a high degree of kin interaction or to be satisfied with extended family relationships, (3) to receive from or give to children various forms of assistance, or (4) to have friends either in or outside of the community or to be satisfied with their opportunities to be with close friends. Further, they were least likely to be church members or to attend church services, or to belong to and participate in formal organizations or groups. Obviously, the cumulative consequences of these conditions would lead to an insufficient amount of stimulating and rewarding social interaction. As we shall note in a moment, the *younger* male survivors usually are able to avoid these problems through remarriage.

Indeed, there are some sociologists who suggest that it is the wife and not the husband who faces the greatest difficulties in returning to the single status. Bell, for example, feels that the role of the widow may be socially and psychologically more difficult than that of the widower for a variety of reasons.[19] He argues that in American society (1) marriage is generally more important for the woman than the man and, therefore, when it is terminated by death she loses a role more basic to the wife than may be the case for the surviving husband; (2) the widow is more apt to be forced to"go it alone" because in comparison to the widower she receives less encouragement from family and friends to remarry; (3) the widow faces much more difficulty in providing and caring for herself and her children because her financial resources usually are considerably less than those of a widower; and (4) there are far greater numbers of widows than widowers and the majority of them are widowed at advanced ages; therefore it is much more difficult for a surviving wife than for a surviving husband to change her status through remarriage. In the following sections, we want to take up each of these issues in detail, beginning with the last first.

Widowhood and Remarriage

Not only are more widows than widowers created each year as a result of the factors previously mentioned, but in addition the annual proportion of female survivors who remarry is considerably lower. In every decade since the turn of the century the remarriage rate for widowers has been more than double that of widows; and with each

---

[19]Robert R. Bell, *Marriage and Family Interaction* (Homewood, Ill.: Dorsey Press, 1963), pp. 412–416.

Table 23.3

Chances Per 100 for Marriage and Remarriage, by Marital Status, Age, and Sex

| Age | Men | | | Marital Status | Women | |
	Single	Divorced	Widowed	Single	Divorced	Widowed
20	97	99	97	97	100	97
25	93	99	97	88	99	93
30	82	99	96	70	98	81
40	45	92	85	30	83	50
50	18	71	62	10	53	20
60	5	42	29	3	23	6
65	3	29	16	1	13	3

ADAPTED FROM Paul H. Jacobson, *American Marriage and Divorce* (New York: Rinehart and Co., 1959), pp. 78, 80, 82–87.

successive increment in age this disparity widens, so that for persons fifty-five years or older, the remarriage rate for widowers is approximately five times as great.[20] This is perhaps most clearly illustrated by the data presented in Table 23.3, which indicates the statistical probabilities for first and subsequent marriages according to age, sex, and marital status. Several rather interesting patterns become apparent from the distribution of these statistical probabilities. First, the divorced are more apt to remarry than widowed persons and, except at the very young ages, the latter have greater prospects of marriage than the single. Second, regardless of marital status, males obviously have a higher probability of remarriage than females, and this advantage becomes increasingly apparent with advances in age. Third, when marital categories are compared, the largest differences between the sexes in terms of their chances for remarriage occur between widows and widowers. The age factor, then, is important to an understanding of the disparity in remarriage rates between wife and husband survivors. A woman who has been widowed at age twenty-five may find some small comfort in the knowledge that she has more than a 90 per cent chance for remarriage. At age forty-five, however, this probability is reduced to one in three, and at age sixty-five it drops to one in thirty-two.

One factor at work here is the traditional and still prevalent taboo in American society against young men's dating or marrying older women.[21] Ellis has reviewed the pros and cons associated with this

[20]Jacobson, op. cit., p. 68, Table 28. Jacobson also notes that the remarriage rate for all widowed persons has been declining proportionately over the past several decades. This trend reflects the lower incidence of widowhood at earlier ages in the United States.

[21]Albert Ellis, with Lester David, "Should Men Marry Older Women?" in *Marriage and Family in the Modern World,* 2nd ed., ed. by Ruth S. Cavan (New York: Thomas Y. Crowell Company, 1965), pp. 164–165.

606

particular restriction and has argued that the social pressure for men to wed women younger than themselves is both irrational and prejudicial in view of sociological and psychological evidence that "older wives" are frequently found to be the happiest. Moreover, he suggests that there are several distinct advantages to such unions. For the female it would mean first of all a lessened likelihood of prolonged widowhood. We have already noted that as a consequence of her longevity, coupled with her younger age at first marriage, the modern American wife can look forward to many more years of survival than her husband. Conceivably, the period of widowhood could be considerably reduced if not entirely eliminated through a reversal of the current age differentials between spouses. Secondly, elimination of the taboo presumedly would give many facing lifelong spinsterhood a second chance to find husbands. Women who have not married by age thirty find that their chances for marriage to a similarly aged or slightly older male sharply diminish with each passing year because of the reduction in the number of available unmarried men. (Of all men who eventually marry about nine tenths do so before age thirty). If, however, marriages to younger men were made acceptable, this would greatly enlarge the pool of potential spouses because there are many more single males in the younger age groups. One final advantage to a woman who marries a younger man is that the latter is perhaps less likely to be set in his ways and to have a rather rigid personality than, for instance, the older bachelor. Because of his greater flexibility the younger man can presumably adapt to the temperament and idiosyncrasies of an older woman, thereby easing the adjustments necessitated by the marriage.

For the male Ellis posits at least three advantages to be derived from wedding an older female spouse. First, she is more likely to be in a better economic situation than a younger woman; for example, she will have been working longer and accumulated larger savings. As a result, she can ease the economic burdens that typically face the modern couple in the early years of marriage. Similarly, many young men postpone marriage because they are not in a position to support a wife and children. Here again the economic situation of the older woman could help eliminate this barrier. Finally, it is argued, an older woman is more apt to be a more mature person with a realistic outlook on life.

A separate but related factor that helps to account for the surplus of unattached female survivors has to do with the period of time that elapses between bereavement and remarriage. Evidence from various sources indicates that the chances for remarriage for the widowed population are most favorable within a few years immediately following bereavement.[22] Thus, among all widowed persons who eventually

[22]Paul C. Glick, *American Families* (New York: John Wiley & Sons, 1957), pp. 138–139.

607

remarry more than two fifths do so within two years following the death of the spouse; within three years this proportion rises to one half. However, we have previously shown that the chances for remarriage for older persons is considerably less for widows than for widowers. When this knowledge is coupled with the fact that the majority of females in our society become widowed at advanced ages, it becomes apparent that in the case of the woman who has reached middle age a delay for even a few years brings her closer to an age at which she is more likely to be passed over by men who would have married her at an earlier period but who now are seeking younger women as wives. It is not unusually difficult for an older man, especially one who has substantial income, to find a woman approximately his own age or several years younger who would be willing to marry him. The aged woman, on the other hand, has much less of an opportunity for a second marriage.

OLDER MARRIAGES INCREASING In the latter connection, however, it may be worth mentioning that marriages of persons sixty-five years of age and older have shown a substantial rise in recent decades. For example, in one ten-year period such unions of older brides or grooms increased by more than one third and involved a total of 35,200 marriages in which either partner or both were sixty-five years of age or older.[23] Among the total number of such marriages, 78 per cent of the brides and 73 per cent of the grooms were widowed. This trend toward increased incidence of late marriages has been observed by a number of sociologists, although there has been relatively little systematic investigation of the courtship and mate-selection processes involved in such unions. McKain found that although courtship among older couples performed many of the same functions as it did for the young, there were important differences. Older couples recognized that societal attitudes toward their courtship activities were not as permissive as in the case of young persons. Moreover, unlike the latter, they were not blinded by the intensity of romantic love and, therefore, were more cognizant of the reactions of friends and relatives. Consequently, they were more sensitive to signs of community approval and family pressures, especially those emanating from their adult children. Thus, "the courtship pattern of older men and women tends to be more circumspect, their judgements more carefully weighed, and their decisions more responsive to outside influence."[24] Visiting with children, attending church together, going to the movies, attending social events, and frequently the bride-to-be's cooking dinner for the groom-to-be constituted their major courtship activities.

---

[23]"Trends in Number of Marriages of Older Persons, 1949–59, and Characteristics of Older Brides and Grooms, 1959," *Facts on Aging*, No. 2 (Jan. 1963), Office of Aging, U.S. Department of Health, Education, and Welfare, Washington, D. C.
[24]McKain, op. cit., p. 21.

Older marriages, of course, are by no means devoid of romance. Indeed, as Bernard has observed,

love in the middle and later years offers an opportunity to express deep emotions which a first marriage may have dulled to staleness. It may be a love that not only is reassuring and supporting but also brings with it euphoria. It is likely to have wider dimensions than love in youth and may perhaps be treasured even more, because the partners have experienced the deprivation of love. Although the sexual element is still present and important, later love tends to be less dependent upon the sexual relationship alone.[25]

Family sociologists for the most part have concentrated on youthful romance and love, and it is only within recent years that they have begun to direct some attention to the heterosexual attractions of older couples and late marriage.

IDEALIZATION AND REMARRIAGE There are certain subtle but recognizable psychological processes in operation during bereavement that seem to account in part for the comparatively low remarriage rate of widows. In terms of sex differential, it may be, as Waller and others have suggested, that wives often tend to idealize their former marriages in such a manner that they then are rendered incapable of entering a second union—at least in the immediate future. In such instances the deceased husband is, in a sense, placed so high on a pedestal that no potential suitor can offer comparable attributes. "The widow tends to think of her husband as young and virile, and her own spontaneous love interests are likely to go out strongly to men of this type; this interferes strongly with remarriage."[26] It is this type of emotional involvement with the deceased husband that must eventually be resolved if the surviving wife is to make a satisfactory adjustment to her changed status. If she remarries without making this necessary emotional transition, the probability of marital conflict is thereby increased because of the perhaps inevitable but unrealistic comparisons she may feel compelled to make between her new husband and her former spouse.

Idealization appears to be particularly detrimental to the establishment of new and intimate heterosexual relationships between the formerly married, that is, the separated and divorced, and the widowed person. In Hunt's investigation of the experiences of these two groups, he found that the formerly married reported their dating experiences with widows and widowers to be the least satisfactory. The formerly married male dating a widow quickly became aware that it was a distinctly different experience from dating a divorced woman.

[25]Jessie Bernard, *Remarriage: A Study of Marriage* (New York: The Dryden Press, 1956), pp. 119–124.
[26]Waller, op. cit., pp. 520–521.

The widow may be friendly and talkative on the surface, but there is an almost tangible barrier between her and the man, she is insulated, and no current of feeling flows between them . . . there is something about her that is not so much fearful as hostile. . . . She wears her loyalty to the dead man like a mask over her face; it is as though any show of interest or warmth would be a betrayal of her own love—especially if directed toward a man who, himself, had broken up his own marriage, instead of having it broken up, as hers was, by Fate.[27]

Similarly, it was not uncommon for a divorced or separated woman who had dated a widower to discover the latter's attitude toward her to be cold and condescending, and she would frequently feel as if he were making a critical judgment of her. Hunt concludes that the formerly married and the widowed are generally antagonistic toward each other and exhibit a distinct preference for dating persons of a similar marital status. This is, of course, later reflected in the rather well-established homogamous principle of assortive mating that "likes tend to select likes." It is not surprising, therefore, to learn that in general widowed persons most frequently marry each other. Likewise, the divorced and single, when they marry, predominantly choose mates within their own marital status.

It is not uncommon for well-meaning friends and relatives to view the single status for survivor spouses as unfortunate and/or unnecessary. Consequently, they experience a certain compulsion or sense of social obligation to play the role of matchmaker, and subsequently engage in the arrangement of "chance" meetings between unattached persons. These "accidental" encounters are often characterized by strain and embarrassment on the part of the couple involved. Not only are the matchmakers aware of the purpose of such encounters, but the real reason may also become painfully apparent to either or both of the parties involved, in which case an atmosphere of distrust and uncomfortableness may ensue. Perception of the situation often leads to resentment on the part of either party over the attempts of others to consciously manipulate their social relationships. Older survivors are particularly apt to resent having their courtship activities arranged. There are a number of other potentially negative consequences that might result from these "forced" encounters that the reader could no doubt think of. At the same time one cannot deny that, given the proper circumstances, prearranged contacts may have positive and long-lasting outcomes.

On the other hand, there are instances in which widows and widowers are explicitly excluded from social gatherings by friends and relatives because his or her presence is interpreted as a threat to their

---

[27]Morton M. Hunt, *The World of the Formerly Married* (New York: McGraw-Hill Book Company, 1966), pp. 122–125.

610

own marital situation. This suspicion seems to be especially true of some married women who suspect that the widow is "after" their husband or fear that he will be tempted into an extramarital affair with this "other woman." Although there is little empirical evidence to support their assumptions, the fact remains that in American society widows occasionally find themselves being suspected of being if not labeled as promiscuous.

In America, most social participation occurs in pair relationships. The widowed, therefore, by virtue of their single status, often find themselves barred from such participation through either neglect of noninvitation.[28]

Stability of Remarriage Following Widowhood

Sociologists generally have utilized two types of evidence to evaluate the marital success of second marriages: (1) the rate of divorce that occurs among such unions; and (2) measures of marital adjustment, including the ratings by couples of their satisfaction with the new marriage. In either instance, studies have shown that the remarriages of widowed persons exhibit a high degree of stability, especially in comparison to remarriages involving individuals who have been divorced.

With regard to the first criterion, the divorce rate, a study by Monahan is perhaps most illustrative. Comprehensive data according to previous marital status for persons divorcing in the state of Iowa were examined and yielded the results presented in Figure 23.2. It can be seen that marriages in which both partners have been widowed once exhibit the lowest proportion of divorces, whereas those in which both parties have been divorced twice or more have the highest. Even in those cases in which a once-widowed person has married a single person, the percentage divorced is considerably less than in any of the remaining combinations examined. As a matter of fact, in those rare instances of a marriage involving couples who have been widowed twice or more, only two out of every one hundred such unions are terminated by divorce. Monahan cautions, however, that the widowed generally remarry at much older ages and, therefore, their low divorce rates may be due largely to the effect of joint mortality.[29] In any event, it

---

[28]The organization Parents Without Partners (PWP) has been one solution to this problem. Incorporated in 1958, it now has chapters in nearly every state and in Canada and is devoted to the welfare and interests of single parents and their children. See Jim and Janet Engleson, *Parents Without Partners* (New York: E. P. Dutton & Co., 1961).

[29]Thomas P. Monahan, "The Changing Nature and Instability of Remarriage," *Eugenics Quarterly,* **5** (June 1958), pp. 83–85. Bernard, op. cit., p. 112, also found that marriages involving a widowed person and a single or also widowed person exhibited the most favorable "success ratio."

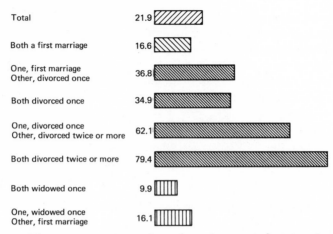

Figure 23.2 Divorce per 100 marriages by prior marital status, Iowa, 1953–1955. Divorce-widowed combinations excluded. [From Thomas P. Monahan, "The Changing Nature and Instability of Remarriage," *Eugenics Quarterly,* **5** (June 1958), pp. 73–85. Reprinted by permission.]

is safe to conclude that the remarriage of the widowed has approximately the same probabilities of success as have first marriages.[30]

In terms of the more subjective aspects of marital adjustment (our second criterion), the remarriages of the widowed again appear to be more successful when compared to those of the divorced. In Bernard's study, for example, almost two thirds of the widowed remarriages were rated by informants as either "very happy" or "happy," whereas slightly over half of the divorced remarriages were rated as such.[31] McKain used five criteria to develop a subjective evaluation of the older marriages in his study, namely: (1) whether the couple showed affection and respect for each other; (2) whether they obviously enjoyed each other's company; (3) whether the couple made serious complaints about each other; (4) whether the husband and wife were genuinely proud of each other; and (5) whether the spouses were considerate of each other. In addition to these evaluations made by the interviewer, the couple were also asked a number of questions that were also useful in indicating whether the marriage was a success. For example, they were asked which one was the head of the family and which one made the decisions on major purchases, menus, religious affiliation, and the extent of social activity. On the basis of these and other data, McKain concluded that nearly three fourths of these widowed remarriages could be rated as successful.[32]

[30]Thomas P. Monahan, "The Duration of Marriage and Divorce: Second Marriages and Migratory Types," *Marriage and Family Living,* **21** (May 1959), pp. 134–138.
[31]Bernard, op. cit., p. 111, Table IV-3.
[32]McKain, op. cit., pp. 41–50.

Inasmuch as the majority of the widowed who eventually remarry do so at older ages than the divorced or the single, it has been previously suggested that they probably enter into such unions with less in the way of romantic expectations. That is, it is possible that their first marriages may have provided sufficient satisfaction of earlier romantic needs and that the new marital bond may therefore be established on a more rational basis. Thus, older persons are not apt to demand as much from marriage as they might have when they were younger. For them, the companionship and security of married status takes greater priority than the fulfillment of romantic aspirations.

The findings concerning the stability and happiness among the widowed remarriages are illuminating in view of the many important areas of potential conflict that often accompany such relationships. Take for example, the case of a second wedding in which at least one of the couple was formerly widowed. In such instances, the widowed spouse may be unable to inhibit the tendency to idealize the deceased mate. Under such circumstances, it becomes difficult to appreciate fully the positive attributes of the new spouse. Bernard has noted that often where

idealization exists, the present wife is at a great disadvantage in competition with the former wife. She cannot prove to her husband that her cooking is better, her housekeeping more competent, her budgeting more efficient, or her sexual appeal greater than that of her rival, and she herself has no way of knowing whether or not she is superior to the first wife, especially if the second wife has come to live in the widowed man's home. And the husband may, consciously or unconsciously, play upon his advantage. His manner may imply that his former marriage set a high standard which the present marriage is not achieving. Without saying anything at all, he may communicate an invidious contrast between his former and his present wife.[33]

Another potential problem arises from the recognition on the part of the new spouse that the partner's first marriage was involuntarily terminated by death. For example, the new husband may feel uncomfortable with the knowledge that he is a second choice. Should he dwell on the possibility that if the first husband had survived he never would have been considered this could lead to feelings of anxiety and uncertainty regarding his present marriage relationship. It may introduce a good deal of tension into the new marriage that would have to be resolved if relationships are to be harmonious and secure.

The new marital partner sometimes discovers that he is initially resented by friends and relatives of the widowed spouse and her former husband. They may find it difficult to reconcile their established relationships with the deceased spouse with the presence of the second

---

[33]Bernard, op. cit., pp. 199–202.

husband. The uneasiness caused by the situation may lead them to cast the new husband in the role of an intruder. Special efforts may have to be made in order to overcome the notion that he is an "outsider" and to gain his acceptance as a legitimate member of the group.[34] A related factor here is that additional in-law relationships are established as a result of remarriage and this may further necessitate some type of readjustment. The remarried widow, for example, must adjust to her new in-laws while at the same time appeasing her old ones.[35] The family of the deceased spouse may claim that she has not mourned for a sufficient period of time and therefore the second union is disrespectful to the deceased and inconsiderate of their own feelings. The new marriage may be viewed by them as an act of disloyalty, and hostilities toward the second spouse may ensue.

Despite these and other potential problems, we have seen that the majority of widowed remarriages are successful. Consequently, although the chances for marital and familial conflict exist, they are evidently surmountable and therefore do not necessarily and unequivocally produce negative outcomes.

In an earlier period of American history negative community attitudes toward second marriages were frequently pervasive and of sufficient influence to delay if not completely discourage individuals, especially widows, from entering another union. This type of resentment apparently has subsided over the years. Even at the time of Bernard's study she observed that the conditions surrounding remarriages were in the process of redefinition in the direction of a more favorable community attitude.[36] Although there are no doubt wide differences from community to community, as well as from one social class to another, the individual prerogatives of persons contemplating second marriages have gained increasing recognition in this country as well as abroad.[37] The trend seems highly desirable, for remarriage often serves to alleviate some of the major complaints voiced by the widowed, namely, loneliness, a sense of isolation, and an unacceptable dependency status.[38]

Maternal and Paternal Orphanhood

Currently over 9 million youngsters in the United States are living in homes with only one parent present. Among these are nearly 1.5

---

[34]Ibid., p. 214.

[35]Ibid., p. 196.

[36]Ibid., p. 36.

[37]Goode has presented a cogent argument with supporting cross-cultural evidence for a general trend toward the relaxation of the mores regarding remarriage of the widowed. William J. Goode, *World Revolution and Family Patterns* (New York: The Free Press, 1963), pp. 199–200, 265–269.

[38]Helena Z. Lopata, "Loneliness: Forms and Components," *Social Problems,* **17** (Fall 1969), pp. 248–262.

million *paternal* orphans, that is, children who have lost their fathers through death, and about .25 million *maternal* orphans. Recent estimates indicate that of all orphans in the nation, approximately 71 per cent have deceased fathers only and about 27 per cent have lost their mothers only. Less than 3 per cent have experienced the death of both parents.[39] That the burdens of orphanhood are borne primarily by women is illustrated rather clearly in Table 23,4. There, for example, it can be seen that the number of children under eighteen orphaned by the death of a mother was only half those who lost a father. The chances of paternal orphanhood are, then, considerably greater than those of maternal orphanhood. For instance, the probability that a father aged twenty-five will die before his newborn child reaches age eighteen is close to five in one hundred. This probability increases to ten in one hundred when the father is thirty-five, and rises to twenty-three in one hundred when he is forty-five. On the other hand, the chances of the mother's dying before the newborn child reaches age eighteen are only about half those for the father of the same age.[40]

Table 23.4
Husbands and Wives Dying and Own Children Under Age 18 Surviving
United States, 1964 (Numbers in Thousands)

Age of Husband at Time of His or Wife's Death	Husbands		Wives	
	Number Dying	Number of Own Children Surviving	Number Dying	Number of Own Children Surviving
All Ages	594.2	282.3	251.3	141.1
Under 25	4.5	4.5	1.8	1.8
25–34	13.6	29.9	8.5	18.7
35–44	33.9	84.8	19.5	48.8
45–54	77.9	93.4	36.6	43.9
55–64	137.7	46.8	55.4	18.8
65 and over	326.7	22.9	129.4	9.1

Note: Each figure has been independently rounded; hence, the sums of parts may differ slightly from the totals.
SOURCE: Metropolitan Life Insurance Company, "Orphanhood—A Continuing Problem," *Statistical Bulletin,* **47** (Dec. 1966), p. 4. Reprinted by permission.

Children who have experienced the trauma of bereavement and/or have been reared in a one-parent household have typically been depicted as occupying a particularly disadvantaged position because of the presumed family disruption engendered by such circumstances.

[39]Metropolitan Life Insurance Company, "Orphanhood—A Continuing Problem," *Statistical Bulletin,* **47** (Dec. 1966), pp. 3–5.
[40]Metropolitan Life Insurance Company, "Chances of Dependency," *Statistical Bulletin,* **50** (Jan. 1969), pp. 10–11.

The dysfunctional consequences for personality development and social adjustment of the children involved have been especially emphasized. Researchers sharing this perspective, such as Landis, have often "assumed as a working hypothesis that the young person in the broken home who does not go to the extreme of delinquency may still experience problems in his adjustment with peers and teachers, in school relationships, and in the community which are not experienced by young people living in families with both parents present."[41] A related assumption underlying this viewpoint relevant to the paternal orphan is that the absence of a proper sex-role model, represented by the father, results in inadequate socialization. Similarly, it is assumed that because the mother is forced to shoulder dual role obligations, such as the breadwinner role, she is not able to supervise and control her children adequately. These circumstances are said to result in a variety of negative consequences, such as delinquency, mental illness, sex-role inadequacy, sexual maladjustment, and so on.

For some time then the major sociological opinion endorsed the attributes of a complete family environment. This somewhat traditional viewpoint, however, was subsequently challenged by investigators who stressed that the presence of both parents does not automatically guarantee a better child-rearing situation. It does not necessarily mean, for instance, that the interaction between parents and children will be of sufficient intensity and quality to produce positive results. Rather, it is argued that "the crucial factor in the adjustment of children is the social-psychological success or failure of the family, not whether or not it is legally and physically broken."[42] Nye, for example, compared the adjustment of children in *broken* and *unhappy unbroken* homes and found that adolescents from the broken homes exhibited a more successful pattern of adaptation. That is, they showed less psychosomatic illness, less delinquency, and better adjustment to parents. Moreover, he found no evidence of greater problems in "mother only" homes than in remarried or unhappy unbroken homes. As a matter of fact, parent-child relationships were superior in the "solo" mother homes in almost every area of adjustment measured. Perry and Pfuhl also compared the adjustment of adolescents in homes broken by death or divorce with that of youngsters in remarried homes.[43] They found no

[41]Paul H. Landis, "The Broken Home in Teenage Adjustments," Washington Agricultural Experiment Station Bulletin 542 (June 1953), State College of Washington (now Washington State University), Pullman.

[42]F. Ivan Nye, "Child Adjustment in Broken and in Unhappy Unbroken Homes," *Marriage and Family Living,* **19** (Nov. 1957), pp. 356–361; also see Lee Burchinal, "Characteristics of Adolescents from Unbroken, Broken, and Reconstituted Families," *Journal of Marriage and the Family,* **26** (Feb. 1964), pp. 44–51.

[43]Joseph B. Perry, Jr., and Erdwin H. Pfuhl, Jr., "Adjustment of Children in 'Solo' and 'Remarriage' Homes," *Marriage and Family Living,* **25** (May 1963), pp. 221–223.

significant differences between the two groups in terms of delinquent behavior, psychoneurotic tendencies, and school grades. The results of these and similar studies have thrown into question the assumption that the effects of family dissolution on children are necessarily adverse. They suggest, on the contrary, that family dissolution, per se, is not the most important factor influencing the lives of the young survivors. In addition to the social-psychological climate mentioned earlier, the question of whether or not and how the absence of a parent through death affects children has been found to depend on a combination of variables, including the age, number, and sex of the children, the duration of the marriage up to the time of dissolution as well as the age of the surviving parent at that moment, and a variety of social-class and ethnic factors.[44]

Spousal Demise and Economic Deprivation

Because the majority of the widowed are aged, their economic circumstances are usually far below average, particularly in the case of surviving wives and their families. A special survey by the insurance industry of widows fifty-five years of age and older, for example, revealed that almost 67 per cent of the deceased husbands left their families a sum total of assets (including cash, savings, life insurance, property value of the home, and other assets) of less than $10,000; indeed, 44 per cent left assets of less than $5,000. Equally significant, almost 75 per cent of the husbands owned less than $5,000 in life insurance at the time of their death, and an additional 20 per cent owned less than $10,000. Moreover, many of their widows had to use what small amounts of insurance their husbands did carry to pay for funeral expenses, medical bills, taxes, mortgages, and so on, leaving them with only small savings, if any. Their economic plight is further revealed by the fact that the median income of these wives in the year preceding the survey was less than $2,000.[45]

A nationwide survey of younger widowed mothers and their dependent children who were receiving survivor benefits under the Social Security program showed that the median income of these families was only slightly above the poverty level.[46] The low income level of these

---

[44]Part of the problem with achieving a definitive answer to the question has to do with certain methodological problems associated with studying one-parent families. See Jetse Sprey, "The Study of Single Parenthood: Some Methodological Considerations," *The Family Life Coordinator,* **16** (Jan.–Apr. 1967), pp. 29–34.

[45]Institute of Life Insurance, *Some Data on Life Insurance Ownership and Related Characteristics of the Older Population* (New York: Institute of Life Insurance, Nov., 1965, Mimeographed).

[46]Erdman Palmore, Gertrude L. Stanley, and Robert H. Cormier, *Widows with Children Under Social Security,* U.S. Department of HEW, Office of Research and Statistics, Social Security Administration, Research Report No. 16 (Washington, D.C.: Government Printing Office, 1966).

widowed families affected their consumption patterns and living arrangements in various ways. For example, they spent considerably more of their total income on food and housing than the average family, and this meant there was less money available for other needs. Thus, fewer of them had cars, health or life insurance, and so on. Moreover, in comparison to normal families these beneficiary families were much more likely to share their households with others, both as a means of reducing expenses and as a means of obtaining aid in child care. Nevertheless, many employed widows found it necessary to leave their school-age children uncared for while they worked.[47]

Life insurance has become a principle defense against the insecurity and risk of widowhood in our urban industrial society with its attendant nuclear family system. It is a concrete form of security that in many instances may help the bereaved family to avoid an embarrassing dependence on relatives and the state in the case of untimely death. However, as we have seen, the amount of insurance obtained is often insufficient to meet the needs of the surviving family. Even in those instances in which adequate assets have been accumulated, many surviving wives find that they are incapable of handling the economic responsibilities brought about by the husband's death, inasmuch as they know very little about matters of real estate, titles, mortgages, contracts, stocks, bonds, and other such matters or property.[48]

Actually the economic dilemma in which widows often find themselves is frequently brought about as a direct result of the failure of husbands to plan their estates and advise their wives.

The truth is that most men leave their affairs in a jumble. This is not because their lives are unduly complicated, but simply because they can't seem to get around to the task of setting up a program for their families that would automatically go into operation upon their death. Death is unpleasant to think about and always seems remote. The tendency is to put the problem off and plan "to get to it one of these days."[49]

Moreover, some husbands themselves are incapable of making sensible financial decisions, as the following example illustrates:

A young widow came into the insurance office to collect the proceeds of her husband's policies. She had three children aged 4, 6, and 8. There were three $5,000 policies and one $2,000 policy. Her husband had made each $5,000

---

[47]Ibid., p. 65.

[48]Pertinent illustrations of the dilemma faced by widows regarding economic responsibilities may be found in "A Widow and Her Money," *Changing Times* (Aug. 1961), pp. 25–29.

[49]"How to Help Your Widow," *Changing Times* (Nov. 1961), pp. 9–14, contains many useful suggestions for "putting one's house in order" in preparation for the untimely death of the family breadwinner.

618

policy payable to one child upon the child's reaching age 17 and furnishing proof of being in college. The money with which the widow was expected to raise the children to age 17 and get them into college was—you guessed it—$2,000.[50]

It should be obvious that these and similar decisions reflect inadequate preparation on the part of families for dealing with the contingencies of death. As a result, economic dilemmas are often created for the surviving family members that can be resolved only through the aid, sometimes elusive and expensive, of a competent lawyer or other person.

Because they frequently encounter serious economic problems soon after their husbands have passed away, many wives find it necessary to seek employment, particularly in the case where dependent children are involved. Thus, in the survey of widow-child beneficiary families mentioned previously, it was found that widowed mothers were more than twice as likely as wives whose husbands were still living to be in the labor force. However, most of these were employed only part time and many who sought employment were unsuccessful in obtaining a job. Indeed, the survey revealed that unemployment among these widowed mothers was about three times as high as that of other women. The majority of those who did find jobs worked in low-skilled occupations.[51]

Although wives entering widowhood at the older ages are not as likely to have dependent children in the home, nevertheless, they often face a similar problem of self-support because Social Security benefits provide only for the minimum necessities. Moreover, the obstacles to securing employment at this stage of the life cycle are often rather difficult to overcome. Typically, these wives have been absent from the labor market for several years and are, therefore, at a disadvantage with respect to the educational and occupational demands of the labor market. In addition, they frequently are confronted with a pervasive discrimination on the part of employers who are not in favor of hiring older persons, let alone older women. In spite of these handicaps, many older surviving wives do manage to become a part of the labor force. Like their younger counterparts, however, they are heavily concentrated in the low-paying jobs.[52]

Research indicates that playing a role in the productive economy is predictive of favorable adjustment to widowhood status. Specifically, an employed widow in later life tends to be better adjusted—that is, to

[50]*Changing Times* (Aug. 1961), op. cit., pp. 25–29.
[51]Palmore et. al., op. cit., pp. 64–65.
[52]It is clear, however, that because the majority of surviving wives, but in particular the aged widows, are unemployed, they are unable to support themselves and consequently are partly or wholly dependent on the assistance of children and relatives, and on public or private funds.

have higher morale—than either a housewife who has never worked or a retired widow. It is suggested that if giving employment status to the older widow permits her to manipulate her environment (entertain friends, purchase books, go to the movies or the theater, travel, and so on), then this will produce higher morale. The acts of preparing for work, carrying out one's tasks on the job, and returning home appear to be intimately connected to feelings of personal worth, self-esteem, and significance in life. Thus, researchers have concluded that

for widowed women, there is a need for a service that will provide occasional jobs, such as babysitting, service as companions for bedridden persons, and occasional light housekeeping tasks. Many widows have never been in the labor force and have never acquired skills in any other line. These kinds of jobs frequently coincide with their experiences as homemakers.[53]

FOSTER GRANDPARENTS A federally sponsored program that dovetails rather nicely with the employment needs of older survivors who lack specialized technical skills is the Foster Grandparent program developed by the Office of Economic Opportunity. Under this program, the federal government awards grants of money to the states to be used to employ older people as "foster grandparents" to work with and serve as companions for the mentally retarded, the physically handicapped, the delinquent, the emotionally disturbed, and dependent and neglected children in institutions, day-care centers, and homes. Potential foster grandparents are carefully screened and, if selected, undergo a brief training course as well as in-service training designed to familiarize them with the complexities of working with institutionalized children. The foster grandparents visit five days a week with their young charges and receive remuneration for their work. Participation in such a program often meets the strong needs of older persons to feel useful and to be loved.

The Foster Grandparent program appears to have been very successful since its inception in 1965 and has been rapidly implemented in various places across the nation. Preliminary research indicates that experience in the program has aided many persons to adjust to the problems of later maturity and survivorship. Gray and Kasteler, for example, compared a group of foster grandparents with a similar group of persons who were not employed in the program and found the grandparents to be better adjusted both personally and socially as well as being more satisfied with their lives.[54]

[53]Kutner et al., op. cit., p. 254.
[54]Robert M. Gray and Josephine M. Kasteler, "An Evaluation of the Effectiveness of a Foster Grandparent Project," *Sociology and Social Research,* **54** (Jan. 1970), pp. 181–189. See also Genevieve M. Thompson, "Foster Grandparents," *Child Welfare,* **48** (Nov. 1969), pp. 546–568.

620

Part VI

Postscript on the Family

24

The Future Family

Throughout this text we have been examining the contemporary family in terms of its organization and relationships, and frequently we have compared the family structure and functions of the past with those of the present. In these final pages, we shift the perspective forward beyond the horizon and discuss the family yet to come—the family of the future. We will explore, from a sociological viewpoint, the directions in which the modern family seems to be heading, the forms it is apt to assume, and the functions it is likely to be performing in the not distant future.

Sociological prognostications about the future of the family, like most if not all scientific forecasting, must of necessity be framed in terms of degrees of probability. In the more so-called exact sciences, the accuracy of prediction about future events is often high, either because the scientist can exert control over the phenomena being studied, or because what he is studying is affected little or not at all by human intervention.[1] By way of illustration, the astronomer can make fairly accurate approximations about the path of the earth's orbit or the movement of celestial bodies; they exhibit such statistical regularities over time that this makes for rather precise forecasting. It is not a matter of luck that space engineers can establish with almost pinpoint accuracy the impact time and location of a rocket landing on the moon!

The social scientist, on the other hand, deals with variable social phenomena over which he has little or no control, and his projections are subject to change by a multiplicity of factors. For example, the family sociologist might predict, on the basis of declining birth rates,

[1] Lest we overstate this point, it is perhaps worth remembering that the physical sciences do have their problems with prediction, as in the case of the forecasts of the meteorologist!

623

that the family of the future will be smaller in size. Birth rates and family size, however, do not show the statistical regularity of the nightly appearance of the stars. They are influenced by a host of dynamic forces, not the least of which are unanticipated fluctuations in the economic order. The rapid and accelerated increase in the proportion of employed mothers in America further illustrates the difficulty of sociological forecasting.

During World War II, when much was made of the fact that "Rosie" was riveting, everybody assumed that after the war she would go back home and never rivet again. But the number of working mothers today is greater than the wartime peak when a shortage of men in the labor force and the urgent demands of the war machine created practical and patriotic motives for working. Now, under ordinary peace-time conditions, voluntarily and in full competition with men, millions of married women have gone back to work.[2]

This change has profoundly affected not only the economic system but family relations as well; yet it was largely unpredicted. Few could have foreseen the dramatic increase in employment opportunities available to women created by the demands of a new and vast technology, or the removal of the traditional obstacles to their seeking employment outside of the home.

Long-range forecasting about the future development of the family, therefore, must be approached cautiously and stated with somewhat less certainty than might be desired.[3] Nevertheless, although exact and detailed predictions about the family in the far distant future are not feasible, *if* present trends continue, then certain predictions are possible.

It is within the context of these short-range trends that forecasts about the future are most likely to attain a reasonable degree of accuracy rather than being mere uneducated conjecture. Longer-range predictions are both less accurate and more intriguing.

Social Change and Family Adaptation

Most of this chapter will be concentrated on large-scale changes occurring in contemporary American society and the impact they are expected to have in shaping family life in the next few decades. In any

[2]Robert O. Blood, Jr., "Long-Range Causes and Consequences of the Employment of Married Women," *Journal of Marriage and the Family,* **27** (Feb. 1965), pp. 43–47.

[3]For a brief discussion of some of the methods used by sociologists to project contemporary family life into the future, and the hazards associated with them, see Reuben Hill, "The American Family of the Future," *Journal of Marriage and the Family,* **26** (Feb. 1964), pp. 20–28.

discussion of social change, however, it is necessary to keep in mind the complex and reciprocal nature of the relationships between the family system and other institutional structures. Traditionally, socio-logical analyses and interpretations of these interrelationships have generally treated the family as a *dependent* variable. That is, the family is seen primarily as being affected by and responding to the changing requirements of other social institutions.

Conceptions of the family system as an *independent* variable respon-sible for producing major alterations in other aspects of the social structure are given much less recognition. Nimkoff explains the basic rationale for this in terms of the differential dynamic qualities of institutions.

The economic and political systems are more dynamic than the family, and the economic order is the most dynamic of all in Western society. An important factor here is that economic production, being based upon science, is subject in the West to the process of rationalization, and the family is not. If science can be said to have a motto, it is: there is always a better way. Obsolescence and innovation are encouraged. But the family, like religion, is designed to afford stability to social life. We may be interested in a new model of car every year but not in a new model of family life.[4]

Vincent provides a related rationale when he suggests that the family system is the least organized of the several social systems that make up our society. Unlike the various segments of the religious, educational, professional, recreational, political, and occupational worlds, which have strong and powerful spokesmen at all levels of society, the "family system has no collective representative, no lobbyist, no official spokesman," and because it is "*un*organized as a family system beyond each individual family, it is easily divided and its resistance con-quered."[5] Consequently, it can be argued that the family system is more likely to adapt to changes in other institutional structures than to effect changes in them.

At the same time, the reciprocal role of the family system in exerting significant influences on other social systems should not be underesti-mated. For example, the so-called population explosion, which is partly a result of changes in family values, has compelled drastic expansion of the educational system, has effected numerous changes in the economy, and has stimulated a variety of governmental programs and activities. It is important, therefore, in discussing the impact that

---

[4]Meyer F. Nimkoff (ed.), *Comparative Family Systems* (Boston: Houghton Mifflin Company, 1965), pp. 33–35.

[5]Clark E. Vincent, "Family Spongia: The Adaptive Function," *Journal of Marriage and the Family*, **28** (Feb. 1966), pp. 29–36.

625

large-scale shifts in the American social structure are expected to have in shaping the future family, that we keep in mind this mutual adaptation of institutions to one another. In some instances, shifts in one or more institutions have an impact on the family as an institution and on the relationships of its members. In other cases, changes in the family due to broad economic, social, or ideological reasons will have an influence on other areas of the social order. In any event, it should be noted that the family *must* adapt to the changing social milieu in which it lives and works. Such adaptation must not be taken as evidence of family demoralization or as an indication that the family as an institution is about to disappear.

Some Recent Forecasts

Sociological forecasting of the future of the family has a long and interesting history that can, depending on one's point of view, be dated back several centuries. Predictions about the eventual courses family life would follow can be found in many of the works of the early social philosophers, anthropologists, historians, political scientists, and many others. Although it would be of value to examine such material in depth, such a task is beyond the scope of the present work. We do think it necessary and relevant, however, to take a brief look at a few selected predictions about the American family made by contemporary social scientists writing in the second half of the twentieth century. This survey will provide a wider and more meaningful framework within which to present our own discussion.

1. Sociologists have developed a variety of methods for making predictions. One method, reported by Hill and his colleagues, utilizes generational changes as a basis for identifying the family of the future. "The method consists of examining the consistent differences which persist over three generations into the married-child generation— regarding the families of this latter generation as the best indication of what the American family of the future will be like."[6] Hill's analysis involved 300 intact and generationally linked nuclear families: 100 married child families (ages twenty to thirty), 100 parental families (ages forty to sixty), and 100 grandparental families (ages sixty to eighty). The contemporary generation exhibited a more developmental ideology with respect to parenthood, were most likely to share household tasks, and showed less specialization of husband-wife roles. They were also more future oriented. "From this analysis a picture emerges of increasing effectiveness, professional competence, and economic

---

[6]Hill, op. cit., pp. 21–22. See also: Reuben Hill, et al., *Family Development in Three Generations* (Cambridge, Mass.: Schenkman Pub. Co., 1970).

well-being, of greater courage in risk-taking accompanied by greater planning, of greater flexibility in family organization with greater communication and greater conflict."[7] On the basis of this and additional evidence derived from other methods of prediction, Hill rejects the notion that the family is becoming a functionless and disintegrated unit in society.

2. Farber has predicted that at least six major trends will be evident in the American social structure in the next decade and a half, each of which he feels will significantly influence family life: a decline of manpower in agriculture; increased automation; more manpower in service occupations; increasingly high social density through rising urbanization, geographical mobility, and expanded communication and transportation networks; increased employee-entrepreneur ratio, i.e, more employees, less entrepreneurs, with a concomitant emphasis on large-scale, bureaucratic economic organizations and control; and, continued advances in medicine leading to greater control of illness and disease.[8] On the basis of these trends, Farber offers a number of specific forecasts regarding developments that will affect the family of the future. Some of these forecasts closely parallel those presented later in this chapter and therefore will be discussed subsequently.

3. More recently, Christensen has attempted to project a picture of the American family in 1980.[9] He recognizes four basic social trends that are now affecting and will continue to have profound influences upon our family structure: increasing rates of technological innovations, which are continually raising the level of living and allowing more and more families to obtain material comforts; population growth and its attendant developments, such as the search for new contraceptives, migration from rural to urban centers, and so on; increasing democratization and individualism and a decline in families; and increasing secularism and materialism, including a decline in religious values and a growing faith in science. In attempting to sketch some of the features of the future family, Christensen states:

it will not be replaced by state-controlled systems of reproduction and childbearing. It will persist because it is needed for both personal contentment and social stability. Its stability, nevertheless, will depend even more than at present upon the strength of its interpersonal bonds, rather than upon kinship loyalty or social pressures from without; and upon how well it performs the

---

[7]Ibid., p. 24. With respect to marital conflict, the married child generation was also most likely to conclude their disagreements with consensus and gestures of affection (p. 23).

[8]Bernard Farber, *Family: Organization and Interaction* (San Francisco: Chandler Publishing Co., 1964), pp. 232–281.

[9]Harold T. Christensen, "Changing Roles of Family Members," paper presented in the fall of 1965 at a workshop at Michigan State University, pp. 1–25.

627

personality functions still left to it. It will be the nuclear family essentially, therefore, organized around affectional ties and the socialization processes.[10]

There are certain similarities in the works of Nimkoff, Hill, Farber, and Christensen. They all see the family as a highly adaptable institution, capable of withstanding tremendous alterations in the social structure and of continuing to function as a viable institution. Although they all recognize that the family will experience a variety of problems in the years ahead, and that these problems will cause a certain amount of disruption, though not necessarily disorganization, they all remain essentially optimistic with respect to the future role the family institution will play in society. Finally, and particularly in the case of Farber and Christensen, there is general agreement as to the major social trends that are expected to be especially influential in shaping the family of tomorrow.

Social Trends and the Future Family

We have seen that there are several broad social and technological developments in American society that are having and will continue to have direct and indirect consequences for the family. In our discussion we will not try to cover all of them but will concentrate on three broad-scale trends that we feel will be most intimately connected with family living in the next decade or two. We have labeled these trends the demographic, the cybernetic, and the human rights revolutions. Moreover, it is necessary to point out that these trends are by no means mutually exclusive. They are interdependent and, therefore, a change in any one of them will to some extent modify the others.

The Demographic Revolution

World population has been multiplying at an unprecedented rate. "From the time of the first man and woman it took thousands of years for the race to reach the number of one billion living people. That occurred around 1830. It required only one century to add the second billion—around 1930—about 30 years for world population to add a third billion."[11] World population now stands at 3.4 billion, and if present growth rates continue, the number of people on this planet is expected to reach 6 or 7 billion by the year 2000. In the United States, an equally dramatic population increase has been occurring. Whereas our total population was 76 million in 1900, in 1967 it passed the 200 million mark, and if present trends continue, by the year 2000 our population is expected by some analysts to be between 350 million and

---

[10]Ibid., p. 19.
[11]*The Population Bomb,* a pamphlet issued by the Hugh Moore Fund, 51 E. 42nd St. New York, N.Y.

375 million.[12] The major causes of this population explosion can be traced to medical discoveries and widespread advances in sanitation, which have drastically reduced the death rate.

If the growth rate continues, it could lead to absolute government regulation of the size of families.[13] A number of methods have been suggested as a means of introducing economic persuaders aimed at encouraging young couples to postpone marriage and to limit births within marriage: charging substantial fees for marriage licenses, levying a "child tax," taxing single persons less than married persons, eliminating tax exemptions for children, or legalizing abortion and sterilization.[14]

The tremendous reductions in morbidity and mortality over the past several decades has extended the average life expectancy from less than fifty years at the turn of the century to more than seventy years for the present generation. As we noted in Chapter 21, this means greater numbers of surviving generations within families and a growing population of postparental couples, both consequences calling for continuing readjustments in family relationships in the future.

The demographic revolution has witnessed a major transformation both in agricultural technology and in agricultural manpower, as the United States has shifted from a predominantly rural to urban society.

The urbanization and suburbanization of America continue apace, and with them come new family problems and adjustments.[15] These changes from rural to urban milieu have and will continue to reduce further the proportion of children who work at economically productive tasks, will facilitate the movement of married women into paid employment, and will further discourage large families.

---

[12]U.S. Bureau of the Census, *Current Population Reports,* Series P-25, No. 388, "Summary of Demographic Projections" (Washington, D.C.: U.S. Government Printing Office, 1968).

[13]William B. Shockley, a Nobel Laureate, has proposed a plan for government-administered birth control that has some rather Orwellian overtones. He proposes that the public ballot on the rate of population growth it wants, and then the Census Bureau would use that decision to determine how many children each couple would have without exceeding the predetermined growth rates. Each couple would be issued a certificate for each child it could have. All girls would be temporarily sterlized with a mechanical contraceptive. When a couple wanted a child, they would present one of their certificates to a public health agency, and the contraceptive device would be removed to permit conception. After the child was born, the woman would be resterilized. Shockley believes couples not wishing children or wanting less than they were entitled to should be permitted to sell their surplus certificates on the open market.

[14]Kingsley Davis, "Population Policy: Will Current Programs Succeed?" *Science,* **158** (Nov. 10, 1967), p. 730.

[15]Ewan Clague, "Demographic Trends and Their Significance," in *The Changing American Population,* ed. by Hoke S. Simpson (New York: Institute of Life Insurance, 1962), p. 1920. In 1870, 58 per cent of the employed males in the American labor force were in agricultural occupations, but by 1966 less than 7 per cent were so employed.

The Cybernetic Revolution

In 1955, Ogburn and Nimkoff advanced the thesis that of the various causes producing changes in family life, the influence of scientific discoveries and inventions is far and away the most outstanding. They traced the far-reaching consequences of technological innovations for family life since the Industrial Revolution. They viewed change in terms of a chainlike sequence of events, in which several events converged to produce a certain result; the effects of this result were then dispersed outward into many areas of life. For example,

the increased use of mechanical power developed by the steam engine dispersed its effects upon innumerable activities. Its influence, among other things, was felt, for instance, on (1) home production, (2) jobs for men outside the home, (3) jobs for women for pay, (4) the growth of cities, (5) the increase of governmental functions, (6) the development of commercial recreation, and on many other activities. Thus the dispersed effect of the steam engine were varied and many. Now these same effects resulting from dispersion converged in turn as causes of changes in the family. Thus the authority of the husband in the family is less because of (1) the loss of production from the home of which he was boss, (2) the creation of jobs for men away from home where for many hours of the day they are not in a position to exercise authority over their families, (3) the trend of women to work not for their husbands but for others for pay which brought them independence from their husband's authority, and rights not allowed them in the authoritarian family, (4) the increase of governmental functions which provided protection and services to women and children which husbands formerly provided, and (5) the development of recreation in commercial places that took the members of the family away from home. Thus, an invention, which has many dispersed effects on various activities which later converge to produce a single change in the family, becomes a very important cause of family change.[16]

The United States is just beginning to move into a "cybercultural era," that is,

the era of human civilization that is evolving since the discovery of cybernetics and the invention of the computer machine and cybernation. . . . Cybernation is the science of relationships—its realm is the vast and complex, but unified system we call the universe. One of the applications of cybernetics has resulted in the technology of cybernation—the production system consisting of machine systems under the control and direction of a computing machine.[17]

This would be an era of full automation in which computer-directed

---

[16]W. F. Ogburn and M. F. Nimkoff, *Technology and the Changing Family* (Cambridge, Mass.: Houghton Mifflin Company, 1955), p. 254.

[17]Alice M. Hilton, "The Family in a Cybercultural Era," paper presented at the Oct. 1966 annual meeting of the National Council on Family Relations at Minneapolis and published that same month in their *Annual Meeting Proceedings*.

machinery would do all the labor and all that would be required in the way of human effort would be supervisory and maintenance personnel.

Although there is a good deal of disagreement among social scientists as to the ultimate consequences of a cybernated economy and widespread automation—for example, whether it will lead to greater rates of unemployment or not, whether it will produce greater abundance and leisure or not—there is no doubt that such a development will have tremendous influences on family life in the future. Hilton, who feels that cybernated production will inevitably lead toward the disemployment of human beings and at the same time produce unprecedented abundance and leisure, offers the following picture:

In a cybercultural era, the basic condition of family life will change. The job will become less important, less demanding, and will eventually disappear—at least as a source of sustenance. In an abundant society, the job-income link makes no sense at all and will be obsolete. The "jobs" individuals hold will be the means for them to accomplish the work they wish to do, rather than the labor they must perform. The "job" will no longer be held under the threat of capital punishment—for in our society losing a job is almost tantamount to capital punishment by means of starvation and/or disgrace—but through the free choice of the individual. Thus, the husband's job will be no more important to the survival of the family than the wife's—the children can be educated, rather than trained for their future employment; and the whole fabric of which the family structure is woven will change. . . . It might be very different from any family structure we recognize now. It might, for example, be a flexible structure whose members are free to stay or leave, to return, to take a vacation. Children may stay with their parents, or possibly live with relatives and friends for a year or more. . . . In a free, dynamic family structure, it will be possible to permit a variety of family combinations that is unthinkable now. In an age of abundance and leisure, where everyone's needs are generously provided for, the stigma of not providing adequately for one's children will be unknown.[18]

Whether societal values or family life will ever move in the directions suggested by Hilton is, of course, very debatable. Only time will tell. To date, automation has *not* substantially increased leisure time—rather, the increased productivity has been utilized to produce an ever-larger volume of goods and services. Future productivity may be used to increase leisure or goods and services, or both. But it is certainly premature to assume a future epoch dominated by leisure.[19]

[18]Ibid., p. 37. For a related but somewhat different view of technological change and the future quality of life, see John R. Platt, "The Step to Man," *Science,* **149** (Aug. 6, 1965), pp. 607–613.

[19]Gilbert Burck, "There'll Be Less Leisure Than You Think," *Fortune* (March 1970), pp. 86–89, 162–65.

The Human Rights Revolution

The United States continues to witness a long and exciting history of citizens struggling toward the attainment of a more full and complete democratic way of life, and in the process family relationships have been dramatically altered.[20] The economic and political democracy of men has been followed by increasing freedom for women (and children). The right of individual choice in marriage is now the accepted heritage of both sexes. "In democratic courtship, two persons with equal political rights, equal economic status, and equal educational opportunity choose each other without interference (often without guidance) of family, church, or state."[21] The emphasis on individualism inherent in the pursuit of the democratic ideal is increasingly being reflected in our system of courtship, marriage, and family life.

The vast civil rights legislation of the sixties moved the country further along the road to democratic equalitarianism. Historical bases of discrimination and prejudice are being removed, emancipating minority groups not only of ethnic and religious backgrounds, but on the basis of age and sex as well. Discriminatory state laws, such as those prohibiting intermarriage or the dissemination of contraceptive information and devices, continue to crumble as their constitutionality is challenged in the courts. The value placed on personal freedom and individual rights is reflected in the recent recommendations of the Task Force on Family Law and Policy. The stated fundamental principle underlying the considerations of the Task Force "is that men and women are entitled to equal rights in regard to marriage and the family as well as in all other aspects of American life."[22] If their very specific recommendations with respect to marital property rights, alimony and child support, financial responsibility to aged parents, the protection of the rights of children, and personal rights relating to pregnancy, illegitimacy, and abortion, as well as divorce and desertion, are accepted and passed into law, the impact on our current system of marriage and the family will be extraordinary.

This "Democratic Revolution," as Christensen refers to it, reflects a long-time trend in the shift from familism to individualism.

---

[20]Alexis de Tocqueville, the keen observer of the nineteenth century, had already noted the trend: "In America, the family, in the Roman and aristocratic signification of the word, does not exist. All that remains of it are a few vestiges in the first years of childhood, when the father exercises, without opposition, that absolute domestic authority which the feebleness of his children renders necessary, and which their interest, as well as his own incontestable superiority, warrants. But as soon as the young American approaches manhood, the ties of filial obedience are relaxed day by day; master of his thoughts, he is soon master of his conduct." *Democracy in America* (New York: The Century Co., 1898) Vol. 2, p. 233.

[21]Francis E. Merrill, *Courtship and Marriage* (New York: Holt, Rinehart and Winston, Company, 1959), p. 27.

[22]*Report of the Task Force on Family Law and Policy,* Citizens' Advisory Council on the Status of Women, U.S. Department of Labor, Washington, D.C. (Apr. 1968). p. v.

Familism refers to the traditional type of social organization in which family values are uppermost and considerations of personal advantages are ruled out, or at best come secondary. Individualism reverses these emphases; and, since contemporary American culture is more individualistic than formerly, it is commonplace now to think of marriage in terms of personal happiness and to turn quickly to divorce if this isn't readily found.[23]

Christensen feels that although the current trends are desirable and worthwhile, their immediate effects will be to disorganize the family, and they will be reflected in high rates of divorce and separation.

Predictions of the Future

In the previous pages we have very briefly sketched three major social trends—in technology, in population, and in human rights—that are expected to have dramatic repercussions for family life. It is within the context of these trends that we now attempt some specific predictions about the characteristics of American family life in the not-too-distant future.

Family Affluence

The economic expansion in the United States resulting from technological advances will continue and will be paralleled by increasing family incomes. Current trends indicate a steady decline in the incidence of poverty and a rise in family income.[24] In 1941, for example, only one American family in twenty had an income of $5,000 or more a year; now more than fifteen out of twenty earn that much. Our nation is entering an era of mass high income, and it has been estimated that by 1975 the average family income after federal taxes will be about $10,000.[25] This means that many families will move beyond the point where spending must go entirely for necessities and will be able to exercise broad options about what they buy. There will be more two-income families. Families will spend more on alcoholic beverages, recreation, education, clothing, eating out, and travel. They will spend proportionately less on food, housing, and so on.

The reduction in economic pressures created by the rising affluence will have a number of positive benefits for the internal relationships of the family. For example, women will increasingly enter the labor force on a voluntary basis rather than out of sheer necessity to avoid poverty.

[23]Christensen, op. cit., pp. 7–8.

[24]R. Ferguson, "Employment and the War on Poverty in the United States," *International Labour Review*, **101** (March 1970), pp. 247–269.

[25]Lawrence A. Mayer, "The Diverse $10,000-and-over Masses," *Fortune* (December, 1967), pp. 114–220. More than 20 million families already have incomes over $10,000 and they account for well over half of the total income in the U.S.

"When poverty forces women to work, they are liable to resent it and to take their resentment out on their husband and children. They are not very nice people for any members of the family (including themselves!) to live with."[26]

Employed Wives

The number of employed wives entering the labor force will continue to increase. Moreover, there will be an increasing number of women with young children going to work outside of the home. Married women in paid employment already constitute a large majority—59 per cent—of all working women. Of the more than 30$\frac{1}{2}$ million working women sixteen years of age and over, almost three out of five are married and living with their husbands.[27] It has been estimated that the annual average number of employed women will grow to 36 million by 1980 and that the majority of these will be married. This trend is expected to continue because of greater employment opportunities, the higher educational attainment and occupational training of women, increased efficiency in housework activities, and changing attitudes toward the participation of married women in the paid labor force. The information explosion, the changing nature of occupations, and other factors mean that continuing education will be especially important to mothers seeking employment in the near future.[28]

Child Care

There will be an increase in child-care (day care, nursery centers) services. Paralleling the increase in the number of employed mothers since World War II, there has been a slow but growing concern and recognition of the need for child-care services in all communities for children from all types of families who may require day care, after-school care, and so on. In response to this need, a national conference regarding child-care services was held in 1960 under the joint sponsorship of the Children's Bureau and the Women's Bureau. The conference

---

[26]Blood, op. cit., pp. 45–46.

[27]Women's Bureau, Wage and Labor Standards Administratron, U.S. Department of Labor, *Background Facts on Women Workers in the United States,* Washington, D.C., 1970.

[28]These trends have led one sociologists to speculate that in the future:

"women will be divided into two categories. One category will be the no career women who have too little education to break into the occupational system. They will be trapped in domesticity with no way out. In families with large numbers of children closely spaced together, mothers may be eager to earn multiple tuition costs. But women who never got an adequate education in the past and do not manage somehow to pick up one in the future will be unable to find a job.The second category will be a growing group of career women. More college girls will be interested in a foundation for future work. They will not earn a teacher's certificate simply as a "life insurance policy" against the husband's premature death." Blood, op. cit., pp. 43–47.

officially endorsed day care as a necessary and integral part of the entire range of child-welfare services.[29] The President's Commission on the Status of Women made the following recommendation in this regard:

For the benefit of children, mothers, and society, child care services should be available for children of families at all economic levels. Proper standards of child care must be maintained, whether services are in homes or in centers. Costs should be met by fees scaled to parents' ability to pay, contributions from voluntary agencies, and public appropriations.[30]

Federal legislation, such as the Public Welfare Amendments of 1962, which permitted up to $10 million of federal child-welfare funds to be earmarked for day care for the fiscal year 1964 and each year thereafter, provided a great potential impetus for day care and was a first step in raising its provision to the level of national policy.[31]

In 1970, approximately 43 per cent of all wives were in the labor force (over 18 million wives). In husband-wife families with children under six years of age present, 32 per cent of the mothers worked; and if there were children six to seventeen years old only, 52 per cent worked.[32] Many of the children in both types of homes were young enough to require some type of after-school care. Mothers can truly be free to decide whether to work outside of the home or not, however, only when adequate substitute care that safeguards their children during the working day is available. Currently, however, such facilities are not available. The most recent estimates place only 475,000 of the nation's children in licensed day-care facilities.[33] One study estimates that there are 1 million children without any supervision while their mothers are at work.[34]

---

[29]Alfred Kadushin, *Child Welfare Services* (New York: The Macmillan Company, 1967). Kadushin, in commenting on the history of day-care centers in the United States, notes that "widespread support of day care facilities did not result primarily in response to the needs of children, but in response to the needs and demands of adult society—to increase job possibilities during the Great Depression, to increase the availability of woman power during periods of critical labor shortage such as occurred during war periods" (p. 307).

[30]Margaret Mead and Frances B. Kaplan (eds.), *American Women: The Report of the President's Commission on the Status of Women and Other Publications of the Commission* (New York: Charles Scribner's Sons, 1965), p. 38.

[31]Kadushin, op. cit., p. 307, however, notes that although all the states have developed approved day-care service plans, Congress had only appropriated about half of the $10 million authorized.

[32]*Handbook on Women Workers,* Women's Bureau, U.S. Department of Labor, Bulletin 294, 1969, pp. 37, 39.

[33]"Women and Their Families in Our Rapidly Changing Society," *Report of The Task Force on Health and Welfare,* to the Citizens' Advisory Council on the Status of Women, U.S. Department of Labor, Washington, D.C., April, 1968, p. 18.

[34]"Child Care Arrangements of the Nation's Working Mothers, 1965," Children's Bureau, U.S. Department of Health, Education, and Welfare, and Women's Bureau, U.S. Department of Labor, p. 4.

Adequate day or home care increases the alternative solutions to a variety of family problems, of which only a few will be mentioned here. Mothers in low-income families would be able to supplement the family income by taking employment and thereby providing the necessary increment of income desired to promote and maintain family stability. Adequate day care permits the mother to explore various job openings and to find the most suitable one. Some women are happier and more effective mothers by virtue of the fact that day-care services make it possible for them to work outside the home.[35]

Children who might not otherwise have a safe, stimulating place available for play are provided such a facility; children who might otherwise be deprived of an experience in group interaction under guided supervision are provided with this kind of enriching experience; and children who might otherwise be left to care for themselves, or left to haphazard, uncertain arrangements for care, are more adequately, more safely cared for as a result of the availability of day care facilities. . . . Day care as a supplementary service, then, has a great preventive value. It acts to prevent breakup of families, separation of children from their parents, increased dependency on public aid, and dangers and hazards of children.[36]

Family Life Styles

Convergence of family consumer habits and styles of living will continue. People from all social classes will eat out, will buy the same kinds of apparel, will have at least one car, will purchase outdoor play equipment for children, and will possess the paraphernalia for lawn care and outdoor cooking.[37] A number of sociologists have commented on the homogenization of tastes and style that is taking place—at least among the middle classes—in this country.[38] This standarization of consumer habits and styles of life will be accompanied by a convergence in family values regarding such things "as sex behavior, birth control, size of family, treatment of children, et cetera—and this drawing together is taking place among religious groups, racial groups, and social classes; between the two sexes, youth and the older generation, and such sociological divisions as rural and urban."[39] Thus, we would expect the families among the several subcultures to become more standardized. This is not to deny that a growing segment of our young, and particularly our college-educated population, will continue to experiment with divergent life-styles.

[35]Kadushin, op. cit., pp. 325–328.

[36]F. Ivan Nye and Lois Wladis Hoffman, *The Employed Mother in America* (Chicago: Rand McNally & Co., 1963), Chapter 24.

[37]*Fortune*, op. cit., p. 218.

[38]George Katona, *The Mass Consumption Society* (New York: McGraw-Hill Book Company, 1964); David Riesman and Howard Roseborough, "Careers and Consumer Behavior," in *Consumer Behavior*, Vol. 2, ed. by Lincoln H. Clark, "The Life-Cycle and Consumer Behavior" (New York: New York University Press, 1955).

[39]Harold T. Christensen, op. cit., pp. 1–25.

More Families

There will be an increase in the marriage rate and more families. There has been a substantial and uninterrupted rise in the marriage rate in the United States every year since 1962, and this upward trend is expected to continue. The high birth rates during and after World War I are now being reflected in the greater proportion of young people reaching the peak ages for marriage. In 1970 alone, well over 2 million marriages were recorded. In addition, the ages at which future husbands and wives first marry will be in closer proximity; that is, the young couple will be nearer in age to one another.[40] The smaller age differences between the new spouses will mean, other things being equal, a greater probability of joint survival. This will lead to a substantial future increase in the proportion of persons living with their spouses in late middle age and old age.

Divorce and Remarriage

The trend toward increasing divorce and remarriage rates will continue. An estimated 728,000 decrees of divorce or annulments were granted in the United States in the year ending April, 1971, and the divorce rate of 3.3 per 1,000 population was the highest national divorce rate since 1949 (but still substantially below the 1946 rate of 4.3).[41] The annual total *number* of divorces, however, far exceeds the 1946 all-time high of 600,000 divorces. At the same time, there has been and will continue to be an increase in remarriage rates. More and more marriages in the future will be second marriages for one or both spouses and will involve as well greater numbers of children.

Some sociologists have predicted that in the long run more marriages will remain intact. Parke and Glick, for example, reason that (1) the recent reductions in the age differences between spouses will reduce the extent to which marital dissolution will occur as a result of widowhood, and (2) the trend toward upgrading the economic position of the population will continue and therefore lessen the chances of divorce. "Barring a rise in the divorce rate or major changes in the pattern of divorce and separation by socio-economic status," they say, "the reduction of poverty should result in a substantial long-term improvement in the average stability of marriages."[42]

Age at Marriage

Age at marriage will increase. As women move toward greater equality, the range of alternatives open to them in the occupational world will expand. The possibilities of embarking on a full-time career

---

[40]Robert Parke, Jr., and Paul C. Glick, "Prospective Changes in Marriage and the Family," *Journal of Marriage and the Family,* **29** (May 1967), pp. 249–256.

[41]*Monthly Vital Statistics Reports,* **20** (June 30, 1971).

[42]Parke and Glick, op. cit., pp. 253–254.

are increasing. The passage of federal civil rights legislation to guarantee equal opportunity to women will contribute to this trend. And as more and more women recognize the utility of completing their educations for entering the occupational world, there will be postponement in marriage plans for large numbers of them, although we cannot say with any exactness what the proportion will be. A job or a career means, for many women, financial independence, travel, and so on, and a number of other rewarding alternatives to marriage, child-rearing, and economic dependence on a husband. Research may play a part, too, in that it has shown that early marriages are characterized by very high divorce rates (Chapter 9). As women become aware of this fact, they may be less eager to enter an early marriage.

Family Power

The family of the future will be more equalitarian. The continued rise in the employment of wives will further accentuate the companionate type of family, which only recently came into existence and which is characterized by equalitarian norms with respect to the family power structure and the divison of labor:

the shape of the American family is being altered by the exodus of women into the labor market. The roles of men and women are converging for both adults and children. As a result, the family will be far less segregated internally, far less stratified into different age generations and different sexes. This will enable family members to share more of the activities of life together, both work activities and play activities. The old symmetry of male dominated, female-serviced family life is being replaced by a new symmetry, both between husbands and wives and between brothers and sisters. To this emerging symmetry, the dual employment of mothers as well as fathers is a major contributor.[43]

Whether this trend will result in greater clarity of familial roles and increased joint decision-making, as Christensen has suggested,[44] remains to be seen.

At the same time, the emerging *colleague family,* suggested by Miller and Swanson, will become more prevalent. The colleague family is similar to Burgess and Locke's companionate family with its emphasis on equalitarianism and shared affection. In addition, however, it recognizes that partners to a marriage have individual competencies that may contribute to the marriage. The colleague family draws upon the specialized skills and interests of its members; partners are willing to relinquish authority to each other in areas in which one or the other has

---

[43]Blood, op. cit., p. 47.
[44]Christensen, op. cit., p. 22.

certain assumed role competencies. Moreover, there is explicit recognition that absolute equality among the members in every area of activity is not possible. Although children are not as subordinate to their parents as in the past, and their opinions are more likely to be sought and given serious consideration, nevertheless they must acquiesce to parents and older siblings. Moreover, they must have demonstrated the ability to assume adult role responsibilities before being admitted to full participation in family decision-making.[45]

Sexual Intercourse

The sex norms will more closely approximate a single standard for both men and women. The increasing autonomy of the courtship institution in America means less supervision and control by parents and greater opportunity for sexual intimacy among young couples prior to marriage. It appears safe to predict wider acceptance of sexual intimacy between engaged couples.[46]

Women will increasingly accept sexual equality with men. Technological innovations in contraception have succeeded in separating sex from reproduction, and now

women will demand that they have equal rights with men to decide their actions as regards sex without consideration of reproductivity. They will demand, that, like the male, they be allowed the right of individual choice in this area; that, like him, their choice now can be made with regard to what is moral for them, not what are the procreative consequences. We do not believe that the moral fiber of girls will suddenly crumble en masse or that they will become different people by *swallowing* the pill.[47]

However, nonmarital sexual intercourse of all types except prostitution is likely to increase. The knowledge that pregnancy can be prevented and venereal disease controlled reduces the social stigma associated with nonmarital intercourse. This knowledge and the relaxation of abortion laws reduce the cost to women of nonmarital intercourse; therefore, more of this activity is likely to occur.

Fertility Control

The family of the future will be in a position to exert much greater control over its own biological processes. Nearly two decades ago, Nimkoff advanced the thesis that discoveries in human biology were

[45]Daniel R. Miller and Guy E. Swanson, *The Changing American Parent* (New York: John Wiley & Sons, 1958), p. 200–201.

[46]Walter R. Stokes, "Sex in the World of Tomorrow," *Sexology,* **32** (June 1966), pp. 748–751.

[47]Miriam Birdwhistell, "Adolescents and the Pill Culture," *The Family Coordinator,* **17** (Jan. 1968), pp. 27–32.

potentially more significant for the social psychological aspects of family life than technological developments, and future events may prove this thesis to be sound.[48]

The safe, effective, convenient, and inexpensive contraceptives will undoubtedly become available to all in the not-too-distant future. A reversible contraceptive substance that would provide sterility for extended periods of time has already been developed and is now awaiting approval from the Food and Drug Administration. Advances are being made in experiments with organ banks and transplants, the preservation of human spermatozoa through freezing, the manipulation and control of sex chromosomes affecting hereditary traits, and hormonal therapy for modifying the secondary sex characteristics. Techniques for determining and controlling the sex of animals have already been achieved, and similar control and determination of the sex of human offspring is not unlikely in the distant future.[49]

The federal government will play an increasing role in these developments, especially in the area of family planning, through appropriations for research and services designed to provide more effective measures for the voluntary control of human fertility.[50] As a result, families can be expected to receive greater assistance in extending control over their biological processes. Such developments, along with the trend toward more liberalized abortion laws, potentially mean that there will be fewer unwanted children.

Family Leisure

In their book *The Year 2000,* Herman Kahn and Anthony J. Wiener contemplate the possibility of a "leisure-oriented" work pattern, with a seven-and-a-half-hour day, a four-day week, thirteen weeks a year off, and ten legal holidays. Although this may be an overoptimistic forecast, there is no doubt that the average work week will shrink in the future, a trend that has been going on for one hundred years. It has been suggested that if a husband worked a four-day week,

his family could live where they chose within a 200-mile or greater radius of his office; he could come in Monday (or Tuesday) morning, have his own living

---

[48]Meyer F. Nimkoff, "Biological Discoveries and the Future of the Family," *American Journal of Sociology,* **58** (July 1958), pp. 20–26; "Biological Discoveries and the Future of the Family: A Reappraisal," *Social Forces,* **41** (Dec. 1962), pp. 212–217.

[49]"Drama of Life Before Birth," *Life* (Apr. 30, 1965); "Control of Life," a four-part series, (September 10, 17, 24, and October 1, 1965); "Choosing the Sex of Rabbits," *Time* (June 7, 1968). For a more detailed discussion of biological discoveries and their potential implications for the family, see W. F. Ogburn and M. F. Nimkoff, *Technology and the Changing Family* (Boston: Houghton Mifflin Company, 1955), Chapter 13, "Scientific Discoveries and the Future of the Family."

[50]Carl Djerassi, "Birth Control After 1984," *Science,* **169** (September 4, 1970), pp. 941–951.

quarters in the city, and travel home again Thursday (or Friday) night. But increased leisure on an annual basis, and especially longer periods of leisure at longer intervals, would have much greater opportunities for travel, education, public service, and other activities as well as for sheer play. It too, would surely have a major impact upon community activities and business.[51]

If such a situation emerged, the family of the future will have to learn how to deal with this new leisure time as a means of creating a more gratifying existence for its members. Moreover, it is predicted that an increasing proportion of total consumer income will be given to leisure-related expenditures, such as sporting goods or camping equipment, travel, and cultural events. In this connection it is expected that more families will be acquiring second homes for weekend or vacation use.[52]

Early retirement as a result of both mandatory and voluntary actions will become more prominent. When couples have a longer life span, they will have longer periods of leisure time together after the children have left the parental home.

Future Family Roles

Finally what is likely to happen to the family roles that have been analyzed in previous chapters? In offering some predictions we shall try to anticipate the meaning and impact of the social trends described in the first part of this chapter.

Provider Role

The future seems to hold "more of the same" for men. The provider role will continue to be prescribed for men with no normatively acceptable alternatives. Even if production becomes predominantly automated, service, recreational, governmental, and religious organizations are expanding and will continue to expand. Given materialistic values, added efficiency in a society seems likely to produce a continually increasing volume of goods and services, rather than much less work.

If innovations are made in the economic institutions to increase the number of jobs, the future male provider may not have to contend with unemployment, but he will continue to compete with his fellow men (and women) for the better-paid and more powerful positions.

---

[51]Marion Clawson, "How Much Leisure, Now and in the Future?" in *Leisure in America: Blessing or Curse?* ed. by James C. Charlesworth, Monograph 4, in a series sponsored by the American Academy of Political and Social Science, Philadelphia, Apr. 1964, pp. 1–20.

[52]Mayer, op. cit., p. 220.

641

At present the only females clearly obligated to earn a living are adult single women. Their parents would reject the idea that they should support a physically able adult daughter all her life. There is some noticeable social pressure on young married women with no children to take paid employment, and such pressure is expected to increase as women's housekeeper tasks become fewer. It is anticipated that the same will become true for the mother with no preschool children and only one or two of school age. Likewise, in the family headed by a widow or a divorcee, it seems probable that these women will be expected to enact the provider role while society furnishes some assistance in the child-care role through subsidized day-care centers. In short, within a decade or two it is expected that all adult, able-bodied women, except those married with preschool children, will be expected to enter paid employment. Doubtless, some will resist such pressure just as in the early period of employed mothers, some resisted the pressure to keep mothers out of employment.

As noted in Chapter 10, many women will become more effective in the provider roles than their husbands and will contribute more to the family income. Men will, however, find it difficult to relinquish a provider role and assume the housekeeper role because there will be too little left of the housekeeper role to constitute a full-time occupation for anyone.

As women enter more fully into occupational life, they will secure more of the higher professional, business, and governmental positions. Prejudice against women in such positions will decline and perhaps eventually disappear completely.

Housekeeper Role

Housekeeper tasks have been moving to specialized factories and service establishments. Most meals are still cooked and served at home, but this is likely to change drastically in the next decade. The emergence of the cafeteria and the buffet makes it possible to prepare meals at a cost close to that of home-cooked meals. As more of these establishments open and as their volume increases, there will be little reason, other than personal preference, for preparing food in the house or the apartment. Likewise, professional cleaners are likely to take over that last housekeeper task, cleaning the home. The wife of the future, employed at an equitable salary will feel no special pressure to do her own housecleaning or to prepare or serve meals.

Of those housekeeper tasks that are performed by the couple, the husband is likely to do more, in recognition of the wife's employee responsibilities, but his tasks are likely to be light and voluntary, because neither he nor his wife need perform them.

642

Child Care

The daytime care of the child is likely to be performed by a day-care center for preschool children or by the school for school-age children. The school or some new agency is likely to have the child for a longer day to correspond with the working day of his parents. Child care at home is likely to be shared by the father, either as a positive preference or as an equitable arrangement for sharing the task. Parents who have few if any housekeeping tasks will have more time and energy to care for their children.

Child Socialization

The development of generally available day-care centers will give these centers a considerable share of the responsibility for the socialization of young children. This socialization will differ from current patterns in that the child will adapt to many other young children and to more adults at an early age. This would appear to provide a more continuous type of socialization from infancy, through childhood, and into the adult occupational and recreational world.

Parents are likely to "relax" a little as the fallacies of theories that predicted personality malformation in children as a result of any word or gesture of parents becomes generally obvious. A degree of relaxation is likely to decrease the nervous strain on parents. Disciplinary techniques are likely more nearly to approximate those of the prescientific period; that is reward for achievement, punishment for deviance. However, because learning theory emphasizes rewarding acceptable behavior rather than punishing undesired behavior, discipline is unlikely to rely as much on corporal punishment as was true in prescientific epochs.

Differences in the content of socialization for boys and girls is expected to continue to decrease. Girls are less likely to be discouraged from aspiring to careers in politics, engineering, medicine, and other professions that have been dominated by men. Boys are less likely to be discouraged from interests in cooking, cleaning, and caring for children.[53] Socialization for sexual and therapeutic roles is likely to become more similar. However, it does not seem to follow that boys and girls will be encouraged to look alike. Sexual attraction is based on the differences between the sexes. Clothing acknowledges and accentuates these differences. In a society in which sexual activity and gratification are highly valued, socialization seems more likely to continue to

[53]For an imaginative discussion of the future socialization of children for adult (including marital) roles, see Alice S. Rossi, "Equality Between the Sexes: An Immodest Proposal," *Daedalus*, **93** (Spring 1964), pp. 607–652. See also Margaret Mead, "Marriage in Two-Steps," *Redbook Magazine* (July, 1966).

643

emphasize sexual differences.[54] It is possible that differential socialization for males and females may cease to exist, except in personal appearance.

It is unclear at this time how the adolescents of the future are to be reared. It has been pointed out that they are physically, and often intellectually, adults rather than children (Chapter 8). Current socialization, based on the assumption that they are children, and the attempt to meet their needs by giving them things are not proving satisfactory to adults or adolescents. In Chapter 8 two social structural changes were outlined that would redefine adolescence as a period of adult life: (1) Acknowledge that the student role is a work role, expand it to a full work day and provide pay for it, graded to accomplishment in the role. Considering the need for physical activity of adolescents, an expanded physical recreation program would seem appropriate to accompany this plan. (2) The alternative outlined was to provide part-time paid employment for adolescents so that they attend school for about five hours, then work for three or four. Either plan would occupy more of their time and energy under supervised conditions and would provide a chance for them to earn what they spend. Either would provide socialization experiences to prepare them for adult work roles.

Whether one or the other of these structures for socializing adolescents is used or some other innovation will occur cannot be predicted because each involves a major social innovation, rather than the extension of a trend already discernible.

Sexual Role

The sexual role has been treated as an established role for wives and an emerging one for husbands (Chapter 10). There is evidence that it has emerged in the middle class, and it can be expected to spread to the lower classes. As women accept full responsibilities as providers, they can expect equality in sexual gratification and it will be the duty of husbands to try to provide it. It is a little less certain that wives will have the additional duty to respond in intercourse rather than merely being sexually available, but this seems to follow as part of the reward for the husband's efforts. Whether the enlarged role for wives will also include stimulating the sexual interest of their husbands is unclear at this time, but because women are increasingly considered to have positive sexual interests and needs, this enlarged role also seems to follow.

[54]Hippies may seem to contradict this prediction, but these are the drop-outs from the society, not the bearers of its dominant values and norms.

644

Therapeutic Role

In a society increasingly complex, the need for assistance in problem-solving and tension management is likely to become greater. To the extent that spouses can learn to listen and to respond effectively, they can function in a therapeutic capacity.[55] With the geographical dispersion of the extended family, kin are less available as confidants. The number and availability of professional counselors is limited and their help is costly. The need felt for help in problem-solving and tension management will increase. Spouses are likely to enact therapeutic roles more and more, first in the middle class but probably eventually in all classes.

Final Comments

In this final chapter we have tried to anticipate some future changes in the family. That there will be major changes is almost as certain as it is that changes in the family have occurred in the past. Some of the anticipated changes will be essentially extensions of past trends, but as noted earlier some trends have been reversed. For example, we have seen small families in the thirties, and now smaller families again. Likewise, as an established trend is followed, at some point a real breakthrough occurs. It has been predicted that this will occur in two areas: the establishment of preschool day-care centers and the establishment of truly economical food preparation and service in eating establishments.

Forecasting is obviously hazardous and the reader is again cautioned that no more than a tentative acceptance of these forecasts is warranted. Implicit in the writing of a chapter on the future of the family is the recognition that one's perspective is more likely to be useful if he tries to look ahead to anticipate the future than if he only looks to the past to see what has happened.

Will there, then, *be* a family of the future? There is good reason to believe so. Most of the child-care and socialization functions will still remain in the family. A permanent relationship between a man and a woman is an effective arrangement for meeting sexual needs, of providing affection, and for meeting the therapeutic needs of each, and of providing a partner for recreational activity. These are important needs, and the marriage that provides well for them surely will be highly

---

[55]Irving Tallman, "The Family as a Small Problem Solving Group," a paper presented at the annual meeting of the National Council on Family Relations, New Orleans, La., Oct. 18, 1968.

valued. Indeed, the institution of the family, pessimists notwithstanding, will persist as the most fundamental unit of society.

There is little doubt that the institution of the family *is here to stay,* not because this basic unit of social structure is valuable, *per se,* but because it is instrumental in maintaining life itself, in shaping the infant into the person, and providing for the security and affectional needs of people of all ages. In fact, the family is so central to the fulfillment of several central intrinsic values, that [it can] be anticipated that it will become an even more competent instrument for meeting human needs, and as a consequence, will become more highly and generally valued throughout society in that fascinating and ever more rapidly changing world of tomorrow.[56]

---

[56]F. Ivan Nye, "Values, Family, and a Changing Society," *Journal of Marriage and the Family,* **29** (May 1967), pp. 241–248.

Author Index

647

Subject Index